Canadian Studies

An Introductory Reader

Renée Lafferty
Brock University

KENDALL/HUNT PUBLISHING COMPANY
4050 Westmark Drive   Dubuque, Iowa 52002

Contents

Introduction

One of the long-standing lessons of the Canadian experience has been the importance of living on several levels at once.

—John Ralston Saul[1]

For Canadians, questions of identity have been constant companions to the substance of politics, culture, and society since the earliest moments of contact between Aboriginal and European societies. What is Canada? *How* is it? Is it English or French—or American? Is it a 'home and native land' or a home on native land? Is it multicultural or without cultural substance? Is it a place of infinite promise, or a place teetering on the edge of self-destruction? These kinds of questions have lurked in the shadows of military conflict, flirted with the fathers of Confederation, inspired citizens to rebellion and celebration, and manipulated—for good and ill—the contours of the country's cultural and political landscape. At times, seeking answers can be a melancholy exercise ending in bleak predictions of separation or annexation—the erasure of the country from the global gazetteer. Other times, the exercise is less melancholy than gormless, falling back on the hackneyed stereotypes so popular with advertisers of beer and doughnuts: we are a polite nation of beer-drinking, hockey playing, middle-grounders. But as the above reflection from John Ralston Saul suggests, Canada and the Canadian experience cannot be understood by seeking seamless answers to knotty and demanding questions. Canada is a place and an experience that is fundamentally multi-dimensional, a "celebration of overlap" whose "very originality . . . has always been to stay out of step with the norm. That's what makes it interesting."[2]

The present collection of documents, essays and poems is a species of historical topography. It attempts to map—and perhaps at times to celebrate—the overlapping contours of the nation by excavating certain key events and ideas which lie beneath the skin of its history. These are moments of creation, conflict, and compromise that have, undoubtedly, inspired those melancholy predictions of Canada's demise and supported the vacuous stereotypes of its people. But they also have resulted, ultimately, in the place called Canada and the often confusing experience of being Canadian. The hope is that these readings will point the way to a more meaningful understanding of Canada, and of the challenges facing the people who live within its borders.

The timeline represented by these documents—stretching as far back as Champlain (and farther, even, with George Sioui's exploration of Aboriginal belief and culture)—is an acknowledgement that Canada did not arrive on the world map, fresh and newborn, on 1 July 1867. The country's roots are buried in centuries of history rather than decades, and too many of our present mythologies draw their inspiration from this deep past to ignore it in favour of a discussion of contemporary events alone. Many of the texts are primary documents that invite the reader to step directly into the past, through the words and ideas of those who witnessed or experienced a given event themselves. Others offer contemporary interpretations of Canada's past and, more importantly, suggest what that past means (or should mean) to Canadians today. Whether these documents are primary or secondary, however, none of them lack bias, and none of them present a whole truth or a complete picture. For this reason, wherever possible, readers are given a variety of interpretations and viewpoints—historic and contemporary—on a given topic. The intended effect of this variety is to complicate the question of national identity, and to promote the sort of critical thinking and reflection necessary to the formation of any thoughtful understanding of Canada's past, present, and future. The topics for discussion in this reader make the transient nature of supposedly concrete definitions very clear. At the same time, it also is hoped that they will illuminate some of the important aspects and moments of the journey itself. This tactic is inspired by the clichéd, yet still elemental credo, that the journey itself is more important than the destination. It also is based on the belief that *lacking* a uniform definition of nation is perhaps not such a bad thing, after all.

This journey begins with "Discovery"—the now controversial term used to describe the first meetings between European explorers and the Aboriginal peoples. The theme of European-Aboriginal interaction threads its way throughout the rest of the reader—from the poignant poetry of Tekahionwake (Pauline Johnson), to the impassioned 1969 "Red Paper" of the Indian Chiefs of Alberta. But silences often speak louder than words. Readers should be keenly aware of those times when the Aboriginal voice—or indeed the voice of any socially or economically marginalized group, be it Aboriginal, female, immigrant, or working class, is absent or silenced by the country's social and political elite.

Other prominent themes explored in this reader involve the always fraught and challenging world of French-English relations, Canada's position on the world stage, and a number of crucial landmarks in its cultural and political development. While these themes can be arranged with strict divisions between what constitutes politics and what culture, such divisions would not reflect a more accurate sense that Canadian politics and culture are inseparable—they exist together in that realm of overlap so central to the Canadian experience. Critical issues of political identity frequently become icons of popular culture, while elements of the country's cultural identity are just as frequently politicized. Confederation, healthcare, the Riel Rebellions, peacekeeping, Conquest, multiculturalism, the building of the Railway, the Charter,—even the National Anthem—exist as both political and cultural entities. It is hoped that casting such a wide net across Canada's past will allow those interested in its future to see how, and why, these events and ideas have such a complicated and imperative position in the nation. It also is hoped that readers will understand what is effectively lost in translation when the cultural becomes political, and politics becomes culture.

The assembly of a collection such as this one is a daunting task—even more so when, after it is completed, the compiler recognizes how much has ultimately been left out. A dozen—even a hundred—similar collections could not begin to do justice to the range of stories, good and bad, that can be told about this country. Any omissions or errors, however, are entirely the fault of the editor. And, undoubtedly, many more omissions and errors would have occurred, if not for the excellent advice and thoughtful contributions of my friends and colleagues at Brock University, and for the patience and perseverance of the excellent team of people at Kendall/Hunt. Thanks especially to Carmela Patrias, Mike Funke, Michelle Bahr, Renae Horstman, Mark Sawyer, and those most indefatigable supporters, critics, and explorers, my students. I am, as P.E.I., *parva sub ingenti.*

References

1. John Ralston Saul, *Reflections of a Siamese Twin: Canada at the End of the Twentieth Century* (Penguin Books, 1997), 411
2. *Ibid,* 411, 10

1

Natives and Newcomers

Introduction

Did Europeans, like the famous explorer Samuel De Champlain, "discover" North America? From their own perspective, they did: Everything from the vast tracks of forests to the lakes, rivers, and mountains—even the bogs and the icebergs—were empty and unclaimed. For Champlain, whose 1615/16 letter is the first of two readings in this chapter, everything he saw around him in the territory we now call Ontario belonged to his employer, the King of France. And part of his duty, as the "discoverer" of this territory, was to report back to the King all that he observed in the land, to detail what precisely it was that the king "owned."

Champlain, and other explorers like him, clearly disregarded the fact that there were already people living in North America—people who had lived there for centuries. This disregard was based on the culturally arrogant and mistaken belief that Aboriginals were less "civilized"—that they were, as Champlain describes them, "savages," who lacked the capacity, and even the right, to dispute the claims of the King of France. Indeed, as Champlain makes clear, he and his European counterparts believed they had a God-given responsibility to civilize, educate, and "improve" the lives of the "savages" they encountered.

Georges Sioui's essay on the Huron/Wendat people whom Champlain encountered, presents a sharp contrast to the perceptions of these European explorers. He describes a sophisticated, creative, and complex society—one vastly different from that of the European arrivals, and one clearly misunderstood and misrepresented by them. These misunderstandings, these European claims to "ownership" and "discovery," their belief that it was their responsibility to bring religion and civilization to a "savage" people, resulted in centuries of violence, destruction and mistrust between Aboriginal people and the immigrants from Europe.

A Letter to the King
Samuel de Champlain
1615/16

TO THE KING: Sir, here is the third volume of my account of the most interesting and important things that happened on my voyages to New France. I think you will find this volume even more enjoyable to read than the first two, for there I was chiefly concerned with ports, harbours, latitudes, magnetic variations and other matters of greater interest to seamen and navigators than to laymen. In this book you will learn something of the manners and customs of the savages—their weapons, their strategy in the field, their methods of travel—all set down with enough detail to satisfy the most curious reader.

You will soon see that these people are by no means so ignorant that in course of time they cannot be taught the arts of civilization. You will see how for fifteen long and arduous years we have nourished the hope of planting the cross in the New World, knowing that our first duty was to treat the savages with patience and charity and seeking above all to bring the miserable creatures to a knowledge of God and their Saviour. It is true that some of our people think only of profit, but I am convinced that their greed is nothing more than a means to an end and part of God's holy plan.

When a tree brings forth fruit, the fruit belongs to the owner of the land, who has watered the tree and cared for it. The fruit of our labours belongs by right to your Majesty, not only because New France is part of your dominions but also because you have given us the benefit of your protection. Certain persons were unfriendly to our aims and ambitions and they used every means at their disposal to hinder the success of our expedition. Whatever we have achieved we owe to the support of your Majesty and the wisdom of the Council, which gave us the authority to act in your name.

This only makes us the more eager to establish new colonies overseas, so the savages may learn not only of the glory of God but also of the power and greatness of your Majesty. Once the savages have been taught to speak French they will soon learn to think and feel like Frenchmen, and then they will want nothing so much, after the love of God, as to serve France. If we succeed, your Majesty will share the honour and glory with God alone.

Your name will always be blessed as that of the man who brought so many wretched creatures to a knowledge of their Saviour. You will always be famous for having carried the sceptre of France farther west than all your ancestors carried it to

The excerpts from *Samuel de Champlain—Voyages to New France 1615–1618,* translated by Michael Macklem, are reprinted by permission of Oberon Press.

3

the east, so that now we hold sway over the whole known world. You alone of all kings are entitled to call yourself Most Christian. This great enterprise shows that you deserve the tide not only by right of inheritance but also by right of achievement. For despite all your other cares you have taken pains to see to the preaching of the gospel in many a land where the name of God had never been heard before. In course of time these people will join us in praying for the Kingdom of God and like us will bless the name of France.

I am, Sir, your most humble, faithful and obedient servant and subject, CHAMPLAIN

To the east the country is already well-known, extending as it does to the shores of Labrador, Newfoundland, Cape Breton, Acadia and New England. I have already described this part of the country in the journals of my previous voyages and I won't say anything more about it now, since I want to tell you as much as I can of what I saw in the interior.

The Huron country lies in latitude 44° 30' and is seven hundred miles from east to west and thirty from north to south.[1] Like Brittany, it is almost completely surrounded by water. The land is fertile and most of it is cleared. There are about eighteen villages, of which six are really fortified towns, with stockades surrounding the living quarters. The stockades are made of wooden stakes set in three rows and lashed together, with galleries behind from which the defenders can throw boulders down on the enemy or pour water on him if he tries to set fire to the defences.

The population of the country is about thirty thousand, of which two thousand are warriors. They live in lodges made of bark. These lodges are about twelve yards wide and up to fifty or sixty yards long, with a gangway a foot or two across running down the middle from one end to the other. On each side there is a sort of bench about four feet high, where they sleep in summer to get away from the fleas. In winter they sleep on mats on the floor near the fire, where it is warmer. They gather dry wood all summer and pile enough in the lodges to last the winter. At one end of each lodge there is an open space where they store their Indian corn in large casks made of bark. Mice are everywhere and everything they want to keep safe, such as food or clothing, has to be hung up on wooden pegs. The average lodge will have a dozen fires and two dozen families. The smoke inside is thick and blinding and diseases of the eyes are common, in fact many of the older people have lost their sight altogether. The trouble is that there are no windows and so there is no way for the smoke to escape except through a single hole in the roof. Each lodge is built three or four yards from the next, in case one should catch fire from another. Often they will live in one place for ten, twenty or even thirty years and then move to a new site six or eight miles away. If they are driven out by their enemies they may move to a distance of a hundred and twenty miles or more, as the Onondagas once did.

They are a happy people, even though their life is wretched by comparison with ours. They have never known anything better, so they are content with what they have. The staple of their diet is Indian corn mixed with red beans and cooked in a variety of different ways. First they pound the corn and beans with a wooden mortar to make flour, then they winnow the flour with pieces of bark. To make bread they boil the dough, as if they were making corn soup. This makes it easier to whip. After it is thoroughly boiled they sometimes add blueberries or dried raspberries or occasionally (for it is very scarce) pieces of suet. After moistening the batter with warm water they make it up into loaves or biscuits which they bake under hot coals. Then when the loaves are ready they take them out and wash them.

Sometimes they take the meal and wrap it in corn leaves, fasten it together and put it into boiling water. More often they make it into a dish they call Migan. To make Migan they take two or three handfuls of corn, pound it and put it into an earthenware pot. Then they add water without removing the husks and bringing it to the boil, stirring the meal from time to time to make sure it doesn't stick to the pot and burn. Finally, they add a little fresh or dried fish, depending on the season, to give it flavour. They eat a lot of Migan, especially in winter. It usually smells foul and tastes worse, either because they don't know how to make it or because they don't bother to make it properly. They can prepare it well enough when they want to take the trouble, and when they cook it with venison it tastes all right. Usually they simply put the fish into the pot in small pieces, without bothering to remove the bones, scales or insides, and this is what gives it a bad taste. Then when it is ready they all simply help themselves from the common pot. Migan is thin enough to drink but there isn't much to it. Sometimes they make the same dish by roasting unripe corn. This they preserve and later cook whole with fish or, when they have it, with meat. Or they take dried corn and roast it over hot coals, then pound it and make it into flour. This is the way they make it when they are on the move and it's the way I like it best.

For banquets and other special occasions they take a quantity of fish and meat, cut it up into pieces and boil it in big kettles. After it has been boiled for some time they skim off the fat with a spoon. Then they add the roasted meal and stir it in until the mixture is like a thick soup. Each person gets a helping from the pot, along with a spoonful of fat, which is their idea of a delicacy. Sometimes they add beans and boil them up with the roasted meal, with a little fat and some fish stirred in. They often give banquets in winter, when they have time on their hands, and dogs are kept busy eating up the scraps. They save up their fish and game for these occasions and the rest of the time they live on thin Migan, which is no better than pig swill.

There is another dish they make with Indian corn. They take the ears and bury them in the mud and leave them to soak for two or three months. When they are good and rotten they dig them up and boil them with meat or fish and then eat them just as they are. Sometimes they roast the corn instead of boiling it and that tastes better, but I can assure you that nothing could smell worse than the ears of corn when they come up all covered with mud. However, there's nothing they like better. The women and children suck the rotten ears as if they were sugar-cane. They also eat a lot of squash, which they boil or roast over hot coals. Usually they have only two meals a day. We ourselves fasted during Lent, partly to give them an example, but it was a waste of time.

We noticed that they kept bears in captivity for two or three years at a time, to fatten them for the slaughter. I have no doubt that if they had livestock they would have no difficulty in caring for it, once they had learned how. There is plenty of good land for pasture and all they need is suitable stock—horses, cows or pigs. Without stock they will always be poor. However, they seemed to me happy enough. They live from hand to mouth but they are better off than the savages who have no permanent settlements and roam the countryside like wild animals.

Their clothing is made from skins of all sorts. Some of these they get by skinning their own game; others they get in exchange for corn, meal, beads and fish-nets from the Algonkins and Nipissings, who are great hunters. Everything they wear is cut to the same design, so there isn't any variety of style or colour, but they take great pains with the skins when they cure them. Their loincloth is usually made out of a piece of deerskin. So are their leggings, which hang in folds and come up to the waist. Moccasins they commonly make out of deerskin, bearskin or beaver. Beaver is in great demand, for they use it to make robes, which they wear like a cloak in the Irish or Egyptian fashion, with sleeves tied behind with a cord. When they go out into the bush they wrap themselves up in their furs, but when they are at home they loosen the sleeves and wear their cloak open.

They decorate their clothes with coloured bands made out of glue and strips of skin. Sometimes you will see bands painted red or brown alternating with bands of glue, which always keep their shape and colour no matter how dirty and worn they get. Some of the tribes are more skillful in dressing skins than others, and more ingenious in decorating them. The Montagnais and the Algonkins take more pains with it than any of the others. They decorate their skins with bands of porcupine quills, which they dye a bright scarlet. They prize these trimmings and when they discard a skin they take the trimmings off and use them over again. They even use them to adorn their faces when they want to look their best. Usually they paint their faces black and red, mixing the pigment with vegetable oil (sometimes made from sunflower seeds) or animal fat. They also dye their hair, which some of the men grow long; others grow it short, while still others grow it on one side of the head only. The women and girls all do their hair the same way, keeping it well combed, oiled and dyed. When they go to a dance they put it up in a tuft at the back, bound with an eelskin thong, or else in heavy plaits hung with beads. They dress just like the men except that they always keep their robe, which comes down to the knee, fastened around them. For though they aren't ashamed to show their bodies above the waist and below the knee, they always keep the rest covered. They like to wear bracelets and ear-rings and often have beads hanging from their belt. I have often seen girls at dances, where the elders take pride in showing off their daughters at their best, wearing more than twelve pounds of beads, to say nothing of the rest of the finery they had on.

For the most part the people are cheerful and good-natured, though some are surly enough. Both men and women are strong and well—built. Many of the women and girls are attractive and have good figures, clear skin and regular features. Most of the young girls have good breasts. The women do much of the work around the house and in the fields, sowing the corn, gathering the wood, stripping and spinning the hemp, making fishnets. They are expected to harvest the corn and store it, cook the meals and take care of the house. They are in fact no better than beasts of burden. As for the men, they do nothing but go hunting and fishing, build the lodges and fight the wars. When they have nothing else to do, they go trading in other parts of the country. On their return they eat and drink and dance until they can stay awake no longer. This is all they know of work.

They have a kind of marriage ceremony, which works like this. When a girl turns 'thirteen or fourteen, boys will begin to notice her, if she is attractive. Eventually one of them will ask the girl's parents for her hand. (Sometimes the girl doesn't wait for her parents' consent, but the wisest and best of them do.) Next the suitor will give the girl a present of beads, perhaps a necklace or a bracelet. If she likes him she will accept the present. He will then come and sleep with her for three or four nights and they will enjoy each other as if they were man and wife. If they don't get on well with each other, the girl will leave her lover, but she will keep his presents in return for the pleasure she has given him. The disappointed suitor is then free to look for another girl and the girl is free, if she likes, to look for another suitor. This goes on till they find what they are looking for. Some girls spend their whole youth like this, so that by the time they are married they have had twenty or more suitors. Not that these will be their only lovers. For no matter how many suitors they have, the girls go about from one lodge to another after nightfall and so do the boys, making love whenever they feel like it to any girl who will have them. The married men do the same and nobody thinks the worse of them for it, for that is the custom and everybody expects it.

The only time a woman will stay with her suitor is when she is with child. Then her most recent suitor will return and treat her with all the tenderness and affection he used to feel for her. Usually he will claim the unborn child as his and often another man will say the same. In the end it is up to the woman to decide which of them she will marry and she will choose the one that pleases her most. By that time she will have amassed a great quantity of necklaces and beads of all sorts. She will also have had the privilege of marrying the husband of her choice. Once married, the women stay with their husbands and never leave them without some very good reason. There is, of course, never any question of impotence, for each suitor must prove himself before he is married. Nevertheless, the women aren't any more particular where they find their pleasure after they are married than they were before, so long as they keep up appearances. This means that there is no way of knowing whether or not the children are the lawful issue of a man and his wife. For the same reason children never inherit property or titles from their fathers. Since there is no way for a man to know who his children are, he will choose his heirs from among his nephews and nieces, for he can be sure they are his sisters' children if not his own.

The children are fed and cared for by the women. During the day they bind the child to a piece of wood and wrap him in furs or skins, leaving an opening through which he can urinate. With girls they twist a leaf of corn and put it between their thighs in such a way that one end presses against their crotch while the other remains outside their clothing. The leaf carries off the urine and keeps the child dry. Under the child they spread the silk of a special kind of reed—the one we call hare's foot—which is soft for it to lie on and helps to keep it clean. They decorate the backboard with beads and the smallest of children wear necklaces. At night they put the child to bed with nothing on, between its father and mother. It's a wonder they don't get hurt or smothered while their parents are sleeping, but this seldom seems to happen. When they get old enough the children run free. They are never punished and for this reason are often naughty. You often see them strike their mother and sometimes, when they get big enough, they will even strike their father if he does anything they don't like. It's almost as if they were a curse from on high.

They have no laws, so far as I could see. They have no idea of justice, except to take an eye for an eye and a tooth for a tooth, so naturally they are always having quarrels and blood feuds.

They have no gods and no forms of worship and live like animals. They do have some respect for the devil, or for something of the same name, but it's hard to say what it is. The word they use means several different things, so one can't make out whether they are talking about the devil or about something else. I think it's the devil they mean, because I've noticed that when they see a man do something extra—ordinary, something more courageous or cunning than usual, or when they see a man in a frenzy or out of his mind, they address him as Oqui, that is, great all-knowing spirit or devil.

Some of them deliberately play the part of an Oqui, or Manitou as the Algonkins and Montagnais call them. They serve as medicine-men, healing the sick, caring for the wounded and foretelling the future. In other words, they practice all the tricks and deceptions of the devil in order to confuse and mislead the people. For instance, they persuade the sick that they won't recover unless they go through certain ceremonies and invite everybody to great banquets. Then, of course, the Oquis come to the banquets and make sure they get the best of it. Not satisfied with that, they will convince their patients that they have to go through further ceremonies, which I will describe more fully later on, if they hope to make a quick recovery. But though the people trust their medicine-men, you seldom see any of them actually possessed by the devil, as you do farther inland. This is why I have always felt it wouldn't be too hard to teach them the essential truths of the Christian religion, if only one was willing to take the trouble. But there's no point in sending out a few priests without adequate backing, for though the savages are eager enough to learn about God today, tomorrow, when they find out they have to give up some of their filthy habits, their bad manners and their dissolute conduct, they will change their minds. What we need are people who can keep them up to the mark, people who can set an example and encourage them to mend their ways.

Father Joseph and I often went to their councils and talked to them about their customs and their beliefs, and they always listened carefully. They couldn't always understand what it was we were trying to tell them. It wasn't always something you could put in words. More than once they suggested that if we really wanted to help them we should bring our women and children and settle down among them. Then they could see for themselves how to serve God and obey His laws. They could see how we lived out our daily lives, how we sowed the seed and tilled the soil, how we fed and cared for our stock, how we made all the many things they had seen and envied. They felt sure, they said, that they would learn more this way in one year than they would learn in twenty years of listening to us talk. If necessary, we could take their children and bring them up as our own. Seeing their life was so wretched in comparison with ours, the children would certainly make no bones about adopting our customs in preference to their own. This seemed sensible to me and showed, I felt, that they were genuinely anxious to know and understand the truth. It's a shame to let so many of our fellow-men be lost, to let them perish as it were on our doorstep, without doing what we can to save them. Surely this of all things is a work fit for kings, princes and prelates, and they alone are equal to the task, the task of establishing the Christian faith in a wild, unknown country. After all, these poor people ask for nothing but to be told what to do and what not to do. It is up to those who have the wealth and power for such a work to take it upon themselves, for one day they will have to answer to God for all the souls they, in their negligence and greed, have allowed to perish. This great work will be accomplished in due course, God willing, and the sooner the better, for it will bring glory to God, honour to the King and lustre to the good name of France.

I promised to say more about the ceremonies they use to heal the sick. The sick person sends for an Oqui. The Oqui comes and asks him to describe his symptoms. Then he sends for a number of men, women and girls, along with three or four old women, sometimes more. They all come dancing into the sick man's lodge, each wearing the head of some wild beast—usually that of a bear, since it is the most terrifying to look at. Two or three of the old women go to the sick man, who usually isn't sick at all but only thinks he is or pretends to be. In any case he is soon cured and then he usually arranges a feast at the expense of his friends and relatives. Each of them has to give something to put in the pot. The dancers also bring presents—a string of beads perhaps or some other such trinket. These they give to the old women, who take turns singing until all the presents have been handed over. Then they all join in, beating time with sticks on pieces of dry wood. At this point all the women and girls go to one end of the lodge, as if they were about to act out a ballet or a masquerade. The old women walk out in front with their bearskins on their heads and the rest bring up the rear. They have only two ceremonial dances, one of four steps, the other of twelve like the Breton *trioly*. Sometimes the young men join in and many of them dance quite gracefully. When the sick man sees that he has made all he can out of his sickness he gets up. The old women lead him out. At first he pretends to be unwilling, but once he starts to dance he soon gets into the swing of it and has as much fun as any of the others. It goes without saying that most of the sufferers aren't really sick at all. Those who are sick don't get much good out of such foolishness.

However that may be, the Oquis are often renowned for their cures. This in spite of the fact that their treatment usually does more harm than good, for sometimes they keep up their racket from dawn until two o'clock the next morning, by which time the sick man is almost out of his mind. Sometimes they get the women and girls to dance together, but only if the Oqui gives the word. Sometimes the Oqui or Manitou will get together with several of the others and start making faces and casting spells. Soon they are writhing and twisting and before long they are beside themselves. Then they will start scattering brands all over the place like madmen, swallowing hot coals or holding them in their hands and throwing red-hot cinders into the eyes of the onlookers. Anyone who saw them in such a state would think they were possessed by the devil, that is, by the great Oqui or Manitou.

When the dancing is over and the noise has died down they each go back to their own quarters. The wives of the Oquis have the worst of it, for the Oquis are quite mad by that time and will set fire to anything they can lay their hands on. Usually the women hide everything they can. The Oqui will come in with eyes flashing and stand there until the fancy strikes him, when he will start throwing things all over the place. Then just as suddenly he will lie down and sleep for a while. Before long he will wake up with a start and seize some hot coals or stones and start throwing them about. When he gets tired of that he will go off to sleep again. In time the madness passes off. To bring on a cure, the Oqui will go and sweat himself with several of his friends. For two or three hours they will steam themselves under long strips of bark, wrapped up in skins with stones heated in the fire. They sing the whole time, stopping only to catch their breath or to take a drink of water, for of course they get extremely thirsty. Eventually they become themselves again.

Usually two or three of the sick recover, more by luck than good management, and this encourages the people to believe in the Oquis. They forget that for every two that get better ten die of the noise, which is more likely to kill a sick man than to cure him. We know that a sick man needs rest and quiet, but they think they can cure him by making a racket. This just shows how the devil turns everything upside down.

Sometimes the women will go into a frenzy like the men, but they do less harm. They get down on all fours like animals. At this point the Oqui starts to sing. Then he makes a face and breathes on the woman, telling her to drink certain waters and to feast on fish or meat, no matter how scarce it is. When the feast is finished they all go back to their lodges until the Oqui comes again. This time he brings a number of other people with him. They all sing and breathe on the woman. Each of them has a dried tortoise-shell filled with pebbles, which they shake in her ear. They tell her to hold a dance and three or four feasts. The Oqui will then order costumes and masquerades, like those you see during the Mardi Gras in France, and the girls will come elaborately painted and dressed. While they are making ready for the masquerade, the

Oqui will go and sing by the litter of the sick woman and then will go up and down the length of the village, singing and chanting the whole way. When it's all over everyone is hungry and they sit down and eat up all the Migan in the pot.

According to custom, each family must live on what it can get by farming and fishing. They have all the land they can use, but they find it hard to clear without proper tools. This is how they go about it. First they strip the trees of their branches. Next they burn all the cuttings at the foot of each tree, so as to kill it. Then they clean up the ground between the trees and sow their corn. They set out about ten grains to a clump, leaving a yard between clumps, and sow enough to last for three or four years, in case they have a bad season. The women sow the seed and harvest the grain, as I've already explained. They also collect wood for the winter. This they do in March or April, and by all working together they finish the job in two or three days. Each family gathers enough for its own needs. If a girl gets married, every woman in the village has to give her a load of firewood to get her started, since she wouldn't be able to get enough for herself out of season.

This is how their government works. The elders and chiefs meet in council and make all decisions necessary for the welfare of the village. Normally they act by majority vote, but sometimes they defer to someone they have special reason to respect. Such a man may be asked by the others to give his opinion on the point at issue and in that case his advice, once given, is followed to the letter. None of the chiefs has any authority over the rest, though as a mark of respect the oldest and bravest among them are known as captains. There are usually several such men in each village. They are treated with deference and respect, but they aren't allowed to put on airs.

They have no laws and no punishments. The elders make long speeches and give their opinion when asked for it, but they have no authority to enforce their decisions. Everyone has a right to speak in council and if anyone makes a proposal that pleases the others he is expected to come forward and offer to carry it out. They tell him that he is a brave man and worthy of the enterprise in hand, and say that such a work will bring him new honour and add new lustre to his name. He can excuse himself if he likes, but few do, for they are anxious to make a name for themselves.

When they decide to make war, two or three of the oldest and bravest captains will volunteer to lead the expedition. Before they start they send messengers to all the neighbouring villages with presents, to let them know their plans and to ask for help. The captains choose the time and place where they will meet the enemy, as our generals do. They also dispose of prisoners and attend to all other matters of importance, for the captains are the only superiors these people are willing to recognize and obey. If things turn out well they get all the praise; if they turn out badly they take all the blame.

So much for their councils. They also have general assemblies to which delegates come each year from distant parts of the country, one from each district. They meet in a village chosen for the purpose. This is an opportunity to renew old friendships and take whatever steps may be necessary for the defence of the country against the common enemy. The meetings last three weeks or a month and there is constant feasting and dancing. When the meetings are over they exchange presents and then each man sets out for his own district.

When a man dies and is to be buried, they take the body, wrap it in skins, cover it carefully with bark and then raise it up on four posts, over which they build a shelter roofed in with strips of bark. Sometimes they bury the body in the ground, in which case they first dig the grave and then shore up the sides to prevent it from falling in. Then they lower the body and cover it with bark before filling the grave with earth. Finally they build a small shelter over the top.

The bodies are left like this for eight or ten years, until the next festival of the dead. What happens then is that they summon a general assembly at which, among other things, the delegates decide when and where the next festival of the dead will be held. Then they each return to their own district and uncover the bones of those who have died since the last festival. These are carefully cleaned and preserved, though they smell like newly—buried bodies. At the appointed time the relatives and friends of the dead bring the bones, together with necklaces, skins, tomahawks, pots and other valuables, and a quantity of food, to the chosen place. There they lay down their burdens and give themselves up to dancing and feasting for the ten days of the festival. Tribes come from all over the country to take part in the ceremonies. The dancing, the feasting, the general councils all serve to renew and strengthen old friendships. As a symbol of goodwill they mingle the bones of their relatives and friends one with another, saying that just as the bones of the dead are gathered in one place, so also the living will be united in friendship, as one people, as long as they live. They make a number of speeches over the bones and then after making certain faces and signs they dig a big trench sixty feet square and bury all the bones in it, together with the necklaces, beads, tomahawks, pots, knives and other trinkets they have brought with them. This they cover with earth and on top of that they build a wooden canopy supported on four posts. The burial of the dead is the most solemn of all their festivals. Some of them believe in the immortality of souls; some doubt it and say that after their death they are more likely to turn into crows than angels.

So far I have said nothing about how these people spend their time in winter, that is, from the beginning of December to the end of March, when the snow melts and spring begins. Ordinary life continues in winter as in summer, with its feasts and dances for the sick. They also have festivals of song and dance called *tabagies,* to which they invite people from other villages. Sometimes there are five hundred men, women and girls at these festivals, all dressed in their best clothes. On special days they hold masquerades and go about from lodge to lodge, asking for anything that takes their fancy. So-and-so gave me this, they sing, and so—and—so gave me that— or something to that effect. Everybody gives what they have to give. If anyone refuses, the masquers get angry and make a sign: they go and find a stone and leave it, as an insult and mark of contempt, beside the man or woman who refused them. This goes on until some of them—women as well as men—have asked for and been given skins of all sorts, along with fish, Indian corn, tobacco and even such things as cauldrons, kettles, pots, tomahawks, sickles and knives. Some of the villages have clowns like the ones we have for the Mardi Gras in France, and from time to time they challenge the clowns of other villages to a contest. And so ,they spend the winter.

There's also work to do: the women spin and grind meal and the men go off to trade in other parts of the country. We noticed that they were always careful to leave enough men to defend each village in case of attack. By custom—for they have no laws—no-one is supposed to leave his village without the consent of the council of chiefs. The men also make their own nets and fish right through the winter. This is how they go about it. First they make a number of holes in the ice, one about five feet long and three feet wide. They fasten the net to a wooden pole six or seven feet long and lower it through the ice. Then they pass the pole under the ice from one hole to the next, until they come to the large opening. Here they let the net, which is weighted down with small stones, sink to the bottom. After leaving it for some time they will suddenly pull up both ends and bring the fish that are caught in the net to the surface.

Winter closes in during November and lasts until the beginning of April,[2] when the sap starts to rise and the buds begin to show. On the twenty-second we received our first news of Brule, who, you may remember, had set out for Carantouan. A party of savages had met him and brought word that he had turned back, why they didn't know. On the twentieth of May we ourselves set out for the habitation with several savages who had promised to show us the way. The journey took forty days. We caught fish of all sorts on the way and killed a lot of game. This gave us fresh food to eat and besides we enjoyed the hunting and fishing. We reached St. Louis toward the end of June and there I found the Sieur du Pont waiting for me with two ships. The savages had told him I had been killed and he had just about given me up for lost. Some of the priests were at St. Louis and we were very happy to see each other again. As soon as we had greeted each other, however, I made arrangements to leave for the habitation with Darontal, my host. Before saying goodbye to the savages I promised to visit them again as soon as I could and to bring them presents. I begged them to forget their quarrels and they promised they would.

We set out on the eighth of July and reached the habitation on the eleventh. There the priests led us in giving thanks to Almighty God for having preserved us from all the dangers we had passed through.

When the first excitement was over I introduced Darontal to the others. He admired the buildings and our way of life, and when we had seen everything there was to see he told me privately that he wouldn't rest until as many of his people as possible had come to live with us, so they could learn to worship our God and live as we lived. He much preferred our way of life to his own and realized that his people could learn our ways more easily by living with us than by waiting for us to come and teach them. He had already pointed out to Father Joseph that if they were slow to learn, their children would be quicker. He now suggested that we build another habitation at St. Louis to secure the river from enemy attack. He assured me they would join us there as soon as there were quarters for them to live in and promised that from then on we would live together like brothers. I thought this was a good idea and told him we would build a habitation for them as soon as we could.

I entertained Darontal for four or five days and before he left I gave him a number of presents to mark the occasion. He was very pleased. I urged him not to forget what had passed between us and suggested that before long he come to see us again with some of his people. With that he rejoined his companions, who were waiting for him at St. Louis.

After his departure we enlarged the habitation by at least a third and strengthened the fortifications, for as it was it wasn't fit to live in. For the buildings we used limestone, which is an excellent material and plentiful in those parts.

Father Denis and Father Joseph had both made up their mind to return to France. They planned to take with them the story of what they had seen in the New World, in the hope of persuading more of their brethren to devote their lives to service among the savages.

Before leaving, we harvested some corn we had brought out from France. The seeds had come up well and I wanted to take some of the grain back with me to show how fertile the country is. By now our gardens were lovely. We had some fine Indian corn and some young trees and grafts that de Monts had given me in Normandy. We also had peas, beans, squash, cabbages, white beets and a number of other vegetables and herbs.

We left in the long—boats on the twentieth of July. Two of the priests, Father Jean Delbeau and Father Pacifique, stayed on at the habitation. They seemed pleased with what they had accomplished so far and now planned to wait at the habitation for Father Joseph, who was expected back the following year.

We reached Tadoussac on the twenty-third. There we found du Pont, ready and waiting for us. On the third of August we set sail. The winds were favourable and we reached Honfleur on the tenth of September, 1616. As soon as we landed we gave thanks to God for having brought us safely back to our native land. We prayed also that He would move the hearts of the King and Council to do what was necessary to nourish and succour the savages and bring them to a knowledge of the holy catholic faith, for the greater glory of God and the honour of the crown of France.

Endnotes

1. By Huron country Champlain here means the whole of what is now Ontario, south of the Ottawa River. From east to west this area measures about 500 miles; from north to south it varies from a few miles to 175 miles or more. In the next sentence Champlain seems to be referring to only a part of the region, namely the Bruce Peninsula.
2. Champlain says that winter lasts *until April,* but since in a previous paragraph he spoke of winters as lasting *until the end of March* he must mean *the beginning of April.*

Origins and Mythology
Georges Sioui
1999

Wendat, pronounced approximately as "one dot," was the word used by the five con-federated nations of Wendake to describe themselves. Wendake was the Wendat name for Huronia, the Ontario territory that the French—mainly the Jesuits—knew and described between 1615,[1] when the Recollet Joseph Le Caron and Samuel de Champlain arrived, and 1649, when the Wendat confederacy collapsed.

The word was first recorded as houandate in 1623 by the Recollet historian Gabriel Sagard.[2] Despite his relatively short time in Wendake, he has handed down to us a surprising number of details about different facets of life in the territory, describing fauna and flora, various objects, domestic organization, voyages, relationships among people, and so on—the kind of information that was of little interest to sub-sequent chroniclers.

Samuel de Champlain, by contrast, was never aware that the people of Wendake referred to themselves as Wendats, although he spent thirty years in New France. He was the first to make consistent use of the disparaging term "Huron" in naming the Wendats.[3] It is astonishing to find that the man who founded the city of Quebec learned little about the social and political organization of this people, even though, as a leader and trading partner, he was one of the rare Europeans to be officially invited to visit each of the main Wendat villages (Trigger 1987: 300, 327–8).[4]

The Jesuits, who were the last religious observers to come to Wendake after the Recollets, gave far less meticulous accounts of Wendat life and society. Although the two orders were fairly equal in their religious fanaticism, the Jesuits were far more experienced and direct in their methods for replacing Amerindian culture (Trigger 1987: 490–2).

The Jesuits' French translation of Wendat, "the inhabitant of an island," seems correct, but apparently there were many other connotations that necessarily escaped these missionaries. Heidenreich has established that the territory of Wendake was an "island" for all practical purposes in the precontact period, being surrounded on three sides by bodies of water (two bays and Lake Simcoe), in addition to a large stretch of swamp land. Similarly, Wendat cosmology viewed the world as an island carried on the back of a turtle (Trigger 1990a: 12). Moreover, the Wendats believed they were the first people created on this island and were placed hierarchically in the centre of the other nations. "When the tribes were all settled, the Wyandots were placed at the head," said Oriwahento, Wendat chief from Amherstburg (Ontario) in 1837.[5]

This idea is directly related to the fact that the Wendats occupied the position of chief people in the political hierarchy of a group of Northeastern Native peoples that formed one of the most widespread and unified trading networks in North America. Sagard, in his *Journey to the Huron Country* provides a major clue to the origin of the Wendats' geopolitical importance, noting in the 1620s that the Wendat language was the lingua franca of interethnic trade and diplomacy for at least fifty non-Wendat nations. The Jesuits were also quick to realize that Wendake lay at the heart of the Amerindian Northeast. "The Missionaries," wrote the Jesuit priest and historian Pierre-Francois-Xavier de Charlevoix in 1744, were persuaded that "in fixing the Centre of their Missions in a Country [Wendake] that was also the Centre of Canada, they would easily be able to bring the light of the Gospel to all parts of this vast Continent" (Charlevoix 1976: 1: 186; trans. J. Brierley).

The Wendats' oral tradition is eloquent on the subject of their central position in the Amerindian Northeast. Chief Oriwahento stated in 1837 that after the tribes were settled, "[The Wendats] were the first tribe of old [that is, first among the tribes], and had the first [principal] chieftainship." Then, speaking of how the Wendats retained this position throughout the dispersals experienced by these tribes, Oriwahento added, "We were followed [that is, driven] from the east and went up north away to Michilimackinac, but as we had the right before, so when we came back, the tribes looked up to us, as holding the council fire."[6]

Wendat Creation Myths and the Wendat Conception of Morality

There are several versions of the Wendat Creation myth recorded in Barbeau and other sources. Although they vary in detail, in essence they tell the same story.

The Wendats believed, as did the Iroquois, that the land on which all humankind lived was an island[7] to which a woman named Aataentsic had descended from a celestial world.[8] This island was the back of the Big Turtle who, at the request of the animals (all aquatic at this time), provided a landing place for Aataentsic. The humblest of these animals, the Toad, was able to dive deep enough to gather some silt, which the Small Turtle then spread over the Big Turtle's shell. This island grew until it formed the world (the Americas) as known to the Amerindians (Barbeau 1915: 37–40).

Aataentsic explored the island and found a lodge lived in by an old woman whom she spontaneously called Shutai, meaning grandmother (Barbeau 1915: 306). Aataentsic had been pregnant when she left her sky-world, and it was in this house that she waited to give birth to her daughter. The daughter soon became a young woman, courted by many suitors who were in fact male spirits. On the advice of her mother, the young woman chose a turtle spirit.[9] This being placed an arrow beside his sleeping lover and returned to fetch it without her knowledge. He never appeared again. Aataentsic's daughter later gave birth to twin boys. The first was Tsestah

("Man of Fire"), destined to be the benevolent spirit creator who worked for the Wendats' good.[10] The other was Tawiskaron ("Man of Flint"), who created traps and sowed danger and difficulty in the Wendats' lives and environment.

Ataentsic's daughter died in childbirth. Tawiskaron refused to come into the world in the natural way. He tore a path through to his mother's armpit, killing her as he emerged (Barbeau 1915: 44). Historians have traditionally seen the twins as symbols of good and evil—a kind of pagan distortion of the Christian God and Satan. Actually, Amerindians in general, and the Wendats and Iroquois in particular, have a sense of morality that differs completely from the Christian tradition. Christian morality advocates and seeks an absolute good, while Amerindian morality sees absolute good and absolute evil as equally dangerous concepts for the human conscience.

Tsestah wished to make life easier for the Wendats by making it free of dangers and difficulties. Being the firstborn, he was also the first to prepare the world for human arrival and settlement. His idea was that each river would have "a twofold channel (or rather, perhaps, a double channel), in which the streams should flow in opposite directions" (Barbeau 1915: 302) so that people could come and go easily and not have to carry heavy loads over long distances. "The maple was made so that syrup would just drip out when the tree was tapped," and "blackberries, strawberries, and raspberries" grew on luxuriant bushes within easy reach (Barbeau 1915: 45). Such abundance would produce plump, succulent animals with little fear of the hunter's arrow or snare. The land consisted of "gentle undulations" (Barbeau 1915: 307).

Tawiskaron, who was to do his share of the work after Tsestah, found all this "too good for the people. 'Let them at least: he said, 'have to work one way upstream.'" (Barbeau 1915: 302). The malevolent twin began sabotaging his brother's fine innovations, diluting the maple syrup into watery sap throughout the tree, shrinking the various fruits to a fraction of their original size, and wilfully creating numberless difficulties (such as steep mountains, dangerous rapids, and enormous insects) to a degree that made war with the benevolent brother inevitable (Barbeau 1915: 46, 308).

The Man of Fire and the Man of Flint challenged each other to a duel (a formal combat in one version, a race in another). In deciding which weapons to use, each asked the other what he found most terrifying. "Buck's horns," replied Tawiskaron truthfully.[11] Tsestah, however, tricked his brother by saying that "Indian grass braid" was what he dreaded most.[12] Each twin gathered large quantities of the weapon feared by the other and spread it over a course of epic length. Tsestah kept up his strength by eating the Indian grass braid and was able to outlast his brother, who was not only exhausted but terrified by the constant sight of buck horns. Finally, Tawiskaron fell onto a heap of sharp antlers and soon died of his wounds.[13]

Tawiskaron's spirit lived on, however. He went to the "northwest" (Barbeau 1915: 298) where, according to the Wendats, he had deliberately created a harsh, ugly land of monotonous prairies and impenetrable mountains (Barbeau 1915: 308). The

Wendats believed that Tawiskaron's spirit continued to visit his grandmother Aataentsic, who always appeared to be fonder of Tawiskaron than of Tsestah, his too-benevolent brother.

Tawiskaron had tricked Aataentsic as to the real culprit in her daughter's death. We may wonder, nevertheless, whether she was really deceived. She braided the Indian grass (something manifestly good and sacred) for Tawiskaron to help him triumph over Tsestah (Barbeau 1915: 298), knowing in advance who would actually win (since life must always triumph over death). Tawiskaron being really the weaker of the two, was she not acting as do all loving grandmothers and mothers? Was it not normal and natural for her to help the more vulnerable grandson?

My point is that the two brothers (the twin forces of Creation) were recognized as equally necessary to world order and equilibrium. "The works of each were to be subject to the modification of the other, but neither was to absolutely change the character of any work of the other, nor was he to totally destroy it," wrote Wyandot historian William E. Connelley in 1899. "Each brother now went his way, and did that which was proper in his own eyes. They were engaged in this work for untold ages. When their works were finished, they met again as they had agreed."[14]

Aataentsic, in accordance with the Wendats' matricentric social outlook, saw beyond the present moment and established a balance between the two essential forces. Nevertheless, conventional ethnohistory has associated her with the latter. She is portrayed as being in league with her malevolent grandson, using all her ingenuity to counteract the benevolent Tsestah's projects.

At this point I would like to put forward a hypothesis on the differences between the Creation myths that developed in Christian and Wendat contexts, as well as the effect of such differences on the social philosophies of these traditions. This is a hypothesis that could certainly be expanded on more universal lines, although I am limiting it to the Northeast.

Briefly stated, the patricentric Judeo-Christian tradition developed a myth that deals in absolutes (good and evil), whereas the matricentric Wendat tradition developed a myth that reflects the more complex interaction of real life.

We can already see two major similarities in these myths: the woman who comes from a paradise and founds a human race in a world that is a testing ground fraught with danger; and the presence of two brothers, one of whom kills the other. Let us now look at the basic differences. Both male and female are equally represented in the Wendat twins. Tawiskaron displays brutal masculine force, but also innocence. He loses the duel because he isn't devious enough to lie.[15] Yet Tawiskaron has the gift of clairvoyance possessed by his mother and grandmother, as shown by his opposition to the infinite and unthinking benevolence of his brother.[16] Humans need adversity in order to live.

Similarly, death must be the lot of humankind. In what I call heterohistorical interpretations,[17] Aataentsic is always seen as presiding over the reign of death, and as having assumed the macabre function of making humans die, a task in which she is assisted by the equally sinister Tawiskaron. In fact, however, an immoral world would be one without death, pain, or adversity, for these three are sources of compassion, the fountain of all social virtues, or in other words of society itself.

Note that the dying Tawiskaron, whose blood turned to flint as it touched the ground, gave humankind a material vital to its subsistence (Barbeau 1915: 307). Similarly, animals give their blood (that is, sacrifice themselves) so that human life may continue.

If men kill, thereby providing subsistence and material culture, women nurture, providing spiritual culture. Tsestah supplies fire, a gift more useful to women and without which the human condition would be no different from that of animals. Nevertheless, Tsestah does not have the intuitive powers that distinguish women. As in patricentric societies, his sense of morality raises facility to the level of an absolute value, helping to make humankind soft and weak. In this sense, he is certainly as "bad" as Tawiskaron.

For Wendats, and for circular thinkers generally, life triumphs without eliminating death. Tawiskaron does not die, despite being killed. The world is supremely beautiful and good, but also harsh, mysterious, and dangerous.

For Christians, evil triumphs over good. Abel (who corresponds to the feminine aspect of humankind, implied in the Wendats' Tawiskaron) is killed. Cain (Tsestah), embodying the masculine aspect of humankind, is the absolute victor. Brutality is therefore more powerful than intelligence. Christian morality, being patriarchal, advocates a single God who is infinitely good and *who crushes evil*. The Wendats have Aataentsic and Tawiskaron, who protect them *against absolute good*.[18]

Monotheism and Animism

The Europeans who first encountered the Wendats viewed all non-Christian peoples as barbarians and infidels and considered it their duty to convert them. This great task, which Europe had taken upon itself, was already well under way in the other "Indian" parts of the world. "Christianity," wrote Sagard in his prefatory note to the reader in his *Long Journey to the Country or the Hurons,* "has made little advance in that country in spite of the labours, care, and diligence which the Recollects have brought to it, with results far below the ten millions of souls whom our friars have baptized in the course of years in the East and West Indies" (Sagard 1939: 9).

Indians therefore meant—for the clerics at any rate—the *infidels* of the entire known world. Since the Wendats were also Indians, they were naturally viewed as pagans, that is to say people with a very flawed idea of the Godhead and an even more flawed sense of their duty toward it. (An outright denial of the Amerindians' sense of the supernatural was not acceptable, since this would have invalidated the evangelical mission that constituted moral justification for the actual process of invasion.)

The Animist Conception

Peoples of animist religion are always considered backward compared to those with "real" religions. By *religion* I mean spiritual world view; *animist* is the general term for natural or circular peoples. Such societies, based on kinship systems, are seen as evolving toward a "true" form of government by the state. And yet, in contrast to so-called developed societies, animist societies display significantly greater respect for the rights of the human individual and other beings, and consider equality and plenty for all as the norm.[19]

Animism is the spiritual world view of societies with a circular vision of the world. The characteristic attachment of animists to their social vision—a consequence of the moral security and moral well-being that they derive from it—depends directly on their capacity to perceive the soul (anima) inhabiting all beings and all things, material or immaterial.[20] This capacity was the spiritual heritage of the entire New World civilization. In other words, in its original state (before the shock of European contact), this civilization was unaware of the concept of human and non-human exploitation aimed at the accumulation of power by certain groups within a society, to the detriment of the majority, whose lot in life, condition, and even religion must therefore be that of acquiescence, or indeed the culture of poverty and destitution.

Circle societies[21] view life as a universal reality, not divisible into classes or various other classifications. Each expression of this reality is a product of the whole. Nothing exists by and for itself. Good is partly the product of evil, as evil is partly the product of good, which means that neither quality exists as an absolute. There is only the mystery of life, unfathomable to humankind but evident in its infinitely perfect order.

Human Beings Are *Ongwe*

The Wendats did not believe they were placed on the Great Island to dominate the rest of Creation. Rather, as their mythology shows, they believed they were created to bear witness to the infinite grandeur and wisdom of the Master of the Universe and his co-creators, and therefore to live in harmony with the multitude of other beings, who greeted the arrival of this contemplative predator with boundless joy (Barbeau 1915: 311).

The Wendats and all human peoples were *ongwe*.[22] The Tuscarora ethnologist John N.B. Hewitt, who worked for the Smithsonian Institution in the first quarter of the twentieth century, defined ongwe as meaning more than "human being." It denoted "all beings that assumed human shapes or attributes, and in the primitive [that is, circular] world of thought all beings could upon occasion assume the human form and characteristics, and man shared with them these attributes . . . *Ongwe* signifies 'man-being,' that is to say, the being which is of the substance of which all beings are formed."[23]

Animals, trees, insects, stones, and so on constitute families and peoples, as worthy of living as are humans, since they too are expressions of the great creative will. Through rituals, offerings, and expressions of gratitude, human beings must consciously and frequently acknowledge these other peoples who, directly or indirectly, contribute to their subsistence, education, well-being, and happiness.

In discussing the Iroquois concept of society[24] as reflected in their oral tradition, Dennis remarked that while the Iroquois shared the world with other humans—members of their family, clan, tribe, and the confederated nations of their league, as well as other Iroquoians and Algonkians—their world was also inhabited by the beaver and ondathra (muskrat)[25] people (as well as those of other animal species). These animals didn't merely symbolize humans. The accounts should be interpreted quite literally: ondathras, beavers, and other animals were *people* of a non-human kind (Dennis: 1986: 35).

The Moral Aspect of Wendat Stories

Wendat and Amerindian stories[26] in general have a moral—so much so that one could say their only function is to constitute a moral code.[27] Since life (good) triumphs, the Wendat accepts fate gracefully, no matter what it brings. A figure such as Satan, who is the accomplice of the "good" Christian God, is not only useless but impossible in the Wendat cosmology.

Legends and tales constitute history in that they contain the wisdom of a people, Wendat or otherwise, acquired since its genesis. We should first realize that for peoples without writing (a characteristic of Circle societies, generally speaking), life cannot and should not be a purely material and temporal venture. History that fails to address the human spirit and conscience is of no use. According to J.S. Boston, writing on the subject of African peoples, "Each people's oral traditions have their own kind of historical perspective, and . . . the historian's first task is to understand this perspective before trying to fit the traditions into a unilinear time scale" (Boston 1969: 10: 35).

Stories with a moral go hand in hand with the type of education favoured by the Wendats—what observers have characterized as respect for and belief in the individual's freedom and inalienable rights (Tooker 1964: 124 n. 27; Trigger 1987: 47). In this type of education, children, as developing individuals, do not see or hear themselves being told how to think and behave by people invested with arbitrary powers, or by a system. Instead they simply have access to the abundant source of wisdom available to all, which comes from the ancient spirit of the people. Children can draw on it when and how they wish.

Barbeau, whose *Huron and Wyandot Mythology* included material collected from the Wyandots of Oklahoma and the Huron-Wendats of Lorette in the years immediately preceding publication, noted that "the present body of Huron-Wyandot myths, tales, and traditions constitutes only a small fraction of what it formerly was"

(Barbeau 1915: 35). Nevertheless, his collection provides a remarkable number of stories that indicate how the Wendats envisaged human morality. The principal points of this morality are as follows:

1. We must love and care for our own children or those entrusted to us, otherwise they may be taken from us and returned to the world of souls, like the seven boys who, because they were not fed, at last rose up to the sky and disappeared, becoming *Hutiwatsija*, "the Cluster," the constellation of the Seven Stars ("Origin of the Seven Stars," Barbeau 1915: 58–9).

2. The harm we do children always becomes known in the end, even though we believe it to be well hidden. This is the lesson to be learned from stories of children abandoned by their human parents and cared for by animals, especially bears (116–28).

3. We are always punished for the harm we do others. Everything becomes known in the end, after which natural justice takes effect. A woman who tried to murder her stepson was killed by her husband, and no one intervened to save her (128–31). (Among Wendats, punishment by death was reserved for cases of betrayal or witchcraft.) A man was saved and cared for by the animals after his wife had tried to starve him to death by tying him up in the forest. The woman was described as "worthless"

4. We should not look down on the poor and the powerless. Power, fame, and fortune may one day knock at the door of the most wretched beings. as in the case of a poor man to whom the Beaver gave the power of discovering hidden objects and mysterious causes. A poor man was given healing powers by a supernatural being with whom he shared his food, and as a result soon became prosperous (115–6). A boy named Tawidia was so simple-minded that everyone laughed at his blunders. However, he grew up to be a great hunter and an influential man (224–33).

5. We must not fight fire with fire. It is far more effective to use finesse and display a positive attitude than to resort to confrontation. Many of the animals were jealous of the Big Turtle's success in marathon races, both on land and in the water, as well as other triumphs resulting from his incomparable wisdom. His enemies captured him and tried to destroy him by burning, beating, and losing him in the forest. The Turtle pretended to enjoy it and laughed at all these torments. When finally the other animals decided to throw him into the water to drown, he pretended to be "most frightened and begged for mercy." The animals tossed him into a river and left him for dead, but the Big Turtle swam to the other shore from where he could taunt his persecutors with impunity (72–7).

6. Recognizing the place of animals in human existence is not only a matter of ethics but a question of survival. Animals must be continually thanked, and pleasing

offerings constantly given to animal spirits. Animals have powers that humans do not. Humans can enter into animal secrets if they adopt the required spiritual means of communication by fasting, meditating, and performing rituals. Animals speak to humans through dreams and visions, which can be induced by self-imposed privations and trials. The speech of human beings who beings to the Circle constantly reflects their humility toward the animal-peoples on whom they depend for survival.

7. Generous acts that reciprocate animal generosity in fact reflect a highly ecological form of thought. However, such acts have often been interpreted as wasteful, thus fuelling assumptions of the Amerindian as irrational, destructive, and anti-ecological. By generous acts, I am referring mainly to Amerindian hunters sharing their catch with animals, as the latter frequently request. In a typical Wendat story, a wolf/protector asks his hunter/protege to cut open the first deer killed and leave it for his fellow wolves (Barbeau 1915: 103–5). A final example is the frog who appears to a captive Wendat woman in a dream and shows her how to escape (335–6). Here again, gratitude is the motivation, for, as the frog says to the woman, "Your race have often rescued some of our kind from the jaws of the snake."

8. Animals are not the only non-humans to give messages or special powers to their human kin. Plants and minerals do this as well. Plants appear to have a closer bond with women, most especially in horticultural, matricentrist cultures where as much as 80 percent of the food consumed is the fruit of a very intimate woman-Mother Earth relationship and spiritual collaboration.

9. One must not attempt to recall to earth those who have departed for the soul world. The Wendats developed social rituals designed to prevent grief for the death of kinsfolk from becoming socially disruptive. "journey to the World of Souls" shows the futility and danger of excessive grief on the part of a man who tries to bring back his dead sister (Barbeau 1915: 327–9). "The Stars Dehndek and Mahohrah" (318–20) tells how a highly respected man, Dehndek, overcome by grief, follows his dead daughter Mahohrah "to the Land of the Little People." Using a sledge drawn by three (or possibly four) stags, he flies up into the sky in eternal pursuit of Mahohrah. Dehndek and his stags form the stars of Orion's belt, and Mahohrah with her torches is Orion's sword. In contrast, "How the Wyandots Obtained the Tobacco Plant" (325) tells of an even more grief-stricken man who, despite losing his wife and two daughters, devotes the rest of his life to the happiness and well-being of his people. Through a supernatural agency, his elder daughter appears to him and gives him the tobacco plant—which all Amerindians came to regard as possibly their most sacred possession.

Endnotes

1. Bruce Trigger (1987: 261–2) gives 1610 as the year that the young French adventurer Etienne Brule went to live among the Wendats, All quotations from Trigger, *Children of Aataentsic*1987 (2nd ed.) appear by permission of McGill-Queen's University Press.
2. The word *Houandate* is included in the dictionary (first published in 1636) prepared by Sagard, who was a lay brother in the Recollet order (Sagard 18'66: 4, under "Nations, de quelle nation"; see also Trigger 1987: 436-7, n. 3). In addition to its interest as a rare linguistic reference work, Sagard's dictionary presents a unique source of ethnological information.
3. *Huron* initially described all the sedentary peoples of the Nadouek family. The word is derived from the French *hure* (boar's head), an image evoked by their frequent habit of leaving a central band of hair from front to back of their shaven heads, reminiscent of a boar's mane (Trigger 1987: 27). "Huron" was also used in the French of the day to designate an individual who was boorish, unmannerly, and "savage."
4. Gabriel Sagard (1866: 2: 444) notes that the Amerindians reproached Champlain for never acquiring any knowledge of their languages after twenty years of continued life in their country,
5. Barbeau 191$: 299-300. The spelling of *Wyandot* follows the English pronunciation of the word Wet/dat as pronounced by the Wendats themselves. The Wyandots are descendants of the Wendats, Tionontates. Atliwandaronks, and Eries who migrated westward after the destruction of their homelands in the middle of the seventeenth century,
6. Barbeau 1915: 300. Just as certain chiefs acted as spokesmen for the group on the level of clan, tribe, federation, or confederacy, some chiefs of nations acted as the principal spokesmen for all, and usually were also custodians of the archives for treaties between nations.
7. The relationship between the Creation myth of the original island and the quasi-insular nature of Wendake is considered plausible, even though the Wendats only settled there in the fourteenth century, mainly for trade reasons (Trigger 1990a: 4-6).
8. Possible translations for the word *Aataentsic* are "her-body-is-wise" or "witch" (Barbeau 1915: 65, n. 6), Seneca tradition gives basically the same meaning (Hewitt 1974: 228).
9. The mention of a turtle-spirit comes from the Mohawk tradition, which clearly supplies details of the Wendat myth that have not been otherwise preserved. In the Jesuit reserves created after the destruction of Wendake, Huron-Wendats and Mohawks developed a culture and traditions that were often identical (Hewitt 1974: 225–337).
10. Barbeau 1915: 306-8. Tsetsah is also called Yoskaha, Jouskeha, or Tijuskaa (possibly from a root signifying benevolent). See Barbeau 1915: 6, n. 6; 301, n. 1.
11. Barbeau 1915: 298, The antlers of the white-tailed deer symbolize justice and authority among the Wendats and Iroquois. A chief who has been dismissed is described as having been *dehorned.*
12. Barbeau 1915: 298. Other versions replace Indian grass braid with sacks of corn and beans (Barbeau 1915: 302), with "the flowering branch which he had torn from the wild apple tree [that] fell down from heaven with his Mother" (Barbeau 1915: 310), or with "some fruits of the wild rosebush" (Brebeuf, as quoted in Barbeau 1915: 293). All these "weapons" involve gentle, edible things. Mohawk tradition reveals that Tsestah (Oterontonnia) was secretly receiving instruction in warfare from his father, the Big Turtle (Hewitt 1974: 302).

13. Barbeau 1915: 46. Other versions mention that wherever Tawiskaron's blood fell on the island, it became flint, a substance vital to hunting peoples (Barbeau 1915: 293, 310),

14. Barbeau 1915: 307. When the time came to populate the island, the two brothers again worked together (309).

15. In the same way, a Wendat story shows the Turtle triumphing by tricking his many enemies, who are jealous of his intelligence (Barbeau 1915: 72-5), Similar accounts reveal a moral that can be applied on a more practical level: in a confrontation, intelligence is more important than sheer strength.

16. Typically, Amerindians do not deny the worth or selfhood of other beings, even when the latter are particularly odious and hateful. This was illustrated 111 a conversation I had in 1972 with an elderly Montagnais woman from the Maliotenam Indian reserve in Quebec. She spoke to me with her grandson acting as interpreter (my friend John D. Thomas, also from Maliotenam, and a law student at the time), and had this to say on how lice viewed their fate in modern times. "The lice say that in the old days they took great care of people's hair," she explained, gently smoothing her own hair. "They made it beautiful and shiny. The people began getting soap and washing their hair with things like that. The lice were very offended at being treated in this way, 'Humans want to kill us with these things they put in their hair. They're trying to get rid of us now, but they'll never be able to do it. We'll always survive.'"

17. The word *heterohistorical* implies interpretations made from a standpoint outside the culture being studied, whereas the auto historical method (Sioui 1992: ix–xiii, xxi–xxiv) is based on acquiring an understanding of Amerindian vision from within the culture.

18. For another view of the Wendat Creation myth and its implications see Trigger 1987: 77–8.

19. For an excellent discussion of the negation of the civilization of societies of circular thought, see Marshall D. Sahlins, *Stone Age Economics* (1974).

20. In the 1620s the Wendats explained to Sagard that "dogs' souls will still serve the souls of their masters in the other life, or at least will stay with the souls of other animals in this beautiful [Sagard applies the adjective ironically] country of Youskeha where they [the souls] will all go—this country being only inhabited by the souls of both domestic and wild animals, and the souls of axes, knives, kettles, and other things given to the dead person" (Sagard 1866: 2: 458; trans. J, Brierley), Interestingly, modern Western industrial society is beginning to demonstrate an awareness of rights belonging to non-human beings and entities: animals, the land, water, air, and so forth. Basically, before speaking of any form of conservation, must there not be overt recognition of kinship, and therefore of mutual responsibilities?

21. See "The Sacred Circle of Life," discussed in Sioui 1992: 8–19.

22. For Wendats and Iroquois, *Ongwe* meant human being; its more profound significance is dealt with in this section, Sagard's dictionary (1636) gives *Honhouoy.*

23. J.N.B. Hewitt, "Cosmology notes," Hewitt Papers, N,A,A. M.S. 3693, quoted in Dennis (1993: 21). *Ongwe* in Wendat, like *innu* in Montagnais, *anishnabe* in Algonkian, and similar instances, refers only to Amerindians, that is, those who have similar thinking and beliefs or who do not doubt them.

24. I have already remarked that one of the fundamental traits of Amerindian philosophy is the capacity of almost all Amerindians to agree on their social concepts. (Sioui 1992: 23) The Iroquois are especially close to the Wendat5 in this respect.

25. *Ondathra*: One of the rare Wendat animal names that passed into the French language, and that ought to replace the more common translation of *rat musque* in French or muskrat in English, which is zoologically incorrect.
26. Rather than using the terms *tales* or *legends,* in general refer to the Wendat material quoted from Barbeau and other sources as *stories* (in the sense that these are stories/histories of the people/nation, thus expressing Wendat and Amerindian logic and therefore belief in the importance of stories/histories as a spiritual and moral record).
27. The descriptions 'of Wendat moral and spiritual ideas given here are in general applicable to all Amerindians.

Focus Questions

1. How does the fact that Champlain is writing to the King possibly affect the content of his letter?

2. How does Champlain portray Aboriginal people? What does this portrayal tell you about *Champlain*? What does it tell you about the Huron?

3. How does the Huron/Wendat conception of life differ from the European view expressed by Champlain?

4. How did the Huron/Wendat conception/way of life make them vulnerable to the Europeans?

5. Do the Huron/Wendat people have any power in their relationship with Europeans? What is this power?

6. Why do you think this topic is still relevant to Canada/Canadians today?

2

Building a British Colony

PART ONE:
THE EXPULSION OF THE ACADIANS

Introduction

The Acadians were an agricultural people of French Catholic origin, who settled around the Bay of Fundy beginning in 1604. In 1710, the territory in which they lived, once controlled by the French, was captured by the English and renamed Nova Scotia. Initially, the Acadians managed to remain disconnected from the politics and wars between these two imperial powers (France and Britain), and made oaths of neutrality to their British rulers—they would not take up arms on behalf of the French, nor the English, but wished only to be left alone.

By the 1750s, however, as the English began a more intensive campaign to capture all the French territories in North America (including Quebec—see Part 2), the presence of this community, now about 13,000 strong, grew increasingly irksome. When a group of Acadians were found alongside French troops within the walls of Fort Beausejour in present-day New Brunswick, the decision was made by officials in Halifax to deport the entire population. Almost three-quarters of them were eventually expelled and scattered throughout various landings in Europe and the southern English colonies (present-day United States). At least part of the goal of this dispersal was to loosen the cultural ties that bound the Acadians together, and to facilitate their assimilation into English culture—in essence, to ensure that the population of the colonies in North America would be English in character, language, and culture.

This goal was not realized. While the community was seriously damaged, Acadian culture has survived, and even thrived in parts of North America. This persistence was aided, at least in part, by the enormously popular, romantic poem by

American poet Henry Wadsworth Longfellow. No fan of the English himself, Longfellow dramatized and romanticized the deportation through the fictional story of a young woman, Evangeline, who was separated from her fiancé, her family, and her community, by the Expulsion. Longfellow's poem has only grown in popularity since it was first penned in 1847, and it is his vision of the expulsion which has become the standard, popular interpretation of that event.

In recent years, the descendants of the original Acadians deported by the British, have demanded an apology—and in some cases compensation—from the British crown, and the Canadian government, for the Expulsion. Along with the brief extract from Longfellow's *Evangeline,* the second and third excerpts in this chapter outline these current debates and controversies as they have played out in the press and the House of Commons.

Evangeline: A Tale of Arcadie
Henry Wadsworth Longfellow
1893

THIS is the forest primeval. The murmuring pines and the hemlocks,
Bearded with moss, and in garments green, indistinct in the twilight,
Stand like Druids of eld, with voices sad and prophetic,
Stand like harpers hoar, with beards that rest on their bosoms.
Loud from its rocky caverns, the deep-voiced neighboring ocean
Speaks, and in accents disconsolate answers the wail of the forest.
This is the forest primeval; but where are the hearts that beneath it
Leaped like the roe, when he hears in the woodland the voice of the huntsman?
Where is the thatch-roofed village, the home of Acadian farmers—
Men whose lives glided on like rivers that water the woodlands,
Darkened by shadows of earth, but reflecting an image of heaven?
Waste are those pleasant farms, and the farmers forever departed!
Scattered like dust and leaves, when the mighty blasts of October
Seize them, and whirl them aloft, and sprinkle them far o'er the ocean.
Naught but tradition remains of the beautiful village of Grand-Pré.

Part the First
I

IN the Acadian land, on the shores of the Basin of Minas,
Distant, secluded, still, the little village of Grand-Pré
Lay in the fruitful valley. Vast meadows stretched to the eastward,
Giving the village its name, and pasture to flocks without number.
Dikes, that the hands of the farmers had raised with labor incessant,
Shut out the turbulent tides; but at stated seasons the flood-gates
Opened, and welcomed the sea to wander at will o'er the meadows.
West and south there were fields of flax, and orchards and corn-fields
Solemnly down the street came the parish priest.
Spreading afar and unfenced o'er the plain; and away to the northward
Blomidon rose, and the forests old, and aloft on the mountains

From *Evangeline: A Tale of Arcadie* by Henry Wadsworth Longfellow, 1893 Cambridge Edition.

Sea-fogs pitched their tents, and mists from the mighty Atlantic
Looked on the happy valley, but ne'er from their station descended.
There, in the midst of its farms, reposed the Acadian village.
Strongly built were the houses, with frames of oak and of chestnut,
Such as the peasants of Normandy built in the reign of the Henries.
Thatched were the roofs, with dormer-windows; and gables projecting
Over the basement below protected and shaded the doorway.
There in the tranquil evenings of summer, when brightly the sunset
Lighted the village street, and gilded the vanes on the chimneys,
Matrons and maidens sat in snow-white caps and in kirtles
Scarlet and blue and green, with distaffs spinning the golden
Flax for the gossiping looms, whose noisy shuttles within doors
Mingled their sound with the whir of the wheels and the songs of the maidens.
Solemnly down the street came the parish priest, and the children
Paused in their play to kiss the hand he extended to bless them.
Reverend walked he among them; and up rose matrons and maidens,
Hailing his slow approach with words of affectionate welcome.
Then came the laborers home from the field, and serenely the sun sank
Down to his rest, and twilight prevailed. Anon from the belfry
Softly the Angelus sounded, and over the roofs of the village
Columns of pale blue smoke, like clouds of incense ascending,
Rose from a hundred hearths, the homes of peace and contentment.
Thus dwelt together in love these simple Acadian farmers—
Dwelt in the love of God and of man. Alike were they free from
Fear, that reigns with the tyrant, and envy, the vice of republics.
Neither locks had they to their doors, nor bars to their windows;
But their dwellings were open as day and the hearts of the owners;
There the richest was poor, and the poorest lived in abundance.

Somewhat apart from the village, and nearer the Basin of Minas,
Benedict Bellefontaine, the wealthiest farmer of Grand-Pré,
Dwelt on his goodly acres; and with him, directing his household,
Gentle Evangeline lived, his child, and the pride of the village.
Stalworth and stately in form was the man of seventy winters;
Hearty and hale was he, an oak that is covered with snow-flakes;
White as the snow were his locks, and his cheeks as brown as the oakleaves.
Fair was she to behold, that maiden of seventeen summers.
Black were her eyes as the berry that grows on the thorn by the way-side,
Black, yet how softly they gleamed beneath the brown shade of her tresses!
Sweet was her breath as the breath of kine that feed in the meadows.
When in the harvest heat she bore to the reapers at noontide
Flagons of home-brewed ale, ah! fair in sooth was the maiden.

Fairer was she when, on Sunday morn, while the bell from its turret
Sprinkled with holy sounds the air, as the priest with his hysop
Sprinkles the congregation, and scatters blessings upon them,
Down the long street she passed, with her chaplet of beads and her missal,
Wearing her Norman cap, and her kirtle of blue, and the ear-rings,
Brought in the olden time from France, and since, as an heirloom,
Handed down from mother to child, through long generations.
But a celestial brightness—a more ethereal beauty—
Shone on her face and encircled her form, when, after confession,
Homeward serenely she walked with God's benediction upon her.
When she had passed, it seemed like the ceasing of exquisite music.

Thus, at peace with God and the world, the farmer of Grand-Pre
Lived on his sunny farm, and Evangeline governed his household.
Many a youth, as he knelt in the church and opened his missal,
Fixed his eyes upon her, as the saint of his deepest devotion;
Happy was he who might touch her hand or the hem of her garment!
Many a suitor came to her door, by the darkness befriended,
And as he knocked and waited to hear the sound of her footsteps,
Knew not which beat the louder, his heart or the knocker of iron;
But, among all who came, young Gabriel only was welcome;
Gabriel Lajeunesse, the son of Basil the blacksmith,
Who was a mighty man in the village, and honored of all men;
For since the birth of time, throughout all ages and nations,
Has the craft of the smith been held in repute by the people.
Basil was Benedict's friend. Their children from earliest childhood
Grew up together.

He was a valiant youth, and his face, like the face of the morning,
Gladdened the earth with its light and ripened through into action.
She was a woman now, with the heart and hopes of a woman.
"Sunshine of Saint Eulalie" was she called; for that was the sunshine
Which, as the farmers believed, would load their orchards with apples;
She, too, would bring to her husband's house delight and abundance,
Filling it full of love and the ruddy faces of children.

II

Now had the season returned, when the nights grow colder and longer,
And the retreating sun the sign of the Scorpion enters.
Birds of passage sailed through the leaden air, from the ice-bound,
Desolate northern bays to the shores of tropical islands.

Harvests were gathered in; and wild with the winds of September
Wrestled the trees of the forests, as Jacob of old with the angel.
All the signs foretold a winter long and inclement.
Bees, with prophetic instinct of want, had hoarded their honey
Till the hives overflowed; and the Indian hunters asserted
Cold would the winter be, for thick was the fur of the foxes.
Such was the advent of autumn.

In-doors, warm by the wide-mouthed fireplace, idly the farmer
Sat in his elbow-chair; and watched how the flames and the smoke-wreaths
Struggled together like foes in a burning city. Behind him,
Nodding and mocking along the wall, with gestures fantastic,
Darted his own huge shadow, and vanished away into darkness.
Faces, clumsily carved in oak, on the back of his arm-chair
Laughed in the flickering light, and the pewter plates on the dresser
Caught and reflected the flame, as shields of armies the sunshine.
Fragments of song the old man sang, and carols of Christmas,
Such as at home, in the olden time, his fathers before him
Sang in their Norman orchards and bright Burgundian vineyards.
Close at her father's side was the gentle Evangeline seated,
Spinning flax for the loom, that stood in the corner behind her.
Silent awhile were its treadles, at rest was its diligent shuttle,
While the monotonous drone of the wheel, like the drone of a bagpipe,
Followed the old man's song, and united the fragments together.
As in a church, when the chant of the choir at intervals ceases,
Footfalls are heard in the aisles, or words of the priest at the altar,
So, in each pause of the song, with measured motion the clock clicked.
Thus as they sat, there were footsteps heard, and, suddenly lifted,
Sounded the wooden latch, and the door swung back on its hinges.
Benedict knew by the hob-nailed shoes it was Basil the blacksmith,
And by her beating heart Evangeline knew who was with him.
"Welcome!" the farmer exclaimed, as their footsteps paused on the threshold,
"Welcome, Basil, my friend! Come, take thy place on the settle
Close by the chimney-side, which is always empty without thee;
Take from the shelf overhead thy pipe and the box of tobacco;
Never so much thyself art thou as when through the curling
Smoke of the pipe or the forge thy friendly and jovial face gleams
Round and red as the harvest moon through the mist of the marshes."
Then, with a smile of content, thus answered Basil the blacksmith,
Taking with easy air the accustomed seat by the fireside—
"Benedict Bellefontaine, thou hast ever thy jest and thy ballad!
Ever in cheerfulest mood art thou, when others are filled with

Gloomy forebodings of ill, and see only ruin before them.
Happy art thou, as if every day thou hadst picked up a horseshoe."
Pausing a moment, to take the pipe that Evangeline brought him,
And with a coal from the embers had lighted, he slowly continued—
"Four days now are passed since the English ships at their anchors
Ride in the Gaspereau's mouth, with their cannon pointed against us.
What their design may be is unknown; but all are commanded
On the morrow to meet in the church, where his Majesty's mandate
Will be proclaimed as law in the land. Alas! in the mean time
Many surmises of evil alarm the hearts of the people."
Then made answer the farmer: "Perhaps some friendlier purpose
Brings these ships to our shores. Perhaps the harvests in England
By the untimely rains or untimelier heat have been blighted,
And from our bursting barns they would feed their cattle and children."
"Not so thinketh the folk in the village," said, warmly, the blacksmith,
Shaking his head, as in doubt; then, heaving a sigh, he continued—
"Louisburg is not forgotten, nor Beau Sejour, nor Port Royal.
Many already have fled to the forest, and lurk on its outskirts,
Waiting with anxious hearts the dubious fate of to-morrow.
Arms have been taken from us, and warlike weapons of all kinds;
Nothing is left but the blacksmith's sledge and the scythe of the mower."
Then with a pleasant smile made answer the jovial farmer:
"Safer are we unarmed, in the midst of our flocks and our cornfields,
Safer within these peaceful dikes, besieged by the ocean,
Than were our fathers in forts, besieged by the enemy's cannon.
Fear no evil, my friend, and to-night may no shadow of sorrow
Fall on this house and hearth; for this is the night of the contract.
Built are the house and the barn. The merry lads of the village
Strongly have built them and well; and, breaking the glebe round about them,
Filled the barn with hay, and the house with food for a twelvemonth.
Rene Leblanc will be here anon, with his papers and inkhorn.
Shall we not then be glad, and rejoice in the joy of our children?"
As apart by the window she stood, with her hand in her lover's,
Blushing Evangeline heard the words that her father had spoken,
And as they died on his lips the worthy notary entered.

III

BENT like a laboring oar, that toils in the surf of the ocean,
Bent, but not broken, by age was the form of the notary public;
Shocks of yellow hair, like the silken floss of the maize, hung
Over his shoulders; his forehead was high; and glasses with horn bows

Sat astride on his nose, with a look of wisdom supernal.
Father of twenty children was he, and more than a hundred
Children's children rode on his knee, and heard his great watch tick.
Four long years in the times of the war had he languished a captive,
Suffering much in an old French fort as the friend of the English.
Now, though warier grown, without all guile or suspicion,
Then up rose from his seat by the fireside Basil the blacksmith,
Knocked from his pipe the ashes, and slowly extending his right hand,
"Father Leblanc," he exclaimed, "thou hast heard the talk in the village,
And, perchance, canst tell us some news of these ships and their errand."
Then with modest demeanor made answer the notary public—
"Gossip enough have I heard, in sooth, yet am never the wiser;
And what their errand may be I know not better than others.
Yet am I not of those who imagine some evil intention
Brings them here, for we are at peace; and why then molest us?"
"God's name!" shouted the hasty and somewhat irascible blacksmith;
"Must we in all things look for the how, and the why, and the wherefore?
Daily injustice is done, and might is the right of the strongest!"
But, without heeding his warmth, continued the notary public—
"Man is unjust, but God is just; and finally justice
Triumphs; and well I remember a story, that often consoled me,
When as a captive I lay in the old French fort at Port Royal."
This was the old man's favorite tale, and he loved to repeat it
When his neighbors complained that any injustice was done them.
"Once in an ancient city, whose name I no longer remember,
Raised aloft on a column, a brazen statue of Justice
Stood in the public square, upholding the scales in its left hand,
And in its right a sword, as an emblem that justice presided
Over the laws of the land, and the hearts and homes of the people.
Even the birds had built their nests in the scales of the balance,
Having no fear of the sword that flashed in the sunshine above them.
But in the course of time the laws of the land were corrupted;
Might took the place of right, and the weak were oppressed, and the mighty
Ruled with an iron rod. Then it chanced in a nobleman's palace
That a necklace of pearls was lost, and ere long a suspicion
Fell on an orphan girl who lived as maid in the household.
She, after form of trial condemned to die on the scaffold,
Patiently met her doom at the foot of the statue of Justice.
As to her Father in heaven her innocent spirit ascended,
Lo! o'er the city a tempest rose; and the bolts of the thunder
Smote the statue of bronze, and hurled in wrath from its left hand

Down on the pavement below the clattering scales of the balance,
And in the hollow thereof was found the nest of a magpie,
Into whose clay-built walls the necklace of pearls was inwoven."
Silenced, but not convinced, when the story was ended, the blacksmith
Stood like a man who fain would speak, but findeth no language;
All his thoughts were congealed into lines on his face, as the vapors
Freeze in fantastic shapes on the window-panes in the winter.

IV

PLEASANTLY rose next morn the sun on the village of Grand-Pré.
Pleasantly gleamed in the soft, sweet air the Basin of Minas,
Where the ships, with their wavering shadows, were riding at anchor.
Life had long been astir in the village, and clamorous labor
Knocked with its hundred hands at the golden gates of the morning.
Now from the country around, from the farms and the neighboring hamlets,
Came in their holiday dresses the blithe Acadian peasants.
Many a glad good-morrow and jocund laugh from the young folk
Made the bright air brighter, as up from the numerous meadows,
Where no path could be seen but the track of wheels in the greensward,
Group after group appeared, and joined, or passed on the highway.
Long ere noon, in the village all sounds of labor were silenced.
Sat in the cheerful sun, and rejoiced and gossiped together,
Every house was an inn, where all were welcomed and feasted;
For with this simple people, who lived like brothers together,
All things were held in common, and what one had was another's.
Yet under Benedict's roof hospitality seemed more abundant:
For Evangeline stood among the guests of her father;
Bright was her face with smiles, and words of welcome and gladness
Fell from her beautiful lips, and blessed the cup as she gave it.

Under the open sky, in the odorous air of the orchard,
Bending with golden fruit, was spread the feast of betrothal.
There in the shade of the porch were the priest and the notary seated;
There good Benedict sat, and sturdy Basil the blacksmith.
Not far withdrawn from these, by the cider-press and the beehives,
Michael the fiddler was placed, with the gayest of hearts and of waistcoats.
Shadow and light from the leaves alternately played on his snow-white
Hair, as it waved in the wind; and the jolly face of the fiddler
Glowed like a living coal when the ashes are blown from the embers.
Gayly the old man sang to the vibrant sound of his fiddle,

Tous les Bourgeois de Chartres, and *Le Carillon de Dunkerque,*
And anon with his wooden shoes beat time to the music.
Merrily, merrily whirled the wheels of the dizzying dances
Under the orchard-trees and down the path to the meadows;
Old folk and young together, and children mingled among them.
Fairest of all the maids was Evangeline, Benedict's daughter!
Noblest of all the youths was Gabriel, son of the blacksmith!

So passed the morning away. And lor with a summons sonorous
Sounded the bell from its tower, and over the meadows a drum beat.
Thronged ere long was the church with men. Without, in the churchyard,
Waited the women. They stood by the graves, and hung on the headstones
Garlands of autumn leaves and evergreens fresh from the forest.
Then came the guard from the ships, and marching proudly among them
Entered the sacred portal. With loud and dissonant clangor
Echoed the sound of their brazen drums from ceiling and casement—
Echoed a moment only, and slowly the ponderous portal,
Closed, and in silence the crowd awaited the will of the soldiers.
Then uprose their commander, and spake from the steps of the altar,
Holding aloft in his hands, with its seals, the royal commission.
"You are convened this day," he said, "by his Majesty's orders.
Clement and kind has he been; but how you have answered his kindness,
Let your own hearts reply! To my natural make and my temper
Painful the task is I do, which to you I know must be grievous.
Yet must I bow and obey, and deliver the will of our monarch;
Namely, that all your lands, and dwellings, and cattle of all kinds
Forfeited be to the crown; and that you yourselves from this province
Be transported to other lands. God grant you may dwell there
Ever as faithful subjects, a happy and peaceable people!
Prisoners now I declare you; for such is his Majesty's pleasure!"
As, when the air is serene in the sultry solstice of summer,
Suddenly gathers a storm, and the deadly sling of the hailstones
Beats down the farmer's corn in the field and shatters his windows,
Hiding the sun, and strewing the ground with thatch from the house-roofs,
Bellowing fly the herds, and seek to break their inclosures;
So on the hearts of the people descended the words of the speaker.
Silent a moment they stood in speechless wonder, and then rose
Louder and ever louder a wail of sorrow and anger,
And, by one impulse moved, they madly rushed to the doorway.
Vain was the hope of escape; and cries and fierce imprecations
Rang through the house of prayer; and high o'er the heads of the others
Rose, with his arms uplifted, the figure of Basil the blacksmith,

As, on a stormy sea, a spar is tossed by the billows.
Flushed was his face and distorted with passion, and wildly he shouted—
"Down with the tyrants of England! we never have sworn them allegiance!
Death to these foreign soldiers, who seize on our homes and our harvests!"
More he fain would have said, but the merciless hand of a soldier
Smote him upon the mouth, and dragged him down to the pavement.

In the midst of the strife and tumult of angry contention,
Lo! the door of the chancel opened, and Father Felician
Entered, with serious mien, and ascended the steps of the altar.
Raising his reverend hand, with a gesture he awed into silence
All that clamorous throng; and thus he spake to his people;
Deep were his tones and solemn; in accents measured and mournful
Spake he, as, after the tocsin's alarum, distinctly the clock strikes.
"What is this that ye do, my children? what madness has seized you?
Forty years of my life have I labored among you, and taught you,
Not in word alone, but in deed, to love one another!
Is this the fruit of my toils, of my vigils and prayers and privations?
Have you so soon forgotten all lessons of love and forgiveness?
This is the house of the Prince of Peace, and would you profane it
Thus with violent deeds and hearts overflowing with hatred?
Lo! where the crucified Christ from His cross is gazing upon you!
See! in those sorrowful eyes what meekness and holy compassion!
Hark! how those lips still repeat the prayer, 'O Father, forgive them!'
Let us repeat that prayer in the hour when the wicked assail us,
Let us repeat it now, and say, 'O Father, forgive them!'"
Few were his words of rebuke, but deep in the hearts of his people
Sank they, and sobs of contrition succeeded that passionate outbreak;
And they repeated his prayer, and said, "O Father, forgive them!"

Meanwhile had spread in the village the tidings of ill, and on all sides
Wandered, wailing, from house to house the women and children.
Long at her father's door Evangeline stood, with her right hand
Shielding her eyes from the level rays of the sun, that, descending,
Lighted the village street with mysterious splendor, and roofed each
Peasant's cottage with golden thatch, and emblazoned its windows.

Ah! on her spirit within a deeper shadow had fallen,
And from the fields of her soul a fragrance celestial ascended—
Charity, meekness, love, and hope, and forgiveness, and patience!
Then, all-forgetful of self, she wandered into the village,
amid the gloom, by the church Evangeline lingered.

All was silent within; and in vain at the door and the windows
Stood she, and listened and looked, until, overcome by emotion,
"Gabriel!" cried she aloud with tremulous voice; but no answer
Came from the graves of the dead, nor the gloomier grave of the living
Slowly at length she returned to the tenantless house of her father.
Smouldered the fire on the hearth, on the board stood the supper untasted,
Empty and drear was each room, and haunted with phantoms of terror.
Sadly echoed her step on the stair and the floor of her chamber.
In the dead of the night she heard the whispering rain fall
Loud on the withered leaves of the sycamore-tree by the window.
Keenly the lightning flashed; and the voice of the echoing thunder
Told her that God was in heaven, and governed the world he created!
Then she remembered the tale she had heard of the justice of heaven;
Soothed was her troubled soul, and she peacefully slumbered till morning.

V

FOUR times the sun had risen and set; and now on the fifth day
Cheerily called the cock to the sleeping maids of the farmhouse.
Soon o'er the yellow fields, in silent and mournful procession,
Came from the neighboring hamlets and farms the Acadian women,
Driving in ponderous wains their household goods to the seashore,
Pausing and looking back to gaze once more on their dwellings,
Ere they were shut from sight by the winding road and the woodland.
Close at their sides their children ran, and urged on the oxen,
While in their little hands they clasped some fragments of playthings.

There to the Gaspereau's mouth they hurried; and there on the sea-beach
Piled in confusion lay the household goods of the peasants.
All day long the wains came laboring down from the village.
Late in the afternoon, when the sun was near to his setting,
Echoing far o'er the fields came the roll of drums from the churchyard.
Thither the women and children thronged. On a sudden the church-doors
Opened, and forth came the guard, and marching in gloomy procession
Followed the long-imprisoned, but patient, Acadian farmers.
Even as pilgrims, who journey afar from their homes and their country,
Sing as they go, and in singing forget they are weary and wayworn,
So with songs on their lips the Acadian peasants descended
Down from the church to the shore, amid their wives and their daughters.
Foremost the young men came; and, raising together their voices,
Sang they with tremulous lips a chant of the Catholic Missions—

"Sacred heart of the Saviour! O inexhaustible fountain!
Fill our hearts this day with strength and submission and patience!"
Then the old men, as they marched, and the women that stood by the wayside
Joined in the sacred psalm, and the birds in the sunshine above them
Mingled their notes therewith, like voices of spirits departed.

Half-way down to the shore Evangeline waited in silence,
Not overcome with grief, but strong in the hour of affliction—
Calmly and sadly waited, until the procession approached her,
And she beheld the face of Gabriel pale with emotion.
Tears then filled her eyes, and, eagerly running to meet him,
Clasped she his hands, and laid her head on his shoulder and whispered—
"Gabriel! be of good cheer! for if we love one another,
Nothing, in truth, can harm us, whatever mischances may happen!"
Smiling she spake these words; then suddenly paused, for her father
Saw she slowly advancing. Alas! how changed was his aspect!
Gone was the glow from his cheek, and the fire from his eye, and his footstep
Heavier seemed with the weight of the weary heart in his bosom.
But with a smile and a sigh she clasped his neck and embraced him,
Speaking words of endearment where words of comfort availed not.
Thus to the Gaspereau's mouth moved on that mournful procession.

There disorder prevailed, and the tumult and stir of embarking.
Busily plied the freighted boats; and in the confusion
Wives were torn from their husbands, and mothers, too late, saw their children
Left on the land, extending their arms, with wildest entreaties.
So unto separate ships were Basil and Gabriel carried,
While in despair on the shore Evangeline stood with her father.
Half the task was not done when the sun went down, and the twilight
Deepened and darkened around; and in haste the refluent ocean
Fled away from the shore, and left the line of the sand-beach
Covered with waifs of the tide, with kelp and the slippery seaweed.
Farther back in the midst of the household goods and the wagons,
Like to a gypsy camp, or a leaguer after a battle,
All escape cut off by the sea, and the sentinels near them,
Lay encamped for the night the houseless Acadian farmers.
Back to its nethermost caves retreated the bellowing ocean,
Dragging adown the beach the rattling pebbles, and leaving
Inland and far up the shore the stranded boats of the sailors.
Then, as the night descended, the herds returned from their pastures;
Sweet was the moist still air with the odor of milk from their udders;

Lowing they waited, and long, at the well-known bars of the farmyard—
Waited and looked in vain for the voice and the hand of the milkmaid.
Silence reigned in the streets; from the church no Angelus sounded,
Rose no smoke from the roofs, and gleamed no lights from the windows.

But on the shores meanwhile the evening fires had been kindled,
Built of the driftwood thrown on the sands from wrecks in the tempest.
Round them shapes of gloom and sorrowful faces were gathered,
Voices of women were heard, and of men, and the crying of children.
Onward from fire to fire, as from hearth to hearth in his parish,
Wandered the faithful priest, consoling and blessing and cheering,
Like unto shipwrecked Paul on Melita's desolate sea-shore.
Thus he approached the place where Evangeline sat with her father,
And in the flickering light beheld the face of the old man,
Haggard and hollow and wan, and without either thought or emotion,
E'en as the face of a clock from which the hands have been taken.
Vainly Evangeline strove with words and caresses to cheer him,
Vainly offered him food; yet he moved not, he looked not, he spake not,
But, with a vacant stare, ever gazed at the flickering firelight.

Suddenly rose from the south a light, as in autumn the blood-red
Moon climbs the crystal walls of heaven, and o'er the horizon
Titan-like stretches its hundred hands upon mountain and meadow,
Seizing the rocks and the rivers, and piling huge shadows together.
Broader and ever broader it gleamed on the roofs of the village,
Gleamed on the sky and the sea, and the ships that lay in the roadstead.
Columns of shining smoke uprose, and flashes of flame were
Thrust through their folds and withdrawn, like the quivering hands of a martyr.
Then as the wind seized the gleeds and the burning thatch, and, uplifting,
Whirled them aloft through the air, at once from a hundred housetops
Started the sheeted smoke with flashes of flame intermingled.

These things beheld in dismay the crowd on the shore and on shipboard.
Speechless at first they stood, then cried aloud in their anguish,
"We shall behold no more our homes in the village of Grand-Pre!"
Then rose a sound of dread, such as startles the sleeping encampments
Far in the western prairies or forests that skirt the Nebraska,
When the wild horses affrighted sweep by with the speed of the whirlwind,
Or the loud bellowing herds of buffaloes rush to the river.
Such was the sound that arose on the night, as the herds and the horses
Broke through their folds and fences, and madly rushed o'er the meadows.

Overwhelmed with the sight, yet speechless, the priest and the maiden
Gazed on the scene of terror that reddened and widened before them;
And as they turned at length to speak to their silent companion,
Lo! from his seat he had fallen, and stretched abroad on the seashore
Motionless lay his form from which the soul had departed.
Slowly the priest uplifted the lifeless head, and the maiden
Knelt at her father's side, and wailed aloud in her terror.
Then in a swoon she sank, and lay with her head on his bosom.
Through the long night she lay in deep, oblivious slumber;
And when she woke from the trance, she beheld a multitude near her.
Faces of friends she beheld, that were mournfully gazing upon her,
Pallid, with tearful eyes, and looks of saddest compassion.
Still the blaze of the burning village illumined the landscape,
Reddened the sky overhead, and gleamed on the faces around her,
And like the day of doom it seemed to her wavering senses,
Then a familiar voice she heard, as it said to the people—
"Let us bury him here by the sea. When a happier season
Brings us again to our homes from the unknown land of our exile,
Then shall his sacred dust be piously laid in the churchyard."
Such were the words of the priest. And there in haste by the seaside,
Having the glare of the burning village for funeral torches,
But without bell or book, they buried the farmer of Grand-Pré.
And as the voice of the priest repeated the service of sorrow,
Lo! with a mournful sound, like the voice of a vast congregation,
Solemnly answered the sea, and mingled its roar with the dirges.
'T was the returning tide, that afar from the waste of the ocean,
With the first dawn of the day, came heaving and hurrying landward.
Then recommenced once more the stir and noise of embarking;
And with the ebb of that tide the ships sailed out of the harbor,
Leaving behind them the dead on the shore, and the village in ruins.

Acadian Gives Queen Earful Over 1755 Deportation

Kevin Cox, Moncton

2002

The Queen left New Brunswick without saying anything to the people of the province but at least one Acadian woman, upset about the way her ancestors were forced out of their homes by the British, had lots to say to the monarch.

"Give us back the land that you stole from my ancestors in 1755," Marie-Claire Dugas shouted, waving her Acadian flag in the crowd in downtown Moncton as the Queen walked past on her way to a luncheon Saturday.

Ms. Dugas's shouts were drowned out by the music of a handbell ensemble and the cheering from the several thousand people who crowded the courtyard outside a downtown hotel to get a glimpse of the Queen.

Her one-person protest drew angry glares from the pro-monarchy crowd and some people jeered at reporters who went to talk to Ms. Dugas.

Ms. Dugas said the Queen should have used her visit to New Brunswick to apologize formally for British expulsion of thousands of the original French settlers from the lands of Acadie—now part of New Brunswick and Nova Scotia—in 1755.

Ms. Dugas, whose ancestors lost their homes and land, were forced by deportation to live in the United States and France before returning to the Maritimes, said the British Crown should compensate Acadians for the losses of their ancestors.

"She should say she's sorry about the deportation. That would be a start," Ms. Dugas said in an interview.

"But at this point she is not saying anything."

Several Acadian groups sent a request to the Queen in July asking her to recognize formally the suffering caused by the deportation and dispersion of their ancestors. But Acadian leaders said they had not expected an answer during the Queen's Golden Jubilee tour.

"They {the British soldiers} committed a crime against British subjects so they owe us something," Ms. Dugas said. "It was illegal genocide."

Bloc Québécois MP Stéphane Bergeron came to Monoton to hear what the Queen might say about the Acadians, but said he wasn't disappointed by her silence.

"Acadian Gives Queen earful over 1755 deportation" by Kevin Cox, *The Globe and Mail,* October 14, 2002. Reprinted by permission of The Globe and Mail.

Mr. Bergeron, who is pushing the federal government and the British Crown for recognition of the suffering of his ancestors, hopes the Queen will address the issue before the 250th anniversary of the deportation of the Acadians.

He said the expulsion is still an emotional issue.

"It's the same as the passion that many people feel for the monarchy and the Queen," Mr. Bergeron said.

"It's because of their roots. They find their roots when they find the Queen. For the same reason people are so passionate about recognition from the Crown for what was done to the Acadian people."

While the Queen attracted several thousand people earlier in the day when she visited the small rural town of Sussex, fewer than 1,000 people attended a civic ceremony at the Monoton International Airport in Dieppe, which has a large Acadian population.

Ms. Dugas said many of her Acadian friends preferred to stay home and rake leaves on the balmy fall day.

But another Acadian, Phyllis LeBlanc, said she is still fascinated by royalty and she didn't want her moment with the monarch tarnished by the debate over the treatment of her ancestors.

"To me {the expulsion} was in the past. Our ancestors went through it and life goes on," she said.

In Sussex, the Queen did stop to talk to some elementary-schoolchildren who were planting a red New Brunswick maple tree to mark her visit.

Inside the school she had seen a computer image of how the tree would grow.

"She was pretty proud that this was a real maple tree and she said to water it and take care of it," said Chelsea Coates, 10.

Private Members' Business: The Acadians

Hansard, 37th Parlament, 3rd Session, Number 008, February 2004

Mr. Stéphane Bergeron (Verchères—Les-Patriotes, BQ) moved:

That a humble Address be presented to Her Excellency praying that, following the steps already taken by the Société Nationale de l'Acadie, she will intercede with Her Majesty to cause the British Crown to recognize officially the wrongs done to the Acadian people in its name between 1755 and 1763.

He said: As a result of procedural circumstances, I am once again in a position where I have to initiate debate on Motion No. 382.

Following the unexpected events of last December, when Her Excellency signed a royal proclamation creating a National Acadian Day commemorating the deportation of Acadians, I pondered for a long time what should become of this motion.

I talked about the issue with several individuals and I must say that not everyone was of the same opinion about this. However, I have to recognize that the fate of this motion does not rest with me alone, but with all the members of this House.

That is why I have launched a series of consultations with colleagues to settle the issue, because clearly, the problem is now quite different from what it was when we first wrote the motion.

These consultations are continuing and will, I am absolutely certain, enable us to reach consensus before the motion is put to a vote. Perhaps we will be able to finally write an ending to this troubling chapter of our collective history.

As you are probably aware, right before the holiday period, December 9 of last year to be precise, the previous government unexpectedly made public a royal proclamation. It established July 28 each year as "A Day of Commemoration of the Great Upheaval."

The proclamation is to take effect on September 6, 2004, and the day will be commemorated for the first time on July 28, 2005. I was totally amazed to learn that the former heritage minister and the former intergovernmental affairs minister had taken this initiative with their colleagues in order to achieve this reversal. It was as unexpected as it was spectacular.

It is regrettable that so much time and energy was required to get my Liberal colleagues to finally take the necessary steps to achieve formal acknowledgment of these tragic events. These are the same people who, not so long ago, were fighting tooth and nail to defend their categorical refusal to do such a thing. They spared no sarcasm in

From *Hansard (edited)*, 37th Parliament, 3rd Session, Number 008, Wednesday, February 11, 2004.
Reprinted by permission of the Canadian House of Commons.

their remarks to me, claiming that looking back into the past was futile and the Acadians would gain nothing from it.

I must admit that I have always known, deep down in my heart, that the time would come when truth and justice would prevail. This action by my Liberal colleagues was all the more remarkable and praiseworthy. Although the date of July 28 is not unanimously accepted by the community of historians and specialists in Acadian history, I am still extremely pleased that the federal government has finally decided to have a day to commemorate the deportation of the Acadians. In this way, the Governor General, on behalf of the Crown of Canada, henceforth recognizes the suffering inflicted upon the Acadians by the Great Upheaval.

There is no doubt whatsoever that such a gesture of major historical significance has a symbolic value that cannot be denied or downplayed. From now on, the Great Upheaval can no longer be considered a non-event or a myth, believed by some never to have occurred.

For the first time in the history of Canada, we have official acknowledgment that the Acadians were the victims of a great tragedy which changed the face of Acadia and Canada forever.

The deportation is now acknowledged to be an undeniable historical fact, as stated in the Royal Proclamation, which reads:

> We (the Governor General) acknowledge these historical facts and the trials and suffering experienced by the Acadian people during the Great Upheaval.

As Mr. Euclide Chiasson, President of the Société Nationale de l'Acadie, said on December 10 in a speech in Ottawa:

> What we are celebrating today is not a rewriting of history nor a revision of history. What we are celebrating is the validation of a chapter in our history. The royal proclamation, ratified by the cabinet on December 2, simply attests to the universally recognized historical facts.

I would be remiss in not mentioning the enormous amount of work done by the Société Nationale de l'Acadie, which took on this cause and unflaggingly sought recognition by the British Crown of the wrongs done to the Acadian people during the Great Upheaval.

Having said that, I must admit that I was pleasantly surprised by the clear, frank, direct and uncompromising wording of the proclamation's preamble. When I first heard vague rumours that such a proclamation was being secretly prepared in the back rooms of government, I suspected trickery, bad faith and machinations.

Considering the acrimonious tenor of the debate to that point, I feared that they would try to cloud the issue by resorting to the convenient euphemism of the Great Upheaval, and limit themselves to sickeningly inoffensive generalities.

But that is not the case, indeed it is quite the opposite. The text of the proclamation spells out the story of the deportation and the considerable suffering caused to the Acadian people. The proclamation even goes so far as to recognize that the decision to deport the Acadians was not made by the colonial authorities in Nova Scotia, Massachusetts and Maine alone, as some have claimed even in this House, but in fact by the Crown itself.

Even for that reason alone, we must recognize that this is an unprecedented gesture. Still, the reasons for rejoicing and satisfaction end there. While it is undoubtedly a significant step forward, the proclamation does not deal with the root of the problem, which remains untouched, because this is the Crown of Canada recognizing the facts of the deportation. The British Crown, which ought at least to assume moral responsibility for these tragic events, has not yet officially recognized them.

It may seem like a subtle distinction, but it is not. The fact that the Crown of Canada, like that of Australia or even New Zealand, followed suit and did what the legislative assemblies in Louisiana and Maine have done, is certainly very comforting and nice, but nothing can replace recognition directly from the British Crown.

The Crown of Canada should not have to recognize wrongs for which it bears no responsibility, and should certainly not have to do instead of an entity that still exists, namely the British Crown.

It is very clear to me, and I believe I have demonstrated this many times in this House, that the Crown was not only well aware of what was afoot in Acadia, but was at the heart of the operation that had been brewing for a number of years to allow British and American settlers to occupy fertile Acadian lands.

Until then, Acadians were allowed to stay on their land so that they would not pack up their belongings and livestock and increase the ranks of the French settled on Ile Royale, further strengthening the influence of the Fortress of Louisbourg in the region. That is why Acadian neutrality suited the British so well. But then again, they took exception to it many times and in the end they used it as an excuse to justify the Deportation.

However, in 1720, the Governor-in-chief of Nova Scotia, Colonel Philipps, taking into consideration these military and economic imperatives, expressed a wish in a letter to London:

> —a plan needs to be made in the motherland to populate this land with people from Great Britain . . . Until then, the inhabitants will not even think about leaving, . . . until I have received your new instructions.

At the end of that year, Philipps received a response from the Bureau des colonies:

> —The French in Nova Scotia will never become good subjects of His Majesty . . . That is why they should be expelled as soon as the forces we plan to send you arrive in Nova Scotia . . . Do not yourself undertake such an expulsion without a specific order from His Majesty to that effect.

A few years later, in 1747 to be more precise, the governor of Massachusetts, William Shirley, assured Acadians that they could remain peacefully on their own land, while he was negotiating with London to have them deported. In response to a proposal from him to that effect, the Secretary of State said:

> Although the removal of these inhabitants from the province is desirable, His Majesty has decided that it would be better to postpone this project. However, His Majesty requests that you examine how such a project could be carried out at a suitable time.

Then, in 1753, Charles Lawrence was appointed governor of Nova Scotia. A year later, he would send a letter to London about Acadians, in which he said:

> Their land holdings are the largest and the richest in the province. As long as that situation remains, no settlement would be successful—

Soon after Vice-Admiral Boscawen arrived from England, on July 8, 1755, with "secret instructions signed by His Majesty," the decision was finally made, and on the 28th of the same month, the removal of Acadians was carried out.

Since there is no longer any doubt in my mind about the direct involvement of the British Crown in this upheaval, there is a questionable and quite surprising substitution in the proclamation issued in December. To follow up on a point the Liberals have used recently to criticize my initiative, the proclamation stipulates that Canada is a sovereign state and that, with regard to Canada, the Crown in right of Canada and of the provinces succeeded to the powers and prerogatives of the Crown in right of the United Kingdom.

Need I remind the House that the Crown in right of Canada and Canada itself, as we know it today, did not exist in 1775.

Moreover, as Université de Moncton professor Kamel Khiari pointed out, in crimes such as this great upheaval that could be compared to the ethnic cleansing occurring these days, responsibility cannot be transferred to the successor state but remains in perpetuity with the predecessor state. If the predecessor state still exists, it is responsible for those crimes.

Also, the Canadian royal proclamation only affects, so to speak, Acadians in Canada. Although it is not trivial, this action has officially no effect on Acadians in Louisiana or in Belle-Île-en-Mer, for example. Indeed, it is not the federal government, or the Société nationale de l'Acadie, or even this Bloc member that started this whole saga to seek official recognition of the wrongs done to the Acadian people during the deportation, but a lawyer from Louisiana, Warren Perrin, to whom I want to pay tribute today.

I suggest that the argument that it was incumbent upon the Canadian government, and not the British Crown, to take formal action to recognize the facts surrounding the deportation was only a legal and constitutional manoeuvre to set the process in motion for what appears to several people as a rather surprising flip flop by a faction that was heretofore vehemently opposed to such an action.

I recognize that, under the circumstances, this was a fair political manoeuvre and the government now had to oppose the very mechanism provided in the wording of the motion. In this regard, I want to say that the motion was initially written with the cooperation of the clerk of the House and his staff, following thorough research on relevant precedents.

The Canadian government understood well the limits of the action that it took, since it announced at the same time that an "unofficial" invitation had been extended to Her Majesty so that she could personally read this proclamation in Grand-Pré, a highly symbolic place for the Acadian people.

It would be very sad to try to lead the Acadian people to believe that, by this proclamation, the page has definitely been turned and this saga is finally over. I sincerely believe that this royal proclamation would only be truly meaningful if Her Majesty herself would read it. The Canadian government even provided for this possibility in the proclamation.

This historic event could take place next September 5, during the celebrations surrounding the 400th anniversary of the foundation of Acadia, or on July 28, 2005, which will be the first Day of the Commemoration of the Great Upheaval. The reading of the proclamation by Her Majesty would have the effect, to paraphrase the president of the Société Nationale de l'Acadie, of "crowning" the representations made to seek official recognition of the wrongs done to the Acadian people during the deportation.

This action by Her Majesty, who embodies the authority of the two Crowns, could then be interpreted as a de facto recognition, by the British Crown, of the terms of the proclamation signed by the Canadian Crown.

So, the House of Commons must support the December 9 royal proclamation and formally invite Her Majesty to come and read this proclamation in Canada, preferably in Acadia, in a place and at a time to be determined by Buckingham Palace, the Canadian government and the Société Nationale de l'Acadie. We could then put closure on the parliamentary aspect of this saga, which has already had a very positive impact.

It is my hope that, this time, we will leave partisanship aside and think about the best interests of the Acadian people, and that all of us will gather here in this House to salute and applaud the action taken by the government in December, and will join our voices to that of the government to formally invite Her Majesty to come to read the proclamation.

Lynne Yelich (Blackstrap, CPC): Mr. Speaker, the member for Lanark—Carleton could not be present today, so he has asked me to deliver the speech that he has researched and written. On behalf of the member for Lanark—Carleton, I begin.

Mr. Speaker, it is with regret that I will be voting against Motion No. 382. My reasons for doing so are twofold. First, I feel that this motion is based on a faulty premise, that being that guilt can be collective and can be passed on from one generation to the next.

Second, despite the good intentions of those who drafted it, the motion seems to attribute alternate responsibilities for the expulsion of the Acadians to the crown which is not an accurate reading of the events of 1755. A more historically accurate reading would lay blame with the colonial governors of New England and the pioneers they represented.

I will begin with the historical argument and come back later to the philosophical one. Many of the facts surrounding the deportation of the Acadians are unchallenged. In 1755 the colonial authorities began a process of uprooting and deporting the part of the Acadian population which had settled on British lands beginning with the centre of the Acadian colony along the east shore of the Bay of Fundy.

Nova Scotia's Governor Lawrence and Governor Shirley, commander in chief of the British forces in New England, began by seizing colonists' firearms to prevent them from using force to resist. Then they took a large number of adult males hostage in order to guarantee the docility of their families at the time of deportation.

In the years which followed, approximately three-quarters of the total Acadian population, or 13,000 people, were deported. Some of these people were sent to England, others to Louisiana and still others were returned to France. Although we know with certainty the degree of suffering caused by the deportations between the years 1755 and 1763, it is much more difficult to pin down historic responsibility for them.

One thing is certain and that is the governors Lawrence and Shirley were at the heart of the decision making and must bear ultimate responsibility. But nothing proves that they acted with the approval of the Parliament of Westminster. According to the most commonly accepted version of events, Lawrence acted with the authorization of the local council in Nova Scotia and parliament and King George did not take part in the planning of the deportations.

As I will discuss momentarily, I emphasize that I will not support the notion of a collective or hereditary guilt, but even if I did support it, I think that the first collective excuses that should be conveyed to the Acadian people should come from the government of Maine.

Nonetheless, the Queen recently chose to address this issue, deferring a decision on any apology to the Canadian cabinet. As we are all aware, cabinet recently dealt with this issue and this past December, the Governor General signed a royal proclamation regarding this issue. Excerpts from the proclamation read as follows:

Whereas on July 28, 1755, the Crown, in the course of administering the affairs of the British colony of Nova Scotia, made the decision to deport the Acadians;

Whereas the deportation of the Acadian people, commonly known as the Great Upheaval, continued until 1763 and had tragic consequences, including the deaths of many thousands of Acadians;

Whereas the Crown acknowledges these historical facts and the trials and suffering experienced by the Acadian people during the Great Upheaval;

Therefore, Her Excellency the Governor General in Council, on the recommendation of the Minister of Canadian Heritage, directs that a Proclamation do issue designating July 28 of every year as "A Day of Commemoration of the Great Upheaval".

I commend the decision of the government to issue this proclamation, one which seems entirely appropriate to me.

I believe there is a legitimate expectation that all participants in the public life of a civilized society should adopt a moral attitude toward the past. A moral attitude involves recognizing and embracing those past actions which are regarded as good and just and rejecting those which are regarded as unjust or monstrous.

The acknowledgement of the trials and suffering experienced by the Acadian people and the designation of an annual day to commemorate this unfortunate chapter in our history is an appropriate way to address this unfortunate episode.

In contrast to the proclamation issued by the Crown, however, the motion before the House explicitly requests an apology for this historical wrong. This is quite a different concept. It rests on the idea that actual guilt for past injustice can be passed on institutionally and collectively in precisely the same way that the residual effects of that wrong continue to have some impact on the descendants of those who suffered the initial wrong. This is simply untrue.

I do not accept the notion that an institution can maintain a heritage or a collective guilt that is imposed upon successive generations of those who become members of that institution or who fall under its protection.

An attitude of collective guilt or responsibility, or worse yet, of expecting others to accept a mantle of guilt, or responsibility for acts in which they themselves did not take part strikes me as being of no utility at all.

A debate similar to the one taking place today took place in the House 20 years ago on Pierre Trudeau's last day as prime minister. He was asked by Brian Mulroney in question period to issue an apology for the war time internment of Canadians of Japanese descent. Trudeau's response reveals a subtle grasp to the distinction that I am attempting to draw here today. He said:

I do not see how I can apologize for some historic event to which we... were not a party. We can regret that it happened. But why...say that an apology is much better than an expression or regret?

I do not think that it is the purpose of a Government to right the past. It cannot re-write history. It is our purpose to be just in our time...

I agree with the reasoning of this statement. In the case of the great upheaval, the wronged parties are long dead. Those who committed the wrong are long dead. The British Empire, by whose power the wrongs were perpetrated, no longer exists and the principle of mercantilism on which it was founded has been firmly and absolutely rejected by the present British Crown and state.

Most important of all, perhaps, the British colonies of New England, in whose interest the wrongs were committed, ceased to exist as political entities over two centuries ago, with the coming of American independence.

So no individual is left, nor even any corporate entity, which can truthfully and honestly accept guilt in its own name, or serve as the justified target of the indignation of others.

This does not excuse us from a responsibility to adopt a moral attitude of condemnation toward this great wrong any more than we can adopt an attitude of moral neutrality toward the monstrous evils of more recent times.

As moral actors, we need to recognize the existence of these past wrongs, to identify them to our fellow citizens and to do all we can to ensure that no modern version of this wrong can occur.

As such, I would like to applaud the sincere efforts of the hon. member for Verchères—Les-Patriotes to ensure that this episode in our history is not forgotten.

Nonetheless, I believe that the recent proclamation, which acknowledges this issue without extending an official apology, is sufficient to express our sorrow for this past wrong. It allows us, without condemning others, to indicate our determination that no such future wrong will ever be tolerated on Canadian soil.

Hence, I disagree on both historical and philosophical grounds with the fundamental assumption on which Motion No. 382 rests, that the Crown bears a further responsibility.

First, I take issue with the historical claim that the British Crown, past or present, bears the ultimate responsibility for the great upheaval.

Second, I disagree with the philosophical claim that we can inherit a collective guilt which places on us a responsibility to apologize for events which took place over two centuries ago.

Therefore, I must vote against this motion and encourage others to do so as well.

Focus Questions

1. How does Longfellow's portrayal of Evangeline's character and behaviour turn the English into villains?

   - She is protrayed as an innocent lady of the house
     ↳ modest, calm, worried
   - b/c of all the emphasis on her being good the English who are doing bad to her get protrayed as villans.
   - Alagory of Acadians
   - Saint-like
   - She contrasts the soldiers

2. Why do you think that the story became so popular?

   - b/c it was an interesting story based on a historicle event
     ↳ Acadians shared the feeling of evangeline and
     ↳ it rose contreversy ∴ everyone wanted to read it
   - romantism /tragity

3. What does the Expulsion tell us about Canada's origins?

- politicaly noetral
- Americas speaking on behalf of Acadians

- cness board

4. Should the Federal Government be obliged to issue an apology?   Should the Queen? Why or why not?

No
→ time has passed and what would an apology do?
    ↳ from ppl who weren't there to other ppl who
    weren't there

shows weakness

PART TWO:
THE CONQUEST

Introduction

The conquest of New France by the British in the middle of the 18th century is perhaps one of the most crucial turning points in Canadian history—at least according to some. For many years, the British and French had been battling for control of North America, and on 13 September 1759 the English, under the direction of James Wolfe, won a crucial battle on the now-famous Plains of Abraham, just outside the walls of Québec City. They defeated the French troops led by Louis-Joseph, the Marquis de Montcalm, but both Wolfe and Montcalm were killed in the battle. The population of French Catholic settlers—known as the Canadians—were, like the Acadians, now under the power of English, Protestant rulers.

The capture of Quebec, while it did not end the fighting, was considered the pivotal battle in the war overall—the stronghold of French power in North America had been defeated, and it would never again come under French control. In the aftermath of this war, however, the new English rulers did not (as some people had expected, and wished them to do), outlaw the French language or the customs and laws of the population. Instead, it was believed that over time, the French Canadians would come to see English ways as superior, and they would assimilate. Clearly, this did not happen.

Because the French colonists in Quebec were allowed to maintain their religion, their laws, and their language, some historians look at Conquest as just another battle between imperial powers, and one which did not truly affect the course of history for the French in Quebec. For most, however, Conquest is seen as a profound turning point, inspiring Quebec nationalism and separatist politics right up to the present day. And, as these two primary documents suggest, even in 1759, both the French and English were very aware that the transfer of power from the French to the English was momentous. The first extract was written by a French Catholic nun (whose name is not known) living and working in the Hospital in Quebec at the time of the battle. The second was written by a British soldier, Captain John Knox, who fought alongside James Wolfe in the campaigns against the French.

Siege of Quebec in 1759
Translated from the French

NARRATIVE of the doings during the SIEGE OF QUEBEC, and the conquest of CANADA; by a NUN of the General Hospital of Quebec, transmitted to a religious Community of the same order, in France.

My very reverend Mothers,

As our constitution requires us to consult the other establishments of our Congregation, in any difficulties that may occur, tending to impede the progress of our holy Institution, it must also give you the same power, I imagine, when necessary to promote our edification. The simple narration, which I am about to give you, of what passed since the year 1755, when the English determined to use every effort to acquire this colony; the part we took, by the immense labours which were consequently imposed upon us, will be the subject.

The General Hospital is situated in the outer limits of Quebec, about half a mile from the walls.

Let us now, dear Mothers, endeavor to give you some details of a war and captivity, which our sins have drawn upon us. Heaven, so far favorable to our supplications, preserved us on several occasions. The most holy Virgin, patroness of this, country, having baffled the efforts of the enemy enabled our vessels to escape their vigilance, and the tempests and storms of the ocean. But alas! want of sufficient gratitude, deprived us of a continuation of her protection. Still, during the first attacks of our enemy, we continued to enjoy it; every where they appeared, they were beaten and repulsed with considerable loss. The taking of ————[1] of Fort St. George and several others, of which they were deprived, are proofs. The victories we obtained at Belle Rivière and at Carillon, were most glorious; our warriors returned crowned with laurels. They probably, did not return thanks to the God of armies, to whom they were indebted for success, as it was miraculous; their small numbers, without heavenly aid, could not so completely have accomplished it. Thereupon, the enemy, despairing of vanquishing us, ashamed to retreat, determined to fit out a formidable fleet, armed with all the artillery that the infernal regions could supply for the destruction of human kind. They displayed the British flag in the harbour of Quebec on the 26th June, 1759. On the receipt of intelligence of their arrival, our troops and

From *Narrative of the Doings During the Siege of Quebec and the Conquest of Canada* by Nun of the General Hospital of Quebec, Quebec, 1855.

militia came down from above. Our Generals left garrisons in the advanced posts, of which there is a great member above Montreal, in order to prevent the junction of their land forces, which it was understood were on the march, Our Generals did not fail to occupy most points where the enemy might land; but they could not guard them all. The sickness suffered by our troops, lately from France, and the losses they sustained in two or three recent actions with the enemy, though victorious, weakened us considerably; and it became necessary to abandon Point Levi, directly opposite to and commanding Quebec. The enemy soon occupied it and constructed their batteries; which commenced firing on the 24th July, in a manner to excite the greatest alarm in our unfortunate Communities of religious ladies.

It now became necessary to ascertain how we should accommodate ourselves. On the arrival of the English fleet, all the families of distinction, merchants, &c. capable of maintaining themselves, were removed to Three Rivers and Montreal, thereby relieving the garrison during the seige. Several members of our families and others whom we could not refuse, sought shelter with us, being at hand to succour their husbands and sons who might be wounded. As our house was beyond the range of the enemy's artillery, the poor people of the city did not fail to seek refuge there. All the out-houses, stables, barns, garrets, &c. were well filled.

The only consolation we enjoyed was that of daily seeing our Bishop, tho' in a dying state, exhorting and encouraging us not to relax in our good works. He was induced to retire from his capital, his palace and cathedral being reduced to ashes. He would not quit his flock while any hope remained of saving them; he lived with the curate of Charlesbourgh, three miles from Quebec. He permitted the several Almoners to celebrate Mass in our Choir, the Church being occupied by the wounded. Most people of the neighbourhood assisted at Mass, so that we were extremely crowded. It was consolatory to us -that we were enabled to have divine service during the siege, without interfering with the attentions to the sick and wounded. The only rest we partook of, was during prayers, and still it was not without interruption from the noise of shells and shot, dreading every moment that they would be directed towards us. The red-hot shot and carcasses terrified those who attended the sick during the night. They had the affliction of witnessing the destruction of the houses of the citizens, many of our connexions being immediately interested therein. During one night, upwards of fifty of the best houses in the Lower Town were destroyed. The vaults containing merchandise and many precious articles, did not escape the effects of the artillery. During this dreadful conflagration, we could offer nothing but our tears and prayers at the foot of the altar at such moments as could be snatched from the necessary attention to the wounded.

In addition to these misfortunes, we had to contend with more than one enemy; famine, at all times inseparable from war, threatened to reduce us to the last extremity; upwards of six hundred persons in our building and vicinity, partaking of our small means of subsistence, supplied from the government stores, which were likely soon to be short of what was required for the troops. In the midst of this desolation, the Almighty, disposed to humble us, and to deprive us of our substance, which we had probably amassed contrary to his will, and with too great avidity, still mercifully preserved our lives, which were daily periled, from the present state of the country.

Our enemy, informed of our destitute condition, was satisfied with battering our walls, despairing of vanquishing us, except by starvation. The river was the only obstruction we could oppose to the enemy; it likewise interfered to prevent our attacking them. They remained long under our eyes, meditating a descent; finally they determined upon landing at Beauport. Our army, always on the alert, being apprised by the advanced guard, immediately rushed to the spot, with that ardour natural to the French nation, without calculating upon the many causes likely to wrest the victory from their grasp.

The enemy, more cautious in their proceedings, on observing our army, hesitated in landing all their forces. We drove them from our redoubts, of which they had obtained possession. They became overwhelmed, and left the field strewed with killed and wounded. This action alone, had it been properly managed, would have finally relieved us from their invasion. We must not, however, attribute the mismanagement solely to our Generals; the Indian tribes, often essential to our support, became prejudicial to us on this occasion. Their hideous yells of defiance tended to intimidate our foes, who instead of meeting the onset, to which they had exposed themselves, precipitately retreated to their boats, and left us masters of the field. We charitably conveyed their wounded to our hospital, notwithstanding the fury and rage of the indians, who, according their cruel custom, sought to scalp them. Our army continued constantly ready to oppose the enemy. They dared not attempt a second landing; but ashamed of inaction, they took to burning the country places. Under shelter of darkness, they moved their vessels about seven or eight leagues above Quebec. There they captured a great number of prisoners, including women and children, who had taken refuge in that quarter. There again they experienced the valour of a small garrison of invalides, commanded by an officer, having one arm only, placed there in charge of military stores. The enemy, after a severe struggle, succeeded in capturing them.

After remaining in vain nearly three months at anchor in the Port, they appeared disposed to retire, despairing of success; but the Almighty, whose intentions are beyond our penetration, and always just, having resolved to subdue us, inspired the English Commander with the idea of making another attempt before his departure, which was done by surprise during the night. It was the intention, that night, to send supplies to a body of our troops forming an outpost on the heights near Quebec. A miserable deserter gave the information to the enemy, and persuaded them that it would be easy to surprise us, and pass their boats by using our countersign. They profited by the information, and the treasonable scheme succeeded. They landed on giving the password; our officer detected the deceit, but too late. He defended his post bravely with his small band, and was wounded. By this plan the enemy found themselves on the heights near the city. General De Montcalm, without loss of time, marched at the head of his army; but having to proceed about half a league, the enemy, had time to bring up their artillery, and to form for the reception of the French. Our leading battalions did not wait the arrival and formation of the other forces to support them, they rushed with their usual impetuosity on their enemies and killed a great number; but they were soon overcome by the artillery. They lost their General and a great number of officers. Our loss was not equal to that of the enemy; but it was not the less serious. General De Montcalm and his principal officers fell on the occasion.[2]

Several officers of the Canadian Militia, fathers of families, shared the same fate. We witnessed the carnage from our windows. It was in such a scene that charity triumphed, and caused us to forget self-preservation and the danger we were exposed to, in the immediate presence of the enemy. We were in the midst of the dead and the dying, who were brought in to us by hundreds, many of them our close connexions; it was necessary to smother our griefs and exert ourselves to relieve them. Loaded with the inmates of three convents, and all the inhabitants of the neighbouring suburbs, which the approach of the enemy caused to fly in this direction, you may judge of our terror and confusion. The enemy masters of the field, and within a few paces of our house; exposed to the fury of the soldiers, we had reason to dread the worst. It was then that we experienced the truth of the words of holy writ: "he who places his trust in the Lord has nothing to fear."

But tho' not wanting in faith or hope, the approach of night greatly added to our fears. The three sisterhoods with the exception of those who were dispersed over the house, prostrated themselves at the foot of the altar, to implore Divine mercy. The silence and consternation which prevailed, was suddenly interrupted by loud and repeated knocks at our doors. Two young Nuns, who were carrying broth to the sick, unavoidably happened to be near when the door was opened. The palor and fright which overcame them, touched the officer, and he prevented the guard from entering; he demanded the appearance of the Superiors, and desired them to assure us of protection; he said that part of the English force would entour and take possession of the house, apprehending that our army, which was not distant, might return and attack them, in their intrenchments;—which would certainly have taken place had our troops been enabled to reassemble before the capitulation. Soon after we saw their army drawn up under our windows. The loss we had, sustained the day before led us to fear, with reason, that our fate was decided, our people being unable to rally. General De Lévi, second in command, who became chief on the death of De Montcalm, had set out, some days previous, with about 3000 men, to re-inforce the upper posts, which were daily harassed by the enemy.

The loss we had just sustained, and the departure of that force, determined the Marquis De Vaudreuil, Governor General of the Colony, to abandon Quebec, being no longer able to retain it. The enemy having formed their entrenchments and their Camp, near the principal gate; their fleet commanding the Port, it was impossible to convey succour to the garrison. Mr. De Ramsay, who commanded, with a feeble garrison, without provisions or munitions, held out to the last extremity.

The principal inhabitants represented to him that they had readily sacrificed their property; but with regard to their wives and children, they could not make up their minds to witness their massacre, in the event of the place being stormed; it was therefore necessary to determine on capitulation.

The English readily accorded the articles demanded, religious toleration and civil advantages for the inhabitants. Happy in having acquired possession of a country, in which they had on several previous occasions failed, they were the most moderate of conquerors. We could not, without injustice, complain of the manner in which they treated us. However, their good treatment has not yet dried our tears. We do not shed them as did the good Hebrews' near the waters of Babylon, we are still in the land of promise; but our canticles will not again be heard until we can shake off this medley of nations, and until our temples are re-established; then we will celebrate, with the utmost gratitude, the merciful bounty of the Lord.

Let us now return to the French. Our Generals not finding their force sufficient to undertake the recovery of their losses, proceeded to the construction of a Fort, about five leagues above Quebec, and left a garrison therein, capable of checking the enemy from penetrating into the country. They did not remain inactive, but were constantly on the alert, harassing the enemy. The English were not safe beyond the gates of Quebec. General Murray the commander of the place, on several occasions was near being made a prisoner; and would not have escaped if our people had been faithful. Prisoners were frequently made, which so irritated the Commander, that he sent out detachments to pillage and burn the habitations of the country people.

The desire to recover the country and to acquire glory, was attended with great loss to our citizens. We heard of nothing but combats throughout the winter; the severity of the season had not the effect of making them lay down their arms. Wherever the enemy was observed, they were pursued without relaxation; which caused them to remark, "that they had never known a people more attached and faithful to their sovereign than the Canadians."

The English did not fail to require the oath of allegiance to their King; but, notwithstanding this forced obligation, which our people did not consider themselves bound to observe, they joined the flying camps of the French, whenever an opportunity offered.

Reverend Mothers,—as I give you this account, merely from memory, of what passed under our eyes, and with a view to afford you the satisfaction of knowing that we sustained with fortitude and in an edifying manner the painful duties, imposed upon us by our vocation; I will not undertake to relate to you all the particulars of the surrender of the country. I could do it but imperfectly, and from hearsay. I will merely say that the majority of the Canadians were disposed to perish rather than surrender; and that the small number of troops remaining were deficient of ammunition and provisions, and only surrendered in order to save the lives of the women and children, who are likely to be exposed to the greatest peril where towns are carried by assault.

Alas! Dear Mothers, it was a great misfortune for us that France could not send, in the spring, some vessels with provisions and munitions; we should still be under her dominion. She has lost a vast country and a faithful people, sincerely attached to their sovereign; a loss we must greatly deplore, on account of our religion, and the difference of the laws to which we must submit. We vainly flatter ourselves that peace may restore us to our rights; and that the Almighty will treat us in a fatherly manner, and soon cease to humble us; we still continue to experience his wrath. Our sins, doubtless, are very great, which leads us to apprehend that we are doomed to suffer long; the spirit of repentance is not general with the people, and God is still offended. We, however, yet entertain the hope of again coming under the dominion of our former masters.

You must, no doubt, have learnt that the English, moved by our importunities, have granted us a Bishop for this unfortunate colony. The choice of both governments has fallen upon the reverend Jean Olivier Briand. It is unnecessary that I should dwell upon his merits; they are well known. Without his protection and intercession our convent and property would have been sold to satisfy the debts, contracted to support the French troops; our creditors were compelled by order of the English Governor, to desist from their prosecutions. To him our establishment is indebted for its present existence. The French government is indebted to us in the sum of one hundred and twenty thousand livers, for expenses incurred in the maintenance of French troops. We look for no compensation for our services, He to whom we devote ourselves will recompence us amply. It is said that we will have to depend upon the public for support: we cannot believe it, as the English government, having witnessed the expenses we have incurred, will plead our cause with France, and not allow us to suffer such serious loss.

Endnotes

1. Fort Chouagen probably.
2. It is the memorable battle of the 13th September, 1759, which took place on the Plains of Abraham, that is alluded to. The Official account of the English loss on this occasion, is as follows:

Officers, Serjeants and privates killed	61
Officers, Serjeants, Drummers and privates wounded	598
Soldiers missing	5
Total	664

After the battle, several French officers admitted their loss amounted to nearly 1500 men, killed, wounded and prisoners.

An Historical Journal of the Campaigns in North America
Captain John Knox
For the years 1757, 1758, 1759, and 1760

While our Brigade halted at Beaumont, brigadier Monckton was pleased to order a manifesto in the French language to be fixed on the door of the church, of which the following is an exact translation:

> By his Excellency James Wolfe, Esq; Colonel of a Regiment of Infantry, Major-General and Commander in Chief of his Britannic Majesty's Forces in the River St. Lawrence, &c. &c.

"The formidable sea and land armament, which the people of Canada[1] now behold in the heart of their country, is intended by the King, my master, to check the insolence of France, to revenge the insults offered to the British colonies, and totally to deprive the French of their most valuable settlement in North America. For these purposes is the formidable army under my command intended.—The King of Great Britain wages no war with the industrious peasant, the sacred orders of religion, or the defenceless women and children: to these, in their distressful circumstances, his Royal clemency offers protection. The people may remain unmolested on their lands, inhabit their houses, and enjoy their religion in security; for these inestimable blessings, I expect the Canadians will take no part in the great contest between the two crowns. —But if, by a vain obstinacy and misguided valour, they presume to appear in [304] arms, they must expect the most fatal consequences; their habitations destroyed, their sacred temples exposed to an exasperated soldiery, their harvest utterly ruined, and the only passage for relief stopped up by a most formidable fleet. In this unhappy situation, and closely attacked by another great army, what can the wretched natives expect from opposition?—The unparalleled barbarities exerted by the French against our settlements in America might justify the bitterest revenge in the army under my command.—*But Britons breathe higher sentiments of humanity, and listen to the merciful dictates of the Christian religion.* Yet, should you suffer yourselves to be deluded by any imaginary prospect of our want of success, should you refuse those terms, and persist in opposition, then surely will the law of nations jus-

Excerpts from *An Historical Journal of the Campaigns in North America, Vol. I & II* by Captain John Knox, Toronto: The Champlain Society, 1914.

tify the waste of war, so necessary to crush an ungenerous enemy; and then the miserable Canadians must in the winter have the mortification of seeing the very families, for whom they have been exerting but a fruitless and indiscreet bravery, perish by the most dismal want and famine. In this great dilemma let the wisdom of the people of Canada shew itself; Britain stretches out a powerful, yet merciful, hand: faithful to her engagements, and ready to secure her in her most valuable rights and possessions: France, unable to support Canada, deserts her cause at this important crisis, and, during the whole war, has assisted her with troops who have been maintained only by making the natives feel all the weight of grievous and lawless oppression.——Given at Laurent in the island of Orleans, this 28th day of June, 1759.[2]

Ja. Wolfe.

Endnotes

1. The etymologies given to the name of this country are various; that which Monsieur Hennepin[1] has transmitted to us in his History of Canada,—(and dedicated to William the Third, of immortal memory) seems to be the most natural. He says, the Spaniards, who were the first discoverers, expected to have found some valuable mines there, and, being disappointed, called that part of it, on which the upper town of Quebec is now partly situated,—*il capo-di-nada,* 'a cape of nothing, or barren cape:' whence, adds this writer, the name of Canada has been corrupted. Others say, that, upon the Spaniards' first landing, they were accosted by the natives with the words *hah-ca-nah-dah,* which implies—'there's nothing here.' It is not a matter of great consequence to us; but, I think, Dr. Douglas's definition of it, in his American History, is very absurd;—for he pretends that it derives its name from Monsieur Kane, or Cane, who he advances to have been the first adventurer in the river St. Lawrence.—*Note by author.*
2. On the previous day Wolfe had issued a longer and much more boastful proclamation. (See *Siege of Quebec,* vol. ii. pp. 67–70.) If he thought that the Canadians would heed the menacing invitation he gave them to remain neutral, he did not understand their character. It is probable that he did not feel the confidence he expressed in his manifesto, and that it was prepared for its moral effect and with a view to further operations. The people removed the notice from the church door, carried it to Vaudreuil, and paid no further heed to it. It is true that they were wretched and oppressed, but with all her faults France—*la belle France*—was firmly planted in their affections.

7 August 1759

No alteration in wind or weather. Some sailors and marines strayed to-day into the country, contrary to repeated orders, to seek for vegetables: they were fired upon by a party of the enemy, and three were killed and scalped; the remainder, being ten in number, made their escape; two of them, however, were slightly wounded. Three Indians showed themselves to the westward of our batteries, and set up a war-shout; whereupon an Officer and thirty rangers, being detached to that quarter, scoured the environs for several miles, without making any discovery. All is quiet to-day between our batteries and the town. We esteem ourselves very happy in this country, having no fogs as in Nova Scotia, nor are we tormented with musketa's: we have myriads of the common black window fly, which, though they have no sting, are nevertheless troublesome in tainting our victuals. We are now tolerably well provided with the conveniencies of life; at times butchers' meat is scarce, but that is supplied by young horse-flesh; a loin of a colt eats well roasted, and there are many other parts of the carcase, which, if disguised in the same manner that one meets with other victuals at table, may deceive the nicest palate. I shall here annex the prices of the several under-mentioned articles, which only vary as there is plenty or otherwise.

A deserter surrendered yesterday to the north camp; the enemy fired many signals last night from their batteries, and other works, nearest to Charles's river; it was apprehended they would have sent [12] down some fire-rafts, as there are many of them floating at the entrance of that river;—the transports, traders, and other small craft, fell down a–stern of the fleet to be out of danger, and the men of wars' boats were instantly spread over the bason, in readiness to receive and grapple them. Three frigates and two transports are to pass the town with the first fair wind, they being for some time under orders for that purpose. A flag of truce was sent to the Point de Lest, with directions to the French General to return an answer from the same quarter; that for the future no regard will be paid to those that may be sent from the town, as the enemy take indirect advantages of them. Captain Ouchterlony, who is wounded and a prisoner, had the good fortune to be protected from the savages by a French grenadier, to whom it is confidently reported that General Wolfe sent twenty guineas, as a reward for his humanity: M. Montcalm returned the money, saying, 'the man had not particularly merited such a gratuity, having done no more than his duty, and what he hoped every Frenchman in his army would do under the like circumstances: '—This is an absurd piece of ostentation which the enemy greatly affect upon particular occasions.[1]—Ships are arrived with stores and provisions, under convoy of a frigate, who has brought some money for the subsistence of the army. Two of our twenty-four pounders are disabled at the batteries, whence we still maintain a brisk fire against the town, which appears to be in a most ruinous condition. In the evening Mr. Wolfe cannonaded and bombarded the left of the enemy's camp for above an hour; they were erecting some traverses to prevent his enfilading that flank, but were obliged to desist. A drunken Indian,[2] who crossed the river Montmorencie to-day, was surrounded and made prisoner by some centinels of the thirty-fifth regiment; he had no other weapon than a scalping knife, and has confessed that his intention was to surprise two or three centries, and carry back their scalps, in order to recover his credit with Monsieur [13] Montcalm, who had punished him for some misdemeanor.[3] We are now preparing a quantity of combustible materials, which are to be sent by the first opportunity to Admiral Holmes in the upper river.

9 August 1759

About one o'clock this morning a fire broke out in the lower town, and, by the wind's freshening, the flames spread with great rapidity, and continued burning until ten, by which the greatest part of that quarter was destroyed [4]: it communicated to one of their batteries, blew up a small magazine or powder-chest, burned their platforms and carriages, and discharged some of their guns. Another fire was perceived to burst forth in the upper town at the same time, which [14] was extinguished in less than an hour. Our artillery Officers observe, that they can now reach the north suburbs, where the Intendant's superb palace is situated; and this quarter they hope they shall soon put on the same romantic footing with the rest.—*A plan was this day sent over to General Wolfe for a fort, which, it is pretended, will be constructed on the island of Coudre, to contain fifteen hundred men, who are to garrison it this winter, in case we cannot become masters of Quebec.* A great smoke is perceived this morning on the north side, at a distance below Orleans: this is supposed to be occasioned by Captain Goreham's detachment, who are burning the settlements a-breast of the isle of Coudre. When the lower town was in flames early this morning, Mr. Wolfe ordered the piquets and grenadiers to march down to the beach, and make a feint to cross the ford leading to the Point de Lest; which the enemy perceiving, beat instantly to arms, and lined their works; whereupon the General gave them a spirited discharge from all his cannon and howitzers, and did great execution among them. The batteries of the town have re-assumed a little vigour to-day, in dealing their shot and shells with great profusion, and to as little purpose as heretofore. When the last flag of truce came from the enemy, the bearer of it was told, that we were surprised at their silence, and that we took unkind our not hearing from their batteries as often of late as usual. To which Monsieur replied-'they had intelligence from our deserters that they did no execution, and would therefore reserve their ammunition for another occasion.' He then demanded, why we did not fire as briskly on the garrison for some time past as before? And was answered to this effect:—"We have sufficiently damaged your town already, and we not chose to destroy all its buildings, as we hope soon to be in possession of it."

11 August 1759

ORDERS.
Camp at Montmorencie.

"When any detachment either sees or hears notice of the enemy, the Commander must send immediate advice of it to the General. When the escorts that cover the working parties are posted, they are to receive the enemy in that situation till the Commander thinks proper to reinforce them or call them off: in the mean time the working men are to get under arms, and wait for such orders as the Commanding Officer thinks proper to give. The General was extremely surprised to see the disorder that seemed to run through the working party this morning; and foresees, that, if a stop is not immediately put to such unsoldiery proceedings, they may have very dangerous consequences. The men fired this day upon one another, and upon the light infantry; and were scattered in such a manner, that a few resolute people would easily have defeated them; it is therefore ordered and commanded, that, when there is any alarm of this kind, every soldier shall remain at his post till ordered to march by the proper Officer: if any man presumes to detach himself, and leave his platoon, division, or party, the Officer will make an immediate example of him.—Divine service will be performed to-morrow morning at half past ten, for Bragg's, Monckton's, artillery, light infantry, and rangers; in the afternoon at five, for Anstruther's, Otway's, Lascelles's, marines, and Lawrence's grenadiers."

This morning[5] some working parties were detached from the troops in the north camp into the woods, to cut fascines and palisadoes, with light infantry to cover them. After being settled at [17] work, they spied a body of Indians creeping towards them; whereupon they ran in confusion to their arms, and, without any kind of order, fired impetuously at every thing they saw, whether friends or enemies; the General, hearing the alarm, flew to their assistance, leaving orders for an artillery Officer and two six-pounders to follow without delay. Upon the appearance of the General, the men recovered themselves, and vigorously attacked the savages in front; another body of them attempted to flank our parties, which an Officer suspecting, by an excellent disposition, anticipated their scheme, and repulsed them; by this time the field-pieces came up, just as the Indians were seemingly about to rally; which completely put an end to the affair, and drove the rabble across the river with great loss;[6] we had about fifteen men wounded, though none killed. Captain Goreham has sent an express to the General to acquaint him, that he has burned a large settlement, and made some prisoners; that his rangers met with some Canadians dressed like Indians, had routed them, and took a few scalps.

12 August 1759

[19] This morning, at day-break, our weather changed to uncommon heavy rain, which continued several hours without intermission; the wind is still fair, and blows fresh. A command of Highlanders is to go out this night, to distress the country. The town and our batteries have been respectively complaisant to-day. By deserters we are informed, that, a few days after the affair of the 31st of July, at the Point de Lest, the Sieur de Montcalm, in discourse with some of the Indian Chiefs, told them,—'You see we beat the English, we drove them away, we conquered them, we defeated them, &c. &c.,' to which the savages replied, 'Conquered them, and defeated them,—we will never believe that, until you drive them back to their ships; are they not still firing against Quebec, and are they not as unconcerned in their camps, as if nothing had happened?'—This anecdote evinces that, though illiterate, as these unhappy people are, they are not deficient in good natural parts, or so easily to be imposed upon, as some travellers insinuate. At night our weather cleared up, and the wind came right a-head; the detachment intented to reinforce Brigadier Murray still remain on board of the ships.

General Wolfe is preparing to withdraw his troops from the ground eastward of the cataract; for this purpose he has sent over all his artillery, stores, baggage, tents, &c. Some of the regiments will incamp here, and others are to remain on the island of Orleans until farther orders: the settlements on that agreeable spot have, for the most part, shared the same fate with the rest of the country, wherever our light troops have been detached. Two French regulars deserted across the rivulet of Montmorencie. We fired vigorously on the town last night. The enemy cannonaded our boats passing between this point, the west of Orleans, and the shore occupied by General Wolfe; they beat one of them to pieces, in which were seven men, six of whom were drowned. The wind still continues favourable for ships to pass the town. The garrison are making merlins and embrasures to their great barbet battery next the bason; our batteries retard these works considerably. A sloop of war is under orders to sail to England with dispatches from the Admiral and General. General Wolfe is endeavouring to draw the flower of the French Army, from their strong intrenched camp, to an engagement on his own ground, before he abandons it.

[41] The killed, wounded, and missing of this army, in the different services where we have been employed, since our arrival before Quebec, amount to:

	K.	W.	M.	
Commissioned Officers	10	47	...	Total of every
Serjeants	9	26	...	Rank, Regulars,
Drummers	...	7	...	Marines, Artillery,
Rank and File	163	575	17	and Rangers.
Total	182	655	17	854

Being now come to that period at which the General drew up a summary of the various transactions of this armament, since our arrival before Quebec, I take the liberty, *in compliance with the particular desire of several gentlemen, whose names are prefixed to this work,* to annex here a transcript of that review comprehended in his Excellency's letter to the Ministry, as it is not only the best and most lively recapitulation that can be made of our sundry proceedings to this day, but also demonstrates, in a great measure, the authenticity of my labours:

'The obstacles we have met with, in the operations of the campaign, are much greater than we had reason to expect, or could foresee; not so much from the number of the enemy (though superior to us) as from the natural strength of the country, which the Marquis de Montcalm seems wisely to depend upon. When I learned that succours of all kinds had been thrown into Quebec; that five battalions of regular troops, completed from the best of the inhabitants of the country, some of the troops of the colony, and every Canadian that was able to bear arms, besides several nations of savages, had taken the field in a very advantageous situation; I could not flatter myself that I should be able to reduce the place.

7 September 1759

Fine warm weather: Admiral Holmes's squadron weighed early this morning; at six o'clock we doubled the mouth of the Chaudiere, which is near half a mile over; and at eight we came to an anchor off Cape Rouge; here is a spacious cove, into which the river St. Michael disembogues, and within the mouth of it are the enemy's floating batteries; a large body of the enemy are well intrenched round the cove,[7] (which is of a circular form) as if jealous of a descent in those parts: they appear very numerous, and may amount to about one thousand six hundred men, besides their cavalry, who are cloathed in blue, and mounted on neat light horses of different colours; they seem very alert, parading and counter-marching between the woods on the heights in their rear, and their breast-works, in order to make their numbers shew to greater advantage. The lands all round us are high and commanding, which gave the enemy an opportunity of popping at our ships, this morning, as we tacked in working up: I did not hear of any damage sustained, though they were a little troublesome. Upon our coming to an anchor, they turned out their floats, and ranged them in great order; their cavalry then dismounted, formed on the right of the infantry, and their whole detachment ran down the precipice with a ridiculous shout, and manned their works. I have often reflected upon the absurdity of this practice in the French, who entertain a high opinion of their own discipline and knowledge in the art of war; [57] there is nothing that can be more absurd than such noises in engaging an enemy; I think it expressive of the greatest diffidence, and must tend to defeat all regularity and good order among themselves, because their men arc thereby confused, and are rendered incapable of paying attention to their Officers or their duty;—it is a false courage. How different, how nobly awful,[8] and expressive of true valour is the custom of the British troops! they do not expend their ammunition at an immense distance; and, if they advance to engage, or stand to receive the charge, they are steady, profoundly silent and attentive, reserving their fire until they have received that of their adversaries, over whom they have a tenfold advantage; there are cases where huzzaing may be necessary, but those are very rare; the practice is unmilitary in an army or body of regulars; and experience plainly shows us, that the troops, who, in perfect silence, engage an enemy, waiting for their first fire, will always preserve a superiority. This afternoon, at two o'clock, the Seahorse, Leostaff, and two floating batteries, that were lately taken, were ordered to edge into the cove, and attack the enemy's armed floats; at the same time the troops put into their boats, and rowed up and down, as if intending to land at different places, to amuse the enemy; the Brigadiers, no doubt, knew this was intended only as a *finesse,* but the corps thought they were, in reality, going a-shore; and such was their zeal, that they were much disappointed, when, after parading some time in this manner, they were ordered back to their ships; this seems calculated to fix the attention of the enemy on that particular part, while a descent is meditated elsewhere, perhaps lower down.[9]

11 September 1759

An Officer of the forty-third regiment was sent a-shore to St. Nicholas, to endeavour to procure some fresh provisions, but could not succeed, the troops not having sufficient for themselves; the party that went in search of cattle found only seven cows and two sheep, guarded by a few Indian men and women, upon whom our advanced-guard too eagerly fired, before they were within reach, by which the rabble made their escape, shouting and yelling in their flight, intending thereby to alarm the country. Great preparations are making, throughout the fleet and army, to surprise the enemy, and compel them to decide the fate of Quebec by a battle: all the long-boats below the town are to be filled with seamen, marines, and such detachments as can be spared from Points Levi and Orleans, in order to make a feint off Beauport and the Point de Lest, and endeavour to engross the attention of the Sieur de Montcalm, while the army are to force a descent on this side of the town. The Officer of our regiment, who commanded the escort yesterday on the reconnoitring party, being asked, in the General's hearing, after the health of one of the gentlemen who was reported to be ill, replied,—'he was in a very low indifferent state;' which the other lamented, saying, 'he has but a puny, delicate constitution.'—This struck his Excellency, it being his own case, who interrupted, 'Don't tell me of constitution, that Officer has good spirits, and good spirits will carry a man through every thing.'

12 September 1759

A soldier of the Royal Americans deserted this day from the south shore, an one came over to us from the enemy, who informed the General, 'that he belonged to a detachment (composed of two Officers and fifty men, who had been sent across the river to take a prisoner; [66] that the French Generals suspect we are going higher up, to lay waste the country, and destroy such ships and craft as they have got above; and that Monsieur Montcalm will not be prevailed on to quit his situation, insisting that the flower of our army are still below the town; that the reduction of Niagara has caused great discontent in the French army, that the wretched Canadians are much dissatisfied, and that Monsieur de Levis is certainly marched, with a detachment of the army, to Montreal, in order to reinforce Mr. Bourlemacque, and stop General Amherst's progress.' This fellow added, 'that if we were fairly landed on the north side of the river, an incredible number of the French regulars would actually desert to us.'—In consequence of this agreeable intelligence, the following orders were this day issued to the army.

ORDERS.
On board the Sutherland.

"The enemy's force is now divided, great scarcity of provisions now in their camp, and universal discontent among the Canadians; the second Officer in command is gone to Montreal or St. John's, which gives reason to think, that General Amherst is advancing into the colony: *a vigorous blow struck by the army at this juncture may determine the fate of Canada.* Our troops below are in readiness to join us; all the light artillery and tools are embarked at the point of Levi, and the troops will land where the French seem least to expect it. The first body that gets on shore is to march directly to the enemy, and drive them from any little post they may occupy; the Officers must be careful that the succeeding bodies do not, by any mistake, fire upon those who go on before them. The battalions must form on the upper ground with expedition, and be ready to charge whatever presents itself. When the artillery and troops are landed, a corps will be left to secure the landing-place, while the rest march on, and endeavour to bring the [67] French and Canadians to a battle. *The Officers and men will remember what their country expects from them, and what a determined body of soldiers, inured to war, is capable of doing, against five weak French battalions, mingled with a disorderly peasantry.* The soldiers must be attentive and obedient to their Officers, and resolute in the execution of their duty."

The Brigadiers Monckton and Murray, with the troops under their command, reimbarked this day, from the parish of St. Nicholas, and returned to their ships. This evening all the boats of the fleet below the town were filled with marines, &c. &c. covered by frigates and sloops of war, worked up, and lay half-channel over, opposite to Beauport, as if intending to land in the morning, and thereby fix the enemy's whole attention to that quarter; the ships attending them are to edge over, at break of day, as near as possible without grounding, and cannonade the French intrenchments. At nine o'clock this night, our army in high spirits, the first division of them put into the flat-bottomed boats, and, in a short time after, the whole squadron moved up the river with the tide of flood, and, about an hour before day-light next morning, we fell down with the ebb. Weather favourable, a star-light night.

Battle of Quebec

Thursday, September 13, 1759

Before day-break this morning we made a descent upon the north shore, about half a quarter of a mile to the eastward of Sillery; and the light troops were fortunately, by the rapidity of the current, carried lower down, between us and Cape Diamond; we had, in this debarkation, thirty flat-bottomed boats, containing about sixteen hundred men. This was a great surprise on the enemy, who, from the natural strength of the place, did not suspect, and consequently were not prepared against, so bold an attempt. The chain of centries, which they had posted along the summit of the [68] heights, galled us a little, and picked off several men[10], and some Officers, before our light infantry got up to dislodge them[11]. This grand enterprise was conducted, and executed with great good order and discretion; as fast as we landed, the boats put off for reinforcements, and the troops formed with much regularity: the General, with Brigadiers Monckton and Murray, were a-shore with the first division. We lost no time here, but clamoured up one of the steepest precipices that can be conceived, being almost a perpendicular, and of an incredible height. As soon as we gained the summit, all was quiet, and not a shot was heard, owing to the excellent conduct of the light infantry under Colonel Howe; it was by this time clear day-light. Here we formed again, the river and the south country in our rear, our right extending to the town, our left to Sillery, and halted a few minutes[12]. The General then detached the light troops to our left to route the enemy from their battery, and to disable their guns, except they could be rendered serviceable to the party who were to remain there; and this service was soon performed. We then faced to the right, and marched towards the town by files, till we came to the plains of Abraham;[13] an even piece of ground which Mr. Wolfe had made choice of, while we stood forming upon the hill. Weather showery: about six o'clock [69] the enemy first made their appearance upon the heights, between us and the town; whereupon we halted, and wheeled to the right, thereby forming the line of battle.

The enemy had now likewise formed [70] the line of battle, and got some cannon to play on us, with round and canister-shot; but what galled us most was a body of Indians and other marksmen they had concealed in the corn opposite to the front of our right wing, and a coppice that stood opposite to our center, inclining towards our left; but the Colonel Hale, by Brigadier Monckton's orders, advanced some platoons, alternately, from the forty-seventh regiment, which, after a few rounds, obliged these sculkers to retire: we were now ordered to lie down, and remained some time in this position. About eight o'clock we had two pieces of short brass six-pounders playing on the enemy, which threw them into some confusion, and obliged them to alter their disposition, and Montcalm formed them into three large columns; about nine the two armies moved a little nearer each other. The light cavalry made a faint attempt upon our parties at the battery of Sillery, but were soon beat off, and Monsieur de Bougainville, with his troops from Cape Rouge, came down to attack the flank of our second line, hoping to penetrate there, but, by a masterly disposition of Brigadier Townshend, they were forced to desist, and the third battalion of Royal Americans was then detached to the first ground we had formed on after we gained the heights, to preserve the communication with the beach and our boats. About ten o'clock the enemy began to advance briskly in three columns, with loud shouts and recovered arms, two of them inclining to the left of our army, and the third towards our right, firing obliquely at the two extremities of our line, from the distance of one hundred and thirty—, until they came within forty yards; which our troops withstood with the greatest intrepidity and firmness, still reserving their fire, and paying the strictest obedience to their Officers: this uncommon steadiness, together with the havoc which the grape-shot from our field-pieces made among them, threw them into some disorder, and was most critically maintained by a well-timed, regular, and heavy discharge of our small arms, [71] such as they could no longer oppose; hereupon they gave way, and fled with precipitation, so that, by the time the cloud of smoke was vanished, our men were again loaded, and, profiting by the advantage we had over them, pursued them almost to the gates of the town, and the bridge over the little river, redoubling our fire with great eagerness, making many Officers and men prisoners. The weather cleared up, with a comfortably warm sun-shine: the Highlanders chased them vigorously towards Charles's river, and the fifty-eighth to the suburb close to John's gate,[14] until they were checked by the cannon from the two hulks; at the same time a gun, which the town had brought to bear upon us with grape-shot, galled the progress of the regiments to the right, who were likewise pursuing with equal ardour, while Colonel Hunt Walsh, by a very judicious movement, wheeled the battalions of Bragg and Kennedy to the left, and flanked the coppice where a body of the enemy made a stand, as if willing to renew the action; but a few platoons from these corps completed our victory. Then it was that Brigadier Townshend came up, called off the pursuers, ordered the whole line to dress, and recover their former ground. Our joy at this success is inexpressibly damped by the loss we sustained of one of the greatest heroes which this or any other age can boast of,—GENERAL JAMES WOLFE, who received his mortal wound, as he was exerting himself at the head of the grenadiers of Louis-[72] bourg; and Brigadier Monckton was unfortunately wounded upon the left of the forty-third, and right of the forty-seventh regiment, at much the same time; whereby the command devolved on Brigadier Townshend, who, with Brigadier Murray, went to the head of every regiment, and returned thanks for their extraordinary good behaviour, congratulating the Officers on our success. There is one incident very remarkable, and which I can affirm from my own personal knowledge,—that the enemy were extremely apprehensive of being rigorously treated; for, conscious of their inhuman behaviour to our troops upon a former occasion, the Officers who fell into our hands most piteously (with hats off) sued for quarter, repeatedly declaring they were not at Fort William Henry (called by them Fort St. George[15]) in the year 1757. A soldier of the Royal Americans, who deserted from us this campaign, and fought against us to-day, was found wounded on the field of battle; he was immediately tried by a general court-martial, and was shot to death, pursuant to his sentence. While the two armies were engaged this morning, there was an incessant firing between the town and our south batteries. By the time that our troops had taken a little refreshment, a quantity of intrenching tools were brought a-shore, and the regiments were employed in redoubting our ground, and landing some cannon and ammunition. The Officers who are prisoners say, that Quebec will surrender in a few days: some deserters, who came out to us in the evening, agree in that opinion, and inform us, that the Sieur de Montcalm is dying, in great agony, of a wound he received to-day in their retreat. Thus has our late renowned Commander, by his superior eminence in the art of war, and a most judicious *coup d'etat,* made a conquest of this fertile, healthy, and hitherto formidable country, with a handful of troops only, in spite of the political schemes, and most vigorous efforts, of the famous Montcalm, and many other Officers of rank and experience, at the head of an army considerably more numerous. My pen is too feeble to draw the character of this *British Achilles;* but [73] the same may, with justice, be said of him as was said of Henry IV. of France: *He was possessed of courage, humanity, clemency, generosity, affability, and politeness.* And though the former of these happy ingredients, how essential soever it may be in the composition of a soldier, is not alone sufficient to distinguish an expert Officer; yet, I may, with strict truth, advance, that Major General James Wolfe, by his great talents, and martial disposition, which he discovered early in life, was greatly superior to his experience in generalship, and was by no means inferior to a Frederic, a Henry, or a Ferdinand.

> "When the matter match'd his mighty mind,
> Up rose the Hero: on his piercing eye
> Sat observation, on each glance of thought
> Decision follow'd, as the thunderbolt
> Pursues the flash."

14 September 1759

The Sieur * de Montcalm[16] died late last night; when his wound was dressed, and he settled in bed, the Surgeons who attended him were desired to acquaint him ingenuously with their sentiments of him, and, being answered that his wound was mortal, he calmly replied, 'he was glad of it :' his Excellency then demanded,—'whether he could survive it long, and how long?' He was told, 'about a dozen hours, perhaps more, peradventure less.' 'So much the better,' rejoined this eminent warrior; 'I am happy I shall not live to see the surrender of Quebec.' He then ordered his Secretary into the room to adjust his private affairs, which as soon as they were dispatched, he was visited by Monsieur de Ramsey, the French King's Lieutenant, and by other principal Officers, who desired to receive his Excellency's commands, with the farther measures to be pursued for the defence of Quebec, the capital of Canada. To this the Marquis made the following answer,—'I'll neither give orders, nor interfere any farther; I have much business that must be attended to, of greater moment than your ruined garrison and this wretched country: my time is very short,—therefore pray leave me—I wish you all comfort, and to be happily extricated from your present perplexities.' He then called for his Chaplain, who, with the Bishop of the colony, remained with him till he expired.

Endnotes

1. There does not seem to have been any "ostentation" on the part of the Marquis de Vaudreuil in returning the twenty guineas sent by General Wolfe to the soldier of the Regiment of Guienne who conveyed the wounded Captain Ochterloney to the General Hospital. The man, as Vaudreuil said, simply did his duty. It would be, no doubt, dangerous to allow men to receive gifts from the enemy. Ochterloney was cared for most tenderly by Madame de Ramezay, directress of the hospital, "who wept when he died." Ochterloney died on August 23, and all his effects, which had been sent to him from the British camp, were returned. General Wolfe addressed a letter to Madame de Ramezay thanking her for her kindness to his officer and assuring her that he would protect the community if fortune favoured his arms. (*British Magazine,* 1761: see Wright's *Life of Wolfe,* p. 540, note.) This promise was faithfully carried out by General Townshend.
2. The advent of this drunken Indian is responsible for a choice entry in the *Journal* of Townshend, Wolfe's second brigadier, on the 8th: "This morning an Indian Swam over the ford below the Falls with an Intention as we supposed to scalp a Centry, but on the Centry running up to him and presenting his piece to his breast he got down on his knees, threw away his knife and delivered himself up, he was a very savage looking brute & naked all too an arse Clout, he seem'd to be very apprehensive of putting him to Death, altho' there was several in the Camp that spoke Indian Language we cou'd not get him to understand any sort of Languages . . . Most Nights we hear the Indians Hollow in the Woods all about us." (*Siege of Quebec,* vol. v. p. 257.)
3. It is not probable that Montcalm punished the Indian in any way, except in limiting his supply of rum. On this occasion he had imbibed a sufficient quantity to render him incapable of understanding any "sort of Languages."
4. The low town, in the center of which stood l'eglise de la Sainte Victoire,[1] was completely destroyed by this conflagration: it was occasioned by one of our shells, which forced its way into a vaulted cellar, hitherto deemed bombproof, wherein were twenty pipes of brandy, and several smaller casks of other spirituous liquors; this was the richest and best

inhabited part of the whole city, and contained the most magnificent houses, churches and public buildings excepted.—*Note by author.*

5. The order previously quoted was issued after the events here described by the author. Wolfe, who was present, notes the "bad disposition of our people, loss sustained on that account." (*Journal.*) The order was evidently issued in consequence.

6. Wolfe says that the enemy escaped "with little damages to them."

7. Bougainville had strong entrenchments on the summit of the cliff on the east side of the river Cap Rouge, which commanded the river St. Lawrence. He also had a redoubt on the north side of the road leading to Sillery.

8. The author is evidently profoundly impressed with the superiority of British methods.

9. These various movements were designed, as the author states, to draw the attention of the enemy from the real place of attack, which the Brigadiers proposed to make between the Cap Rouge River and St. John.

10. In the boat where I was, one man was killed; one seaman, with four soldiers, were slightly, and two mortally wounded.—*Note by author.*

11. Captain Donald M'Donald, a very gallant Officer, of Fraser's Highlanders, commanded the advanced-guard of the light infantry, and was, consequently, among the foremost on shore; as soon as he and his men gained the height, he was challenged by a centry, and, with great presence of mind, from his knowledge of the French service, answered him according to their manner: it being yet dark, he came up to him, told him he was sent there, with a large command, to take post, and desired him to go with all speed to his guard, and to call off all the other men of his party who were ranged along the hill, for that he would take care to give a good account of the B——Anglois, if they should persist; this *finesse* had the desired effect, and saved us many lives, &c.—*Note by author.*

12. *The hill they climb'd, and halted at its top, of more than mortal size: Tow'ring they seem'd, an host angelic, clad in burning arms!*-Note by author.

13. It is interesting to observe that while the French always refer to the "Heights," the British speak of the "Plains" of Abraham. This is probably due to the fact that the place chosen by Wolfe was a level piece of ground much lower than the lands surrounding the walls of the city. The history of the Heights or Plains of Abraham began 124 years before the siege of Quebec. On December 4, 1635, while Champlain, the founder of Quebec, was confined to his bed in the Château St. Louis, a piece of land not far from the site of the battle of the Plains was given to Abraham Martin, a pilot of Scotch descent, who had settled in Quebec. Thirteen years later he obtained a further grant near by, in all thirty-two acres, not far from the Martello tower on the north. Claire Fontaine Street, Quebec, derived its name from a spring on the property, officially described as the *Fontaine d'Abraham.* Martin used the land for pasturage, and, as little of the ground in the vicinity was under cultivation, Martin's cattle wandered at pleasure over the adjoining fields, and thus the name of the Heights of Abraham was given to a far larger tract of land than that within the boundaries defined by the concession. At the time of the siege of Quebec all the ground on the plateau between the town walls and Sillery was commonly referred to as the Heights of Abraham.

14. It was the Canadians who made this gallant stand in the wood surrounding St. John's Gate. They were driven over the cliff, but still disputed every inch of the retreat to the bat-

tery at the foot. Over two hundred were killed in this encounter. Many of the French regulars escaped the fury of the Highlanders in consequence of this resistance.

15. "Fort George": see Errata.

16. Montcalm, already slightly wounded at the beginning of the battle, was endeavouring with his face to the foe to rally his troops, when he received a fatal wound in the loins. Two grenadiers hastened to his side, and supported by them the General entered the city through St. Louis Gate. As he rode down the street on his black horse some women began to weep, exclaiming, "Oh mon Dieu! Mon Dieu! le Marquis est tué!" Montcalm, concealing his sufferings, tried to reassure them. "Ce n'est rien! Ce n'est rien! Ne vous affligez pas pour moi, mes bonnes amies." He was taken to the house of Mr. Arnoux, the surgeon; that gentleman himself was on duty at Lake Champlain, but his younger brother attended to the wound and saw at once that it was fatal.

"He begged Arnoux to be so kind and outspoken as to tell him how many hours he might yet live. Arnoux answered him that he might live till three in the morning. 'So much the better,' returned Montcalm, 'I am happy that I shall not live to see the surrender of Quebec.'"

Focus Questions

1. Consider how and why these two accounts from New France differ in their portrayal of the French Canadians, Native people, and Conquest itself?

   [handwritten] non - Canadians / Qebec won most battles but not the
   won that counted. letter, civilian, - religious

   captain- won the battle!, journal, soldier
   - order, detail
   - Conquest war; stratigy
   - tackficks
   natives- savages

   → destroyed
   → knowledgeable
   nurse - Natives
   → loud & disadvantage

2. What effect do these differences have on your ability to understand what really happened? What does this say, overall, about what history is and how it works?

   [handwritten] - different prespectives= us less bias = manipulitive

   - non made you feer bad, she was writing to superior
   → 'God has a better plan'
   → we need money

3. What sorts of challenges were facing the French Canadians and the English forces, respectively, as outlined in these accounts? (and what can you learn about their lives from them?)

- lack of food (both) ⚡

French could attack at any time

- landscape - cliff/river
  - winter is on its way

- English burned farms

- Traders

- issue of moral btw English

4. If you were an English-Canadian historian using these two documents to write about Conquest, what would you find most useful in each one, and what would you ignore? What if you were a French Canadian historian?

- conditions
- emphasis on battles won

AN ADDENDUM

Introduction

Along with its political effects, Conquest had enormous cultural ramifications, and not just for French Canada. As the account of Captain Knox implies, it was a moment of enormous pride for the English—and that pride transferred itself into the cultural vocabulary of English Canada as demonstrated by the lyrics of Alexander Muir's 1867 song, *The Maple Leaf Forever.* Taking inspiration from the thing which eventually becomes the defining symbol of Canada itself—the maple leaf—Muir's song was considered for decades to be the country's national anthem—at least by English Canadians. Notably, the French element of Canada's cultural landscape is almost entirely absent from the lyrics (the thistle, shamrock and rose referred to Scotland, Ireland, and England, respectively). French Canada appears in this song only by inference—as the conquered people of "Wolfe, the dauntless hero."[1]

Cultural differences—albeit much more subtle ones—also made their way into the French and English versions of Canada's now-official national anthem, *O Canada!* Although the modern lyrics to the anthem have changed slightly, those originally penned by French Canadian Adolphe-Basile Routhier in 1882, and later by English Canadian R. Stanley Weir (1908), demonstrate how music could become instrumental to politics.

[1] Some later accounts of this song claim that Muir's original lyrics included reference to the Lily (France), although the song is most often reproduced as it appears here.

The Maple Leaf Forever
Alexander Muir
1867

The Maple Leaf Forever

In days of yore, from Britain's shore,
Wolfe the dauntless hero came,
And planted firm Britannia's flag,
On Canada's fair domain.
Here may it wave, our boast, our pride,
And joined in love together,
The Thistle, Shamrock, Rose entwine
The Maple Leaf for ever!

The Maple Leaf, our emblem dear,
The Maple Leaf for ever!
God save our Queen, and Heaven bless
The Maple Leaf for ever!

At Queenston Heights and Lundy's Lane,
Our brave fathers, side by side,
For freedom, homes, and loved ones dear,
Firmly stood and nobly died;
And those dear rights which they maintained,
We swear to yield them never!
Our watchword ever more shall be,
The Maple Leaf for ever!

[Chrous]

Our fair Dominion now extends
From Cape Race to Nootka Sound;
May peace for ever be our lot,
And plenteous store abound:

And may those ties of love be ours
Which discord cannot sever,
And flourish green o'er Freedom's home,
The Maple Leaf for ever!
The Maple Leaf, our emblem dear,
The Maple Leaf for ever!
And flourish green o'er Freedom's home,
The Maple Leaf for ever!

On merry England's far-famed land
May kind Heaven sweetly smile;
God bless Old Scotland evermore,
And Ireland's Emerald Isle!
Then swell the song, both loud and long,
Till rocks and forest quiver,
God save our Queen, and Heaven bless
The Maple Leaf for ever!

[Chorus]

O Canada!
Adophe-Basile Routhier
1882

O Cananda!

O Canada! land of our sires,
Whose brow is bound with glorious bays,
The sword thy valorous hand can wield
And bear the Cross that faith inspires,
What mighty deeds hast thou beheld,
An epogee of glorious sights!
The faith, thy shield through all thy days,
Shall still protect our homes and rights,
Shall still protect our homes and rights.

By the broad river's giant stream,
Beneath God's ever-watchful sights,
Canadians thrive in Hope's bright gleam,
Sprung from a great and noble race,
Cradled by self-denial's hand,
In the new world high Heaven did trace
The pathway of their progress grand,
And ever guided by its light
They'll guard the banner of their land,
They'll guard the banner of their land.

Christ's forerunner, their patron saint,
From him they bear a crown offire,
Enemies of the tyrant's base restraint
The depths of loyalty their deeds inspire.
And their proud liberty they would keep
With never-ending concord blest,

While by their genius sown deep
Upon our soil the truth shall rest,
Upon our soil the truth shall rest.
O sacred love of altar and of throne,
May thy immortal breath our spirits fire!
'Midst other races as we hold
Thy law whose sway we ever own,
May we as brethren all aspire,
With faith's control, while clear shall ring,
As from our sires in days of old,
The conquering cry, "For Christ and King,"
The conquering cry, "For Christ and King."

O Canada!
R. Stanley Weir
1908

O Cananda!

O Canada! Our Home and Native Land!
True patriot-love in all thy sons command;
With glowing hearts we see thee rise,
The True North, strong and free,
And stand on guard, 0 Canada,
We stand on guard for thee.
O Canada, glorious and free!
We stand on guard for thee!
O Canada! Where pines and maples grow,
Great prairies spread and lordly rivers flow,
How dear to us thy broad domain,
From East to Western Sea;
Thou land of hope for all who toil!
Thou True North, strong and free!
O Canada, glorious and free!
We stand on guard for thee!

O Canada! Beneath thy shining skies
May stalwart sons and gentle maidens rise,
To keep thee steadfast through the years,
From East to Western Sea.
Our Fatherland, our Motherland!
Our True North, strong and free!
O Canada, glorious and free!
We stand on guard for thee!

Focus Questions

1. What sort of picture do the lyrics of *The Maple Leaf Forever* draw about Canada in the late nineteenth century? Why do you think the song remained (and remains) so popular?

2. What are the differences between the lyrics of the two versions (French and English) of "O Canada!" What do these differences mean?

3. Who or what do the lyrics of these two versions of the anthem exclude? What do these exclusions, if they exist, say about Canada as a whole?

4. Do you think that governments/citizens should change the words and meaning of their national anthems to better reflect the country's social or political realities, or should tradition take precedence?

5. Do you think the current national anthem best reflects an understanding of Canada today? How would you change it?

3

Rebellions and Responsibilities: The Durham Report

Introduction

In the late 1830s, the British colonies of Upper and Lower Canada (Ontario and Québec, respectively) both experienced violent rebellion. These rebellions came on the heels of nearly two decades of vocal, and sometimes violent, opposition to colonial governance. In both cases, the majority of the population had been denied any form of effective voice within the political system, and had found themselves subjected, instead, to leadership and rule from the social and economic elites of their communities—the so-called Family Compact of Upper Canada, and the *Chateau Clique* of Lower Canada. In Lower Canada, the fact that the members of this so-called *Chateau Clique* were almost exclusively English, only added to the tensions (French Canadians very rarely held positions of any importance in the administration of their colony).

In Upper Canada, the most vocal reformer was a man called William Lyon Mackenzie (the grandfather of later Prime Minister William Lyon Mackenzie King). Mackenzie, an admirer of the political system in the United States, led a short-lived and poorly executed rebellion in December 1837. In Lower Canada, Louis Joseph Papineau led the French-Canadian rebels in a much more deadly series of battles against British troops, wherein over three-hundred people were killed. While at the time, the violence perpetrated by Mackenzie and Papineau lost them support amongst their followers, both have since emerged in the historical record as folk heroes.

In the immediate aftermath of these uprisings, the British crown sent John George Lambton, otherwise known as Lord Durham, to conduct an investigation into the causes and possible solutions to political unrest in the Canadian colonies. Durham's report is one of the most significant political documents in Canadian history. While its major recommendations, most notably for Responsible Government, would take many more years (and the now famous coalition between Baldwin and LaFontaine) to come to fruition, the content of the report captures quite clearly the attitudes of the British crown to the Canadian colonies. In particular, its recommendations and desire for the assimilation of French Canadians into the apparently 'superior' culture of the English, and its belief that Responsible Government would actually *strengthen,* rather than weaken, the ties of the Canadian people to the British Empire, are particularly telling of attitudes of the time. The Durham report has been said by some to show evidence of extraordinary prejudice against French Canadians, further proof that Canada simply could not work as a "bi-national" nation. Others see the document as a pragmatic response to the difficulties of governing the colony. As you read this extract, consider which of these two interpretations you think best reflects the content of the Report itself.

Report on the Affairs of British North America from the Earl of Durham

1839

On Responsible Government

I have now brought under review, the most prominent features of the condition and institutions of the British Colonies in North America. It has been my painful task to exhibit a state of things which cannot be contemplated without grief, by all who value the well-being of our colonial fellow-countrymen, and the integrity of the British empire. I have described the operation of those causes of division which unhappily exist in the very composition of society; the disorder produced by the working of an ill-contrived constitutional system, and the practical mis-management which these fundamental defects have generated in every department of government.

It is not necessary that I should take any pains to prove, that this is a state of things which should not, which cannot, continue. Neither the political nor the social existence of any community, can bear much longer the operation of these causes which have; in Lower Canada, already produced a long practical cessation of the regular course of constitutional government; which have occasioned the violation, and necessitated the absolute suspension, of the provincial constitution—and which have resulted in two insurrections—two substitutions of martial for civil law—and two periods of a general abeyance of every guarantee that is considered essential for the protection of a British subject's rights. I have already described the state of feeling which prevails among each of the contending parties, or rather their races; their all-pervading and irreconcilable enmity to each other; the entire and irremediable disaffection of the whole French population, as well as the suspicion with which the English regard the imperial government; and the determination of the French, together with the tendency of the English to seek for a redress of their intolerable present evils in the chances of a separation from Great Britain. The disorders of Lower Canada admit of no delay; the existing form of government is but a temporary and forcible subjugation. The recent constitution is one of which neither party would tolerate the re-establishment, and of which the bad working has been such that no friend to liberty or to order could desire to see the province again subjected to its mischievous influence. Whatever may be the difficulty of discovering a remedy, its urgency is certain and obvious.

Nor do I believe that the necessity for adopting some extensive and decisive measures for the pacification of Upper Canada, is at all less imperative. From the account which I have given of the causes of disorder in that province, it will be seen that I do not consider them by any means of such a nature as to be irremediable, or even to be susceptible of no remedy that shall not effect an organic change in the existing constitution. It cannot be denied, indeed, that the continuance of the many practical grievances which I have described as subjects of complaint, and above all, the determined resistance to such a system of responsible government, as would give the people a real control over its own destinies, have, together with the irritation caused by the late insurrection, induced a large portion of the population to look with envy at the material prosperity of their neighbours in the United States, under a perfectly free and eminently responsible, government; and, in despair of obtaining such benefits under their present institutions, to desire the adoption of a Republican Constitution, or even an incorporation with the American Union. But I am inclined to think, that such feelings have made no formidable or irreparable progress; on the contrary, I believe that all the discontented parties, and especially the reformers of Upper Canada, look with considerable confidence to the result of my mission. The different parties believe that when the case is once fairly put before the mother country, the desired changes in the policy of their government will be readily granted: they are now tranquil, and I believe loyal; determined to abide the decision of the home Government, and to defend their property and their country against rebellion and invasion. But I cannot but express my belief, that this is the last effort of their almost exhausted patience—and that the disappointment of their hopes on the present occasion, will destroy forever their expectation of good resulting from British connection. I do not mean to say that they will renew the rebellion, much less do I imagine that they will array themselves in such force as will be able to tear the government of their country from the hands of the great military power which Great Britain can bring against them. If now frustrated in their expectations, and kept in hopeless subjection to rulers irresponsible to the people, they will, at best, only await in sullen prudence the contingencies which may render the preservation of the province dependent on the devoted loyalty of the great mass of its population.

With respect to the other North American provinces, I will not speak of such evils as imminent, because I firmly believe that, whatever discontent there may be, no irritation subsists which in any way weakens the strong feelings of attachment to the British Crown and Empire. Indeed, throughout the whole of the North American provinces, there prevails among the British population an affection for the mother country, and a preference for its institutions, which a wise and firm policy on the part of the Imperial Government may make the foundation of a safe, honourable, and enduring connexion. But even this feeling may be impaired, and I must warn those in whose hands the disposal of their destinies rests, that a blind reliance on the all-enduring loyalty of our countrymen may be carried too far. It is not politic to waste and cramp their resources, and to allow the backwardness of the British provinces everywhere to present a melancholy contrast to the progress and prosperity of the United States.

It is time to reward this noble confidence of the colonists by showing that men have not indulged in vain the hope that there is a power in British institutions to rectify existing evils, and to produce in their place a well-being which no other dominion could give. It is not in the terrors of the law or in the might of our armies that the secure and honourable bond of connexion is to be found. It exists in the beneficial operation of those British institutions which link the utmost development of freedom and civilization with the stable authority of an hereditary monarchy, and which, if rightly organized and fairly administered in the colonies, as in Great Britain, would render a change of institutions only an additional evil to the loss of the protection and commerce of the British Empire.

But while I count thus confidently on the possibility of a permanent and advantageous retention of our connexion with these important colonies, I must not disguise the mischief and danger of holding them in their present state of disorder. I rate the chances of successful rebellion as the least danger in prospect. I do not doubt that the British government can, if it choose to retain these dependencies at any cost, accomplish its purpose. I believe that it has the means of enlisting one part of the population against the other, and of garrisoning the Canadas with regular troops sufficient to awe all internal enemies. But even this will not be done without great expense and hazard. The experience of the last two years furnishes only a foretaste of the cost to which such a system of government will subject us, On the lowest calculation, the addition of £1,000,000 a year to our annual colonial expenditure will barely enable us to attain this end. Without a change in our system of government, the discontent which now prevails, will spread and advance. As the cost of retaining these colonies increases, their value will rapidly diminish; and if by such means the British nation shall be content to retain a barren and injurious sovereignty, it will but tempt the chances of foreign aggression, by keeping continually exposed to a powerful and ambitious neighbour, a distant dependency, in which an invader would find no resistance, but might rather reckon on active co-operation from a portion of the resident population.

When I look on the various and deep-rooted causes of mischief which the past inquiry has pointed out as existing in every institution, in the constitutions, and in the very composition of society throughout a great part of these provinces, I almost shrink from the apparent presumption of grappling with these gigantic difficulties. Nor shall I attempt to do so in detail. I rely on the efficacy of reform in the constitutional system, by which these colonies are governed, for the removal of every abuse in their administration, which defective institutions have engendered. If a system can be devised which shall lay, in these countries, the foundation of an efficient and popular government—insure harmony, in place of collision, between the various powers of the state—and bring the influence of a vigorous public opinion to bear on every detail of public affairs, we may rely on sufficient remedies being found for the present vices of the administrative system.

It is not by weakening, but strengthening the influence of the people on its government; by confining within much narrower bounds than those hitherto allotted to it, and not by extending the interference of the Imperial authorities in the details of colonial alfairs, that I believe that harmony is to be restored, where dissension has so long prevailed, and a regularity and vigour hitherto unknown introduced into the administration of these provinces. It needs no change in the principles of government, no invention of a new constitutional theory, to supply the remedy which would, in my opinion, completely remove the existing political disorders. It needs but to follow out consistently the principles of the British constitution, and introduce into the government of these great colonies those wise provisions, by which alone the working of the representative system can in any country be rendered harmonious and efficient. We are not now to consider the policy of establishing representative government in the North American colonies. That has been irrevocably done; and the experiment of depriving the people of their present constitutional power is not to be thought of. To conduct their government harmoniously, in accordance with its established principles, is now the business of its rulers; and I know not how it is possible to secure that harmony in any other way, than by administering the government on those principles which have been found perfectly efficacious in Great Britain. I would not impair a single prerogative of the Crown; on the contrary, I believe that the interests of the people of these colonies require the protection of prerogatives, which have not hitherto been exercised. But the Crown must, on the other hand, submit to the necessary consequences of representative institutions: and if it has to carry on the government in unison with a representative body, it must consent to carry it on by means of those in whom that representative body has confidence.

In England this principle has been so long considered an indisputable and essential part of our constitution, that it has really hardly ever been found necessary to inquire into the means by which its observance is enforced. When a ministry ceases to command a majority in parliament, on great questions of policy, its doom is immediately sealed; and it would appear to us as strange to attempt, for any time, to carry on a government by means of ministers perpetually in a minority, as it would be to pass laws with a majority of votes against them. The ancient constitutional remedies, by impeachment and a stoppage of the supplies, have never, since the reign of William III, been brought into operation for the purpose of removing a ministry. They have never been called for: because; in fact, it has been the habit of ministers rather to anticipate the occurrence of an absolutely hostile vote; and to retire, when supported only by a bare and uncertain majority. If colonial legislatures have frequently stopped the supplies—if they have harassed public servants by unjust or harsh impeachments—it was because the removal of an unpopular administration could not be effected in the colonies by those milder indications of a want of confidence, which have always sufficed to attain the end in the mother country.

It is said that it is necessary that the administration of a colony should be carried on by persons nominated without any reference to the wishes of its people; that they have to carry into effect the policy, not of that people, but of the authorities at home and that a colony which should name all its administrative functionaries would, in fact, cease to be dependent. I admit that the system which I propose would, in fact, place the internal government of the colony in the hands of the colonists themselves; and that we should thus leave them to the execution of the laws, of which we have long intrusted the making solely to them. Perfectly aware of the value of our colonial possessions, and strongly impressed with necessity of maintaining our connexion with them, I know not in what respect it can be desirable that we should interfere with their internal legislation in matters which do not affect their relations with the mother country. The matters which so concern us are very few. The constitution of the form of government—the regulation of foreign relations, and of trade with the mother country, the other British colonies, and foreign nations, and the disposal of the public lands, are the only points on which the mother country requires a control. This control is now sufficiently secured by the authority of the Imperial legislature, by the protection which the colony derives from us against foreign enemies, by the beneficial terms which our laws secure to its trade, and by its share of the reciprocal benefits which would be conferred by a wise system of colonization. A perfect subordination on the part of the colony on these points is secured by the advantages which it finds in the continuence of its connection with the empire. It certainly is not strengthened, but greatly weakened; by a vexatious interference on the part of the home government with the enactment of laws for regulating the internal concerns of the colony, or in the selection of the persons intrusted with their execution. The colonists may not always know what laws are best for them, or which of their countrymen are the fittest for conducting their affairs; but at least, they have a greater interest in coming to a right judgment on these points, and will take greater pains to do so, than those whose welfare is very remotely and slightly affected by the good or bad legislation of these portions of the empire. If the colonists make bad laws, and select improper persons to conduct their affairs, they will generally be the only, always the greatest, sufferers; and, like the people of other countries, they must bear the ills which they bring on themselves, until they choose to apply the remedy. But it surely cannot be the duty or interest of Great Britain to keep a most expensive military possession of these colonies, in order that a Governor or Secretary of state may be able to confer colonial appointments on one rather than another set of persons in the colonies, for this is really the only question at issue. The slightest acquaintance with these colonies proves the fallacy of the common notion, that any considerable amount of patronage in them is distributed among strangers from the mother country. Whatever inconvenience a consequent frequency of changes among the holders of office may produce, is a necessary disadvantage of free government, which will be amply compensated by the perpetual harmony which the system must produce between the people and its rulers. Nor do I fear that the character of the public servants will, in any respect, suffer from a more popular tenure of office. For I can conceive no system so calculated to fill important posts with inefficient persons as the present, in which public opinion is too little consulted in the original appointment, and in which it is almost impossible to remove those who disappoint the expectations of their usefulness, without inflicting a kind of brand on their capacity or integrity.

I am well aware that many persons, both in the colonies and at home, view the system which I recommend, with considerable alarm, because they distrust the ulterior views of those by whom it was originally proposed, and whom they suspect of urging its adoption with the intent only of enabling them more easily to subvert monarchical institutions, or assert the independence of the colony. I believe, however, that the extent to which these ulterior views exist has been greatly overrated. We must not take every rash expression or disappointment as an indication of a settled aversion to the existing constitution; and my own observation convinces me that the predominent feeling of all the English population of the North American Colonies is that of devoted attachment to the mother country. I believe that neither the interests nor the feelings of the people are incompatible with a colonial government wisely and popularly administered. The proofs, which many who are much dissatisfied with the existing administration of the government, have given of their loyalty, are not to be denied or overlooked. The attachment constantly exhibited by the people of these provinces towards the British crown and empire, has all the characteristics of a strong national feeling. They value the institutions of their country, not merely from a sense of the practical advantages which they confer, but from sentiments of national pride; and they uphold them the more because they are accustomed to view them as marks of nationality, which distinguish them from their republican neighbours. I do not mean to affirm that this is a feeling which no impolicy on the part of the mother country will be unable to impair: but I do most, confidently regard it as one which may, if rightly appreciated, be made the link of an enduring and advantageous connexion. The British people of the North American colonies are a people on whom we may safely rely, and to whom we must not grudge power. For it is not to the individuals who have been loudest in demanding the change that I propose to concede the responsibility of the colonial administration, but to the people themselves. Nor can I conceive that any people, or any considerable portion of a people, will view with dissatisfaction a change, which would amount simply to this, that the crown should henceforth consult the wishes of the people in the choice of its servants.

On the Future of French Canada

A plan by which is proposed to insure the tranquil government of Lower Canada, must include, in itself, the means of putting an end to the agitation of national disputes in the legislature, by settling, at once and for ever, the national character of the province. I entertain no doubts as to the national character which must be given to Lower Canada; it must be that of the British empire—that of the majority of the population of British America—that of the great race which must, in the lapse of no long period of time, be predominant over the whole North American continent. Without effecting the change so rapidly or so roughly as to shock the feelings and trample on the welfare of the existing generation, it must henceforth be the first and steady purpose of the British government to establish an English population, with English laws and language, in this province, and to trust its government to none but a decidedly English legislature.

It may be said, that this is a hard measure to a conquered people—that the French were originally the whole, and still are the bulk, of the population of Lower Canada—that the English are new-comers, who have no right to demand the extinction of the nationality of a people among whom commercial enterprise has drawn them. It may be said, that if the French are not so civilized, so energetic, or so money-making a race as that by which they are surrounded, they are an amiable, a virtuous, and a contented people, possessing all the essentials of material comfort, and not to be despised or ill-used, because they seek to enjoy what they have, without emulating the spirit of accumulation which influences their neighbours. Their nationality is, after all, an inheritance—and they must be not too severely punished, because they have dreamed of maintaining, on the distant banks of the St. Lawrence, and transmitting to their posterity, the language, the manners, and the institutions of that great nation, that for two centuries gave the tone of thought to the European continent. If the disputes of the two races are irreconcilable, it may be urged that justice demands that the minority should be compelled to acquiesce in the supremacy of the ancient and most numerous occupants of the province, and not pretend to force their own institutions and customs on the majority.

But, before deciding which of the two races is now to be placed in the ascendant, it is but prudent to inquire which of them must ultimately prevail; for it is not wise to establish to-day that which must, after a hard struggle, be reversed to-morrow. The pretensions of the French Canadians to the exclusive possession of Lower Canada, would debar the yet larger English population of Upper Canada, and the townships, from access to the great natural channel of that trade which they alone have created, and now carry on. The possession of the mouth of the Saint Lawrence concerns not only those who happen to have made their settlements along the narrow line which borders it, but all who now dwell, or will hereafter dwell, in the great basin of that river. For we must not look to the present alone. The question is, by what race is it likely that the wilderness which now covers the rich and ample regions surrounding the comparatively small and contracted districts in which the French Canadians are located, is eventually to be converted into a settled and flourishing country?

The whole interior of the British dominions must, ere long, be filled with an English population; every year rapidly increasing its numerical superiority over the French. Is it just that the prosperity of this great majority, and of this vast tract or country, should be for ever, or even for a while, impeded by the artificial bar which the backward laws and civilization of a part, and a part only, of Lower Canada, would place between them and the ocean? Is it to be supposed that such an English population will ever submit to such, a sacrifice of its interests?

The French Canadians are but the remains of an ancient colonization, and are, and ever must be, isolated in the midst of an Anglo-Saxon world. Whatever may happen, whatever government shall be established over them, British or American, they can see no hope for their nationality. They can only sever themselves from the British empire, by waiting till, some general cause of dissatisfaction alienates them, together with the surrounding colonies, and leaves them part of an English confederacy; or, if they are able, by effecting a separation singly, and so either merging in the American Union, or keeping up for a few years a wretched semblance of feeble independence, which would expose them more than ever to the intrusion of the surrounding population. I am far from wishing to encourage indiscriminately these pretensions to superiority on the part of any particular race; but while the greater part of every portion of the American continent is still uncleared and unoccupied, and while the English exhibit such constant and marked activity in colonization, so long will it be idle to imagine that there is any portion of that continent into which that race will not penetrate, or in which, when it has penetrated, it will not predominate. It is but a question of time and mode—it is but to determine whether the small number of French, who now inhabit Lower Canada, shall be made English under a government which can protect them, or whether the process shall be delayed, until a much larger number shall have to undergo, at the rude hands of its uncontrolled rivals, the extinction of a nationality strengthened and embittered by continuance.

And is this French Canadian nationality one which, for the good merely of that people, we ought to strive to perpetuate, even if it were possible? I know of no national distinctions marking and continuing a more hopeless inferiority. The language, the laws, the character of the North American continent are English; and every race but the English (I apply this to all who speak the English language) appears there in a condition of inferiority. It is to elevate them from that inferiority that I desire to give to the Canadians our English character. I desire it for the sake of the educated classes, whom the distinction of language and manners keeps apart from the great empire to which they belong.

I desire the amalgamation still more for the sake of the humbler classes. Their present state of rude and equal plenty is fast deteriorating under the pressure of population in the narrow limits to which they are confined. If they attempt to better their condition, by extending themselves over the neighbouring country, they will necessarily get more and more mingled with an English population; if they prefer remaining stationary, the greater part of them must be labourers, in the employ of English capitalists. In either case it would appear, that the great mass of the French Canadians are doomed, in some measure, to occupy an inferior position, and to be dependent on the English for Employment. The evils of poverty and dependence would merely be aggravated in a ten-fold degree, by a spirit of jealous and resentful nationality, which should separate the working class of the community, from the possessors of wealth and employers of labour.

There can hardly be conceived a nationality more destitute of all that can invigorate and elevate a people, than that which is exhibited by the descendants of the French in Lower Canada, owing to their retaining their peculiar language and manners. They are a people with no history, and no literature.

. . . In these circumstances I should be indeed surprised, if the more reflecting part of the French Canadians entertained at present any hope of continuing to preserve their nationality. Much as they struggle against it, it is obvious that the process of assimilation to English habits is already commencing. The English language is gaining ground, as the language of the rich and of the employers of labour naturally will. And there are about ten times the number of French children in Quebec learning English, as compared with English children who learn French. A considerable time must, of course elapse, before the change of a language can spread over a whole people; and justice and policy alike require that while the people continue to use the French language their government should take no such means to force the English language upon them. But I repeat, that the alteration of the character of the province ought to be immediately entered on, and firmly, though cautiously, followed up; that in any plan which may be adopted for the future management of Lower Canada, the first object ought to be that of making it an English province; and that, with this end in view, the ascendancy should never again be placed in any hands but those of an English population. Indeed, at the present moment this is obviously necessary; in the state of mind in which I have described the French Canadian population, as not only now being, but as likely for a long while to remain, the trusting them with an entire control over this province would be, in fact, only facilitating a rebellion. Lower Canada must be governed now as it must be hereafter, by an English population; and thus the policy which the necessities of the moment force on us is in accordance with that suggested by a comprehensive view of the future and permanent improvement of the province.

On the Benefits of Union

The only power that can be effectual at once in coercing the present disaffection, and hereafter obliterating the nationality of the French Canadians, is that of a numerical majority of a loyal and English population.

On these grounds, I believe that no permanent or efficient remedy can be devised for the disorders of Lower Canada, except a fusion of the government in that of one or more of the surrounding provinces; and as I am of opinion, that the full establishment of responsible government can only be permanently secured by giving these colonies an increased importance in the politics of the empire, I find in union the only means of remedying at once, and completely, the two prominent causes of their present unsatisfactory condition.

Two kinds of unions have been proposed—federal and legislative. By the first, the separate legislature of each province would be preserved in its present form, and retain almost all its present attributes of internal legislation—the federal legislature exercising no power, save in those matters of general concern which may have been expressly ceded to it by the constituent provinces. A legislative union would imply a complete incorporation of the provinces included in it under one legislature, exercising universal and sole legislative authority over all of them, in exactly the same manner as the parliament legislates alone for the whole of the British Isles.

On my first arrival in Canada, I was strongly inclined to the project of a federal union; I was fully aware, that it might be objected that a federal union would, in many cases, produce a weak and rather cumbrous government; that a colonial federation must have, in fact, little legitimate authority or business, the greater part of the ordinary functions of a federation falling within the scope of the Imperial legislature and executive; and that the main inducement to federation, which is the necessity of conciliating the pretensions of independent states to the maintenance of their own sovereignty, could not exist in the case of colonial dependencies, liable to be moulded according to the pleasure of the supreme authority at home.

I am aware also of great practical difficulties in any plan of federal government, particularly those that must arise in the management of the general revenues. But I had still more strongly impressed on me the great advantages of a united government; and I was gratified by finding the leading minds of the various colonies strongly and generally inclined to a scheme, that would elevate their countries into something like a national existence. I thought that it would be the tendency of a federation, sanctioned and consolidated by a monarchical government, gradually to become a complete legislative union; and that thus, while conciliating the French of Lower Canada, by leaving them the government of their own province, and their own internal legislation, I might provide for the protection of British interests by the general government, and for the gradual transition of the provinces into an united and homogeneous community.

But the period of gradual transition is past in Lower Canada. In the present state of feeling among the French population, I cannot doubt that any power which they might possess would be used against the policy and the very existence of any form of British government. I cannot doubt that any French assembly that shall again meet in Lower Canada, will use whatever power, be it more or less limited, it may have to obstruct the government, and undo whatever has been done by it. Time, and the honest co-operation of the various parties, would be required to aid the action of a federal constitution; and time is not allowed, in the present state of Lower Canada, nor co-operation to be expected from a legislature of which the majority shall represent its French inhabitants. I believe that tranquility can only be restored, by subjecting the province to the vigorous rule of an English majority; and that the only efficacious government would be that formed by a legislative union.

If the population of Upper Canada is rightly estimated at 400,000, the English inhabitants of Lower Canada at 150,000, and the French at 450,000, the union of the two provinces would not only give a clear English majority, but one which would be increased every year by the influence of English emigration; and I have little doubt that the French, when once placed, by the legitimate course of events and the working of natural causes, in a minority, would abandon their vain hopes of nationality. I do not mean that they would immediately give up their present animosities, or instantly renounce the hope of attaining their end by violent means. But the experience of the two unions in the British Isles may teach us how effectually the strong arm of a popular legislature would compel the obedience of the refractory population; and the hopelessness of success would gradually subdue the existing animosities, and incline the French Canadian population to acquiesce in their new state of political existence. I certainly should not like to subject the French Canadians to the rule of the identical English minority with which they have so long been contending; but from a majority emanating from so much more extended a source, I do not think they would have any oppression or injustice to fear; and in this case the far greater part of the majority never having been brought into previous collision, would regard them with no animosity that could warp their natural sense of equity.

But while I convince myself that such desirable ends would be secured by the legislative union of the two provinces, I am inclined to go further, and inquire whether all these objects would not more surely be attained by extending this legislative union over all the British provinces in North America; and whether the advantages which I anticipate for two of them, might not, and should not in justice, be extended over all. Such an union would at once decisively settle the question of races; it would enable all the provinces to co-operate for all common purposes; and, above all, it would form a great and powerful people, possessing, the means of securing good and responsible government for itself, and which, under the protection of the British empire, might in some measure counterbalance the preponderant and increasing influence of the United States on the American continent. I do not anticipate that a colonial legislature thus strong, and thus self-governing, would desire to abandon the connexion with Great Britain. On the contrary, I believe that the practical relief from undue interference, which would be the result of such a change, would strengthen the present bond of feelings and interests; and that the connexion would only become more durable and advantageous, by having more of equality, of freedom, and of local independence.

I am, in truth, so far from believing that the increased power and weight that would be given to these colonies by union would endanger their connexion with the empire, that I look to it as the only means of fostering such a national feeling throughout them as would effectually counterbalance whatever tendencies may now exist towards separation. No large community of free and intelligent men will long feel contented with a political system which places them, because it places their country, in a position of inferiority to their neighbours [ie., the United States]. The colonist of

Great Britain is linked, it is true, to a mighty empire, and the glories of its history, the visible signs of its present power, and the civilization of its people, are calculated to raise and gratify his national pride. But he feels, also, that his link to that empire is one of remote dependence; he catches but passing and inadequate glimpses of its power and prosperity; he knows that in its government he and his own countrymen have no voice—While his neighbour on the other side of the frontier assumes importance, from the notion that his vote exercises some influence on the councils; and that he himself has some share in the onward progress of a mighty nation, the colonist feels the deadening influence of the narrow and subordinate community to which he belongs. In his own, and in the surrounding colonies, he finds petty objects occupying petty, stationary, and divided societies; and it is only when the chances of an uncertain and tardy communication bring intelligence of what has passed a month before on the other side of the Atlantic, that he is reminded of the empire with which he is connected. But the influence of the United States surrounds him on every side, and is forever present. It extends itself as population, augments and intercourse increases; it penetrates every portion of the continent into which the restless spirit of American speculation impels the settler or the trader; it is felt in all the transactions of commerce, from the important operations of the monetary system down to the minor details of ordinary traffic: it stamps on all the habits and opinions of the surrounding countries the common characteristics of the thoughts, feelings and customs of the American people. Such is necessarily the influence which a great nation exercises on the small communities which surround it. Its thoughts and manners subjugate them, even when nominally independent of its authority. If we wish to prevent the extension of this influence, it can only be done by raising up for the North American colonist some nationality of his own, by elevating these small and unimportant communities into a society having some objects of a national importance, and by thus giving their inhabitants a country, which they will be unwilling to see absorbed even into one more powerful.

Focus Questions

1. To what does Durham attribute the cause of the Rebellion in Lower Canada?

   - French were to assimilate → difference in culture
     ↳ French had no say

   upper
   - Apointed not elected

2. What role did the United States play in Durham's interpretation of the two Rebellions?

   - rebellions looked up to U.S and their government

   - Durham
     ↳ Anti French - pro English
   - p 99
     ↳ give them more political power to the ppl
     ↳ combine Upper and lower Canada more English ppl
       ↳ if combined there will be

3. Why does he propose Responsible Government as a solution to the troubles in the colonies? How would it operate? What did he consider to be its chief benefits for the Empire? Who was opposed to the scheme, and why?
   ↳ French

   Key elements - Lord Durham
   → his opinion of combining Upper and Lower Canada
   → the election of representatives
       ↳ responsible government
   → step up towards confederation
   → tensions of French and English
   → shows arrogance of english

103

4

Confederation

Introduction

Throughout the early 1860s, colonial politicians from Nova Scotia, New Brunswick, Prince Edward Island, Ontario, and Quebec, began negotiating the terms of Confederation—an agreement to unite—politically and legally—most of the remaining British colonies of North America. As this series of extracts from the Confederation debates make clear, they had many good reasons for uniting—and perhaps just as many good reasons for remaining independent of each other. In the end, through a remarkably—and perhaps even uniquely—peaceful process, the decision was made in favour of unity (though P.E.I. did not initially sign on). Importantly, however, for these men, Confederation was not necessarily about *independence*: many of them saw the deal as something which would naturally strengthen their ties to the British Empire and their beloved Mother country, England. It was also a proposal which was intended, or so they believed, to strengthen the French Canadian nation within the bonds of Confederation.

As Ramsay Cook explains in the first of two contemporary discussions in this chapter, the meaning of Confederation to a citizen of 1867 was perhaps *not* the same as it is today—and this shift in meaning has important consequences. In the final reading, Irving Layton, renowned Canadian poet, reflects on the Canadian nation in his rather acerbic 1967 poem, "Centennial Ode."

ARGUMENTS IN FAVOUR

Address to the Legislative Assembly
Sir John Alexander Macdonald
Monday, 6 February 1865

. . . only three modes that were at all suggested, by which the dead-lock in our affairs, the anarchy we dreaded, and the evils which retarded our prosperity, could be met or averted. One was the dissolution of the union between Upper and Lower Canada, leaving them as they were before the union of 1841. I believe that that proposition, by itself had no supporters. It was felt by everyone that, although it was a course that would do away with the sectional difficulties which existed,—though it would remove the pressure on the part of the people of Upper Canada for the representation based upon population,—and the jealousy of the people of Lower Canada lest their institutions should be attacked and prejudiced by that principle in our representation; yet it was felt by every thinking man in the province that it would be a retrograde step, which would throw back the country to nearly the same position as it occupied before the union,—that it would lower the credit enjoyed by United Canada,—that it would be the breaking up of the connection which had existed for nearly a quarter of a century, and, under which, although it had not been completely successful, and had not allayed altogether the local jealousies that had their root in circumstances which arose before the union, our province, as a whole, had nevertheless prospered and increased. It was felt that a dissolution of the union would have destroyed all the credit that we had gained by being a united province, and would have left us two weak and ineffective governments, instead of one powerful and united people. (Hear, hear.) The next mode suggested, was the granting of representation by population. Now, we all know the manner in which that question was and is regarded by Lower Canada; that while in Upper Canada the desire and cry for it was daily augmenting, the resistance to it in Lower Canada was proportionably increasing in strength. Still, if some such means of relieving us from the sectional jealousies which existed between the two Canadas, if some such solution of the difficulties as Confederation had not been found, the representation by population must eventually have been carried; no matter though it might have been felt in Lower Canada, as being a breach of the Treaty of Union, no matter how much it might have been felt by the Lower Canadians that it would sacrifice their local interests, it is certain that in the progress of events representation by population would have been carried; and, had it been carried—I speak here my own individual sentiments—I do not think it would have been for the interest of Upper Canada. For though Upper Canada would have felt that it had received what it claimed as a right, and had succeeded in establishing its right, yet it would have left the Lower Province with a sullen feeling of injury and injustice. The Lower Canadians would not have worked cheerfully under such a change of system, but would have ceased to be what they are now—a nationality, with representatives in Parliament, governed by general principles, and dividing according to their political opinions—and would have been in great danger of becoming a faction, forgetful of national obligations, and only actuated by a desire to defend their own sectional interests, their own laws, and their own institutions. (Hear, hear.) The third and only means of solution for our difficulties was the junction of the provinces either in a Federal or a Legislative union. Now, as regards the comparative advantages of a Legislative and a Federal union, I have never hesitated to state my own opinions. I have again and again stated in the House, that, if practicable, I thought a Legislative union would be preferable. (Hear, hear.) I have always contended that if we could agree to have one government and one parliament, legislating for the whole of these peoples, it would be the best, the cheapest, the most vigorous, and the strongest system of government we could adopt. (Hear, hear.) But, on looking at the subject in the Conference, and discussing the matter as we did, most unreservedly, and with a desire to arrive at a satisfactory conclusion, we found that such a system was impracticable. In the first place, it would not meet the assent of the people of Lower Canada, because they felt that in their peculiar position—being in a minority, with a different language, nationality and religion from the majority,—in case of a junction with the other provinces, their institutions and their laws might be assailed, and their ancestral associations, on which they prided themselves, attacked and prejudiced; it was found that any proposition which involved the absorption of the individuality of Lower Canada—if I may use the expression—would not be received with favor by her people. We found too, that though their people speak the same language and enjoy the same system of law as the people of Upper Canada, a system founded on the common law of England, there was as great a disinclination on the part of the various Maritime Provinces to lose their individuality, as separate political organizations, as we observed in the case of Lower Canada herself. (Hear, hear.) Therefore, we were forced to the conclusion that we must either abandon the idea of Union altogether, or devise a system of union in which the separate provincial organizations would be in some degree preserved. So that those who were, like myself, in favor of a Legislative union, were obliged to modify their views and accept the project of a Federal union as the only scheme practicable, even for the Maritime Provinces. Because, although the law of those provinces is founded on the common law of England, yet every one of them has a large amount of law of its own—colonial law framed by itself, and affecting every relation of life, such as the laws of property, municipal and assessment laws; laws relating to the liberty of the subject, and to all the great interests contemplated in legislation; we found, in short, that the statutory law of the different provinces was so varied and diversified that it was almost impossible to weld them into a Legislative union at once. Why, sir, if you only consider the innumerable subjects of legislation peculiar to new countries, and that everyone of those five colonies had particular laws of its own, to which its people have been accustomed and are attached, you will see the difficulty of effecting and working a Legislative union, and bringing about an assimilation of the local as well as general laws of the whole of the provinces. (Hear, hear.) We in Upper Canada understand from the nature and operation of our peculiar municipal law, of which we know the value, the difficulty of framing a general system of legislation on local matters which would meet the wishes and fulfill the requirements of the several provinces. Even the laws considered the least important, respecting private rights in timber, roads, fencing, and innumerable other matters, small in themselves, but in the aggregate of great interest to the agricultural class, who form the great body of the people, are regarded as of great value by the portion of the community affected by them. And when we consider that every one of the colonies has a body of law of this kind, and that it will take years before those laws can be assimilated, it was felt that at first, at all events, any united legislation would be almost impossible. I am happy to state—and indeed it appears on the face of the resolutions themselves—that as regards the Lower Provinces, a great desire was evinced for the final assimilation of our laws. One of the resolutions provides that an attempt shall be made to assimilate the laws of the Maritime Provinces and those of Upper Canada, for the purpose of eventually establishing one body of statutory law, founded on the common law of England, the parent of the laws of all those provinces. . . .

As I stated in the preliminary discussion, we must consider this scheme in the light of a treaty. By a happy coincidence of circumstances, just when an Administration had been formed in Canada for the purpose of attempting a solution of the difficulties under which we labored, at the same time the Lower Provinces, actuated by a similar feeling, appointed a Conference with a view to a union among themselves, without being cognizant of the position the government was taking in Canada. If it had not been for this fortunate coincidence of events, never, perhaps, for a long series of years would we have been able to bring this scheme to a practical conclusion. But we did succeed. We made the arrangement, agreed upon the scheme, and the deputations from the several governments represented at the Conference went back pledged to lay it before their governments, and to ask the legislatures and people of their respective provinces to assent to it. I trust the scheme will be assented to as a whole. I am sure this House will not seek to alter it in its unimportant details; and, if altered in any important provisions, the result must be that the whole will be set aside, and we must begin *de novo*. If any important changes are made, everyone of the colonies will feel itself absolved from the implied obligation to deal with it as a Treaty, each province will feel itself at liberty to amend it *ad libitum* so as to suit its own views and interests; in fact, the whole of our labors will have been for nought, and we will have to renew our negotiations with all the colonies for the purpose of establishing some new scheme. I hope the House will not adopt any such a course as will postpone, perhaps forever, or at all events for a long period, all chances of union. All the statesmen and public men who have written or spoken on the subject admit the advantages of a union, if it were practicable: and now when it is proved to be practicable, if we do not embrace this opportunity the present favorable time will pass away, and we may never have it again. Because, just so surely as this scheme is defeated, will be revived the original proposition for a union of the Maritime Provinces, irrespective of Canada; they will not remain as they are now, powerless, scattered, helpless communities; they will form themselves into a power, which, though not so strong as if united with Canada, will, nevertheless, be a powerful and considerable community, and it will be then too late for us to attempt to strengthen ourselves by this scheme, which, in the words of the resolution, "is for the best interests, and present and future prosperity of British North America." If we are not blind to our present position, we must see the hazardous situation in which all the great interests of Canada stand in respect to the United States. I am no alarmist. I do not believe in the prospect of immediate war. I believe that the common sense of the two nations will prevent a war; still we cannot trust to probabilities. . . .

The Conference having come to the conclusion that a Legislative union, pure and simple, was impracticable, our next attempt was to form a government upon federal principles, which would give to the General Government the strength of a legislative and administrative union, while at the same time it preserved that liberty of action for the different sections which is allowed by a Federal union. And I am strong in the belief that we have hit upon the happy medium in those resolutions, and that we have formed a scheme of government which unites the advantages of both, giving us the strength of a Legislative union and the sectional freedom of a Federal union, with protection to local interests. In doing so we had the advantage of the experience of the United States. It is the fashion now to enlarge on the defects of the Constitution of the United States, but I am not one of those who look upon it as a failure. (Hear, hear.) I think and believe that it is one of the most skilful works which human intelligence ever created; is one of the most perfect organizations that ever governed a free people. To say that it has some defects is but to say that it is not the work of Omniscience, but of human intellects. We are happily situated in having had the opportunity of watching its operation, seeing its working from its infancy till now. It was in the main formed on the model of the Constitution of Great Britain, adapted to the circumstances of a new country, and was perhaps the only practicable system that could have been adopted under the circumstances existing at the time of its formation. We can now take advantage of the experience of the last seventy-eight years, during which that Constitution has existed, and I am strongly of the belief that we have, in a great measure, avoided in this system which we propose for the adoption of the people of Canada, the defects which time and events have shown to exist in the American Constitution. . . . They commenced, in fact, at the wrong end. They declared by their Constitution that each state was a sovereignty in itself, and that all the powers incident to a sovereignty belonged to each state, except those powers which, by the Constitution, were conferred upon the General Government and Congress. Here we have adopted a different system. We have strengthened the General Government. We have given the General Legislature all the great subjects of legislation. We have conferred on them, not only specifically and in detail, all the powers which are incident to sovereignty, but we have expressly declared that all subjects of general interest not distinctly and exclusively conferred upon the local governments and local legislatures, shall be conferred upon the General Government and Legislature.—We have thus avoided that great source of weakness which has been the cause of the disruption of the United States. We have avoided all conflict of jurisdiction and authority, and if this Constitution is carried out, as it will be in full detail in the Imperial Act to be passed if the colonies adopt the scheme, we will have in fact, as I said before, all the advantages of a legislative union under one administration, with, at the same time, the guarantees for local institutions and for local laws, which are insisted upon by so many in the provinces now, I hope, to be united. . . .

As may be well conceived, great difference of opinion at first existed as to the constitution of the Legislative Council. In Canada the elective principle prevailed; in the Lower Provinces, with the exception of Prince Edward Island, the nominative principle was the rule. We found a general disinclination on the part of the Lower Provinces to adopt the elective principle; indeed, I do not think there was a dissenting voice in the Conference against the adoption of the nominative principle, except from Prince Edward Island. The delegates from New Brunswick, Nova Scotia and Newfoundland, as one man, were in favor of nomination by the Crown. And nomination by the Crown is of course the system which is most in accordance with the British Constitution. We resolved then, that the constitution of the Upper House should be in accordance with the British system as nearly as circumstances would allow. An hereditary Upper House is impracticable in this young country. Here we have none of the elements for the formation of a landlord aristocracy—no men of large territorial positions—no class separated from the mass of the people. An hereditary body is altogether unsuited to our state of society, and would soon dwindle into nothing. . . .

I shall not detain the House by entering into a consideration at any length of the different powers conferred upon the General Parliament as contradistinguished from those reserved to the local legislatures; but any honorable member on examining the list of different subjects which are to be assigned to the general and local legislatures respectively, will see that all the great questions which affect the general interests of the Confederacy as a whole, are confided to the Federal Parliament, while the local interests and local laws of each section are preserved intact, and entrusted to the care of the local bodies. As a matter of course, the General Parliament must have the power of dealing with the public debt and property of the Confederation. Of course, too, it must have the regulation of trade and commerce, of customs and excise. The Federal Parliament must have the sovereign power of raising money from such sources and by such means as the representatives of the people will allow. It will be seen that the local legislatures have the control of all local works; and it is a matter of great importance, and one of the chief advantages of the Federal union and of local legislatures, that each province will have the power and means of developing its own resources and aiding its own progress after its own fashion and in its own way. Therefore all the local improvements, all local enterprises or undertakings of any kind, have been left to the care and management of the local legislatures of each province. (Cheers.) . . .

One of the great advantages of Confederation is, that we shall have a united, a concerted, and uniform system of defence. (Hear.) We are at this moment with a different militia system in each colony—in some of the colonies with an utter want of any system of defence. We have a number of separate staff establishments, without any arrangement between the colonies as to the means, either of defence or offence. But, under the union, we will have one system of defence and one system of militia organization. In the event of the Lower Provinces being threatened, we can send the large militia forces of Upper Canada to their rescue. Should we have to fight on our lakes against a foreign foe, we will have the hardy seamen of the Lower Provinces coming to our assistance and manning our vessels. (Hear, hear.) We will have one system of defence and be one people, acting together alike in peace and in war. (Cheers.) The criminal law too—the determination of what is a crime and what is not and how crime shall be punished—is left to the General Government. This is a matter almost of necessity. It is of great importance that we should have the same criminal law throughout these provinces—that what is a crime in one part of British America, should be a crime in every part—that there should be the same protection of life and property as in another. It is one of the defects in the United States system, that each separate state has or may have a criminal code of its own,—that what may be a capital offence in one state, may be a venial offence, punishable slightly, in another. But under our Constitution we shall have one body of criminal law, based on the criminal law of England, and operating equally throughout British America, so that a British American, belonging to what province he may, or going to any other part of the Confederation, knows what his rights are in that respect, and what his punishment will be if an offender against the criminal laws of the land. I think this is one of the most marked instances in which we take advantage of the experience derived from our observations of the defects in the Constitution of the neighboring republic. (Hear, hear).

I shall not go over the other powers that are conferred on the General Parliament. Most of them refer to matters of financial and commercial interest, and I leave those subjects in other and better hands. Besides all the powers that are specifically given in the 37th and last item of this portion of the Constitution, [it] confers on the General Legislature the general mass of sovereign legislation, the power to legislate on "all matters of a general character, not specially and exclusively reserved for the local governments and legislatures." This is precisely the provision which is wanting in the Constitution of the United States. It is here that we find the weakness of the American system—the point where the American Constitution breaks down. (Hear, hear.) It is in itself a wise and necessary provision. We thereby strengthen the Central Parliament, and make the Confederation one people and one government, instead of five peoples and five governments, with merely point of authority connecting us to a limited and insufficient extent. . . .

In conclusion, I would again implore the House not to let this opportunity to pass. It is an opportunity that may never recur. At the risk of repeating myself, I would say, it was only by a happy concurrence of circumstances, that we were enabled to bring this great question to its present position. If we do not take advantage of the time, if we show ourselves unequal to the occasion, it may never return, and we shall hereafter bitterly and unavailingly regret having failed to embrace the happy opportunity now offered of founding a great nation under the fostering care of Great Britain, and our Sovereign Lady, Queen Victoria. (Loud cheers, amidst which the honorable gentleman resumed his seat.)

Address to the Legislative Assembly
George Brown
Wednesday, 8 February 1865

Here is a people of two distinct races, speaking different languages, with religious and social and municipal and educational institutions totally different; with sectional hostilities of such a character as to render government for many years well-nigh impossible; with a constitution so unjust in the view of one section as to justify any resort to enforce a remedy. And yet, sir, here we sit, patiently and temperately discussing how these great evils and hostilities may justly and amicably be swept away forever. (Hear, hear.) We are endeavouring to adjust harmoniously greater difficulties than have plunged other countries into all the horrors of civil war. We are striving to do peacefully* and satisfactorily what Holland and Belgium, after years of strife, were unable to accomplish. We are seeking by calm discussion to settle questions that Austria and Hungary, that Denmark and Germany, that Russia and Poland, could only crush by the iron heel of armed force. We are seeking to do without foreign intervention that which deluged in blood the sunny plains of Italy. We are striving to settle forever issues hardly less momentous than those that have rent the neighbouring republic and are now exposing it to all the horrors of civil war. (Hear, hear.) Have we not then, Mr. Speaker, great cause of thankfulness that we have found a better way for the solution of our troubles than that which entailed on other countries such deplorable results? And should not every one of us endeavour to rise to the magnitude of the occasion, and earnestly seek to deal with this question to the end in the same candid and conciliatory spirit in which, so far, it has been discussed? (Loud cries of hear, hear.)

The scene presented by this chamber at this moment, I venture to affirm, has few parallels in history. One hundred years have passed away since these provinces became by conquest part of the British Empire. I speak in no boastful spirit—I desire not for a moment to excite a painful thought—what was then the fortune of war of

---

* Brown refers to the Belgian overthrow of Dutch rule in 1830, the Hungarian rising against Hapsburg rule in 1848, the rising of 1863 in Russian Poland, the Danish-German war of 1864 over the provinces of Schleswig and Holstein, the continuing struggle for' Italian unity and independence, and the civil war in the United States. He congratulates Canadians on finding a better way of resolving "national" disputes—a tribute both to their own civility and to the enlightenment of British colonial governance and parliamentary institutions.—PR.

the brave French nation might have been ours on that well-fought field. I recall those olden times merely to mark the fact that here sit today the descendants of the victors and the vanquished in the fight of 1759, with all the differences of language, religion, civil law, and social habits nearly as distinctly marked as they were a century ago. (Hear, hear.) Here we sit today seeking amicably to find a remedy for constitutional evils and injustice complained of—by the vanquished? No, sir—but complained of by the conquerors!* (Cheers by the French Canadians.)

Here sit the representatives of the British population claiming justice—only justice; and here sit the representatives of the French population, discussing in the French tongue whether we shall have it. One hundred years have passed away since the conquest of Quebec, but here sit the children of the victor and of the vanquished, all avowing hearty attachment to the British crown—all earnestly deliberating how we shall best extend the blessings of British institutions—how a great people may be established on this continent in close and hearty connection with Great Britain. (Cheers.)

Where, sir, in the page of history, shall we find a parallel to this? Will it not stand as an imperishable monument to the generosity of British rule? And it is not in Canada alone that this scene is being witnessed. Four other colonies are at this moment occupied as we are—declaring their hearty love for the parent state, and deliberating with us how they may best discharge the great duty entrusted to their hands, and give their aid in developing the teeming resources of these vast possessions.

Address to the Legislative Assembly
George-Étienne Cartier
Tuesday, 7 February 1865

Objection had been taken to the scheme now under consideration because of the words "new nationality." Now, when we were united together, if union were attained, we would form a political nationality* with which neither the national origin, nor the religion of any individual, would interfere. It was lamented by some that we had this diversity of races, and hopes were expressed that this distinctive feature would cease.

The idea of unity of races was utopian—it was impossible. Distinctions of this kind would always exist. Dissimilarity in fact appeared to be the order of the physical world and of the moral world, as well as in the political world. But with regard to the objection based on this fact, to the effect that a great nation could not be formed because Lower Canada was in great part French and Catholic, and Upper Canada was British and Protestant, and the lower provinces were mixed, it was futile and worthless in the extreme. Look for instance at the United Kingdom, inhabited as it was by three great races. (Hear, hear.) Had the diversity of race impeded the glory, the progress, the wealth of England? Had they not rather each contributed their share to the greatness of the empire? . . . In our own federation we should have Catholic and Protestant, English, French, Irish, and Scotch, and each by his efforts and his success would increase the prosperity and glory of the new confederacy. (Hear, hear.) We viewed the diversity of races in British North America in this way: we were of different races, not for the purpose of warring against each other, but in order to compete and emulate for the general welfare. (Cheers.)

Address to the Legislative Assembly
Thomas D'Arcy McGee
Thursday, 9 February 1865

I wish to say a few words in reference to what I call the social relations which I think ought to exist and will spring up between the people of the lower provinces and ourselves if there is a closer communication established between us . . . And first, I will make a remark to some of the Canadian gentlemen who are said to be opposed to our project, on French-Canadian grounds only. I will remind them . . . that every one of the colonies we now propose to re-unite under one rule—in which they shall have a potential voice—were once before united, as New France. (Cheers.) Newfoundland, the uttermost, was theirs, and one large section of its coast is still known as "the French shore"; Cape Breton was theirs till the final fall of Louisbourg; Prince Edward Island was their Island of St. Jean, and Charlottetown was their Port Joli [Port la Joie]; in the heart of Nova Scotia was that fair Acadian land, where the roll of Longfellow's* noble hexameters may any day be heard in every wave that breaks upon the base of Cape Blomedon. (Cheers.) . . . In New Brunswick there is more than one county, especially in the north, where business, and law, and politics require a knowledge of both English and French . . . Well, gentlemen of French origin, we propose to restore these long-lost compatriots to your protection: in the federal union, which will recognize equally both languages, they will naturally look to you; their petitions will come to you, and their representatives will naturally be allied with you.

---

*Henry Wadsworth Longfellow (1807–1882). The reference is to his poem Evangeline, which treats the British deportation of the Acadians from Nova Scotia in 1755 (See Chapter 2, Part One).

ARGUMENTS AGAINST

Address to the Legislative Assembly
Sir Antoine-Aimé Dorion
Thursday, 16 February 1865

Arguments Against

It is but natural that . . . [the] honourable gentlemen opposite want to keep as much power as possible in the hands of the government—that is the doctrine of the Conservative Party everywhere—that is the line which distinguishes the Tories from the Whigs—the Tories always side with the crown, and the Liberals always want to give more power and influence to the people. The instincts of honourable gentlemen opposite, whether you take the Honourable Attorney General East [George-Étienne Cartier] or the Honourable Attorney General West [John A. Macdonald], lead them to this—they think the hands of the crown should be strengthened and the influence of the people, if possible, diminished—and this constitution is a specimen of their handiwork, with a governor general appointed by the crown; with local governors also appointed by the crown; with legislative councils, in the general legislature, and in all the provinces, nominated by the crown; we shall have the most illiberal constitution ever heard of in any country where constitutional government prevails. (Hear.)

---

* The lack of aristocracy was considered a special political problem in North America because of the belief that a balanced mixture of the three principles of monarchy, aristocracy, and democracy would produce the best government of all, on the British model, as reflected in a king/queen, a senate/house of lords, and a house of commons. This balanced system had been made widely desirable to the reading public by Montesquieu in his Spirit of the Laws (1748). But absence of a traditional aristocracy in North America meant that a defence of a "natural aristocracy" composed of good and wise people was required. The contrast is between inherited, unearned, aristocratic privilege and earned privilege.—WDG

Address to the Legislative Assembly
Henri Joly
Monday, 20 February 1865

What then are the aspirations of the French Canadians? I have always imagined, indeed I still imagine, that they centre in one point, the maintenance of their nationality* as a shield destined for the protection of the institutions they hold most dear. For a whole century this has ever been the aim of the French Canadians; in the long years of adversity they have never for a moment lost sight of it; surmounting all obstacles, they have advanced step by step towards its attainment, and what progress have they not made?

What is their position today? They number nearly a million; they have no longer, if they are true to themselves, to fear the fate of Louisiana, which had not as many inhabitants, when it was sold by Napoleon to the United States, as Canada had in 1761. A people numbering a million does not vanish easily, especially when they are the owners of the soil. Their numbers are rapidly increasing. New townships are being opened in every direction and peopled with industrious settlers. In the Eastern Townships, which it was thought were destined to be peopled entirely by English settlers, these latter are slowly giving way to French Canadians. There is a friendly rivalry between the two races, a struggle of labour and energy; contact with our fellow-countrymen of English origin has at last opened our eyes; we have at last comprehended that in order to succeed, not only labour is needed, but well-directed and skilled labour, and we profit by their example and by the experience they have acquired in the old countries of Europe.

Agriculture is now becoming with us an honourable pursuit; the man of education is no longer ashamed to devote himself to it. Our farmers feel the necessity and desire of attaining perfection in the art. We possess magnificent model farms, in which we can learn the science of agriculture. We are entering a new era of prosperity. The French Canadians hold a distinguished position in the commerce of the country; they have founded banks and savings banks; on the St. Lawrence between Quebec and Montreal, they own one of the finest lines of steamboats in America; there is not a parish on the great river which has not its steamboat; the communications with the great towns are easy; we have railways, and we now measure by hours the duration of a journey which formerly we measured by days; we have foundries and manufactories, and our shipbuilders have obtained a European renown.

We have a literature peculiarly our own; we have authors, of whom we are justly proud; to them we entrust our language and our history; they are the pillars of our nationality. Nothing denotes our existence as a people so much as our literature; education has penetrated everywhere; we have several excellent colleges, and an university in which all the sciences may be studied under excellent professors. Our young men learn in military schools how to defend their country. We possess all the elements of a nationality. But a few months ago, we were steadily advancing towards prosperity, satisfied with the present and confident in the future of the French-Canadian people. Suddenly discouragement, which had never overcome us in our adversity, takes possession of us; our aspirations are now only empty dreams; the labours of a century must be wasted; we must give up our nationality, adopt a new one, greater and nobler, we are told, than our own, but then it will no longer be our own. And why? Because it is our inevitable fate, against which it is of no use to struggle. But have we not already struggled against destiny when we were more feeble than we are now, and have we not triumphed? Let us not give to the world the sad spectacle of a people voluntarily resigning its nationality . . .

I object to the proposed Confederation, first, as a Canadian, without reference to origin, and secondly, as a French Canadian. From either point of view, I look upon the measure as a fatal error; and, as a French Canadian, I once more appeal to my fellow-countrymen, reminding them of the precious inheritance confided to their keeping—an inheritance sanctified by the blood of their fathers, and which it is their duty to hand down to their children as unimpaired as they received it. (Cheers.)

Address to the Legislative Assembly
Christopher Dunkin
Tuesday, 28 February 1865

The people of the United States, when they adopted their constitution, were one of the nations of the earth. They formed their whole system with a view to national existence. They had fought for their independence and had triumphed; and still in the flush of their triumph, they were laying the foundations of a system absolutely national. Their federal government was to have its relations with other nations, and was sure to have plenty to do upon entering the great family of nations.

But we—what are we doing? Creating a new nationality, according to the advocates of this scheme. I hardly know whether we are to take the phrase as ironical or not. Is it a reminder that, in fact, we have no sort of nationality about us, but are unpleasantly cut up into a lot of struggling nationalities, as between ourselves? Unlike the people of the United States, we are to have no foreign relations to look after or national affairs of any kind; and therefore our new nationality, if we could create it, could be nothing but a name. I must say that according to my view of the change we ought to aim at, any idea of federation that we may entertain had need take an imperial direction. Whenever changing our institutions, we had need develop and strengthen . . . the tie, not yet federal as it ought to be, between us and the parent state. (Hear, hear.)

It is the entire empire that should be federalized and cemented together as one, and not any mere limited number of its dependencies here or there. A general, or so-called general, government, such as we are here proposing to create, will most certainly be in a false position. As I said just now, the federal government of the United States was to take its place in the great family of the nations of the earth; but what place in that family are we to occupy? Simply, none. The imperial government will be the head of the empire as much as ever, and will alone have to attend to all foreign relations and national matters; while we shall be nothing more than we are now. Half-a-dozen colonies federated are but a federated colony after all . . . The real difficulty in our position is one that is not met by the machinery here proposed. What is that difficulty? In the larger provinces of the empire we have the system of responsible government thoroughly accorded by the imperial government and thoroughly worked out; and the difficulty of the system that is now pressing, or ought to be, upon the attention of our statesmen is just this—that the tie connecting us with the empire, and which ought to be a federal tie of the strongest kind, is too slight, is not, properly speaking, so much as a federal tie at all. These provinces, with local responsible government, are too nearly in the position of independent communities; there is not enough of connection between them and the parent state to make the relations between the two work well, or give promise of lasting long . . . What is wanting, if one is to look to the interest of the empire, which is really that of all its parts—what is wanting, as I have said, is an effective federalization of the empire as a whole, not a subordinate federalization here or there, made up out of parts of it.

Address to the House of Assembly of Nova Scotia
Archibald McLelan
Tuesday, 17 April 1866

Turn to the map of the world and you will find every country, occupying a first-class position, compact in shape, and just as the country departs from that it descends in the scale of nations. England has been styled "the tight little isle of the sea." There is in her a compact territory, which affords that blending of interests which heads to a harmonious co-operation for the good of the whole. We have been frequently reminded since this question arose of the heptarchy in England* and the great results of her union. Union for her was a natural act, and so may it be said of England and Scotland. The boundary line is wiped out by the dense population which flows back and forth, that the influence of the interest of each extends into and operates upon the other, forming a strong and enduring union. Ireland has not this territorial connection. The influence of her interests is bounded by the sea-shore, and naturally seeks a centre within her own territory. There is not the same interweaving of interests, and consequently the bond of union is acknowledged to be weaker than between England and Scotland.

England grew in greatness and power by every union which combined territory and people and interests, having for each a natural affinity, but when she went beyond that she gained only elements of weakness. She crossed the channel† into France and attempted to draw that people and country to her, but the more territory she acquired the weaker she became, and eventually yielded to the inflexible law of nature that the drawings of all people are to their natural centre of interest. Look at France upon the map. No straggling arms or long jutting headlands, but all compact, and forming a country which claims and holds a first position among empires. Go over the map of Europe, and just as you find countries departing from that compact shape you find them descending in the scale of nations.

But I may be referred to England's colonies scattered all over the globe and having no territorial connection with England, and be asked how she has held them without their being a source of weakness? Simply by permitting them to manage all matters of internal policy as suited themselves; attempting no action affecting the internal interests of a colony further than was compensated for by a protection of her external interests. By this wise and liberal policy she has seen her colonies grow and prosper in a remarkable degree. She departed from this policy when she proposed to tax the thirteen New England states,* but the people regarded it as a violation of their chartered rights and they severed the connection with the parent state. England saw the mistake Lord North[†] committed and compelled him to repeal the act imposing a tax on colonists, and from that time to the present the policy pursued by England towards her colonies has been growing more enlightened and liberal . . .

The honourable member for Richmond, Mr. [William] Miller, in calling for this resolution, told us how proud he is of Nova Scotia. It is not he alone who is proud of her. We are proud of being British subjects, of being British Americans, but not less so of being called Nova Scotians. That gentleman, however, seeks to blot out this name. Whilst he addressed the house I thought of that anecdote told . . . of the cod-fishing captain on a voyage to Newfoundland who, on going down to the cabin to consult his chart and finding it in shreds and tatters, told his men they might as well turn about, for the rats had eaten Newfoundland. I do not mean to say that Nova Scotia will be literally devoured, but rats are striving to eat out the name from the map of North America.

Sir, if this proposition be carried into effect without consulting the people, I anticipate the most serious results. There is in the breast of every man claiming British allegiance a principle—a feeling—implanted by God himself that he should be consulted in all changes affecting his rights and privileges and the constitution under which he lives. In no part of the British Empire is that feeling more strong and irrepressible than in this country, and if the provincial secretary carries out his proposition without consulting the people, this province will rebel against the act. I have no hesitation in telling the honourable gentleman that he is tampering with the loyalty and allegiance of the people. He knows our attachment to the mother country is strong, but he must not count too much on it.

---

* Wellington commanded the British, Portuguese, and Spanish forces in the Peninslar War against Napoleon between 1808 and 1813.

[†]Lord North (1732–1792), British prime minister during the American War of Independence.

REFLECTION

The Meaning of Confederation
Ramsay Cook

As the fiftieth anniversary of Confederation approached, in 1917, a Canadian historian faced with the task of explaining the meaning of Confederation might have concluded that his country's founders intended to build a nation capable of assisting Great Britain and her allies in their magnificent effort to make the world safe for democracy. Ten years later, the historian, basking in the glories of the Balfour Declaration, might well have replied that the objective of Confederation was to lay the foundations of a nation capable of winning full autonomy within the British Commonwealth. Another historian, in the midst of the Great Depression, would probably have insisted that the intention of the founders was to establish a nation with a central government strong enough to guarantee all Canadians a reasonable standard of living and social welfare. At the end of the Second World War, yet another practitioner of this sensitive craft might have claimed that the far-seeing statesmen of 1867 had intended to build a nation capable of interpreting Europe to America, and vice versa. A decade ago the answer would certainly have been that the great object of Confederation was to build a nation in the northern half of the North American continent strong enough to resist annexation to the United States. Perhaps in the 1970s some particularly perceptive reader of the *Confederation Debates* will be able to conclude that the real intention of those serious, if not always sober, Victorian gentlemen who sat around the tables at Charlottetown, Quebec, and London was to build a nation scientific enough to launch a bilingual astronaut on his travels to the moon.

Each of those historians, it should be noted, would be English-speaking. A French-speaking historian would in some cases have given those same answers. But he would also have insisted that there was another objective equal to if not prior to the ones emphasized by his English-speaking colleagues. The French-speaking historian would have maintained, at each of the dates mentioned, that the objective of Confederation was to guarantee the survival of *la nation canadienne-française*. He

From "The Meaning of Confederation" from *Canada and the French-Canadian Question* by Ramsay Cook. Reprinted by permission of the author.

would then have gone on either to defend or to criticize Confederation according to his view of how fully this objective had been served.*

While each of these interpretations, in its French and English variations, is based with a greater or lesser degree of accuracy, the answer of the mid 1960s must place the emphasis on yet another interpretation. This interpretation stems from the most permanent theme in Canadian history: the relations between French- and English-speaking Canadians. Among the several objectives of the architects of the Canadian constitution, none was more important than the effort to accommodate the needs of the two cultural communities that had been made co-inhabitants of British North America by the Seven Years' War and the American Revolution. In the minds of the men of 1867, that accommodation was to be achieved by the founding of a new nation. But the important question relates to their definition of the form of that nation.

Several years ago a young French-Canadian intellectual began his explanation of his position as a Quebec separatist with some lines that go directly to the heart of the meaning of the word 'nation' in the context of Confederation. In his tract *J' ai choisi l' indépendance,* Raymond Barbeau wrote:

> The national thought of French Canadians has always seemed ambiguous to me; most of those who defend our interests remain undecided before the following question: does the French-Canadian nation exist? According to the response that we give, our political and patriotic activity will be centered on the state of Quebec or, inversely, on Canada and the federal government. If the Canadian 'nation' exists, the French-Canadian 'nation' has never existed, or exists no longer, either in theory or in practice.

That claim represents the fundamental assumption of the separatist thesis in the current debate over the future of Confederation. It is that a nation must express itself through a sovereign state. A nation that lacks a state of its own is a colony and therefore must, like other colonies, win its independence.

The view that state and nation must be coterminous represents a form of political orthodoxy that finds its roots in the French Revolution, was nurtured by the accidental alliance of liberals and nationalists in the nineteenth century, and flowered under the warm sun of Wilsonianism at Versailles in 1919. That the plant has now clearly produced bitter, even poisonous, fruit has not greatly decreased its apparently habit-forming attractions. Indeed, in the 1960s ideological nationalism, with its emphasis on cultural homogeneity and the right of self-determination, is perhaps more alive and more inebriating than at any time since 1848.

Yet despite the nineteenth-century origins of what is perhaps best called the ideal of the nationalist-state, it was a different ideal that motivated the founders of the

---

*French-Canadian historians have not written much of a scholarly kind about Confederation, but two rather different approaches can be found in Lionel Groulx, *La Confédération canadienne* (Montreal, 1918), and Thomas Chapais, *Cours d'histoire du Canada* (Quebec, 1934), Vol. VIII.

Canadian nation. That is why any answer to the question of the meaning of Confederation must be both exceedingly simple and extremely complex. If it were just one or the other we would almost certainly not have had that apparently endless search for the elusive Canadian identity, and French-Canadian identity, which has characterized so much writing about Canada. Nor would we have had the ever-repeating debate about the functions of the various levels of government in Canada if the men of 1864–7 had given us a statement of intention either so simple that every schoolboy could grasp it or so complex that only a philosopher-king could interpret it. But Sir John A. Macdonald's merry men did neither. Hence the debate and hence also the fascination of Canadian history.

The meaning of Confederation was, first, simple. There cannot be the slightest doubt that the intention of the Fathers of Confederation was, in Macdonald's words, the 'founding of a great nation.' Here on the northern half of the North American continent 'a new nationality' was being founded. Not one of the supporters of the scheme, English- or French-speaking, contended otherwise. The opponents of the scheme, from whatever part of British North America they came, recognized the nation-building objective of the proposals. For various reasons they thought that the new nation was either impractical or undesirable or both.

But what kind of a nation could be built out of four or five scattered colonies which knew either too little about one another, as was the case of the Maritimes and Canada, or too much about one another, as was the case of Canada East (as Quebec was then called) and Canada West (later Ontario)? It is in answering this question that the originality and deviationism of the founders of Canada become clear and the complexity of the problem becomes obvious. While the Fathers of Confederation were intent upon establishing a 'nation-state,' they were equally forthright in their rejection of the ideal of the 'nationalist-state.' The nation whose foundations were being laid was not culturally homogeneous. Nor was it the objective of the politicians of the Great Coalition to build a structure that would enforce or produce ultimate homogeneity. In the house of the Fathers of Confederation there were to be many mansions. In explaining why he had forsaken his ideal of a single, unitary legislative union in favour of a federal system, Macdonald, who understood every detail of the scheme, had this to say:

> In the first place it [legislative union] would not have met the assent of the people of Lower Canada, because they felt that in their peculiar position—being a minority with a different language, nationality and religion from the majority—in case of a junction with the other provinces, their institutions and their laws might be assailed, and their ancestral associations, on which they prided themselves, attacked and prejudiced; it was found that any proposition which involved the absorption of the individuality of Lower Canada—if I may use the expression—would not be received with favour by her people.

Macdonald, who had successfully trod through the no-man's-land of sectional, religious, and cultural quarrels for twenty years before Confederation, knew that the key to political success and constitutional stability was harmony between French and English Canadians. He defined his formula in 1856 when he told an English-speaking Montrealer: 'Treat them [the French Canadians] as a nation and they will act as a free people generally do—generously. Call them a faction and they become factious.'

But how could one build a 'nation' and yet treat the French Canadians as a 'nation'? Macdonald supplied his answer in the Confederation debates. The British constitutional system was one that required no enforced uniformity, but rather provided for the protection of minority rights. 'We will enjoy here,' Macdonald claimed, 'the great test of constitutional freedom—we will have the rights of the minority respected.' This point was explained more fully by George Etienne Cartier, the leading French Canadian among the Fathers. Cartier was naturally very sensitive to the charge made by his opponents that the much-talked-about 'new nationality' would engulf the French-Canadian nationality. Had not Lord Durham been one of the first to propose federation of all British North America? And for what purpose? None other than to erase the French-Canadian nation from the face of British North America. Cartier made it plain, however, that the nation whose birth he was attending would be the very antithesis of the Anglo-Saxon nationalism that Durham had supported:

> Now when we were united together, if union were attained, we would form a political nationality with which neither national origin, nor the religion of any individual would interfere. . . . In our federation we should have Catholic and Protestant, English, French, Irish, Scotch, and each in his efforts and success would increase the prosperity and glory of our new Confederacy.

Thus while it is true that in 1867 the political leaders of Canada were engaged in that characteristic nineteenth-century activity, the building of a nation-state, it is likewise true, and highly significant, that they were rejecting that equally characteristic nineteenth-century phenomenon, the nationalist-state. Their concept of Canada was of a community based on political and juridical unity, but also on cultural and religious duality. And the key to that unity in duality was the rejection of the intolerant, conformist, ideological nationalism that was, in these same years, shaking the foundations of Europe and also providing the drive that led to the destruction of the Southern Confederacy by the North in the American Civil War.

The second key to the meaning of Confederation was that the new union was to be a federal one. In this fashion, diversity was to be given specific institutional guar-

---

*For an account of federal ideas in Canada, see Peter B. Waite, *The Life and Times of Confederation* (Toronto, 1962), and Jean-Charles Bonenfant, 'L'Idée que les Canadiens français de 1864 pouvaient avoir du fédéralisme', *Culture*, Vol. XXV, December 4, 1964, pages 307–22.

antees. Federalism, as has often been remarked, was not a very well understood system of government in the nineteenth century.* And where it was known, in the United States, it did not provide a very encouraging example. Yet federalism was indispensable if there was to be a union of British North America. The Maritime Provinces were quite unwilling to be completely absorbed into the upstart culture of Canada. More important, the French Canadians refused to give up the relative security of the union where Canada East and Canada West enjoyed equal representation for a new union based on representation by population unless they were given the means of protecting their individuality. Arthur Gordon, the Governor of New Brunswick, watched the preliminary discussions on the projected union and reported to the Colonial Secretary, 'The aim of Lower Canada is a local independence as complete as circumstances will permit, and the peculiarities of race, religion and habits which distinguish its people render their desire respectable and natural.' And when Lord Carnarvon, the Colonial Secretary, presented the British North America Act to the House of Lords in February 1867 he noted that 'Lower Canada now *consents* to enter into this Confederation because its peculiar institutions were to be given effective guarantees.' The great compromise of 1867, and at the same time the great victory for the French Canadians, was the federal system of government. Had there been only one 'nation' involved in the negotiations that preceded the establishment of Confederation, the proponents of legislative union would doubtless have fought harder for their viewpoint. Since there was not one nation but two, the result was federalism.

What is perhaps not often enough emphasized in discussions of Confederation is that while the events of 1864 to 1867 produced a union, they also produced a division. From 1841 to 1865 Canada East and Canada West had been united in a theoretically unitary, but practically federal, state. The experience had been less than satisfying. Moreover, it was not only, or even chiefly, the French Canadians who were anxious to bring this unhappy condition to an end. Indeed, throughout the last years of the union the loudest complaints came from the Liberals in Canada West. Led by George Brown, the Grit party practically made its fortune on two cries: 'French domination' and 'rep by pop.' The federal system adopted in 1867 provided the means whereby this so-called French domination could be ended and representation by population implemented with the approval of the French Canadians. This explains the exuberant tone of the letter George Brown scribbled to his wife at the end of the Quebec Conference in 1864. 'All right!!' he whooped. 'Confederation through at six o'clock this evening—constitution adopted—a creditable document—a complete reform of all the abuses and injustices we have complained of! Is it not wonderful? French Canadianism entirely extinguished.' That last line about 'French Canadianism' speaks volumes about the history of the United Canadas! In the debates that took place in the Parliament of the Canadas on the subject of the Quebec Resolutions, speaker after speaker, in more restrained terms than the editor of the Toronto *Globe,* noted that the proposed Confederation was 'a separation of the provinces,' as the venerable Sir E. P. Taché put it. Once more the complexity of Confederation is obvious: to unity in duality has been added unity in separation.

To the English-speaking Fathers, unity was all-important. Macdonald repeatedly emphasized his preference for a legislative union—which he evidently thought was compatible with cultural duality. Each of the supporters of the scheme emphasized the necessity of a strong central government if the new nation-state was to survive in the face of a rapidly changing world. In the newly emerging balance of world power, Britain seemed anxious to retreat from her costly commitments in North America at a time when the United States, the traditional enemy of British North America, was giving proof of its enormous military strength. Both French and English supporters of the Confederation scheme were agreed that a central government capable of initiating effective military and economic policies was necessary if British North America was to survive. Every nation is founded on a will to survive. Canada was no exception and it was that will which united French- and English-speaking British North Americans in 1867. In 1940 the report of a royal commission, the Rowell-Sirois Commission, which had been appointed to carry out a full-scale examination of the Canadian federal system, made the point in this way:

> Confederation was conceived as a solution for a number of political and economic difficulties and, therefore, had both political and economic aims. Politically it was designed to establish a new nation to meet the changed conditions of British policy and to brace the scattered provinces against possible American aggression. Economically it was intended to foster a national economy which would relieve dependence upon a few industries and lessen exposure to the effects of the economic policies pursued by the United States and Great Britain.

With these objectives in mind, the men who drafted the British North America Act placed the preponderance of power, including the residual power, in the hands of the central government.*

So broad were the powers of the proposed central government, the critics of the scheme charged that to describe the system as federal was to divest the term of all known meaning. 'I am opposed to the scheme of Confederation,' Eric Dorion, the *enfant terrible* of French Canada, announced, 'because the first resolution is nonsense and repugnant to truth; it is not a federal union which is offered, but a legislative union in disguise.' The fear that disturbed these French-Canadian opponents of the plan was quite simple: had the Macdonalds and Cartiers, in their concern for Canadian survival, produced a system of government that would threaten *la sur-*

---

*Today even French Canadians appear to accept this view of the intention of the Fathers, though traditionally they have been loath to do so. (See Jean-Charles Bonenfant, 'L'Esprit de 1867,' *Revue d'histoire de l'Amérique française,* Vol. XVII, No. 1, June 1963, pages 19–38.)

vivance de la nation canadienne-française? Cartier, of course, said no; but his response failed to convince a significant number of his compatriots.†

This sharp difference of opinion is another reminder of the duality of the country and also of the duality of the motives that lay behind the union of 1867. Therefore, just as the Rowell-Sirois Report stressed the theme of Canadian survival as the central factor in Confederation, a Quebec royal commission in 1956, the Tremblay Commission, stressed the factor of French-Canadian survival. And just as the Rowell-Sirois Commission emphasized the centralized character of the 1867 scheme, so the Tremblay Commission underlined provincial powers. Here is the way the Quebec commissioners concluded their consideration of the events of 1864–7:

> To sum up, the Union of 1867 met the common needs of the provinces. If it assumed a federative character it was doubtless due to their divergencies, but it was especially due to the irreducible presence of the French Canadian bloc which only accepted Confederation because it had been given every conceivable promise that it would be able to govern itself in autonomous fashion and thereby develop, along with all its institutions, according to its special way of life and its own culture.

Those who try to read orthodox nationalist assumptions into Confederation— that is to say, those who argue that Canada is a nationalist-state rather than a nation-state—always fail to realize that survival and *la survivance* are not necessarily interchangeable words. Indeed, rather than being interchangeable, the two realities that the words represent are in a constant state of tension. It was one of the fundamental objectives of the Fathers of Confederation to bring that tension into a state of equilibrium. Confederation was an agreement, pact, or *entente,* whichever of those words best describes the political rather than the legal character of the events of 1864–7. And the terms of that *entente* were that a new nation-state was to be founded on the basis of an acceptance of cultural duality and on a division of powers. The unstated major premise of that *entente* was that both survival and *la survivance* were legitimate objectives and that those objectives could better be achieved within the structure of a single, federal state than in separate states or in a unitary state. The unceasing responsibility of Canadian political leaders since 1867 has been to ensure that the equilibrium between survival and *la survivance,* between the legitimate goals of Canadians and of French Canadians, should not be destroyed. It has never been an easy assignment.

---

†It is, of course, impossible to know the exact strength of the opposition to Confederation since the matter was not put to a popular test. One French-Canadian writer, after a less than exhaustive analysis, has concluded that a majority of French Canadians probably supported the scheme. (See Jean-Charles Bonenfant, 'Les Canadiens français et la naissance de la Confédération,' *Report of the Canadian Historical Association,* 1952, page 45.)

Centennial Ode
Irving Layton
1967

Centennial Ode

Like an old, nervous and eager cow
my country
is being led up to the bull
of history

The bull has something else
on his mind
and ignores her;
still, dazed by her wagging tail, in good time
he must unsheathe
his venerable tool
for the long-awaited consummation

Certainly it will be the biggest
bang-up affair
within the memory of centenarians,
and seismologists have been alerted
everywhere
to record the shocks and tremors

Emissaries
are fanning out to advise
younger and older statesmen around the globe:
take note, finally our brindled Elsie
is mating history

For everyone coming to watch
this extraordinary event
there can be standing room only
for himself
and a single bag of overcharged peanuts
Poor dear
what will she do
the day after
when she looks in a pool
and sees
the same bland face,
the same dull wrinkles between the horns
and the relieved bull
even more indifferent than before?

Focus Questions

1. What were the pro and con arguments for Confederation? When approaching this question, consider how each side stood on the following subjects:
   a. What did they want, and what did they want to *avoid*?
   b. How did the presence and example of the United States affect their opinions?
   c. What were the major points of agreement and disagreement?

2. According to D'Arcy McGee, how would confederation strengthen ties to Empire? How do Dunkin's opinions differ on this subject? Who do you think makes the stronger argument?

3. Given the content of these speeches, what effect, if any, do you think Lord Durham's suggestions had on the colonies? What effect did Conquest have?

4. How was Confederation supposed to protect *la nation canadienne-française?*

5. According to Ramsay Cook, what did Confederation mean to Canadians in the 1960s? What does it mean to you today?

6. What do you think Irving Layton's message is in his poem? Do you agree with it?

5

The North West Rebellion: Canada Confronts Louis Riel

Introduction

Louis Riel is one of the most controversial figures in Canadian history. A member of western Canada's Métis community (a people of mixed Aboriginal and French Catholic origin), he has been called both a hero and a outlaw, a Father of Confederation and a traitorous villain. Many credit him for defending the rights and territory of the Métis against the demands of a rapacious Canadian government which was bent on extending the Dominion *ad mare usque ad mare* (from sea to sea). Indeed, in the late 1860s, Riel and his Métis compatriots organized the National Committee of the Métis of Red River (in present day Manitoba) to present their demands to the Federal Government, who had until that time, blithely ignored the presence of the Métis in their quest to survey and settle the western territories. The result was the creation of the Province of Manitoba in May of 1870. As the Métis were French speaking and Catholic, many French Canadians saw Riel as an heroic figure, who had successfully staked a claim for their people in the west. However, there are also many people who remembered that during this 1869 dispute, Riel ordered the execution of Thomas Scott, an English speaking Protestant from Ontario. Scott had protested Riel's claims to leadership of the Red River community, as well as the actions taken by the National Committee. After a trial conducted according to the Métis tradition, he was executed by firing squad.

When, in 1885, Riel found himself once more in direct conflict with the Federal Government—this time in the North West (present-day Saskatchewan)—this execution returned to haunt him. Riel had been exiled to the United States after the Red River Rebellion, but had returned to Canada at the request of the Métis, who were once more facing pressures from Euro-Canadian settlers on their land. The Canadian government—greatly helped by the now-complete CPR—defeated the Métis at the battle of Batoche. Riel was captured, and in the summer of 1885, was put on trial for treason. While the jury found Riel guilty, they recommended clemency, believing (as

many did, and still do) that he suffered from serious mental illness. Against this recommendation, however, Riel was hanged in November 1885. The resulting outcry
from Quebec was enormous—as outraged and furious as the outcry from Ontario had
been at the time of Scott's execution.

The opinions from both sides—English Ontario and French Quebec—are
exposed in the following series of letters and newspaper articles published shortly
after the 1885 North West Rebellion (some of them before Riel's execution took
place). These documents starkly reveal both the linguistic and religious dimensions
to the controversy. Notably, however, they reveal very little about who Riel actually
was. As George F. G. Stanley reveals, this challenge—defining and redefining the
events and the man—have been done in vastly different ways, over time, by historians and the Canadian public.

But what about the Métis themselves? In many ways, they are a forgotten people,
and rarely are their voices heard in the grand debates about their former leader. The
Métis themselves have not forgotten, however, and their memory and interpretation
of the North West Rebellion is retold and remembered in very interesting ways, as
revealed here in the story of the recent theft—or was it a liberation?—of the Batoche
Bell.

THE ONTARIO PERSPECTIVES

Petition of Ontario Orangemen, Regarding the Sentence Against Riel

1885

Dear Sir,—The Orangemen of this district would respectfully approach you, as our representative in Parliament, concerning the case of Riel, now under sentence of death, for his recent acts of violence, bloodshed and treason. . . .

The fact that public meetings have been called in favour of Riel, in defence of his conduct, in the Lower Province, and especially by the Roman Catholics, and that the most strenuous efforts are being put forth by these parties and by Riel's friends to secure a commutation of his sentence, renders it imperative upon us as a loyal and Protestant association, that we should express to the Government our views and deep convictions on this subject. The pardon of Riel was resorted to before. The exile of Riel from Canada was tried before. . . .

His murderous intentions have only been intensifying. The pardon but emboldened him to treat British laws and British leniency with contempt, and the slaughter of loyal and law-abiding British subjects has been ten-fold more appalling than on the former occasion. . . .

We trust that you will entreat of the Government not to allow any petitions, requests, or influences from Riel's friends, or from any other source, to prevail on them to commute the sentence, postpone the same, or in any way alter the just sentence that now hangs over this self-doomed man.

From *La Mort de Riel et la Voix du Sang* (undated pamphlet, pp. 4–5. (trans.) in *The North-West Rebellion* edited and translated by A.I. Silver and Marie-France Valleur, The Copp Clark Publishing Company, 1967, pp. 52.

The Toronto Evening News
Editorial
18 May 1885

The full significance of the prompt and effective suppression of the half-breed rebellion in the Northwest is hardly yet realized. . . .

The echoes of the Gatling gun and the ringing cheers of our men in the assault of the rebel position at Batoche sounded the death-knell of French ascendancy. Behind the rebel rifle-pits were entrenched not merely the sharpshooters of Gabriel Dumont, but the long and warmly cherished aspirations of the entire French-Canadian race—the hope of building up on the prairies a second Quebec. The secret underlying motive of the half-breed uprising was to preserve intact for the French "their laws, their language, and their institutions". . . .

The one all-absorbing idea of the leading spirits among the French-Canadians, to which they adhere with a singular tenacity, amid all minor plunder-grabbing projects, is the complete reconquest of Canada, the establishment on a firm and lasting basis of French ascendancy throughout the Dominion. . . .

They saw in the few thousand half-breeds of French origin a possible nucleus around which French institutions could be crystallized. . . . It has always been our misfortune in dealing with the French that what we have gained in battle we have lost by political concessions. Will history repeat itself in the present case? Will our rulers throwaway the results of Batoche . . . by concessions . . . which will inspire the Quebec visionaries with new hopes? . . . The volunteers of Ontario who have won this fight ought to make the powers that be clearly understand that they fought for national unity and Anglo-Saxon institutions and do not mean to be cheated of the legitimate fruits of their victory.

Excerpts from the Toronto Evening News, May 18, 1885.

THE QUEBEC PERSPECTIVES

Question Nationale du Nord-Ouest

1886

The North-West affair is a decisive question on which depends, perhaps, both the future of our race, and the role we will have to play on this continent.

Not just because Riel was executed: the interests and the fate of a single individual are, after all, quite secondary in a question of this nature. But because the solution applied to the North-West question . . . the lot reserved for several dozen unfortunate Métis who are suffering today in the cells of Regina, show just how much justice and fair dealing they intend to permit to any nationality—even to one of the strongest nationalities in Canada—when it happens to be in the minority. . . .

The great evil working for the ruin of Canada—and it has always been the same—is a rabid and dishonest francophobia. What would have been the progress of Canada if the development of our rich North-West had been opened loyally and impartially to all honest competition, to all enterprise! . . . They wanted to make the North-West essentially Anglo-Saxon in race and in language, and to drive out of it every French-Catholic element. But, since the majority of the population already established there was French and Catholic, it was necessary to destroy or expel it. . . .

Excerpts from the *Toronto Evening News,* May 18, 1885.

La Mort de Reil at la Voix du Sang

Riel is dead, and the cursed city which has drunk his blood, the hordes of sectarians who demanded it with foaming mouths, with sinister, execrable cries, are still plunged in an infernal orgy of fanaticism and hatred against the French name, against the French province, which they imagine they have destroyed and trampled under foot by destroying and stamping upon the livid corpse of the poor Metis leader, the tortured immortal of Regina. . . .

The rope that strangled him strangles and garrots the province of Quebec in the minds of the thousands of spectators who savoured his death rattle; it strangles, it garrots the French-Canadians in the minds of the Ontario fanatics who at this very moment are celebrating their victory over us, over our ministers, over our representatives.

Why is Riel dead? Why? Because he was French.

From *La Mort de Riel et la Voix du Sang* (undated pamphlet) pp. 4,5. (trans.) in *The North-West Rebellion* edited and translated by A. I. Silver and Marie-France Valleur, The Copp Clark Publishing Company, 1967

HISTORICAL PERSPECTIVES

The Last Word on Louis Riel—
The Man of Several Faces
George F. G. Stanley
1986

"La question Métisse est comme une charrette.
Pour la faire marcher, il faut deux roues et dans le moment,
il nous en manque une. Si no us la voulons, il nous faut aller
la chercher dans le Montana,
le long du Missouri." (Charles Nolin, 1884)[1]

1

Louis Riel! The name evokes a variety of images in the minds of Canadians. Of the many people who have played a role on the historical stage in Canada, Louis "David" Riel has, in the last fifty years, become one of the most popular and most publicized. And yet this has not always been true. Admittedly Riel's trial and execution, a century ago, produced a spate of political pamphlets and polemics. But then the poor man lapsed into obscurity. Canadians focussed their attention on the politicians, the men who brought the Canadian Confederation into being, and those who tried to prevent it from becoming a vital political reality. During the first half century of our national existence as a federal union, Riel did have his place in our history texts, but it was a very small place indeed. French-speaking Canadians felt sympathy for him, but it was a sympathy frequently marred by the recollection of his apostasy; English-speaking Canadians never could, never did overlook the execution of the Ontario Orangeman, Thomas Scott, by a Metis court-martial in 1870, and held Riel responsible for it.

"The Last Word on Louis Riel—The Man of Several Faces" by George F.G. Stanley reprinted from *1885 and After: Native Society in Transition,* F. Laurie Barron and James B. Waldram, eds., University of Regina, 1986 with permission of Ruth L. Stanley.

2

Since the conclusion of World War II, Canadian attitudes have undergone a change. Riel's life has become the subject of biographies, academic and popular, documented and otherwise, of poems and plays, in English and French, of an opera—probably the most ambitious and best produced by a Canadian musician—and an overture. His statue has been erected in two provincial capitals,[2] although not yet in Ottawa, the capital city from which he fled in 1874, when expelled from Parliament. His grave in St. Boniface has become a site visited annually by pilgrims and political radicals, most of whom he would probably have repudiated in the days when he presided over the Provisional Government of Assiniboia. The University of Alberta, with monies from the Social Science Federation of Canada, a body funded by Ottawa, has published a complete annotated edition of his writings. And on the political scene, efforts are being made to secure for him a posthumous pardon for the "treason" for which he was hanged one hundred years ago.

Why this change? Because historical writing, like history itself, does not stand still. It is subject to intellectual influences which mould its shape and content. Historical events and institutions must be considered against the background of the changing cultural and intellectual foci that have conditioned their evolution. Historians live in what Rudy Wiebe has called a "fictive present," collecting past facts in order to create an understanding of the world in the light of the "expected future."[3] In simply worlds, this means that, since the events of Canadian history were dominated in the second half of the nineteenth century by the imperial idea, historical writing reflected the idea of empire as a creative, philosophical, political and religious force. The Canadian Confederation was the imperial idea in action; Canada's expansion from sea to sea was natural and irresistible. Natural, because it was part of the expansion of the British Empire. Irresistible, because Empire was part of the divine plan, whether it was British, French or American; because imperial expansion brought peace, order, justice, liberty and Christianity to troubled lands, and, above all, to the benighted Natives of the world. The "white man's burden"; how often we used to hear those words from pulpit and platform. And we, white Canadians, were expected to bear our share of that burden, in the West and in the North. I am not being cynical. French men and English men in British North America might disagree on points of detail as to what their share of the burden would be; what kind of Christianity, for instance, they would take to the heathen; but they were all agreed on the general principle. White expansion was, therefore, a matter of religious faith, an obligation. It was also a matter of scientific faith. During the nineteenth century, evolution, biological and social, was gradually gaining acceptance in academic circles. What a combination of strengths; doctors of Divinity allied with doctors of Science. Nothing could resist it! Natives of any colour or race who tried, could and would be swept away. It was the Will of God and His prophet, Charles Darwin. Riel, Indians, Métis, what chance had they of standing by themselves against the inevitable? Of course they failed, as one would have expected them to fail. Why then, should history students spend much time on Riel and his rebellions? A footnote in recorded history; that would be sufficient.

The next question is obvious. Why then, have Riel and his adherents once more seized the public imagination in Canada, as they have done in recent years? I suggest that every period in history has, within itself, not only its heritage of values carried forward from the past, its haunting ghosts of former empires, but also the seeds of future change. And of these seeds of change, the most important is that of new ideas imported or intruding from outside the confines of the national group. In Canada, as elsewhere in the early years of the twentieth century, the imperial idea was beginning to lose some of its vitality and popularity. That was one of the legacies of World War I. Woodrow Wilson talked about "clearly recognizable lines of nationality" and "the freest opportunity of autonomous development."[4] The Treaty of Versailles administered the knockout blow. Even the British dominions, Canada included, were on the way to becoming national entities. In 1926 the term "British Empire" was replaced by "British Commonwealth"; and in 1931 the Statute of West minster gave nation status to the Dominions. By the end of World War II, imperialism was dead: long live the nation state![5] The British Empire, over the dissolution of which Winston Churchill had declared he would never preside, simply ceased to exist. Canadians generally were aware of what had happened and recognized that the old spiritual cupboard was bare: that the concept of Empire could never again provide them with intellectual nourishment. It had changed from a living thing into an historical artifact.

The sequel was that Canadians became aware of the irrelevance of their earlier attitudes towards Native peoples, those "lesser breeds without the law." It was hard to regard as inferior a Native Indian who fought beside you in the ranks.[6] Or who might carry the King's commission. Is it surprising that some Canadians at least should begin to wonder if the pale-faced nations were really as God-blessed, as high-minded and as altruistic as they previously had thought them to be? Were the white man's social institutions, his mores, his forms of government, his jurisprudence, his educational theories as superior as the whites had always taken for granted?

Perhaps the people who resisted denationalization and cultural assimilation in Europe were the real heroes. Is it to be wondered at, under the impact of these changing ideas, that white Canadians should begin to take another look at Riel, to reconsider his role in western Canadian history, and look upon the Métis leader as a hero, a kind of a "resistance" hero, and the Métis insurrection as the armed protest of a small national group struggling against cultural absorption? It can be argued that to picture the Métis as "freedom fighters" and Riel as a hero-figure in this sense, is going too far. But I do suggest that, even if the comparison is overdrawn, this is a view that is widespread today in Canada, certainly among the Native people themselves and among a not inconsiderable number of whites as well. That is why, I suggest, historical writing about Riel has, of necessity, become contemporary in its outlook.

3

Historical research in recent years has not added greatly to our knowledge of the details of Riel's career. The sources have, on the whole, been within comparatively easy reach of scholars for many years. We have long known that he was born in St. Boniface, 22 October 1844; that he was educated at the local school in St. Boniface and then sent to the Sulpician-managed Collège de Montréal to be educated for the priesthood; that he left in his final year of formal schooling without graduating, tried his hand at law, and at writing poetry, became engaged, only to have his engagement broken by his fiancée's parents, apparently on racial grounds, and finally returned to St. Boniface in 1868. We know that he had been exposed in Montreal to the wordy, emotional controversies over the union proposals which ended in Confederation in 1867. We know that on his return to Red River, he placed himself at the head of a group of Métis, concerned about their future under Canadian rule and that he occupied Fort Garry with an armed force, ignoring the decrepit administration of the Hudson's Bay Company.

Having refused to accept as the political head of state a Canadian-appointed Lieutenant-Governor, William MacDougall, Riel called for an election and formed a Métis Provisional Government. During the next few months, he carried on official talks with Canadian emissaries from Ottawa; suppressed the armed efforts of a group of Canadians resident in the settlement to overthrow his Provisional Government; executed one Thomas Scott, an Ontario Orangeman and malcontent; and sent delegates to Canada to negotiate the entry of the Red River Settlement into the Canadian federation as a province. In this sense Riel may legitimately be looked upon as the father of Manitoba.

Meanwhile, however, the federal authorities despatched a military force to Manitoba, and Riel, trusting Bishop Alexandre Taché to obtain an amnesty for him, offered no armed resistance, but distrusting the troops, fled from Red River. A Canadian Lieutenant-Governor, Adams Archibald of Nova Scotia, took over the provincial administration. Elected several times to the federal Parliament, Riel was never able to take his seat. Instead, he took refuge in asylums, first in Montreal and later in Québec. On his release he made his way to the western United States where he became an American citizen in 1883, finally settling down as a school teacher in Montana.

In 1884, on the invitation of the French and English half-breeds of the North Saskatchewan valley, Louis Riel returned to Canada to organize and lead a political agitation designed to secure for the half-breed population titles to the lands they already occupied. Following the pattern of action he had adopted in Manitoba in 1870, Riel sent a petition to Ottawa, formed a Provisional Government, and waited to be invited to negotiate with Ottawa. But 1885 was not 1869–70. This time the federal authorities sent a military force to the West before, not after, opening negotiations with the Native peoples. Riel met force with force and was defeated. His prayers and hopes for divine intervention were of no avail. Not God but a stipendiary magistrate sat in judgement upon him. Riel was charged with and convicted of treason in Regina and condemned to death. Despite every effort on the part of Québec politicians and, despite even the threats of the collapse of the Anglo-French *modus vivendi* that had been Sir John A. Macdonald's source of strength before and after Confederation, Riel was hanged at Regina, 16 November 1885.

4

That, in outline, is the biography of Louis Riel. There is little or no controversy about the facts. They are available to any historian who takes the trouble to find them in libraries and archival establishments; but the facts, by themselves, don't do very much to broaden our understanding of the man himself and what motivated him. History is more than a chronicle of facts and dates. That is history devoid of meaning. A suitable comparison would be a statue lacking facial features. As Francis Bacon put it, "that part being wanting which doth most show the spirit and life of the person."[7] Obviously, if the details of the face be unknown, the sculptor must add them in such a way as to give an element of personality to the figure carved in stone or cast in bronze. By the same token, the historian is obliged to portray his subject in a manner that will convey the significance of his subject's being to his readers. In other words, he must portray his subject's face in a credible fashion.

To Riel's own contemporaries the Métis leader's face was clear and unmistakable. They believed they knew who Riel was: a western Métis who reflected, in his career, the Anglo-French politico-cultural conflict imposed on this country by the defeat of France by Great Britain in 1763 and by the defeat of Great Britain by the United States in 1783. By defeating France in the Seven Years' War, Great Britain acquired a body of French (Canadian) subjects and by losing to the Americans, Britain acquired a body of English (American) subjects, who, whether they liked it or not, were compelled by defeat and common misery to become co-partners in a new colonial venture. English and French, Protestant and Catholic, the products of different cultural and political systems, but living within the boundaries of British North America, thus became uneasy and contentious rivals, ever on the offensive and on the defensive against each other. A happy situation for the United States, which as long as the Franco- and Anglo-Canadians squabbled with each other, would have little to fear economically or politically from the British colonies on the eastern shore of the St. Lawrence.

Given the traditional rivalries of French and English Canadians, exacerbated by arguments over Confederation, it was not unreasonable for historians and novelists, as well as for politicians, to see the events which transpired in the Red River and Saskatchewan River valleys as western manifestations of the same rivalries that existed in the valleys of the Ottawa and the St. Lawrence. That is why events in western Canada, whether related by historians, novelists or poets, appear as little more than the projection to the prairies of the religious and political quarrels of central Canada. Given a knowledge of their traditional outlooks, was it unreasonable for Ontario writers in 1870 to see Riel as the "murderer" of Thomas Scott, the Ontario Orangeman; was it unreasonable for Quebec writers to see him as a defender of French rights and separate schools in Manitoba? Riel's Provisional Government was legitimate or illegitimate, according to the cultural and national background of the beholder. This interpretation of the Red River troubles carried over to the North–West rising in 1885. To one group Riel appeared as the "rebel" solely responsible for the outbreak, and for the killings that followed, perpetrated by Indians and Métis alike; a man inspired by personal ambition; a cold-blooded murderer, and, particularly a French, Catholic murderer. To the other group, Riel was seen as a poor, pathetic madman struggling to help his people or as a brave persistent champion of the French fact in the West, resisting the assimilation of his culture by the English, and the destruction of his faith by Pope-hating Protestants. These contrasting views are to be found in the speeches delivered on the floor of the House of Commons, in newspaper editorials, in the poems and in the novels of the day.

In February 1870, the editor of *The Globe* of Toronto referred to Riel as "The Great Potentate of the North," increasing the volume of his criticism in April to include Fathers Ritchot and Lestanc and suggesting Riel was only the "front" man in Bishop Taché's "political game of chess" with Canada; the clergy had "deeper designs than the uneducated French were aware of" letting loose "a monster whose craft, condition and ferocity are greater than any one supposed." *La Minerve*'s characterization of Riel was rather different. To the French language newspaper of Montréal, Riel was "un jeune homme de grande abilité ... éloquent dans ses discours." *La Minerve* accepted Sir John A. Macdonald's assurance that the military expedition being sent to Red River was bound on a mission of peace. In fact, said *La Minerve,* "L'envoi des troupes lui répugnait."[8] The same positions were taken in 1885. The English-language *Gazette* declared that "when Riel is captured he ought to be strung up on the first convenient tree without ceremony." *La Minerve* replied by asking if Riel was "Suffisamment équilibre pour comprendre toute la responsabilité de ses actes." Thus while the English language journals demanded that Riel "be hanged, or —!," the francophone newspapers were crying that Riel "shall not be hanged, or —!" An anonymous letter sent to Macdonald put the issue in these terms: "If the French of Montreal and Quebec think that he [Riel] is a marter [*sic*] and that he is sure of going strait [*sic*] to Heaven the sooner he goes there the better."[9]

That was how the popular press portrayed Riel. The poets and novelists followed the same line, reflecting their racial bias. Louis Fréchette, said by some to have been an associate of Riel in the years prior to the latter's return to Red River in 1868, included two poems in his epic *La Légende d'un Peuple* entitled "Le Dernier Martyr" and "Le Gibet de Riel."[10] Across the Ottawa River, in Ontario, an obscure novelist by the name of J. E. Collins, wrote a fictional account, *The Story of Louis Riel, the Rebel Chief,* in which Métis were described as "a debased sort and unfit socially to mix with those who had kept their race free from taint." Elsewhere he refers to Riel as "the wily traitor" and "the arch agitator . . . foaming with rage" at any opposition and whose sneer, when his advances were rejected by a Métisse girl, "sounded like an envenomed hiss." Collins overworked his adjectives, portraying Scott as a "noble" and "heroic" figure when encountering the "craven," "foul," miscreant Riel. The Indians too are said to have had "fiendish faces" and "wolf-like eyes." Collins saw the Abbé Ritchot, Riel's ecclesiastic adviser, only as a "great swaggering, windy" priest, and O'Donoghue as "coarse and loud-mouthed." After such a dose of venom, the reader is relieved to find that the women, Métis or Indian, are invariably "beautiful with dusky eyes."[11]

Even musicians got into the act. But their efforts are now long, perhaps happily, forgotten. Do you suppose any militia units that took part in the events of 1885 still march to the tune of J. E. Whitney's *The Otter Grand March,* or can anybody remember or has anybody today ever danced to fiddles scratching out the melody of Annie Delaney's *Batoche Polka*?[12]

Canadian historians reflected much the same views as the writers of fiction, although, of course, in more restrained and dignified prose. The elements of racial and religious controversy were still there. And they continued to dominate our historical writing until the nineteen thirties. Certainly this is true of Georges Dugast's *Histoire Véridique,* published in Montréal in 1905. Dugast, who was personally acquainted with Riel in St. Boniface, portrayed the Métis chief as a martyr whose actions were understandable and excusable. It was still the Riel, the victim of prejudice, who appeared in Jean Bruchési's *Histoire du Canada pour tous.*[13] This is also the Riel the Abbé Lionel Groulx saw when he visited St. Boniface in 1944, the centenary of Riel's birth, and used the occasion to attack the "destructive" public school system and the myopic vision of English-speaking Manitobans.[14] The visage of Riel, the defender of French, Catholic rights was the one seen by the Catholic priest, Adrien Morice,[15] and the French historian, Auguste-Henri de Trémaudan. Trémaudan shared Groulx's view that Riel was the foremost defender of French culture in western Canada. In the "Avertissement" to his *Histoire de la Nation Métisse,* he wrote, "La race française peut être fière de ce rameau qui, dans l'Ouest canadien, fut fidèle à sa mission civilisatrice."[16] He closed his book reiterating the same theme, Quant au grand martyr qu'il avait donné à cette cause sacrée, le peuple métis resta longtemps seul à révérer, seul à voir se dresser, à l'horizon, l'ombre de l'Emancipateur et du libérateur."[17]

In the minds of English Protestant writers, at least those close to the times about which they wrote, such as George Bryce and R. G. MacBeth, Riel's actions never had any legitimacy. The man was a demagogue, a demagogue inspired by self-interest or misled by an ambitious Roman clergy. Perhaps the Métis did have grievances; but nothing, absolutely nothing could justify the "wanton murder" of Thomas Scott[18] or give legitimacy to Riel's governments, either in Manitoba or Saskatchewan. Indeed, the general impression the reader gets from MacBeth is one of a simple people misled by Riel and the Roman Church. The only thing to be said for Riel was that he was a "madman." His defeat, even his execution, were necessary for the development and progress of the country. Later writers were inclined to be less outspoken. This was true of Schofield in Manitoba, Black in Saskatchewan[19] and George Wrong and Chester Martin in Ontario. The latter, writing in *Canada and its Provinces*[20] gives a calm, well-written and, by his own standards, balanced account of both the Red River and North Saskatchewan troubles. A.R.M. Lower, one of Canada's most perceptive as well as outspoken historians, put his views in these words when dealing with Riel's trial and execution: "Riel in 1885 symbolized to Frenchmen the blood lust of Orangeism, its determination to take away from French Catholics all their rights, to oppress and destroy them. The execution took on a highly representative character; a whole people was on trial. It was taken as a direct challenge to the whole French race, just as Scott's execution had been a challenge to Protestantism. Wherever justice lay, from the deed the curse descended once more upon Canada, the curse of division and of racialism."[21]

Carefully avoiding the extremism and special pleading of a de Trémaudan or a MacBeth, but still within the framework of the now traditional thesis of the Riel troubles as a western expression of the stresses and strains of Canadian binationalism and biculturalism, was a doctoral dissertation written by J.A. Jonasson at the University of California. ThIs thoroughly professional piece of work, however, failed to find a publisher, either in Canada or in the United States. All that appeared in print was an article published by the *Pacific Historical Review* in 1934.[22] This essay gave an excellent academic summary of what was, by this time, the well-accepted interpretation of Riel. The American historian, Mason Wade, who carefully avoided identifying himself with either side in the Canadian controversy, followed the traditional line of thought. In his *French Canadian Outlook,* he saw French Canadian history as enshrining Riel as a martyr of French and Catholic culture in Canada. Wade followed the same interpretive approach to Riel in his voluminous work, *The French Canadians 1760–1945,* published in Toronto several years later.[23]

By the 1930s, however, a new face began to emerge on Louis Riel. This was the one I saw as I pursued my doctoral studies at Oxford University. Having, as a small boy in southern Alberta, read Fenimore Cooper's Leatherstocking tales and Francis Parkman's *Oregon Trail,* and listened to stories about Indians, half-breeds and mounted policemen, I was familiar at least with the outlines of western Canadian history before I ever went to university. And it was not a hostile or critical picture that emerged in my mind. My father was disposed to regard the Indians with a sympathetic eye, and although my mother—she too had moved to the West from Ontario in the late years of the nineteenth century, spending some time in Fort Macleod and in Lethbridge—was afraid of Indians (after all, the fires had been extinguished only a few years earlier at Wounded Knee) she too was not hostile. How could I help but be interested when Indians drove each day in front of our house in Calgary on their way from Sarcee to the city, and when as a small boy, I had a chance to meet not only

Father Lacombe, but Colonel James Walker, who made the march with the Mounted Police in 1873, and others, including Robert Armstrong to whom Riel surrendered on 16 May 1885, and William Cameron, who had narrowly escaped death at Frog Lake.

Even so, the most decisive influence shaping my view of Riel came from my experience at Oxford. I included British colonial policy among my undergraduate studies, and read widely about Native problems in South Africa, Australia and New Zealand. When I went on to graduate work, Dr. Vincent Harlow, the Rhodes House Librarian, encouraged me to take a look at Riel. And when I gained permission to work in the Hudson's Bay Company archives, the subject of my thesis was settled. But there was more to it than that. My undergraduate reading had prompted an interest in the problems arising out of the cultural conflict between Native peoples and European immigrants during the British colonial period. And this interest was further stimulated by Dr. E.P. Morrell, a New Zealander, then Beit Lecturer in Colonial History at Oxford, who suggested to me the possibility of a parallel between the Indians in Canada and the Maoris of his own country. In consequence, when I wrote my doctoral thesis, this idea of cultural conflict was uppermost in my mind. The traditional French-English, Catholic-Protestant approach to western Canadian history appeared to me to be purely coincidental. Instead, I saw the Riel issues as a Canadian example of a far wider problem which was, in brief, the inevitable clash arising out of the expansion of an industrialized civilization into regions inhabited by peoples whose culture-pattern was still based upon a hunting or rudimentary agricultural economy. In every instance the more primitive people were compelled to pay a heavy price for the alleged "benefits" of "civilization."

Later I found myself, for some reason or other, labelled as a "frontier" historian by some of my contemporaries.[24] I know that A.L. Burt, my professor at the University of Alberta in the nineteen twenties, was a strong supporter of Turner's "frontier thesis"; but, I believe the key to my interpretation of Riel is to be found in my Oxford rather than in my Alberta experience. This surely must be apparent to anyone who takes the trouble to read two articles over my signature written in 1940 and in 1947.[25] I have always tended to see Turner's thesis simply as a scholarly effort to bolster American nationalism by attributing democracy, not to the fertilization of American political thinking by eighteenth century European writers, but to purely indigenous influences, in particular, to the "open frontier, the hither edge of free land." Turner's interpretation of American history was and still is, to my mind, an oversimplification, an effort, not wholly successful, to isolate the United States from the general course of civilization; a kind of political parthenogenesis.

My Oxford doctoral thesis was published by Longmans, Green, in London, England, in 1936, under the title of *The Birth of Western Canada*. It was well reviewed. *John O'London* even made it "the book of the week."[26] Some British people even purchased copies. But in Canada the book was largely ignored, despite a moderately favourable review in the *Canadian Historical Review* by R.O. MacFarlane.[27]

Am I presumptuous in claiming to have pointed the way to a new interpretation of Riel and the Métis risings? I can point out that my "cultural-conflict" theory was adopted by the French ethnologist-historian, Marcel Giraud. Giraud was familiar with my book and with A.S. Morton's *History of the Canadian West* (1936).[28] He had studied the Canadian historical scene in depth, and was free, during the years of World War II, to put his researches on paper and to secure publication in 1945 by the Institut d'Ethnologie de l'Université de Paris. Giraud adopted my cultural-conflict thesis interpretation and added the strength of his vast researches to it. However, neither *The Birth of Western Canada, Le Métis Canadien* nor *The History of the Canadian West* made much impact upon the general book-buying, or even book-reading public. To interpret Riel as the defender of a Native culture rather than as a rebel against constituted authority was to imply, on my part, a degree of sympathy unacceptable at that time to many Canadians. I was dismayed but not discouraged. The revival of interest in Riel in the middle fifties, which led to the re-publication of *The Birth of Western Canada,* by the University of Toronto Press in 1960, prompted me to do what I had long wanted, to write a full-dress biography of Louis Riel. For several years, I assumed that the late William Morton of the University of Manitoba, who had already published his *History of Manitoba* and a lengthy introduction to the *Alexander Begg Journal,*[29] would probably undertake that task. Finally, when the late Lorne Pierce of the Ryerson Press asked me to write the biography, I put the question fairly to Professor Morton. He replied that he had taken it for granted that I would do it. And so I did. The book was published in 1963 and met with a good response.[30] However, after the Ryerson Press was taken over by the American firm of McGraw-Hill, I ceased to be one of their favoured authors.

There was a step-up of Canadian interest in Riel during the post-World War II years, partly, I think, because of his discovery by the Americans. In 1952, Riel emerged from the pens of Kinsey Howard and Bernard de Voto as "the American primitive," the hero, the forlorn hope, the right stuff.[31] There were no grey tones here, no shades of meaning. It was all white and black; liberty and death; gallantry and cowardice; good and evil; freedom and oppression. Everything required for a popular consumption. Charles Dickens used the theme of heroic self-sacrifice in *A Tale of Two Cities.* Do we see Louis Riel as a Sydney Carton? Of course the academic historian does not, in all conscience, attempt to match this; even though he knows that his reading public likes its history simple and direct, with good guys and bad guys clearly delineated. What does it matter if historical truth, or what passes for historical truth, is touched up a bit? Photographers do it all the time. A portrait is all the more pleasing if the warts are removed. The old western movies may not have portrayed accurate history, but they followed a sure-fire box-office formula. In academic terms, we could sum up the formula as "romantic primitivism."

It was this "romantic primitivism" that appealed to the imaginative writers in Canada. The most significant of these was the Irish Canadian playwright, John Coulter, whose two-part play *Louis Riel* is a dramatic portrayal of a man trying to preserve the way of life of a minority against overwhelmIng odds. Riel, according to Coulter, was "The most theatrIcal character in Canadian history, and probably in American history as well. He rides the political conscience of the nation after nearly three-quarters of a century, and is manifestly on his way to becoming the tragic hero at the heart of the Canadian myth."[32] Played first in Toronto in 1950 by the New Play Society, Coulter's *Riel* was broadcast by the Canadian Broadcasting Corporation (CBC) with Bruno Gerussi playing the role of Louis Riel—a far better production incidentally, than the CBC's fictional effort in 1979. The producer, in this latter instance, would have done better had he repeated the original Coulter production or at least given his viewers something that would have adhered more accurately to historical and geographical truth.[33]

Of much less significance as a work of dramatic art than Coulter's was a play written by Charles Bayer and E. Parage. The piece was published originally in Montreal in 1886 and re-published at St. Boniface in 1984. It has not been produced and has little to commend it historically or theatrically. Also lacking both literary or historical merit, other than as evidence of the interest aroused by the execution of Riel, are Elzéar Paquin's *Riel, tragédie en quatre actes* (Montréal, 1886), and F.G. Walsh's *The Trial of Louis Riel*, published in Fargo, North Dakota, in 1965. More satisfying is Mavor Moore's libretto for the Harry Somers opera, *Riel,* produced in the O'Keefe Centre in Toronto in 1967. Bernard Turgeon played the lead role. A television version of Somers's opera was later produced making this magnificent production heard elsewhere in Canada and in Europe.

In the field of historical fiction, here are a few random examples: J.E. Collins's *Annette the Métis Spy: A Heroine of the N.W. Rebellion* (Toronto, 1886); Joseph Emile Poirier's *La Tempète sur le Fleuve* (Paris, 1931); Edward McCourt's *Buckskin Brigadier* (Toronto, 1955); and R.D. Symon's *Still the Wind Blows* (Saskatoon, 1971). None of these works has, however, the strong emphasis on Riel to be found in Rudy Wiebe's *The Scorched Earth People* (Toronto, 1977). Making allowances for his fictional projection of Gabriel Dumont into the Red River story and his idealization of Riel, Wiebe is unquestionably the most skillful novelist to address himself to the problems posed by the Métis risings in Manitoba and Saskatchewan. Even a cursory glance at this book will reveal the mighty gap that exists between Collins's *The Story of Riel, the Rebel Chief* and Wiebe's *The Scorched Earth People.* More people will read Wiebe, despite or perhaps because of his romantic liberalism, than are likely to read the more complicated, professional studies by academic historians.

6

Meanwhile, however, Riel has taken on a new face. Today he appears to some historians and would-be historians alike, not as a French Catholic leader, nor as the representative leader of a cultural minority, nor as a romantic hero, but as the first of a long line of prairie political patriots, extending from John Norquay to Peter Lougheed, seeking to give coherence to western regional identity.[34] Stretching their imaginations a little farther, some westerners profess to see Riel as the father-founder of western separatism; not just the voice of the land-robbed Métis and Indians, but the voice of every prairie farmer and prairie oil investor resenting the economic domination, real or imaginary, of those grasping, federal politicians located somewhere in "Eastern Canada." Sir John A. Macdonald, now long in his grave, has been forgotten as the object of western reproach; his place has been taken by Pierre Trudeau.

The face of Louis Riel, the progenitor of western radicalism, is not without its appeal to historians. After all, are not radicals and revolutionaries the stuff to give liveliness to political history? The late Professor William Morton had caught a dim glimpse of this new face of Riel when he wrote his introduction to *Alexander Begg's Red River Journal.* Professor Douglas Owram made this point in his paper on "The Myth of Louis Riel," in the *Canadian Historical Review* in September 1982.[35] And it is a legitimate point. A Manitoba Anglophone, Morton was inclined towards a mild sympathy with the Métis as westerners, suggesting that Riel's basic aim had been to obtain a position for the Métis "similar to that which the French of Quebec had won for themselves in Canada." As a Manitoban, of rural origin, Morton was also inclined towards a suspicion of Ottawa and federal politicians. He did not see Riel as the precursor of Manitoba's New Democratic Party leader, Howard Pawley, but he did see him as resembling Alberta's evangelistic Social Credit founder, William Aberhart. Both, he wrote, "were prairie politicians."[36]

Morton, even if he did react in typical western fashion to the arrogance of Upper Canadians and try to see in Riel a western Canadian political prototype, was too cerebral and too conservative to share Howard Adams's opinions about Riel. A Métis and a great-grandson of Maxime Lepine, one of Riel's supporters both in 1869–70 and in 1885, Adams, in his *Prison of Grass,* runs the gamut of tendentious phraseology, accusing the Canadian government of "racism"; declaring that parliament's action in 1874 in expelling Riel from the House of Commons "leads me to wonder whether the electoral system will ever work for the Indians and Métis."[37] Adams presents a more interesting speculation when he describes the events in the Saskatchewan valley in 1884–85 as the "culmination of a complex struggle that had arisen over the previous two decades between the people of the Northwest and the industrial rulers of Ottawa." Adams's book is a passionate work; scholarly, I suppose, within the framework of his political radicalism. The people of the North-West, the farmers, settlers, workers, white, Indian and Métis alike, were, according to Adams, doing no more than struggling for economic and land reforms and responsible government. Riel, he writes, was "murdered . . . on the colonizers' scaffold."[38] This kind of thesis fits neatly into the Marxist stereotype. Adams sees the Riel movement of 1884–85 as a secessionist movement and argues that it was federal policy deliberately to allow the situation to degenerate to the point at which troops could justifiably be sent to western Canada to subdue the Indians and the Métis by force of arms. According to Adams, Father André, Charles Nolin and Philippe Garnot were *agents provocateurs;*

the Métis and Indian fighters were "champions of freedom and democracy"; and those who suffered death were "uncomparable heroes."

Another popular, politically-minded if not politically active writer like Adams, who works over the same left-wing themes, is Peter Charlebois. His *The Life of Louis Riel,* however, lacks Adams's liveliness, and his restrained approach excites little in the way of strong support. Charlebois believes that the mistakes of the Riel story are still being repeated in the Northwest Territories and argues that unless another Riel appears on the horizon, the Indians and the Métis of the North will become "beggars in their own homeland."[39] Charlebois and Adams, if nothing else, have helped to make Louis Riel into a relevant figure in the eyes of those who would never have become interested in his career had they seen him only as a protagonist of French language rights, as a Native cultural leader, as just another prairie politician. Political parties of every stripe and hue must inevitably establish their own calendar of saints and martyrs, as well as sinners. But, to me, it remains an oddity to see Riel, the man who contested elections as a Conservative and who envisioned a theocratic state for western Canada, so readily welcomed to the ranks of left-wing Socialists.

Is it an error to try to read modern secularist politics back into the events of the North-West Rebellion? Is there justification for those communists who used to meet annually—and may still do for all I know—at Riel's grave implying they and Riel emerged from the same political mould? To wish to establish roots in the past and thereby gain respectability, is understandable, but that does not make it commendable. To ask me to believe that there is an intellectual affinity between Riel, Lepine, Dumont with Engels, Marx or Lenin is to ask me to stretch my imagination beyond the breaking point, to accept political cliches as revealed truth. Quite frankly, I am more inclined towards the fourth visage of Riel, that is Riel the millenarian, the man who believed change would come as a matter of divine revelation, by a holy miracle.

7

Radicalism is not limited to politics. Throughout history, there have been groups of people, shepherds, bandits, Robin Hoods as it were, members of religious sects who usually expressed their aspirations in cults and rituals, but also at times in acts of violence.[40] All of these groups had one thing in common, namely a deep-seated religious conviction that, with God's help, they could remake the world. How and when was usually unclear. Seldom did they ever have a definite programme of action, a positive time-table for the transfer of power, They believed that God was on their side. With His aid they would attain the millenium. Some such movements still exist. They are usually composed of impractical people, unrealistic, utopian, who speak and think in terms apocalyptic. Does this pattern fit Riel? It follows, therefore, that we must look more closely at Riel, the man with a sense of divine mission; the man who saw a new heaven and a new earth on the North American continent; the man who talked of a reformed Papacy in the New World; the man who proclaimed his hope the western plains would be peopled by the oppressed thousands of Europe. This new and currently popular visage of Riel is that of Riel the Millenarian, the Prophet who spoke the language of apocalyptic religion.

That Riel held strange views and held them strongly was well known to his contemporaries. And has been to historians. Indeed that is why many people have argued that he was insane. When I wrote my biography of Riel, I was inclined to see him as "unstable," but I could not bring myself to use the word "insane." I read many of Riel's prophecies, prayers, supplications, letters. I regarded his actions as irrational; but I did not, could not say positively, "this man is insane."[41] And for my indecision I was roundly accused of lack of decisiveness by those critics who like positive assessments. As if this were always easy or always possible. The fact was that I harboured a certain sympathy for the Court, bound as it was, by the McNaghten Rules, a certain sympathy for the physicians, doctors Lavell, Valade and Jukes, who examined Riel. And not least, for the convicted man himself.[42]

My studies at Oxford had not pointed me in the direction of millenarianism, as the explanation of the Riel risings of 1869 and 1885; but those of Gilles Martel, studying for the priesthood, did give him a new standpoint from which to look at Riel. He saw Judeo-Christian messianism as one of the main features of the historical phenomenon of millenarianism, and concluded Riel's strong religious upbringing and his clerical schooling in Montreal at the hands of the Sulpicians may well have left the young Métis open to the influence of messianic theories. Martel, therefore, undertook to trace the development of Riel's messianic ideas.[43] The first phase covered the years 1870 to 1875. These were the years when Riel went into hiding to escape his suspected assassins; when he attempted to enter the field of federal politics and was defeated; when he was banished from Canada by parliamentary edict. In 1875 he experienced his first vision, while in Washington, and became convinced that God had singled him out for a special mission to the Métis people. The second phase covered the years 1875 to 1878, the years Riel spent in the mental hospitals of St. Jean de Dieu in Montréal and Beauport in Quebec. During these years Riel saw himself as the "Prophet of the New World" in communication with God Himself. He envisioned the Old World as suffering under the domination of heretical and heathen nations. This tired Old World was nearing collapse. The third phase, 1878 to 1884, saw the development of Riel's concept of the Métis as God's Chosen People and the establishment of the Kingdom of God in North America. The Papacy would leave a corrupt Rome and move to Montreal and later to St. Vital in Manitoba. The last phase, 1884 to 1885, saw the expansion of Riel's concept of North America as a continent filled with peoples of various nations who, while retaining the memories of their origin, would, however, become assimilated by the Métis, if necessary by introducing polygamous marriages. Unity in diversity. The Indians Riel regarded as of Hebrew origin, "du plus pur sang d'Abraham."[44] Presumably they were the lost ten tribes of Israel. The theory of the Hebraic origin of the Indians was suggested in the Book of Mormon.

Professor Thomas Flanagan of the University of Calgary subsequently joined forces with Martel. In an analysis of Riel's thought in his *The Diaries of Louis Riel* and *Louis "David" Riel: Prophet of the New World*,[45] Flanagan expanded on Martel's work and, in so doing, revealed Riel as the visionary, the prophet in arms, the priest stretching forth his arms to the millenium. Flanagan discards the familiar symbols and slogans attached to Riel by earlier historians, martyr, murderer, leader, radical, and replaces them with new ones. New in the sense of their application to the western Canadian scene. But old in the sense that they derive from earlier European, even African, examples.[46] Flanagan sees the Riel movements as much religious as political in inspiration; as one more example of a pattern of social behaviour deriving from the past history of millenarianism and revealing recognizable similarities. Another example of the fact that historians, like history itself, are part of a recurring intellectual kaleidoscope?

If I cannot go the full course with Flanagan, it is because, while accepting the mental agility of Louis Riel, I am still a little suspicious of the mental stability of prophets proclaiming the imminence of the egalitarian millenium. Perhaps, too, I remain puzzled by the ambiguities of motive which seem to attend so many of Riel's actions. Sometimes I speculate on what might have been the outcome of a meeting between the "Young Politician" Riel and the wily "Old Chieftain" Macdonald. Of one thing only am I certain. That is, the impossibility of understanding the history of Canada during the last hundred years without a thorough study of the personalities, thoughts and actions of both these men.

8

There you have the four faces of Riel—Riel, the defender of French language and religious rights; Riel, the half-breed patriot; Riel, the first western Canadian leader; Riel, the prophet and visionary. Which is the true face? For each Canadian, the true face of Riel is the one he or she recognizes. Is it not like the old tale of the blind men describing the elephant by that particular portion of the animal each happened to touch? Perhaps we historians are the blind men. We know Riel only from the sources we consult. Perhaps each one of us is right. Again, perhaps Riel is a composite of everything we discover in our sources.

Following his execution, the ghost of Riel returned to haunt the political platforms in Québec and Ontario for many years. Today, Riel's ghost still haunts our poets, playwrights, air waves and universities. He has become a Canadian legend, if not the Canadian legend. He is our Hamlet, the personification of the great themes of our human history. Mavor Moore, the librettist of Harry Somers's opera, put it this way in a recent contribution to the *Globe and Mail:* "The young idealist, driven mad by constant betrayal at the hands of cynical realists . . . The thinker paralysed by thinking about what action to take. The half-breed, the member of the 'society of neithers,' . . . The lunatic who is framed by an unjust 'sane' society. The warrior entering battle with a cross . . . in his hand, instead of a gun . . . The leader of a small victimized group that stands in the way of the majority. The petty tyrant given comeuppance by a bigger one. The God-intoxicated human who tries to play God."[47] These are themes basic to the political and human drama of the Riel story. And they are all universal themes. Not just Canadian themes. They apply to Riel's era and to our own. They are timeless. Just as Riel is timeless. He is the patriotic myth of Canada: the haunting disquietude of our history.

Phantasmagoria! The ever-changing scene. In our efforts to reconcile the past with the present, do we reveal the truth or create more illusions? At least the next generation of students and historians will have the advantage of ready access to all of Riel's writings still extant. The Riel Project, started in 1978, by the University of Alberta, and comprising Professor Raymond Huel (University of Lethbridge), Gilles Martel (Université de Sherbrooke), Glen Campbell (University of Calgary), Thomas Flanagan (University of Calgary), under my direction as General Editor—and including Dr. Claude Rocan as co-ordinator—has finally completed its work. The result is the publication by the University of Alberta of five volumes entitled, *The Complete Writings of Louis Riel*. These volumes do not impose anyone particular point of view upon the reader. The editors envisioned their task as one of ensuring the accuracy of each item, and the widest possible coverage of the subject by publishing all of Riel's writings, even those in draft form. The editors also limited their introductions to explaining how the project was carried out, and to discussing some of the problems of identification. The Riel Project is not, therefore, an academic effort to exorcise the haunting phantom of Riel. We simply hope that our publications will enable historians, artists, poets and novelists to make up their own minds about the visage of Riel that is most recognizable to him or her.

As far as I am concerned personally, the paper I have read to you tonight is my last statement on Louis Riel. Hence the title of my address. After fifty years of working on Riel's life and thoughts, off and on, it is time that I devoted my days to other Canadian historical topics. I leave any further analysis of the Métis leader to others.

La patrie est la plus importante de toutes les choses de la terre, et, de plus, elle est sainte par les ancêtres qui la transmettent. (Louis Riel)

Notes

1. Guillaume Charette, *L'Espace de Louis Goulet* (Winnipeg: Editions Bois-Brûlés, 1976), 137.
2. Winnipeg and Regina.
3. Rudy Wiebe, *My Lovely Enemy* (Toronto: McClelland and Stewart, 1983), 3.
4. See IX and X of President Wilson's "Fourteen Points," outlined in his speech to Congress, 8 January 1918. See *Readings in the History of Modern Europe*, Department of Social Sciences, United States Military Academy, West Point, N.Y., 1959.
5. The shedding of imperial ties came more readily to the former colonies and dominions than to the imperial powers themselves. The latter could not easily forget that they had,

at one time, shaped history and directed the course of civilization. Frenchmen, Englishmen, Americans and Russians are still inclined, each in their own way, to see their nation as bearing the light of the world to come.

6. Over 3,000 treaty Indians enlisted during World War II. It is impossible to determine how many Métis served in the Canadian Armed Forces. One Indian, Oliver Martin, a veteran of World War I, became a brigadier commanding the 13th Brigade. Among the junior officers, Lieutenants Greyeyes and Victor Moore of Saskatchewan were among the best known. I am grateful to Mr. Fred Gaffen of the Canadian War Museum for this information.

7. H.E. Barnes, *A History of Historical Writing* (New York: Dover, 1962), 296. Barnes quotes from Francis Bacon's *De Augmentis.*

8. These quotations from *The Globe* and *La Minerve* are taken from R.E. Lamb *Thunder in the North—Conflict over the Riel Risings, 1870–1885* (New York: Pageant Press, 1957), 81, 82, 75, 101.

9. Ibid., 185, 198, 209, 202.

10. Henri d'Arles, *Louis Fréchette* (Toronto: Ryerson, 1924), 69. The author wrote "Le genre épique demande un recul dans le temps et dans l'espace. Il faut laisser aux événements le loisir de prendre la perspective nécessaire. Pour cette raison, et pour d'autres encore, son *Gibet de Riel* et son *Dernier Martyr* n'auraient pas dû trouver leur place dans cette oeuvre."

11. *The Story of Louis Riel, the Rebel Chief* (Toronto: J.S. Robertson & Bros., 1885). The author's name is not given but the book is generally attributed to Joseph Edmund Collins (1855–1892) who also wrote *Annette the Métis Spy: A Heroine of the N.W. Rebellion* (Toronto: Rose Publishing Co., 1886). See R.E. Watters, *A Check-list of Canadian Literature and Background Materials, 1628–1960* (Toronto: University of Toronto Press, 1972). The quotations are to be found on pp. 24, 38, 42, 65, 144, 47, 48, 131. In view of recent writings about Riel, it is interesting to note that Collins compared Riel with Mohammed and El Madhi and "other great patrons of race and religion," 49.

12. Mrs. J.E.M. Whitney's "The Otter Grand March" was published by Lamplough in Montreal in 1885, and Annie Delaney's "Batoche Polka" was published by Nordheimer in Toronto in 1885. For other "Rebellion" music, see Alan Mills: *Canada's Story in Song,* published by Folkway Records and Service Corp., New York, and Margaret A. Macleod: "Songs of the Insurrection," *Beaver* 287 (Spring 1957): 18–23.

13. Jean Bruchesi, *Histoire du Canada pour Tous, 2 Vols.* (Montréal: Editions Beauchemin, 1940).

14. In his *Le Français au Canada* (Paris: Delagrave, 1932), 157–59, Groulx argues that Riel fought to defend "son individualizé ethnique" which he (Groulx) saw as French rather than as Métis. In his *Histoire du Canada Français* (Montreal: Fides, 1962), 4:141–42, Groulx refers to the " Affaire Riel" as a Canadian "Affaire Dreyfus," and maintained that Riel "n'expie pas seulement le crime d'avoir réclamé les droits de ses compatriotes, il expie surtout et avant tout le crime d'appartenir à notre race . . ."

15. Rev. A.G. Morice, *A Critical History of the Red River Insurrection after Official Documents and non-Catholic Sources* (Winnipeg: The author, 1935). This book according to Giraud (*Le Métis Canadien* Paris: Institut d'Ethnologie, 1945, 51) although "bien documenté . . . apparait trop souvent comme un ouvrage de polémique." See also *La race métisse, étude critique en marge d'un livre récent* (Winnipeg: L'Auteur, 1938).

16. A-H. de Trémaudan, *Histoire de la Nation Métisse dans l'Ouest canadien* (Montréal: A. Lévesque, 1935), 28. Giraud wrote of this book, "C'est une apologie de l'oeuvre de L.D. Riel," 51. See also, *Riel et la naissance de Manitoba* (N.p., 1924).

17. Ibid., 376.

18. George Bryce, *A Short History of the Canadian People* (London: S. Low, Marston, Searle and Rivington, 1887); R.G. MacBeth, *Making the Canadian West* (Toronto: W. Briggs, 1905), and *The Romance of Western Canada* (Toronto: William Briggs, 1920). The words are MacBeth's. *Canadian West*, 81.

19. F.H. Schofield, *The Story of Manitoba*, 3 Vols. (Winnipeg: S.J. Clarke Pub. Co., 1913), and Norman F. Black, *A History of Saskatchewan* (Regina: North West Historical Company, 1913).

20. The completion of this twenty-three volume work under the general editorship of Drs. Adam Shortt and Arthur Doughty in 1913 was a major achievement on the part of Canadian historians which was not equalled by *The Canadian Centenary Series* directed by W.L. Morton and D.G. Creighton. The latter is already eighteen years behind schedule. The contributions to *Canada and its Provinces,* while spotty, are generally good. They still serve Canadian historians. Chester Martin's work was always well written and reliable; although out-of-date, it should not be ignored.

21. A.R.M. Lower, *Colony to Nation, A History of Canada* (Don Mills, Ont.: Longmans, 1964), 389.

22. J.A. Jonasson, "The Background of the Riel Rebellions," *Pacific Historical Review* 3 (1934):3.

23. Mason Wade, *The French Canadian Outlook* (New York: Viking, 1946). Peter Waite in his *Canada 1874–1896* (Toronto: McClelland and Stewart, 1971) described this as "a water-bug kind of book, skimming across the surface." Much more significant a contribution to Canadian historiography is Wade's *The French Canadians, 1760–1945* (Toronto: Macmillan, 1955).

24. Duke Redbird, *We are Métis: A Métis View of the Development of the Canadian People* (Willowdale, Ont.: Ontario Métis and Non-status Indian Association, 1980), 4. See also Gerald Friesen, *The Canadian Prairies: A History* (Toronto: University of Toronto Press, 1984), 232.

25. G.F.G. Stanley, "Western Canada and the Frontier Thesis," *Annual Report, The Canadian Historical Association,* ed. R.G. Riddell (Toronto, 1940) and G.F.G. Stanley, "The Métis and the Conflict of Cultures in Western Canada," *The Canadian Historical Review* 28, no. 4 (December 1947).

26. See Edward Shanks in *John O'London's Weekly,* 1 August 1936.

27. *The Canadian Historical Review* 17, no. 4 (December 1936): 454–57.

28. In *Le Métis Canadien* (Paris: Institut d'Ethnologie, 1945), 4, Giraud wrote "The Birth of Western Canada, Londres—Toronto, 1936 contient l'exposé le plus sûr, le plus complet et le plus scientifique." Of Morton's book he wrote "A History of the Canadian West to 1870–71, fournit une excellente mise au point de l'insurrection de 1869–70."

29. W.L. Morton, *Manitoba: A History* (Toronto: University of Toronto Press, 1957); Alexander Begg's *Red River Journal and Other Papers Relative to the Red River Resistance of 1869–1870* (Toronto: Champlain Society, 1956).

30. Some of the old attitudes were still apparent even at this late date. When the Canadian Historical Association brought out my booklet *Louis Riel: Patriot or Rebel* in 1954, the Department of Education in Ontario was the only provincial Education Department in Canada to refuse to buy any copies for the provincial schools! In 1963 Dr. Wilhelmina Gordon, reviewing my *Louis Riel* for *Echoes,* limited herself to two sentences. I quote from memory, "Dr. Stanley seems to like Riel. There were a lot of soldiers out in 1885 who didn't." A sympathetic revisionist manuscript prepared some years before World War II by W.M. Davidson of Calgary, could not find a publisher. It was finally printed in 1955, some years after Davidson's death, by his old newspaper, *The Albertan,* with a "stimulation grant" provided by his widow.

31. Joseph Kinsey Howard, *Strange Empire: A Narrative of the Northwest* (New York: Morrow, 1952). Riel has fallen victim to several popularizers, whose works sometimes pass for history, such as Frank Rasky, *The Taming of the Canadian West* (Toronto: McClelland and Stewart, 1967). Taming? *Mon oeil!*

32. John Coulter, *Riel a play in two parts* (Toronto: Ryerson, 1962), dust cover quoting the author. This work was followed by D.G. Gutteridge's five-part narrative poem, *Riel A Poem for Voices,* Toronto, 1972. The work is built around two basic conflicts: the struggle between the Métis, who hold tenaciously to the land, and the Anglo-Saxon Canadians who wish to dispossess them, and the inner turmoil of a man (Riel) of two bloods and two cultures. This is a humane piece of work that sees the Riel issue in terms of the clash of cultures. Gutteridge acknowledged his debt to G.F.G. Stanley, *Louis Riel* and to J.K. Howard's *Strange Empire.*

33. Truth may be stranger than fiction; certainly it is no less interesting or dramatic. An adaptation of the screen play by Roy Moore in narrative form by Janet Rosenstock and Dennis Adair deserves Donald Swainson's comment that it "Harlequinized" history. See Donald Swainson's "Rielana and the Structure of Canadian History," *Journal of Popular Culture* 14, no. 2 (Fall 1980): 295.

34. Native ancestors are to be found in the family trees of both Norquay and Lougheed. Does this give strength to the idea of classifying Riel, the Métis, as the first prairie political patriot?

35. Douglas Owram, "The Myth of Louis Riel," *Canadian Historical Review* 63, no. 3 (September 1982): 329. This excellent article should be read as a corrective, shall I say, to my paper.

36. W.L. Morton, "The Bias of Prairie Politics" *Transactions of the Royal Society of Canada* 44 (1955): 57. It is interesting to note that one of the most recent publications by a Manitoba historian, Gerald Friesen, follows Morton's lead in portraying the West as a federal colony. Friesen does not refer to Riel as a prairie patriot but entitles one of his chapters "Canada's Empire," 1984.

37. Howard Adams, *Prison of Grass* (Toronto: New Press, 1975), 63.

38. Ibid., 137.

39. Peter Charlebois, *The Life of Louis Riel* (Toronto: New Canada Publications, 1975), 239.

40. See E.J. Hobsbawm, *Primitive Rebels, Studies in Archaic Forms of Social Movement in the 19th and 20th Centuries* (New York: Praeger, 1963).

41. I was more positive when I wrote Historical Booklet No. 2 for the Canadian Historical Association in 1954, *Louis Riel: Patriot or Rebel.* But after I had spent more time studying Riel, I became less certain. That is why I avoided any positive statement in my 1963 biography about the state of Riel's mind.

42. In 1947, I talked with Walter Allison Cooke in Vancouver (the man with the bald head, with his back to the camera in the familiar photograph illustrating Riel's trial at Regina—see Stanley, *Riel,* opposite p. 338). He told me that he found the trial an exhausting emotional experience, that he felt sympathetic towards the prisoner in the dock and did not believe him to be insane. Such was the attitude of a young protestant minister who, sixty-two years later, had not changed his mind. His father's views were confirmed in a letter from his son, retired Professor Albert C. Cooke, dated 7 February 1985.

I think it is worth recording that, quoting from memory a conversation with J.N. Greenshields, one of Riel's lawyers, the late Edward Shanks attributed to Greenshields the statement that Riel was "a religious fanatic, but very reasonable and far-seeing in particular matters." Still quoting Greenshields on Riel, Shanks continued, "His religious views were universal, though not unique. He wanted a Pope for the American continent, which lost him the support of the Church, though not that of his Catholic followers. In practical matters he was far too practical to be practical. He wanted a gradual development from the mixture of two races in the unexploited continent instead of the results produced by Western impatience to get the utmost out of the soil and the animals at once. Had the luck of the historical process been with him, he might have made a great nation out of the Métis of the North-West. It was against him, and so he is a curiosity, tucked away in the annals of the British Empire. Yet, when you think it over coolly, what he tried to do for Canada was in essence as finely constructive as many things done by men who we commonly reckon to be statesmen of genius." (See Edward Shanks, "The Rebel of the North-West," *John O'London's Weekly,* 1 August 1936, 626).

43. Gilles Martel, *Le Messianisme de Louis Riel* (Waterloo: Wilfrid Laurier University, 1984). This book was prepared as a doctoral thesis for the University of Paris in 1976.

44. Martel, "Les Indiens dans la pensée messianique de Louis Riel," in A.S. Lussier, *Riel and the Métis: Riel Mini-Conference Papers* (Winnipeg: Manitoba Métis Federation Press, 1979), 36–38.

45. Thomas Flanagan, *Louis "David" Riel: Prophet of the New World* (Toronto: University of Toronto Press, 1979).

46. See Norman Cohn, *The Pursuit of the Millennium, Revolutionary messianism in medieval and Reformation Europe and its bearing on modern totalitarian movements* (New York: Harper and Row, 1957).

47. Mavor Moore, "Haunted by the ghost of a rebellious upstart," *Globe and Mail,* 9 March 1985, E2.

Unearthing the Trail of Riel Rebellion's Twice-Stolen Relic

Katherine Harding and Dawn Walton

October 8, 2005

As Gary Floyd Guiboche lifted the Bell of Batoche out of the glass container that long guarded this Canadian trophy of war, he was struck by the mystique surrounding the relic.

The silver sparkled. Métis leader Louis Riel was connected to it. It embodied 106 years of resentment toward the Canadian government for quashing a Métis uprising.

"To me, it looked really wonderful," Mr. Guiboche recalls now, 14 years after that night when he first laid eyes on the bell. He remembers thinking: "I'm actually right here where the bell is."

Then the Métis from Manitoba went right back to work stealing—or in his view liberating—one of the most storied artifacts of the Riel rebellions. It's a secret he kept from the public until recently, when he was contacted by The Globe and Mail.

"It's not what it's worth," explains Mr. Guiboche. "It's what it means."

In 1885, Canadian soldiers from small-town Ontario were summoned to the Prairies in what is now Saskatchewan to crush a Métis revolt led by Riel. They also plundered the bell from the church in Batoche during what was the war's final skirmish.

The soldiers smuggled the bell home to Millbrook, southwest of Peterborough, where it was considered *the* prize of the battle, and was eventually put proudly on display at the local Royal Canadian Legion branch.

Until 1991, when it was stolen a second time. Mr. Guiboche says he and another man broke into the legion to reclaim the bell in honour of Riel and with an eye to displaying it somewhere more befitting a Métis icon.

Mr. Guiboche was never charged with theft in the disappearance of the Bell of Batoche.

Nobody was. The case is still open; but police say with no suspects and no evidence, the trail has gone cold.

After all this time, few care about charges anyway. What most people want—Métis leaders, historians, politicians, members of the legion and police—is to see the bell returned to public view.

"Unearthing the trail of Riel rebellion's twice-stolen relic" by Katherine Harding and Dawn Walton, *The Globe and Mail,* October 8, 2005. Reprinted with permission from The Globe and Mail.

Over the years, there have been promises of no criminal charges in exchange for the bell, and even a cash reward offered, but attempts by the governments of Manitoba and Saskatchewan, police and Métis leaders to recover it have failed.

Some say police have not treated the case seriously. Others say Métis officials haven't done their part to turn up the heat on the culprits long thought to be in their midst. And now Mr. Guiboche says his partner in crime—whom he won't identify— has kept the bell hidden too long for no reason. It should surface, he says, and together they should be treated as heroes, not thieves.

"I think we should be recognized as a legend in our people, in our history."

* * *

The silver-plated, 40-kilogram bell baptized Marie Antoinette was purchased for $25 in 1884. About 30 cm high, it hung for nine months in the steeple of the white clapboard St. Antoine-de-Padoue parish at Batoche, a thriving Métis community about 85 kilometers northeast of Saskatoon.

It beckoned residents to prayer. It also rang out in times of celebration and mourning.

It was Batoche that Riel had hoped would become the headquarters for his provisional government of Saskatchewan.

The Battle of Batoche began on May 9, 1885, and ended three days later in a bloodbath.

The Métis led by Gabriel Dumont found themselves outmanned by the Canadian soldiers 800 to 300. Mr. Dumont managed to escape what would be the last conflict of the North-West Rebellion.

But Riel, who had returned from exile in Montana to help the Métis cause, surrendered. He was hanged for treason.

A group of soldiers from Ontario's Midland Provisional Battalion, Sergeant Ed McCorry among them, plucked the bell from its perch—along with a host of other objects—and wrapped it in a blanket and took it home to Protestant Ontario as a spoil of war.

It hung in the Millbrook fire hall before being moved to the legion branch on the town's main street. A picture window was eventually constructed for passersby to view the war trophy.

In the fall of 1991, a group of Métis leaders went to see the bell and drank and chatted with legion members. They posed for pictures with the bell, which was in a locked glass display case, and left.

Not long after that visit, the legion was robbed. During the break-in, medals awarded to Sgt. McCorry disappeared. So did the bell.

* * *

Gary Floyd Guiboche is a burly yet soft-spoken man with greying hair and mustache who was raised in Swan River, Man., a community not far from the Saskatchewan boundary that was first settled around the fur trade.

He's handy with tools. He's also strong. Both are skills he developed from holding a variety of jobs between moves to Winnipeg and his home town over the years.

He turned 46 this week. It was another birthday spent at Stony Mountain Institution, a medium-security prison just north of Winnipeg that is home to 549 inmates. There he is serving a life sentence with no chance of parole for 10 years for beating his common-law wife to death with a baseball bat after a night of heavy drinking in 1999.

It's a crime he says he didn't commit. His first conviction was overturned on appeal. He was convicted at a second trial, and the Supreme Court of Canada refused to hear his appeal.

Métis leaders believe his story about the bell.

Mr. Guiboche was working in home construction in Winnipeg in 1991 when his telephone rang. The voice of a long-time friend who had nurtured bitterness about government treatment of the Métis was on the other end.

"'I need help,' he said. 'I know you're good with a lot of stuff. I can't do this alone. We can succeed,'" Mr. Guiboche recalls.

The man said he had already "scoped out" the target. They would do it by Oct. 22—in honour of Riel's birthday. Mr. Guiboche, who was sympathetic to the cause, didn't hesitate.

He jumped in the friend's Jeep Cherokee—a vehicle chosen because it could traverse dodgy terrain if they needed to outrun the law and carry supplies in case they had to lie low in the woods—and they left Winnipeg bound for Millbrook.

They took turns driving, and along the way witnessed a series of "spiritual helpers." A moose lumbering beside the highway. Eagles flying overhead. A cougar milling around in a ditch.

"We took it as a good sign," Mr. Guiboche says.

They arrived at Millbrook in the dark. The town was asleep. They decided to park at the back door of the legion to save them from heaving the small but heavy bell very far.

They donned gloves, tuques and went to work popping the back door open with a crowbar. Once inside, they went straight for the bell.

Emboldened by the lack of activity in the sleepy town, they even switched on the light. They removed the top of the glass case. They brought along an air jack, and as they were about to use it to pry apart the two steel bars that held the bell in place, they noticed an elderly woman walking outside.

They held their breath as she passed by, oblivious to the crime that was taking place inside.

It took only seconds for a few pumps on the jack to dislodge the bell. In one swift motion, Mr. Guiboche pulled the bell out and placed it in a hockey bag they had brought along.

"Once we got it in the bag, we were kind of shaky," he says, eyes widening with pride. "We did it."

They stuffed shirts, sweaters, whatever they had brought along, inside the bell to prevent it from changing. Before leaving, Mr. Guiboche noticed some war medals on display. He looked at them and then to his friend before returning his gaze to the medals.

He says his friend shoved them in the bag.

"It was payback," the pair agreed. They left the building and loaded their cargo into the Jeep. As a final insult, they drove by the legion on their way out of town, waved and said, "See, ya."

Later, they would get rid of their clothes, right down to their shoes. They drove all day until they were just outside Thunder Bay, when the vehicle, which had been struggling for the duration of the trip, finally died.

Parts, and repairs would take time. They weren't about to hang around an unfamiliar town with stolen goods.

They rode a bus home to Winnipeg, an eagle following them along the way. The bell, stashed in the hockey bag, was stowed underneath with the rest of the passengers' luggage.

Mr. Guiboche says they had a lawyer on standby in case they needed advice.

* * *

Bradford Morse, a University of Ottawa law professor who specializes in aboriginal law, says he was brought into the saga shortly after the bell vanished from the legion.

Mr. Morse says he was hired for a dollar by a "person who had direct information" about the bell's removal and whereabouts.

The people who took the bell did it with the belief it could become a "positive emotional, political and cultural achievement" for the Métis, he says.

It was to be a rallying cry for the country's estimated 350,000 to 400,000 Métis people.

"You have to remember what was happening in 1991," he explains.

The 1990 Oka crisis, triggered when Mohawk Warriors shot an officer of the *Sûreté du Québec* (the provincial police) to death during a raid, was still fresh.

At the same time, the Métis were worried that they were going to be shut out of constitutional discussions the Mulroney government was holding.

"This was seen as a way to put Métis front and centre on the national stage and remind people of their history," Prof. Morse says.

For months, there was an attempt, through his client and intermediaries, to broker a formal transfer of the bell to the Métis nation and its return to Batoche.

To help speed up the, negotiations, Yvon Dumont, then president of the Manitoba Métis Federation who went on to become the province's lieutenant -governor, wrote a letter offering to pay reparations for the break-in, such as damage done to the legion's back door.

Prof. Morse had hoped that if the bargaining succeeded, there would be a "celebration" at which the bell would be "greeted with open arms," not with criminal charges or civil litigation. Legion members were asked to be guests of honour at the ceremonial returning of the bell.

But Millbrook legion members weren't interested in co-operating and talks dissolved, Prof. Morse recalls.

Retired Ontario Provincial Police detective Gary Katz vividly remembers when the Bell of Batoche case landed on his desk in the late 1990s.

"You can't forget a case like that because of the politics involved," he says.

Mr. Katz, who left the force in 1999, says he too worked hard to broker a settlement so the file could finally be closed.

"The break and enter in the policing business is very serious," he says. "But if you can negotiate something and it was a prized possession to someone, then you wheel and deal with the bad guy and do what you have to do."

Mr. Katz says he thought a deal had been arranged through a "well-connected man" in Winnipeg whose name he has forgotten.

If the bell reappeared and the medals were returned to the Millbrook legion, then no charges would be laid. He said the offer was necessary because the police didn't have suspects or leads in the case.

"We really wanted those medals back," he says. "I can't even remember why it went sour because we had everything ready to go."

Jack Hillson was Saskatchewan's minister of intergovernmental and aboriginal affairs in 2000 when he got involved in the case. He says he managed to lift the threat of charges in exchange for the bell. Through intermediaries, a hand over was arranged, to be carried out in a July, 2000, ceremony at Batoche, and the missing medals were to be returned to the legion.

"The guy presumed to have the bell was there [at the ceremony], then the moment presented itself, but [the bell] didn't."

Mr. Hillson, still smarting from his failure to recover the bell, blames the Métis community for not demanding the bell be returned.

"The Métis never miss an opportunity to miss an opportunity," he says. "It's up to the Métis community to resolve it. It's time to get real."

David Chartrand, president of the Manitoba Métis Federation, says the people who stole the bell are thieves just like the soldiers who pilfered it in 1885. It's a serious crime that should be punished, he says, but the police haven't given the case the national attention it deserves.

Under Métis law, he says, the culprits would be "blackballed by the Métis nation as a whole."

He even reiterated the offer of a "substantial amount" of money—tens of thousands of dollars—for the bell's return. But he's not optimistic after so many failed chances.

"These individuals are selfish and greedy. They're keeping it for their own political or personal gain or spiritual gain if you want to call it that," he says.

The pressure is on from within the Métis community for whoever has the bell to give it up, but to no avail.

"I know how these people operate, and the more you give it significance or importance, the more they toy with you. They'll use it to some kind of gain and wait and wait and wait if they have to," he says.

* * *

Métis leader BillyJo DeLaRonde, a former head of the Manitoba Métis Federation who was ousted during an internal feud in the 1990s, says when the bell was stolen in 1885, it was a test of the Métis people. He calls the 1991 disappearance a "repossession."

Mr. DeLaRonde was recently elected chief of Pine Creek First Nation, about 450 kilometers northwest of Winnipeg. Last December, he moved to a modest trailer, which is not far from the shore of Lake Winnipegosis and is across the road from his community's new school.

His next door neighbour says the chief is a busy man who's often away at meetings, but describes him as "the best chief we've had."

But not everybody shares that opinion. Mr. DeLaRonde, who lived in Winnipeg yet was invited to run for chief after a visit to the reserve, faced opposition from a group of band members and councillors who protested against his election. But during a meeting with members, he smoothed things over.

He is a slow and colourful speaker. He denies he had anything to do with the disappearance of the bell, but he is not short on opinions about it.

The people who took the bell are not thieves, he explains.

"Actions speak louder than words. They are people of action."

Mr. DeLaRonde also says he hopes the bell will eventually surface, but that whoever has it is just "laying low."

"There's a time and a place for everything. When the time is right, it should be on display somewhere," he says, "I hope it does happen."

* * *

If the bell does return to Batoche, it would be going home to a very different place.

The site of the failed Métis rebellion is a national historic site that now resembles a mom-and-pop type theme park where visitors can snack on French fries and buy Batoche memorabilia, including shirts ($10.64) and tall beer glasses ($6.99).

The battleground on the banks of the meandering South Saskatchewan River that was once pocked with rifle pits, trenches and bodies is now a peaceful pastoral field.

And instead of soldiers, tourists, schoolchildren and tour guides riding golf carts trample the wild grass leading up to the Roman Catholic mission church and rectory at the rate of about 20,000 people a year.

Even the church steeple in which the silver bell hung for only nine months before being swiped is gone; it was replaced long ago by a taller version that soars high into the bright blue Prairie sky. A bell almost six times the size of the original is now placed there.

In the distance is a tiny museum that details how the course of the country's history changed here more than a century ago. The story of the church's stolen bell is a mere sidebar.

"[The bell] hasn't seen this place for a long, long time," says William Paintednose. The 65-year-old Cree man's two-room grey-sided house looks onto Batoche from the fringes of the One Arrow First Nations reserve.

"That there is a sacred place, but maybe they should put that bell somewhere where more people can see it," he says. "Lots of buses go down this here road, but it's still out of the way."

Even the manager of the historic site isn't sure that a "repatriated" bell should return to the church from which it was pillaged.

Fern Armstrong, president of the Millbrook legion, says the branch would like to see the bell placed somewhere meaningful to the Métis people. Her members would like the medals returned. If that happened, the legion would not press for charges.

Peterborough County OPP Inspector Ed Robertson says that while the case is still open, the crime is not being investigated, and there has never been enough evidence to solve it or lay charges.

The veteran officer paused for a long time when asked whether charges would be laid if the force was presented with new evidence to support them.

"I think we would have to look at the circumstances as they were presented to us should they arise," he says. "Reopening the investigation would all depend on how the bell reappeared."

The power to grant immunity to those involved may lie with the federal justice minister, he says. Justice officials in Manitoba and Ontario say they would look at any new evidence presented to them.

For now, Insp. Robertson says, the case remains a "very interesting piece of history."

* * *

Mr. Guiboche says he knows where he last saw the bell, but he's not sure where it is now.

Over the years, they moved it among hiding places and even once buried it under an above ground swimming pool, which police say is not an uncommon place to stash things that people don't want to be found.

Interestingly, the soldiers who took the bell in 1885 also once buried the bell in a creek out of fear it would be reclaimed.

More than 10 years ago, two people told police they saw the bell at a Winnipeg home. Rumours persist that it has been the main attraction at drunken parties where it is "gonged." Most say it is still somewhere in Winnipeg.

It saddens Mr. Guiboche to think about the bell being somewhere underground. He also worries that the stolen medals have been lost forever.

When the bell surfaces, he would like it displayed at Riel's birthplace in St. Boniface, Man., with the other artifacts and memorials dedicated to his controversial life.

But he also wants to be honoured for his role in righting a historic wrong.

As he is about to be escorted back to his cell, Mr. Guiboche says one more thing: "I hope I don't get into any trouble for saying this. But I'm here for life. What are they going to do to me?"

Justice once judged Riel a traitor. Now that history has had time to reassess him, many Canadians consider the man a patriot and hero. Riel simply believed his actions were just. But he also knew when to surrender the cause.

Focus Questions

1. How are French and English accounts of Riel and the Rebellion different? Are there any *common* themes between them? What do these differing opinions tell you about the state of the country in 1885?

   [handwritten notes:]
   English- Villan
   French - Hero pg142

   common
   - leader!   - Charasmatic way
   - Greator of manitoba
   . 1885
   - Imperilism! - Religion!
   - tense state

2. Why does Riel become such a popular historical figure after World War Two? How is he remembered, and why?

   [handwritten notes:]
   - moving away from Imperilism
   - his discovery by Americans
   - home grown figuers
   memorial
   → moder statue
   - opera
   - songs   - comic book

   History changes w changes in culture

3. Should Riel be considered a Father of Confederation?

   [handwritten notes:] Yes

4. What do changed attitudes about Riel say about the state of the country?

- Imperialism and Religion - goneish
- more facts - educated opinion

- Freedom fighter
- less emotionally attached ⁖ educated opinion

5. Do you thing the Métis should return the Batoche Bell?

- no, because they were rightfully their
- symbolic of victory,

6

The Ties that Bind? A National Railway and the National Myth

Introduction

The readings in this chapter explore both the history and the mythology of the Canadian Pacific Railway. Completed in 1885, stretching from the Atlantic to the Pacific, it was envisioned as the physical tie that would bind the entire country together. As well as the enormous technological prestige its completion conferred upon the young country, the railway also carried enormous national and economic importance. It was the mechanism by which Canada could claim definitive ownership over the vast expanse of the western territories, the means by which the Prairies would be settled, and the indispensable trade link between the provinces.

As these readings demonstrate, the railway's economic, political, and symbolic importance is both deeply embedded in the nation's identity, and deeply controversial. From disagreement over who should get credit for building it, to its real benefits for the country's economy and political culture, to its wider significance as a Canadian icon, the railway can simultaneously be a symbol of Canada's progress and unity, as well as its divisions and disputes.

The Last Spike

Ceremonial Photograph of the "Last Spike," Craigellachie, British Columbia, 7 November 1885

The Last Spike: The Great Railway, 1881–1885
Pierre Berton
1971

The Great Canadian Photograph

The men in the picture are like old friends, even though their names may not be familiar. There they stand in their dark and shapeless clothing, frozen for all time by the camera's shutter, the flat light of that wet November morning illuminating an obvious sense of occasion as they lean forward to watch a white-bearded old gentleman hammer home an iron railroad spike.

The setting is spectral. In the background the blurred forms of trees rise like wraiths out of a white limbo. The picture might have been taken anywhere, for there are no identifiable natural features. But, as every school child knows, the time is 1885 and the place is Craigellachie in the mountains of British Columbia.

It is not just the school children who know this picture; every Canadian knows it. Banks feature it on calendars; insurance companies reproduce it in advertisements; television documentaries copy it; school pageants reenact it. But who remembers that just seven years before the photograph was taken, Sir John A. Macdonald called that same old gentleman the greatest liar he had ever known and tried to punch him in the nose? Probably very few; but then, the Prime Minister himself forgave and forgot. The old gentleman's name is Donald A. Smith and here, among the shrouded mountains in a damp clearing bearing a strange Gaelic name, he has managed once again to get himself into the foreground of the picture. That act will link him for all time with the great feat of railroad construction though, in truth, his has not been a major role.

George Stephen ought to be driving the final spike, but George Stephen is not even in the photograph. The CPR president is eight thousand miles away, in London, resting briefly after his four-year battle to keep the struggling railway solvent.

But Van Horne is there. The general manager stands directly behind Donald Smith, hands thrust deep in side pockets. John A. Macdonald once called him a sharp Yankee, but he has become more Canadian than any native. With his Homburg-style hat, his spade beard, and his heavy-lidded Germanic eyes, he looks remarkably like Bertie, the Prince of Wales, for whom he is occasionally mistaken. His poker face, so valuable in those legendary all-night card games, betrays no expression of triumph, jubilation, or sense of drama—only a slight impatience. "Get on with it," Van Horne seems to be saying. After all, the first transcontinental train in Canadian history is waiting to take him on to the Pacific.

Sandford Fleming stands to Van Horne's left. With his stovepipe hat and his vast beard, he almost dominates the photograph and perhaps that is as it should be; after all, it was he who made the first practical suggestion for a Pacific railroad nearly a quarter of a century before. Because of Fleming, the railroad engineer, the country runs on railroad time, so that now when it is noon in Toronto it is not 12.25 in Montreal.

Andrew Onderdonk is not in the picture. The man who brought the Chinese coolies to British Columbia to help build the railroad through the canyon of the Fraser is as elusive as ever. He has sent, in his place, his reckless Irish superintendent, Michael Haney, who can be seen craning his neck over Van Horne's great bulk, his handlebar moustache giving him the look of a Tammany politician. Not far away is another of Onderdonk's men, Henry Cambie, the engineer who hung by ropes to plot the railway's location along the walls of that same black canyon. He is standing a row or two behind the small boy, his long beard already whitening, a bowler tilted forward over his eyes. On his left, also bearded and bowlered, is one of the men chiefly responsible for the crazy-quilt pattern of Regina, John McTavish, the CPR'S land commissioner; on McTavish's left, wearing a floppy hat, is the railway's western superintendent, John Egan, perhaps the only man ever to see Van Horne shed a tear.

Directly across from Donald Smith, hands plunged into the pockets of his short coat, eyes twinkling, is the stocky, black-bearded figure of James Ross, the man in charge of the CPR'S mountain construction. He looks no different from the other roughly dressed labourers around him, but he will shortly become one of the richest and most powerful capitalists in Canada—a coal and steel baron, a utilities magnate, a financial wizard.

There are others present, though not all can be seen. Sam Steele of the Mounted Police, fresh from his pursuit of Big Bear, the rebellious Cree chieftain, is present but not in the picture. Young Tom Wilson, the packer who discovered Lake Louise, is just identifiable at the very rear in his broad-brimmed cowboy hat. And that most unconventional of all surveyors, the peripatetic Major Rogers, holds the tie bar as Smith strikes the spike. In a less familiar photograph, taken a moment before, the Major can be seen quite clearly, white mutton chops, black string tie, gold watch chain and all; but in most school books only his boot is showing. He does not need the immortality of this picture; his name is already enshrined on the long-sought pass in the Selkirks.

Do they realize, as the shutter closes, that this is destined to be the most famous photograph ever taken in Canada? Perhaps they do, for Canada, with their help, has just accomplished the impossible. In 1875, Alexander Mackenzie, then Prime Minister, declared that such a task could not be completed in ten years "with all the power of men and all the money in the empire." Now it is 1885 and the job has been done with precious little help from the empire at all through a remarkable blend of financial acumen, stubborn perseverance, political lobbying, brilliant organization, reckless gambling, plain good fortune, and the hard toil of a legion of ordinary workmen.

It is these nameless navvies who really dominate the Great Canadian photograph. Few of them have ever been identified and perhaps that is fitting. They have become symbolic figures, these unknown soldiers in Van Horne's army, standing as representatives for the thirty thousand sweating labourers—French and English, Scots and Irish, Italians and Slavs, Swedes and Yankees, Canadians and Chinese—who, in just four years and six months, managed to complete the great railway and join the nation from sea to sea.

North West

Edward Mallandaine wanted to fight the Indians. When the news of the rebellion reached Victoria, where he lived and went to school, there was no holding him; and his father, a pioneer architect and engineer, did not try to hold him. He booked passage to New Westminster, got aboard the new CPR line out of Port Moody, and took it as far as Eagle Pass Landing. He was just seventeen years old, small for his age, with a thin, alert face, half-hidden by a black cap. He trudged over the line of the partly finished road until he reached Golden, at the foot of the Kicking Horse, and there he learned, to his intense disappointment, that the rebellion was over and that the troops from eastern Canada, which had had all the adventure and all the glory, were already on their way home.

He was disappointed and disgusted. He headed west again, through the Rogers Pass and into Farwell, with its single street lined with log and frame shacks. There was a feeling of excitement in Farwell that summer of 1885. The town was the halfway point between the two Ends of Track: freight outfits bustled in from the Rogers and the Eagle Passes; boats puffed into the new docks from the mines at the Big Bend of the Columbia; a new post office was opening. Young Mallandaine decided to stay for a while in Farwell and go into business for himself. He opened a freighting service between the town and Eagle Pass Landing, taking a pony through the Gold Range twice each week along the tote road carved out by the railway contractors and soliciting orders for newspapers and supplies from the navvies along the way. It was hard going but it made a profit.

For a teenage boy it was an exciting time in which to live and an exciting place in which to be. Mallandaine was bright enough to realize that history was being made all around him and he noted it all in his mind for later reference: the spectacle of fifty men hanging over the face of the cliffs at Summit Lake, drilling holes in the rock; the sound of thunder in the pass as hundreds of tons of rock hurtled through the air; the sight of a hundred-foot Howe truss put together in a single day; the long, low huts where the navvies, mostly Swedes and Italians, slept "huddled in like bees in a hive with little light and ventilation;" the accidents, brawls, drinking, and gambling in the camps, "with men of all nationalities throwing away their hard-earned pay at faro, stud poker and other games of chance;" a gun battle with two men shot in a gambling den not far from the Farwell post office; and, towards the end of the season, the rough pageantry of the Governor General, Lord Lansdowne himself, riding on horseback through the gap between the two lines of steel on his way to the coast.

Each time Mallandaine made his way through Eagle Pass, that gap was shorter. He noted "day by day the thousands of feet of earth removed and . . . the swarms of men slaving away like ants for the good of the gigantic enterprise." By October it became clear that the road would be finished by first snow. The mushroom towns began to lose their inhabitants and a general exodus took place as the contractors discharged more and more men. Now, as the boy moved through the mountains, he noticed the wayside houses shut up and deserted, contractors' equipment being shifted and carted away, and hundreds of men traveling on foot with all their belongings to the east or to the west. Some of the rougher characters, who had operated saloons and gambling dens, became road agents, "and many a poor man who had been toiling all summer, was obliged to deliver up his earnings."

All the activity that had excited Edward Mallandaine on his arrival began to die away, and an oppressive silence settled on the pass—a silence broken only by the hideous shrieking of the construction locomotives echoing through the hills, as they rattled by with flat cars loaded with steel rails. Mallandaine felt a kind of chill creeping into his bones—not just the chill of the late October winds, sweeping down through the empty bunkhouses, but the chill of loneliness that comes to a man walking through a graveyard in the gloom.

"It seemed as though some scourge had swept this mountain pass. How ghostly the deserted camps would look at night! How quiet it all seemed!"

The pass became so lonely that Mallandaine almost began to dread the ride between Farwell and the Landing. There was something eerie about the sight of boarded-up buildings, dump cars left by the wayside, and portions of contractors' outfits cast aside along the line of the tote road. And the silence! Not since the days of the survey parties had the mountains seemed so still. Mallandaine decided to pack it in; there was no business left to speak of anyway. He made plans to return to his parents' home in Victoria. There was, however, one final piece of business, which he did not want to miss. He was determined to be on hand when the last spike on the Canadian Pacific Railway was driven.

On the afternoon of November 6, the last construction train to load rails—an engine, a tender, and three flat cars—left Farwell for Eagle Pass. Mallandaine was one of several who climbed aboard and endured the "cold, cheerless, rough ride" that followed. A few miles out of Farwell, it began to snow. The rails became so slippery that when one gumbo grade was reached the locomotive could not creep over it and, after three attempts in which the train slid backwards down the incline, one car had to be abandoned.

Far into the darkness of the night the little train puffed, its passengers shivering with cold. Mallandaine, lying directly upon the piled-up rails and unable to sleep, was almost shaken to pieces as the train rattled over the unballasted roadbed. Finally it came to a stop. The youth tumbled off the flat car in the pitch dark, found an abandoned box car, and managed a short sleep. At six that morning the track crews were on the job. By the time Mallandaine awoke, the rails had almost come together.

At nine o'clock, the last two rails were brought forward and measured for cutting, with wagers being laid on the exact length that would be needed: it came to twenty-five feet, five inches. A peppery little man with long white whiskers, wearing a vest with a heavy watch-chain, cut the final rail with a series of hard blows. This was the legendary Major Rogers. One of the short rails was then laid in place and spiked; the second was left loose for the ceremony. The crowd, which included Al Rogers, Tom Wilson, Sam Steele, and Henry Cambie, waited for the official party to appear.

It is perhaps natural that the tale of the driving of the last spike on the CPR should have become a legend in which fancy often outweighs fact; it was, after all, the great symbolic act of Canada's first century, a moment of solemn ritual enacted in a fairyland setting at the end of a harrowing year. Two days before the spike was driven, George Stephen had cabled in cipher from England: "Railway now out of danger." The bonds had risen to 99, the stock to 52 1/2. Nine days after the spike was driven, Louis Riel kept his rendezvous with the hangman at Regina. In more ways than one the completion of the railway signalled the end of the small, confined, comfortable nation that had been pieced together in 1867.

It is not surprising, then, that some who were present that day in the mountains—a construction boss named George Munro was one—should have recalled half a century later that the spike was made of gold. Munro claimed that it was pulled out and taken east. The Perthshire *Advertiser* of Scotland, in a special issue honouring Alexander Mackenzie, "a Perthshire lad who rose to eminence," stated that the former prime minister's widow drove the spike, which was "of 18 carat gold with the word Craigellachie in diamonds. It was replaced almost immediately with a serviceable one of steel and the first presented to Mrs. Mackenzie who afterward wore it as a brooch." But Mrs. Mackenzie was not a widow in 1885 and there was no golden spike. The Governor General had had a silver spike prepared for the occasion; it was not used, and His Excellency, who had expected to be present, had been forced to return to Ottawa from British Columbia when weather conditions caused a delay in the completion of the line.

"The last spike," said Van Horne, in his blunt way, "will be just as good an iron one as there is between Montreal and Vancouver, and anyone who wants to see it driven will have to pay full fare." He had toyed with the idea of an elaborate celebration and excursion but found it impossible to fix limits on the necessary invitations. It would have resulted "in a vast deal of disappointment and ill feeling"—not to mention expense.

The truth was that the CPR could not afford a fancy ceremony. It had cost the Northern Pacific somewhere between $175,000 and $250,000 to drive its golden spike. The CPR might be out of danger, but it had enormous expenditures facing it.

Stephen proposed paying off the five-million-dollar temporary loan almost immediately. Van Horne's whole purpose was to get a through line operating to the Pacific so that he could tap the Asian trade. There would be time for ceremonies later on.

The very simplicity and near spontaneity of the scene at Eagle Pass—the lack of pomp, the absence of oratory, the plainness of the crowd, the presence of the workmen in the foreground of the picture—made the spectacle an oddly memorable one. Van Horne and a distinguished party had come out from Ottawa, Montreal, and Winnipeg for the occasion. The big names, lounging at their ease in the two parlour cars "Saskatchewan" and "Matapedia," included Donald A. Smith, Sandford Fleming, John Egan, John McTavish, the land commissioner, and George Harris, a Boston financier who was a company director. Because of the incessant rains the party was held up for several days at Farwell until the work was completed.

Meanwhile, on the far side of the mountains, Andrew Onderdonk's private car "Eva" came up from Port Moody with Michael Haney aboard, pulling the final load of rails to the damp crevice in the mountains which the general manager, with a fine sense of drama, had decided years before to name Craigellachie. The decision predated Stephen's memorable telegram to Donald A. Smith. When Van Horne first joined the company the word was in common use because of an incident in 1880, when the Syndicate was being formed out of the original group that had put the St. Paul railway together. One of the members had demurred at the idea of another railway adventure and suggested to Stephen that they might only be courting trouble. Stephen had replied with that one word, a reference to a Scottish poem which began with the phrase: "Not until Craigellachie shall move from his firm base. . . . " Van Horne, healing of the incident, decided that if he was still with the CPR when the last spike was driven, the spot would be marked by a station called Craigellachie.

It was a dull, murky November morning, the tall mountains sheathed in clouds, the dark firs and cedars dripping in a coverlet of wet snow. Up puffed the quaint engine with its polished brass boiler, its cord wood tender, its diamond-shaped smokestack, and the great square box in front containing the acetylene headlight on whose glass was painted the number 148. The ceremonial party descended and walked through the clearing of stumps and debris to the spot where Major Rogers was standing, holding the tie bar under the final rail. By common consent the honour of driving the connecting spike was assigned to the eldest of the four directors present—to Donald A. Smith, whose hair in five years of railway construction had turned a frosty white. As Fleming noted, the old fur trader represented much more than the CPR. His presence recalled that long line of Highlanders—the Mackenzies and McTavishes, Stuarts and McGillivrays, Frasers, Finlaysons, McLeods, and McLaughlins—who had first penetrated these mountains and set the transcontinental pattern of communication that the railway would continue.

Now that moment had arrived which so many Canadians had believed would never come—a moment that Fleming had been waiting for since 1862, when he placed before the government the first practical outline for a highway to the Pacific. The workmen and the officials crowded around Smith as he was handed the spike hammer. Young Edward Mallandaine was determined to be as close to the old man as possible. He squeezed in directly behind him, right next to Harris, the Boston financier, and directly in front of Cambie, McTavish, and Egan. As the little hunchbacked photographer, Ross of Winnipeg, raised his camera, Mallandaine craned forward so as to see and be seen. Fifty-nine years later, when all the rest of that great company were in their graves, Colonel Edward Mallandaine, stipendiary magistrate and Reeve of the Kootenay town of Creston, would be on hand when the citizens of Revelstoke, in false beards and borrowed frock-coats, re-enacted the famous photograph on that very spot.

The spike had been hammered half-way home. Smith's first blow bent it badly. Frank Brothers, the roadmaster, expecting just such an emergency, pulled it out and replaced it with another. Smith posed with the uplifted hammer. The assembly froze. The shutter clicked. Smith lowered the hammer onto the spike. The shutter clicked again. Smith raised the hammer and began to drive the spike home. Save for the blows of the hammer and the sound of a small mountain stream gushing down a few feet away, there was absolute silence. Even after the spike was driven home, the stillness persisted. "It seemed," Sandford Fleming recalled, "as if the act now performed had worked a spell on all present. Each one appeared absorbed in his own reflections." The spell was broken by a cheer, "and it was no ordinary cheer. The subdued enthusiasm, the pent-up feelings of men familiar with hard work, now found vent." More cheers followed, enhanced by the shrill whistle of the locomotives.

All this time, Van Horne had stood impassively beside Fleming, his hands thrust into the side pockets of his overcoat. Though this was his crowning moment, his face remained a mask. In less than four years, through a miracle of organization and drive, he had managed to complete a new North West Passage, as the English press would call it. Did any memories surface in that retentive mind as the echoes of Smith's hammer blows rang down the corridor of Eagle Pass? Did he think back on the previous year when, half-starved and soaking wet, he had come this way with Reed and Rogers? Did he reflect, with passing triumph, on those early days in Winnipeg when the unfriendly press had attacked him as an idle boaster and discussed his rumoured dismissal? Did he recall those desperate moments in Ottawa and Montreal when the CPR seemed about to collapse like a house of cards? Probably not, for Van Horne was not a man to brood or to gloat over the past. It is likelier that his mind was fixed on more immediate problems: the Vancouver terminus, the Pacific postal subsidy, and the Atlantic steamship service. He could not predict the future but he would help to control it, and some of the new symbols of his adopted country would be of his making: the fleet of white Empresses flying the familiar checkered flag, the turreted hotels with their green chateau roofs, boldly perched on promontory and lakefront; and the international slogan that would proclaim in Arabic, Hindi, Chinese, and a dozen other languages that the CPR spanned the world.

As the cheering died the crowd turned to Van Horne. "Speech! Speech!" they cried. Van Horne was not much of a speechmaker; he was, in fact, a little shy in crowds. What he said was characteristically terse, but it went into the history books: "All I can say is that the work has been done well in every way."

Major Rogers was more emotional. This was his moment of triumph too, and he was savouring it. In spite of all the taunts of his Canadian colleagues, in spite of the skepticism of the newspapers, in spite of his own gloomy forebodings and the second thoughts of his superiors, his pass had been chosen and the rails ran directly through it to Craigellachie. For once, the stoic Major did not trouble to conceal his feelings. He was "so gleeful," Edward Mallandaine observed, "that he upended a huge tie and tried to mark the spot by the side of the track by sticking it in the ground."

There were more cheers, some mutual congratulations, and a rush for souvenirs—chips from the tie, pieces of the sawn rail. Young Arthur Piers, Van Horne's secretary, spotted the first, twisted spike lying on the track and tried to pocket it. Smith, however, told him to hand it over; he wanted it as a souvenir. Smith had also tossed the sledge aside after the spike was driven but, before he left, one of the track crew, Mike Sullivan, remembered to hand it to him as a keepsake. Then the locomotive whistle sounded again and a voice was heard to cry: "All aboard for the Pacific." It was the first time that phrase had been used by a conductor from the East, but Fleming noted that it was uttered "in the most prosaic tones, as of constant daily occurrence." The official party obediently boarded the cars and a few moments later the little train was in motion again, clattering over the newly laid rail and over the last spike and down the long incline of the mountains, off towards the dark canyon of the Fraser, off to the broad meadows beyond, off to the blue Pacific and into history.

CPR Workers Posing for their own version of the "Last Spike" (1885)

Making Tracks
The Myth of the CPR
Daniel Francis
1997

On the morning of November 18, 1993, as I sat over my morning cereal reading the *Globe and Mail,* I was startled to encounter columnist Michael Valpy's outrage at the desecration of a Canadian symbol. Canadian Pacific had just announced that it was introducing a new corporate logo which would include the American Stars and Stripes along with the familiar maple leaf. "I have a message for those soul-shrivelled, dreary, thick, witless people at Canadian Pacific Railway," Valpy wrote. "You are pathetic."

According to Valpy, CPR was "flushing away" a great Canadian tradition for the sake of making a few more dollars. The railway was, said Valpy, a "wonderful romantic notion," a magnificent technical achievement and one of the enduring symbols of Canadian identity. It had been built in order to preserve the country from the Americans. It was one of the truly great things Canadians had done together as a nation. Yet the "grey faceless bean-counters" in the corporate head offices now planned to betray that legacy by painting the dreaded Stars and Bars on the sides of their rail cars.

In his outrage, Michael Valpy was expressing a common view of the CPR and its relationship to the country. This view holds that without the railway there would be no Canada, certainly not as it exists today. The railway was built chiefly on the backs of Chinese coolie labour, using land obtained for almost nothing from the Indians and capital raised for the most part in Britain. Nevertheless, for many people, it has become over the years a great "Canadian" achievement and a symbol of the bonds which unite us as a people. In 1990, when the Mulroney government introduced drastic cutbacks to national rail service, including an end to the historic route north of Superior known as *The Canadian*, the disappointment and anger were widespread. "It's one of the most famous trains in the world," wrote one mourner about *The Canadian*, "right in there with the Orient Express, the Trans-Siberian, the Indian-Pacific. They can't be serious. The history of *The Canadian* is our history."[1] It seemed as if the government was giving up on a noble dream, the National Dream, that once gave meaning to the country. In Canada, a train is, or at least was, much more than a

"Making Tracks: The Myth of the CPR," reprinted with permission from *National Dreams: Myth, Memory, and Canadian History* by Daniel Francis (Arsenal Pulp Press, 1997).

train. It is seen as a visible expression of the determination to exist as a country, against the logic of the geographers and the accountants, Michael Valpy's "grey faceless bean-counters."

"Study the railways and you learn about our people," Silver Donald Cameron once wrote.[2] Where does this idea come from? Most recently it comes from Pierre Berton, who mythologized the history of the railway during the 1970s in three books and a popular television series. Berton's narrative presents the CPR as a heroic endeavour which united the disparate regions of the country in a single, bold dream of nationhood, making Canada "a rare example of a nation created through the construction of a railway."[3] In this narrative, Prime Minister John A. Macdonald is presented as a visionary politician who recognized that Canada was a nation in name only until its two ends were united by the iron road. W. Kaye Lamb, another historian of the railway, agrees. "If he [Macdonald] had not found ways and means of constructing it when he did, Canada would almost certainly not extend today from sea to sea."[4] In the pantheon of nation builders, Macdonald holds front rank, and the railway was his chosen instrument.

The myth of the CPR was in the air long before Berton and Lamb began writing it. Almost every book written about the railway has made the argument that, as R.G. MacBeth put it in 1924, "the country and the railway must stand or fall together."[5] When the Newfoundland poet Ned Pratt was casting about for a suitable epic theme to cap his distinguished career, he saw that the story of the CPR had the necessary ingredients.

> The east-west cousinship, a nation's rise,
> Hail of identity, a world expanding,
> If not the universe: the feel of it
> Was in the air
>
> —*"Union required the line."*

His Governor-General's Award-winning epic, *Towards the Last Spike*, presents the railway as a symbol for the completion of the nation.

The myth of the CPR as creator of the country is, in fact, as old as the railway itself, which is not surprising given that it was the railway itself which created the myth. Once the CPR had built the line, it set about promoting its achievement in countless books, pamphlets, stories, and movies. "The construction of the Canadian Pacific consummated Confederation," the company crowed in one of its early publications. The mundane act of constructing a railway was transformed into a heroic narrative of nation building. After a while it was almost impossible to imagine one without applauding the other.

I

Canada is a country without an independence day. Our history reveals no single moment at which the country gained its autonomy.[6] "We cannot find our beginning," Robert Kroetsch writes. "There is no Declaration of Independence, no Magna Carta, no Bastille Day."[7] Canada began as a collection of separate colonies belonging to Great Britain, then evolved by stages into an independent nation. During the 1840s, responsible government brought a modicum of independence to the local legislatures. In 1867, Confederation united these legislatures into a single colony, but one which remained under the protective wing of the Mother Country. The Balfour Report (1926) declared that Canada was an "autonomous community within the British Empire," and we began establishing our own embassies in foreign countries, but the British Privy Council was still our court of last resort, and the constitution was still amendable only in London. Perhaps we were not truly independent until 1982, when Canadians attained the power to amend their own constitution.

Canada accepted its autonomy as a country gradually, almost tentatively, as opposed to many other countries which seized it enthusiastically and proclaimed it defiantly. As a result, we have no myth of creation, no narrative which celebrates the birth of the nation, not even a central image like Uncle Sam or John Bull to personify the community and sum up what it stands for. We have no Founders, at least none whom we celebrate. In the absence of a defining moment, various symbolic ones have been proposed. For the sake of convenience we celebrate our national birthday on July 1, implying that Confederation Day, 1867, is Canada's true independence day, even though it is not. (To make matters more complicated, Quebec celebrates its "national" day on June 24, St. Jean Baptiste Day.) One familiar narrative suggests that Canada "came of age" during World War I, that the country attained a new maturity and the right to speak for itself in the world because of the carnage suffered by our young soldiers. On the other hand, I remember getting the impression when I was at school that Canada became independent with the Statute of Westminster in 1931, even though that legislation continued to leave important powers in British hands.

One of the most popular candidates for Canadian Independence Day has been November 7, 1885, the day on which a party of CPR navvies and notables watched company president Donald Smith drive the last spike at Craigellachie deep in the mountains of British Columbia. Histories of this event declare that the two photographs taken at Craigellachie are the most famous in Canadian history. In his 1924 book about the railway, R.G. MacBeth suggests that a Last Spike photograph belongs on the wall of every schoolroom in the country because it captures "the birth of a nation."[8] A much more recent book about the company calls the Last Spike "the most important single event in Canadian history."[9] Other countries have produced romantic images of citizens storming the barricades clutching the flag of freedom. Canada's version is apparently these photographs, showing a man in a top hat and a wool suit banging at a nail.

If the photographs of the Last Spike are going to be taken as symbolic representations of the moment of our independence as a nation, it is worth inquiring how they came to be taken. Textbooks tell us that CPR general manager William Van Horne wanted a modest ceremony, mainly because it was all the railway could afford. Chief engineer Sandford Fleming was there, as was Van Horne, Major A.B. Rogers, discoverer of Rogers Pass, and a few other company officials. So were the men who had been busy completing the last stretch of track through Eagle Pass. Otherwise, Van Horne supposedly said, "anyone who wants to see it driven will have to pay full fare."[10] Donald Smith's first blow with the hammer glanced away and merely bent the spike. Another was quickly substituted and, this time more carefully, Smith drove it home. The original, bent spike was taken by Smith and cut up into brooches for the wives of company officials. The second last spike was pulled out following the ceremony to prevent its removal by over-zealous souvenir hunters; it eventually ended up in the possession of Edward Beatty, a later president of the CPR.

The man who took the famous photographs was Alexander J. Ross, a photographer from Calgary. Berton describes him as a hunchback. Beyond that nothing is known about why he was chosen to capture this historic moment on film. Ross remained in the photography business for a few years, then turned to ranching before he died in 1894.[11]

No public officials were present at the Last Spike ceremony, no representative of the country which, myth has it, the railway made possible. (The Governor-General, Lord Lansdowne, had planned to be there, but was called back to Ottawa on more pressing business.) The Last Spike was an event staged by a group of capitalists to celebrate the completion of a privately-owned railway, albeit one which was generously supported with public land and cash. For them the "trail of iron" was a money-making proposition, not a national dream. "The Canadian Pacific was built for the purpose of making money for the share-holders and for no other purpose under the sun," stated Van Horne.[12] Yet within a few years myth had transformed the railway from a triumph of private capitalism into a triumph of patriotic nation-building. The backers of the CPR were "Empire-builders," not "money-makers," wrote MacBeth.[13] The implication to be drawn is that the real Fathers of Confederation were William Van Horne, Donald Smith, and George Stephen, the men who built the railway.

The narrative of nation-building was reinforced by the fascination which railways exerted over the public imagination during the last half of the nineteenth century. Railways were the emblem of an age which believed fervently in progress and technological achievement. Their promoters presented them as miracle workers. This "apparently impossible project," MacBeth called the CPR; "this modern wonderwork."[14] Railways seemed capable of transforming the world like magic, spreading wealth, settlement, and industry in their wake. George Ham, an early CPR publicist, marvelled at how the road "magically transformed a widely scattered Dominion into a prosperous and progressive nation."[15] The railway, proclaimed another enthusiast, is "the magical wand which is destined to people the Great North West."[16]

Despite all this rhetoric, in the spring of 1885 the yet-to-be-completed CPR was teetering on the verge of bankruptcy, in desperate need of another injection of capital. But the patience of the government was wearing thin, and most observers expected the half-finished project to collapse. Then a group of disaffected Metis led by Louis Riel and Gabriel Dumont in the Saskatchewan River country decided to take up arms in support of their land grievances. They declared a provisional government and routed a party of Mounted Police, raising the spectre of an all-out frontier war. The CPR offered its partially-completed line to move a force of almost 3,000 soldiers quickly westward from Ontario to quell the insurrection. After the Metis and their Indian allies were defeated, the CPR could claim a share in saving the country, and in return a grateful government saved the CPR by approving the money necessary to finish the road.

This co-dependency between the railway and the politicians whose survival depended on its completion goes some way toward explaining the origins of the CPR myth. The railway needed Prime Minister Macdonald and his party to ensure the provision of public funds. Macdonald needed the railway to prolong his political survival and to complete his vision of a transcontinental nation. CPR contributions to the Conservative Party during the 1880s totalled somewhere between $15 and $25 million in today's money.[17] This was taxpayers' money, of course, paid over to the CPR by the government, and then given back to the Conservatives to use to fight their political battles. Locked in such a mutually rewarding embrace, it was not hard for the railway and the Party to convince themselves that the country depended on their success. No wonder the destiny of one became so thoroughly confused with the destiny of the other.

II

The railway preceded settlement, it did not follow it, which meant that once it was completed, there was no one to ride on it. In 1885, the great boom in prairie settlement was still a decade in the future, and almost nobody had any reason to take a train ride across the country. Faced with the challenge of paying for itself, the CPR did two things. First of all, it developed an immigration program for the Prairie West, and secondly it began a campaign to convince travellers that western Canada, and particularly the Rocky Mountains, were attractive tourist destinations. Both objectives could only be achieved by creating a favourable image of western Canada and marketing it around the world. So the CPR embarked on a mammoth selling job, which succeeded beyond its wildest dreams.

In return for building the railway, the CPR had obtained from the government about ten million hectares of land between Ontario and the Rocky Mountains (along with $25 million and a variety of other concessions). The company was expected to finance the railroad by selling the land to new settlers. To do so, it created an immigration department which produced a flood of posters, pamphlets, maps, and books in a variety of languages for distribution across Europe and in the United States. This material extolled the Canadian West as a paradise where newcomers would find every opportunity to achieve the good life. Lecturers toured Europe with slide shows designed to impress viewers with the wealth and fertility of the region. In England the railway created a Travelling Exhibition Van which toured the back-country roads like an itinerant circus, carrying the message of the Canadian Eden to all the tiny hamlets where future immigrants might be found. The agent who accompanied the van set up shop in the village market; distributing pamphlets, showing photographs, displaying samples of grain and other produce. Similar exhibition cars were dispatched to eastern Canada and through the United States, and foreign journalists were conducted across the Prairie at no expense to see for themselves the prairie wonderland. The company even employed the new technology of moving pictures as early as 1902, by commissioning Charles Urban, a British producer, to make a series of thirty-five short films, collectively called *Living Canada*, intended to encourage travel and immigration. A few years later the company ordered a series of thirteen dramatic films, made on location by the Edison Company using a special train placed at its disposal. The films featured melodramatic plots set against the impressive scenic backdrops which were their real subject matter.[18]

This massive sales campaign, reinforced by the government immigration program, paid enormous dividends. By the end of 1883 the company had already made $6.6 million on land sales.[19] Crop failures and government land policies combined to create a slump in the market for a few years, but when the great immigration boom began in 1896, the CPR was nicely situated to profit from its real estate holdings. Much of this valuable land was located in the downtown core of burgeoning western cities like Winnipeg, Calgary, and Vancouver, where even today the CPR continues to profit from the original deal it made well over a century ago.

The efforts which the CPR put into selling western Canada contributed to a new image of the prairie region, which prior to the 1880s had been considered a desert unfit for agricultural settlement. In 1880, a botanist named John Macoun toured the southern prairies on behalf of the federal government and returned to declare that the desert was in fact fertile and just waiting for the farmer's plow to transform it. Immigration promoters, the CPR among them, seized on this revised estimate of the West's potential and spun it into an aggressive campaign to attract settlers. In the process, they manufactured a new identity for the region. No longer was the central interior a barren wasteland better left to the Indians who inhabited it. Now the West was a sunny paradise of grassy meadows, broad rivers, and fertile soil, breadbasket to the world, "the last, best West."

Immigrants were not the only target of CPR propaganda. Tourists were another source of revenue for the railway and a lot of effort went into presenting an image of the West, and particularly of the Rocky Mountains, that would attract visitors. As William Van Horne put it: "Since we can't export the scenery we shall have to import the tourists."[20] In 1884, he engaged the well-known Montreal photographic firm, William Notman and Son, to travel west at the railway's expense to make photographs of the prairie and mountain sections of the railroad. William McFarlane Notman, eldest son of the founder, made a total of eight forays out west, and the photographs he made were used extensively in CPR promotional material and sold separately as postcards, prints, and viewbooks. CPR patronage was extended to other photographers, including Oliver Buell, who used his photographs as lantern slides in his travelling lectures, as well as to several painters who received free rail passes which allowed them to discover the mountains as a new subject matter for their art. The resulting "Railway School" of painters—John Fraser, Lucius O'Brien, Thomas Mower Martin, F.M. Bell-Smith, to name a few—produced a steady stream of mountain portraits. Some of these paintings found their way into the CPR'S publicity, as well as into the homes of company executives.

The CPR publicity machine succeeded in turning the country into story. With the help of the company's promotional material, the rail journey unfolded like a book, leaving thoughtful travellers to contemplate the rise of civilization and the majesty of wild nature. The transcontinental trip became a narrative by which visitors interpreted the country as they passed through it, beginning in the settled East where cultivated farms and growing industrial cities gave evidence of a long history of occupation, and progressing onto the plains, which were being transformed into a world granary. Everywhere the signs of industry and growth indicated a prosperous future, while here and there a picturesque Indian village exposed vestiges of me "primitive" peoples who first occupied the region. Finally, visitors arrived at the wilderness of mountains, the ultimate scenic experience.

A further consequence of the CPR'S corporate agenda was the system of national parks. The railway created the idea of western Canada as a scenic theme park, promising visitors the chance to see "mighty rivers, vast forests, boundless plains, stupendous mountains and wonders innumerable."[21] Canada was "a paradise for sportsmen," a rare challenge for hikers and trailriders, an unparalleled experience even for someone who just wanted to sit at the window of the observation car and watch the scenery go by. The CPR was involved from the very beginning in the creation of national parks. It pressed the federal government to take control of the hot springs at Banff in order to develop a fashionable spa resort there. Once the government established the Rocky Mountain parks, the CPR took full advantage by touting these wilderness preserves as offering the most spectacular mountain scenery in the world, "1000 Switzerlands Rolled into One" in Van Horne's memorable phrase. It was the CPR which came up with the novel idea of turning the natural wilderness into a profit centre, with great success. By the outbreak of World War I the railway estimated that the Rockies were attracting about $50 million worth of tourism into the country each year.[22] The commercialization of the western mountains persists today in the way we imagine and utilize that part of the country.

The railway also created another narrative; western Canada as Indian Country. Photographs of Native people and their villages sold briskly to travellers wishing mementoes of their visit. Tourists with their own cameras had lots of opportunity to

"Kodak the Indians" at stops along the way. "The Indians and the bears were splendid stage properties to have at a station," remarked the English traveller Douglas Sladen.[23] In 1894, the CPR inaugurated Banff Indian Days, an annual summer festival featuring displays of traditional Native cultural practices. The railway realized that wild Indians were a surefire tourist attraction, every bit as exciting as the tribes of darkest Africa, yet available from the safety and convenience of a railway car.

III

The myth of the CPR—the myth that was created by the company and reiterated by most historians ever since—is that the railway made Canada. And perhaps it did. We cannot really know for sure what would have happened had the railway not been built, or not been built as speedily as it was. Without the iron road, the "spine of Canada," the West may well have been absorbed by the United States. Regardless, what remains unarguable is that the CPR did play a leading role in imagining the country into being, which is an entirely different thing. The photographs, paintings, and other images produced by the railway's publicity machine provided the first look most people had of the "New Canada" west of Manitoba. It was impossible even to see the country except by rail; until World War I, the CPR was the only way to do it. Travellers rode in CPR trains, stayed at CPR hotels, ate in CPR restaurants and understood what they were seeing through a veil of CPR promotional material. The CPR "created" Canada not by binding it together with steel rails, but by inventing images of it that people then began to recognize as uniquely Canadian. Canada was the last, best West. Canada was an exotic wilderness. Canada was the breadbasket of the world. Canada was Indian Country. Canada was an imperial highway linking Britain and its distant colonies in a new northwest passage. All mese Canadas were conjured into being by the CPR as part of its strategy for becoming the leading transportation and real estate conglomerate in the land.

By 1990, when the federal government closed down most passenger rail service, Canadians had long since given up taking the train. Rail was too slow, too inconvenient, for the modern traveller. But strong public reaction to the cuts demonstrated that the railway nevertheless continues to play an important role in the national fantasy life. We know that the railway no longer holds the country together in fact, but we suspect that it is one of the things which hold it together in our imaginations. Still revered as a fabulous technical achievement, completed against enormous odds, the railway is for many people—Michael Valpy among them—a symbol of our unity, sea to sea. Canadians take pride in the railway as a way of taking pride in the country. You don't just shut down symbols. The protests were expressing a real anxiety, not about the loss of a money-losing rail network, but about the loss of a sense of nation.

Endnotes

1. Jo Davis, ed., *Not a Sentimental Journey* (Goderich, Ont.: Gunbyfield Publishing, 1990), p.9.
2. Ibid., p. 17
3. Pierre Berton, *The Great Railway, 1871–1881* (Toronto: McClelland & Stewart, 1970), p. 12.
4. W. Kaye Lamb, *History of the Canadian Pacific Railway* (New York: Macmillan, 1977), p. 436
5. R.G. MacBeth, *The Romance of the Canadian Pacific Railway* (Toronto: The Ryerson Press, 1924), p. 172.
6. Robin Winks, *The Relevance of Canadian History* (Toronto: Macmillan, 1979), p. 47.
7. Robert Kroetsch, "Canada is a Poem," in Gary Geddes, ed., *Divided We Stand* (Toronto: Peter Martin Associates, 1977), p. 14.
8. MacBeth, p. 139
9. David Cruise and Alison Griffiths, *Lords of the Line* (Toronto: Viking Penguin, 1988), p. 1
10. Lamb, p. 135.
11. Hugh A. Dempsey, "Catching the Sunbeams: An Inventory of Canadian Prairie Photographers to 1900," unpublished paper, Glenbow Museum, 1993.
12. Lamb, p.1.
13. MacBeth, p. 73.
14. Ibid., p. 9.
15. George Ham, *Reminiscences of a Raconteur* (Toronto: The Musson Book Co., 1921), p. 265.
16. Cited in Doug Owram, *Promise of Eden: The Canadian Expansionist Movement and the Idea of the West, 1856–1900* (Toronto: University of Toronto Press, 1980), p. 123.
17. Michael Bliss, *Right Honourable Men* (Toronto: McClelland & Stewart, 1995), p. 22.
18. Sam Kula, "Steam Movies," in Hugh Dempsey, ed., *The CPR West* (Vancouver: Douglas & McIntyre, 1984), pp. 247–57.
19. Lamb, p. 219.
20. John Murray Gibbon, *Steel of Empire* (New York: Bobbs-Merrill Co., 1935), p. 304.
21. Cited in E.J. Hart, *The Selling of Canada* (Banff: Altitude Publishing, 1983), p. 25.
22. C. James Taylor, *Negotiating the Past: The Making of Canada's National Historic Parks and Sites* (Montreal: McGill-Queen's University Press, 1990), p. 27.
23. Douglas Sladen, *On the Cars and Off* (London: Ward, Lock & Bowden Ltd., 1895), p. 306.

Focus Questions

1. How and why does the CPR become a symbol of Canadian greatness and prosperity? What did it contribute to the "building" of Canada?

-trade w/in eachother

- unity

- increase settlement in west
  ↳ more jobs
      ↳ gold mines

- tourist industry

- cities are build where transportation is
  available

2. How does Pierre Berton's history contribute to the creation of these myths?

Myths
- Edward reps Canada
  ↳ From the top down
    ↳ Capitalists

→ was built to create Canada /nationalizm

3. How—and why—does Daniel Francis seek to dissect the myths of the CPR? How does he explain the anxiety that Canadians feel about alterations to the Railway's logo?

- we would still be a country, maybe woot the west
- it was built for capitalists to make money
- includes U.S. flag " the 50 stars
- they accomplished unity through the train
- built by chinese /italians /irish, not canadians
- we no longer use the rail way
- he tries to bring these things forward.

pg 191
- constructions of Capitalists trying to make the money back they used on the railway.

4. What are the contrasts between the two photographs of the "last spike" and what do these differences tell you about the myth and history of the CPR?

- alot more people in the fake last photo
- 1st pic
  - no chinese
  - clothing!
- funding

7

Canada's "Indians" at the Turn of the Twentieth Century: Cultural Imagination and Historical Realities

Introduction

In this chapter, the issue of Aboriginal identity is placed front and centre through a series of readings from the late nineteenth and early twentieth centuries. In each case, the author was attempting to depict some part of their vision of what they believed to be true about Canada's native peoples. But in each case, their vision was deeply coloured by politics or culture, by convention or stereotype—even by an awareness of audience. Together, these readings present a broad spectrum of opinion about Canada's aboriginal people before the mid-twentieth century.

The first piece is drawn from the work of Duncan Campbell Scott, a well-known poet and, between 1913 and 1932, government minister responsible for Indian affairs. The second selection, "A Cry From an Indian Wife," was written by E. Pauline Johnson, the daughter of a Mohawk chief and English woman, and one of Canada's first real celebrities. Despite the implicit critique of white society's treatment of Natives in her poetry, Johnson generated enormous fame with white audiences during her late nineteenth century career. As Daniel Francis has argued, her popularity rested in part on her adoption of stereotypically "Indian" garb and name (Tekahionwake) during her performances. Although neither were authentic, they appeared so to a white audience, which made her recitations all the more intriguing. Equally important, while Johnson *critiqued,* her poetry did not demand change or reparation—only sympathy.

"Tolerance," the brief essay by Grey Owl, shares a reliance on image and stereotype with Johnson. Grey Owl, whose real name was Archie Belaney, was not an Indian, but a disaffected Englishman who abandoned his life in England in favour of a career as a trapper in Northern Ontario. His real identity was not revealed until his death in 1938, but in the meantime, he achieved remarkable popularity through his writings about conservation and environmental protection. Like Johnson, this popularity rested largely on a belief that he spoke with authentic "Indian" wisdom—he looked and acted just as a "real" Indian was supposed to look and act. Also included in this chapter is the haunting story "D'Sonoqua" by Canadian painter and author Emily Carr. Carr's paintings are now well known and sought after, but during her life, she often struggled for recognition. She was deeply sympathetic with the plight of the Native tribes whose lives so often intersected with hers, perhaps because she felt an affinity with their marginal status, and with the disregard they'd been shown by the rest of Canadian society.

The Red Indian and The Aboriginal Races
Duncan Campbell Scott
1920

The Red Indian

It may be conceded that the typical Canadian Indian is the hunter and trapper, and, when one thinks of him, buckskins and beadwork and feathers still cloak him with a sort of romance. But these are rarely seen, except in pageants and on holidays, when the superior race must be amused by a glimpse of real savages in war-paint. The Indian hunter and trapper follows the craft of his ancestors, clothed as you and I, his wife and children likewise. His domestic surroundings grow less and less savage. The rabbit-skin robe yet holds its own, and the snow-shoe; but the birch-bark canoe is supplanted by the basswood or cedar variety; as likely as not he has a sewing machine and a gramophone in his tent. The aboriginal hunter is supreme no longer in his own craft; gone is the fiction that he is superior in these pursuits. The white man equals him as a trapper and holds his own on the trail and in the canoe. But as the margin of the wilderness recedes, it is difficult for comparisons of this kind to find the Indian of pure blood. There has been through all these years a great interfusion of white blood by lawful union and by illicit intercourse; legally a man may be an Indian with but a small trace of native blood, if his Indian descent is through the male line. If an Indian woman marries a white man she ceases to be an Indian in the eye of the law, and her children take the status of their father.

For 70 years after the cession of Canada, Indian administration was in the hands of the Imperial military authorities; it was not until 1835 that the responsibility was transferred to the Province of Canada. The military policy had looked upon the Indians as potential allies or foes, and, during the pioneer days, the feeling was balanced between hope and apprehension. They were kept quiet by presents of scarlet cloth, silver gorgets, brass kettles, and ammunition, with an occasional ration of rum. The fur-traders used the latter fluid as the most precious means of exchange and barter, and the restless, dejected people that were handed over to the province were indeed a problem. One Governor of Upper Canada, seeing them so wretched, resolved

From *The Times,* London, May 25, 1920.

to send them back to Nature for healing, and to remove them to hunting grounds where they might recuperate or die away unseen. But better counsels prevailed. The missionaries claimed them as material ready for evangelization, and protested that they were capable of lasting improvement. Upper and Lower Canada, not long after that, began a systematic endeavour to educate the Indians, supported by zealous missionary effort. This informal union between Church and State still exists, and all Canadian-Indian schools are conducted upon a joint agreement between the Government and the denomination as to finances and system. The method has proved successful, and the Indians of Ontario and Quebec, in the older regions of the provinces, are every day entering more and more into the general life of the country. They are farmers, clerks, artisans, teachers, and lumbermen. Some few have qualified as medical doctors and surveyors; an increasing number are accepting enfranchisement and taking up the responsibilities of citizenship.

Although there are reactionary elements among the best educated tribes, and stubborn paganism on the most progressive reserves, the irresistible movement is towards the goal of complete citizenship. At least 25 per cent of the Indians of Eastern Canada are hunters, and must remain so until settlement filters slowly into their country.

Last year the value of fur and fish taken by the Indians of Canada was $1,626,890; this year it will be larger, as the value of raw furs rapidly increases. Measured by even a low standard, the life of these hunting Indians is not enviable, and a condition almost of slavery exists. By the very circumstances of their lives they are bound to their masters, the traders, and are in a position of debt and obligation that cannot be thrown off. The methods of the hunt are often beset with privation, but the Indian has no longer the old stamina of the race to fall back upon.

The larger portion of the Indian population of Canada is west of Lake Superior, and it was adopted in a primitive state by the Dominion shortly after Confederation. The aboriginal title to the vast areas east of the Rocky Mountains was extinguished; annual gifts of cash, special reserved lands, assistance in agriculture, and education, were promised by the Government. For a time the Plains Indians had to be fed, owing to the disappearance of the buffalo, but gradually stock-raising and agriculture were introduced, and now hardly a pound of gratuitous food is issued. Residential schools were established, which have influenced beneficially the life on the reserves, and, now that they are educating the children of former pupils, the progress will be more rapid and stable. The older school buildings are gradually being replaced by modern structures, which are built with the sense of civic pride which should always influence the establishment of public institutions. Many of these schools are models of what such institutions should be, and are exerting a constant influence on the character of their pupils. The graduates are either formed into so-called colonies on the reserves, or are encouraged in making practical use of the knowledge gained at school.

The Indians of Canada may look with just pride upon the part played by them in the great war, both at home and on the field of battle. They have well and nobly upheld the loyal traditions of their gallant ancestors who rendered invaluable service to the British cause in 1776 and in 1812, and have added thereto a heritage of deathless honour which is an example and an inspiration for their descendants. According to the official records of the department more than 4,000 Indians enlisted for active service with the Canadian Expeditionary Forces. This number represents approximately 35 per cent of the Indian male population of military age in the nine Provinces.

The situation of the British Columbia Indians is unique.

Anthropologists have found in their myths and religious ceremonies an inexhaustible field for investigation, and volumes have been written in elucidation of their manners and customs. Civilization also came to this people not in the guise of an evangel, but with a sinister aspect. It struck at the very root of the tribal existence. For years the women were sacrificed to the licence of the white men of the coast, often with the connivance of the native males: disease and whiskey worked swiftly, and destroyed them. After these staggering blows the race is only now beginning to recover. A population which was variously estimated at from 40,000 to 50,000 in about the year 1871, when British Columbia came into Confederation, has now dwindled to 26,000. Nowhere in Canada are the Indians a greater factor in the labour market than in this province. They are the mainstay of the fisheries of the Fraser and Skeena rivers. The labour of the women is valued in the fish canning factories, and an Indian fisherman is always sure of employment if he has a number of women who can be useful in packing the fish. The men themselves are excellent fishermen, but not without the usual native failing, lack of steadiness. They are excellent boatbuilders, and can readily manage gasoline boats and engines. In the high and lonely parts of this wonderful Province there are Indians who are as primitive as those who first looked upon Capt. Vancouver.

Although no cession of the Indian title in British Columbia has ever been sought or obtained, the Provincial Government has set apart adequate reserves, and the Dominion Government has extended to the natives the same system of education, agricultural assistance, and administrative supervision as in the prairie Provinces. Many of the reserves are suitable for stock-raising, and some Indians have been successful in breeding cattle and horses, while in other localities fruit culture and the cultivation of beans and peas offers suitable employment. The outlook in British Columbia is certainly encouraging; there is fine material among the natives to make good British citizens, and in two or three decades we may expect that a large number of Indians will have been absorbed into the ordinary life of the Provinces.

The Indian population of Canada is fairly stable at about 100,000. Among the less civilized groups, the high birth-rate balances the high death-rate; but in the civilized tribes, who have withstood the first shock of contact with civilization, there is an appreciable gain, not only in numbers, but in physical standards. These latter people have long ago proved their worth, and only need to develop and mature under protection until they, one and all, reach their destined goal, full British citizenship.

The Aboriginal Races

Any comprehensive or reliable information as to the aboriginal population of British North America at the time of Champlain, or at the date of the Conquest, is non-existent, and there is no basis for a comparison between the native population of today and that of past times.

We state roughly that our natives, recognized legally as Indians and Eskimos, number 105,000 persons, whose descent is through the male line. This population includes many of mixed blood but excludes the progeny of legal marriages between white men and Indian women, the offspring of such unions being counted as citizens. They do not receive the protection of such special legislation as exists for Indians. This round number of 105,000 must be much smaller than any figures representing the population of an earlier day. If we could know accurately the number of natives living at the time of Confederation, the comparison would show a material decrease. The native population of British Columbia at the time of the union with the Dominion was stated, with fair accuracy, to be about 70,000; it is now counted as 25,000. The decrease of 64 per cent in fifty years was very rapid, assuredly more rapid than in any other province, but there has been undoubtedly a very heavy loss of native population in all provinces since Confederation.

Ravages of Disease

It is to be hoped that the lowest point of the general ebb has been reached, but it may be said at once that even now the birth rate is the important factor in stabilizing the population. The death rate is abnormally high. The inroads of tuberculosis and the losses by epidemics constantly operate to counteract the increases which might be expected from the favorable birth rate. During the epidemic of influenza, 1918–19, we lost 6,000 Indians, and such diseases as smallpox and measles take annual toll, but tuberculosis is the real foe of the aborigine. It is possible to fight this scourge in some measure in certain localities, but the conditions of aboriginal life are so varied that it is impossible to meet them all with effective methods. In Indian communities, close to civilization, there is a constant education going on in the schools; the nature and the danger of the disease is known to the Indians, and they have recourse to the sanitaria provided for the white population, but it is impossible to follow with prophylactic advice and remedies Indians whose livelihood is gained by hunting and fishing. Exposure, irregular and often sparse food supply, crowded, overheated shacks and other departures from the older and more sanitary life of the wigwam and teepee, all these aid the development and hasten the progress of the disease.

The Reserve System

The location of Indians on special Reserves of land has been the practice from the earliest times in this country. This system was designed to protect them from encroachment and to establish for them a sort of sanctuary where they could develop unmolested, until advancement had rendered possible their absorption with the general citizenship. The Reserve System was intended to insure the continuation of the tribal life and the life of the individual as an Indian, as well as to render possible a continuous and consistent administrative policy directed toward civilization. If there had been strict confinement to Reserve limits, the system would have had many objectionable features, but neither officials nor Indians considered the Reserve as more than a "pied de terre." The Indians wandered away from it and returned to it as the nomadic instinct prompted, no doubt bringing back much undesirable knowledge and experience. But this mingling with the outside world was less undesirable than a strict confinement within boundaries would have been, even had such confinement been possible. We can now see the results in the older provinces of such an interplay of forces and tendencies. We find a native population to a certain degree intimate with the usages of civilized life. The individual Indian is either maintaining himself and his family away from his tribal reserve by mercantile or industrial pursuits, or living upon the Reserve and obtaining his subsistence from its soil.

Enfranchisement

The social condition of the Reserve Indians does not differ materially from the social conditions of those who have separated themselves from the tribal relationship. Intermarriage with white persons has affected both classes and has prevented the evils of marriage in closely related family groups. Enfranchisement, that is the removal of all the civil disabilities which are borne by the Indian, and his mergence in the general citizenship, is the goal of all administrative effort. It is possible, under the present law, to enfranchise Indians of both classes, but the problem of enfranchisement is less difficult for those who own no land upon a Reserve. These are readily merged in the ranks of full and free citizens by the payment to them of their share of the capital funds of their tribe or band. When enfranchisement involves the allotment of land in fee simple and the disintegration of the Reserve, the matter is not so free from complications, but through enfranchisement the Indians and the Indian problem disappears and the effort towards civilization is consummated. The older sections of the Dominion exhibit the process towards enfranchisement in action from day to day, but it has hardly begun to work in the newly settled districts or in the old provinces among hunting and fishing Indians. Enfranchisement is sometimes confused with the exercise of the franchise. In provincial elections no Indian residing in Manitoba, Saskatchewan, Alberta, British Columbia, or New Brunswick, has the right to vote, but in the other provinces, if he does not reside on a Reserve, and is otherwise qualified, he may vote. In Dominion elections those Indians only who served in the late war can vote.

Effect of Competition on Indians

It will be observed that Ontario has the largest Indian population, at least 50 per cent of the total of Indians in that province being dependent for a livelihood to a greater or lesser degree on hunting and fishing. A variable percentage in all the provinces is likewise so dependent. This is the natural manner of life and although the Indian is by no means superior to the white man in this, his native pursuit, he is yet the most important source of supply to the fur trader. In British Columbia he is a highly important factor in the labor of the salmon fishery, not only in the taking of the fish but in the preparation in the canneries of the product for the market.

Of late the presence of competition in the hunt has begun to bear heavily upon the Indian and his maintenance problem becomes more difficult as the years go by. In the old days, when Indians alone were in the woods, fur was taken with care and with due concern for the future. The established traders took a paternal interest in the hunters, an interest perhaps not more elevated than their interest in the beavers or foxes, considering the animals who trapped and the animals who were trapped as of equal importance to a successful business venture, but the interest evoked by the situation at least ensured a fair supply of food and clothing for the Indian. The condition was a condition of bondage without evitable hardship, but the competition of rival traders brought a new element into the problem. Allegiance to the rivals was set up and therefore discrimination and jealousy, and the lot of the Indian became harder. Now that the petty trader has invaded the field,—the foreigner without a permanent establishment and with only cash in hand,—further difficulties have arisen and the incursions of white trappers have put a last tangle into the involved interests. No stringency of regulations can do more than postpone the disappearance of the fur-bearing animals and the complete alteration in the source of native livelihood. In some districts the day is far off, in others it is near, and the Government has now to supplement the food supply which has failed for all but the more vigorous hunters.

It will be gathered from this sketch that the policy is to protect the Indian, to guard his identity as a race and at the same time to apply methods which will destroy that identity and lead eventually to his disappearance as a separate division of the population. This policy might be frustrated by the gradual extinction of the race while yet in the tutelary stage. But that is hardly to be feared. The Indian has proved that he can withstand the shock of contact with our civilization, that he can survive the manifold evils of that contact, and transfer his native energy into the channels of modern life. The original stamina of the tribe to which he belongs is the root factor in his survival. Certain tribes have proved to be too feeble in their resistance to the new influences and will disappear, while others have overcome the initial evils and have increased and flourished.

A Cry from an Indian Wife
E. Pauline Johnson (Tekahionwake)
1885

My Forest Brave, my Red-skin love, farewell;
We may not meet tomorrow; who can tell
What mighty ills befall our little band,
Or what you'll suffer from the white man's hand?
Here is your knife! I thought 'twas sheathed for aye.
No roaming bison calls for it to-day;
No hide of prairie cattle will it maim;
The plains are bare, it seeks a nobler game:
'Twill drink the life-blood of a soldier host.
Go; rise and strike, no matter what the cost.
Yet stay. Revolt not at the Union jack,
Nor raise thy hand against this stripling pack
Of white-faced warriors, marching West to quell
Our fallen tribe that rises to rebel.
They all are young and beautiful and good;
Curse to the war that drinks their harmless blood.
Curse to the fate that brought them from the East
To be our chiefs—to make our nation least
That breathes the air of this vast continent.
Still their new rule and council is well meant.
They but forget we Indians owned the land
From ocean unto ocean; that they stand
Upon a soil that centuries agone
Was our sole kingdom and our right alone.
They never think how they would feel to-day,
If some great nation came from far away,
Wrestling their country from their hapless braves,
Giving what they gave us—but wars and graves.
Then go and strike for liberty and life,
And bring back honour to your Indian wife.

Your wife? Ah, what of that, who cares for me?
Who pities my poor love and agony?
What white-robed priest prays for your safety here,
As prayer is said for every volunteer
That swells the ranks that Canada sends out?
Who prays for vict'ry for the Indian scout?
Who prays for our poor nation lying low?
None—therefore take your tomahawk and go.
My heart may break and burn into its core,
But I am strong to bid you go to war.
Yet stay, my heart is not the only one
That grieves the loss of husband and of son;
Think of the mothers o'er the inland seas;
Think of the pale-faced maiden on her knees;
One pleads her God to guard some sweet-faced child
That marches on toward the North-West wild.
The other prays to shield her love from harm,
To strengthen his young, proud uplifted arm.
Ah, how her white face quivers thus to think,
Your tomahawk his life's best blood will drink.
She never thinks of my wild aching breast,
Nor prays for your dark face and eagle crest
Endangered by a thousand rifle balls,
My heart the target if my warrior falls.
O! coward self I hesitate no more;
Go forth, and win the glories of the war.
Go forth, nor bend to greed of white men's hands,
By right, by birth we Indians own these lands,
Though starved, crushed, plundered, lies our nation low . . .
Perhaps the white man's God has willed it so.

Original Ending, 1885 Edition

A Cry from an Indian Wife
Copytext: Flint and Feather.

First published in *The Week* 18 June 1885, and revised for *WW*, this was one of Johnson's most effective recital pieces. It was frequently reprinted in newspaper accounts of her performances from 1892 onward. The last four lines originally read:

O! coward self—I hesitate no more.
Go forth—and win the glories of the war.
O! heart o'erfraught-O! nation lying low-
God, and fair Canada have willed it so.

This poem appeared during the course of the Northwest Rebellion of 1885, between the surrender of Poundmaker on 26 May and the surrender of Big Bear on 2 July. The major confrontation involved Métis and Indians, led by Louis Riel and Gabriel Dumont, who rallied in protest against the land policies of the dominion government. They were opposed by forces assembled under Major-General Frederick Middleton, which included some three thousand volunteers from Eastern Canada who joined another seventeen hundred from the west.

D'Sonoqua
Emily Carr
1941

I was sketching in a remote Indian village when I first saw her. The village was one of those that the Indians use only for a few months in each year; the rest of the time it stands empty and desolate. I went there in one of its empty times, in a drizzling dusk.

When the Indian agent dumped me on the beach in front of the village, he said "There is not a soul here. I will come back for you in two days." Then he went away.

I had a small Griffon dog with me, and also a little Indian girl, who, when she saw the boat go away, clung to my sleeve and wailed, "I'm 'fraid."

We went up to the old deserted Mission House. At the sound of the key in the rusty lock, rats scuttled away. The stove was broken, the wood wet. I had forgotten to bring candles. We spread our blankets on the floor, and spent a poor night. Perhaps my lack of sleep played its part in the shock that I got, when I saw her for the first time.

Water was in the air, half mist, half rain. The stinging nettles, higher than my head, left their nervy smart on my ears and forehead, as I beat my way through them, trying all the while to keep my feet on the plank walk which they hid. Big yellow slugs crawled on the walk and slimed it. My feet slipped, and I shot headlong to her very base, for she had no feet. The nettles that were above my head reached only to her knee.

It was not the fall alone that jerked the "Oh's" out of me, for the great wooden image towering above me was indeed terrifying.

The nettle bed ended a few yards beyond her, and then a rocky bluff jutted out, with waves battering it below. I scrambled up and went out on the bluff, so that I could see the creature above the nettles. The forest was behind her, the sea in front.

Her head and trunk were carved out of, or rather into, the bole of a great red cedar. She seemed to be part of the tree itself, as if she had grown there at its heart, and the carver had only chipped away the outer wood so that you could see her. Her arms were spliced and socketed to the trunk, and were flung wide in a circling, compelling movement. Her breasts were two eagle-heads, fiercely carved. That much, and the column of her great neck, and her strong chin, I had seen when I slithered to the ground beneath her. Now I saw her face.

From *Klee Wyck* by Emily Carr. Clarke, Irwin & Company Limited (Canadaian Classics Edition), 1951, pp. 40-50.

The eyes were two rounds of black, set in wider rounds of white, and placed in deep sockets under wide, black eyebrows. Their fixed stare bored into me as if the very life of the old cedar looked out, and it seemed that the voice of the tree itself might have burst from that great round cavity, with projecting lips, that was her mouth. Her ears were round, and stuck out to catch all sounds. The salt air had not dimmed the heavy red of her trunk and arms and thighs. Her hands were black, with blunt finger-tips painted a dazzling white. I stood looking at her for a long, long time.

The rain stopped, and white mist came up from the sea, gradually paling her back into the forest. It was as if she belonged there, and the mist were carrying her home. Presently the mist took the forest too, and, wrapping them both together, hid them away.

"Who is that image?" I asked the little Indian girl, when I got back to the house.

She knew which one I meant, but to gain time, she said, "What image?"

"The terrible one, out there on the bluff." "I dunno," she lied.

I never went to that village again, but the fierce wooden image often came to me, both in my waking and in my sleeping.

Several years passed, and I was once more sketching in an Indian village. There were Indians in this village, and in a mild backward way it was "going modern." That is, the Indians had pushed the forest back a little to let the sun touch the new buildings that were replacing the old community houses. Small houses, primitive enough to a white man's thinking, pushed here and there between the old. Where some of the big community houses had been torn down, for the sake of the lumber, the great corner posts and massive roof-beams of the old structure were often left, standing naked against the sky, and the new little house was built inside, on the spot where the old one had been.

It was in one of these empty skeletons that I found her again. She had once been a supporting post for the great centre beam. Her pole-mate, representing the Raven, stood opposite her, but the beam that had rested on their heads, was gone. The two poles faced in, and one judged the great size of the house by the distance between them. The corner posts were still in place, and the earth floor, once beaten to the hardness of rock by naked feet, was carpeted now with rich lush grass.

I knew her by the stuck-out ears, shouting mouth, and deep eye-sockets. These sockets had no eye-balls, but were empty holes, filled with stare. The stare, though not so fierce as that of the former image, was more intense. The whole figure expressed power, weight, domination, rather than ferocity. Her feet were planted heavily on the head of the squatting bear, carved beneath them. A man could have sat on either huge shoulder. She was unpainted, weatherworn, sun-cracked, and the arms and hands seemed to hang loosely. The fingers were thrust into the carven mouths of two human heads, held crowns down. From behind, the sun made unfathomable shadows in eye, cheek and mouth. Horror tumbled out of them.

I saw Indian Tom on the beach, and went to him. "Who is she?"

The Indian's eyes, coming slowly from across the sea, followed my pointing finger. Resentment showed in his face, greeny-brown and wrinkled like a baked apple,—resentment that white folks should pry into matters wholly Indian.

"Who is that big carved woman?" I repeated.

"D'Sonaqua." No white tongue could have fondled the name as he did.

"Who is D'Sonoqua?"

"She is the wild woman of the woods."

"What does she do?"

"She steals children." "To eat them?"

"No, she carries them to her caves; that," pointing to a purple scar on the mountain across the bay, "is one of her caves. When she cries 'OO-oo-oo-oeo', Indian mothers are too frightened to move. They stand like trees, and the children go with D'Sonoqua."

"Then she is bad?"

"Sometimes bad . . . sometimes good," Tom replied, glancing furtively at those stuck-out ears. Then he got up and walked away.

I went back, and sitting in front of the image, gave stare for stare. But her stare so over-powered mine, that I could scarcely wrench my eyes away from the clutch of those empty sockets. The power that I felt was not in the thing itself, but in some tremendous force behind it, that the carver had believed in.

A shadow passed across her hands and their gruesome holdings. A little bird, with its beak full of nesting material, flew into the cavity of her mouth, right in the pathway of that terrible OO-oo-oo-oeo. Then my eye caught something that I had missed—a tabby cat asleep between her feet.

This was D'Sonoqua, and she was a supernatural being, who belonged to these Indians.

"Of course," I said to myself, "I do not believe in supernatural beings. Still—who understands the mysteries behind the forest? What would one do if one did meet a supernatural being?" Half of me wished that I could meet her, and half of me hoped I would not.

Chug—chug—the little boat had come into the bay to take me to another village, more lonely and deserted than this. Who knew what I should see there? But soon supernatural beings went clean out of my mind, because I was wholly absorbed in being naturally seasick.

When you have been tossed and wracked and chilled, any wharf looks good, even a rickety one, with its crooked legs stockinged in barnacles. Our boat nosed under its clammy darkness, and I crawled up the straight slimy ladder, wondering which was worse natural seasickness, or supernatural "creeps." The trees crowded to the very edge of the water, and the outer ones, hanging over it, shadowed the shoreline into a velvet smudge. D'Sonoqua might walk in places like this. I sat for a long time on the damp, dusky beach, waiting for the stage. One by one dots of light popped from the scattered cabins, and made the dark seem darker. Finally the stage came.

We drove through the forest over a long straight road, with black pine trees marching on both sides. When we came to the wharf the little gas mail-boat was waiting for us. Smell and blurred light oozed thickly out of the engine room, and except for one lantern on the wharf everything else was dark. Clutching my little dog, I sat on the mail sacks which had been tossed on to the deck.

The ropes were loosed, and we slid out into the oily black water. The moon that had gone with us through the forest was away now. Black pine-covered mountains jagged up on both sides of the inlet like teeth. Every gasp of the engine shook us like a great sob. There was no rail round the deck, and the edge of the boat lay level with the black slithering horror below. I t was like being swallowed again and again by some terrible monster, but never going down. As we slid through the water, hour after hour, I found myself listening for the OO-oo-oo-oeo.

Midnight brought us to a knob of land, lapped by the water on three sides, with the forest threatening to gobble it up on the fourth. There was a rude landing, a rooming-house, an eating-place, and a store, all for the convenience of fishermen and loggers. I was given a room, but after I had blown out my candle, the stillness and the darkness would not let me sleep.

In the brilliant sparkle of the morning when everything that was not superlatively blue was superlatively green, I dickered with a man who was taking a party up the inlet that he should drop me off at the village I was headed for.

"But," he protested, "there is nobody there."

To myself I said, "There is D'Sonoqua."

From the shore, as we rowed to it, came a thin feminine cry—the mewing of a cat. The keel of the boat had barely grated in the pebbles, when the cat sprang aboard, passed the man shipping his oars, and crouched for a spring into my lap. Leaning forward, the man seized the creature roughly, and with a cry of "Dirty Indian vermin!" flung her out into the sea.

I jumped ashore, refusing his help, and with a curt "Call for me at sun-down," strode up the beach; the cat followed me.

When we had crossed the beach and come to a steep bank, the cat ran ahead. Then I saw that she was no lean, ill-favoured Indian cat, but a sleek aristocratic Persian. My snobbish little Griffon dog, who usually refused to let an Indian cat come near me, surprised me by trudging beside her in comradely fashion.

The village was typical of the villages of these Indians. It had only one street, and that had only one side, because all the houses faced the beach. The two community houses were very old, dilapidated and bleached, and the handful of other shanties seemed never to have been young; they had grown so old before they were finished, that it was then not worth while finishing them.

Rusty padlocks carefully protected the gaping walls. There was the usual broad plank in front of the houses, the general sitting and sunning place for Indians. Little streams ran under it, and weeds poked up through every crack, half hiding the companies of tins, kettles, and rags, which patiently waited for the next gale and their next move.

In front of the Chief's house was a high, carved totem pole, surmounted by a large wooden eagle. Storms had robbed him of both wings, and his head had a resentful twist, as if he blamed somebody. The heavy wooden heads of two squatting bears peered over the nettle-tops. The windows were too high for peeping in or out. "But, save D'Sonoqua, who is there to peep?" I said aloud, just to break the silence. A fierce sun burned down as if it wanted to expose every ugliness and forlornness. It drew the noxious smell out of the skunk cabbages, growing in the rich black ooze of the stream, scummed the water-barrels with green slime, and branded the desolation into my very soul.

The cat kept very close, rubbing and bumping itself and purring ecstatically; and although I had not seen them come, two more cats had joined us. When I sat down they curled into my lap, and then the strangeness of the place did not bite into me so deeply. I got up, determined to look behind the houses.

Nettles grew in the narrow spaces between the houses. I beat them down, and made my way over the bruised dank-smelling mass into a space of low jungle.

Long ago the trees had been felled and left lying. Young forest had burst through the slash, making an impregnable barrier, and sealing up the secrets which lay behind it. An eagle flew out of the forest, circled the village, and flew back again.

Once again I broke silence, calling after him, "Tell D'Sonoqua—" and turning, saw her close, towering above me in the jungle.

Like the D'Sonoqua of the other villages she was carved into the bole of a red cedar tree. Sun and storm had bleached the wood, moss here and there softened the crudeness of the modelling; sincerity underlay every stroke.

She appeared to be neither wooden nor stationary, but a singing spirit, young and fresh, passing through the jungle. No violence coarsened her; no power domineered to wither her. She was graciously feminine. Across her forehead her creator had fashioned the Sistheutl, or mythical two-headed sea-serpent. One of its heads fell to either shoulder, hiding the stuck-out ears, and framing her face from a central parting on her forehead which seemed to increase its womanliness.

She caught your breath, this D'Sonoqua, alive in the dead bole of the cedar. She summed up the depth and charm of the whole forest, driving away its menace.

I sat down to sketch. What was the noise of purring and rubbing going on about my feet? Cats. I rubbed my eyes to make sure I was seeing right, and counted a dozen of them. They jumped into my lap and sprang to my shoulders. They were real—and very feminine.

There we were—D'Sonoqua, the cats and I—the woman who only a few moments ago had forced herself to come behind the houses in trembling fear of the "wild woman of the woods"—wild in the sense that forest-creatures are wild—shy, untouchable.

Tolerance
Grey Owl (Wa-sha-quon-asin)
1936

"The brute tamer stands by the brutes,
by a head's breadth only above them!
A head's breadth, ay, but therein is hell's
depth and the height up to Heaven."

—Padriac Colum

Thus says the poet. But with all due regard for his meaning, if I understand him aright, I am inclined to disagree with him. There is not so wide a difference between man and beast as all that. Often I think that the term "brute" as applied to a dissolute fellow is somewhat of a misnomer. Brutes are rarely depraved, and at least with animals you do not have to watch for symptoms of an overdeveloped business instinct, nor is it necessary to guard against the double dealings of self-interest. There is nothing much to fear save a little wilful mischief and the odd misunderstanding. These cerebral shortcomings may perhaps be the result of a lack of imagination, but it is very refreshing to be confronted by constant evidences of sincerity, even if they are at times a little vigorous. Few forms of affection are more genuine than the guileless and intense devotion that is given only by children and some animals.

As a man lives longer and longer in the woods, so he entertains, if he be of an entertaining nature, an ever-increasing respect and love for Wild Life in all its varied forms. He hesitates at last to kill, and even when necessity demands that he take life he does so with feelings of apology, even of regret for the act. So natural and compelling is this instinct for reparation that old Indians, not yet made self-conscious of their pagan customs (many of which, by the way, are rather beautiful and worth perpetuating), have a ritual fitting for such occasions in respect of the more highly esteemed creatures. Years ago I came to this attitude, and it enveloped me so slowly, and yet so surely, that it seemed at last to be the natural outcome of a life spent overmuch in destroying rather than in building. I cannot believe that I am alone in this, but have pretty good evidence that of those whose experience has been such as to

From Tales of An Empty Cabin by (Wa-sha-quon-asin) Grey Owl. Lovat Dickson Limited, 1906, pp. 323–333.

cause them to consider the matter at all, only the ignorant or unthinking or the arrogant, or those governed by selfishness are not so affected, at least to some degree.

A man will always lack something of being a really good woodsman, in the finer sense, until he is so steeped in the atmosphere of the Wild and has become so possessed, by long association with it, of a feeling of close kinship and responsibility to it, that he may even unconsciously avoid tramping on too many flowers on his passage through the forest. Then, and then only, can he become truly receptive to the delicate nuances of a culture that may elude those who are not so tuned in on their surroundings. Many instances have I seen of men who, half-ashamed by the presence of spectators, yet had the courage to save the lives of ants, toads, snakes and other lowly creatures in the face of ridicule. And these were virile, hard-looking "he-men," to whom such abject forms of life should supposedly have been of small consideration. And speaking of toads and harmless types of snakes, and other ill-appearing but inoffensive and often beneficial beasts, their persecution is generally the outcome of fanatical hatred, springing from an unreasoning fear of them on the part of those who know nothing whatever about them.

There are many who walk through the woods like blind men. They see nothing but so many feet of board measure in the most magnificent tree that ever stood, and calculate only so many dollars to each beaver house. (With all due respect for economic necessities, there is, I believe, even a certain amount of sentiment present in some slaughter-houses.) For such the beauties of Nature do not exist, and their reactions to the scenic splendours that surround them are similar to that of a man I once accompanied to the top of an eminence, to view a wide-spread panorama of virgin pine forest that stretched from our feet into the blue distance. He looked at the scene before him—such a one as few men are privileged to see—and I thought him rapt with appreciation, when he presently remarked, "Gosh, wouldn't that look good all piled on skidways!"

The function of the forest is *not* exclusively that of providing lumber, though judicious and *properly controlled* garnering of a reasonable forest crop is essential to industry. There are many reasons, æsthetic, economic and patriotic, for the perpetuation of large tracts of unspoiled, *original* timber-exclusive of re-forestation. This last scheme should be carried on intensively, and commercial concerns should be obliged (and many of them do, to their credit) to plant six or a dozen trees for everyone they cut, thus putting in their own crop, and so be made to keep their acquisitive eyes off some of Canada's remaining beauty spots, which will be irretrievably ruined if commerce has its way with them. There is plenty for all purposes, if patronage does not outdo honesty.

It is said that all creatures are put here for our exclusive use, to be our servants. Perhaps they are. Yet the abuse of servants is no longer popular; and no one will say that the deer are put in the woods expressly for the wolves to eat, or the spruce cones especially for the squirrels. And once in the woods we are apt to be not much greater than the wolves and squirrels, and are often less. Human beings, as a whole, deny to animals any credit for the power of thought, preferring not to hear about it and ascribing everything they do to instinct. Yet most species of animals can reason, and all men have instinct. Man is the highest of living creatures, but it does not follow as a corollary that Nature belongs to him, as he so fondly imagines. He belongs to it. That he should take his share of the gifts she has so bountifully provided for her children, is only right and proper; but he cannot reasonably deny the other creatures a certain portion. They have to live too. And he should at least use some discretion about it and not take the whole works. Proper use should without doubt be made of our natural resources, whether animal or of any other kind, but it could be done more in the spirit of one who, let us say, is walking in a lovely garden where he may gather, by invitation, choice blossoms sufficient for his needs. But only too often we (I say "we" because I too have not been altogether guiltless in the past) have acted like irresponsible children who, not satisfied with the bounty that should suffice them, must needs tramp down what they cannot carry away.

Man's unfair treatment of the brute creation is too well realized to need a great deal of comment. It varies all the way from neglect, and a callous disregard of any claims the animal may have on his (the man's) sense of fair play, to active cruelty. There are those who are able to indulge a craving for a sense of power, only by exercising it over others who cannot retaliate. This is weakness, not strength such as real power bestows, and from it springs the proverbial cruelty of the coward. The bravest men are generally the kindest, as I saw very often proven during the war; and when, on returning from active service, I heard and saw demonstrations of bitter and implacable animosity, I learned that only the weakling or the non-combatant can hate with such terrible intensity. You have to meet the enemy to appreciate him; and the frank hostility that is sometimes seen to exist between some of those belonging to different social strata, could be much ameliorated did each have a chance to cultivate the other. I have met the great, the near great, and the not great. Some say that the higher you go, the simpler and more unassuming they are. I will go further and say that wherever you go, be it up or down, they are quite usually—just people, real folks. Kindness, hospitality and consideration are not the prerogative of any class, and a difference in accent is no indication of any great difference in heart. I have met traffic policemen who were natural born gentlemen, and one of the kindest and most courteous hosts I ever had was an ex-bartender who was also an ex-pugilist; and I have dined with a patrician whose conversation missed on every cylinder. But he was an individual.

Titles can be convenient appendages whereby those who have them may be sufficiently bedeviled by those who have not; though I observe that few refuse them. Certainly, the great ones among us, title or no, once they know that you wish only to talk with them as one human to another, with mutual respect, as we should meet all men—when they find, to their relief, that you do not propose to cross swords with them in a crackling duel of splintery, two-edged trivialities, they can be as simple, kindly and unaffected as any son of the soil. And they have so genuine an interest in what you have to tell them and have, moreover, such very well-considered things to say, and they have, altogether, brought to so fine an art that priceless ability to put at his ease the stranger within their gate, that it is at once ascertained that therein lies the real secret of their greatness. And in this they seem to me to be very close in spirit to those great trees that stand so nobly, and yet so proudly tranquil, who never will offend, and who bring grace and elegance to the landscape that they dominate.

If this tolerant attitude is so desirable, nay essential, in our dealings with our fellow humans of whatever class, race or creed, all of whom can, when put to it, ask our aid if need be, would it not seem to be at least fair, a little like good sportsmanship, to permit ourselves just a little sympathy, to exercise some small amount of thought, in our dealings with those creatures who sometimes stand so badly in need of the consideration for which they cannot ask?

That chivalry towards the weaker in which man so prides himself, does not appear to any large extent, if at all, in his attitude towards dumb animals that are unable to upbraid him, or to contribute verbally to public opinion and so damn him. Man's general reactions to his contacts with the animal world (here I speak only of that unfortunately rather large class to whom these remarks apply) are contempt or condescension towards the smaller and more harmless species, and a rather unreasonable fear of those more able to protect themselves. There are many men who inspire our respect by their love for their horses, dogs and other animal companions; yet we still have the bull fight, which I once saw described as a game in which the whole effort of the human players, they having the odds all on their side, was to commit a series of fouls and expect applause for them. I am given to understand that in at least one country whose people regard with disgust this brutal "sport," certain dealers carryon a trade in old, worn-out horses who, as a reward for their long years of service, are shipped away to be tortured in the bull ring for the satisfaction of audiences whose ancestors for hundreds of years blackened the pages of history with the most fiendish cruelties, and annihilated a whole race of Indian people in the name of God. Dogs are still beaten to death in the harness by their owners, and so-called sportsmen, willing to take a chance which only the animal will have to pay for, take flying shots at distant or moving game, and frequently their only reaction to the knowledge that the beast has escaped to die a lingering death, is one of irritation at losing a trophy or some meat.

I had a hunting partner who in attempting such snap shooting, smashed the bottom jaw of a deer. Some days later we found it dead, on which he looked at the carcase and said" Well, you . . ., I got you anyway." Nor is this an extreme case. All through the woods, in hunting season, careless hunters allow maimed animals to escape them to either die in the throes of suffering, or to slowly starve to death owing to their inability to take care of themselves in a crippled condition. Whole species of valuable and intelligent animals have been exterminated for temporary gain, and useful varieties of birds have been destroyed to the point of annihilation (and in one case completely) to tickle the palates of gourmets.

Kindness to animals is the hall-mark of human advancement; when it appears, nearly everything else can be taken for granted. It comes about last on the list of improvements as a rule, so that by the time animal care has been allowed to assume a place of real importance in the curriculum of human activities, it will generally be found that most other social advancements have already been brought to a high degree of refinement, and it is perhaps not too much to say that, using animal welfare among a people as the lowest level in the gauge of their accomplishments, the degree of culture that they have attained to may be indicated by it.

Much of the cruelty perpetrated to provide fashionable adornment is not realized, or even suspected, by the wearers who, somewhat unjustly, get most of the blame. Few perhaps, if any, of those who wear one type of lamb's wool coat, know that the excellence of texture they demand, and which is merely ornamental, is obtained by beating the pregnant mother with sticks until she, in her terror and pain, gives premature birth to her young, who provide the skins, and I have heard that ranches or sheep farms are maintained to cater to this horrible industry. Not much comment is needed on this except, on my part, that the much played-up ferocity of the North American Indian supplies nothing quite like it, and that I would like very much to believe that the general public, including those who wear the coats, did they know of this most inhuman practice, would no longer countenance it.

It would seem as though the making of money would excuse almost anything, and that nearly any undertaking, however unethical, can be termed " business" and so get itself excused, provided it is successful and does not muscle in on some big-shot monopoly. Sheep, I know, are often skinned alive, and I hear that certain kinds of fish are cut in pieces from the tail to the head, so they will remain alive to the last, in order that jaded appetites may be stimulated by the crimped appearance of the flesh that is thus obtained. Is the mere shape of the food, then, of such consequence? Can anyone really be so childish? And perhaps fish do not feel; I cannot know, but I am pretty sure, from what I have seen, that those to whom these puerilities are of such consuming importance, number such unprofitable speculations among the least of their worries. However, I think we can agree that birds are capable of feeling, and I am given to understand that live ducks are crushed in a press for some outlandish dish designed for connoisseurs of food, and that larks and other song-birds are killed by thousands in some countries, and cooked to feed the delicate sensualism of epicures. I cannot believe that these little songsters were put on earth to feed gross appetites, but to give joy to mankind in another way, and even this gift of song is perverted by the bird-catchers, who have been known to blind the tiny eyes with needles, so the helpless little creatures should sing unceasingly, and then to put them in the nets as bait.

Vivisection may be necessary, lamentably, and medical men of the utmost honesty and sincerity may be working by this means for the good of humanity, and are perhaps as merciful as circumstances allow. We understand that important results are sometimes obtained. Yet the importance of the findings provides little surcease from suffering for the poor dumb brutes that are subjected for hours, even days, to excruciating agonies on our behalf. And many a cold-blooded torturer of sadistic inclinations performs, in the name of research, as has been proved, terrible experiments that are of little or no benefit to the human race. And benefit or no, I think the price is too great for any living creature to be called upon to pay, far greater than we have any right to ask.

Personally, I could not ever feel at ease if I knew that I had prolonged my not so important life by the infliction of long-drawn-out and agonizing pain on perhaps hundreds of helpless and inoffensive creatures, tortured until they died in misery that I might live, who some day must die in any case.

Every living creature is parasitical to some degree, in one way or another, on some other form of life, in order to live; but man extracts tribute from everything, even including the less fortunate of his own kind. Almost always he extorts far beyond his needs, destroying without thought for the future—the parasite supreme of all the earth. And in spite of the high position he has gained, he has still much to learn of tolerance, moderation and forbearance towards not only the lesser of created things, but towards his fellowman.

And now I have discovered, in my slow way, that it is actually necessary in this day and age of our civilization, to enact legislation forbidding the exploitation of children in industry, and that in one year thousands of young people were injured, and not a few killed at their work, whilst profiteers waxed rich on the proceeds of their cheap labour. It is more than a little saddening to find that even children fall a prey to the predatory instincts of a mercenary ogre, and when I first heard of it, I found some difficulty in believing that it could be true and still cannot quite grasp why a *law* should be necessary to put a stop to it.

And now, have I offended you, my readers? It has not been my intention. But if in my ignorance and little knowledge I have erred, it is because in my late travels in the centres of civilization I have seen and heard much that was unexpected, some of it not easy to grasp and leaving me at times a little bewildered. We who live in the woods have different standards—not all of them good.

* * * * * *

I am still a hunter, in a little different way. The camera is my weapon today. It is, after all, more fun, and if sport is the object, a lot harder. Yet hunting calls into play many manly attributes and I would not, if I could, lay a hand to the suppression of this most noble sport (I do not refer here to either fox, stag, or otter hunting with hounds, all of which are, to my way of thinking, grossly unfair and exceedingly unsportsmanlike)—noble, that is, if carried on with at least a reasonable consideration for those creatures that are giving, not for your necessity, Mr. Sportsman, but for your amusement, all they have to give—their lives. I go so far as to say that in most cases, the circumstances of the hunt mean more to the average hunter—if he is a sportsman—than the actual kill itself. The healthful, invigorating exercise, the beauties of the scenic Wilderness, the zest of such achievements as are necessary in order to get around in a rough country, the tonic properties of the pure, fresh air, the association with his guides, the hearty meals over crackling camp fires, the romance and the adventure—all these things go to make a hunt worth while. And if you are lucky, a good, clean, merciful kill is excusable, provided the animal is put to proper use and not killed for the sake of its eye-teeth or a pair of horns, while several hundred pounds of the very best of meat are allowed to lie in the woods to rot. And hunting has this to recommend it, that everything you get you work for.

Me, I kill no more, unless in case of absolute necessity, having had perhaps my share and over. Some prefer to have a den full of trophies; others a hunting-lodge decorated with skins, maybe. Each to his own taste; I like mine alive.

I make no false claims that I am out especially to try and do the public good, or that I have some "message" for the world. I am only trying to do what little is within my power for those creatures amongst whom my life has been passed. And if by so doing I can also be of some little service to my fellow-man, the opportunity becomes a twofold privilege. I do not expect to accomplish much in the short span that is left to me, but hope to assist, even if only in a minor role, in laying a foundation on which abler hands and better heads may later build. In this way I may perhaps be instrumental, at least to some extent, in the work of saving from entire destruction some of those interesting and useful dwellers in our waste places, in whom lie unexpected possibilities that await but a little kindness and understanding to develop—the rank and file of that vast, inarticulate army of living creatures from whom we can never hear.

Quite the most interesting of the developments that have arisen from this self-imposed task of mine, has been the opportunity given me of coming into contact with people from every walk of life. I have been privileged to make many friends, and expect to make some more. These experiences are valuable to me, and apart from their educational angle and the broadening effect they have on my views in general, I enjoy them.

One of my most absorbing tasks is that of answering the letters I receive from schools. Some arc written in a childish scrawl, some are smudged, others extremely neat with the lettering all erect and very soldierly; but everyone is so carefully inscribed, and all bear the signs of the labour that has been put into them by their intensely sincere and hopeful writers labours of love if ever there were any. And in this, above all things, am I greatly honoured. I try to answer them all, either collectively, or through their teachers, or, if the case should call for it, individually; for this is a responsibility I may not shirk.

This is to me my most important correspondence, for I feel that by this means it is given to mc to build, even if only a very little, and to implant in fertile minds, anxious for knowledge, seeds that perhaps will blossom into deeds after the planter has been long forgotten.

Focus Questions

1. How do D.C. Scott's depictions of Aboriginal people compare to those presented by Champlain (see Chapter One)? Why do you think he believed these things about Aboriginal people, and how are his views made more dangerous by his occupation?

   - Champlain thought Aboriginals would assimilate eventually
   - Scott's trying to maintain good appearances but Aboriginals = Assimilated
   "lost child in a whiteman's world"

2. What kinds of messages were Johnson, Grey Owl, and Emily Carr, trying to send to Canadians about Aboriginal peoples?

3. Imagine that these four brief readings, in some far distant future, are all the evidence that remains of Canada and Canadians. What sorts of conclusions and observations would be drawn about the people who wrote them, and about the people they wrote about?

8

A Great War and a Great Divide:
Canadian Voices in
World War I

Introduction

The 'Great War' of 1914–18 is often described as a pivotal moment in the emergence of a distinct and independent national identity—a moment when the country emerged out of its childhood dependence on Great Britain and earned a respected place on the world stage. Historically, this transformation is most often linked to the impressive Canadian victory at Vimy Ridge in April of 1917. The capture of this strategic landmark is arguably the most well known of all battles in which Canadians participated (and in this case led)—and it is certainly the one possessing the most spectacular memorial to Canada's fallen. Through the emphasis on battles like Vimy Ridge, the Great War (or World War I as it is now known) has most often been described through, linked with, and defined by, the experiences of the fighting men. The trenches and gas attacks, the physical and emotional horrors of the battles, stand out as its most vivid features. The final reading in this chapter, an extract from the memoirs of Canadian Lieutenant Colonel D.E. Macintyre, gives one man's vivid memories of these conditions and the sense of triumph and nationalism that he felt after the battle.

But behind the actions of soldiers, pilots, and sailors who fought the war, were many other voices, often silenced by the weight of history and the staggering lists of Canadian combat casualties. It is to these often forgotten voices that this chapter also turns its attentions, in order to present an alternate view of how the Great War was viewed by other Canadians. First, through a series of speeches made by the then-Prime Minister Robert Borden, readers can trace the subtle, but insistent shift in his appreciation of how the war would affect Canada's place in the Empire. While Bordon does not press outright for Canadian independence, it is clear that this idea had been firmly planted in his consciousness over the course of the war. His insistence, at war's end, that Canada be granted its own seat at the League of Nations, is foreshadowed by these early texts. Second, this chapter turns to the voice of a women who was, at the start of the war, a pacifist: Nellie McClung. McClung, however, was also a mother, and like so many other women, she had a son fighting in the war. Here, she presents her opinion on the conflict—"not that it matters"—in a brief essay written in 1915. Both Borden and McClung's voices demonstrate, in very different ways, how the Great War was as divisive as it was unifying.

There is also the impassioned voice of Henri Bourassa, one of Canada's most articulate nationalists. Bourassa believed that the war was contrary to spirit of the nation, and detrimental to the cause of Canada's independence. As a French Canadian, however, his voice was often overpowered or simply dismissed. Indeed, during World War I, tensions between English and French Canadians were at an all time high. Culminating in the Conscription Crisis of 1917, there are some who believed that the Great War brought with it a great divide—a rupture between French and English Canadians that has never been fully repaired.

WAR AS A CATALYST
FOR INDEPENDENCE

Wartime Speeches
Sir Robert Borden

December 29, 1914 Canadian Club, Winnipeg

It is within the bounds of probability that the four free nations of the Overseas Dominions will have put into the fighting line 250,000 men if the war should continue another year. That result, or even the results which have already been obtained, must mark a great epoch in the history of inter-Imperial relations. There are those, within sound of my voice, who will see the Oversea Dominions surpass in wealth and population the British Isles. There are children playing in your streets who may see Canada alone attain that eminence. Thus it is impossible to believe that the existing status, so far as concerns the control of foreign policy and extra-Imperial relations, can remain as it is to-day. All are conscious of the complexity of the problem thus presented, but no one need despair of a satisfactory solution, and no one can doubt the profound influence which the tremendous events of the past few months and those in the immediate future must exercise upon one of the most interesting and far-reaching questions ever presented for the consideration of statesmen.

At a Meeting of the United Kingdom Branch of the Empire Parliamentary Association, House of Commons, July 13th, 1915

I appreciate very sincerely, and very warmly as well, what Mr. Bonar Law said with regard to the part which Canada has played in this great contest. There was no doubt in my own mind as to what that part would be, and I took the responsibility four days before the actual declaration of war of sending a message to His Majesty's Government stating that, if war should unhappily supervene, they might be assured that Canada would regard the quarrel as her own, and would do her part in maintaining the integrity of this Empire and all that this war means to us. We are not a military nation in Canada; we are a peace-loving and peace-pursuing people with great tasks of development within our own Dominions lying before us. Thus, for a struggle such as this, upon so gigantic a scale, we were naturally unprepared. But even so, relatively unprepared as we were, the Minister of Militia and Defence in Canada succeeded in placing upon the Plain of Valcartier, within six weeks of the outbreak of war, a force of 33,000 men, thoroughly armed and equipped in every branch of the Service—artillery, commissariat, Army Service Corps, and all the vast organisation that is necessary in war as carried on in the present day.

We have sent overseas up to the present time nearly 75,000 men, including troops which are doing garrison duty in the West Indies. We have in Canada to-day 75,000 men in training, with organisation being prepared as rapidly as possible for their advent to the front when needed. The response from every province in Canada, indeed, has been so warm, so impressive, so inspiring, that our difficulty has been to secure arms and equipment and material and all that is necessary to enable our men to go to the front. So far as the men were concerned they were there in abundance. So far as the other preparations were concerned we have been very much in the same condition as yourselves, unprepared for war upon so tremendous a scale.

Looking back on what we had to face and upon what we had to contend with, I venture to think that the condition of affairs to-day is one upon which we should rather congratulate ourselves than otherwise. I have no fear for the future, although the struggle may be a long one and may entail sacrifices which we did not anticipate at first. I think I may bring to you from the people of Canada this message, that in whatever is necessary to bring this war to an honourable and triumphal conclusion, Canada is prepared to take her part. And I am sure that is true of every dominion of the Empire.

What a fantastic picture it was that Prussian militarism made for itself before the outbreak of this war. It pictured Canada, Australia, and New Zealand standing aloof and indifferent, or seeking an opportunity to cut themselves aloof from this Empire. What is the actual picture to-day? They are bound to the Empire by stronger ties than ever before, and are prepared to fight to the death for the maintenance of its integrity and for the preservation of our common civilisation throughout the world.

We have nothing to fear at the outcome of this war. We do not and dare not doubt the success of the cause for which the British Empire and the Allied nations are fighting to-day. It is impossible to believe that the democracies of the British Empire, even though unprepared on so tremendous a scale as our opponents for such a war as this, will not prove their efficiency in this day of peril. They have proved it, and I think they will prove it in the future. In the later days when peace comes to be proclaimed, and after the conclusion of peace, it is beyond question that large matters will come up for consideration by the statesmen of the United Kingdom and the Overseas Dominions. It is not desirable, nor perhaps becoming, that I should dwell upon these considerations to-day. I said what I had to say on the subject with considerable frankness and some emphasis three years ago when I had the pleasure of addressing you.

What I said then represents my convictions now. I do not doubt the problems which will be presented, exceedingly difficult and complex as they are, will find a wise and just solution, and in thanking you for the reception which you have accorded me to-day, and for the honour which you have done to the Dominion which I represent as its Prime Minister, let me express the hope and aspiration that in confronting the immense responsibilities which devolve upon those inheriting so great an Empire as ours, and one which must necessarily command so profound an influence on the future of civilisation and the destiny of the world, we shall so bear ourselves, whether in these mother islands or in the Overseas Dominions, that the future shall hold in store no reproach for us for lack of vision, want of courage, or failure of duty.

At the Guildhall, on Being Presented with the Freedom of the City of London, July 29th, 1915.

While it may not be fitting that one of our kindred should speak, of the British people as a great race, I may be permitted to say that it has wrought great things, and that the greatest of all its achievements is the upbuilding of an Empire bound together by such ties as those which unite ours.

In the beginning, in the founding of the nation within these islands, there was need for orderly government, and that made necessary a strong and autocratic system of government. But, as the years rolled on, there came to the people the right to govern themselves. Orderly government, individual liberty, equal rights before the people—upon these secure foundations the fabric of the national life was erected, and in these later days has come the not less noble ideal of a democracy founded upon equality of opportunity for all the people before the conditions of modern life.

In the Dominions beyond the seas, the same ideals of liberty and of justice have led inevitably to the establishment of self-governing institutions. Their development there has been very much the same as within your own islands, and those short-sighted ones who believed that the right to govern themselves would drive the far-flung nations of our Empire asunder, have found that that very circumstance, and that free development, have united them by ties stronger than would be possible under and system of autocratic government.

I have listened with the deepest possible appreciation to the words which have been spoken of the action of Canada in this war. That action was due to no Government, to no statesman or group of statesmen. It was due to the spirit of the Canadian people, a spirit which will make the cause for which we are contending victorious, and which will pervade the Dominions to the end. I do not need to tell you of the part that Canada has played and the part she proposes to play. But it might not be amiss for a moment to allude to the remarkable circumstance that four great Overseas Dominions, self-governing Dominions of the Empire, have been actuated by a common impulse at this juncture—Australia, New Zealand, South Africa, Canada! Why have all these great free nations sent their men from the remotest corners of the earth to fight side by side with you of this island home in this quarrel? Why in Canada do we see those who are the descendants of those who fought under Wolfe, and of those who fought under Montcalm, standing side by side in the battle-line of the Empire? Why, coming down to later days, do we see the grandson of a Durham, and the grandson of a Papineau, standing shoulder to shoulder beyond the Channel in France or Belgium? When the historian of the future comes to analyse the events which made it possible for the Empire to stand like this, he will see that there must have been some over-mastering impulse contributing to this wonderful result.

One such impulse is to be found in the love of liberty, the pursuit of ideals of democracy, and the desire and determination to preserve the spirit of unity founded on those ideals, which make the whole Empire united in aim and single in purpose. But there was, also, in all the Overseas Dominions, the intense conviction that this war was forced upon the Empire—that we could not with honour stand aside and see trampled underfoot the liberties and independence of a weak and unoffending nation whose independence we had guaranteed. And, above and beyond all that, was the realisation of the supreme truth—that the quarrel in which we are engaged transcends even the destinies of our own Empire and involves the future of civilisation and of the world.

Last week I looked into the keen, intent faces, of 10,000 Canadian soldiers, within sound and range of the German guns. Three days ago I looked into the undaunted eyes of 1,000 Canadian convalescents returned from the valley of the shadow of death. In the eyes, and in the faces of those men, I read only one message—that of resolute and unflinching determination to make our cause triumphant; to preserve our institutions and our liberties, to maintain the unity of our Empire and its influence through the world. That message, which I bring to you from those soldiers, I bring you also from the great Dominion which has sent those men across the sea.

While the awful shadow of this war overhangs our Empire, I shall not pause to speak of what may be evolved in its constitutional relations. Upon what has been built in the past it is possible, in my judgment, that an even nobler and more enduring fabric may be erected. That structure must embody the autonomy of the self-governing Dominions and of the British Isles as well, but it must also embody the majesty and power of an Empire united by ties such as those of which I have spoken, and more thoroughly and effectively organised for the purpose of preserving its own existence. Those who shall be the architects of this monument will have a great part to play, and I do not doubt that they will play it worthily. To those who shall be called to design so splendid a fabric, crowning the labours of the past and embodying all the hopes of the future, we all of us bid God speed in their great task.

THE (FRENCH) CANADIAN NATIONALIST PERSPECTIVE

Wartime Editorials
Henri Bourassa,
(translated by Joseph Levitt)
1914

On Canada's Entry into World War I[1]

. . . . To those of my friends who ask me with anguish if I approve to-day of what I had forseen and condemned since 1899—the participation of Canada in English wars, foreign to Canada—I answer without hesitation: no!

Canada as an irresponsible dependency of Great Britain has no moral or constitutional obligation nor any immediate interest in the present conflict.

Great Britain has entered it on her own account, in consequence of an international situation where she took a position only to safeguard her own interests, without consulting her colonies and without regard to their situation or their particular interests.

The Canadian territory is nowhere exposed to the attacks of the belligerent nations. As an independent nation, Canada would to-day enjoy perfect security. The very far-off dangers to her trade may result from the fact that as a British possession she undergoes perforce the counter blows to a policy of which Great Britain is alone mistress and to an intervention for which the British authorities are alone responsible. It is then the duty of England to defend Canada and not that of Canada to defend England.

Moreover in protecting the territory and trade of its colonies England is assuring its own proper subsistance.

Great Britain herself in this war runs a minimum of danger and will gain from it substantial benefits, no matter what happens.

In law and in fact, Canada, a British colony, has then no direct reason to intervene in the conflict. There are many serious ones, for abstaining; and the future will undertake to show, too harshly perhaps, that its military intervention, not very effective for nations at war, will have disastrous consequences for it. . . .

Independent of these colonial "obligations", void by virtue of history, the constitution and the facts, can Canada, as an embryonic nation or if one wishes, as a human community, remain indifferent to the European conflict?

To this question, as to the first, I answer without hesitation: no!

Canada, an Anglo-French nation, tied to England and France by a thousand ethnic, social, intellectual and economic threads, has a vital interest in the maintenance of the prestige, power and world action of France and England.

It is therefore its national duty to contribute, to the measure of its strength and by appropriate means, to the triumph and above all the *endurance* of the combined efforts of France and England.

But to make this contribution effective, Canada must begin by facing resolutely its real situation, by making an exact count of what it can do or not do, and to assure its internal security, before beginning or pursuing an effort which it will not be in a condition to sustain to the end.

On Empires and Nationalities[2]

No race, no nation has the right to claim the supremacy of the world.

England has no more right to appeal to its colonies to ensure its command over the seas than Germany has a right to ask Europe to ensure it the command of the land.

What we formerly claimed for the Boer republic, what we claimed for national Ireland, what we insist on to-day for the French Canadians of Ontario, is the right of all peoples, all nationalities to live. We deny to any race, whatever it may be, we deny to any people, however grand it may be, however high its aspirations, however noble its traditions, however numerous its fleets, however powerful its armies, the right to impose its yoke, beneficial or harmful, on other peoples of the earth; and we say that it is profound hypocrisy to claim to bring about peace and friendship between peoples by opposing the hegemony of one nation to that of another nation. The English yoke is no more legitimate than the German yoke.

One day in 1899 I heard an Englishman claim seriously that England was rendering a real service to the little Dutch republics by imposing its conquest, after having torn up the *scrap of paper* which guaranteed them their independence, under the seal of the English Crown. To become English was in itself such a precious advantage that the Boers could well buy it at the price of any sacrifice. This is what we deny. Neither the France of Louis XIV nor of Napoleon had the right to run her chariot over the peoples of Europe; neither the England of Marlborough, of Nelson, of Chamberlain, had the right to impose the British constitution on those who did not freely wish it; neither Russia nor Germany have the right to aspire to the domination of Europe or Asia; and as a convinced nationalist—a Canadian nationalist and a British nationalist—I assert to-day that it is our right and our duty to fight English imperialism as well as German imperialism: it is our right and duty to affirm that the young Canadian nation, separated by the designs of Providence from the continent of Europe, ought to follow a free course on American soil, a peaceful course, ought to make itself strong, develop its institutions, build its forces and search out its future without tying itself body and soul, without sacrificing the lives and the blood of its children to help settle the world's conflicts.

Ladies and Gentlemen, perhaps I am offending the sentiments of some of you. But look at it from another point of view. Suppose Canada was attacked to-morrow by the United States in a war against England, or even as a result of an act of Canada itself: how many Belgians, how many Frenchmen, how many Germans would come from Europe to fight in the ranks of the Canadian army or those of the American army? We are trying to convince our compatriots that Canadians should put their duty to Canada first, before their responsibilities to England or France. There, in sum, is the reason for our struggles against imperialism.

On French Canadian Enlistment[3]

. . . [Capt. Papineau] takes the French-Canadians to task and challenges their patriotism, because they enlist in lesser number than the other elements of the population of Canada. Much could be said upon that. It is sufficient to signalise one patent fact: the number of recruits for the European war, in the various Provinces of Canada and from each component element of the population, is in inverse ratio of the enrootment in the soil and the traditional patriotism arising therefrom. The newcomers from the British Isles have enlisted in much larger proportion than English-speaking Canadians born in this country, while these have enlisted more than the French-Canadians. The Western Provinces have given more recruits than Ontario, and Ontario more than Quebec. In each Province, the floating population of the cities, the students, the labourers and clerks, either unemployed or threatened with dismissal, have supplied more soldiers than the farmers. Does it mean that the city dwellers are more patriotic than the country people? or that the newcomers from England are better Canadians than their fellow-citizens of British origin, born in Canada? No; it simply means that in Canada, as in every other country, at all times, the citizens of the oldest origin are the least disposed to be stampeded into distant ventures of no direct concern to their native land. It proves also that military service is more repugnant to the rural than the urban populations.

There is among the French-Canadians a larger proportion of farmers, fathers of large families, than among any other ethnical element in Canada. Above all, the

French-Canadians are the only group exclusively Canadian, in its whole and by each of the individuals of which it is composed. They look upon the perturbations of Europe, even those of England or France, as foreign events. Their sympathies naturally go to France against Germany; but they do not think they have an obligation to fight for France, no more than the French of Europe would hold themselves bound to fight for Canada against the United, States or Japan, or even against Germany, in case Germany should attack Canada without threatening France.

English Canada, not counting the *blokes,* contains a considerable proportion of people still in the first period of national incubation. Under the sway of imperialism, a fair number have not yet decided whether their allegiance is to Canada or to the Empire, whether the United Kingdom or the Canadian Confederacy is their country.

As to the newcomers from the United Kingdom, they are not Canadian in any sense. England or Scotland is their sole fatherland. They have enlisted for the European war as naturally as Canadians, either French or English, would take arms to defend Canada against an aggression on the American continent.

If English-speaking Canadians have a right to blame the French-Canadians for the small number of their recruits, the newcomers from the United Kingdom, who have supplied a much larger proportion of recruits than any other element of the population, would be equally justified in branding the Anglo-Canadians with disloyalty and treason. Enlistment for the European war is supposed to be absolutely free and voluntary. This has been stated right and left from beginning to end. If that statement is honest and sincere, all provocations from one part of the population against the other, and exclusive attacks against the French-Canadians, should cease. Instead of reviling unjustly one-third of the Canadian people—a population so remarkably characterised by its constant loyalty to national institutions and its respect for public order,—those men who claim a right to enlighten and lead public opinion should have enough good faith and intelligence to see facts as they are and to respect the motives of those who persist in their determination to remain more Canadian than English or French.

The jingo press and politicians have also undertaken to persuade their gullible followers that the Nationalists hinder the work of recruiters *because* of the persecution meted out to the French minorities in Ontario and Manitoba.* This is but another nonsense. My excellent cousin, I am sorry to say,—or his inspirer—has picked it up.

The two questions are essentially distinct, this we have never ceased to assert. One is purely internal; the other affects the international status of Canada and her relations with Great Britain. To the problem of the teaching of languages we ask for a solution in conformity with the spirit of the Federal agreement, the best interests of Confederation, and the principles of pedagogy as applied in civilised countries. Our attitude on the participation of Canada in the war is inspired exclusively by the constant tradition of the country and the agreements concluded half a century ago between Canada and Great Britain. Even if the irritating bilingual question was non-existent,

*Bourrasa refers here to controversies over the maintenance of French-language schools in these provinces.

our views on the war would be what they are. The most that can be said is, that the backward and essentially Prussian policy of the rulers of Ontario and Manitoba gives us an additional argument against the intervention of Canada in the European conflict. To speak of fighting for the preservation of French civilisation in Europe while endeavouring to destroy it in America, appears to us as an absurd piece of inconsistency. To preach Holy War for the liberties of the peoples overseas, and to oppress the national minorities in Canada, is, in our opinion, nothing but odious hypocrisy.

The Case Against Conscription[4]

Most of the following statement appeared in the *Evening Post* (New York) of July 10. It was published in full in *Le Devoir,* July 12.

We are opposed to further enlistments for the war in Europe, whether by conscription or otherwise, for the following reasons: (1) Canada has already made a military display, in men and money, proportionately superior to that of any nation engaged in the war; (2) any further weakening of the man-power of the country would seriously handicap agricultural production and other essential industries; (3) an increase in the war budget of Canada spells national bankruptcy; (4) it threatens the economic life of the nation and, eventually, its political independence; (5) conscription means national disunion and strife, and would thereby hurt the cause of the Allies to a much greater extent than the addition of a few thousand soldiers to their fighting forces could bring them help and comfort.

1.—Military Effort

Canada has already supplied 420,000 men to the Imperial forces of Great Britain[5]— not counting the numerous French or Italian reservists, who have rejoined their respective colours in their native lands. This is equivalent, in proportion to population, to an army of 2,400,000 men for France, 2,700,000 for Great Britain and Ireland, 6,000,000 for the United States.

If the proportionate cost of the armies is taken into account, as well as the population of the countries, Canada's war expenditure is now equivalent to what France would spend for a fighting force of 9,600,000 men, Great Britain for 8,100,000 and the United States for 7,000,000. Which of those countries has done or *will do* as much?[6]

It should be remembered, also, that over one half of the Canadian contingent is composed of British-born volunteers, who, instead of enlisting in the British section of the Imperial army, have preferred joining the Canadians, thereby receiving from Canada a pay four times as high as that of Great Britain.

Finally, when we know that England is still keeping at home, for profitable purposes, at least three million of her own men, enlisted or serviceable, we sincerely believe that we have done more than, our share.

2.—*Labour and Agricultural Crisis*

To realize the extent of the labour crisis, one must know the conditions of the country. The scanty population of 7,000,000 is scattered over a territory as large as that of the United States. The present army of 420,000, to which must be added at least 20,000 to 30,000 foreign reservists, has been recruited without the slightest regard to local or special conditions, or the technical competency of the recruits. Certain industries, as the extraction of coal, for example, have been disorganized. For want of labour, land under cultivation is much less this year than last,—and this, at the very moment the supply of food is likely to be the main factor of the situation in Europe.

Canadian farming has remained and will remain short of more than 60,000 labourers, the help of whom was considered by our government as *absolutely, necessary* to ensure the required production of foodstuffs. How then can we accept, from the same government, the suggestion of increasing the fatal gap by the further enlistment of 100,000 men for military operations in Europe?

It must not be forgotten that, in England and France, thousands of men are periodically recalled from the trenches and put at work on the farms, during seed and harvest times. This is impossible in Canada. Once in Europe, our soldiers are there to stay till the end of the war, and a good while after. The wounded and the crippled alone are brought back, to help in impoverishing the country.

If Canada persists in her run towards extreme militarism, in order to supply the armies of Europe with a number of men wholly insufficient to influence the fate of arms, she will soon find herself utterly unable to give to the Allied nations the real help which ought to be, and could be, her most valuable contribution to the common cause: nourishment.

3.—*National Bankruptcy*

Canada is a country of immense natural wealth, still undeveloped. But it is poor in money. Even before the war, it was practically living on borrowed money. The highest authority on economics, in the British Empire, Sir George Parish, estimated Canada's total indebtedness, on the eve of the war, at $3,000,000,000—over $400 per head of population. Out of that amount, $300,000,000 represented the federal or national debt, piled up in half a century. Within 3½ years, $1,000,000,000 will have been added to that national debt for war purposes alone. In other words, Canada in less than four years will have borrowed, for destructive purposes, three times as much as in the previous fifty years for constructive work. What the result will be after the war when the transient activity of munition making and army equipping collapses suddenly and entirely is easier to imagine than to cope with. Nothing further at least should be done to make it worse.

4.—*Menace To American Peace*

We, Canadian Nationalists, hold that Canada has not the right to commit suicide for the sake of any European or humanitarian cause, excellent as it may be. It must live and do honour to its own obligations. It must also keep the *pax americana,* and not sow the seeds of future strifes with its only neighbour. British politics brought it twice to war with the United States, in 1774 and 1812, and twice at least on the verge of conflict, during the Secession war and the Venezuela embroilment. We do not want Canada to raise a quarrel of its own; we do not want to see it reduced to such a state of financial despondency that the money lenders of the United States will have to recoup themselves at the expense of our national independence. A free Canada—free politically, free economically—and a peaceful America are more important to us than the establishment of democratic governments in Europe, or the settlement of the Balkan problem.

5.—*National Disunion and Strife*

Conscription is sure to bring serious troubles in the labour circles. Indiscriminate enlistment has already disorganized labour conditions. Rightly or wrongly, labour leaders apprehend that conscription is sought for not so much for military purposes as with the object of controlling wages and work. The enforcement of conscription will certainly be resisted by the organized labour of Canada.

There is also in Canada a large foreign element to which conscription is distasteful to the extreme. Most of these foreigners were invited to come. The government paid premiums to secure them. They were assured that Canada was free from military service. They have therefore against conscription a case much stronger than that of the so-called "hyphenated" Americans.

The situation and sentiments of the French-Canadians, who form between one third and one fourth of the population of Canada, have also to be reckoned with. Such silly things have appeared about them in some of the English-Canadian papers, and occasionally in the American press, that elementary truths have to be recalled.

In spite of all statements to the contrary, the French-Canadians are loyal to Great Britain and friendly to France; but they do not acknowledge to either country what, in every land, is considered as the most exclusively national duty: the obligation to bear arms and fight.

The only trouble with the French Canadians is that they remain the only true "unhyphenated" Canadians. Under the sway of British Imperialism, Canadians of British origin have become quite unsettled as to their allegiance: they have not yet made up their mind whether they are more British than Canadian, or more Canadian than British; whether they are the citizens of a world-scattered empire, or members of an American community. The French-Canadians have remained, and want to remain, exclusively Canadian and American.

Opposition to conscription and warmadness in Canada is not anti-patriotic: it is essentially patriotic and clear-sighted.

Endnotes

1. "On Canada's Entry into World War I," Henri Bourassa, *Le Devoir,* September 8, 1914, in *Issues in Canadian History: Henri Bourassa on Imperialism and Bi-Culturalism, 1900–1918,* edited by Joseph Levitt, The Copp Clark Publishing Company, 1970.
2. "Empires and Nationalities," Henri Bourassa, *Le 5e anniversaire du Devoir,* Montreal, 1915, pp. 44–45 in *Issues in Canadian History: Henri Bourassa on Imperialism and Bi-Culturalism, 1900–1918,* edited by Joseph Levitt, The Copp Clark Publishing Company, 1970.
3. "French Canadian Enlistment" by Henri Bourassa (1868–1952), *Canadian Nationalism and the War,* Montreal, 1916.
4. "The Case Against Conscription" by Henri Bourassa (1868–1952), *Win the War and Lose Canada,* Montreal, 1917.
5. Since this was written, the government has stated that over 60,000 recruits were dismissed as bodily unfit, or for other reasons, and that 10,000 had deserted. This alters the comparison with other nations, as regards the number of troops. But as to cost, it makes the position of Canada worse. The loss of money incurred by the dislocation of regimental units is tremendous.
6. Everything being counted, the basis of comparison with France and Great Britain is below the mark. France pays only 5 cents a day to her troopers, and Great Britain, one shilling.

WAR AND CANADIAN MOTHERS

What Do Women Think of War?
(Not That It Matters)
Nellie McClung
1915

> Bands in the street, and resounding cheers,
> And honor to him whom the army led!
> But his mother moans thro' her blinding tears—
> "My boy is dead—is dead!"

Since the war broke out women have done a great deal of knitting. Looking at this great army of women struggling with rib and back seam, some have seen nothing in it but a "fad" which has supplanted for the time tatting and bridge. But it is more than that. It is the desire to help, to care for, to minister; it is the same spirit which inspires our nurses to go out and bind up the wounded and care for the dying. The woman's outlook on life is to save, to care for, to help. Men make wounds and women bind them up, and so the women, with their hearts filled with love and sorrow, sit in their quiet homes and knit.

> Comforter—they call it—yes—
> So it is for my distress,
> For it gives my restless hands
> Blessed work. God understands
> How we women yearn to be
> Doing something ceaselessly.

Women have not only been knitting—they have been thinking. Among other things they have thought about the German women, those faithful, patient, homeloving, obedient women, who never interfere in public affairs, nor question man's ruling. The Kaiser says women have only two concerns in life, cooking and children, and

From *In Times Like These* by Nellie L. McClung.

the German women have accepted his dictum. They are good cooks and faithful nurses to their children.

According to the theories of the world, the sons of such women should be the gentlest men on earth. Their home has been so sacred, and well-kept; their mother has been so gentle, patient and unworldly—she has never lowered the standard of her womanhood by asking to vote, or to mingle in the "hurly burly" of politics. She has been humble, and loving, and always hoped for the best.

According to the theories of the world, the gentle sons of gentle mothers will respect and reverence all womankind everywhere. Yet, we know that in the invasion of Belgium, the German soldiers made a shield of Belgian women and children in front of their army; no child was too young, no woman too old, to escape their cruelty; no mother's prayers, no child's appeal could stay their fury! These chivalrous sons of gentle, loving mothers marched through the land of Belgium, their nearest neighbor, leaving behind them smoking trails of ruin, black as their own hard hearts!

What, then, is the matter with the theory? Nothing, except that there is nothing in it—it will not work. Women who set a low value on themselves make life hard for all women. The German woman's ways have been ways of pleasantness, but her paths have not been paths of peace; and now, women everywhere are thinking of her, rather bitterly. Her peaceful, humble, patient ways have suddenly ceased to appear virtuous in our eyes and we see now, it is not so much a woman's duty to bring children into the world, as to see what sort of a world she is bringing them into, and what their contribution will be to it. Bertha Krupp has made good guns and the German women have raised good soldiers—if guns and soldiers can be called "good"—and between them they have manned the most terrible and destructive war machine that the world has ever known. We are not grateful to either of them.

The nimble fingers of the knitting women are transforming balls of wool into socks and comforters, but even a greater change is being wrought in their own hearts. Into their gentle souls have come bitter thoughts of rebellion. They realize now how little human life is valued, as opposed to the greed and ambition of nations. They think bitterly of Napoleon's utterance on the subject of women—that the greatest woman in the world is the one who brings into the world the greatest number of sons; they also remember that he said that a boy could stop a bullet as well as a man, and that God is on the side of the heaviest artillery. From these three statements they get the military idea of women, children, and God, and the heart of the knitting woman recoils in horror from the cold brutality of it all. They realize now something of what is in back of all the opposition to the woman's advancement into all lines of activity and a share in government.

Women are intended for two things, to bring children into the world and to make men comfortable, and then they must keep quiet and if their hearts break with grief, let them break quietly—that's all. No woman is so unpopular as the noisy woman who protests against these things.

The knitting women know now why the militant suffragettes broke windows and destroyed property, and went to jail for it joyously, and without a murmur—it was the protest of brave women against the world's estimate of woman's position. It was the world-old struggle for liberty. The knitting women remember now with shame and sorrow that they have said hard things about the suffragettes, and thought they were unwomanly and hysterical. Now they know that womanliness, and peaceful gentle ways, prayers, petitions and tears have long been tried but are found wanting; and now they know that these brave women in England, maligned, ridiculed, persecuted, as they were, have been fighting every woman's battle, fighting for the recognition of human life, and the mother's point of view. Many of the knitting women have seen a light shine around their pathway, as they have passed down the road from the heel to the toe, and they know now that the explanation cannot be accepted any longer that the English women are "crazy." That has been offered so often and been accepted.

Crazy! That's such an easy way to explain actions which we do not understand. Crazy! and it gives such a delightful thrill of sanity to the one who says it—such a pleasurable flash of superiority!

Oh, no, they have not been crazy, unless acts of heroism and suffering for the sake of others can be described as crazy! The knitting women wish now that there had been "crazy" women in Germany to direct the thought of the nation to the brutality of the military system, to have aroused the women to struggle for a human civilization, instead of a masculine civilization such as they have now. They would have fared badly of course, even worse than the women in England, but they are faring badly now, and to what purpose? The women of Belgium have fared badly. After all, the greatest thing in life is not to live comfortably—it is to live honorably, and when that becomes impossible, to die honorably!

The woman who knits is thinking sadly of the glad days of peace, now unhappily gone by, when she was so sure it was her duty to bring children into the world. She thinks of the glad rapture with which she looked into the sweet face of her first-born twenty years ago—the brave lad who went with the first contingent, and is now at the front. She was so sure then that she had done a noble thing in giving this young life to the world. He was to have been a great doctor, a great healer, one who bound up wounds, and make weak men strong—and now—in the trenches, he stands, this lad of hers, with the weapons of death in his hands, with bitter hatred in his heart, not binding wounds, but making them, sending poor human beings out in the dark to meet their Maker, unprepared, surrounded by sights and sounds that must harden his heart or break it. Oh! her sunny-hearted lad! So full of love and tenderness and pity, so full of ambition and high resolves and noble impulses, he is dead—dead already—and in his place there stands "private 355," a man of hate, a man of blood! Many a time the knitting has to be laid aside, for the bitter tears blur the stitches.

The woman who knits thinks of all this and now she feels that she who brought this boy into the world, who is responsible for his existence, has some way been to blame. Is life really such a boon that any should crave it? Do we really confer a favor on the innocent little souls we bring into the world, or do we owe them an apology?

She thinks now of Abraham's sacrifice, when he was willing at God's command to offer his dearly beloved son on the altar; and now she knows it was not so hard for Abraham, for he knew it was God who asked it, and he had God's voice to guide him! Abraham was sure, but about this—who knows?

Then she thinks of the little one who dropped out of the race before it was well begun, and of the inexplicable smile of peace which lay on his small white face, that day, so many years ago now, when they laid him away with such sorrow, and such agony of loss. She understands now why the little one smiled, while all around him wept.

And she thinks enviously of her neighbor across the way, who had no son to give, the childless woman for whom in the old days she felt so sorry, but whom now she envies. She is the happiest woman of all—so thinks the knitting woman, as she sits alone in her quiet house; for thoughts can grow very bitter when the house is still and the boyish voice is heard no more shouting, "Mother" in the hall.

> There, little girl, don't cry!
> They have broken your heart, I know.

WAR AND THE CANADIAN SOLDIER

Canada at Vimy

Lieutenant Colonel D. E. Macintyre, D.S.O., M.C.

The ground to be captured was the height of the ridge and the far slope. A supreme effort was to be made to end the enemy's domination of the high ground from which he threatened Arras and the roads to the Channel ports; but possession of this eminence alone was not enough.

The intention was to inflict a crushing defeat on the German forces, and to demonstrate to the world that we now had the strength in men and munitions to go on and win the war. A victory here would take the pressure off the French forces, which were being readied for a great assault at the Aisne, and help to convince doubtful nations and wavering allies that the might of the supposedly invincible German army could, and would, be broken.

It was to be expected that the enemy would defend this high ground with the utmost tenacity, no matter how dreadful the cost, and this indeed he did.

Zero hour was set for 5.30 a.m. The Artillery program was worked out with minute exactitude. The greatest concentration of guns yet witnessed on the Western front was to deliver the destructive fire that would pave the way for the infantry. Had all the guns on the Canadian side been ranged in one four-mile line, they would have been only 7 yards apart. Their object was to smother all effective opposition in the German front line, by laying down a continuous curtain of fire for three minutes, then lifting the barrage about 100 yards to the support line, with which it would deal thoroughly for five minutes, and so on at intervals of about 100 yards. At each range the fire would continue for from 3 to 6 minutes as it crept across the battlefield like a rain storm crossing a lake, [and] would continue the bombardment with unabated violence for 40 minutes in order to give the infantry time to close up, smash all resistance, mop up the dugouts and the machine gun nests, place blocks in communication trenches and do what they could to reverse the trench against any counterattack.

The operation was timed to be completed at 1.18 p.m. or seven hours and forty-eight minutes from the time the opening gun was fired. When the day of battle came action was related so closely to the time table that the written orders might almost be read as a description of the events which followed.

From "The Plan of Battle" from *Canada at Vimy* by Lieutenant Colonel D. E. Macintyre, D.S.O., M.C., Peter Martin Associates Limited, 1967. Reprinted by permission of the author's son, John Macintyre.

The tunnelers worked in day and night shifts to complete their hard tasks, especially in Zivy Tunnel, so essential for the free movement of our men to their assembly positions. They got it wired for electric light, the power being supplied by gas operated generators. In practice the batteries were not strong enough to supply us with light for more than twelve hours daily so that during the other twelve we burned candles.

The engineers also piped water through the tunnel, which saved an immense amount of labour as compared with the old method of sending tins of water up by carrying parties who often suffered casualties.

Activity in the air increased noticeably, and I saw three planes shot down in one day. One of them came down in flames—a terrible sight. Our observation planes flew many sorties every day when visibility permitted. They were the eyes of the army, reporting movements of troops and trains and sites of batteries. The photography squadrons took the pictures that revealed so much to the Intelligence Branch.

The engineers were pushing ahead with the construction of roads and a light railway system to reach as close to the front as possible.

A number of wide, deep trenches had to be bridged to permit the attacking waves, coming from supporting positions, to reach the front without delay.

Paths had to be cut through our own wire entanglements.

Dumps of all kinds of ammunition and materials were being assembled.

Water supply in the area was limited. Reservoirs, pumping stations and pipe had to be laid on. The Corps' daily consumption of water was 600,000 gallons.

Runners, stretcher bearers, burial parties and carrying parties were organized.

Zivy cave was fitted out with bunks, tables, cooking stoves, telephones, electric lights, running water and anything else that was essential. It would have to accommodate two brigade headquarters and five battalion headquarters, as well as about 400 fighting men, to be held there as a reserve.

Tension mounted as "Z" day approached, but we were all too busy to worry, and the work went forward methodically.

The gun fire on both sides had developed into a crescendo of violence impossible to describe for the intensive phase of the bombardment had opened on April 2nd. Guns fired until they were hot.

The Germans had known for some time that the attack was impending for they could not only see our preparations going forward, but were able to pick up telephone conversations with listening sets by induction through the ground. They could also feel the increasing weight of our gun fire, especially from our heavy batteries. The only uncertainty was the date of the attack so, in order to throw them off balance, heavy barrages were laid down on their front lines from time to time (the usual prelude to an attack) and, when no action followed, they became somewhat careless about the prompt manning of the trenches when the bombardment ceased, thinking it another false alarm.

We settled down as well as we could and I looked around me [in "Zivy" Cave].

The saturated ground above us leaked its moisture through the roof of the cave in a tiresome dribble on everything below—tables, beds and floor—so that there was always an inch or two of greyish white slime underfoot.

Scattered about on the floor, men could dimly be seen by the candle light, their grotesque shadows dancing on the adjoining walls. Some slept, fully clothed, their weapons near at hand, ready to surge upward at the first alarm. Others cleaned their arms while their comrades played cards or made tea over small fires. Numbers of soldiers, with their army clasp knives, carved their names and unit numbers in the firm chalk of the walls. Some of these would die on the morrow, but their names shall live for ever.

There was a constant movement of men entering or leaving the cave. The sound of talking, coughing, spitting and shuffling feet went on without ceasing. Sometimes a wounded man would be brought in by the stretcher bearers and, if his pain was greater than he could bear, his piteous cries would cause the wakeful to turn their heads and the sleepers to stir restlessly.

Carrying parties would arrive from outside and dump their loads; reliefs struggled up to the line, and tired, mud-covered men came back to snatch a little rest. The smell of foul air, mud, cooking, sweat, urine, chloride of lime, tobacco and candle smoke filled the atmosphere and was almost overpowering. And over and beyond all this there was the continuous, sullen rumble of gun fire, like a thunder storm. But with all these discomforts, it was a thousand times better than being outside.

I was worried about getting our troops undetected into their assembly positions, which were the old observation lines in No Man's Land, and two lines close behind it, so after dark I took Captain Jennings, who was acting Intelligence officer, and we went over the whole line, which our men had deepened and cleared of all the old wire obstacles.

There was plenty of water in these trenches and the Germans were so nervous that the noise of splashing often caused them to open fire at the sound. Rocket flares constantly were in the air, rising with a swift rush, then breaking into a bright white light at the summit and floating slowly back to earth, illuminating every detail of the forward area for a few seconds.

The German flares were better than ours, so we saved our taxpayers' money by allowing the Reich to bear most of this expense.

The lines were very close together in places, and when I tripped on a wire and fell awkwardly, we had a potato masher type of bomb thrown at us; but it buried itself in the muck and exploded like a damp squib.

The moon was up and giving a considerable amount of light. I became convinced that, if the moon was shining on the following night, the task of assembling thousands of men of the leading waves in their jumping-off lines without their presence being observed was going to be a very difficult one indeed.

Easter Sunday, the 8th, was a beautiful spring day, and I thought of the people at home going to church, of girls in their Easter finery, and of family gatherings. They could not know what we were to face on the morrow, and it was just as well. To the troops of both sides it was a quiet day and a welcome respite from the incessant noise. Our men knew what was coming and got what rest they could while the Germans were lulled into a false sense of security. Nevertheless, it was nauseating to contemplate the horrors that the representatives of two Christian nations would inflict on each other at this time of the Easter festival, each side believing that he was in the right.

Chaplains conducted services in the field wherever they could, but parades of this kind could not be held in the forward area.

General Rennie and the rest of his staff moved up during the afternoon and evening, and by 9 p.m. the crowd had reached the capacity of the cave.

The battlefield was bathed in moonlight, as I had feared, but the men in long lines in single file moved up steadily, each by his appointed communication trench.

Officers and men were dressed in battle order, with their haversacks strapped to the web equipment on their backs. Each man carried 120 rounds of cartridges, grenades, his rifle, bayonet and entrenching tool. They had no blankets or packs. In many units no greatcoats were worn. This was for ease of movement.

Everyone knew what to do.

Later the sky clouded over and the whole operation was completed in silence without our presence being discovered.

Considering the darkness, the strange surroundings, the water and mud, the great length of our line (four miles) and the means available to the enemy for listening to telephone conversations, and for observation aided by artificial illumination, it was a remarkable performance. If someone fell into a water filled hole with a splash, or snagged his clothing on a strand of barbed wire and expressed his feelings in soldier's language; if steel rifle clanged against steel helmet, or a stray bullet thudded into human flesh and bone and extracted a cry of pain, our presence was not revealed. Either such small sounds, if heard, passed as normal with the Germans or the noise of gunfire covered them up. The men were warned not to talk except in whispers and not to smoke. Our years of training and discipline now paid off—the assembly of four divisions took place undetected within a stone's throw of the enemy.

This was the moment for which the Canadian Corps had been trained; one might almost say that this was the moment for which they had been created. While they were filled with high hope and confidence as they crouched there in the bitter cold before dawn and stared into the darkness, where lay their tenacious and battle-wise enemies, who knows what thoughts passed through their minds. But they were ready, tense and anxious, like players before a big game, as they waited silently for first light and the opening crash of the barrage.

So much for the plan.

Everything that we could think of had been done. All watches had been synchronized, not once but several times. Now all we could do was to wait for the barrage to begin at 5.30 a.m. The minute hand on my watch appeared to be stuck. Five minutes seemed like half an hour. Had anything been overlooked? We did not think so, but there was always the chance of misunderstanding. Anyway, we were committed now, and the whole course of events was out of our hands. The first few minutes would tell a good deal. Guns were firing in a routine way as in normal trench warfare and then it became quiet outside while a man could take two puffs on a cigarette. Now came the massive thunder of the barrage, so well co-ordinated that not one gun fired before the others. First heard were the sharp reports at the muzzles of hundreds of guns, followed abruptly by the ear-splitting, shattering smash and crump of heavy and light explosives falling on the Hun positions, front and rear. Minutes later the enemy, caught by surprise, retaliated with ragged bursts of shell fire as the news, delayed by loss of much of his telephone system, reached his artillery that this was no raid, no false alarm, but an attack in strength.

Hundreds of German flares shot up as the infantry called on their gunners for help. As a pyrotechnic display it was quite a show but it did them little good because as reports of our relentless advance reached them their gunners did not know where to aim for fear of firing on their own troops.

The staccato bark of rifles, the stuttering rivetter-like sound of machine guns and the sharp crack of hand grenades, as well as the boom boom of trench mortar bombs, stepped up in volume as the alarm spread and added to the awful clamour of the drum fire. The sustained uproar of this combined and concentrated bombardment was so violent that it quaked the earth for miles around and could be heard in England. An Air Force observer of this battle later told me that the overhead canopy of our artillery fire was so dense that he saw a number of our low-flying aircraft explode like clay pigeons as they collided with shells in flight. It was like flying through a storm of gigantic and deadly hailstones.

At the first salvo that signalled zero hour, we knew that long lines of Canadian infantrymen, over 20,000 bayonets strong, rose up out of their temporary shelters and commenced a slow but steady walk toward the German lines, and that tens of thousands more would follow closely. In a number of places explosive charges had been laid at the blind end of tunnels ending in No Man's Land. These were detonated at zero hour and parties of our men poured out of the openings, half way to the German front line.

There was a strong northwest wind blowing with occasional snowflurries, which was to our advantage. Later in the day the sun shone.

Reports coming in to us from the rear indicated that everywhere along the line success was attending our efforts. Everyone was jubilant.

Our artillery fire must have been terrible for the Germans to endure, but at many points the resistance was stubborn and exacted its toll. A few stout-hearted men under a tough and experienced sergeant can hold up the advance in any battle at a given spot, especially if they can get themselves sandbagged in with a machine gun in a concrete pit. But our fighters had all been well trained in the methods of dealing with such obstacles, and the waves of men rolled along accepting losses as they went as part of the price to be paid in blood and suffering. They were always in sufficient strength to overcome any opposition and reached all objectives on the minute.

The spectacle of masses of exultant Canadians and British on the sky line, wet bayonets flashing, plunging down on to their positions with a yell only a few hours after the opening of the battle, must have been a terrifying one. Plainly the battle was lost, and although some Germans defended their guns bravely, true to the tradition of the artilleryman, most realized that resistance was useless and either threw up their hands or fled downhill. Few of them reached shelter.

Streams of prisoners began to come back very soon after the battle opened and were hustled to the prisoners' cages in the rear, under the efficient control of the Provost Corps.

On that day and the three days following, the Canadian Corps took 4,016 prisoners. The Germans captured forty-nine Canadians, most of them wounded.

By 3 p.m. I was at last able to leave the cave, and I went forward and walked over that part of the battlefield taken by the 4th Brigade. Our men swarmed everywhere. Telephone lines and light railways were being laid on, and I saw more than one battery blazing away in territory that had been enemy property only a few hours before. Everywhere I looked, men were digging and each one gave me a wide grin as I passed.

The field had been cleared quickly of the wounded, both friend and foe, some carried on stretchers by German prisoners, but many of the dead still lay where they had fallen. Special parties were picking them up now and they would be buried in preselected cemeteries instead of where they had fallen as often used to be the case. In No Man's Land I recognized an officer of the 19th Battalion with whom I had enjoyed dinner a short time before the battle, and with whom I had played basketball in Canada. He lay in that awkward humpbacked posture I had so often observed in the dead, made more conspicuous by the heavy pack on his back as though the load had been too heavy and he had stumbled and fallen face down, his knees buckled under him, his hands spread before him. A gallant officer who died leading his men.

The first dead German I saw was spread-eagled against the parados, or back wall, of his trench, arms flung out as though crucified. Where his head had been was a red pulp like a crushed strawberry. Many of the dead lay as though sleeping without a mark of disfigurement and I am certain felt no pain, but others were disembowelled or with limbs shattered and clothing torn from their bodies by the blast of high explosives. The water in the shell holes was stained blood red; altogether a horrible sight that I shall never forget, but nothing like as bad as the fields of St. Eloi, the Somme or Passchendaele.

However, our losses had been severe, though fewer than we expected, and when the accounts were cast up by war's inexorable method of reckoning, it was found that no fewer than 3,524 Canadians of all ranks had given up their lives, while 7,773 more had been wounded on the day of battle, and up to the 13th of April. The very high proportion of dead to wounded gives some indication of the deadliness of the German fire power. The Germans, too, paid dearly for their defence, and their losses, including prisoners, must have been more grievous than ours, although separate figures for the action at Vimy Ridge are not available. But it is known that of two of the divisions which opposed us one lost 3,133 and the other 3,473 officers and men.

The weather had been cloudy, with squalls of rain and snow, and the men of our brigade now faced several days and nights of discomfort without blankets or great-coats.

And so the day ended, with our troops on their objectives. The main line of the ridge had fallen in one hour and forty-five minutes, and the whole operation completed, as planned, in seven hours and twenty minutes, except on the 4th Divisional front, where they ran into very stiff opposition on the steep slopes; but by the afternoon on the 10th, by desperate hand-to-hand fighting, they had captured Hill 145 and, on the 12th, by a local operation and in a snow storm, the remaining high ground around the "Pimple" and had descended the hill to the village of Givenchy-en-Gohelle.

Afterwards I caught a little sleep, but at 6 a.m. on the 10th, Lindsey and I went up to reconnoitre the 13th Imperial Brigade front, with which I was unfamiliar. Their headquarters was in Paynesley tunnel, which had a widened-out place for working and sleeping. I found and woke up their brigade major and arranged details of the relief with him, and he gave me a guide to take us to the new front. As I left the tunnel, I met Major C. F. Constantine of our 4th Artillery brigade staff, and we all went forward together. "Consy" was a fine soldier and athlete, and went on to become a Major General during World War II.

It was not long before we came upon a young transport driver in trouble. The faithful fellow had stayed beside his horse all night, trying in vain to extricate the poor pack animal from the mud in which it was buried to its belly. The horse was utterly exhausted and far beyond making any further effort and, as there was no hope of saving it, Consy drew his revolver and shot it. A little further on he had to shoot another. This incident illustrates well the condition of the ground.

The ridge remained in British hands until the end of the war. During the great German offensive in the Spring and Summer of 1918 nearly every yard of the Allied front from Rheims to the English Channel was attacked, but they left Vimy Ridge severely alone. The Canadians had carried out stupendous defence works there and it was a matter of pride with every Canadian soldier that the historic ridge should never pass from his hands . . .

I managed to stay indoors all the next day, the 12th, hoping to cure my cold, but I looked out once and saw that it was snowing, great big wet flakes. When we took over this cave, a young German soldier, a mere boy, lay dead near the doorway, and we had been too busy to bury him. Today the snow mercifully had covered him up. I never ceased to wonder how the Germans managed with some of the troops they had.

Admittedly most were well built, hardy men, but amongst the prisoners there were always a good number of undersized youths who looked about 16 or 17 and whose greatcoats almost touched the ground, like boys in men's clothing. They were types that our recruiting officers would have rejected out of hand, but there must be something in the German temperament and in German discipline that made these youths fight so well. Of course, a 120 pound youngster can be taught to handle a machine gun just as well as a husky halfback, but it was always with a sense of disillusion that one saw in the flesh some of these "supermen" who had been holding out against us under weeks of devastating shell fire.

On the 13th

The platoon under Lieutenant Hall came up and halted, strung along in single file in the deep trench. From the opposite direction a Lewis gun crew of five reported. Manion and I stood there between the two groups, talking to Captain Percy Brocklebank of the 21st who was at the top of the steep dugout steps. I had just read the message handed to me by Elmitt's runner, when I heard someone yell "Look out!" and there was a loud crash in our midst.

I had heard no whine like that of an approaching shell, so thought we had been bombed from the air. Later we found that someone had dropped a Mills grenade out of his hand, or his pocket, into the foot-deep mud; the pin had come loose in some unaccountable way, and the deadly little missile had exploded at our feet. Thin blue smoke drifted up through the ooze.

The runner fell face down in the mud. He had taken most of the blast in the belly. The torn blood-stained message lay between us. Manion turned him over and laid him down again, saying that he was dead. Captain Brocklebank suffered severe multiple wounds, and was knocked down the steep flight of steps. Every man in the Lewis gun crew was hit, so that they were out of action. Lieutenant Hall was wounded in the arm.

Captain Manion at once began to give first aid. Fortunately he and I were unhurt. Stretcher bearers arrived from some place nearby and went about their work.

On the 14th

During the afternoon we marched out the ten miles to Maisnil Bouche in clear cool weather. After the trenches, where all vegetation was dead, it was wonderful to see green grass, and buds on the trees; the women and children in the villages. There was no singing and little talk. Everyone was thinking of the last time he had marched up this trail and of the comrades he had left behind on the ridge; but death is an ever-present companion in war, and soldiers cannot spend much time in grieving. No friendships are stronger than those forged on active service, and while pals would be missed as long as life lasted, the struggle had to be continued to the end; new men would be absorbed into the units and new friendships would be formed.

Reaching the hard roads, units formed into column of route, men squared their shoulders and fell into step, their iron-shod boots ringing on the cobblestones.

Onlookers observed that they held their heads proudly, and well they might—they had taken the VIMY.

Focus Questions

1. On what basis did Prime Minister Borden demand greater autonomy for Canada? Why do you think he is not more explicit about these demands?

2. On what basis did Henri Bourassa claim that Canada should stay out of the war? How did he explain low French-Canadian enlistment, and what does his explanation say about the meaning of Canadian nationalism in the early 20th century?

3. According to Nellie McClung, what *do* women think of war—or what *should* they think of war?

4. How does McClung's argument about the war double as an argument for women's equality? What role does she think women should play on the world stage?

5. What does Mcintyre's account of the battle for Vimy Ridge reveal about the conditions faced by Canadian soldiers in the trenches? What do you think is concealed or under-emphasized by its tone?

6. Why is it that conflict and war, in particular, become so significant for national identity (in Canada and elsewhere), as opposed to other sorts of achievements and events? What are the consequences of elevating conflict/war to this status?

9

Canadian Workers in the Interwar Period: The Nation from the Left

Introduction

In Chapter Six, two different photographs of the completion of the CPR were presented—both of them ceremonial, but each drawing a very different picture of how the railway was built. The first was from the perspective of the railway's financiers; the second from the perspective of the navvies who undertook its physical creation. This dual-layered narrative, of the employer and employee, the rich and the poor, the boss and the labourer, underlies the entire span of Canada's past. Today, while poverty continues to be a serious problem for Canadian workers, there are at least some rudimentary protections—such as unemployment insurance, minimum wage regulations, and laws which define workers' rights and set protocols for workplace safety. One doesn't have to dip too far into the past, however, to uncover a vastly different world. The first two documents in this chapter, produced immediately after World War One, demonstrate the violence and uncertainty which often characterized the lives of Canada's working class. That violence and uncertainty was not simply the product of an unpredictable economy, but the result of intransigent employers, complacent governments, racism, poverty, and fear.

The author of one of these documents, J. S. Woodsworth, was a prominent and persuasive social activist. Witness to the desperate poverty of the working class in the west, and convinced that substantial improvements had to be made to wages, working conditions, and the rights of labourers, Woodsworth entered federal politics after the Great War. An avowed socialist at a time when socialism was akin to disloyalty, and considered immoral, scandalous, and even criminal, he sat as an MP for Winnipeg from 1921 until his death in 1942. It was in 1932, one of the worst years of the Great Depression that he, along with other like-minded activists and politicians, penned the "Regina Manifesto"—an enormously significant document in Canada's political landscape. The Manifesto became the basis for a new Cooperative Commonwealth Federation—precursor to today's New Democratic Party (NDP). Its principles continue to inform discussion about the rights and status of Canada's working class.

The Drumheller Strike of 1919
A. B. Woywitka

The year 1919 was a period of industrial unrest in many parts of the world. The war had ended but not the tension nor the anxiety for a better post-war deal. No sooner had World War I ended when the labour war began, accompanied by strikes and violence. In March of 1919, at a Western Labour Conference in Calgary, a new union was organized for Canadian workers. Though the idea for the union originated with the trade unions of Great Britain, the new union itself was to be all-Canadian and for Canadian workers only. The aim of this "One Big Union" was to unite all workers, both white collar and manual, under one leadership. It was to work in the interests of labour and was to be totally disaffiliated from International Unions.

At first, the One Big Union's success was striking. It appealed to the majority of workers. Strong union detachments broke away from parental bodies to join the O.B.U. Among them were the miners of Drumheller Valley who had been members of the United Mine Workers of America, District 18. One of the sore points was the collection of miners' dues which were sent regularly to the head office in the United States leaving a shortage of funds for local union work.

The organizer and secretary of the Drumheller branch or O.B.U. was Jack Sullivan. He was a dynamic man who was liked and respected by the majority of miners. On the other hand the mine operators regarded Sullivan with suspicion and labelled him as a dangerous revolutionary. They refused to have anything to do with the new union that he represented. In their stand against the O.B.U., they had the full support of W. H. Armstrong, Coal Commissioner for Alberta.

Production of coal was interrupted when the Drumheller miners went on strike on May 24, 1919. They requested the mine operators formally recognize the O.B.U. as their legal bargaining agent.

In reply, Coal Commissioner Armstrong said: "I decline to conduct negotiations or enter into negotiations with O.B.U. The present contract is with U.M.W.A. and with them we will conduct business with regard to resumption of work and negotiations of a new agreement." (*Calgary Herald, March 24, 1919*).

The Coal Commissioner's reply became the signal for the start of the war between the unions and was to last through the summer of 1919. When the miners walked out in support of O.B.U. the companies retaliated by closing down the mines. Being in the middle of the slack season, the closing of the mines caused no hardship for the mine operators. But for the miners it was a crucial period; many of them were forced to disperse in search of other work.

"The Drumheller Strike of 1919" by A. B. Woywitka, *Alberta Historical Review* (Winter 1973). Reprinted by permission of the author.

At the same time, the great General Strike of the O.B.U. was underway in Winnipeg, culminating in the so-called Bloody Saturday of June 21st that ended in death for two people and various injuries to thirty others. The strike that paralyzed Winnipeg for more than five weeks ended officially on July 3rd, 1919.

However, by late July the Drumheller lockout was still on when winter orders for coal began to arrive. The mine operators were anxious to resume operations and word went out that the mines were being opened for work again. The miners then called a meeting and the majority voted in favour of continuing the strike for O.B.U. recognition.

The thirteen mine companies, including Drumheller, Newcastle, Western Gem, Manitoba, Atlas, A.B.C., North American, Scranton, Sterling and Midland, joined forces and flatly refused to recognize the O.B.U. They also began to lay plans to break the strike. They asked for and were given official government permission to hire special constables to "protect" their property.

At this time general post-war employment was at a low ebb. The labour market was flooded with returning veterans in search of jobs. Lacking mining experience, the veterans had been by-passed by the mining companies in favour of experienced "foreign" miners—Belgians, Italians, Swedes, Romanians, Ukrainians, Hungarians and Poles—who had kept the mines operating throughout the war.

Playing on the veterans' resentment against aliens, the companies set out to hire a sufficient number of unemployed service men as "protectors of mining property" knowing it would be an important factor in the veterans' dealings with the strikers. The companies paid them $10 a day and let many of them become plied with liquor. Then they gave them pick handles, crowbars and brass knuckles before they sent them out in company cars to round up the strikers for work.

Several old miners who took part in the Drumheller strike of 1919 recall the events that led to the terror that stalked through the Drumheller Valley that summer. One of these men, Nick Gill, had left Drumheller to work on the railroad after the mines closed down in late May. When word reached him that mines were to open again, he returned the first week of August to find the strike still in progress.

Daily, fresh news came of individual miners being picked up for work by force. If they offered no resistance, all was well. They were sent into the mine to work and nothing more was said. But if a striker showed resistance, he was driven out into the country 30 or 40 miles away, beaten and left on the prairies as an example to others.

With each passing day, the atmosphere in the Drumheller Valley grew more tense. The striking miners had to be on the alert at all times. During the day they roamed in packs as there was safety in numbers. At night they slept with one eye open. Living in their small shiplap and tarpaper shacks staggered along the river banks, they soon learned by the grapevine of any happening and in turn, passed it along.

As the struggle progressed, the U.M.W.A. and the mine operators brought in outside agitators able to speak several languages. These silver-tongued orators left no stone unturned in District 18 in favour of the U.M.W.A. Their aim was to turn the "foreign element" against the One Big Union. But the hard-core strikers included not only the foreigners but many English-speaking people, too. These stood fast with the leaders of the O.B.U.

On Saturday, August 9th, Jack Sullivan, who lived in the vicinity of Newcastle mine, was awakened by thunderous knocks on his door. As he dressed hurriedly, five men forced his door open and surrounded him. One of the men grabbed his arm roughly, growled: "You're coming with us, Sullivan!"

Sullivan had no choice but to nod. By his gesture he admitted that he knew he was outnumbered. "Let me wash myself and I'll be with you in a minute," he said quietly.

The men watched him closely as he went to the washstand. Sullivan, scraping the bottom of the pail deliberately with the dipper, filled the basin with cold water. He splashed loudly as he washed. He then wiped himself. Picking up the basin to throw the water out, he took a couple of steps out of the door before he flung the basin away from him. A split second later he was sprinting across the yard to his neighbour's shanty, the ex-soldiers at his heels in pursuit.

"Rogers! Help me!" Sullivan yelled.

Rogers was a Negro fireman in the steam boiler at the Newcastle mine. He had been standing in his doorway wondering what would happen to Sullivan when he saw him come running toward him. As Sullivan rushed past him into the shack, Rogers reacted instantly. He grabbed the gun standing inside his doorway and pointing it at Sullivan's pursuers, he warned them: "Stop! If you come one step closer, I'll shoot! You have no business coming on my property!"

Leaving them no choice, the "special constables" backed away, swearing angrily. Thanks to Rogers, Sullivan was spared that day.

That same morning, word got out that a number of strikers were gathered at Rosedale mine to prevent workers from entering the mine. Two hundred veterans were rushed in touring cars to break up the picketers who were then forced to scatter in all directions.

All day Saturday, August 9th, hundreds of striking miners milled restlessly through the streets of Drumheller. There were frequent exchanges of obscenities and name calling as veterans and strikers stalked around. Tempers flared as the hired strike-breakers taunted the strikers, yelling, "Bohunks, go home! We don't need you here!" The strikers yelled back in return: "You dirty scabs!"

The cauldron bubbled and boiled, fed by hatred and distrust of the opposing factions. On one hand was the veteran glowing with patriotism, returning home after years at the front, expecting a hero's welcome and reward. Instead he found himself facing frustration, unemployment and labour unrest. It angered him to find men of foreign extraction holding jobs while he remained unemployed.

On the other hand, the immigrant who had left the poverty of his homeland and the tyranny of the Austro-Hungarian Empire, arrived in Canada in time to help in developing a raw, new land. He, too, was faced with frustrations and disappointments and the heavy work of opening land, building railroads through the mountains, digging sewers in the cities, mining, etc. When the war began in 1914, he was immediately dubbed an "enemy alien" and required to register with the police and was kept under surveillance. He was sent to fill essential jobs or faced deportation if he refused. Thus each party felt justified in its stand.

The Drumheller police under Sergeant Skelton patrolled the streets and issued repeated warnings to both sides: "Be careful! We will not be responsible if anyone gets hurt or killed!"

The unrest lasted late into the night, when the strikers and the veterans finally dispersed. Early Sunday, August 10th, 500 striking miners gathered in the vicinity of the Newcastle watertank where Sullivan had gone into hiding. To prevent any surprise abduction of Sullivan by the veterans, the strikers took him into their midst and marched with him down the tracks to the Miners Hall.

They found the door padlocked. Refusing to be halted, they lifted one of the men to their shoulders to open a window. After crawling inside, he opened a side door to permit entry of the remaining strikers.

That day, Sullivan, Kent, Browne, Christopher and other O.B.U. leaders addressed the meeting. Discussions followed, touching on many of their problems. In closing the meeting, they passed a resolution to send a telegram to the O.B.U. head office in Calgary for further instructions.

Leaving the hall, the mass of strikers proceeded to the station house where they ordered the stationmaster to send a telegram. He refused, saying it was Sunday and he was not working. But mob pressure changed his mind. The message was sent and instructions were received to hold a special meeting with an O.B.U. representative from Calgary on Monday morning. Once again, the men dispersed for the night.

The miners' shacks were strung along the valley, separated by brush, sometimes a bit of a garden, maybe a fence here and there. In each of them lived at least two or three people, and sometimes as many as could put their bed rolls on the floor.

With Mr. and Mrs. Gill lived an elderly uncle and the old man, being a poor sleeper, was up early Monday morning. He dressed himself and went out into the milky whiteness of early dawn. Except for the singing of the birds, the valley was sleeping peacefully. The old man sighed. At this hour it was hard to believe the harshness of preceding days. As he stood contemplating the austere beauty of hill and valley, his ears caught the laboured chugging of approaching vehicles.

He peered into the valley, waiting. Within minutes, the cars stopped and he heard a commotion as of people thrashing through the brush accompanied by loud whoops and cries of outrage. He did not need to be told what was happening but hurried back to the shack to warn his nephew.

"Wake up, wake up!" he called from the doorway, his voice rising with the sense of approaching danger. "They're coming our way! Hurry!"

Gill was up and dressed in no time. Stepping outside, he heard heavy thrashing through the thick growth of chokecherries and saskatoons that grew along the valley. Presently, he saw men running and recognized his neighbours. Close behind them were their pursuers, rending the morning air with their cries. They were heading in the general direction of Gill's shack.

Halfway between Gill's shack and the bush was Mike Babyn's shanty. Back of it, firewood was stacked neatly making a fence several feet long and four feet high. The fleeing miners headed for this shelter. They were joined by Mr. Gill, his uncle and several other men who'd been drawn there by the early morning disturbance. Each grabbed firewood, rocks or whatever was handy and when the pursuers came into view, they were met by a furious barrage of flying missiles.

The unexpected counterattack was enough to stop the startled pursuers. No doubt the cries of pain accompanied by loud swearing meant that many of the missiles found their targets. Unable to cope with the attack, the ex-servicemen turned about and started running back to their cars. Immediately, the strikers taking advantage of the retreat, started after them in hot pursuit. They headed them off, forcing the veterans to run for the hills.

The chase was finally abandoned when the ex-servicemen scattered in all directions on top of the hills. As the strikers began to make their way back to the valley, they heard rifle shots reverberating through the valley. Realizing that all was not well, they paused on the edge of the hills overlooking the town of Drumheller. It was then they saw that reinforcements had arrived for the ex-servicemen. More cars and men had come and the valley rang with their shouting. They recognized numbers of their own men running for the safety of the hills. Turning on their heels, they headed the exodus.

A number of strikers were captured that morning, but the majority gained the hills. Here they sought vantage points for observation, and hiding places in the deep gullies and crevices scattered over a large territory. It was apparent that the special meeting scheduled in the hall for that day would not take place. However, many of them hoped that a meeting could be organized in the hills. Then, as several hours went by it was apparent that there would be no assembly in the hills after all. Sullivan was nowhere to be seen; sometime during the melee, he had disappeared.

As day drew to a close and night began to fall, men began to emerge warily from gully to hilltop, seeking contact with fellow strikers. With the coming of darkness, several men offered to make their way down for further news of what happened and for food and water.

Eventually, when they came back, they brought with them news that the hired strike breakers had returned to Babyn's shack, hoping perhaps to capture Babyn in retaliation for the attack suffered at his place. Mr. Babyn was not home but his wife fearing an attack on herself, met the intruders with a .22 rifle. She fired two shots which went astray and hurt no one. (Later Mr. Babyn was convicted of illegal possession of arms by an alien and was sentenced to three months in Lethbridge jail.)

Among those captured that day was a man named Thompson. He was taken to a barn at Midland mine, strung up by his feet and offered horse urine to drink. A report in *Calgary Daily Herald* denied mistreatment of captured men but there is a cryptic item in the paper saying: "He (Thompson) was given a drink of water and was told not to spit in it."

In another instance two other men, Gulka and Malowany were assaulted and strung, feet up, in the same barn. Gulka, who was almost totally deaf, was presumed to be stubborn and un-cooperative and was treated accordingly.

The *Calgary Herald,* August 12 observed: "Legally, the course adopted on Saturday, Sunday and Monday last, may be gravely questioned but the valley people are not splitting hairs in connection with this matter."

Those who had gone down into the valley secretly Monday night brought back the news that the mine operators were threatening to run the strikers out of town if they did not return to work by Tuesday morning.

It was a sleepless night for the strikers on the hills. They were cold and tired. By daybreak, the groups began to congregate again. Their spirits were flagging. Left without a leader, they were at loose ends as to their next step. Tuesday morning arrived and from their vantage points, men watched the valley for further developments, half expecting reprisals. The sun rose higher. Thirst and hunger increased as it grew hotter. Disillusionment grew with every passing minute.

Presently, they noticed what appeared to be a party of police officers making their way towards the hills. Word was passed along and soon the men were ready to disperse should it become necessary. They watched warily as the party of ten provincial police officers and a Drumheller constable approached. The striking miners figured that the mine operators knew the strikers did not trust the local police and deemed it advisable to bring in outside help.

The party of policemen spread over a wide area so as to contact as many strikers as possible. Using megaphones, they assured the men there would be no reprisals if they returned to work. "We are here to help you! It is safe for you to return to your homes. There is work for you at the mines. Do not be afraid!"

The message was repeated. Strikers exchanged looks and some nodded. They could not hope to stay there indefinitely. Others withdrew to regroup, preferring to wait for further developments. They did not trust the mine operators' promises nor their "hired constables" who were only too eager to carry out their instructions.

It was noted in *Calgary Daily Herald* that on August 12th, the Drumheller mines were operating at only quarter capacity. This was a long way from full operation which the companies needed in order to fill their winter orders. "So far none of the alien element has returned to work," the newspaper observed. "Those who have returned are the better class miners who up to yesterday have been guided blindly by O.B.U. agitators."

The strikers who returned were soon approached by the companies' "special constables" and were made to sign papers accepting U.M.W.A. as their bargaining agents with the mine operators.

As for the remaining strikers who stayed behind in the hills, it was suggested that they all be run out of the valley. The veterans went to their homes with the message that O.B.U. men had the alternative of signing up with U.M.W.A. or clearing out. On Wednesday, the companies decreed that "preference will be given first, to returned soldiers, next, white men who had mining experience and last, the alien element."

Within a few days, the remainder of striking miners had returned to their homes. The companies had resumed operations with the help of ex-servicemen, their sympathizers and those miners who had given up hope of winning the strike. There was every indication that the strike was broken. However, the "special constables" continued their search for O.B.U. leaders, including Sullivan whom they could not locate. Christopher, Kent and a third unidentified man were captured by five carloads of veterans raiding a secret meeting at Wayne. They brought their prisoners back to Drumheller, held a "court-martial," roughed them up thoroughly and ordered them to clear out of Drumheller.

On August 21st a Drumheller correspondent to the *Calgary Daily Herald* reported, "Considerable excitement prevailed here last Monday when the returned veterans went to the Miners Hall where a meeting was in progress and took Sullivan and Roberts for another ride. Sullivan returned to town on the morning train from Calgary and the vets decided to get rid of him again. Roberts who had also returned, was taken along, too. The two men were taken to Rosedale where the vets at the Moody mine joined forces with the Drumheller boys and set the two men on foot heading towards Calgary."

What the report failed to mention was that Sullivan and Roberts were beaten, tied to telephone poles and then tarred and feathered. They were later released and ordered to make themselves scarce. As the men took off, the mob of veterans howled after them, promising more of the same should they return.

This last incident sounded the final death knell to the O.B.U. in Drumheller. The strike was over. The triple alliance of government, mine companies and U.M.W.A. had triumphed over the wish of the miners for One Big Union. The United Mine Workers of America was again the legal bargaining agent for all the mine workers of District 18.

The veterans who had played the major role of strike breakers were hired by the companies as promised. But in a short time, the majority of them proved to be indifferent miners. The companies, interested only in production and amount of turn-over of coal, soon released many of them from work. The so-called "alien element," being experienced miners, were eventually re-hired under contract with U.M.W.A. and peace returned to the valley.

Besco

J. S. Woodsworth

1924

What is the root of all this trouble in Nova Scotia? Bolshevism among the foreign miners? No, that is not an adequate answer, though an easy way of disposing of any industrial difficulty. The miners in Nova Scotia are chiefly of Scotch-Canadian stock and there was similar trouble long before Lenin came upon the international stage. No case can be summed in a word, yet there is one word that is much nearer than Bolshevism; that is 'Besco'—the common sobriquet of the British Empire Steel Corporation. . . .

Another Royal Commission has reported. It has been studying the miners; only incidentally has it studied Besco. Can its recommendation then prove other than futile? The Commission finds that the military were needed to cope with the situation at Sydney. Property rights were endangered and the Government had to step in. The papers feature this. But what of the primary human rights that have been disregarded until the men are rendered half desperate? On this point the report is couched in the most general terms. Certain obvious reforms are recommended, notably the abandonment of the eleven- and thirteen-hour shifts which involve, every fortnight, twenty-four hours continuous work.

But when the Commission reports to the Federal Government, the Federal Government disclaims any power to enact legislation along these lines, claiming that this is a provincial matter. Possibly growing public opinion may force the Nova Scotia Government to take action. A year ago Besco informed a delegation from a local ministerial association that Nova Scotia would not move until Judge Gary made the change!

Other investigators have reported on the situation but without bringing about material improvements. In 1920 the housing and sanitary conditions were described by a Royal Commission as being 'with few exceptions absolutely wretched.' Two years later a Board of Conciliation admitted that the company's houses were 'not in a satisfactory condition.' The minority report made went further describing the sanitary conditions as 'absolutely wretched.' Another two years and still no change in this or other conditions of life and labour.

From *The Canadian Forum*, Vol. IV, No. 42, March 1924.

In a series of articles which appeared a year ago in the *Toronto Daily Star,* Mr. F. A. Carman puts his finger on one of the sore spots:

> Fourteen companies of various grades of importance go to make up Besco. When the fourteen went into the cauldron they owned in stocks of various kinds a little under $83,000,000. When the merging process had been completed these $83,000,000 had been transmuted into just under $102,000,000. . . . To pay dividends on nearly $102,000,000 of stocks should be a sufficient task for the men who have to manage an industry which must meet the world competition in the steel and coal trade. But before they can begin to do this they have to meet prior charges of over $31,000,000 of mortgages of various sorts. . . . In the Besco process common stocks were reduced from 63 to 24 million while preferred stocks rose from 19 to 77 million. . . . The result of this transformation process has been the addition of charges of over $4,000,000 to the annual liabilities of the industry. . . . The recent watering down of the stock of these companies was not the first operation of the kind. . . . This original $15,000,000 of common 'watered' stock is represented in the existing issues of Besco stock by $6,000,000 of common stock and by $13,500,000 of 7% second preference on which the dividends are a cumulative liability. Which shows us in epitome how what was originally merely a speculative 'flyer' may by skilful financing be transmogrified into the next thing to a bond.

'Skilful financing'—aye, and unscrupulous financing. One transaction has recently been dragged to the light of day. At a time when important negotiations were in progress between the Newfoundland Government and the Company, ex-Premier Squires received $46,000 from funds of the Dominion Steel Co. This action according to the evidence was approved by Roy Wolvin and other high officials (See *Montreal Star,* Jan. 31st, 1924). Such is Besco!

In vain have the workers appealed to Provincial and Federal Parliaments for legal redress or assistance. Besco was well represented in the Government councils. A year ago, when a deputation asked Mr Mackenzie King for the provision of pension for worn-out miners—a part of the pre-election programme of the liberal party—all they received from the Prime Minister was a copy of his book *Industry and Humanity!*

In vain have the workers appealed to Provincial authorities to obtain representation in Parliament; constituencies were gerrymandered, an industrial county being united with a county peopled largely by farmers and fishermen with a two-member constituency. Then on the eve of the election 'roorbacks' were issued—'false tales' concerning the candidate J. B. Maclachlan who went down to defeat.

When two years ago, the miners resorted to the 'strike on the job', the Press entirely misrepresented the situation. Even Mr Meighen recognized the merits of their policy:

> What have these men done? They have been requested, we will put it, to accept a wage reduction of 32-1/2 per cent. They have declined to do it. They say, 'No it is not a living wage, we cannot support our families, we cannot send our children to school, we do not want to go on strike or go out.' . . . They say 'Here you are giving us two-thirds of a day's pay and we will give you two-thirds of a day's work, and only that; we don't pretend to give you any more.' (*Hansard,* March 30th, 1922)

At that time, the Government refused the Royal Commission asked for by the Mayors of the mining towns, but a little later sent down troops notwithstanding the protests of the local authorities that there was no need. So the struggle has gone on with growing bitterness. Last summer driven back to work by starvation, the steelworkers in a notable statement declared that every man's hand was against them. Within the last few weeks the coal miners have been forced into the pits, against their will, by the reactionary American officials at the head of their own union. But that is too long and too complicated a story to be even outlined here.

In the meantime the miners' leader is serving a two-year sentence in Dorchester penitentiary convicted of seditious libel. What had he done? In a circular letter he staged that the Provincial Police had brutally ridden down men, women, and children on a Sunday night when most of them were coming from church.

> One old woman over 70 years of age was beaten into insensibility and may die. A boy of nine years old was trampled under the horses' feet and had his breast bone crushed in. One woman beaten over the head with a police club gave premature birth to a child. The child is dead and the woman's life is despaired of.

The coal operators gave this letter to the papers. Then Maclachlan was arrested and taken to Halifax charged with unlawfully publishing a false tale and also with seditious libel. The charge of publishing a false tale was withdrawn; the tale was all too true. MacLachlan's letter is substantially corroborated by statutory declaration and by the evidence given before the Royal Commission. But in the case of seditious libel, as the Attorney-General pointed out, the truer the statement the worse the libel. So J. B. Maclachlan is behind the bars because he dared to criticize the brutality of the Provincial Police of Nova Scotia.

That is technically true. But under this obsolete and discredited law of seditions any of us might be convicted. Mr Meighen might be sent to the penitentiary for criticizing the Liberal administrations. Why then was MacLachlan the victim? Because in fighting in the cause of the men he had incurred the enmity of the powerful British Empire Steel Corporation. They were out to 'get' him, and since he was irreproachable in his personal character and well within the law in his official activities, they invoked this old law that dates back to witch-burning days.

Even then MacLachlan did not get the fair play of those early times. He was not allowed a trial in his home county but was taken to Halifax where for years the minds of the people have been poisoned against the miners.

When an appeal was taken for another trial, the trial judge was a member of the Court of Appeal. Of the six judges on the Bench, four, before the time of their elevation to the bench, had been connected with the steel or coal companies subsidiary to Besco.

The Regina Manifesto

First CCF National Convention July 19-21, Regina, Saskatchewan

1933

The C.C.F. is a federation of organizations whose purpose is the establishment in Canada, of a Cooperative Commonwealth in which the principle regulating production, distribution and exchange will be the supplying of human needs and not the making of profits.

We aim to replace the present capitalist system, with its inherent injustice and inhumanity, by a social order from which the domination and exploitation of one class by another will be eliminated, in which economic planning will supersede unregulated private enterprise and competition, and in which genuine democratic self-government, based upon economic equality will be possible.

The present order is marked by glaring inequalities of wealth and opportunity, by chaotic waste and instability; and in an age of plenty it condemns the great mass of the people to poverty and insecurity. Power has become more and more concentrated into the hands of a small irresponsible minority of financiers and industrialists and to their predatory interests the majority are habitually sacrificed.

When private profits is the main stimulus to economic effort, our society oscillates between periods of feverish prosperity in which the main benefits go to speculators and profiteers, and of catastrophic depression, in which the common man's normal state of insecurity and hardship is accentuated. We believe that these evils can be removed only in a planned and socialized economy in which our natural resources and the principal means of production and distribution are owned, controlled and operated by the people.

The new social order at which we aim is not one in which individuality will be crushed out by a system of regimentation.

Nor shall we interfere with cultural rights of racial or religious minorities. What we seek is a proper collective organization of our economic resources such as will make possible a much greater degree of leisure and a much richer individual life for every citizen.

This social and economic transformation can be brought about by political action, through the election of a government inspired by the ideal of a Co-operative

"The Regina Manifesto" Programme of the Co-operative Commonwealth Federation, adopted at First National Convention held at Regina, Sask., July, 1933. Reprinted by permission of the Saskatchewan New Democratic Party.

Commonwealth and supported by a majority of the people. We do note believe in change by violence.

We consider that both the old parties in Canada are the instruments of capitalist interests and cannot serve as agents of social reconstruction, and that whatever the superficial difference between them, they are bound to carry on government in accordance with the dictates of the big business interests who finance them.

The C.C.F. aims at political power in order to put an end to this capitalist domination of our political life. It is a democratic movement, a federation of farmers, labour and socialist organizations, financed by its own members and seeking to achieve its ends solely by constitutional methods. It appeals for support from all who believe that the time has come for a far-reaching reconstruction of our economic and political institutions and who are willing to work together for the carrying out of the following policies:

1. PLANNING

The establishment of a planned, socialized economic order, in order to make possible the most efficient development of the national resources and the most equitable distribution of the national income.

The first step in this direction will be the setting up of a National Planning Commission consisting of a small body of economists, engineers and statisticians assisted by an appropriate technical staff.

The task of the Commission will be to plan for the production, distribution and exchange of all goods and services necessary to the efficient functioning of the economy; to co-ordinate the activities of the socialized industries; to provide for a satisfactory balance between the producing and consuming power; and to carry on continuous research into all branches of the national economy in order to acquire the detailed information necessary to efficient planning.

The Commission will be responsible to the Cabinet and will work in co-operation with the Managing Boards of the Socialized Industries.

It is now certain that in every industrial country some form of planning will replace the disintegrating capitalist system. The C.C.F. will provide that in Canada the planning shall be done, not by a small group of capitalist magnates in their own interests, but by public servants acting in the public interest and responsible to the people as a whole.

2. SOCIALIZATION OF FINANCE

Socialization of all financial machinery - banking, currency, credit, and insurance, to make possible the effective control of currency, credit and prices, and the supplying of new productive equipment for socially desirable purposes.

Planning by itself will be of little use if the public authority has not the power to carry its plans into effect. Such power will require the control of finance and of all those vital industries and services which, if they remain in private hands, can be used to thwart or corrupt the will of the public authority. Control of finance is the first step in the control of the whole economy. The chartered banks must be socialized and removed from the control of private profit-seeking interests; and the national banking system thus established must have at its head a Central Bank to control the flow of credit and the general price level, and to regulate foreign exchange operations. A National Investment Board must also be set up, working in cooperation with the socialized banking system to mobilize and direct the unused surpluses of production for socially desired purposes as determined by the Planning Commission.

Insurance Companies, which provide one of the main channels for the investment of individual savings and which, under their present competitive organization, charge needlessly high premiums for the social services that they render, must also be socialized.

3. SOCIAL OWNERSHIP

Socialization (Dominion, Provincial or Municipal) of transportation, communications, electrical power and all other industries and services essential to social planning, and their operation under the general direction of the Planning Commission by competent managements freed from day to day political interference.

Public utilities must be operated for the public benefit and not for the private profit of a small group of owners of financial manipulators. Our national resources must be developed by the same methods. Such a programme means the continuance and extension of the public ownership of enterprises in which most governments in Canada have already gone some distance. Only by such public ownership, operated in a planned economy, can our main industries be saved from the wasteful competition of the ruinous over-development and over-capitalization which are the inevitable outcome of capitalism. Only in a regime of public ownership and operation will the full benefits accruing from centralized control and mass production be passed on to the consuming public.

Transportation, communications and electrical power must come first in a list of industries to be socialized. Others, such as mining, pulp and paper and the distribution of milk, bread, coal and gasoline, in which exploitation, waste, or financial malpractices are particularly prominent must next be brought under social ownership and operation.

In restoring to the community its natural resources and in taking over industrial enterprises from private into public control we do not propose any policy of outright confiscation. What we desire is the most stable and equitable transition to the Co-operative Commonwealth. It is impossible to decide the policies to be followed in particular cases in an uncertain future, but we insist upon certain broad principles. The welfare of the community must take supremacy over the claims of private wealth. In times of war, human life has been conscripted. Should economic circumstances call for it, conscription of wealth would be more justifiable. We recognize the need for compensation in the case of individuals and institutions which must receive adequate maintenance during the transitional period before the planned economy becomes fully operative. But a C.C.F. government will not play the role of rescuing bankrupt private concerns for the benefit of promoters and of stock and bond holders. It will not pile up a deadweight burden of unremunerative debt which represents claims upon the public treasury of a functionless owner class.

The management of publicly owned enterprises will be invested in boards who will be appointed for their competence in the industry and will conduct each particular enterprise on efficient economic lines. The machinery of management may well vary from industry to industry, but the rigidity of Civil Service rules should be avoided and likewise the evils of the patronage system as exemplified in so many departments of the Government today. Workers in these public industries must be free to organize in trade unions and must be given the right to participate in the management of the industry.

4. AGRICULTURE

Security of tenure for the farmer upon his farm on conditions to be laid down by individual provinces; insurance against unavoidable crop failure; removal of the tariff burden from the operations of agriculture; encouragement of producers' and consumers' co-operatives; the restoration and maintenance of an equitable relationship between prices of agricultural products and those of other commodities and services; and improving the efficiency of export trade in farm products.

The security of tenure for the farmer upon his farm which is imperilled by the present disastrous situation of the whole industry, together with adequate social insurance, ought to be guaranteed under equitable conditions.

The prosperity of agriculture, the greatest Canadian industry, depends upon a rising volume of purchasing power of the masses in Canada for all farm goods consumed at home, and upon the maintenance of large scale exports of the stable commodities at satisfactory prices or equitable commodity exchange.

The intense depression in agriculture today is a consequence of the general world crisis caused by the normal workings of the capitalistic system resulting in: (1) Economic nationalism expressing itself in tariff barriers and other restrictions of world trade; (2) The decreased purchasing power of unemployed and underemployed workers and of the Canadian people in general; (3) The exploitation of both primary producers and consumers by monopolistic corporations who absorb a great proportions of the selling price of farm products. (This last is true, for example, of the distribution of milk and dairy products, the packing industry, and milling.)

The immediate cause of agricultural depression is the catastrophic fall in the world prices of foodstuffs as compared with other prices, this fall being due in large measure to the deflation of currency and credit. To counteract the worst effect of this, the internal price level should be raised so that the farmers' purchasing power may be restored.

We propose therefore:

(1) The improvement of the position of the farmer by the increase of purchasing power made possible by the social control of the financial system. This control must be directed towards the increase of employment as laid down elsewhere and towards raising the prices of farm commodities by appropriate credit and foreign policies.

(2) Whilst the family farm is the accepted basis for agricultural production in Canada the position of the farmer may be much improved by: a) The extension of consumers' co operatives for the purchase of farm supplies and domestic requirements; and b) The extension of co-operative institutions for the processing and marketing of farm products.

Both of the foregoing to have suitable state encouragement and assistance.

(3) The adoption of a planned system of agricultural development based upon scientific soil surveys directed towards better land utilization, and a scientific policy of agricultural development for the whole of Canada.

(4) The substitution for the present system of foreign trade, of a system of import and export boards to improve the efficiency of overseas marketing, to control prices, and to integrate the foreign trade policy with the requirements of the national economic plan.

5. EXTERNAL TRADE

The regulation in accordance with the National plan of external trade through import and export boards.

Canada is dependent on external sources of supply for many of her essential requirements of raw materials and manufactured products.

These she can obtain only by large exports of the goods she is best fitted to produce. The strangling of our export trade by insane protectionists policies must be brought to an end. But the old controversies between free traders and protectionists are now largely obsolete. In a world of nationally organized economics Canada must organize the buying and selling of her main imports and exports under public boards, and take steps to regulate the flow of less important commodities by a system of licenses. By so doing she will be enabled to make the best trade agreements possible with foreign countries, put a stop to the exploitation of both primary producer and ultimate consumer, make possible the co-ordination of internal processing, transportation and marketing of farm products, and facilitate the establishment of stable prices for such export commodities.

6. CO-OPERATIVE INSTITUTIONS

The encouragement by the public authority of both producers' and consumers' co-operative institutions.

In agriculture, as already mentioned, the primary producer can receive a larger net revenue through co-operative organization of purchases and marketing. Similarly in retail distribution of staple commodities such as milk, there is room for development both of public municipal operation and of consumers' co-operatives, and such co-operative organization can be extended into wholesale distribution and into manufacturing. Co-operative enterprises should be assisted by the state through appropriate legislation and through the provision of adequate credit facilities.

7. LABOUR CODE

A National Labour Code to secure for the worker maximum income and leisure, insurance covering illness, accident, old age, and unemployment, freedom of association and effective participation in the mazement of his industry or profession.

The spectre of poverty and insecurity which still haunts every worker, though technological developments have made possible a high standard of living for everyone, is a disgrace which must be removed from our civilization. The community must organize its resources to effect progressive reduction of the hours of work in accordance with technological development and to provide a constantly rising standard of life to everyone who is willing to work. A labour code must be developed which will include state regulation of wages, equal reward and equal opportunity of advancement for equal service, irrespective of sex; measures to guarantee the right to work or the right to maintenance through stabilization of employment and through employment insurance; social insurance to protect workers and their families against the hazards of sickness, death, industrial accident and old age; limitation of hours of work and protection of health and safety in industry. Both wages and insurance benefits should be varied in accordance with family needs.

In addition workers must be guaranteed the undisputed right to freedom of association, and should be encouraged and assisted by the state to organize themselves in trade unions. By means of collective agreements and participation in work councils, the workers can achieve fair working rules and share in the control of industry and profession; and their organizations will be indispensable elements in a system of genuine industrial democracy.

The labour code should be uniform throughout the country. But the achievements of this end is difficult so long as jurisdiction over labour legislation under the B.N.A. Act is mainly in the hands of the provinces. It is urgently necessary, therefore, that the RN .A. Act be amended to make such a national labour code possible.

8. SOCIALIZED HEALTH SERVICES

Publicly organized health, hospital and medical services.

With the advance of medical science the maintenance of a healthy population has become a function for which every civilized community should undertake responsibility. Health services should be made at least as freely available as are educational services today. But under a system which is still mainly of private enterprise the costs of proper medical care, such as the wealthier members of society can easily afford, are at present prohibitive for great masses of the people. A properly organized system of public health services including medical and dental care, which would stress the prevention rather than the cure of illness should be extended to all our people in both rural and urban areas. This is an enterprise in which Dominion, Provincial and Municipal authorities, as well as the medical and dental professions, can co-operate.

9. B.N.A. ACT

The amendment of the Canadian Constitution, without infringing upon racial or religious minority rights or upon legitimate provincial claims to autonomy, so as to give the Dominion Government adequate powers to deal effectively with urgent economic problems which are essentially national in scope; the abolition of the Canadian Senate.

We propose that the necessary amendments to the B.N.A. Act shall be obtained as speedily as required, safeguards being inserted to ensure that the existing rights of racial and religious minorities shall not be changed without their own consent. What is chiefly needed today is the placing in the hands of the national government of more power to control national economic development. In a rapidly changing economic environment our political constitution must be reasonably flexible. The present division of powers between Dominion and Provinces reflects the conditions of a pioneer, mainly agricultural, community in 1867. Our constitution must be brought into line with the increasing industrialization of the country and the consequent centralization of economic and financial power—which has taken place in the last two generations. The principle laid down in the Quebec Resolution of the Fathers of Confederation should be applied to the conditions of 1933, that "there be a general government charged with matters of common interest to the whole country and local governments for each of the provinces charged with the control of local matters in their respective sections."

The Canadian Senate, which was originally created to protect provincial rights, but has failed even in this function, has developed into a bulwark of capitalist interests, as is illustrated by the large number of company directorships held by its aged members. In its peculiar composition of a fixed number of members appointed for life it is one of the most reactionary assemblies in the civilized world. It is a standing obstacle to all progressive legislation, and the only permanently satisfactory method of dealing with the constitutional difficulties it creates is to abolish it.

10. EXTERNAL RELATIONS

A Foreign Policy designed to obtain international economic co- operation and to promote disarmament and world peace.

Canada has a vital interest in world peace. We propose, therefore, to do everything in our power to advance the idea of international co-operation as represented by the League of Nations and the International Labour Organization. We would extend our diplomatic machinery for keeping in touch with the main centres of world interest. But we believe that genuine international co-operation is incompatible with the capitalist regime which is in force in most countries, and that strenuous efforts are needed to rescue the League from its present conditions of being mainly a League of capitalist Great Powers. We stand resolutely against all participation in imperialist wars. Within the British Commonwealth, Canada must maintain her autonomy as a completely self-governing nation. We must resist all attempts to build up a new economic British Empire in place of the old political one, since such attempts readily lend themselves to the purpose of capitalist exploitation and may easily lead to further world wars.

Canada must refuse to be entangled in any more wars fought to make the world safe for capitalism.

11. TAXATION AND PUBLIC FINANCE

A new taxation policy designed not only to raise public revenues but also to lessen the glaring inequalities of income and to provide funds for social services and the socialization of industry; the cessation of the debt creating system of Public Finance.

In the type of economy that we envisage, the need for taxation, as we now understand it, will have largely disappeared. It will nevertheless be essential during the transition period, to use the taxing powers, along with the other methods proposed elsewhere, as a means of providing for the socialization of industry, and for extending the benefits of increased Social Services.

At the present time capitalist governments in Canada raise a large portion of their revenues from such levies as customs duties and sales taxes, the main burden of which falls upon the masses. In place of such taxes upon articles of general consumption, we propose a drastic extension of income, corporation and inheritance taxes, steeply graduated according to ability to pay. Full publicity must be given to income tax payments and or the tax collection system must be brought up to the English standard of efficiency.

We also believe in the necessity for an immediate revision of the basis of Dominion and Provincial sources of revenue, so as to produce a co-ordinated and equitable system of taxation throughout Canada.

An inevitable effect of the capitalist system is the debt creating character of public financing. All public debts have enormously increased, and the fixed interest charges paid thereon now amount to the largest single item of so-called uncontrollable public expenditures. The C.C.F. proposes that in future no public financing shall be permitted which facilitates the perpetuation of the parasitic interest-receiving class; that capital shall be provided through the medium of the National Investment Board and free from perpetual interest charges.

We proposed that all Public Works, as directed by the Planning Commission, shall be financed by the issuance of credit, as suggested, based upon the National Wealth of Canada.

12. FREEDOM

Freedom of speech and assembly for all; repeal of Section 98 of the Criminal Code; amendment of the Immigration Act to prevent the present inhuman policy of deportation; equal treatment before the law of all residents of Canada irrespective of race, nationality or religious or political beliefs.

In recent years, Canada has seen an alarming growth of Fascist tendencies among all governmental authorities. The most elementary rights of freedom of speech and assembly have been arbitrarily denied to workers and to all whose political and social views do not meet with the approval of those in power. The lawless and brutal conduct of the police in certain centres in preventing public meetings and in dealing with political prisoners must cease.

Section 98 of the Criminal Code which has been used as a weapon of political oppression by a panic-stricken capitalist government, must be wiped off the statute book and those who have been imprisoned under it must be released. An end must be put to the inhuman practice of deporting immigrants who were brought to this country by immigration propaganda and now, through no fault of their own, to find themselves victims of an executive department against whom there is no appeal to the courts of the land. We stand for full economic, political and religious liberty for all.

13. SOCIAL JUSTICE

The establishment of a commission composed of psychiatrists, psychologists, socially minded jurists and social workers, to deal with all matters pertaining to crime and punishment and the general administration of law, in order to humanize the law and to bring it into harmony with the needs of the people.

While the removal of economic inequality will do much to overcome the most glaring injustices in the treatment of those who come into conflict with the law, our present archaic system must be changed and brought into accordance with a modern concept of human relationships. The new system must not be based, as is the present one, upon vengeance and fear, but upon an understanding of human behaviour. For this reason its planning and control cannot be left in the hands of those steeped in the out-worn legal tradition; and therefore it is proposed that there shall be established a national commission composed of psychiatrists, psychologists, socially-minded jurists and social workers whose duty it shall be to devise a system of prevention and correction consistent with other features of a new social order.

14. AN EMERGENCY PROGRAMME

The assumption by the Dominion Government of direct responsibility for dealing with the present critical unemployment situation and for tendering suitable work or adequate maintenance; the adoption of measures to relieve the extremity of the crisis such as a programme of public spending on housing, and other enterprises that will increase the real wealth of Canada, to be financed by the issue of credit based on the national wealth.

The extent of unemployment and the widespread suffering which it has caused, creates a situation with which provincial and municipal governments have long been unable to cope and forces upon the Dominion government direct responsibility for dealing with the crisis as the only authority with financial resources adequate to meet the situation. Unemployed workers must be secured in the tenure of their homes, and the scale and methods of relief, at present altogether inadequate, must be such as to preserve decent human standards of living.

It is recognized that even after a Co-operative Commonwealth Federation Government has come into power, a certain period of time must elapse before the planned economy can be fully worked out.

During this brief transitional period, we propose to provide work and purchasing power for those now unemployed by a far-reaching programme of public expenditure on housing, slum clearance, hospitals, libraries, schools, community halls, parks, recreational projects, reforestation, rural electrification, the elimination of grade crossings, and other similar projects in both town and country. This programme, which would be financed by the issuance of credit based on the national wealth, would serve the double purpose of creating employment and meeting recognized social needs.

Any steps which the Government takes, under this emergency programme, which may assist private business, must include guarantees of adequate wages and reasonable hours of work, and must be designed to further the advance towards the complete Co- operative Commonwealth.

Emergency measures, however, are of only temporary value, for the present depression is a sign of the mortal sickness of the whole capitalist system, and this sickness cannot be cured by the application of salves. These leave untouched the cancer which is eating at the heart of our society, namely, the economic system in which our natural resources and our principal means of production and distribution are owned, controlled and operated for the private profit of a small proportion of our population.

No C.C.F. Government will rest content until it has eradicated capitalism and put into operation the full programme of socialized planning which will lead to the establishment in Canada of the Co- operative Commonwealth.

Focus Questions

1. Why was there such strong opposition from the Canadian Government and employers to union organizations like the OBU? What does this opposition tell us about the challenges of being a worker? Do you think there is similar opposition to union organization today?

2. What role did veterans play in the Drumheller strike of 1919? Did this surprise you? Why or why not?

3. What did the CCF want to do, and why? Do you find their arguments radical, or do you think they are relatively acceptable/mainstream?

4. What do documents like these tell us about how Canada was formed, and what the country means to different people?

10

Border Politics: American Power and Canadian Sovereignty: the Cold War Precedent

Introduction

During and after the Second World War, Canada's relationship with the United States changed profoundly. The war itself had left Canada's traditional ally, Britain, triumphant but virtually crippled. And as post-war peace transformed into Cold War tensions, concerns about the military security of North America led many Canadians (including those in power) to believe that closer ties with the United States were necessary. Thus, through a series of treaties signed in the early 1940s and continuing into the Cold War, Canada shifted its political, economic, and military attentions to the United States—with results both positive and negative. On one hand, close alliance with the U.S. provided what many believed to be essential military clout and preparedness. On the other, these same ties also made some people increasingly nervous about Canada's sovereignty.

The readings in this chapter, all dating from the period of the Cold War, reflect on Canada's relations with the U.S., and describe what their authors believed to be the chief dangers and benefits of this relationship. The first was written by H. Hume Wrong, an influential Canadian diplomat who served as an ambassador for Canada in the U.S. and on the League of Nations, and who was deeply involved in the negotiations for the North Atlantic Treaty. The second article was written by R. J. Sutherland, a well known and respected defence analyst, and the final by prominent political scientist, Denis Stairs. What is most intriguing and challenging for the historian—as well as anyone interested in probing current relationships with the U.S.—is how similar the concerns of these authors are to Canada's current, post-Cold War relationship with our southern neighbour. While reading these essays, keep these contemporary parallels in mind.

Canada-United States Relations
H. Hume Wrong

In this book on Canada, a great deal has already been said inevitably about the relations between Canada and the United States. This chapter will discuss these relations in the difficult context of Canada's future. The writer is not equipped with the mantle of a prophet; he has no crystal ball nor a convenient oracle to enable him to peer into the future. There is, then, no intention here to attempt the impossible by trying to predict what the relationships between Canada and the United States will be in the years to come. It may, however, serve to cast some light on what the future may bring if, as a point of departure, a description is given of two extreme views, both now current, of the position of Canada in relation to the United States. Later, some thoughts on the realities will be offered.

First let us consider how the relations between Canada and the United States appear to Communist eyes behind the Iron Curtain. According to Communist theory and practice, to judge from what is publicly said and written, and very probably widely believed, Canada can only be a satellite or a victim for the United States, and probably both. The bloodthirsty exploiters of Wall Street, they may say, have stretched their greedy hands across the international boundary in order to exact tribute from the Canadian people who are powerless to resist. The monopolists of American industry and finance, aided by their traitorous Canadian minions, are constantly frustrating developments in Canada which are strongly desired by Canadians in their own national interest. They might conclude that Canadians have nothing to lose but their chains, and that the way to cast off these chains is to transform Canada into what they call a people's democracy.

To the devout Communist peering in the direction of North America through the Iron Curtain, how must the relationships between Canada and the United States appear? He sees two very large countries dividing between them all but the southern extremities of the North American continent. He notes that the boundary between them is of phenomenal length, the longest boundary possibly between any two countries in the world, and that this boundary splits in half four of the five Great Lakes, follows the course of the St. Lawrence, Detroit and other rivers, and for a great stretch of its total length is an arbitrary line marked by no natural features. He concludes, rightly, that the affairs of two countries linked so extensively by geography, must be

From *Canada: Nation on the March*, 1953, pp. 193–197

very much mixed up. He observes that one of the countries is the wealthiest and most productive country in the world, while the other has only about one-eleventh of its population and perhaps one-fifteenth of its production; furthermore, that the resources of the weaker country are very great and in the process of rapid development, a development much aided by the willingness of the capitalists of the United States to invest large sums in Canada. He learns that a substantial portion of Canadian industry is owned or controlled by large concerns in the United States, and he notes the enormous volume of trade that crosses the international boundary and the huge flow of persons constantly going from one country to the other.

Now, all these observations are perfectly true. The list of facts which establish the intimacy of the relations between the two countries could be extended almost *ad infinitum*. Where our faithful Communist would go wrong is in the deductions which he is compelled by his rigid doctrine to draw from the facts. For he is compelled to conclude, or to assert that he concludes lest he be found guilty of the horrid crime of deviation—a crime which may now be in process of redefinition—that Canada is a prime example of the economic imperialism with which he charges the United States. He is compelled to believe therefore that Canadian political independence is only maintained because Canada is an obedient satellite, as ready to obey the master's voice as are the unfortunate Soviet satellites in Europe, and that Canadian independence is nominal, not real, preserved only for the convenience of the American exploiters.

Such Communists would only be confirmed in their mistaken views if they pondered the probable course of future developments. To select two illustrations: try to imagine how they would look at the needs of the United States for raw materials and at the problems of North American defence. They could truthfully note that the need for raw materials to satisfy the huge demand of American industry is steadily increasing, that a growing proportion of these materials must be secured from other countries, and that great new resources are under development in Canada for which the United States will be a principal market. From this must they not deduce, following their mistaken dogma, that Canada must become more and more the servant of the monopolists of the United States?

Turning to defence, the Communists might argue that as the range and destructive power of new weapons increase and as the value of the protection afforded by oceans and icy wastes diminishes, Canada is in process of becoming the front line of defence against attack on the United States from the north, the bastion which protects the heartland of American industry. Surely, then, would they not say, Canada must be under the military direction and control of the United States, for reasons similar to those which have led the Soviet Union to surround itself with a defensive ring of satellites in Europe. Such an interpretation comes naturally to the Communist mind, obsessed with the idea of inevitable conflict.

Let us turn from this extreme view to another but opposite extreme attitude which is closer to the truth but nevertheless requires considerable modification. This view is sometimes expressed in passages of flamboyant oratory, more frequently perhaps in the United States than in Canada. It depicts the cordial relations which exist between the two countries as part of the natural order of things, with the two governments and the two nations bound together indissolubly in brotherly love. Even admitting that this condition has not always existed in the past, these extremists would maintain that a state of opinion and a degree of interdependence have now been developed which guarantee its continuance in perpetuity. So many pleasant and complimentary things are currently being said about Canada in the United States that if one had a really sinister mind one might suspect a concerted American design to infect the Canadian people with a bad case of what the Greeks called *hubris,* a vainglorious pride which would only be a prelude to their destruction. That, of course, is bunkum; but it is both nice and novel to have so much attention paid to Canadian accomplishments and Canadian prospects.

On the one hand we must emphatically reject the Communist interpretation that, no matter what we say, Canada is a victim, willing or unwilling, of American exploitation. On the other hand the opposite error must not be made of assuming that everything will always go well without anyone ever having to do anything very much about it.

The truth is that Canadians and Americans get on well together not because of any superior or inherent national virtue. This state of affairs has not come into existence without a lot of effort, nor will it continue automatically. The two nations do indeed have a great deal in common in their standards of behaviour, their conception of justice, as well as in their national interests. They share a continent which in the dislocated and frenzied world of today is one of the safest places in which to live and also the richest and most comfortable to be found anywhere.

Canada and the United States have indeed reached a position in which their peoples can proudly say that their relationship is a fine example to the rest of the world. That has not always been the case. It has not come about from natural circumstances unassisted by human endeavour. It is the product of many years of development, through many ups and downs, guided by some wise statesmanship and buttressed by tolerant recognition of national interests, national feelings, and, indeed, national prejudices on both sides of the international boundary. The qualities of restraint, imagination and understanding which have helped to produce the present welcome results are still needed just as much as ever to preserve them. These qualities may indeed be needed more than ever today because of the rapidity in this era of technical achievement of the process of shrinkage of space and time.

As mankind progressively masters space and time, so does the area of international relationships automatically expand, and so consequently do the possible sources of international friction increase. For most of the last quarter of a century the present writer has been involved in one capacity or another with a share of the conduct of official business between the governments of the United States and Canada. He has seen that business enlarge greatly, indeed enormously, in extent. Many subjects now of the highest importance and urgency in the official relations of the two countries never entered into them at all twenty-five years ago. Just as there is need to achieve a meeting of minds between Washington and Ottawa on many grave matters which each government once regarded as outside the realm of its international affairs, so new and prickly problems of mutual concern arise which are deeply involved in the domestic politics of both countries.

There still remain the old issues with which the peoples of Canada and the United States have lived for many years. To give a few examples: there are still ancient differences about trade and tariffs, intricate difficulties over customs regulations, though that is predominantly a one-sided issue with the complaints mainly of Canadian origin, still the inability up to the present to arrive at final agreement on how to make joint use of the water power which runs to waste in the international section of the St. Lawrence River and, therefore, the inability to link the inland seas of the Great Lakes with the Atlantic Ocean by an adequate channel of navigation. Such issues as these are old friends, or enemies, perhaps nearer resolution, but as important today as they ever were. They have not been superseded, but they have been supplemented by many newer issues. The outcome is that never have the official relations between Canada and the United States been so close and friendly as they are now, but also never have they been so complicated and so difficult. More than goodwill is required to avoid future irritations, recriminations and disputes. More than ever are needed the stern virtues of sober judgment, hard work, and recognition of the general interest over local pressures and demands.

Of course, the relationships between the two countries involve much more than the dealings between the two governments. They comprise the countless contacts for pleasure and for profit, for friendship and for business, between Americans and Canadians. A continuous effort, both private and public, is needed to bring about a better understanding in both countries of each other's interests, problems and potentialities. The two democracies, while equally based on the will of the people, must reach their governmental decisions independently and by different constitutional methods. It is of high importance to all that they should find their way together in amity and constancy of purpose through the mazes, the entanglements, the frustrations and the perils of today.

Canada's Long Term Strategic Situation
R. J. Sutherland
1962

Since the end of Hitler's war the world has changed almost beyond recognition. The increasing power of weaponry has played a conspicuous role, but developments of a political nature have been equally revolutionary, and are, in the long run, almost certainly more important. This sequence of rapid and dramatic change has led to two results: traditional conceptions of national security and national defence have been called into question, but visibility has been reduced. Nevertheless, security and the protection of vital national interests remain for every nation a constant preoccupation of policy. It is also true that the very concept of national security implies a consistency of purpose and major policy extending over decades and even generations.

The search for stable foundations of policy in the face of drastic and revolutionary change poses a problem of almost excruciating difficulty for all nations, including the two superpowers. We should not be surprised that Canadians find these problems intractable and in some respects insoluble. However, in our case there is a special consideration. Canada has no particular tradition of strategic calculation. Such tradition as we possess seems to be that strategy is a suitable diversion for retired generals who need not be taken very seriously. Yet the increasing attention which is being given to the problems of security and survival by Canadians of the most diverse opinions and backgrounds shows that we too are caught up in the fortunes of a dynamic and dangerous world. We have discovered, as Leon Trotsky once observed, that anyone who desires a quiet life should not have been born in the twentieth century.

To borrow a term from mathematics, there are certain invariants of Canadian strategy. It is worth examining these rather carefully because they shed a great deal of light upon the foundations of Canada's national existence and her place in the world community. They determine, to some very considerable extent, the agenda of Canadian national policy—that is, those major questions with regard to which there is some genuine choice. And they also reveal important areas where there is no choice, however much we as Canadians might like to believe that there is.

"Canada's Long Term Strategic Situation" by R. J. Sutherland, was first published in the *International Journal,* Volume 17, Winter 1961–1962. Reprinted by permission.

Geography

The most important of these invariants is geography. It is a safe prediction that at the end of this century, Canada will occupy the north half of the North American continent and the United States will occupy the south half. This geographical fact has a vitally important strategic consequence. It means that the United States is bound to defend Canada from external aggression almost regardless of whether or not Canadians wish to be defended. We may call this the involuntary American guarantee. For as far ahead as one can possibly foresee, this will be the central fact of Canadian strategy and the basis of Canada's external security.

The involuntary U.S. guarantee to Canada is subject to certain conditions. In 1938, speaking of Canada's relationship with the United States, Prime Minister Mackenzie King had this to say:

> We, too, as a good friendly neighbour, have our responsibilities. One of them is to see that our country is made as immune from possible invasion as we can reasonably be expected to make it, and, that should the occasion ever arise, enemy forces should not be able to make their way, either by land, sea or air, to the United States across Canadian territory.

These are not idle words. What Mackenzie King said was that Canada must not become through military weakness or otherwise a direct threat to American security. If this were to happen, Canada's right to existence as an independent nation would be placed in jeopardy.

When Mackenzie King made this statement, the threat of military operations against the United States via Canadian territory was rather far-fetched. However, the principle was not novel even in 1938. One need only think back to the part played by Canada in the abrogation of the Anglo-Japanese Alliance in 1921. But the principle goes back even further to the Rush-Bagot Treaty in 1817 and the Monroe Doctrine of 1823. One may suggest that in combination these amounted to an outline non-aggression treaty between the United States and Great Britain in right of her American possessions. In the course of almost a century the terms of this treaty were worked out in detail to produce the famous undefended frontier. Mackenzie King was therefore drawing attention to a basic condition of Canada's national existence. If this condition had not been understood and adhered to in the past, there would be, very probably, no British North America and no Canada.

In the final analysis, a Great Power will take whatever action it finds necessary to the maintenance of its security. It must do this or cease to be a Great Power, and the United States is no exception. However, at least for the past half century, relations between Canada and the United States have never approached this brutal basis. It is difficult to believe that they ever will. This is owing to the fundamental community of interests between the two nations. If the United States is bound to defend Canada, it is also true that Canada can never, consistent with her own interests, ignore the requirements of American security; because, in the final analysis, the security of the United States is the security of Canada.

Economic Strength

Now let us turn to economic strength and the raw materials of national power. Canadians are prone to measure themselves against the United States, and by this standard Canada is a rather minor country. By any other standard she is a very powerful nation. The best index of national potential is probably a combination of Gross National Product and technological competence. This is a good measure of the ability of a nation to produce modern military hardware—and military power is still the gold coin of diplomacy. It is equally a good index of a nation's ability to produce the silver coin of diplomacy: to participate in aid programmes, to supply technical assistance, and—most important of all—to engage in old-fashioned international trade. According to these criteria, Canada is somewhere between the seventh and ninth most powerful nation in the world today. This in a field of about 130 political entities which can be regarded as sovereign, and the number is going up from day to day.

In 1945, Canada was, very probably, the fourth most powerful nation in the world. She had a sizable military establishment backed up by a fully intact economy. She was one of four nations which possessed an on-going programme of military research and development, and she had played a subordinate but significant role in the development of the atomic bomb. In the immediate post-war period, Canada's international prestige owed much to the brilliance of her diplomats, but it may be well to remember that in those years Canadian diplomacy could draw upon reserves accumulated during the Second World War. These were in the hardest kind of diplomatic currency—demonstrated military power.

By the year 2000, it is likely that Canada will have slipped a few places as more populous nations gain mastery over modern technology. Nevertheless, Canada will still be at the high end of the international batting order. Of course, Canada is not a super-power in the same category with the United States and Russia. And, unlike such countries as China and India, she cannot reasonably aspire to become a super-power. But she is in the next category along with such nations as Britain, France, Germany, Italy and Japan.

One further point. Owing to the close integration of the American and Canadian economies, an attempt to destroy the productive capacity of the United States would almost certainly result in some Canadian targets being attacked. The two countries constitute a single target system: it would not make sense to attack the United States and leave Canada alone. This has nothing to do with Canada's participation in NATO or NORAD; it is a fact which no treaty can change one way or the other. The same principle applies to any kind of attack aimed at the North American economic system, such as the cutting of sea communications. It is also true of economic warfare pursued by non-violent means, with the reservation that in this respect Canada is substantially more vulnerable than the United States. It is therefore clear that the community of interests between Canada and the United States is much more than a matter of geography. Geography has been the predisposing factor; but economics has forged an even more powerful bond.

Natural Alliances and Alignments

Now let us turn to the subject of alliances and alignments. Friendships between nations are based upon interests in common and enmities are based upon interests in opposition. Among nations, both friendship and enmity are relative. No two nations have precisely the same interests and hence there is no such thing as perfect friendship. Neither is there any such thing as absolute enmity. But there are certain natural alignments based upon a natural community of interests.

In Canada's case, her strongest natural alignment is with the United States. This is based upon close economic ties and the fact that Canada relies upon the United States for her security. But there is also a cultural affinity, a basic compatibility of social institutions and attitudes which goes beyond any ordinary conception of common interests. Canada and the United States are joint participants in the much criticized and greatly envied North American civilization of the twentieth century. As this civilization is their common property, its survival is their common concern.

Canada's second natural affinity is towards Western Europe and especially towards Britain and France. However, it is worth noticing that a sizable proportion of our population comes from such countries as Germany, Italy, Scandinavia and even Central Europe. We share with the nations of Europe a common historical tradition, as well as ties of language, religion and culture. There is also a racial compatibility, and, in spite of what one might wish, race is likely to be a powerful political motive during the next half century.

Canada is also a Pacific power. Her interests in the Pacific area have led her to take part in two wars: the war against Japan and the war in Korea. And, although the Organization of American States is somewhat out of fashion, Canada has a potential role within the Western hemispheric system. We also bear, rather more conscientiously than most, the responsibilities of membership in the United Nations, and participate with conviction in the fraternal association of the Commonwealth.

It is an article of faith with many Canadians that they have some special affinity with the new nations of Africa and Asia based upon the fact that we are a "non-colonial" power. If this were true, a great historic role would be mapped out for Canada: to serve as the link and the interpreter between Western civilization and the cultures of Africa, Asia and Latin America. Unfortunately, it is simply not the case. So far as the Afro-Asians are concerned, Canadians are members of the well-fed white minority. One may hope that Canadians will continue to view the problems of the new nations with sympathy and understanding. However, in the long run our relations with these nations will be governed by interests rather than sentiment; and their interests must figure as prominently as our own.

We should recognize that the new nations are engaged in establishing their historic identity, and they cannot afford to be too choosy about the means. For the moment they are weak. Since they can barely afford penny ante, they naturally disapprove of high stake poker. But one should make no mistake, their aspirations include the full panoply of national power. As they acquire this power they will use it to advance their interests as they see them. Unfortunately, these interests will in some cases not be our interests.

By recognizing this fact now we can at least spare ourselves from severe disillusionment. Well before the end of this century, the problem of accommodating within a genuine world community a number of powerful nations which do not share the traditions and values of European civilization (even in the perverted version of Russian Bolshevism) may well supersede the East-West conflict as the prime problem of international policy.

This point seems to be worth making because there is a persistent idea that aid programmes and similar activities are an alternative to defence. This is simply not true. These programmes are defensible on their merits; but they do not necessarily lead to stability and security. They are all too likely to lay the basis for revolution and turmoil.

The Policy of the Opening Towards Europe

Traditionally, Canada has aimed to off-set excessive influence on the part of the United States by maintaining a close tie with Britain. This was the strategy pursued by Sir John A. Macdonald in creating a single state in the vast expanse of British North America. For the first fifty years of our existence, the "British connection", backed up by the power of the Royal Navy, was the basis of such national security policy as Canada possessed. The tie with Britain was the legal basis and the principal political justification for Canada's participation in the First World War. Between the wars, Canada achieved constitutional independence, but in 1939, it was the historic tie with Britain, more than any other factor, which accounted for Canada's prompt declaration of war.

During the war, there emerged a new conception of Canada's role which was rather flattering to Canada, namely that Canada is the bridge which unites the two great English-speaking democracies and forms with them the North Atlantic Triangle. This idea was given an eloquent formulation by Sir Winston Churchill in a speech in Ottawa in 1943. At that time, it was, beyond doubt, the British belief that after the war the Americans would revert to their traditional isolationism. In this event, a major role would be marked out for Canada—to serve as the vanguard of North American policy and power. It was, it seems clear, the British expectation that Canada would play this role in close association with Britain and to some extent under British tutelage. However, the Americans have not reverted to isolationism; the bridge theory and the concept of the North Atlantic triangle have therefore fallen into some disrepute.

The concept of the North Atlantic Triangle nevertheless plays a certain role in Canadian defence. In 1947, arrangements were entered into between the United States, Britain and Canada in the field of research and development and in certain other important areas. These arrangements have functioned ever since to the very great advantage of Canada. As a result Canada is one of the half dozen nations in the world which possesses a comprehensive and up-to-the-minute understanding of contemporary military technology.

The idea of an opening towards Europe as an off-set to excessive American influence was a powerful factor in Canada's enthusiastic support for NATO. A Canadian statesman might have cribbed from Canning: "I have called into existence the Old World in order to restore the balance of the New." A former Minister of National Defence put it a little differently: with fifteen people in the bed you are less likely to get raped!

Britain's approach to the Common Market has come as a shock to many Canadians, and has tended to call into question the strategy of the opening towards Europe. A clearer reading of Canadian history might at any rate have spared us some surprise. The various fisheries disputes and the Alaska Boundary dispute showed that even in the hey-day of her power Britain had at some point to subordinate Canadian interests to her own. It is not necessarily true that in a bed which contains fifteen other nations Canada is less likely to get raped. One must inquire into motives, and, since all nations have something to gain from the United States, they might possibly be prepared to assist and applaud. It is not necessarily in Canada's interest to involve NATO in the entire agenda of Canadian-American relations.

Does this mean that Canada's membership in NATO is a source of weakness rather than of strength? It depends upon what we expect to gain. If we expect to gather allies against the United States we are going to be disappointed. And this is true of any other forum including the United Nations. However, by participating in NATO, and conceivably other collective defence systems, Canada can achieve two things. Firstly, by being present at the table we can serve as the spokesman for our own interests. If we are not present, our voice will not be heard. Secondly, to the extent that Canada plays a significant role in Western security, she can maintain real influence in Washington. It seems evident that this principle of independent representation is the key to a vigorous Canadian national existence. And although a certain amount can be achieved outside the area of security, in a world as dangerous and dynamic as our own the forum which deals with security will be many times more important than any other.

Collective Defence and Collective Security

The terms collective security and collective defence are often used but seldom defined. It may be worth taking a little time in order to see what they mean. Collective defence is really a somewhat antiseptic term for a military alliance, that is, and association of nations entered into with a view, in some circumstances, to the joint conduct of military operations, or to be blunt about it to war. Whether an alliance as offensive or defensive depends upon political intent.

A collective security system is an association of nations entered into for the purpose of deterring aggression. The basis of the association is that if a member nation were to be the victim of aggression, the other members would form a military alliance in order to wage war on its behalf. Collective security therefore involves two major assumptions:

(a) The members of the association are agreed as to what constitutes aggression; and
(b) If aggression were to occur, member nations would unite in order to wage war.

There is a school of thought which holds that military alliances are nasty and immoral, whereas collective security is upstanding and commendable. The important point is that they are not essentially different. If a collective security system is to provide genuine security it must dispose of force, and it must be based upon a community of interests sufficiently strong to justify member nations, under some circumstances, in going to war. Otherwise, collective security is no more than a facade. This has some bearing upon the U.N. If by a near miracle the U.N. were to become capable of functioning as a collective security system it would begin to look a lot like a collective defence system such as NATO.

Canada's Place in the U.S. Alliance System

Now let us turn to the U.S. alliance system and Canada's place within this system. The United States has formal alliances with some forty odd countries and unwritten alliances with a number of others including such "neutrals" as Yugoslavia, Sweden, Austria and India. At the apex of the hierarchy there are three arrangements involving the U.S.A., Britain and Canada—the North Atlantic Triangle. These are:

(a) The North American defence system which dates from the Ogdensburg agreement of 1940;
(b) The tripartite ABC agreements which operate in the field of research and development and in certain other areas. These were entered into in 1947, but are really a continuation of the war-time partnership;
(c) The U.S.-U.K. system which operates in the area of strategic weapons systems and again goes back to the war-time arrangements .

The Canada-U.S. system is the senior American alliance—the first departure from splendid isolationism. The principal instrument of this alliance is the Permanent Joint Board on Defence which is a "political" body. The role of NORAD has often been misunderstood. The purpose of NORAD is to achieve operational co-ordination of North American air defences and to provide machinery for joint planning. NORAD replaced less formal machinery which had existed for this purpose since 1945. The C.-in-C. NORAD does not exercise "command" over Canadian forces in peace or war. In an err urgency he carries out operational co-ordination in accordance with a directive approved by both Governments. Command of Canadian components is exercised by the Air Officer Commanding Air Defence Command, R.C.A.F., who is responsible to the Government of Canada through the Minister of National Defence.

The U.S. global alliance system includes five regional systems: NATO in Western and Southern Europe; CENTO in the Near East and Middle East; ANZUS in the South-west Pacific; SEATO in South East Asia; OAS in South America. The United States is not formally a member of CENTO, although the alliance depends upon U.S. support. In addition, there is an informal Central Pacific system including Japan, Formosa, South Korea and the Phillipines.

Canada is a member only of NATO. Her role as a Pacific power is to some extent in abeyance. The same is true of OAS. OAS is a good illustration of the dilemma of Canadian policy. Since Punte del Este there has been some tendency for Canadians to congratulate themselves that they are not members of OAS. The fact remains that if one believes that South America is of growing importance to Canada, then Canada's absence from OAS represents a real restriction upon the effectiveness of Canadian diplomacy in South America. This illustrates the principle of the presence at the table. Unless a nation possesses overwhelming power, it cannot play a significant role if it isn't there. In the future, Canada may be faced with a similar dilemma in the Pacific.

Summing Up

There is a fairly common belief in Canada that power politics is a nasty business which we should stay out of. Unfortunately, we have no such option. Calculations of national interest and relative power have figured in Canadian statecraft since the beginning of our history. Barring some total and presently unforseeable transformation in the international order this will continue to be the case.

A few years ago Mr. James M. Minifie wrote a book with the provocative title *Canada, Peacemaker or Powder-Monkey?* The defect in Mr. Minifie's thesis is that these are not real options. Canada does not possess the ability to transform the present system of international politics; nor, indeed, does any other nation. It is also true that prime responsibility for major decisions involving peace and war will not rest with Canada regardless of what we mayor may not do.

What are the real alternatives? It seems evident that in the future as at present Canada will remain an American ally. This is the result of our geography; but in an even more compelling sense it is dictated by our interests. The question is whether we will be a powerful and effective ally or a weak and reluctant one. There is a parallel choice: whether our role in world affairs will be one of dependence upon the

United States or whether we will be effective members of a larger community. This is a genuine choice and one, indeed, which we cannot avoid.

Does this mean that Canada is necessarily a U.S. satellite? No doubt many Canadians will continue to torture themselves with this thought; but the answer is that it is beside the point. In the second half of the twentieth century, no nation, including the United States, can pursue a truly independent policy. By recognizing and acting in accordance with our interests we do not become a U.S. satellite merely because our interests coincide with those of the United States. Instead of lamenting the consequences of our geography we should reflect that it is largely owing to our geography and our uniquely close relationship with the United States that a nation of eighteen millions has been able to achieve so large a share of wealth, power, and constructive influence.

Confronting Uncle Sam: Cuba and Korea
Denis Stairs
1968

Whatever one thinks of the content and execution of Canadian foreign policy, one must grant at least that it adds a little vigour to an otherwise vapid political community. Canadians in general are renowned for the flaccid indifference with which they conduct their political affairs; but raise before them the issue of their relations abroad and they at once assume the guise of warriors in combat. The battle rages with special fury when the influence of Washington over policy-makers in Ottawa is the subject in dispute, and to enter the fray at such a point is therefore to risk the most grievous slings and arrows. The venture is justified, however, by the importance of the issue, for it is a pivotal determinant of Canada's freedom-to-choose in international affairs.

The quarrel actually involves not one question but several. When you ask whether Canada should adopt in a specific case a policy opposed by Washington, the first thing you need to know is whether it will be effective in achieving some or all of its objectives in spite of American hostility. If the answer is No, then the policy presumably must be shelved; but if the answer is Yes, then a second and third question follow: (2) What sacrifices— including sacrifices induced by the disapproval or even in extreme cases the retaliatory action of the United States - will the policy require on the part of Canada? and (3) Do you place a higher value on the objectives you expect to achieve than on the sacrifices your policy will incur? The answers obviously will vary considerably from one case to the next, and the last of the questions is essentially normative in character. The first two are empirical, however, and require judgments about the future consequences of your policy. The accuracy of these judgments will depend upon your understanding of the implications of the international relationships concerned, and this in turn will derive very largely from your knowledge of what happened in previous cases of a similar kind.

Here, then, is the rationale for the case-study approach adopted in this paper. It is true of course that history can be a mischievous teacher and that the precise circumstances of past cases may not be duplicated in the present or future. It is true also that a full and systematic treatment would require the testing of a large number of possible conditions and reference to many more cases than two. Even the two slight cases that follow, however, may cast a little light on the subject and at least draw attention to some of the difficulties it presents. Both have been drawn from the post-1945 period, and they have been selected as tests of the limits of Canada's independence abroad, precisely because in each instance Canadian policy was in diametric conflict with the interests of the United States.

Case I—Canada, the United States and Cuba

In brief outline, the facts are these. Following Fidel Castro's seizure of power in January 1959 the United States imposed a steadily increasing series of restrictions on Cuban-American trade—restrictions which were ostensibly in retaliation for Havana's seizure of American-owned properties in Cuba, but which were given added legitimacy in the United States by the growing conviction that Dr. Castro was guilty of cavorting with "communism." By mid-October 1960 the Washington authorities had declared an embargo on the shipment to Cuba of all commodities except nonsubsidized foodstuffs and medical supplies. Havana responded by nationalizing a large number of American owned companies, by extending and broadening its formal diplomatic relations with the Soviet bloc, and by concluding important agreements for the sale of sugar to the Soviet Union. Official diplomatic relations were finally terminated by President Eisenhower on January 3, 1961. In the following March President Kennedy reduced the quota for Cuban sugar imports to zero and the rupture in Cuban-American relations was complete.

Since then the relationship has been the source of a number of dangerously volatile international crises. The high points have included the attempted Bay of Pigs invasion in April 1961, the subsequent negotiations for the release of the captured invaders, the expulsion of Cuba in January 1962 from the Organization of American States (OAS), President Kennedy's extension of economic sanctions In February of the same year to include a boycott of all Cuban imports, the Cuban missile crisis of the following autumn, and finally the release in December 1962 of the Bay of Pigs invaders in return for $54 million in drugs, medicines and baby foods. To this day each side accuses the other of fostering sinister and subversive activities in Latin America at large, and there is no immediate prospect of an attempted *approachment.*

Under ordinary circumstances Washington's quarrel with Havana might have had little to do with Canada. The situation was complicated, however, by the fact that the Americans had resorted to economic sanctions as a statecraft technique in the pursuit of their Cuban policy. It is an elementary axiom of international affairs that economic sanctions are effective only to the extent that their application is widely endorsed by the international community. If the Americans were to succeed in intervening Cuba's foreign transactions entirely and not merely divert them to other countries, they had to win the co-operation of other actual or potential participants in Cuban trade. The result was that the US Government exerted considerable pressure on its allies to join in the economic isolation of Dr. Castro's regime.

For a number of reasons the pressure on Canada was particularly intense. Perhaps the most important was the similarity between the Canadian and American economies, for no other country could replace so effectively the United States as Cuba's chief supplier of manufactured goods. The American policy was designed to weaken the foundations of the Castro regime. by undermining the efficiency of the Cuban economy. It could reasonably be expected, for example, that as Cuba's cars, trucks and buses broke down and replacement parts became more difficult to obtain, the Cuban people would suffer some irritating inconveniences. Public transportation systems would cease to function effectively, taxis would begin to disappear, private cars would have to be junked and distribution problems would multiply. In time the Cuban citizenry would become disillusioned with Premier Castro's government, and with luck it would come tumbling down. But clearly this could happen only if no other country replaced the United States as a source (in this instance) of automotive machinery and parts. Of all the possible alternative suppliers Canada was the most threatening because Canadian automotive products were in most cases identical with those manufactured in the United States. A Havana taxi that had been imported from Miami could be repaired or replaced by products obtained from Oshawa and Windsor. If this were to happen on a large scale, the net effect of the American embargo would be the enrichment of Canadian industry.

There was an additional danger that commodities produced in the United States would be exported first to Canada and then re-shipped to the Caribbean. Our famous 4,000 miles of "undefended border" would be transformed into a vast gap in the power of the United States to employ economic sanctions against an "enemy" state. The problem was particularly acute in this instance because scrutiny of the movement of goods between Canada and the US is much more relaxed than in the case of either country's trade with other powers.

The Americans could argue also that even if Ottawa did not believe economic sanctions would weaken Premier Castro domestically, it must certainly agree that they would diminish his impact abroad. Cuba, the Americans maintained, was exporting revolution to Latin America. The Castro regime was therefore a threat to the entire hemisphere since it endangered the "western" diplomatic orientation of the Latin American Republics. Trading with Havana could only fortify the Cubans in the pursuit of their revolutionary task, and surely this was an eventuality that Canada was as eager to avoid as the United States.

For observers who are not privy to the documents of the Department of External Affairs it is difficult to determine precisely how severe the American pressure actually was. There can be no doubt, however, that it was considerable. The Canadian Press reported on December 11, 1960, for example, that Bradley Fisk, the American Assistant Secretary of Commerce for International Affairs, had revealed that Secretary of State Christian Herter had tried in vain to obtain Canadian participation in the October embargo against the Cuban regime. "We will keep working on it," Fisk said. "We will respect Canada's sovereignty in every way, but we will keep reminding Canada of our mutual interests in the fight against communism."

The pressure continued under the Kennedy administration. In February 1962, for example, Secretary of State Dean Rusk indicated that he hoped Canada and other nations would follow the OAS in isolating Havana from the Western Hemisphere. "Dollars and foreign exchange are being used by the Castro Government," he said, "to promote subversion in other countries." In the following March Senator Wayne Morse accused the Canadian government of refusing "to co-operate ... in stopping her trade in strategic goods with Communist Cuba," and Senator Kenneth Keating commented that is was impossible to understand why a country "willing to supply troops for the defence of freedom should not be willing to make economic sacrifices for the same objective." American newspapers were equally critical and Cuban refugees were infuriated. On January 15, 1961, 175 Cubans demonstrated at the Canadian Embassy in Washington against the trade policy of the Diefenbaker Government. In what must have been a refreshing treat for normally neglected Canadian diplomatists they chanted, "Down with Canada," and displayed placards reading, "Free Cuba protests Canada's Aid to Castro." On another occasion a leader of the exiles, Jose Miro Cardona, complained that the Canadians were "the Phoenicians of America. Their ships and their cargoes go where there is business to be done."

In essence Cardona was right. In spite of American pressures to the contrary, the Canadian government has maintained "normal" trading relations with the Cuban Republic, qualified only by regulations designed to prevent the trans-shipment of American goods to Cuban buyers over Canadian soil and by prohibitions on the sale to Havana of certain commodities having an accepted strategic significance. As early as November 22, 1960 about one month after the application of the American embargo the Canadian Minister of Trade and Commerce, George Hees, told the House of Commons that "Canada's trade and trading relations with Cuba are completely normal [except for] the regular restrictions that are placed on strategic materials going to any country." Three weeks later Prime Minister Diefenbaker issued a somewhat longer statement in which he said in effect that Cuba was not being treated as a special case. The government wanted "to maintain the kind of relations with Cuba which are usual with the recognized government of another country," although it would not encourage "the bootlegging of goods of United States origin." It hoped "that in so far as mutually beneficial economic relations are maintained or developed, conditions in Cuba may be eased and the general relations of western countries with Cuba may be promoted."[7]

Here was a fundamental divergence of views. The American position was that the Castro government was beyond redemption and therefore had to be eliminated. Economic sanctions comprised one of the weapons in the US arsenal and moral as well as political and strategic considerations required that it be used. By contrast the Canadian view was that Premier Castro was probably in power to stay and that in any event the most constructive policy would be to maintain friendly relations with the revolutionary government. Nothing could be solved by alienating the Cubans entirely; indeed it was probable that harsh treatment would serve only to drive them even more deeply into the communist camp.

On the other hand the Government refrained from giving Canadian businessmen any special encouragement to engage in Cuban trade. As Mr. Diefenbaker said, they would "have to make their own judgments on the prospects for advantageous transactions." Nor would Ottawa allow this country to become an escape route for American interests wishing to circumvent the regulations of their own government. To that extent Canada's willingness to conduct its policies in opposition to those of the United States was ultimately limited. In the circumstances, however, these were the limitations of neutrality rather than of dependence. Had Ottawa sanctioned the subversion of American policy by allowing Canada to become a smugglers' alley, then even the most virulent critic would have had to admit the justice of any consequent American outcry. Nevertheless Canadian policy was in fundamental conflict with that of the United States and still is. Neither the 1962 missile crisis nor the succession of the Liberal government produced any change in the Canadian position.

Parenthetically it should be observed that the government's policy has not resulted, as many Americans have claimed, in the enrichment of the Canadian economy. It is true that in some years our exports to Cuba have substantially increased, but in 1960, 1962 and 1963 they averaged less than in the years before the revolution. Trade statistics for recent years show very considerable increments over the pre-revolutionary average, but these appear to be the result primarily of wheat-sale agreements with the Soviet bloc, and in any case average less than one-tenth of pre-1959 exports to Cuba by the United States. In all years, moreover, the pattern of trade has been balanced very heavily in Canada's favour, which means that Canadian dollars cannot be helping directly to finance the export of Dr. Castro's revolution. Indeed the lack of foreign exchange has been the main factor limiting the volume of Cuban purchases in Canada.

It is worth noting also that the purely diplomatic aspect of Canada's Cuban policy has similarly differed from the American. Ottawa, unlike Washington, has continued to maintain formal diplomatic relations with Havana, and the publicly available information indicates that communication between the two capitals has been friendly and useful. Canadian business interests in Cuba, for example, have been treated very differently from those owned by Americans. In particular on those occasions when Canadian assets have been nationalized by the Cuban government, the ensuing negotiations have been conducted in an atmosphere of accommodation and the Cuban authorities have granted full compensation in the form of hard American dollars.

Ottawa's independent policy was effective to the extent that its immediate objective of maintaining amicable diplomatic and trading relations with Premier Castro's government was achieved, Whether it also advanced the longer-range purpose of reducing Havana's political and economic dependence upon the Soviet bloc is more doubtful, and certainly the Canadian position has done nothing to mitigate tensions between Cuba and the United States. There is no evidence that Canada's independent views resulted in any permanent damage to Canadian-American relations, although they may have contributed to the general animosity between the Kennedy and Diefenbaker administrations.

Case II—Canada, the United States and UNTCOK

The background for the second case is more remote and so will require more detail. After the end of the war with Japan, the United States and the Soviet Union divided the Korean peninsula for occupation purposes at the 38th parallel, with the Americans in control of the South and the Soviets in charge of the North. Originally it was planned that a united and independent Korea would be established "in due course," but as the cold war grew more bitter cooperation between the two occupation administrations proved impossible. This unfortunate development was embarrassing for the American government, partly because it was under pressure by the South Koreans to make good the wartime promise of genuine independence, and partly because it wanted to withdraw its troops from what had become an expensive and vulnerable theatre. In September 1947, therefore, the Americans took the matter before the United Nations. There, in spite of Soviet opposition, they succeeded in having the General Assembly pass a resolution creating a UN Temporary Commission on Korea (UNTCOK) which would supervise an election throughout the peninsula. The elected candidates would then form an administration and take over the governmental functions of both occupation authorities. Korea would thus become united and independent, the Department of State would be relieved of a distressing political dilemma and the American army could happily withdraw its troops without leaving an inviting vacuum of power in their wake.

What was significant from the Canadian point of view was that the United States, without prior consultation, had included Canada among its nominations for UNTCOK membership. The principal historian of the Commission has suggested not only that the Canadians were startled and surprised when the American list of nominations was read out to the Assembly but also that their decision to accept it was governed by a desire "to save the United States from embarrassment." This may or may not be true. What is certain is that the Americans made the nomination because they felt that Canadian membership would strengthen their hand. Indeed almost all the Commission members appear to have been selected with this purpose in mind. Most were closely tied with the United States, and those that were not were firmly committed to the principle of national self-determination and could be expected to support proposals for a united and independent Korea.

But if the Americans really thought UNTCOK would give them little trouble, they were shortly to suffer a rude surprise. The Commission assembled at Seoul in January 1948 only to discover that the Soviets would not allow it to function north of the 38th parallel. In the light of this development the American Commander suggested on behalf of his government that the necessary elections should take place in South Korea alone. It was at this point that conflict appeared for, while the US position was supported by China, France and the Philippines, it was opposed by Canada, Australia, India and Syria (El Salvador remaining neutral). These four powers insisted that the Commission consult with the Interim Committee of the UN General Assembly in New York before making a decision, clearly expecting that the Committee would advise them not to proceed unless they could operate in both occupation zones.

At the Interim Committee, Philip C. Jessup of the United States argued that UNTCOK should be advised "to implement its programme . . . in such parts of Korea as are accessible to the Commission," and he and other members of his delegation engaged in several days of corridor-to-lounge lobbying for the American position. Leon Gordenker has suggested that the Americans "were especially anxious to convince India, Australia and Canada" to support the US view but in the case of the two Dominions they met with little success. Australia and Canada were the only two countries to persevere in their opposition to the American resolution, and the final vote was 31 to 2 in favour, with 11 abstentions.

In presenting the Canadian case Lester Pearson argued that to hold elections in the South alone would involve changes in the Commission's terms of reference which were beyond the power of the Interim Committee to decide. He appeared to agree with the Australian view that the creation of a separate South Korean regime would tend to harden the 38th parallel into a permanent and therefore disruptive international boundary, and in defence of the Canadian position he commented acidly that it "would at least have the advantage of proving the unwarranted nature of certain allegations to the effect that the Temporary Commission was in the service of the United States of America." More startling still, he warned the Committee that if the advice contained in the American resolution were accepted by the UNTCOK majority, "a new and serious situation would be created which would have to be taken into consideration by the governments who are members of the Commission and who feel that the advice from this committee is unwise and unconstitutional." If this was. a threat that Canada would withdraw from UNTCOK if the Americans had their way, then in terms of the usual interpretation of Canadian subservience to Washington it was a bold stroke indeed.

It was also, however, a futile one. When news of the success of the American resolution reached UNTCOK headquarters in Korea, Dr. Patterson was occupied with other business in Tokyo, and on February 28 the seven remaining members met on an informal basis without him. By now the growing impatience of a number of political groups in South Korea had reached alarming proportions, and with a view to forestalling public demonstrations the seven representatives unanimously decided to announce on March 1 that elections would be held in the American zone not later than May 10. The American Commander promptly issued a declaration setting Sunday, May 9, as the precise date.

On instructions from Ottawa Dr. Patterson immediately journeyed to Korea to protest the Commission's decision. A procedural wrangle ensued with Dr. Patterson arguing that the election announcement was not binding and warning, as he had been authorized to do, that unless the Commission changed its mind he "would be compelled to abstain from further participation in the activities of the Commission until he received further instructions from his Government." Finally he withdrew, and when confronted with his departure the Commission decided by a vote of 4 to 3 to issue a press release stating that the Canadian delegation had questioned the March 1 declaration and that the Commissioners were therefore still considering whether it would be confirmed. For the time being Canada had scored a point: UNTCOK had to consider again the "advice" of the Interim Committee, and American plans for a May 9 election were once more placed in jeopardy.

The victory, however, was small and short. When discussions resumed, Dr. Patterson once again reiterated his position and added that he was haunted by "the terrible doubt that the one and only purpose for which the Commission is in Korea will not be furthered one step but rather perhaps disastrously set back if the advice of the Interim Committee is accepted. . . . If elections in South Korea alone contribute nothing to the unifying of Korea, then the United Nations Commission has no right to participate in them." But in spite of his efforts the final vote was 4-2-2 in favour of proceeding with elections in the South alone, with Australia and Canada opposed, and France and Syria abstaining. Dr. Patterson withdrew once more to await instructions from Ottawa but after an absence of 11 days he returned with orders to co-operate in the task of supervising the elections. Canada had at last capitulated.

Three observations can now be made with regard to this lamentable chronicle. The first is the obvious point that, in spite of the fact that Ottawa had used every diplomatic technique at its disposal from simple persuasion to outright boycott, in the final analysis its policy failed in the face of American opposition. The second is that this failure was due almost entirely to the fact that, in a situation in which Canada and the United States were competing for the support of the same foreign powers, the Canadians were bound to lose; indeed while Dr. Patterson was at first supported by a majority of the UNTCOK membership, by the time the dispute had been debated in the General Assembly's Interim Committee his diplomatic allies had been reduced to one. The third is that there is no evidence anywhere that Canada's relations with the United States were seriously or even temporarily jeopardized by the Canadian role in the UNTCOK episode. It is true, of course, that in view of their ultimate success the Americans had no serious motivation for undertaking retaliatory measures. Nevertheless the Canadians had put up a good fight and Washington must have been irritated as well as surprised; yet so far as is publicly known there were no untoward effects on the Ottawa-Washington connection.

Conclusions

Not forgetting that generalizations drawn from specific cases must be regarded with caution and that a rigorous study would require a far greater number of tests and much more intensive analysis than has been provided here, the two instances of post-war Canadian foreign policy discussed seem to suggest four conclusions,

Firstly, as a matter of historical fact the Canadian government occasionally *has* executed foreign policies which have conflicted with those of the United States. A thorough review of Canada's external relations in the postwar period would probably reveal that these occasions have not been so rare as many Canadians assume.

Secondly, it is in turn possible that the frequent appearance of *identical* Canadian and American policies in foreign affairs need not necessarily be due to the success of irresistible American pressures on Ottawa. It may result instead from the fact that Canadian decision-makers tend to reach similar policy conclusions by independent means. To put it differently, those who are dissatisfied with the conduct of Canada's post-war external affairs would do better to blame the objectives and values of the government in Ottawa rather than the hidden machinations of the American Department of State. A Canadian official has suggested privately that one of the reasons for Canada's independent policy in Cuba was the fear that any other course would arouse an outcry from Canadian nationalists. Ottawa is thus not immune to public pressure and its diplomatists are sometimes able to use the opinions of Canadian electors in bargaining with other powers, the United States included. There is therefore no excuse for Canadians who deplore official policy on Vietnam and other issues and yet refrain from speaking out.

Thirdly, when Canadian policies have in fact collided with those of the United States, they apparently have *not* produced serious or permanent ruptures in the important Washington connection. The threat of American retaliation therefore is probably not as effective a restraint upon the options of Canadian policymakers as some commentators have alleged. Canadians would accordingly do well to view such excuses for governmental inaction with some degree of skepticism, at least in cases where the conflict with the United States is not vital to the American national interest. There are doubtless many theoretical policy options which would indeed invite severe American retaliatory action; the conclusion of a Canadian military alliance with the USSR provides an obvious hypothetical example. But the evidence suggests that within the range of realistic choices Canada enjoys a genuine freedom which she can exercise without fear that her fundamental interests will subsequently be mutilated by Uncle Sam.

Finally, it is probably true to say that the direct influence of Ottawa upon decision-makers in Washington is very slight, and certainly in cases like that of UNT-COK, where Canada and the United States are in competition for the support of other members of the international community, Canada seems destined for defeat. By the same token, however, it is true to say also that an independent Canadian position, as in Cuba, is unlikely to make the Americans more intractable than they already are. The frequently expressed view therefore that Canada should maintain her silence on sensitive issues lest she inflame the emotions of the calculating policy-makers at the Department of State is almost certainly invalid. Canada cannot single-handedly make the world a community of angels, but neither on the other hand is she likely populate it with demons.

Focus Questions

1. In these readings, what do the authors identify as the primary challenges *and* benefits of Canada's relationship with the United States?   Would it have been possible, or beneficial, to pursue a more independent stance?

2. How are these challenges and benefits different, if at all, from the present day?

3. How did Canadian politicians and diplomats of the 1950s and 1960s attempt to offset the influence of the Americans? Are there current comparisons?

11

A Worthy National Achievement: Health Care, Then and Now

Introduction

In November of 2004, in a national competition sponsored by the Canadian Broadcasting Corporation, Canadians from coast to coast weighed in on the identity of the "Greatest Canadian." Their choice was not a war hero, an athlete, or a Nobel Prize winner. It wasn't a former Prime Minister, an artist, or a diplomat—it was not even someone born in Canada. The national choice was instead a man who emigrated as a young boy from Scotland; a man who became a Baptist minister, a socialist, a long-serving Premier of Saskatchewan, and a founding member and first leader of the federal NDP. His name was Tommy Douglas.

Douglas was not granted the title of "Greatest Canadian" because of his religious ministry during the Great Depression, or his legendary eloquence and wit, or his highly successful 44 years as an elected official. It was because, against what seemed impossible odds, Douglas instigated the implementation of a universal health insurance plan in his province, one that would eventually serve as the template for Canada's modern public health care system. The first reading in this chapter, penned by Douglas himself, outlines his motivations and the opposition he faced to the plan in the early 1960s.

In 2002, the Canadian Government launched a Royal Commission into the state and future of health care in Canada, an excerpt of which provides the second reading in this chapter. Headed by Roy Romanow, former leader of the Saskatchewan NDP, this Royal Commission discovered what Tommy Douglas may well have suspected— that Health Care has become a "cherished program" for Canadians. The future of that program, however, has been threatened by rising costs, shifting medical therapies, and ideological opposition to government control of the health care "industry." But as Douglas's crowning as the greatest Canadian reveals, many Canadians— perhaps a majority—do not see health care as an industry, but a *right* which must be protected and guaranteed for each and every citizen in the country. It has become far more than a social service—it has become an integral part of national identity.

Medicare: The Time to Take A Stand
Tommy Douglas
1961

I think it is significant that in his address yesterday the Leader of the Opposition said nothing about the basic principles of medical care. His only references to a medical care program were those which were designed to throw cold water on the idea. First he said, "Why don't we wait for a national plan?" Well, Mr. Speaker, I am sure there were a lot of people in Saskatchewan who heard that and who said to themselves, "How long are we supposed to wait?" The Liberal party at its national convention in 1919 promised a national comprehensive health insurance program. They were in office from 1921 to 1930 and from 1935 to 1957. In 1945, during the election immediately following the war, Liberal candidates went up and down the country waving a copy of the Heagerty Report and waving a copy of the bill which was never put into law, and saying, "You elect us now that the war is over and we're going to have comprehensive health insurance." It's true we had a Hospital Insurance Act. But it was a Hospital Insurance Act which contained within it a "joker", whereby we couldn't get a national health insurance plan until at least Ontario or Quebec along with four other provinces were willing to come into the plan. The Liberal party left office without having contributed one five-cent piece to a national hospital insurance plan.

The Conservatives then came into office. Let it be said to their everlasting credit that one of the first things they did was to take the joker out of the Act, and to make national hospital insurance available to whatever provinces were prepared to proceed with such a plan. But they had promised in 1957 that if they were elected they would not only take the joker out of the Act, but they would extend hospital insurance to cover all hospital cases. This they haven't done. They promised to make hospital insurance applicable to mental hospital patients, and to tuberculosis sanitoria, and this they haven't done. The result is that hospital insurance in Canada today covers only 50 percent of the hospital beds in Canada. We haven't got complete hospital insurance yet. Someone has said that we should wait for the report of the Royal Commission on Medical Care which has been set up by the Government of Canada. Well, first of all, most of us have had some experience about waiting for action to be

Speech given by T.C. (Tommy) Douglas to the House of Commons, October 13, 1961.

taken on the reports of Royal Commissions, and if one looks at the terms of reference of that commission, one can see that it is not specifically beamed at dealing with the problem of setting up a comprehensive health insurance program. Therefore, Mr. Speaker, to say that we should wait for a national plan, is to ask the people of Saskatchewan to drag along and wait, as they have waited for thirty or forty years, for the federal government to act and knowing full well that they are not likely to act unless some province leads the way.

The other thing the Leader of the Opposition said about the medical care program was, "What's the hurry?" He said the government is just hurrying this plan through, for the publicity effect in a federal election. Yet, I remember at the last regular session of the legislature, that at least two or three members opposite asked the government when were we going to get on with the medical care plan. They pointed out that the government had promised it in the election of 1960. They wanted to know what we were waiting for—how long was the medical advisory committee going to take to get a report down—what was holding us up? Mr. Speaker, this is surely a disorganized army. The rank and file are saying forward, and the leader is saying retreat. They had better make up their minds. Does the Liberal party believe we should have a medical care plan? Do they believe we should have it now? Do they want to postpone it? They can't be "forwards-backwards" all the time. They've got to take a stand. I think all the people of this province have a right to know where they stand on this question. When the House votes on this matter they'll have a chance to see, and their constituents will have a chance to see what they think about a medical care plan.

There was one statement made by the Leader of the Opposition about medical care which astonished me. He said, "There's not a shred of evidence to show that any person in the province has been unable to get medical attention." Surely if ever a comment indicated that an individual was out of touch with people, it is that remark. It is like Marie Antoinette at the time of the French Revolution when the people were crying for bread, saying, "Why don't they eat cake?" To say that there is no evidence to show that any person in the province has been unable to get medical attention, is to fly in the face of all the facts.

The Canadian Sickness Report, 1951, conducted by the Government of Canada, shows clearly that the lower income groups in the period under study had more illness and more days of disability than did the higher income groups. It shows, conversely, that the volume of medical care received by the low income groups is much less than that received by higher income groups. The low incomes groups, because of poor diet, poor housing conditions, and harder working conditions, have more illness and more disability. Yet the records show that they are the people who get the least medical care. The Canadian Sickness Report shows that the low income groups spent on an average $58.10 per family, whereas the higher income groups spent on an average $158.70 per family. The higher income groups spent almost three times as much per family on medical care as did the low income groups, despite the fact that the low income groups had more sickness and more disability.

If my honorable friend would take the trouble to turn to page 58 of the Interim Report of the Advisory Committee on Medical Care he would see there a table which shows that in the year 1959, 120,940 persons or families in Saskatchewan had incomes of less then $2,500 per year. Forty-eight percent of the income earners of this province had an income of less than $2500. The same report shows thirty-five percent of the income earners in this province didn't earn enough to pay income tax. They didn't earn $2,000 a year if they were married with no dependent children. Those figures can be duplicated right across Canada as the recent survey will show. It is sheer nonsense therefore to say that there is no evidence that people are not able to get the medical attention they require.

Now I readily grant that no doctor has turned patients away. No doctor could do so without violating his Hippocratic oath. But what happens? First of all, patients are reluctant to go to the doctor if they know they can't pay. People fail to seek medical counsel and medical advice when they should get it and they often times leave it until the situation is serious and even dangerous. The second fact is that many people who do go to doctors incur bills and debts which cripple them for years to come, and this does not just apply to poor people. There are thousands of people in Saskatchewan and across Canada living on reasonably comfortable incomes who are able to make the payments on their houses and their cars and on their television sets and who can get by providing two things: firstly, they don't lose their jobs; and secondly, that the breadwinner doesn't get seriously ill. For such people, doctor bills amounting to large sums of money can put that family in a serious financial predicament for years to come.

The Leader of the Opposition yesterday spent a good deal of time talking about the terrible costs which this would place upon the taxpayers of this province. I thought some of his sentences were gems. He said, "The Liberals believe in a medical care plan if it can be done without hardship to the taxpayer." Now, which taxpayer is he worried about—the ones that are going to be paying less under the plan than they pay now, or the ones that are going to be paying more? Which is he worried about? He goes on and says, "Many people wonder if we can afford $20,000,000 at a time like this for a medical care plan." Many people wonder! Is he one of them? Are the members opposite among those who wonder if we can afford $20,000,000, for a medical care plan? Let them say so.

The *Leader-Post* for three months has been writing editorials telling the people of Saskatchewan they cannot afford a medical care plan. Is the Liberal press speaking for the Liberal party? It is time the Liberal party got off the fence and took a stand. The Leader of the Opposition says the people cannot stand more taxes. He says that land taxes are too high. Mr. Speaker, of course land taxes are too high. I want to point out two things. The CCF government doesn't impose any land taxes. There is no provincial land tax. There was a provincial land tax when we took office, and it was put there by a Liberal government. The CCF government took it off. It was a tax of two mill on every bit of land in Saskatchewan.

I want to remind you, moreover, that by gradually increasing school grants and giving additional help to municipalities for roads, we have saved the municipalities a great deal of money which they would otherwise have had to get by levying land taxes. If we had continued to pay school grants, not in the same amounts, but in the same percentage of the total cost of education that the Liberal party gave, and if we gave assistance for roads to municipalities on the same basis that the Liberal party gave them, the municipalities of this province—rural and urban—would have had to impose another 17½ mill on every bit of land in the province of Saskatchewan. The generous help the municipalities have had from the government has enabled them to keep the land taxes from going any higher than they are now.

I want to point out, Mr. Speaker, that the cost of a medical care plan is not a new cost to the people of Saskatchewan. The people of this province now are spending $18 million to $20 million a year for medical care. This is not a new cost. It is a different distribution of the cost—that is all. This money had to be paid before. Doctors of this province had to be paid. Everything has had to be paid for—their staff, X-ray technicians, lab technicians, these things all had to be paid for. But they have been paid for by those who were unfortunate enough to be ill. We are now saying they should be paid for by spreading the cost over all the people. We propose that the family tax, which we admit is a regressive tax, since there is a flat rate on every family, and therefore bears no relationship to ability to pay, should be kept as small as possible. We propose that the balance of the cost—probably two-thirds of the cost—ought to be raised by factors which have a measure of ability to pay.

Maybe this is why the Liberal press have been so vehement in their attacks on this plan. It may be that some of them begin to suspect that they are going to have to pay a part of the medical bill of some other people who are not able to pay their own.

Yesterday the Leader of the Opposition sneered at the idea of "I am my brother's keeper." He said, "There isn't much cream in Saskatchewan." I want to suggest that the *Leader-Post* and the *Star-Phoenix,* the Sifton interests and the Leader of the Opposition have fattened quite a bit during the term of the CCF government in office, and it will certainly not hurt them at all to make some contribution towards the medical care for those less fortunate than themselves.

The Leader of the Opposition when he began his remarks on Wednesday said, "The member for Regina doesn't know what this medical care plan will cost," and "I doubt if the government knows." This is strange. It's strange in the first place the government wouldn't know what it is going to cost, when the Leader of the Opposition has been going up and down the length and breadth of this province, saying that he knows what it's going to cost because he has the government's secret documents.

If the government has a secret document saying what it is going to cost and the Leader of the Opposition says he's got a copy of it, how can he say the government doesn't know what it's going to cost? . . .

When the Leader of the Opposition says that the government doesn't know the cost, and he doesn't know the cost, I wonder if he read a copy of the Interim Report of the Advisory Planning Committee on Medical Care. This was sent to him the very day it was released to the press. He will find that on page 85 estimates are given. They say it will cost between $19,970,000 and $20,570,000. If you add to that the administrative costs, which they estimate at $1 million, this means somewhere between $21 million and $21.5 million, and if a utilization fee is charged, you can subtract $1,800,000 from these amounts. There isn't much doubt as to what the cost will be. We're talking about a sum of money in the neighbourhood of $20 million—more if you don't impose utilization fees, and slightly less if you do.

It seems to me to be begging the question to be talking about whether or not the people of this province, or the people of Canada can afford a plan to spread the cost of sickness over the entire population. This is not a new principle. This has existed in nearly all the countries of western Europe—many of them for a quarter of a century. It has been in Great Britain since 1948; it has been in New Zealand since 1935; it has been in Australia. The little state of Israel that only came into existence in 1948 has today the most comprehensive health insurance plan in the world. It has more doctors, and nurses and dentists per thousand of its population than any other industrialized country or any country for which we can get statistics.

It is not a new principle. To me it seems to be sheer nonsense to suggest that medical care is something which ought to be measured just in dollars. When we're talking about medical care we're talking about our sense of values. Do we think human life is important? Do we think that the best medical care which is available is something to which people are entitled, by virtue of belonging to a civilized community? I looked up the figures and I found that, in 1959, the people of Canada spent $1,555 million, or eight percent of their personal expenditures on alcohol and tobacco. I would be the last person to argue that people do not have the right, if they want to, to spend part of their income for either alcohol or tobacco or entertainment, or anything else. But in the same period of time, the people of Canada spent $944 million for medical and dental care, or four and one-half percent of their income expenses. In other words, in the year 1959 we spent almost twice as much on luxuries such as tobacco and alcohol as we spent on providing ourselves and our families with the medical and dental care which they require.

If we can afford large sums of money for other such things as horse-racing, and many other things, and we do—I'm not arguing against them—then I say we ought to have sufficient sense of values to say that health is more important than these things, and if we can find money for relatively non-essential things, we can find the money to give our people good health.

The Liberal press in this province have been running editorials regularly for months now against the welfare state, particularly attacking the welfare state in the United Kingdom. The other day they pointed out that the British government was spending more on the welfare state than they were spending on national defence. Well, this to me is not a crushing criticism. As a matter of fact, Mr. Speaker, it shows that the Parliament of Great Britain recognizes that giving people security, giving people good health, giving people the feeling of well-being, is the most important defence there is against communism. Communities where people have security and where care is taken of the needy and unfortunate have the kind of society into which Communism has never been able to infiltrate. They published the figures on what this welfare state is costing the British taxpayer. They quoted them as $2.5 billion and that is approximately correct. But there are 55 million people in Great Britain. If you divide 55 million people into $2.5 billion, this works out at less than $50 per person.

Mr. Speaker, $50 per capita gives every man, woman and child in Great Britain security from the cradle to the grave. It takes care of their doctor bills, dental bills, hospital bills, optometric care and appliances. The only thing for which there is a deterrent fee is drugs, and that is very small. It gives them unemployment insurance, baby bonuses, and pensions when they are physically disabled. It provides benefits in the event of death, and it provides adequate pensions for widows and their children. I say that if any government, of any country, can give its people that kind of security for less than $50 per capita, then it is worth the price, and many times over.

The fact is, Mr. Speaker, that a medical care plan can only be financed out of one or two sources of revenue. The first one is from taxes. Everyone knows you have to pay taxes if you want services. Many people under this plan will pay less than they are paying now if they belong to a private plan. Other people will pay more, because if some of the money is collected on a basis of ability to pay, and if they are in the higher income groups, they may be paying a little more. The important thing for the government to ensure is that the part which must be collected from taxes is collected as equitably as possible in order to distribute the burden as equitably as possible.

The other source from which the government can get money, of course, is resource development. I want to remind you that this government has collected probably $100 for every dollar which a Liberal government ever collected from resource development in this province. Yesterday the Leader of the Opposition again made a sweeping statement. He said that the crown corporations cost the people of this province millions of dollars. The fact is, of course, that the last financial statement showed conclusively that after providing for the losses on the woollen mill and the shoe factory and the tannery, the smaller crown corporations—not including gas and power and telephones—have accumulated over $12 million in surpluses. If you include power, gas, and telephones, the surpluses are over $53 million—$53,804,067 to be exact. The crown corporations have paid into the government treasury in royalties some $7,870,000; they paid to the municipality in lieu of taxes $3,609,000 and have paid out in wages over $181 million.

I believe, Mr. Speaker, that the people of this province want health security. I think hospital insurance proves that. In spite of all the criticism we had when hospital insurance was set up, and in spite of the protest of the Liberal party that we should allow it to be handled by the municipalities, the fact is that today no one in this province in their right mind would suggest abolishing hospital insurance. On the contrary, our pioneering in hospital insurance proved so successful that today our example has been followed in every other province in this Dominion.

I believe that the great bulk of the people of this province support the idea of the medical care plan. I believe they will indicate they are willing to pay for it, providing the cost is spread equitably on the basis of ability to pay. The only ones who are likely to oppose it are those who fear that they will have to help those less fortunate than themselves.

Mr. Speaker, you will note in the Speech from the Throne it says that this medical care plan is to be a province-wide plan, with universal coverage. This was an important decision for the Advisory Planning Committee on Medical Care to make. They had before them briefs from the doctors of the province, and from the Chamber of Commerce, which advocated a partial medical care plan. In very brief terms the recommendation was that the great bulk of the people who were self-supporting would ensure themselves by joining the private plan of their choice, and that the remainder should have an extra premium paid on their behalf to the private plan, providing they could show that they were in need. Private plans ordinarily do not take people who have congenital illnesses. But if these people are in need and if an extra premium is paid on their behalf private plans would accept them. Similarly, people who were over 65 who are not accepted by private plans, if they can show they are in need, and if an extra premium was paid on their behalf by the government, they would get medical care from private plans. Those people generally who, because of low incomes, were not able to pay the private plan premium would also be covered by the private plans if they could show they were in need and if the government would pay their premium.

It was said by those submitting this plan that this could be done for some $3,600,000. This would be so much cheaper than a general plan. Well, the majority report of the Advisory Planning Committee on Medical Care showed that the rest of the Committee were very dubious about this $3,600,000. It also showed that they were convinced the people of Saskatchewan in the aggregate would pay much more to private plans than they are going to pay under a government-sponsored plan.

There are two basic weaknesses in the proposals which were put forward by those who wanted a limited coverage for medical care. The first is the private plans bear no relationship to ability to pay. I want to make it abundantly clear, Mr. Speaker, that the private plans such as Medical Services Incorporated, and Group Medical Services have rendered a marvellous service to the people of Saskatchewan. In the absence of a government plan I have advised people throughout the years, if they can possibly afford it, to join these private plans. They have been well operated, and I hope that much of their experience and their facilities and staff may be made available to those who will be managing the government-sponsored medical care plan. But a private medical care plan can only raise money in one way, and that is by putting a flat premium on every family irrespective of whether the family's income is $20,000 a year or $10,000. They have no way of graduating premiums on the basis of ability to pay.

Only the government is in a position to say that those who have less will pay less, and those who have more will pay more. This is why, in my opinion, and in the opinion, apparently, of the majority of the Committee, the idea of partial coverage was dropped.

The other weakness in the proposal of a partial coverage medical care program is that a great many groups in the province would only get coverage if they could prove need. This means imposing a means test; this means probing into people's affairs, and this is a pretty serious thing to do.

I want to say that the time is surely past when people should have to depend on proving need in order to get services that should be the inalienable right of every citizen of a good society.

It is all very well for some people to say that there is no stigma or humiliation connected with having to prove need. This is always said by people who know that they are in no danger of having to prove need. I am very glad that the Committee recommended and the government decided that there will be no such stigma and that there will be no means test. Every person in the province who is self-supporting and able to pay a relatively small per capita tax, will be eligible for care and those who are not self-supporting will be covered by other programs.

I want to say that I think there is a value in having every family and every individual make some individual contribution. I think it has psychological value. I think it keeps the public aware of the cost and gives the people a sense of personal responsibility. I would say to the members of this House that even if we could finance the plan without a per capita tax, I personally would strongly advise against it. I would like to see the per capita tax so low that it is merely a nominal tax, but I think there is a psychological value in people paying something for their cards. It is something which they have bought; it entitles them to certain services. We should have the constant realization that if those services are abused and costs get out of hand, then of course the cost of the medical care is bound to go up.

I believe, Mr. Speaker, that if this medical care insurance program is successful, and I think it will be, it will prove to be the forerunner of a national medical care insurance plan. It will become the nucleus around which Canada will ultimately build a comprehensive health insurance program which will cover all health services—not just hospital and medical care—but eventually dental care, optometric care, drugs and all the other health services which people require. I believe such a plan operated by the federal and provincial governments jointly will ultimately come in Canada. But I don't think it will come unless we lead the way. I want to say that when the history of our time is written, it may well be recorded that in October 1961, the Saskatchewan legislature and the Saskatchewan people pioneered in this field and took a first step towards ultimately establishing a system of medical care insurance for all the people of Canada. . . .

The government believes that health is too important to be left to the chance that the average family will have the necessary money to buy health services. I believe that if we put this health plan into operation it will have the same history as the Hospital Insurance Plan. I am convinced that inside two or three years both the doctors who provide the service and the people who receive the service will be so completely satisfied with it that no government will dare to take it away.

A Message to Canadians
Roy J. Romanow
2002

In April 2001, the Prime Minister established the Commission on the Future of Health Care in Canada and gave me the privilege of serving as its sole Commissioner. My mandate was to review medicare, engage Canadians in a national dialogue on its future, and make recommendations to enhance the system's quality and sustainability. At the time, I promised Canadians that any recommendations I might eventually propose to strengthen this cherished program would be evidence-based and values-driven. I have kept my word.

My team and I have worked hard to assemble the best available evidence. We began by analyzing existing reports on medicare and by inviting submissions from interested Canadians and organizations. To clarify our understanding of key issues, we organized expert roundtable sessions and conducted site visits, both in Canada and abroad. Where we identified knowledge gaps or needed a fresh perspective, we commissioned independent experts to conduct original research. Finally, I met directly with Canada's foremost health policy experts to hear their views, challenge them and have them challenge me.

We also worked hard to engage Canadians in our consultations, because medicare ultimately belongs to them. We partnered with broadcasters, universities, business and advocacy groups, and the health policy community to raise awareness of the challenges confronting medicare. The contribution of the health research community to this effort has been invaluable. We also established formal liaison contacts with provincial governments to share information, and I spoke with the Premiers and heard from many health ministers. I also had the privilege of leading one of the most comprehensive, inclusive and successful consultative exercises our country has ever witnessed. Tens of thousands of Canadians participated, speaking passionately, eloquently and thoughtfully about how to preserve and enhance the system. We also sought advice from health experts and from Canadians in interpreting the results of our processes. I am proud that respect, transparency, objectivity and breadth of perspective have been hallmarks of this process.

These past 18 months have been among the most challenging and rewarding of my more than three decades in public life. Having examined the research, and having

From *Building on Values: The Future of Health Care in Canada* by J. Romanow, Commissioner, November 2002, pp. xv–xxi.

met with Canadians from sea-to-sea-to-sea, I am more confident than ever in the system's potential to meet the needs of Canadians, now and in the future. Canadians remain deeply attached to the core values at the heart of medicare and to a system that has served them extremely well. My assessment is that, while medicare is as sustainable as Canadians want it to be, we now need to take the next bold step of transforming it into a truly national, more comprehensive, responsive and accountable health care system. Making Canadians the healthiest people in the world must become the system's overriding objective. Strong leadership and the involvement of Canadians is key to preserving a system that is true to our values and sustainable.

Canadians Remain Attached to the Values at the Heart of the System

In their discussions with me, Canadians have been clear that they still strongly support the core values on which our health care system is premised—equity, fairness and solidarity. These values are tied to their understanding of citizenship. Canadians consider equal and timely access to medically necessary health care services on the basis of need as a right of citizenship, not a privilege of status or wealth. Building from these values, Canadians have come to view their health care system as a national program, delivered locally but structured on intergovernmental collaboration and a mutual understanding of values. They want and expect their governments to work together to ensure that the policies and programs that define medicare remain true to these values.

Medicare Has Served Canadians Extremely Well

I am pleased to report to Canadians that the often overheated rhetoric about medicare's costs, effectiveness and viability does not stand up to scrutiny. Our health outcomes, with a few exceptions, are among the best in the world, and a strong majority of Canadians who use the system are highly satisfied with the quality and standard of care they receive. Medicare has consistently delivered affordable, timely, accessible and high quality care to the overwhelming majority of Canadians on the basis of need, not income. It has contributed to our international competitiveness, to the extraordinary standard of living we enjoy, and to the quality and productivity of our work force.

The System Is as Sustainable as We Want It to Be

For years now, Canadians have been exposed to an increasingly fractious debate about medicare's "sustainability." They have been told that costs are escalating and that quality of services is declining. They have heard that insatiable public expectations, an aging population and the costs of new medical technologies and prescription drugs will inevitably overwhelm the system. They have been warned that health spending is crowding out other areas of public investment. Thus one of the fundamental questions my report must address is whether medicare is sustainable? My answer is that it is if we are prepared to act decisively.

Governments talk about sustainability in terms of "costs" and financial impacts. This discussion often has more to do with "who pays" than "how much" we pay. In listening to these debates, it is sometimes hard to realize that health spending in Canada is on par with most countries in the Western world, that it is substantially lower than in the United States, and that we devote a smaller portion of our Gross Domestic Product (GDP) to health care today than we did a decade ago.

More troubling is the notion that somehow our health care system is on "autopilot" and immune to change. I believe this is fundamentally inconsistent with the ingenuity and innovation that has for so long defined the Canadian way. It is baseless and false. Governments can make informed choices about how and where to invest; they are not powerless to change current spending trajectories. Better management practices, more agile and collaborative institutions and a stronger focus on prevention can generate significant savings. Technological advances can also help to improve health outcomes and enable a more effective deployment of scarce financial and human resources. Indeed, our health care system is replete with examples of excellence in innovation, many of them world-class. The bigger issue is whether we have the right information and the courage we need to make the choices that support sustainability.

To be sure, the system needs more money. In the early 1990s, the federal share of funding for the system declined sharply. While recent years have seen a substantial federal reinvestment into health care, the federal government contributes less than it previously did, and less than it should. I am therefore recommending the establishment of a minimum threshold for federal funding, as well as a new funding arrangement that provides for greater stability and predictability—contingent on this replenishment supporting the transformative changes outlined in this report. Money must buy change, not more of the same.

But individual Canadians view sustainability from a very different vantage point. The key "sustainability" question for the average Canadian is, "Will medicare be there for me when I need it?" While it is very clear that a majority of Canadians support medicare in its current form, it is not perfect. Some people, particularly Aboriginal peoples and those in rural and remote parts of the country, cannot always access medical services where and when they need them. There are also inefficiencies and mismatches between supply and demand that have resulted in unacceptable times for some medical procedures. These problems must be tackled on a priority basis or they will eventually erode public confidence in medicare and with it, the consensus that it is worth keeping. I am therefore recommending new initiatives to improve timely access to care, to enhance the quality of care the system provides, a more co-ordinated approach to health human resources planning, and a special focus on the health needs of Aboriginal peoples.

We also need to renovate our concept of medicare and adapt it to today's realities. In the early days, medicare could be summarized in two words: hospitals and doctors. That was fine for the time, but it is not sufficient for the 21st century. Despite the tremendous changes over the past 40 years, medicare still is largely organized around hospitals and doctors. Today, however, home care is an increasingly critical element of our health system, as day surgery has replaced the procedures that once took weeks of convalescence in hospital. Drugs, once a small portion of total health costs, are now escalating and among the highest costs in the system. The expense associated with some drug therapies or of providing extended home care for a seriously ill family member can be financially devastating. It can bankrupt a family. This is incompatible with the philosophy and values upon which medicare was built. It must be changed. I am therefore recommending that home care be recognized as a publicly insured service under medicare and that, as a priority, new funds be invested to establish a national platform for home care services. I am also recommending the creation of a national drug strategy, including a catastrophic drug insurance program to protect Canadian families.

I know these views will provoke a hot debate in Canada, particularly among those who advocate "less government" and less government money in health care. The problem with these arguments is that they are focused on the cost to governments, not Canadians. A more narrowly structured system of medicare might free up governments to spend tax dollars on other priorities, or simply on tax relief. But either way, individual Canadians would still be left to personally bear the costs of services that are not covered. To me, that is contrary to the spirit and intent of medicare. It is not the Canadian way.

Canadians Want and Need a Truly National Health Care System

As I noted earlier, Canadians' attachment to medicare is based on their understanding of it as a right of citizenship. They connect with the values that define medicare, not the particular features of the system in place in their province or territory. Canadians expect the system to guarantee them relatively similar access to a common basket of medicare services of equal quality, regardless of where they live. They expect governments, providers and caregivers to work collaboratively to maintain a system with these attributes.

The fact that Canadians perceive health care as a national endeavour should not be construed as an invitation for federal intrusion into an area of primary provincial jurisdiction. Nor should it be interpreted to mean a "one-size-fits-all" approach to health care delivery. In a country as geographically, economically, regionally and culturally diverse as ours, this is neither realistic nor desirable. Medicare must be constantly renewed and continually refined, if it is to remain relevant and viable. A new common approach is needed to encourage, not constrain, innovation. If we allow medicare to become static, it will become brittle and eventually break.

Canadians realize that illness and injury know few boundaries; they afflict all of us. They understand that organizing health care solely along constitutional lines or provincial boundaries makes little practical sense. They recognize that sometimes by design, sometimes by financial necessity, and more often by default, provinces are increasingly willing to go it alone insofar as their respective health care "systems" are concerned. Today, we sit on the cusp. Left unchecked, this situation will inevitably produce 13 clearly separate health care systems, each with differing methods of payment, delivery and outcomes, coupled by an ever increasing volatile and debilitating debate surrounding our nation, its values and principles.

This is no way to renew a program of such immense personal and national importance and, for sure, it is no way to strengthen those foundations that unify us as a nation. It is time for governments, caregivers and Canadian citizens to embark together on the road to renewal. The reality is that Canadians embrace medicare as a public good, a national symbol and a defining aspect of their citizenship. I am therefore recommending a series of measures to modernize the legislative and institutional foundations of medicare that will better equip governments to move forward together to provide Canadians with the health care system they want.

Canadians Want and Need a More Comprehensive Health Care System

We must transform our health care "system" from one in which a multitude of participants, working in silos, focus primarily on managing illness, to one in which they work collaboratively to deliver a seamless, integrated array of services to Canadians, from prevention and promotion to primary care, to hospital, community, mental health, home and end-of-life care.

Indeed, despite our common use of the term "our health care system," the relevance of this term is increasingly doubtful. A system where citizens in one part of the country pay out-of-pocket for "medically necessary" health services available "free" in others, or where the rules of the game as to who can provide care and under what circumstances vary by jurisdiction, can scarcely be called a "system."

There are many examples of the "disconnect." Elderly people who are discharged from hospital and cannot find or afford the home or community services they need. Women—one in five—who are providing care to someone in the home an average of 28 hours per week, half of whom are working, many of whom have children, and almost all of whom are experiencing tremendous strain. Health professionals, who are increasingly stressed, while performing tasks ill suited to their abilities and training. Patients, who are forced to navigate a system that is a complex and unfriendly mystery, in order to find the right specialist, the nearest facility, and the best treatment. People who are forced to repeat lab tests, and to recount their medical histories time and time again. We need clear and decisive action to modernize the system and make it more durable and responsive. I am therefore recommending a series of measures to create a more comprehensive system whose component parts fit together more seamlessly.

Canadians Want and Need a More Accountable Health Care System

Accountability must also be improved. Health care in this country is now a $100 billion enterprise, one of our society's largest expenditures. Yet no level of government has done a very good job accounting for how effectively that money is spent. Canadians still do not know who to believe in the debate over which level of government is paying what share for health services.

Canadians are the shareholders of the public health care system. They own it and are the sole reason the health care system exists. Yet despite this, Canadians are often left out in the cold, expected to blindly accept assertion as fact and told to simply trust governments and providers to do the job. They deserve access to the facts. Canadians no longer accept being told things are or will get better; they want to see the proof. They have a right to know what is happening with wait lists; what is happening with health care budgets, hospital beds, doctors, and nurses, and whether the gaps in home and community care services are being closed; whether the number of diagnostic machines and tests is adequate; and whether treatment outcomes are improving.

Information is a key ingredient. We live in an age of laser surgery and are unlocking the mystery of the human gene, yet our approach to health information is mired in the past. We gather information on some health issues, but not on others. And much of the information we gather cannot be properly analyzed or shared. Indeed, we know far more about resources and the dollars being spent than we do about the return on those investments. Better information will facilitate evidence-based decision making. How can we hold health care managers accountable if what they are managing cannot be measured? If we are to build a better health system, we need a better information sharing system so that all governments and all providers can be held accountable to Canadians. I am therefore recommending a series of measures to improve transparency across the system, to make decision-making structures more inclusive, to accelerate the integration of health informatics, to provide for a secure electronic health record for Canadians that respects their right to privacy, and to give Canadians a greater say in shaping the system's future.

Making Canadians the Healthiest People in the World

During our public hearings, many presentations focused on the need to improve our understanding of the determinants of health. I heard that the quality of the air we breathe, of the water we drink, and of the food we eat directly affects our health and our health care system. I learned that educated, employed and physically active Canadians are far more likely to be healthy than those who are not, and that spiritual, emotional and physical well-being are often inextricably linked. I also heard that lifestyle changes can markedly reduce the incidence and severity of many major and debilitating diseases. Keeping people well, rather than treating them when they are sick, is common sense. And so it is equally common sense for our health care system to place a greater emphasis on preventing disease and on promoting healthy lifestyles. This is the best way to sustain our health care system over the longer term.

The health care system must be on the front lines of this effort. However, we must also invest in related areas of public life to create community mobilization, a sense of social inclusion and provide the infrastructure that enables healthier lifestyle choices. Investing in public housing, a clean environment and education are all part of the solution leading to a healthier Canada.

But we need more than rhetoric; we need action. I am therefore recommending a greater emphasis on prevention and well ness as part of an overall strategy to improve the delivery of primary care in Canada, the allocation of new moneys for research into the determinants of health, and that governments take the next steps for making Canadians the world's healthiest people.

A System Based on Canadian Values

Early in my mandate, I challenged those advocating radical solutions for reforming health care—user fees, medical savings accounts, de-listing services, greater privatization, a parallel private system—to come forward with evidence that these approaches would improve and strengthen our health care system. *The evidence has not been forthcoming.* I have also carefully explored the experiences of other jurisdictions with co-payment models and with public-private partnerships, and have found these lacking. There is no evidence these solutions will deliver better or cheaper care, or improve access (except, perhaps, for those who can afford to pay for care out of their own pockets). More to the point, the principles on which these solutions rest cannot be reconciled with the values at the heart of medicare or with the tenets of the *Canada Health Act* that Canadians overwhelmingly support. It would be irresponsible of me to jeopardize what has been, and can remain, a world-class health care system and a proud national symbol by accepting anecdote as fact or on the dubious basis of making a "leap of faith."

Some have described it as a perversion of Canadian values that they cannot use their money to purchase faster treatment from a private provider for their loved ones. I believe it is a far greater perversion of Canadian values to accept a system where money, rather than need, determines who gets access to care.

It has been suggested to me by some that if there is a growing tension between the principles of our health care system and what is happening on the ground, the answer is obvious. Dilute or ditch the principles. Scrap any notion of national standards and values. Forget about equal access. Let people buy their way openly to the front of the line. Make health care a business. Stop treating it as a public service, available equally to all. But the consensus view of Canadians on this is clear. No! Not now, not ever. Canadians view medicare as a moral enterprise, not a business venture.

Tossing overboard the principles and values that govern our health care system would be betraying a public trust. Canadians will not accept this, and without their consent, these "new" solutions are doomed to fail. Canadians want their health care system renovated; they do not want it demolished.

But we must also recognize that since the earliest days of medicare, public and private sector care providers (including fee-for-service doctors) have been part of our health care system. Our system was never organized according to a strict protocol; it evolved in accordance with the existing capacity of public and private providers, changing notions of what constitute "core services," and the wishes of Canadians.

One of the most difficult issues with which I have had to struggle is how much private participation within our universal, single-payer, publicly administered system is warranted or defensible. On the one hand, I am confronted by the fact that the private sector is already an important part of our "public" system. The notion of rolling back its participation is fraught with difficulty. On the other hand, I am acutely aware of the potential risks to the integrity and viability of our health care system that might result from an expanded role for private providers.

At a minimum, I believe governments must draw a clear line between direct health services (such as hospital and medical care) and ancillary ones (such as food preparation or maintenance services). The former should be delivered primarily through our public, not-for-profit system, while the latter could be the domain of private providers. The rapid growth of private MRI (magnetic resonance imaging) clinics, which permit people to purchase faster service and then use test results to "jump the queue" back into the public system for treatment, is a troubling case-in-point. So too is the current practice of some worker's compensation agencies of contracting with private providers to deliver fast-track diagnostic services to potential claimants. I agree with those who view these situations as incompatible with the "equality of access" principle at the heart of medicare. Governments must invest sufficiently in the public system to make timely access to diagnostic services for all a reality and reduce the temptation to "game" the system. In order to clarify the situation in regard to diagnostic services, I am therefore recommending that diagnostic services be explicitly included under the definition of "insured health services" under a new *Canada Health Act.*

Conclusion

Canada's journey to nationhood has been a gradual, evolutionary process, a triumph of compassion, collaboration and accommodation, and the result of many steps, both simple and bold. This year we celebrate the 40th anniversary of medicare in Saskatchewan, a courageous initiative by visionary men and women that changed us as a nation and cemented our role as one of the world's compassionate societies. The next big step for Canada may be more focused, but it will be no less bold. That next step is to build on this proud legacy and transform medicare into a system that is more responsive, comprehensive and accountable to all Canadians.

Getting there requires leadership. It requires us to change our attitudes on how we govern ourselves as a nation. It requires an adequate, stable and predictable commitment to funding and co-operation from governments. It requires health practitioners to challenge the traditional way they have worked in the system. It requires all of us to realize that our health and well ness is not simply a responsibility of the state but something we must work toward as individuals, families and communities, and as a nation. The national system I speak about is clearly within our grasp.

Medicare is a worthy national achievement, a defining aspect of our citizenship and an expression of social cohesion. Let's unite to keep it so.

Focus Questions

1. What were the concerns and arguments made by the opposition, in the early 1960s, to Tommy Douglas's plan for universal health care in Saskatchewan? How did Douglas counter them?

- it won't cost extra, just the taxes will be redistributed - $2!
- opposition - were promising - Douglas - I'm here to do it now!
- Doc$, will deter ppl from going b/c of lack of money
  ↳ private plans can only go so far

2. Why did he think the government plan was superior to private insurance? What did it mean, practically and theoretically speaking, to say the plan would be universal?

right not choice

everyone can

3. What does Romanow identify as the problems with the Health Care system today, and how does he recommend they be remedied?

Timely - b/c ppl deal w more emotional

financial issuses - technology is expensive
its awesome but not sustainable
- so not only governments responsibility

4. Why has health care become, as Romanow calls it, a "cherished program" for
    Canadians, and what are the so-called "Canadian values" upon which the system
    is apparently based and maintained?

    -right not advantage

    - socialist - Canada

    capitalist - U·S

5. What do you think Tommy Douglas would think about the state of health care
    today, and the Romanow report?

    health care important

    health and wallet shouldn't

    go hand on hand

12

Have You Really Come A Long Way, Baby? Women and Canadian Politics in the 20th Century

Introduction

After many decades of campaigning and petitioning, Canadian women were finally granted the right to vote in federal elections during the First World War.[1] Their fight for suffrage struggled against a very well-entrenched attitude about what constituted woman's 'proper' sphere in society. Most Canadians—men *and* women—of the late nineteenth and early twentieth centuries, believed that women belonged in a realm of private domesticity which was both divinely and naturally ordained—one in which public, political activity was decidedly improper. The final triumph of women's suffrage was not the result of their persistent campaigning alone, however. In the later years of the war, the federal government, led by Sir Robert Borden, was considering the necessity of conscription for military service. The votes of some women—mothers, wives, and daughters of men serving overseas, and women serving in the armed forces themselves—were seen as crucial to widening political support for this controversial plan. It was to this limited group of women that the federal franchise was first granted, through the Wartime Elections Act of 1917. This same act, however, disenfranchised thousands of Canadians of "enemy alien" birth, who had been

---

[1]Several provinces had already granted suffrage to women in provincial elections, first in Manitoba in January of 1916, followed by Saskatchewan and Alberta later that same year. British Columbia and Ontario granted women the vote in April of 1917, followed by Nova Scotia in 1918, New Brunswick in 1919, P.E.I. in 1922, and in Newfoundland (which was not a province of Canada until 1949), women got the vote in 1925. It was not until 1940, after 20 years of exercising a federal vote, that Québec women were granted the same right at the provincial level.

naturalized after 1902. It was, as historian Susan Jackel has described it, "not an honourable victory for Canadian women."[2] The following year, in May of 1918, the right to vote in federal elections was extended to most women in Canada.

Given that the success of the campaign for federal suffrage was a result of political expediency as much as it was part of a recognition of women's right to vote, it comes as no surprise that the vote itself did not result in an immediate recognition of women's overall political equality with men. Indeed, as the final two readings in this chapter explore, equality in politics remains, even today, an ideal rather than a reality. To begin this chapter, however, is an excerpt from a brief essay by Nellie McClung, who was first introduced in Chapter 8, with her essay on "What Women Think of War." In the present chapter, her well-known essay on women's suffrage, "Hardy Perennials," provides a broad sense of the women's suffrage campaign, the ideas which informed it, and the hopes which were placed by women on the right to vote.

[2]Susan Jackel, "Women's Suffrage," in *The Canadian Encyclopedia* (http://www.thecanadianencyclopedia.com)

Hardy Perennials!
Nellie L. McClung
1915

> I hold it true—I will not change,
> For changes are a dreadful bore—
> That nothing must be done on earth
> Unless it has been done before.
>
> *-Anti-Suffrage Creed.*

If prejudices belonged to the vegetable world they would be described under the general heading of: "Hardy Perennials; will grow in any soil, and bloom without ceasing; requiring no cultivation; will do better when left alone."

In regard to tenacity of life, no old yellow cat has anything on a prejudice. You may kill it with your own hands, bury it deep, and sit on the grave, and behold! the next day, it will walk in at the back door, purring.

Take some of the prejudices regarding women that have been exploded and blown to pieces many, many times and yet walk among us today in the fulness of life and vigor. There is a belief that housekeeping is the only occupation for women; that all women must be housekeepers, whether they like it or not. Men may do as they like, and indulge their individuality, but every true and womanly woman must take to the nutmeg grater and the O-Cedar Mop. It is also believed that in the good old days before woman suffrage was discussed, and when woman's clubs were unheard of, that all women adored housework, and simply pined for Monday morning to come to get at the weekly wash; that women cleaned house with rapture and cooked joyously. Yet there is a story told of one of the women of the old days, who arose at four o'clock in the morning, and aroused all her family at an indecently early hour for breakfast, her reason being that she wanted to get "one of these horrid old meals over." This woman had never been at a suffrage meeting—so where did she get the germ of discontent?

From *In Times Like These* by Nellie L. McClung.

At the present time there is much discontent among women, and many people are seriously alarmed about it. They say women are no longer contented with woman's sphere and woman's work—that the washboard has lost its charm, and the days of the hairwreath are ended. We may as well admit that there is discontent among women. We cannot drive them back to the spinning wheel and the mathook, for they will not go. But there is really no cause for alarm, for discontent is not necessarily wicked. There is such a thing as divine discontent just as there is criminal content-ment. Discontent may mean the stirring of ambition, the desire to spread out, to improve and grow. Discontent is a sign of life, corresponding to growing pains in a healthy child. The poor woman who is making a brave struggle for existence is not saying much, though she is thinking all the time. In the old days when a woman's hours were from 5 A.M. to 5 A.M., we did not hear much of discontent among women, because they had not time to even talk, and certainly could not get together. The horse on the treadmill may be very discontented, but he is not disposed to tell his troubles, for he cannot stop to talk.

It is the women, who now have leisure, who are doing the talking. For generations women have been thinking and thought without expression is dynamic, and gathers volume by repression. Evolution when blocked and suppressed becomes revolution. The introduction of machinery and the factory-made articles has given women more leisure than they had formerly, and now the question arises, what are they going to do with it?

Now politics simply means public affairs—yours and mine, everybody's—and to say that politics are too corrupt for women is a weak and foolish statement for any man to make. Any man who is actively engaged in politics, and declares that politics are too corrupt for women, admits one of two things, either that he is a party to this corruption, or that he is unable to prevent it—and in either case something should be done. Politics are not inherently vicious. The office of lawmaker should be the high-est in the land, equaled in honor only by that of the minister of the gospel. In the old days, the two were combined with very good effect; but they seem to have drifted apart in more recent years.

If politics are too corrupt for women, they are too corrupt for men; for men and women are one—indissolubly joined together for good or ill. Many men have tried to put all their religion and virtue in their wife's name, but it does not work very well. When social conditions are corrupt women cannot escape by shutting their eyes, and taking no interest. It would be far better to give them a chance to clean them up.

What would you think of a man who would say to his wife: "This house to which I am bringing you to live is very dirty and unsanitary, but I will not allow you—the dear wife whom I have sworn to protect to touch it. It is too dirty for your precious little white hands! You must stay upstairs, dear. Of course the odor from below may come up to you, but use your smelling salts and think no evil. I do not hope to ever be able to clean it up, but certainly you must never think of trying."

Do you think any woman would stand for that? She would say: "John, you are an right in your way, but there are some places where your brain skids. Perhaps you had better stay downtown today for lunch. But on your way down please call at the grocer's, and send me a scrubbing brush and a package of Dutch Cleanser, and some chloride of lime, and now hurry." Women have cleaned up things since time began; and if women ever get into politics there will be a cleaning-out of pigeon-holes and forgotten corners, on which the dust of years has fallen, and the sound of the political carpet-beater will be heard in the land.

There is another hardy perennial that constantly lifts its head above the earth, persistently refusing to be ploughed under, and that is that if women were ever given a chance to participate in outside affairs, that family quarrels would result; that men and their wives who have traveled the way of life together, side by side, for years, and come safely through religious discussions, and discussions relating to "his" people and "her" people, would angrily rend each other over politics, and great damage to the furniture would be the result. Father and son have been known to live under the same roof and vote differently, and yet live! Not only live, but live peaceably! If a husband and wife are going to quarrel they will find a cause for dispute easily enough, and will not be compelled to wait for election day. And supposing that they have never, never had a single dispute, and not a ripple has ever marred the placid surface of their matrimonial sea, I believe that a small family jar—or at least a real lively argument—will do them good. It is in order to keep the white-winged angel of peace hovering over the home that married women are not allowed to vote in many places. Spinsters and widows are counted worthy of voice in the selection of school trustee, and alderman, and mayor, but not the woman who has taken to herself a husband and still has him.

What a strange commentary on marriage that it should disqualify a woman from voting. Why should marriage disqualify a woman? Men have been known to vote for years after they were dead!

There is another sturdy prejudice that blooms everywhere in all climates, and that is that women would not vote if they had the privilege; and this is many times used as a crushing argument against woman suffrage. But why worry? If women do not use it, then surely there is no harm done; but those who use the argument seem to imply that a vote unused is a very dangerous thing to leave lying around, and will probably spoil and blow up. In support of this statement instances are cited of women letting their vote lie idle and unimproved in elections for school trustee and alderman. Of course, the percentage of men voting in these contests was quite small, too, but no person finds fault with that.

Women may have been careless about their franchise in elections where no great issue is at stake, but when moral matters are being decided women have not shown any lack of interest. As a result of the first vote cast by the women of Illinois over one thousand saloons went out of business. Ask the liquor dealers if they think women will use the ballot. They do not object to woman suffrage on the ground that women will not vote, but because they will.

Then, of course, on the other hand there are those who claim that women would vote too much—that they would vote not wisely but too well; that they would take up voting as a life work to the exclusion of husband, home and children. There seems to be considerable misapprehension on the subject of voting. It is really a simple and perfectly innocent performance, quickly over, and with no bad aftereffects.

It is usually done in a vacant room in a school or the vestry of a church, or a town hall. No drunken men stare at you. You are not jostled or pushed—you wait your turn in an orderly line, much as you have waited to buy a ticket at a railway station. Two tame and quiet-looking men sit at a table, and when your turn comes, they ask you your name, which is perhaps slightly embarrassing, but it is not as bad as it might be, for they do not ask your age, or of what disease did your grandmother die. You go behind the screen with your ballot paper in your hand, and there you find a seal-brown pencil tied with a chaste white string. Even the temptation of annexing the pencil is removed from your frail humanity. You mark your ballot, and drop it in the box, and come out into the sunlight again. If you had never heard that you had done an unladylike thing you would not know it. It all felt solemn, and serious, and very respectable to you, something like a Sunday-school convention. Then, too, you are surprised at what a short time you have been away from home. You put the potatoes on when you left home, and now you are back in time to strain them.

In spite of the testimony of many reputable women that they have been able to vote and get the dinner on one and the same day, there still exists a strong belief that the whole household machinery goes out of order when a woman goes to vote. No person denies a woman the right to go to church, and yet the church service takes a great deal more time than voting. People even concede to women the right to go shopping, or visiting a friend, or an occasional concert. But the wife and mother, with her God-given, sacred trust of molding the young life of our land, must never dream of going round the corner to vote. "Who will mind the baby?" cried one of our public men, in great agony of spirit, "when the mother goes to vote?"

One woman replied that she thought she could get the person that minded it when she went to pay her taxes—which seemed to be a fairly reasonable proposition. Yet the hardy plant of prejudice flourishes, and the funny pictures still bring a laugh.

Father comes home, tired, weary, footsore, toe-nails ingrowing, caused by undarned stockings, and finds the fire out, house cold and empty, save for his half dozen children, all crying.

"Where is your mother?" the poor man asks in broken tones. For a moment the sobs are hushed while little Ellie replies: "Out voting!"

Father bursts into tears.

Of course, people tell us, it is not the mere act of voting which demoralizes women—if they would only vote and be done with it; but women are creatures of habit, and habits once formed are hard to break; and although the polls are only open every three or four years, if women once get into the way of going to them, they will hang around there all the rest of the time. It is in woman's impressionable nature that the real danger lies.

Another shoot of this hardy shrub of prejudice is that women are too good to mingle in everyday life—they are too sweet and too frail—that women are angels. If women are angels we should try to get them into public life as soon as possible, for there is a great shortage of angels there just at present, if all we hear is true.

Then there is the pedestal theory—that women are away up on a pedestal, and down below, looking up at them with deep adoration, are men, their willing slaves. Sitting up on a pedestal does not appeal very strongly to a healthy woman-and, besides, if a woman has been on a pedestal for any length of time, it must be very hard to have to come down and cut the wood.

These tender-hearted and chivalrous gentlemen who tell you of their adoration for women, cannot bear to think of women occupying public positions. Their tender hearts shrink from the idea of women lawyers or women policemen, or even women preachers; these positions would "rub the bloom off the peach," to use their own elo-quent words. They cannot bear, they say, to see women leaving the sacred precincts of home—and yet their offices are scrubbed by women who do their work while other people sleep—poor women who leave the sacred precincts of home to earn enough to keep the breath of life in them, who carry their scrub-pails home, through the deserted streets, long after the cars have stopped running. They are exposed to cold, to hunger, to insult poor souls is there any pity felt for them? Not that we have heard of. The tender-hearted ones can bear this with equanimity. It is the thought of women getting into comfortable and well-paid positions which wrings their manly hearts.

Another aspect of the case is that women can do more with their indirect influ-ence than by the ballot; though just why they cannot do better still with both does not appear to be very plain. The ballot is a straight-forward dignified way of making your desire or choice felt.

But, of course, popular opinion says it is not "womanly." The "womanly way" is to nag and tease. Women have often been told that if they go about it right they can get anything. They are encouraged to plot and scheme, and deceive, and wheedle, and coax for things. This is womanly and sweet. Of course, if this fails, they still have tears—they can always cry and have hysterics, and raise hob generally, but they must do it in a womanly way. Will the time ever come when the word "feminine" will have in it no trace of trickery?

Women are too sentimental to vote, say the politicians sometimes. Sentiment is nothing to be ashamed of, and perhaps an infusion of sentiment in politics is what we need. Honor and honesty, love and loyalty, are only sentiments, and yet they make the fabric out of which our finest traditions are woven. The United States has sent carloads of flour to starving Belgium because of a sentiment. Belgium refused to let Germany march over her land because of a sentiment, and Canada has responded to the SOS call of the Empire because of a sentiment. It seems that it is sentiment which redeems our lives from sordidness and selfishness, and occasionally gives us a glimpse of the upper country.

There are people who tell us that the reason women must never be allowed to vote is because they do not want to vote, the inference being that women are never given anything that they do not want. It sounds so chivalrous and protective and high-minded. But women have always got things that they did not want. Women do not want the liquor business, but they have it; women do not want less pay for the same work as men, but they get it. Women did not want the present war, but they have it. The fact of women's preference has never been taken very seriously, but it serves here just as well as anything else. Even the opponents of woman suffrage will admit that some women want to vote, but they say they are a very small minority, and "not our best women." That is a classification which is rather difficult of proof and of no importance anyway. It does not matter whether it is the best, or second best, or the worst who are asking for a share in citizenship; voting is not based on morality, but on humanity. No man votes because he is one of our best men. He votes because he is of the male sex, and over twenty-one years of age. The fact that many women are indifferent on the subject does not alter the situation. People are indifferent about many things that they should be interested in. The indifference of people on the subject of ventilation and hygiene does not change the laws of health. The indifference of many parents on the subject of an education for their children does not alter the value of education. If one woman wants to vote, she should have that opportunity just as if one woman desires a college education,' she should not be held back because of the indifferent careless ones who do not desire it. Why should the mentally inert, careless, uninterested woman, who cares nothing for humanity but is contented to patter along her own little narrow way, set the pace for the others of us? Voting will not be compulsory; the shrinking violets will not be torn from their shady fence-corner; the "home bodies" will be able to still sit in rapt contemplation of their own fireside. We will not force the vote upon them, but why should they force their votelessness upon us?

I remember when I was a little girl back on the farm in the Souris Valley, I used to water the cattle on Saturday mornings, drawing the water in an icy bucket with a windlass from a fairly deep well. We had one old white ox, called Mike, a patriarchal-looking old sinner, who never had enough, and who always had to be watered first. Usually I gave him what I thought he should have and then took him back to the stable and watered the others. But one day I was feeling real strong, and I resolved to give Mike all he could drink, even if it took every drop of water in the well. I must admit that I cherished a secret hope that he would kill himself drinking. I will not set down here in cold figures how many pails of water Mike drank—but I remember. At last he could not drink another drop, and stood shivering beside the trough, blowing the last mouthful out of his mouth like a bad child. I waited to see if he would die, or at least turn away and give the others a chance. The thirsty cattle came crowding around him, but old Mike, so full I am sure he felt he would never drink another drop of water again as long as he lived, deliberately and with difficulty put his two front feet over the trough and kept all the other cattle away. . . . Years afterwards I had the pleasure of being present when a delegation waited upon the Government of one of the provinces of Canada, and presented many reasons for extending the franchise to women. One member of the Government arose and spoke for all his colleagues. He said in substance : "You can't have it so long as I have anything to do with the affairs of this province—you shall not have it!" . . .

Did your brain ever give a queer little twist, and suddenly you were conscious that the present mental process had taken place before? If you have ever had it, you will know what I mean, and if you haven't I cannot make you understand. I had that feeling then. . . . I said to myself: "Where have I seen that face before? . . . Then, suddenly, I remembered, and in my heart I cried out: "Mike!—old friend, Mike! Dead these many years! Your bones lie buried under the fertile soil of the Souris Valley, but your soul goes marching on! Mike, old friend, I see you again—both feet in the trough!"

Women and Political Participation in Canada
Manon Tremblay
2001

A study of women's participation in Canadian politics might be said to be the study of its absence. Historically, women have been excluded from political institutions, and according to the Royal Commission on Electoral Reform and Party Financing, they remain the group with the most pronounced disparity between demographic weight and representation on decision-making bodies (Lortie Commission, 1991: 97). While it is true that women have been and continue to be excluded from political institutions, it is less true to say that they have refrained from political activity. But their political participation has been—as it continues to be—in areas traditionally considered non-political, such as social movements.

This article reviews the involvement of women in formal political institutions, such as political parties and the House of Commons. Any study of this subject is quickly confronted with the following question: is a woman in this context just "one of the boys," or different from them? This is what Carole Pateman (1989) calls "the Mary Wollstonecraft dilemma:" should women demand full participation in political life based on the common humanity they share with men, or based on their differences from men? In the former case, women's participation in politics stems from universal democratic rights. In the latter, this involvement is to be assessed in terms of their differences: it is because they are different from men that women must participate in politics—with the probable consequence of changing the very nature of politics and public decisions.

The Mary Wollstonecraft dilemma—Universality versus Difference—will guide our examination of the participation of women in Canadian politics. We shall deal with the following themes in succession: women as electors, as members of political parties, as candidates, and finally as parliamentarians, i.e. MPs or senators.

Women as Electors

The first suffragette organizations emerged in Canada in the late 1870s. However, it was not until 1917 that women employed by the army and those with a close male relative in the Canadian Forces obtained the right to vote in federal elections. The following year, this right was extended to most Canadian women, in recognition of their contribution to the war effort. However, a closer examination of the arguments developed during the 1918 debates reveals the Universality vs. Difference dilemma, particularly among those advocating women's suffrage. For example, one line of reasoning associated with the Universality option was that Canada was entering an age of modernization, and that the enfranchisement of women was part and parcel of this forward-thinking approach. Others, arguing for the Difference option, maintained that women ought to be able to vote because Canadian society needed their particular skills to meet the new challenges ahead, notably in the area of social reform.

The Universality-Difference dilemma also generated many questions about the electoral behaviour of these new citizens. Would women be as interested in politics as men? Would they be as assiduous as men in exercising their right to vote? Would they vote like men, or vote as women? Studies today show that women demonstrate somewhat less interest in politics. But the indicators used are still relatively blind to the fact that socialization and social roles differ along gender lines. There are, in fact, very few models, even now, that allow girls to see politics as a sphere that is accessible to them. And Statistics Canada data show that women continue to be the ones primarily responsible for housework and child care, and they are also poorer than men. Consequently, they have less time than their partners to stay abreast of current events and invest effort in political parties, as well as less money to devote to political ends. However, research shows that women are as assiduous in fulfilling their electoral obligations as men. Finally, with regard to voting habits, the results of Canadian studies suggest certain gender-based differences. For instance, in the 1993 federal election, women were more attracted than men to the two parties then led by women (O'Neill 1998); in 1997, women were less inclined than men to vote for the Reform Party and more inclined to vote for the New Democratic Party (Nevitte, Blais, Gidengil and Nadeau 2000: 110–115). Research also shows that women and men react differently to various issues. For example, women are more resistant than men to the idea of curbing the welfare state; something no doubt related to the fact that, all other things being equal, their quality of life is often more closely linked to government's redistribution policies than is men's. In short, while the concept of Universality helps us to define certain aspects of the electoral behaviour of women, that of Difference is more often useful.

Women as Members of Political Parties

Although most political parties claim a balance between men and women in their ranks, women's relationships to political parties are different from men's. Even when they had not yet secured the right to vote and stand for office, women were a significant presence in the parties in an organizational support or "pink-collar" capacity: making coffee, taking minutes, licking stamps, answering the telephone, etc. Today's reality is, of course, less stereotypical, but the same model of participation applies: the higher one looks in the party hierarchy, the fewer women one finds. Sylvia Bashevkin (1993) has shown that, in the early 1990s, about 30 percent of the riding association presidents in the Progressive Conservative and Liberal parties (the only two that have formed a federal government since 1867) were women. However, women were a distinct majority in secretarial positions—a primarily operational role.

Women as Candidates in Federal Elections

Canadian women acquired the right to stand as candidates in federal elections in 1919. However, this was not enough to make them citizens on the same footing as men, for only four women actually campaigned at the time, and only one entered the House of Commons. There have always been fewer women than men seeking seats in the Commons. As recently as the 1997 federal election, 1,672 persons stood as candidates, 1,264 men and 408 women—but only 286 female candidates were members of the five parties represented in the 35th Parliament. What is more, it used to be that women candidates would find themselves in ridings that were lost in advance, although it seems that this is no longer the case (Pelletier and Tremblay 1992, Studlar and Matland 1994, 1996).

Various factors explain why there continue to be fewer female than male candidates: socialization, social gender roles and so-called systemic barriers. In the latter category is the nomination process, which clearly appears to be problematical for women. Despite repeated appeals from certain national elites to increase the number of female candidates, some local elites remain reluctant to entrust women with the party colours on election day, a resistance that was identified even in the early 1970s by the Royal Commission on the Status of Women in Canada. The argument is that the electorate would not be ready to elect a woman. And yet an analysis of the votes obtained by male and female candidates in a Quebec riding in federal elections from 1945 to 1993 clearly shows that, with the same qualifications, women receive more votes than men (Tremblay 1995). Furthermore, the nomination campaign represents a major financial obstacle for women (Brodie 1991), especially since this stage of access to political institutions is still not controlled by the *Canada Elections Act.* Another factor that limits the number of female candidates is the nature of our electoral system: under our electoral rules, each party endorses just one person per riding. Although proportional representation does not guarantee an increase in the number of women candidates, there is no doubt that if a party can expect to elect more than one person in the same riding, it becomes more embarrassing if they are all men.

Women as MPs and Senators

Are the women in Parliament like the men, or different from them? In 2001, they still account for less than a quarter of MPs; this puts Canada far behind Sweden, where parity is on the verge of being achieved. Paradoxically, it appears that the national elites are fairly comfortable with this situation: unlike numerous countries which have developed various strategies to encourage women candidates, the Canadian government has yet to adopt any significant measure to this end (the most recent electoral reform recognized child care costs as campaign expenses, which is certainly a positive step, but plainly insufficient to increase the number of female MPs in the Commons). In this connection, an important issue for future electoral reform would be to place limits on spending during nomination campaigns. However, such an initiative is opposed by some, who see it as an impediment to the free play of democracy—a democracy that has so far functioned more on the model of exclusion than inclusion.

The presence of women in the House of Commons can be understood in terms of a double division, one that is vertical as well as horizontal. The former would suggest that the real positions of power are beyond the access of women, who remain at the bottom of the ladder of political influence. This is probably less true today, since certain women have held positions of great influence in recent Canadian governments. The horizontal division implies a separation of portfolios by gender, men being assigned those associated with production (such as finance, industry or commerce) and women assigned those associated with reproduction (such as justice, immigration or children). This too is tending to change, although this model continues to be a fairly good guide to the composition of parliamentary committees.

Some recent research (Tremblay 1998, 1999; Trimble 1993, 1997) has shown that women could bring about certain changes in political life, notably by placing issues on the political agenda which, in their absence, might be ignored (such as the recent establishment of a parliamentary committee to study women's demands in the context of the World March of Women); by changing political style (e.g. in terms of language); and by taking a different approach to public policy (e.g. by adopting a more humanistic viewpoint). Further research is necessary to lend more force to these observations.

The Senate of Canada offers an interesting laboratory in this regard, since women there have now achieved a critical mass, i.e. 33 percent (34/103, with two seats vacant at the time of writing). There is a good deal of research that tends to demonstrate that, to have a significant impact on the culture of an organization (such as Parliament), women must occupy at least a third of the available space. Even though the Senate has specifically resisted the advent of women in its midst, it might become an important ally for a feminist project for the political representation of women.

Conclusion

Women remain on the margins of federal Canadian politics, at least in terms of their presence in political institutions. Whereas the Mary Wollstonecraft dilemma opposes Universality and Difference, I propose instead that these two aspects be reconciled as one, using the notion of parity. Parity assumes that democratic forums should be composed of roughly half women and half men. Certain opposing voices suggest that citizenship is universal, and has no gender, no skin colour, no age, and so on. But a mere glance at the sociodemographic composition of the House of Commons is sufficient to reveal that, on the contrary, the citizen representative is usually a white male, in the prime of life, etc. In calling for democratic institutions that harmonize rather than exclude differences, notably by including a more or less equal proportion of women and men, parity stands forth as the royal road to Universality.

Spice Girls and Old Spice Boys: Getting There is Only Half the Battle

Linda Trimble and Jane Arscott

2003

Introduction

Frustrated with heckling directed at him during a spring 1998 session of question period in the Alberta legislature, Acting Premier (and then Treasurer) Stockwell Day complained, "It's sometimes difficult to maintain a focus with all the *chirping from the Spice Girls* over there" (emphasis ours).[1] Day's likening of female members of the Liberal opposition to the "girls" in the then popular British band was not well received by the women he targeted. Liberal MLA Colleen Soetaert felt the comment showed "a lack of respect for women in the legislature." Her colleague Sue Olsen summarized her reaction this way, "I'm getting tired of the sexist comments that are being made." Day's remarks came close on the heels of heated personal invective directed at newly elected Liberal leader Nancy MacBeth, including pointed observations about repeated changes to her hairstyle.[2] The media loved the hairdo comments and ran with the Spice Girls story by linking female opposition MLAs with the appropriate band members. Laurie Blakeman, with her red hair, had a clear resemblance to Ginger Spice, but was Colleen Soetaert Baby or Scary? Soetaert, master of the quick quip, responded later in question period by calling a government member "Old Spice," referring to a cologne marketed to the over-50 crowd as an aftershave for the "man's" man.

This incident, and the media response to it, reveals a great deal about the circles of constraint that continue to restrict the advancement of women legislators. The Spice Girls, female newcomers to political office, women with ideas, energy, and confidence, represent a new generation of women politicians who, like the flamboyant pop group, are not afraid to claim "girl power." On the other hand, the Old Spice Boys—men with legislative experience and an expansive sense of entitlement "earned" by dint of hard work and decades of male dominance of political office—have various ways of expressing their discomfort with these female upstarts and their "chirping." Female legislators are quite routinely shouted down, verbally and sexually harassed, heckled, and ridiculed because they are women. The proverbial battle of the sexes continues to be fought between the new Spice Girls and the Old Spice Boys, with the media eager to report every verbal jab, personal insult, and personality clash.

Legislatures remain, much as they have long been, men's clubs. Women intrude at their peril. Their presence is annoying but tolerable so long as they keep to their place on the sidelines. After all, women are not typically contenders for positions of leadership. Women who do contest the top jobs quickly discover that they are intruding on masculine turf. Sheila Copps learned this lesson in her bid for the leadership of the Ontario Liberals. She lost, but surprised many observers by posing a solid challenge to the victor, David Peterson. After the convention, Copps was treated differently by the male powerbrokers in the party.

> Funny—when I had been the "sweet young thing" from Hamilton Centre, the only woman in caucus, I'd been no great threat. But the leadership convention changed that. For the first time, the men in my caucus realized that women could be more than tokens in our party, that we could wield influence—even power. That notion frightened a number of my colleagues. . . . While I had failed in my bid to lead our party, I had shown that it might be possible for another woman at another time. That realization threatened men who might themselves seek greater political roles.[3]

No longer formally excluded from legislatures, women are still seen as outsiders, strangers in a foreign culture, aliens in the "testosterone tabernacles"[4] that make political judgments and direct policy decisions. This chapter begins by exploring the assumptions and attitudes that underlie the construction of politics as a man's game. We then look at the consequences for female political aspirants, including barriers to engaging fully in political debate, the role conflict faced by female legislators with children, and sexist behaviour in legislatures. While some women legislators manage to take up the Spice Girl challenge and rise above the petty politics of the Old Spice Boys, gender-based circles of constraint tend to make legislatures difficult and even unsafe work environments for female legislators. As a result, those women who stay in the game a long time demonstrate considerable courage, persistence, and fortitude.

A Man's Game

One of the very few women who sought a party nomination to run for a seat in the PEI legislature in the 1950s said the male activists in her party "didn't want women mixed up in it. It was a man's legislature."[5] This is a consistent refrain, even by women who have broken into these formerly men-only environments.[6] Canada's legislatures were indeed originally constituted as men's legislatures. They were developed at a time when women were expressly denied not only the right to membership in them, but even to vote for the men seeking political office.

In the beginning, the seats of power were fashioned for a very select group of men. The first federal electoral law denied all but white male property owners the right to vote and singled out women and "mental incompetents" as particularly undeserving of this privilege. A varied and formidable list of reasons was offered to support the exclusion of women from the vote: women were too weak to participate in the excitement of elections; they lacked the mental acuity necessary to comprehend political issues; woman suffrage defied Biblical teachings; the vote would "unsex and degrade women, destroy domestic harmony and lead to a decline in the birth rate;" women could better achieve their goals by means other than the vote, especially by their use of "loving persuasion;" women were said not to want the vote; and, finally, even if granted the right to vote, women would not bother to cast ballots.[7] The very idea of granting women political rights was considered so radical that the first group devoted to winning the female franchise, formed in 1876, felt compelled to disguise its intentions with the moniker "Toronto Women's Literary Club." After seven years of subterfuge, emboldened by an Ontario law that gave property-owning spinsters and widows the right to vote on municipal by-laws, the club unveiled its true intentions by renaming itself the Canadian Woman Suffrage Association.[8]

Many Canadians, including women, were denied political rights on the grounds that they did not possess the necessary qualities to exercise the duties and enjoy the privileges of citizens.[9] The "ideal of citizenship" resulted from a process that systematically excluded all but "an elite class of male landowners [who] . . . first laid claim to the reasoning faculties that alone, in their view, made them competent to influence policy."[10] For much of our post-Confederation history, Canadians were legally or logistically excluded from voting and running for political office simply because they were women, Aboriginal, poor, members of ethnic minority groups, or disabled. Women were neither regarded as a category of person worthy of positive recognition in the eye of the law and in policy, nor were they treated as a unified category . . . some women won the vote federally in 1918, but other women (and men) waited considerably longer for their franchise to be granted. For some—Canadians of Asian or East Indian origins—the vote was not achieved until the late 1940s; for most Aboriginal Canadians the franchise was won in the 1960s; and for persons with disabilities it did not come until the early 1990s.

Politics was designed as a (white, able-bodied) man's game. As its masculinist ethos was consolidated, women were excluded from political activity, including entry to legislatures, on the basis of their sex, ethnicity, class, and mental/physical ability. Notions about a woman's "proper place" included assumptions that lingered long after most women were accorded the right to vote and run for office. After all, women were seen as biologically destined for the domestic household, not the houses of Parliament. In the first few decades after Confederation, political, scientific, and clerical elites clearly delineated a woman's place with statements like "woman's first and only place is in the home" and "woman exists for the sake of the womb."[11] A woman's true calling was to be a good wife and mother. Given attitudes like these, it is not surprising that when Canada's first female MP, Agnes Macphail, tried to enter the House of Commons in 1921, an employee blocked her way. "You can't go in there, Miss!" she was told.[12] In she went. Since Macphail's entry, 154 more women have won admission to the national legislature where formerly they could not go.

Since the social context was pervasively sexist, it is not surprising that several of the first women legislators were elected as replacements for male parliamentarians. In her memoirs, the late Judy LaMarsh, Liberal MP from 1960 to 1968, recalled: "throughout my years in the Liberal party, I never saw evidence that any real attention was paid to seeking out and grooming women as . . . parliamentary material, except in one area and that was the importuning of fresh widows of Members of Parliament to seek their husbands' unexpired terms."[13] The first woman elected in BC, Mary Ellen Smith, replaced her late husband in a by-election held in 1918.[14] Nine women have been elected to the House of Commons as political substitutes for male relatives, one as recently as 1982. Between 1921 and 1970, only 17 women were elected to the House of Commons, taking 74 out of 3,821 seats (2 percent); seven of them took over the role from recently deceased husbands. At the provincial and territorial level, at least six, and likely many more, women were chosen by party gatekeepers to substitute for their departed spouses or fathers. Why? Party officials figured the pity factor could easily be parlayed into a by-election win, and the grieving but grateful widows or daughters would faithfully carry on in the tradition of their departed relatives. Electing women family members also "solved" in the short term the problem of providing for the family of a loyal party man. Ordinarily a suitable male candidate could then be vetted and nominated in the lead-up to a general election. However, not all surrogates stepped aside graciously.

New Brunswick's Margaret Rideout, the first woman from the province to win election federally or provincially, typifies this path for early women politicians. Rideout's husband, Sherwood, had been the Liberal MP for Westmorland when he died of a heart attack. His death left the Liberal minority government in a precarious position; thus, the 1964 by-election was both very important and hotly contested by opposition parties with "no intention of allowing this election to be given away to a grieving widow."[15] But Margaret Rideout's campaign posters and pamphlets suggested that this was precisely why voters should support her, and she won quite handily. As "Mrs. S.H. Rideout," the traditional homemaker, she posed no threat to the male powerbrokers of the day. Electing her provided needed support to the status quo. The women who entered legislatures on their own terms were not welcomed, for they threatened entrenched attitudes and structures of privilege.

In an exchange that took place in 1985 between then President of the National Action Committee on the Status of Women, Judy Rebick, and Newfoundland Conservative John Crosbie, he irreverently needled, "We can't have women representing themselves or the next thing you know we'll have to have the crippleds and coloureds."[16] Crosbie later said he thought his comment was funny. Occasionally persons with disabilities and non-white individuals have been elected, but not consistently or in large numbers.[17] Members of newly enfranchised or politically active groups disrupt established patterns when they speak out about their collective under-representation or other matters affecting the fairness and equity of the political system. Not only women but members of racial minority groups, persons with disabilities, and members of Aboriginal communities have great potential to expose and challenge taken-for-granted notions about who should hold power. A few legislators have commented openly about the potential and actual power of elected members of underrepresented groups to bring attention to injustices.

For example, in the early 1970s BC NDP Rosemary Brown had reservations about seeking elected office. Encouraged by NDP leader Dave Barrett to contest a nomination, Brown said she and her husband laughed at the idea. "We both knew that no Vancouver riding would choose a person who was Black, female and an immigrant to be its elected representative." The couple had experience that supported their prediction. Brown recalled, "It made very little sense to me that people who had for years refused to rent me accommodation or hire me for employment would entrust me with the responsibility of representing them in the place of power, where laws governing their lives were drafted and enforced."[18] However, events took a different turn. A majority of voters was persuaded that she was the right candidate for Vancouver-Burrard, where she won a provincial seat in 1972. Nevertheless, in anticipating negative reactions to her candidacy due to her race and heritage, Brown had not miscalculated the negative reception typically given those who challenge the status quo.

In another tightly fought contest, this one for the Liberal nomination in Rosedale prior to the general election of 1979, social worker and community activist Anne Cools, herself an immigrant, saw her campaign for the nomination marred by racial slurs. The National Film Board documentary, *The Right Candidate for Rosedale,* collected images that used negative racial stereotypes to depict the candidate. Cools lost the nomination to an eminent male candidate, John Evans, President of the University of Toronto; he subsequently was defeated in the election by Conservative incumbent David Crombie.

The reaction to women who entered legislatures at a time when female representatives were few in number clearly illustrates the patriarchal presumptions of the Old Spice Boys. Sheila Copps, freshly elected to the Ontario legislature in 1981 as one of only six women in the House and the only female member of the Liberal caucus, found that her colleagues "clearly saw me as an ornament to the party—nice to have around as long as I knew my place." At least one cabinet minister saw her proper place as the domestic sphere. Irritated by her persistent questioning, he suggested she go "back to the kitchen."[19] When Alexa McDonough was the lone female MLA in the Nova Scotia legislature in the early 1980s, her son received telephone calls from drunks demanding to know why Alexa "wouldn't just do the proper thing and keep to the kitchen."[20] Below the surface but still readily apparent runs the message: "You do not belong here; in this arena you have no merit."

Have attitudes and behaviours changed since women began winning election to legislatures in more than token numbers? Much of the evidence, empirical and anecdotal, suggests that female politicians continue to experience resistance to their inclusion, not just as tokens, but as leaders and decision-makers. Claims for substantive power for women invariably smash up against two sides of the merit argument. First, there is the idea that women have not earned, and thus do not merit, more power. Secondly, merit in electoral politics operates in a gender-specific manner. While women's merit is questioned, most men have their merit taken for granted. Merit has long been used in political circles as a code word for those who have power. And because traditional gender roles have been challenged but not fully uprooted by the women's movement, the assumption persists that women belong in the household, performing duties as wives and mothers. Women are mired in the muck of the traditional dichotomy of gender *versus* politics.

"Are You a Politician or a Woman?"

In the 1970s, the notion that political careers and traditional feminine roles were mutually exclusive options was epitomized by a question frequently posed by reporters to MPs Flora MacDonald and Judy LaMarsh: "Are you a politician or a woman?"[21] It is still often presumed that parenting and governing are incompatible roles, at least for women. Mothering, as it is socially constituted, does impose internal and external constraints on women's political participation. Because child bearing and rearing are seen as the responsibility of women, it is

> assumed that family constraints are irrelevant for male candidates but relevant for females. Males are expected to act in the worlds of business or politics, and the factors that would constrain them become someone else's responsibility, usually the candidate's spouse's. It is often assumed that men have a stable support system within the home; the wife's contribution to the man's candidacy is taken for granted. Obviously, family constraints cannot be so easily minimized for most female candidates because the sexual division of labour denies them the same support system.[22]

A double standard emerges, one that was pointedly summed up by Sheila Copps in her book *Nobody's Baby*. "If a young man ascends the political ladder and successfully combines that effort with a happy family life, he becomes complete. If you are a woman, there is always the question, 'How can you look after your children?'"[23] BC MLA Judy Tyabji found this out the hard way when she was denied custody of her three children because the judge felt her political ambition was incompatible with parenting.[24] In reaction to the decision, outraged women politicians asked why the same reasoning was not applied to former Prime Minister Pierre Trudeau, who, as a single father of three young boys, governed the entire country.[25]

The role conflict experienced by women politicians is not simply a reflection of the actual demands of the job. After all, lots of women combine paid work with child-rearing, and most male politicians have children. But social expectations of fathers remain modest, while mothers are still expected to put their children, husbands, and domestic duties first. As Janine Brodie suggests, "the supposed incongruence between the role of homemaker or mother and the role of politician is imposed as much by the idealization of motherhood as by the actual demands of motherhood." After all, "'good wives' or 'good mothers' do not abandon their husbands, homes or children to pursue political careers."[26] Again, Sheila Copps provides a pithy take on this presumption:

> When I married in the summer of 1985, I had already been working full-time in politics for eight years, yet an amazing number of people asked me whether I planned to quit my job. The unstated reason was that I had now snagged a man and should get down to the real business of woman-hood, having babies. And everyone knows that babies and politics don't mix.[27]

Despite the fact that some or even a great deal of this role conflict is socially constructed, women politicians are greatly affected by it. Iris Evans, now a cabinet minister in Alberta, says women with political ambitions used to be relegated to the local school board. "The attitude was, 'Dearie, we'll take care of the important stuff [namely provincial and national politics] and you look after the kids;" Evans recalls.[28] Some women politicians have described the guilt and anxiety they endure as a legacy of the traditional sexual division of labour in Canadian society.[29] In her memoirs, Rosemary Brown related this story about how the "are-you-a-politician-or-a-mother?" conflict affected her first campaign for a BC legislative seat in 1972:

> The only hostile questions directed at me concerned the hypocritical fear that my children would suffer as a result of my political activities, and accusations of their impending neglect. At first the question made me defensive because I shared these concerns myself. I felt guilty about spending a lot of time away from the children, aged fourteen, twelve and five, so I handled the question badly. In time it became clear that they realized they had found my Achilles' heel. I was not fooled. I knew that the questioners cared not one whit about my children, but they saw that their questions wounded me and so, smelling blood, they kept tearing away, heckling, questioning and accusing me every chance they got.[30]

Brown struggled with her guilt, recognized that similar attacks would not be directed to a male candidate, and in the end used humour to deflect the criticisms. She also pointed to her child-rearing work as invaluable experience for a legislator.

Female politicians without husbands or children are not exempt from traditional assumptions. Those who eschew marriage and motherhood are questioned about their femininity. Kim Campbell was criticized by members of her own party because, when she sought the Conservative leadership, she was single and had no children. Indeed, unmarried women politicians are often assumed to be lesbians.[31] The subtext conveyed by these examples is clear; a "womanly" woman doesn't enter the aggressive and competitive political arena. Pauline Jewett's biographer says this trail-blazing MP, who served for the Liberals in the 1950s and the NDP in the 1980s, was questioned about her femininity and single status: "Her independent spirit and firm opinions were perceived as unwomanly and masculine; she was not seen as a 'real' woman."[32] Power-seeking women are, therefore, considered unfeminine, perhaps abnormal, and certainly a threat to the status quo.

Role conflict for women politicians is about much more than sexual innuendo and feelings of guilt. There are tangible barriers to blending parenting and politicking for male and female politicians alike, but women in the political realm are more likely to point them out. According to a BC study, many female MLAs say long hours, the lack of a fixed schedule during legislative sessions, and night sittings make the Legislative Assembly less than woman-friendly.[33] The sheer unpredictability of the legislative schedule makes it difficult to integrate work and family life, arrange child care, and find time for friends and family.[34] Travel is also a burden, especially for female legislators whose homes are geographically distant from the capital. For example, Conservative MP Pat Carney, then a single parent, was told in 1984 that the MP's family travel benefit was only for spouses. Consequently, she could not use the fund to fly her 15-year old son to Ottawa. Carney protested by refusing to perform her duties until the rule was changed. When that tactic failed, she appealed to the first woman Speaker of the House, Jeanne Sauve, who agreed to extend travel allowances to "designated next of kin."[35]

Now, many Canadian parents cope with long hours spent on the job, but in the public and private sectors, employees can predict their working hours and plan ahead for their time off. Provincial and territorial politicians often do not have this luxury. A sudden election call or a prolonged legislative session plays havoc with the lives of elected representatives, their friends, and their families. These problems are easily addressed, as changes to House of Commons rules made in the mid-1980s show. MPs now have a fixed schedule, no night sittings, an on-site day care centre, and the predictability that results from a parliamentary calendar set months in advance. Kim Campbell wrote that the regular hours in particular "were a boon to the family life of all MPs."[36] But it seems that, although these simple provisions make life so much easier for both male and female representatives, women politicians at the provincial and territorial level have not been able to find support for the necessary changes that improve the work environment all around. The underlying assumptions about the incompatibility of parenting and politics remain uncontested.

Sexist Circles of Constraint

In 1997, the Angus Reid polling firm, in collaboration with the CBC, conducted telephone interviews with 102 female politicians across Canada.[37] Most of the women legislators agreed patriarchal attitudes constrained their political careers. Eighty-one per cent said it is accurate to describe politics as an "old boys" club. Many reported personal experiences with sexist behaviour: 60 per cent had fielded inappropriate or demeaning gender-based remarks, and 31 per cent dealt with unwanted sexual advances or propositions. Almost one-third, 30 percent, said they were held back in their political careers because of their sex. They agreed *en masse* that women politicians face gender-related personal pressures resulting from scrutiny by colleagues, the press, and voters of their private lives, their appearance, wardrobe, family responsibilities, weight, and age. These women also expressed the opinion that the style of politics would change with more women in the legislature: 63 percent believed that with more women elected, legislatures would become more civilized and respectful environments for discussion and debate.

The survey confirmed what many women politicians had been thinking. It certainly codified the sexist circles of constraint women politicians confront regardless of their stance on feminism. In autobiographies and interviews, women legislators have related their first-hand experiences involving sexist attitudes, assumptions, and behaviours. The similarities in their narratives about the job and its perils are striking. Two key themes emerge. First, women politicians say it is unpleasant to work within such a masculine and adversarial environment as legislatures, especially because they find it difficult to reject traditional aggressive and conflict ridden approaches and participate on their own terms. Secondly, they describe a working environment at times so hostile to their participation that it is experienced as emotionally abusive. In particular, women legislators who advocate for women's rights, especially those who identify themselves and their policy goals as feminist, have been ridiculed, heckled, mocked, and harassed.

Entering the "Testosterone Tabernacle"

Many women have commented on the masculine and war-like trappings of Parliament. A central symbol is the mace, a ceremonial staff originally designed as a medieval war club. Seating in legislative chambers was designed to keep opposing sides two sword-lengths apart. The Speaker of the House is still afforded ceremonial protection against the once very real danger of having his head lopped off. And titles like the "Gentleman Usher of the Black Rod"[38] and "Sergeant-at Arms" continue to evoke a "men's club" atmosphere. Even the artwork speaks to the glory days of gory battle. Trudeau-era Liberal cabinet minister Iona Campagnolo had this to say about the paintings decorating the House of Commons: "they're all men and war and swords and blood."[39] Male heroes abound in portraits and statues, while the only women to adorn the halls and grounds of Parliament are a few female monarchs and, as of October 2000, the "famous five" women from Alberta who secured legal person status for women.[40] The memoirs of female politicians express their dismay at this old-fashioned and (to them) arcane institutional culture. Former NDP leader Audrey McLaughlin devoted an entire chapter of her autobiography to her experiences in "the men's club;" likewise Sheila Copps called one chapter "When a House is Not a Home." Former Manitoba Liberal leader Sharon Carstairs titled her book *Not One of the Boys*. Spoken as well as unspoken rules of the parliamentary "men's club" result in the exclusion of women.

Women politicians who are new to the legislative arena arrive full of optimism and enthusiasm. They are keen to voice their own ideas and their constituents' needs, but often have a rude awakening when they begin their jobs as political representatives. They soon discover that the true role of the legislator is not all they hoped it would be. Parliamentary representatives act neither as idealized political representatives, wisely discerning the best ideas and the common interest, nor as the community's liaisons for constituent ideas and opinions. Rather, the legislator's principal job is to champion his or her party and critique the opposing group, regardless of the issue, its nuances, and complexity. The rules of political discourse are, therefore, simple us versus them, no holds barred. The parliamentary system of government is an intrinsically adversarial contest, with opposing "teams" (parliamentary parties) engaging each other in rhetorical battles. Sometimes, the conflicts verge on the physical, as when Reform MP Darrel Stinson stepped away from his desk, rolled up his sleeves, and invited a Liberal member to duke it out. In the end, fisticuffs were not the order of the day, but at least one of the combatants declared himself ready, willing, and able.

Journalist Sydney Sharpe maintains the institution itself is designed to facilitate verbal battles. "In the Commons, enemy MPs are staked in rows on either side of a wide, carpeted isle, a psychological moat across which they fire their modern versions of the flaming arrow-epithets like 'liar,' 'jerk,' 'scumbag,' and 'asshole.'"[41] Liberal cabinet minister Sheila Copps agrees that the "traditions of the House create an atmosphere which is combative, not conciliatory; aggressive not consultative—a forum in which many women feel there is no place for them."[42] Pat Duncan, former premier of the Yukon, said "the high testosterone level in our Legislative Assembly gets to me at times."[43] It is no wonder many women describe the atmosphere as alienating and off-putting. Indeed, "Put Off by Parliament" is the title of an article in *Elm Street* that described federal politics as "Ottawa's macho game." In the piece, journalist Susan Delacourt wrote, "politics functions along the same lines as a sports team or a military unit, emphasizing discipline, tradition, loyalty and bravura performance. The cliche 'Politics is a blood sport' is simply accepted as a fact of life."[44] But for women in the House of Commons this so-called "fact of life" often prevents them from doing the job in their own way, with a lower profile and less confrontational strategies.

The highest profile parliamentary battleground is the daily question period, where ministers are grilled by opposition members with the intent of catching them off guard or exposing government errors. Some women have gone on record as disliking question period because of the hyper-confrontational style and vitriolic tone adopted by many legislators in an effort to score points with their parties and secure ten-second sound bites on TV and radio. Seasoned Liberal cabinet minister Anne McLellan refers to it as a brand of torture equivalent to dental work without Novocaine: "It's about 'gotcha' and 'ha ha.' And I hate that. I hate that."[45] In her autobiography, written while she was leader of the federal NDP, Audrey McLaughlin said: "I remember how amazed Marion [Dewar, also an NDP MP] and I were when we sat through our first Question Period. The posturing, the banging on desks, and the shouting made us think of school kids. And like children in the school yard, the men seemed to be constantly jockeying for territory and dominance."[46]

For women politicians whose job experience is in the professions, particularly health care, teaching, and social service, and who are trained to take a more collegial, holistic approach to decision-making, the political landscape seems alien, riddled with landmines, and difficult to navigate. Many women do not want to play the game by the age-old masculinist rules; it is just not their style. A female legislator in BC explained the atmosphere this way: "it functions on anger, pure and simple, and the ability to control, manipulate, use, display anger, and of course, along with anger goes a big, loud, voice, being tall, being imposing, all of those things which obviously play to male experience, male strengths, male conditioning."[47]

In this sense, then, women politicians are damned if they do, damned if they don't. If they avoid the fray, they may be squeezed out of important discussions, overlooked, or not taken seriously. They may not be able to get the job done. On the other hand, if they embrace the aggressive and adversarial techniques typical of parliamentary exchanges, they run the risk of being labelled unwomanly. The classic example is the much-broadcasted and pilloried image of Liberal "rat packer" Sheila Copps leaping over chairs to confront Sinclair Stevens, a Conservative cabinet minister caught out in a conflict-of-interest scandal and bent on avoiding questions from a parliamentary committee. This "chair hopping" incident happened almost 20 years ago but is still used to brand Copps's behaviour as hyperaggressive and unseemly. And it has served to caution other female aspirants, as political scientist Don Desserud's interviews with women politicians in New Brunswick found. Two female politicians told him that it was important "for women not to be too aggressive."[48]

Babes in Boyland:49 A Hostile Working Environment

The CBC-Angus Reid survey discussed earlier in this chapter provided statistical verification of women politicians' experiences with sexism and sexual harassment in Canada's legislatures. The majority of female legislators, 60 percent, said they had endured inappropriate or demeaning gender-based remarks, and 31 percent reported fending off unwanted sexual advances or propositions. First in the capacity of an MPP and, later, as an MP, Sheila Copps experienced it all, wrote journalist Sydney

Sharpe: "Copps came in for a special brand of sexist insult. Over the years, she was called 'baby,' 'slut,' 'witch' and 'a goddamn ignorant bitch.'" So Copps reported in her autobiography that government members of the Ontario legislature regularly commented on her looks, weight, bra size, and voice.[51] The 1980s were a particularly difficult time for women politicians; although they were relatively few in number, they seemed poised to challenge the complacency of the old boy's clubs. Alexa McDonough still has the nasty notes male MLAs passed to her when she was the lone woman in the Nova Scotia legislature in the early 1980s.[52]

Some of the maltreatment women experience includes sexual harassment and sexual assault. A fellow MPP attempted to sexually attack Sheila Copps, then a member of the Ontario legislature, a move Copps referred to as a "pass."[53] In the late 1980s, Alberta NDP MLA Pam Barrett was aggressively "hugged" by a succession of male Conservative MLAs; a female Conservative cabinet minister was groped by a cabinet colleague, and another female minister was demeaned with the label "Miss Pretty Minister."[54] Manitoba's Sharon Carstairs received the tired, cliched, sexist message directed at "uppity" women:

> Shortly after I was elected leader of the opposition, a card arrived at my
> office. [My assistant] assumed that it contained a congratulatory message,
> so she put it on my desk unopened. I took the card out of the envelope
> and read the outside message which said, "WHAT IS AN EIGHT LET-
> TER WORD FOR WHAT YOU NEED?" Inside it read, "AGOODLAY."[55]

In the Ontario legislature in the early 1990s, opposition members demeaned female members of the Rae government by mocking their voices and blowing kisses at them, prompting cabinet minister Marion Boyd to observe: "I work in a very hostile workplace." Another NDP MPP said she experienced the angry and antagonistic legislative culture, particularly the constant yelling, "almost as abuse or violence."[56] Marion Boyd was so concerned about negative working conditions for women in the Ontario legislature that she made a submission to the Standing Committee on the Legislative Assembly in 1992. In her report, Boyd highlighted the incidence of "language demeaning to women; efforts to humiliate and intimidate women; the use of sexist language; and a general mood of disrespect in the House."[57] This type of behaviour has not disappeared along with the twentieth century. In the BC legislature, when NDP leader Joy MacPhail "rises to challenge Campbell's government during Question Period, Liberal MLA's behind her whisper obscenities and other rude comments."[58]

MP Barbara Greene told the House of Commons in 1991 that "systemic sexual discrimination and harassment are rampant."[59] Greene and the late *Toronto Star* columnist Carol Goar had both been physically assaulted in a poorly-lit Commons parking lot, prompting women MPs and staff to approach the Speaker's office and demand better lighting in the parking area. These and other incidents involving lack of safety and chauvinism, including the misogynist comments, rudeness, and outright harassment such as that experienced by Sheila Copps and others, prompted female

MPs to cross party lines and form the Association of Women Parliamentarians (AWP) in 1990. The AWP sprang into action in 1991 when a Conservative MP called Sheila Copps a "slut" during a Commons debate. The AWP condemned the remark, countering with a proposal to increase the power of the Speaker of the House to discipline MPs who make sexist, homophobic, or racist comments. While the association lasted only as long as the thirty-fourth Parliament, it brought together women from the three major parties to address matters of mutual concern, especially the obstacles to women's participation in political life. Cross-party cooperation among legislators is very rare indeed, especially in parliamentary systems.[60] The creation of the AWP is itself evidence of the severity of the problems it sought to address as all women legislators felt their negative experiences demonstrated the need for reforms.

Women politicians often find support and encouragement inside their party caucuses from both male and female colleagues, but encounter hostility and harassment in their interactions with members of opposing parties. Women in the NDP caucus of Saskatchewan's Romanow government reported that, while the relatively large number of women in caucus provided a supportive atmosphere, interactions between parties remained unchanged.[61] For instance, male NDP MLAs called Liberal leader Lynda Haverstock the "princess of darkness;" A legislative reporter described their highly personalized attacks on the opposition leader as vicious and disrespectful. Similarly, Manitoba MLAs related positive, collegial relationships within caucus, regardless of party, and said the increased numbers of women prompted new standards of behaviour in the House, including replacing the traditional desk-thumping with clapping. However, the women legislators also endured sexist comments and behaviours in the legislature. In the 1980s, a male MLA suggested "that a female member deserved a slap." As recently as the early 1990S, male MLAs made gun-shooting gestures and pelvic thrusts at women when they rose to speak. Manitoba NDP politician Judy Wasyliycia- Leis recalled that the harassment became more overt and opposition MLAs more hostile when members spoke in support of women's issues.[62]

Female politicians who adopt the label "feminist" or voice women's policy demands often come in for a particularly nasty brand of criticism. "In the 1970s, Flora MacDonald was regularly heckled in the House—sometimes by her own Tory colleagues—for raising women's concerns, such as the unfairness of laws that robbed women of pensions after their husband died."[63] Marie Laing, who served in the Alberta legislature from 1986 to 1993, persisted in raising women's experiences with discrimination and demanded policy changes to raise the status of women. She reported at times feeling personally attacked in the legislature because of her support for women. For instance, (then) Conservative backbencher Stockwell Day accused Laing of "browbeating" members of the assembly with her "irresponsible" views on women's rights."[64] Years later, Laing recalled feeling emotionally battered when she left the chamber at the end of sessions.

Catch-22: How to Entice More Women without More Women?

The perils of the "testosterone tabernacle" create a dilemma. According to federal cabinet minister Anne McLellan, "More women aren't going to go into politics until they start to see a more constructive tone, less about theatre, less about scoring points and more about actually working on the issues of the day in a constructive way that gets things done."[65] Alberta Liberal MLA Laurie Blakeman agrees, arguing that the competitive and nasty elements of political life may discourage some women from contemplating a political career: "Do they really want to put themselves in a position where they are heckled about their weight, their looks, whether they are wearing makeup or not?"[66] The CBC-Angus Reid survey of women politicians found widespread agreement that electing more women would help make legislatures more civilized and respectful places in which to work.

There is some evidence to suggest that electing more women can change the tone and style of legislative debate. For example, during the period from the mid-1960s to the mid-1980s in PEI, "the mood among the major parties and in the Assembly remained chilly, and at times hostile, toward participation by and representation of women." But the presence of more women in the PEI assembly in the early 1990s led one MLA to say that decorum had improved and that the language had become more gender-neutral.[67] NDP women in Ontario succeeded in achieving a more collegial atmosphere, at least for the duration of the Rae government. Pat Duncan reported that the Yukon legislature, while home to the highest percentage of women representatives, agreed to adopt nonsexist language. As well, while Premier, she pressed for consensus on the need to avoid violent terms and images in parliamentary debates.[68]

But these types of changes will not happen unless more women are represented. But, the numbers are not going up. Herein lies the classic catch-22. As former BC MLA Rosemary Brown puts it, because "both the hierarchical structure and the patriarchal history and nature of politics make it a hostile profession for women, it has for too long been the private and exclusive domain of men."[69] Journalist Susan Delacourt agrees the system needs to be fixed before many more women will be enticed to enter legislatures, but is unlikely to be renovated by men. And the "cost of *not* fixing it could be a political world that alienates everyone except the old boys who created it."[70]

Conclusion

Canada's newly elected women—the "Spice Girls" who claim "girl power" in the political arena—enter legislatures full of optimism, bursting with ideas and potential, and eager to make change. Flush with success in their personal and professional lives outside politics, empowered by their electoral victories, they may believe they can accomplish whatever they set their minds to do. And perhaps some of them can, despite the circles of constraint drawn by a legacy of institutionalized sexism and gender-based assumptions about a woman's proper place. The continued bad behaviour of the "Old Spice Boys"—men who resist women's entry into political life because it challenges their own power and privilege-enervates some women legislators. Sexist assumptions, verbal and sexual harassment, and anti-feminist rhetoric serve notice to women politicians that they have overstepped time-honoured gender boundaries. But often the biggest obstacle to women seeking a place in political life is resistance to change. Change, much needed though it is, has been slow and piecemeal. The lack of meaningful social change designed to make elected office more women-friendly continues to buttress a destructive form of circular reasoning: "Politics is a man's game; that's just the way things are." Knowing all this, why would women choose a career in politics? The answer is simple. Many do not.

As long as the behaviour inside legislatures is allowed to continue, as long as the media persist in questioning the competence of women politicians,[71] and as long as the public is encouraged by politicians and the media alike to evaluate women legislators according to a gendered double-standard, women will not take their rightful place in public life. Comments on women's looks, personalities, and sex lives litter women's experiences with electoral politics. Observations about Ellen Fairclough's hats in the 1950s, Judy LaMarsh's favourite recipes in the 1960s, the "**Flora Syndrome**" in the 1970s (where party members promised to support Tory MP Flora MacDonald's leadership bid but did not actually vote for her), Sheila Copps's assertive style in the 1980s, and Kim Campbell's love life in the 1990s—all illustrate a pattern of inappropriate scrutiny of female politicians' personal lives.[72] Until sexism is seen for what it is, challenged, and changed, this socially inappropriate behaviour will continue to prevent women from receiving balanced, equitable, and fair treatment in electoral politics in Canada.

Endnotes

1. Jerry Ward, "Spicing Up the House;' *Edmonton Sun* 28 April 1998: 5·
2. Steve Chase, "MacBeth's Return Greeted with Jeers;' *Calgary Herald* 21 April 1998: AI, A2.
3. Copps 50.
4. This term was coined by Sydney Sharpe. In *The Gilded Ghetto* she devotes a chapter to the travails of women politicians in male-dominated legislatures (see 34–52).
5. Crossley 282.
6. Sheila Copps, Audrey McLaughlin, Sharon Carstairs, and many others make this point in their autobiographies.
7. Catherine Cleverdon, *The Woman Suffrage Movement in Canada*, 2nd ed. (Toronto: University of Toronto Press, 1974) 5–7·
8. Alison Prentice, et al., *Canadian Woman: A History,* 2nd ed. (Toronto: Harcourt Brace, 1996) 195–96.
9. For a brief discussion of women's citizenship, see Linda Trimble, "The Politics of Gender; *Critical Concepts: An Introduction to Politics,* 1st ed., ed. Janine Brodie (Scarborough: Prentice-Hall, 1999) 307–10.

10. Mark Kingwell, *The World We Want: Virtue, Vice, and the Good Citizen* (Toronto: Penguin, 2000) 10–11.
11. Prentice 143, 146. 12 Sharpe 36.
13. Judy La Marsh, *Memoirs of a Bird in a Gilded Cage* (Toronto: McClelland and Stewart, 1968) 283·
14. Erickson, "Parties, Ideology and Feminist Action" III.
15. Desserud 261–62.
16. Sharpe 45.
17. See Jerome H. Black, "Representation in the Parliament of Canada: The Case of Ethnoracial Minorities;' Everitt and O'Neill 355–72.
18. Brown 94,119.
19. Copps 25, 28.
20. Anderssen A4.
21. Robinson and Saint-Jean 136.
22. Brodie, *Women and Politics in Canada* 79.
23. Copps 85.
24. Quoted in Sharpe 152.
25. Robert Matas, "Women Politicians Called Backlash Victims," *Globe and Mail* 10 June 1993: A3.
26. Brodie, *Women and Politics in Canada* 81.
27. Copps 85.
28. Johnsrude, "In Politics, Being a Woman is a Drag" AI, A2.
29. Sec Sharpe 144–63, for accounts of role strain experienced by women politicians. 30 Brown 126.
31. Sharpe 47. Indeed, when 29-year old Sheila Copps ran for the leadership of the Ontario Liberal party opponents circulated anonymous notes accusing her of "lesbian tendencies." See Copps 45.
32. McKenzie 59.
33. Erickson, "Parties, Ideology and Feminist Action" 121.
34. At a June 2002 Edmonton YWCA "One Woman One Vote" brainstorming session attended by Linda Trimble, women politicians discussed the dilemma posed by breakfast meetings for women responsible for seeing their young children off to day care or school. One municipal politician said that, when her children were small, she insisted on scheduling meetings at "child friendly" hours.
35. Pat Carney, *Trade Secrets: A Memoir* (Toronto: Key Porter, 2000) 191–93.
36. Campbell 122.
37. Downloaded from Angus Reid, www.angusreid.com/wip/sldo02.htm. 10 May 1997.
38. "Gentleman" was removed from the title when, for the first time, a woman (Mary McLaren) assumed the post, in 1997. Now the position is referred to as "Usher of the Black Rod" or just "Black Rod."
39. Sharpe 37.
40 The monument was unveiled on 18 October, 2000, over 70 years after the Judicial Committee of the Privy Council declared that women could be considered persons under the law. See the Famous Five Foundation website www.famous5.org/htmIlfamous5.html for a photograph of the monument, a history of the Persons Case, and biographies of the Famous Five.

41. Sharpe 35. Calling another member a "liar" is against parliamentary rules, but the same rule book is silent about many of the epithets thrown at women legislators.
42. Copps 93.
43. Hayden 634.
44. Delacourt, "Put Off by Parliament" 53-62. 45 Delacourt, "Put Off by Parliament" 54.
46. McLaughlin 27–28.
47. Erickson, "Parties, Ideology and Feminist Action" 121. 48 Desserud 270.
49. When Linda Trimble was trying to come up with a title for a paper on women in the Alberta Legislature, her colleague Fred Judson offered, not very seriously, "Babes in Boyland." She decided on "A Few Good Women," but Fred's suggestion was not forgotten. This phrase seems an apt description of the legislative climate for women.
50. Sharpe 44.
51. Copps 24–27; 74. 52 Anderssen A4.
53. Copps 29.
54. Sharpe 216. These events led Sharpe to label the Alberta legislature the most sexist in the country.
55. Carstairs 217.
56. Sharpe 185, 187.
57. Burt and Lorenzin 211.
58. Sam Schecter, "Political Stonecutters: Joy MacPhail and Jenny Kwan," *Forward Magazille,* 27 August 2001, http:/www.forwardmagazine.org/articles/PoliticalStonecutters.html (downloaded 12 December 2001).
59. Sharpe 48.
60. Lisa Young, "Fulfilling the Mandate of Difference: Women in the Canadian House of Commons," Arscott and Trimble, *In the Presence of Women* 92-93·
61. Carbert 163–64.
62. Brock 190–193, "94, 195.
63. Sharpe 38.
64. Linda Trimble, "Feminist Politics in the Alberta Legislature, 197Z-1994." Arscott and Trimble, *In the Presence of Women* 143.
65. Delacourt, "Put Off by Parliament" 62.
66. Johnsrude, "In Politics, Being a Woman is a Drag," A2.
67. Crossley 284,304.
68. Hayden 638.
69. Brown 141.
70. Delacourt, "Put Off by Parliament" 62.
71. Susan Carroll and Ronnee Schreiber, "Media Coverage of Women in the 103rd Congress," Norris 132; Kim Fridkin Kahn, "The Distorted Mirror: Press Coverage of Women Candidates for Statewide Office," *Journal of Politics* 56:1 (1994): 170–71.
72. The Flora Syndrome refers to Conservative MP Flora MacDonald's bid for the Tory leadership in the 1970s; numerous activists and party members promised to support MacDonald but failed to deliver their votes; according to some observers, many delegates could not bring themselves to support a woman. Regarding Kim Campbell and the double standard, see Lysiane Gagnon, "Why Isn't Campbell Judged by the Same Yardstick as Male Politicians?" *Globe and Mail* 5 June 1993: D3.

Focus Questions

1. After reading McClung's "Hardy Perennials," return to her essay on "What Women Think of War" (Chapter 8). What sort of picture of women suffragists emerges from these two essays?

2. What type of argument is made by McClung to justify women's suffrage? Would the same arguments be acceptable in today's society?

3. What are the barriers to women's full participation in Canadian politics today? How do they compare to the barriers faced by women like McClung in the early twentieth century?

4. What are the larger consequences—for women and men—of this limited participation?

5. Why does the vote hold such pride of place in definitions of citizenship?

13

The Politics of Culture: Quebec's Quiet (and not so quiet) Revolution

Introduction

Stuart MacLean, the host of CBC's "Vinyl Café," recently referred to conflict between French and English Canadians as the country's "big bang"—the moment at which the basic elements of the country's past, present, and future, were created. In many ways (and setting aside, momentarily, what is perhaps the bigger bang of contact between Europeans and Aboriginals), this assessment of the effects of French-English conflict is an insightful one. From Conquest, through to the Riel Rebellions, and even Henri Bourassa's impassioned plea for abstinence from war, French Canadians have often found themselves on the margins of Canada's political mainstream. After World War II and up to the present day, however, within the borders of *la belle province,* Quebeckers have articulated an increasingly nationalistic vision of their territory, resurrecting the spirit of independence which had inspired people like Louis-Joseph Papineau. Québec separatism, a distressing idea for many Canadians outside of Quebec (and at least some within it), is the product of this history and this vision.

The following chapter presents several diverse articulations of this spirit of independence, beginning with artist Paul-Émile Borduas' *Refus Global,* or "Total Refusal." Written in company with fifteen fellow artists in 1948, it expressed decidedly anti-establishmentarian ideals, encouraging Quebeckers to throw off the shackles of history and religion, and to embrace magic, imagination, and innovation. Often identified as an inspiration for the massive social and political transformation that would occur in the province in the 1960s—the so-called "Quiet Revolution"—*Refus Global* provides a crucial insight into a crucial moment of Quebec's history.

This document is followed by another manifesto, but one which is decidedly contrary to Borduas'. In the early 1960s, a violent left-wing organization, the *Front de libération du Québec* (Quebec Liberation Front, or FLQ), began a campaign of domestic terrorism in hopes of overthrowing the government and achieving independence. Their campaigns climaxed in October of 1970, when they kidnapped two politicians, James Cross and Pierre Laport (who was subsequently killed by his captors). One of the FLQ's demands for the release of their prisoners was that their manifesto be read out over the airwaves—which it was. The October Crisis ended soon afterward, greatly assisted by the fact that Prime Minister Trudeau put the War Measures Act into effect in the province, bringing in the Army to help put an end to the movement's activities.

The FLQ's demand for independence from Canada was not unique, although their means and methods certainly were. Throughout the crisis, in fact, other separatists, including René Lévesque, leader of the *Parti Québecois,* took great pains to separate themselves from the FLQ's methods—if not their underlying message of independence. Lévesque began his career as a war correspondent in Germany, and later became a popular television host in the province. His vision of an independent Québec is articulated here in a brief article written in 1976, the year he was elected Premier of the Province. Only four years later, he led Quebeckers into their first referendum on separation (which did not, obviously, succeed).

The final reading in this chapter was written by Leonard Cohen, one of Canada's most well-known and beloved poets, authors, and musicians. Taking a profoundly sardonic approach to French-English conflict, Cohen's poem puts the issues of language and culture into sharp, and decidedly refreshing relief.

Refus Global
Paul-Emile Borduas
(1905–1960)

We are the offspring of modest French-Canadian families, working-class or lower-middle-class, who, ever since their arrival from the Old Country, have always remained French and Catholic through resistance to the Conquest, through arbitrary attachment to the past, by choice and sentimental pride, and out of sheer necessity. We are the settlers who, ever since 1760, have been trapped in the fortress of fear—that old refuge of the vanquished—and there abandoned. Our leaders set sail to sell themselves to a higher bidder, a practice they have continued to follow at every opportunity.

We are a small people sheltering under the wing of the clergy—the only remaining repository of faith, knowledge, truth, and national wealth; isolated from the universal progress of thought with all its pitfalls and perils, and raised (since complete ignorance was impossible) with well-meaning but grossly distorted accounts of the great historical facts.

We are a small people, the product of a Jansenist colony, isolated, defeated, left a powerless prey to all those invading congregations from France and Navarre that were eager to perpetuate in this holy realm of fear (fear-is-the-mother-of-wisdom!) the blessings and prestige of a Catholic religion that was being scorned in Europe. Heirs of papal authority, mechanical, brooking no opposition, past masters of obscurantist methods, our educational institutions had, from that time on, absolute control over a world of warped memories, stagnant minds, and crooked intentions.

We are a small people, who yet grew and multiplied in number, if not in spirit, here in the north of this huge American continent; and our bodies were young and our hearts of gold, but our minds remained primitive, with their sterile obsession about Europe's past glories, while the concrete achievements of our own oppressed people were ignored.

It seemed as if there were no future for us.

But wars and revolutions in the outside world broke the spell, shattered the mental block.

Irreparable cracks began to appear in the fortress walls.

"Refus Global" by Paul-Emile Borduas as appeared in *French-Canadian Nationalism,* Ramsay Cook (editor), Toronto: Macmillan, 1969.

Political rivalries became bitterly entrenched, and the clergy unexpectedly made mistakes.

Then came rebellions, followed by a few executions, and the first bitter cases of rift between the clergy and a few of the faithful.

Slowly the breach widened, then narrowed, then once again grew wider.

Foreign travel became more common, with Paris as the centre of attraction. But The distance being almost prohibitive, and the city too active for our timid souls, the trip was often no more than an opportunity for a holiday spent in improving a retarded sexual education or in acquiring, through the prestige of a prolonged stay in France, the necessary authority whereby better to exploit the masses on one's return home. With a very few exceptions, the behaviour of members (travelled or not) of our medical profession, for instance, tends to be scandalous (how-else- is-one- to- finance- these-long- years-of-study?).

Revolutionary publications, if they ever attracted any attention at all, were considered as the virulent outpourings of a group of eccentrics. With our usual lack of discernment we condemned such publications as devoid of any academic merit.

Travel was also, at times, an unhoped-for opportunity for a new awakening. Minds were growing restless, and everywhere the reading of forbidden books brought a little hope and soothing comfort.

Our minds were enlightened by the *poetes maudirs* who, far from being monsters of evil, dared to give loud and clear expression to those feelings that had always been shamefully smothered and repressed by the most wretched among us, in their terror of being swallowed up alive. New vistas were opened to us by those literary innovators who were the first to challenge the torments of the soul, the moral turpitude of modern life. How stirring was the accuracy, the freshness of their answers, and how different from the hackneyed old lectures delivered in Quebec and in seminaries the world over.

We began to aspire to greater expectations.

We giddily watched the worn and tattered boundaries of our old horizons vanishing into space. Instead of the humiliation of perpetual slavery there came new pride in the knowledge that freedom could be won.

To hell with Church blessings and parochial life! They had been repaid a hundredfold for what they originally granted.

We had our first burning contact with the brotherhood of man to which Christianity had barred the door.

And fear in all its facets no longer ruled the land.

Its facets were legion, and in an attempt to expel them from memory, I shall enumerate them:

fear of prejudice—fear of public opinion, of persecution, of general disapproval

fear of being abandoned by God and by a society that invariably leaves us

to our lonely fate

fear of oneself, of one's brothers, of poverty

fear of the established order—fear of absurd laws fear of new acquaintances

fear of the irrational

fear of needs to be met

fear of opening the flood-gates of our faith in man—fear of the society of the future

fear of the unsettling experience of love

deadly fear—holy fear—paralysing fear: so many links to our chains

Gone were the days of debilitating fear as we entered the era of anguish.

It would take an iron constitution to remain indifferent to the sadness of those who grimly assume an artificial gaiety, of the psychological reactions to the refinements of cruelty that are but the transparent cellophane wrappings to our current anguished despair. (How can one stop screaming upon reading the account of that horrible collection of lampshades pieced together out of tattooed skin stripped from the flesh of wretched prisoners on the request of some elegant lady; how can one stifle one's groans at the long list of concentration-camp tortures; how can one stop one's blood from curdling at the description of those Spanish prison cells, those meaningless reprisals, those cold-blooded acts of vengeance?) How can one fail to shudder at the cruel lucidity of science?

And now, after the reign of overpowering mental anguish, comes the reign of nausea.

We have been sickened by man's apparent inaptitude to remedy such evils, by the futility of our efforts, by the shattered vanity of our past hopes.

For centuries the many sources of poetic inspiration have been doomed to total failure in a society that tossed them overboard, and then tried to retrieve them and force them into the mould of integration, of false assimilation.

For centuries lusty, seething revolutions have been crushed after one brief moment of delirious hope during their fatal fall:

the French revolutions

the Russian Revolution

the Spanish Revolution

all ended in international confusion, despite the vain hopes of countless simple souls throughout the world.

There again, fatality was stronger than generosity.

It is nauseating that fat rewards should be handed out to practitioners of gross cruelty, to liars, to forgers, to those who manufacture abortive projects, to the plotters of intrigue, to the openly self-seeking, to the false counsellors of humanity, to those who pollute the fountain of life.

It is nauseating to realize our own cowardice, our helplessness, our weakness, our bewilderment.

Our ill-starred loves . . .

And the constant cherishing of vain delusions rather than enigmatic realities.

Where is the cause for man's self-imposed efficacy for evil to be found, if not in our stubborn purpose to defend a civilization that ordains the destinies of our leading nations?

The United States, Russia, England, France, Germany, Italy, and Spain: all of them heirs to the same Ten Commandments, to the same gospel.

The religion of Christ has dominated the world. See what has been made of it: a communal faith exploited for the satisfaction of personal ambitions.

Abolish the individual thirst for competition, natural riches, prestige, authority, and these countries will be in perfect agreement. But whichever of them were to gain total supremacy over the world, the general result would be the same.

Christian civilization has reached the end of its tether.

The next world war will cause its total collapse, when international competition is no longer possible.

Its moribund condition will strike those who are still blind to it.

The least sensitive natures will be nauseated at the sight of the gangrene that has been setting in since the fourteenth century.

The despicable way they have been exploited so effectively, for so many centuries and at the cost of life's most precious values, will at last become obvious to its countless victims, to all of its submissive slaves who, the more wretched they were, the more they strove to defend it.

But then: there will be an end to torture.

The downfall of Christianity will drag down with it all the people and all the classes that it has influenced, from the first to the last, from the highest to the lowest.

The depth of its disgrace will be equal to the height of its success in the thirteenth century.

In the thirteenth century, once man's spiritual awareness of his relations with the universe had been allowed to develop within permissible limits, intuition gave way to speculation. Gradually the act of faith was replaced by the calculated act. Exploitation fed on the very heart of religion by turning to its own advantage the limitations of man's reasoning powers; by a rational use of the holy texts for the maintenance of its easily-won supremacy.

This systematic exploitation spread slowly to all levels of social activity, expecting maximum returns for its investment.

Faith sought refuge in the heart of the populace and became their last hope, their only consolation. But there, too, hope began to fade.

Among the learned the science of mathematics took over from the outmoded tradition of metaphysical speculation.

The process of observation followed that of transfiguration.

Method paved the way toward the elimination of restrictions. Decadence became convivial and necessary, prompting the advent of agile machines moving at frightening speeds, enabling us to harness our riotous rivers pending the day when the planet will blow itself up. Our scientific instruments are wonderful devices for the study and control of size, speed, noise, weight, or length. We have unlocked all the gates of the world with our rational thinking; but it is a world where we are no longer united.

The growing chasm between spiritual and rational powers is stretched almost to breaking-point.

Through systematically controlled material progress—the privilege of the affluent—we were able, with the help of the Church (and later without it), to secure political progress; but we have not been able to renew our basic sensibility, Our subconscious impulses; nor have we been capable of seizing our only chance of emancipation from the grip of Christianity by allowing for a free development of man's true feelings.

Society was born through faith, but will perish through reason: A DELIBERATE PROCESS.

The fatal disintegration of collective moral strength into strictly individual self-indulgence has lined the formidable frame of abstract knowledge with a patchwork quilt under which society is snuggling in concealment for a leisurely feasting on its ill-gained prize.

It required the last two wars to achieve this absurd result. The horror of the third war will be decisive. We are on the brink of a D-day of total sacrifice.

The European rat-race has already started across the Atlantic. But events will catch up with the greedy, the gluttonous, the sybarites, the unperturbed, the blind, the deaf.

They will be swallowed up mercilessly.

And a new collective hope will dawn.

We must make ready to meet it with exceptional clear-sightedness, anonymously bound together by a renewed faith in the future, faith in a common future.

The magical harvest magically reaped from the field of the Unknown lies ready for use. All the true poets have worked at gathering it in. Its powers of transformation are as great as the violent reactions it originally provoked, and as remarkable as its later unavailability (after more than two centuries, there is not a single copy of Sa de to be found in our bookshops; Isidore Ducasse, dead for over a century, a century of revolution and slaughter, is still, despite our having become inured to filth and corruption, too powerful for the queasy contemporary conscience).

All the elements of this treasure as yet remain inaccessible to our present-day society. Every precious part of it will be preserved intact for future use. It was built up with Spontaneous enthusiasm, in spite of, and outside, the framework of civilization. And its social effects will only be felt once society's present needs are recognized.

Meanwhile our duty is plain.

The ways of society must be abandoned once and for all; we must free ourselves from its utilitarian spirit. We must not tolerate our mental or physical faculties' being wittingly left undeveloped. We must refuse to close our eyes to vice, to deceit perpetrated under the cloak of imparted knowledge, of services rendered, of payment due. We must refuse to be trapped within the walls of the common mould—a strong citadel, but easy enough to escape. We must avoid silence (do with us what you will, but hear us you must), avoid fame, avoid privileges (except that of being heeded)—avoid them all as the stigma of evil, indifference, servility. We must refuse to serve, or to be used for, such despicable ends. We must avoid DELIBERATE DESIGN as the harmful weapon of REASON. Down with them both! Back they go!

make way for magic! make way for objective mystery!

make way for love!

make way for what is needed!

We accept full responsibility for the consequences of our total refusal. Self-interested plans are nothing but the still-born product of their author. While passionate action is animated with a life of its own.

We shall gladly take full responsibility for the future. Deliberate, rational effort can only fashion the present from the ashes of the past.

Our passions must necessarily, spontaneously, unpredictably forge the future. The past must be acknowledged at birth—but it is far from sacred. We have paid our debt to the past.

It is naive and unsound to consider famous men and events in history as being endowed with a special quality unknown to us today. Indeed, such quality is automatically achieved when man follows his innermost inclinations; it is achieved when man recognizes his new role in a new world. This is true for any man, at any time.

The past must no longer be used as an anvil for beating out the present and the future.

All we need of the past is what can be put to use for the present. A better tomorrow will emerge imperceptibly from the present.

We need not worry about the future until we come to it.

The Final Squaring of Accounts

The social establishment resents our dedication to our cause, our uninhibited expression of concern, our going to extremes, as an insult to their indolence, their smugness, their love of gracious living (the meaning of a rich, generous life, full of hope and love, has been lost).

Friends of the prevailing political system suspect us of being promoters of the 'Revolution'. Friends of the 'Revolution' suspect us of being downright rebels: '. . . we protest against the established order of things, but reform is our sole objective, not complete change'.

However tactfully it may be worded, we believe we understand what they are getting at.

It is all a matter of class.

It is being conjectured that we are naïvely trying to 'change' society by substituting other, similar men for those currently in power. If that were the case, then why not keep the present ones?

Because they are not of the same class! As if a difference in class implied a difference in civilization, a difference in aspirations, a difference in expectations!

They dedicate themselves, at a fixed salary plus a cost-of-living allowance, to organizing the proletariat; they are absolutely right. The only trouble is that once they have strengthened their positions, they will want to add to their slender incomes, and, at the expense of that self-same proletariat, they will always be demanding more and more, ever and always in the same manner, brooking no rebuttal.

Nevertheless, we recognize that they follow a time-honoured tradition. Salvation can only come after an unbearable exploitation.

These men will be the excess.

They will inevitably become so without anyone's assistance. Their plunder will be plentiful. We shall want none of it.

That is what our 'guilty abstention' will consist in.

We leave the premeditated carnage to you (premeditated like everything else that belongs to complacent decadence). As for us, give us spirited action, and the full responsibility of our total refusal.

(We cannot help the fact that various social classes have superseded each other at government level without any of them being able to resist the compelling pull of decadence. We cannot help the fact that history teaches that only through the full development of our faculties, and then through the complete renewal of our sources of emotional inspiration, can we ever hope to break the deadlock and make way for the eager passage of a new-born civilization.)

All those who hold power or are struggling for it would be quite happy to grant our every wish, if only we were willing to confine our activities to the cramping limitations of their cunning directives.

Success will be ours if we close our eyes, stop up our ears, roll up our sleeves, and fling ourselves pell-mell into the fray. We prefer our cynicism to be spontaneous and without malice.

Kindly souls are apt to laugh at the lack of financial success of joint exhibitions of our work. It gives them a feeling of satisfaction to think they were the first to be aware of its small market-value.

If we do hold countless exhibitions, it is not with the naive hope of becoming rich. We know that there is a world of difference between us and the wealthy, who are bound to suffer something of a shock from their contact with us.

It is only through misunderstanding that such sales have, in the past, brought in big profits.

We hope this text will avoid any such misunderstandings in the future.

If we work with such feverish enthusiasm, it is because we feel a pressing need for unity.

Unity is the road to success.

Yesterday we stood alone and irresolute.

Today we form a group with strong, steady, and already far-reaching ramifications.

We must also share the glorious responsibility of preserving the valuable treasure that history has bequeathed to us.

Its tangible values must constantly be reinterpreted, be compared and considered anew. Such interpretation is an exacting, abstract process that requires the creative medium of action.

This treasure is the poetic source of supply, the fountain of youth for our creative impulses. that will inspire the generations of the future. It must be ADAPTED to suit circumstances if it is to serve its rightful purpose.

We urge all of those who are moved by the spirit of adventure to join us. Within a foreseeable future, man will be able to develop, untrammelled, his own individual skills, through impassioned, impulsive action and glorious independence.

Meanwhile we must work without respite, hand in hand with those who long for a better life; together we must persevere, regardless of praise or persecution, toward the joyful fulfilment of our fierce desire for freedom.

Paul-Emile Borduas
Magdeleine Arbour
Marcel Barbeau
Bruno Cormier
Claude Gauvreau
Pierre Gauvreau
Muriel Guilbault
Marcelle Ferron-Hamelin
Fernand Leduc
Therese Leduc
Jean-Paul Mousseau
Maurice Perron
Louise Renaud
Françoise Riopelle
Jean-Paul Riopelle
Françoise Sullivan.

Manifesto
Front du Libération du Quebec
1970

The Front de liberation du Quebec is not a messiah, nor a modern-day Robin Hood. It is a group of Quebec workers who have decided to use every means to make sure that the people of Quebec take control of their destiny.

The Front de liberation du Quebec wants the total independence of all Quebecois, united in a free society, purged forever of the clique of voracious sharks, the patronizing "big bosses" and their henchmen who have made Quebec their hunting preserve for "cheap labour" and unscrupulous exploitation.

The Front de liberation du Quebec is not a movement of aggression, but is a response to the aggression organized by high finance and the puppet governments in Ottawa and Quebec (the Brinks "show," Bill 63, the electoral map, the so-called social progress tax, Power Corporation, "Doctors' insurance," the Lapalme guys . . .)

The Front de liberation du Quebec finances itself by "voluntary taxes" taken from the same enterprises that exploit the workers (banks, finance companies, etc. . . .)

"The money power of the status quo, the majority of the traditional teachers of our people, have obtained the reaction they hoped for; a backward step rather than the change for which we have worked as never before, for which we will continue to work" (René Lévesque, April 29, 1970)

We believed once that p[...] *things were going* [...] :hannel our energy and our impatience, as René Lévesq *great until Liberal* Quebecois, but the Liberal victory clearly demonstrate *party won and* :cracy in Quebec is nothing but the democracy of the ric *Quebec lashes out* vas nothing but the victory of the Simard Cotroni elect *b/c of this* itish parliamentary system is finished and the Front de [...] ver allow itself to be fooled by the pseudo-elections tha[...] oss to the people of Quebec every four years. A number [...] d and will act. In the coming year Bourassa will have to face reality; 100,000 revolutionary workers, armed and organized.

Yes, there are reasons for the Liberal victory. Yes, there are reasons for poverty, unemployment, slums, and for the fact that you, Mr Bergeron of Visitation Street and you, Mr Legendre of Laval who earn $ 10,000 a year, will not feel free in our country of Quebec.

"Manifesto of the FLQ (1970)" by Claude Bélanger. From Claude Bélanger's Quebec History website at http://www2.marianopolis.edu/quebechistory. Reprinted by permission.

Yes, there are reasons, and the guys at Lord know them, the fishermen of the Gaspé, the workers of the North Shore, the miners for the Iron Ore Company, Quebec Cartier Mining, and Noranda, also know these reasons. And the brave workers of Cabano that you tried to screw again know lots of reasons.

Yes, there are reasons why you, Mr Tremblay of Panet Street and you Mr Cloutier, who work in construction in St Jerome, cannot pay for "Vaisseaux d'or" with all the jazz and oom-pa-pa like Drapeau the aristocrat, who is so concerned with slums that he puts coloured billboards in front of them to hide our misery from the tourists.

Yes, there are reasons why you, Mrs Lemay of St Hyacinthe, can't pay for little trips to Florida like our dirty judges and parliamentary members do with our money.

The brave workers for Vickers and Davie Ship, who were thrown out and not given a reason, know these reasons. And the Murdochville men, who were attacked for the simple and sole reason that they wanted to organize a union and who were forced to pay $2 million by the dirty judges simply because they tried to exercise this basic right—they know justice and they know the reasons.

Yes, there are reasons why you, Mr Lachance of St Marguerite Street, must go and drown your sorrows in a bottle of that dog's beer, Molson. And you, Lachance's son, with your marijuana cigarettes. . . .

Yes, there are reasons why you, the welfare recipients, are kept from generation to generation on social welfare. Yes, there are all sorts of reasons, and the Domtar workers in East Angus and Windsor know them well. And the workers at Squibb and Ayers, and the men at the Liquor Board and those at Seven-Up and Victoria Precision, and the blue collar workers in Laval and Montreal and the Lapalme boys know those reasons well.

The Dupont of Canada workers know them as well, even if soon they will only be able to express them in English (thus assimilated they will enlarge the number of immigrants and New Quebeckers, the darlings of Bill 63).

And the Montreal policemen, those strongarms of the system, should understand these reasons—they should have been able to see we live in a terrorized society because, without their force, without their violence, nothing could work on October 7.

We have had our fill of Canadian federalism which penalizes the Quebec milk producers to satisfy the needs of the Anglo-Saxons of the Commonwealth; the system which keeps the gallant Montreal taxi drivers in a state of semi-slavery to shamefully protect the exclusive monopoly of the nauseating Murray Hill and its proprietor—the murderer Charles Hershorn and his son Paul, who, on the night of October 7, repeatedly grabbed the twelve-gauge shot gun from his employees hands to fire upon the taxi drivers and thereby mortally wound corporal Dumas, killed while demonstrating.

We have had our fill of a federal system which exercises a policy of heavy importation while turning out into the street the low wage-earners in the textile and shoe manufacturing trades, who are the most ill-treated in Quebec, for the benefit of a clutch of damned money-makers in their Cadillacs who rate the Quebec nation on the same level as other ethnic minorities in Canada.

We have had our fill, as have more and more Quebecois, of a government which performs a-thousand-and-one acrobatics to charm American millionaires into investing in Quebec, La Belle Province, where thousands and thousands of square miles of forests, full of game and well-stocked lakes, are the exclusive preserve of the almighty twentieth century lords.

We have had our fill of a hypocrite like Bourassa who relies on Brinks armoured trucks, the living symbol of the foreign occupation of Quebec, to keep the poor natives of Quebec in the fear of misery and unemployment in which they are accustomed to living.

We have had our fill of taxes which the Ottawa representative to Quebec wants to give to the Anglophone bosses to encourage them to speak French, old boy, to negotiate in French: Repeat after me: "Cheap labour means manpower in a healthy market."

We have had our fill of promises of jobs and prosperity while we always remain the cowering servants and boot-lickers of the big shots who live in Westmount, Town of Mount Royal, Hampstead, and Outremont; all the fortresses of high finance on St James and Wall streets, while we, the Quebecois, have not used all our means, including arms and dynamite, to rid ourselves of these economic and political bosses who are prepared to use every sort of sordid tactic to better screw us.

We live in a society of terrorized slaves, terrorized by the big bosses like Steinberg, Clark, Bronfman, Smith, Neaple, Timmins, Geoffrion, J. L. Levesque, Hershorn, Thompson, Nesbitt, Desmarais, Kierans. Compared to them Remi Popol the lousy no-good, Drapeau the Dog, Bourassa the lackey of the Simards, and Trudeau the fairy are peanuts.

We are terrorized by the capitalist Roman church, even though this seems less and less obvious (who owns the property on which the stock exchange stands); by the payments to pay back Household Finance; by the publicity of the overlords of retail trade like Eaton, Simpson, Morgan, Steinberg, and General Motors; we are terrorized by the closed circles of science and culture which are the universities and by their bosses like Gaudry and Dorais and by the underling Robert Shaw.

The number of those who realize the oppression of this terrorist society are growing and the day will come when all the Westmounts of Quebec will disappear from the map.

Production workers, miners, foresters, teachers, students, and unemployed workers, take what belong to you, your jobs, your right to decide, and your liberty. And you, workers of General Electric, it's you who makes your factories run, only you are capable of production; without you General Electric is nothing!

Workers of Quebec, start today to take back what is yours; take for yourselves what belongs to you. Only you know your factories, your machines, your hotels, your universities, your unions. Don't wait for an organizational miracle.

Make your own revolution in your areas, in your places of work. And if you don't do it yourselves, other usurpers, technocrats and so on will replace the handful of cigar smokers we now know, and everything will be the same again. Only you are able to build a free society.

We must fight, not singly, but together. We must fight until victory is ours with all the means at our disposal as did the patriots of 1837-38 (those whom our sacred Mother church excommunicated to sell out to the British interests).

In the four corners of Quebec, may those who have been contemptuously called lousy French and alcoholics start fighting their best against the enemies of liberty and justice and prevent all the professional swindlers and robbers, the bankers, the businessmen, the judges, and the sold-out politicators from causing harm.

We are the workers of Quebec and we will continue to the bitter end. We want to replace the slave society with a free society, functioning by itself and for itself; a society open to the world.

Our struggle can only lead to victory. You cannot hold an awakening people in misery and contempt indefinitely. Long live Free Quebec!

Long live our imprisoned political comrades. Long live the Quebec revolution!

Long live the Front de liberation du Quebec.

For An Independent Québec
René Lévesque
1976

What does Quebec want? The question is an old cliche in Canadian political folklore. Again and again, during the more than 30 years since the end of World War II, it's been raised whenever Quebec's attitudes made it the odd man out in the permanent pull and tug of our federal-provincial relations. In fact, it's a question which could go back to the British conquest of an obscure French colony some 15 years before American Independence, and then run right through the stubborn survival of those 70,000 settlers and their descendants during the following two centuries.

By now, there are some six million of them in Canada, not counting the progeny of the many thousands who were forced by poverty, especially around the turn of the century, to migrate to the United States, and now constitute substantial "Franco" communities in practically all the New England states.

But Quebec remains the homeland. All along the valley of the St. Lawrence, from the Ottawa River down to the Gaspe peninsula and the great Gulf, in the ancient settlements which grew into the big cities of Montreal and Quebec, in hundreds of smaller towns and villages from the American border to the mining centers and power projects in the north, there are now some 4.8 million "Quebecois." That's 81 percent of the population of the largest and second most populous of Canada's ten provinces.

What does this French Quebec want? Sometime during the next few years, the question may be answered. And there are growing possibilities that the answer could very well be—independence.

Launched in 1967-68, the Parti Quebecois, whose platform is based on political sovereignty, now fills the role of Her Majesty's Loyal Opposition in the National Assembly—as we nostalgically designate our provincial legislature. In its first electoral test in 1970, it already had had 24 percent of the votes. Then in 1973, a second general election saw it jump to 30 percent, and, although getting only six out of 110 seats, become what our British-type parliamentary system calls the Official Opposition, i.e., the government's main interlocutor and challenger.

The next election might come any time now; this year in the fall, just after the Montreal Olympics, or at the latest in the fall of 1977. Whenever it does, all available indicators, including an impressive series of public opinion polls, tell us that for the first time the outcome is totally uncertain. The present provincial government, a branch of that same Liberal Party which also holds power at the federal level under Pierre Elliott Trudeau, is obviously on the way out. It has been in power for six years, and ever since its second and Pyrrhic victory in 1973 (102 seats) it has been going steadily downhill. Apart from a host of social and economic troubles, some imported but many more of its own making, there is around it a pervasive smell of incompetence and corruption. The scandal-ridden atmosphere surrounding the Olympic construction sites, and the incredible billion-dollar deficit which is now forecast, are just the most visible aspects of a rather complete political and administrative disaster.

Looking for an alternative, the French voter is now leaning quite clearly toward the Parti Quebecois. In that "national" majority, we are at least evenly matched with Premier Robert Bourassa's Liberals, and probably ahead. As for the Anglophone minority of over a million people, whose natural attachment to the status quo normally makes them the staunchest supporters of the reigning federalist party, they are confused as never before. Composed of a dwindling proportion of Anglo-Saxon descendants of eighteenth-century conquerors or American Loyalists, along with those of nineteenth-century Irish immigrants, and a steadily growing "ethnic" mosaic (Jewish, Italian, Greek, etc.), in the crunch most of this minority will probably end up, as usual, supporting the Liberals. But not with the traditional unanimity. Caught between the Charybdis of dissatisfaction and the Scylla of secessionism, many are looking for some kind of "third force." Others, especially among younger people, are ready to go along with the Parti Quebecois, whose minority vote should be a little less marginal next time than last.

So, all in all, there is quite a serious possibility that an "independentist" government will soon be elected in Quebec. At first sight, this looks like a dramatically rapid development, this burgeoning and flowering over a very few years of a political emancipation movement in a population which, until recently, was commonly referred to as quiet old Quebec. But in fact, its success would mean, very simply, the normal healthy end result of a long and laborious national evolution.

II

There was the definite outline of a nation in that small French colony which was taken over, in 1763, by the British Empire at its apogee. For over a century and a half, beginning just before the Pilgrim Fathers landed in the Boston area, that curious mixture of peasants and adventurers had been writing a proud history all over the continent. From Hudson Bay to the Gulf of Mexico, and from Labrador to the Rockies, they had been the discoverers, the fur-traders, the fort-builders. Out of this far-ranging saga, historically brief though it was, and the tenacious roots which at the same time were being sunk into the St. Lawrence lowlands, there slowly developed an identity quite different from the original stock as well as from France of the *ancien regime;* just as different, in its way, as the American identity had become from its own British seeds. Thus, when the traumatic shock of the conquest happened, it had enough staying power to survive, tightly knit around its Catholic clergy and its country landowners.

Throughout the next hundred years, while English Canada was being built, slowly but surely, out of the leftovers of the American Revolution and as a rampart against America's recurrent attacks of Manifest Destiny, French Quebec managed to hang on—mostly because of its "revenge of the cradles." It was desperately poor, cut off from the decision-making centers both at home and in Great Britain, and deprived of any cultural nourishment from its former mother country. But its rural, frugal society remained incredibly prolific. So it grew impressively, at least in numbers. And it held on obstinately, according to its lights and as much as its humble means made it possible, to those two major ingredients of national identity—land and language. The hold on land was at best tenuous and, as in any colonial context, confined to the multitude of small farm holdings. Everything else—from the growth of major cities to the setting-up of manufacturing industries and then the rush of resource development—was the exclusive and undisputed field of action of "les Anglais," the growing minority of Anglo-Saxon and then assimilated immigrant groups who ran most of Quebec under the compact leadership of Montreal-based entrepreneurs, financiers and merchant kings.

As for the French elite, it remained mostly made up of doctors, lawyers, and priests—"essential services" for the bodies and souls of cheap labor, whose miraculous birthrate kept the supply continuously overabundant. And naturally, there were politicians, practically all of that typical colonial breed which is tolerated as long as it keeps natives happily excited about accessories and divided on essentials.

Needless to say, the educational system was made both to reflect this type of society and to keep it going nicely and quietly. There was a modest collection of church-run seminaries, where the main accent was on recruiting for the priesthood, and which, for over a century, led to just one underdeveloped university. For nine-tenths of the children, there was nothing but grammar school, if that. Read and write barely enough to sign your name, and then, without any time for "getting ideas," graduate to obedient respectful employment by any boss generous enough to offer a steady modest job.

Such was the culturally starved and economically inferior, but well-insulated and thus highly resistant, French Quebec which, 109 years ago, was led into the final mutation of British North America and its supreme defense against American expansionism: Confederation, of four eastern colonies as a beginning, but soon to run north of the border "from sea to sea." Into that impressive Dominion, originally as one of four and eventually one of ten provinces, Quebec was incorporated without trouble and generally without enthusiasm. From now on, it was to be a minority forever, and, with the help of a dynamic federal immigration policy, a steadily diminishing one. In due time, it would probably merge and disappear into the mainstream, or at the most remain as a relatively insignificant and yet convenient ghetto: *la différence.*

As the building of Canada accelerated during the late nineteenth and early twentieth centuries, a tradition was established that Quebec was to get its measured share of the work, anytime there was enough to go around—and the same for rewards. And so, in a nutshell, it went until fairly recently. All told, it hasn't been such a bad deal, this status of "inner colony" in a country owned and managed by another national entity. Undoubtedly, French Quebec was (as it remains to this day) the least ill-treated of all colonies in the world. Under a highly centralized federal system, which is much closer to a unitary regime than American federalism, it was allowed its full panoply of provincial institutions: cabinet, legislature, courts, along with the quasi-permanent fun of great squabbles, usually leading to exciting election campaigns, about the defense or extension of its "state rights!" On three occasions during the last 80 years, one of "its own" has even been called upon-at times when there was felt a particular need to keep the natives quiet—to fill the most flattering of all offices, that of federal Prime Minister. Last but not least of the three, Mr. Trudeau, of whose "Canadian nationalism" it is naturally part and parcel, did as splendidly as was humanly possible for most of the last ten years in this big-chief-of-Quebec dimension of the job. But the law of diminishing returns, along with the inevitable way of all (including political) flesh, has been catching up with his so-called French Power in Ottawa. And no replacement seems to be in sight.

III

But this is getting ahead of our story. To understand the rise of Quebec's own new nationalism and its unprecedented drive toward self-government, we must go back at least as far as World War II. Not that the dream had completely vanished during the two long centuries of survival which have just been described-from an admittedly partisan, but, I honestly believe, not unfair viewpoint. In the 1830S, for instance, there even was an ill-advised and disastrous armed rebellion by a few hundred II Patriots," leading to bloody repression and lasting memories about what not to do. And it is rather significant, by the way, that it took until just now before the poor heroic victims of that abortive rebellion became truly rehabilitated in popular opinion.

Small and impotent though it was, and in spite of feeling that this condition would possibly last forever, French Quebec never quite forgot the potential nation it had once been, never quite gave up dreaming about some miracle which might bring back its chance in the future. In some distant, indescribable future. Now and then, there were stirrings: a writer here, a small political coterie there; a great upsurge of nationalist emotions, in the I 880s, around the Riel affair-the hanging by Illes Anglais" of the French-speaking leader of the Prairie Metis; then in 1917, on the conscription issue, a bitter and frequently violent confrontation between the Empire-minded English and the isolationist" French; faint stirrings again in the Twenties; stronger ones in the Thirties.

Then World War II, with a repeat, in 1944, of the total disagreement on conscription. But mostly, here as elsewhere, this most terrible of all wars was also a midwife for revolutionary change. Thankfully in less disruptive a manner than in other parts of the world, it did start a revolution in Quebec. Wartime service, both overseas and on the industrial home-front, dealt a mortal blow to the old order, gave an irresistible impetus to urbanization and started the breakup of the traditional rural-parish ideal, yanked women by the thousands into war-plant industry and as many men into battle-dress discovery of the great wide world. For a small cooped-up society, this was a more traumatic experience than for most others. And then when the post war years brought the Roaring Fifties, unprecedented mobility, and television along with a consumer society, the revolution had to become permanent.

The beginning of the 1960s saw it baptized officially: the Quiet Revolution, with the adjective implying that "quaint old Quebec" couldn't have changed all that much. But it had. Its old set of values literally shattered, it was feeling collectively naked, like a lobster during its shedding season, looking frantically about for a new armor with which to face the modern world. The first and most obvious move was toward education. After so prolonged and scandalous a neglect of this most basic instrument of development, it was quickly realized that here was the first urgent bootstrap operation that had to be launched. It was done with a vengeance: from one of the lowest in the Western world, Quebec per capita investment in education rapidly became, and remains, one of the very highest. Not always well spent (but who is to throw the first stone?), with many mistakes along the way, and the job still far from complete, which it will never be anyway; but the essential results are there, and multiplying: human resources that are, at long last, getting required development, along with a somewhat equal chance for all and a normal furious rise in general expectations. The same, naturally, is happening also in other fields, quite particularly in that of economics, the very first where such rising expectations were bound to strike against the wall of an entrenched colonial setup, with its now intolerable second-class status for the French majority, and the stifling remote control of nearly all major decisions either in Ottawa or in alien corporate offices.

Inevitably, there had to be a spillover into politics. More than half of our public revenue and most of the decisions that count were and are in outside hands, in a federal establishment which was basically instituted not by or for us, but by others and, always first and foremost, for their own purposes. With the highly centralized financial system that this establishment constitutionally lords over, this means, for example, that about 80 percent of Quebec savings and potential investment capital ends up in banks and insurance companies whose operations are none of our business. It also means, just for example once again, that immigration is also practically none of our business; and this could have, and is having, murderous effects on a minority people with a birthrate, changed like everything else in less than a generation, down from its former prodigious level to close to zero population growth.

Throughout the 1960s, these and other problems were interminably argued about and batted back and forth between federal politicians and bureaucrats ("What we have we hold, until we get more") and a succession of insistent but orthodox, no more than rock-the-boat, nationalists in Quebec. But while this dialogue of the deaf was going on and on, the idea of political independence reappeared as it had to.

Not as a dream this time, but as a project, and very quickly as a serious one. This developed by leaps and bounds from easily ridiculed marginal groups to small semi-organized political factions, and finally to a full-fledged national party in 1967-68. These were the same two years during which, by pure coincidence, Mr. Trudeau was just as rapidly being elevated to the heights as a new federalist champion from Quebec.

But in spite of his best efforts and those of his party's branch-plant in provincial government, and through an unceasing barrage of money, vilification and rather repugnant fear-inducing propaganda, the voters have democratically brought the Parti Quebecois ever closer to power. Which brings us right back to our starting-point . . . .

IV

Let us suppose it does happen, and Quebec peacefully elects such a government. What then?

The way we see it, it would have to go somewhat like this. There is a new Quebec government which is totally dedicated to political independence. But this same Quebec, for the time being, is still very much a component of federal Canada, with its quite legitimate body of elected representatives in Ottawa. This calls, first of all, for at least a try at negotiation. But fruitful talk between two equally legitimate and diametrically opposed levels of government, without any further pressure from the population-that would be a real first in Canadian political history Obviously, there would have to be the referendum which the Parti Quebecois proposes in order to get the decisive yes or-no answer to the tired question: What *does* Quebec want? (This was precisely the procedure by which the only new province to join Confederation during our recent democratic past, Newfoundland, was consulted in 1948-49 about whether or not to opt in. So why not about opting out?) If the answer should be no, then there's nothing to do but wait for the momentum of change to keep on working until we all find out whether or not there is finally to be a nation here. If the answer is yes, out, then the pressure is on Ottawa, along with a rather dramatic surge of outside attention, and we all get a privileged opportunity to study the recently inked Helsinki Declaration and other noble documents about self-determination for all peoples.

Fully confident of the basic integrity of Canadian democracy, and just as conscious that any silliness would be very costly for both sides, we firmly believe that the matter would then be brought to a negotiated settlement. Especially since the Parti Quebecois, far from aiming at any kind of mutual hostility or absurd Berlin Wall, will then repeat its standing offer of a new kind of association, as soon as it is agreed to get rid of our illusion of deep unshakeable national unity, when in fact here are two quite real and distinct entities in an obsolete and increasingly morbid majority/minority relationship. Our aim is simply full equality by the only means through which a smaller nation can reasonably expect to achieve it with a larger one: self-government. But we are definitely not unaware of the shock waves that such a break, after so long an illusion of eternity, is bound to send through the Canadian political fabric.

We do not accept the simplistic domino theory, where Quebec's departure is presented as the beginning of fatal dislocation, with separatism spreading in all directions like a galloping disease until the balkanized bits and pieces are swallowed up by the huge maw next door. In spite of the somewhat unsure character of its national identity and its excessive satellization by the American economic and cultural empire, Canada-without-Quebec has enough "difference" left, sufficient traditions and institutional originality, to withstand the extraction of its "foreign body" and find a way to go on from there. It might even turn out to be a heaven-sent opportunity to revamp the overcentralized and ridiculously bureaucratized federal system, that century-old sacred cow which, for the moment, nobody dares to touch seriously for fear of encouraging Quebec's subversive leanings!

Be that as it may, we know there would be a traumatic moment and a delicate transition during which things might go wrong between us for quite a while, or else, one would hope, start going right as never before. With this strange new-colored Quebec on the map between Ontario and the Maritime provinces, Canada must be kept from feeling incurably "Pakistanized," so we must address ourselves without delay to the problem of keeping a land bridge open with as much free flow of people and goods as is humanly possible; as much and more as there is, I would imagine, between Alaska and the main body of the United States over the western land bridge.

Such a scenario would call, as a decisive first step, for a customs union, as full-fledged as both countries consider to be mutually advantageous. We have, in fact, been proposing that ever since the Parti Quebecois was founded, and naturally meeting with the most resonant silence in all orthodox federalist circles. But in the midst of that silence, not a single responsible politician, nor for that matter a single important businessman, has been heard to declare that it wouldn't happen if and when the time comes. For indisputably such a partnership, carefully negotiated on the basis of equality, is bound to be in the cards. Nothing prevents one envisaging it, for instance, going immediately, or at least very quickly, as far as the kind of monetary union which the European Common Market, with its original six and now nine members, has been fitfully aiming at for so many years. And building on this foundation, it would lead this new "northern tier" to a future immeasurably richer and more stimulating than the 109-year-old bind in which two nations more often than not feel and act like Churchill's two scorpions in the same bottle.

V

What of Quebec's own national future, both internal and international, in this context of sovereignty-cum-interdependence?

The answers here, for reasons that are evident, have to be brief, even sketchy and essentially tentative. The perspective of nationhood, for people who haven't been there yet, is bound to be an uncertain horizon. The more so in a period of history like ours, when so much is changing so fast you get the feeling that maybe change itself is becoming the only law to be counted on. Who can pretend to know exactly what or where his country will be 25 or even just ten years from now?

One thing sure, is that Quebec will not end up, either soon or in any foreseeable future, as the anarchic caricature of a revolutionary banana republic which adverse propaganda has been having great sinister fun depicting in advance. Either-Ottawa-or is very simply inspired by prejudice, the origin of this nonsense mostly to be found in the tragic month of October 1970 and the great "crisis" which our political establishments, under the astutely calculating Mr. Trudeau, managed to make out of a couple of dozen young terrorists, whose ideology was a hopeless hodgepodge of anarcho-nationalism and kindergarten Marxism, which had no chance of having any kind of serious impact. What they *did* accomplish was two kidnappings and, most cynically welcome of all, one murder—highly unfortunate but then also particularly par for the course in the international climate at the time. That was not par at all, however, was the incredible abuse of power for which those events, relatively minor per se, were used as a pretext: the careful buildup of public hysteria, army trucks rolling in during the night, and then, for months on end, the application in Quebec, and solely in Quebec, of a federal War Measures Act for which no peacetime precedent exists in any democratic country. A great spectacle produced in order to terrorize the Quebecois forever back into unquestioning submissiveness, and, outside, to feed the mill of scary propaganda about how dangerous this tame animal could nevertheless be!

In actual fact, French Quebec, with its normal share of troubles, disquiet and, now, the same kind of social turmoil and search for new values that are rampant all over the Western world, remains at bottom a very solid, well-knit and nonviolent society. Even its new and demanding nationalism has about itself something less strident and essentially more self-confident than its current pan-Canadian counterpart. For Quebec has an assurance of identity, along with a relative lack of aggressiveness, which are the result of that one major factor of national durability lacking in the rest of Canada: a different language and the cultural fabric that goes with it.

Now how does the Parti Quebecois see this society begin to find its way as an independent nation? What is the general outline of the political, social and economic structure we hope to bring forth? Serious observers have been calling our program basically social-democratic, rather comparable to the Scandinavian models although certainly not a carbon copy since all people, through their own experiences, have to invent their own "mix."

The way we have been trying to rough it out democratically through half a dozen national party conventions, ours would call for a presidential regime, as much of an equal-opportunity social system as we could afford, and a decent measure, as quickly as possible but as carefully as indicated, of economic "repatriation." This last would begin to happen immediately, and normally without any great perturbation, through the very fact of sovereignty: with the gathering in of all of our public revenues and the full legislative control which any self-respecting national state has to implement over its main financial institutions, banks, insurance companies and the like. In the latter case, this would allow us to break the stranglehold in which the old British-inspired banking system of just a handful of "majors" has always kept the people's money and financial initiative. The dominant position in our repatriated financial circuit would be handed over to Quebec's cooperative institutions, which happen to be particularly well developed in that very field, and, being strongly organized on a regional basis, would afford our population a decent chance for better balanced, responsible, democratic development. And that, by the way, is just one fundamental aspect of the kind of evolution toward a new economic democracy, from the lowest rung in the marketplace up to board-room levels, which all advanced societies that are not already doing so had better start thinking about in the very near future.

As to non-resident enterprise, apart from the universal minimums concerning incorporations and due respect for Quebec taxes, language and other classic national requirements, what we have been fashioning over the last few years is an outline of a policy which we think is both logical and promising. It would take the form of an "investment code," giving a clean-cut picture, by sectors, of what parts of our economic life (e.g., culturally oriented activities, basic steel and forest resources) we would insist on keeping under home ownership, what other parts we would like to see under mixed control (a very few selected but strategic cases) and, finally, the multitude of fields (tied to markets, and to technological and/or capital necessities) where foreign interests would be allowed to stay or to enter provided they do not tend to own us along with their businesses.

In brief, Quebec's most privileged links, aside from its most essential relationship with the Canadian partner, would be first with the United States—where there is no imaginable reason to frown on such a tardy but natural and healthy development (especially during a Bicentennial year). Then Quebec would look to other Francophone or "Latin" countries as cultural respondents, and to France herself who would certainly not be indifferent to the fact that this new nation would constitute the second most important French-speaking country in the world. In brief, such is the peaceful and, we confidently hope, fruitfully progressive state which may very well appear on the map of North America before the end of the decade.

French and English
Leonard Cohen

French and English

I think you are fools to speak French
It is a language which invites the mind
to rebel against itself causing inflamed ideas
grotesque postures and a theoretical approach
to common body functions. It ordains the soul
in a tacky priesthood devoted to the salvation
of a failed erection. It is the language
of cancer as it annexes the spirit and
installs a tumour in every honeycomb
Between the rotten teeth of French are incubated
the pettiest notions of destiny and the shabbiest
versions of glory and the dreariest dogma of change
ever to pollute the simplicity of human action
French is a carnival mirror in which the
brachycephalic idiot is affirmed and encouraged
to compose a manifesto on the destruction of the sideshow

I think you are fools to speak English
I know what you are thinking when you speak English
You are thinking piggy English thoughts
you sterilized swine of a language that has no genitals
You are peepee and kaka and nothing else
and therefore the lovers die in all your songs
You can't fool me you cradle of urine
where Jesus Christ was finally put to sleep
and even the bowels of Satan cannot find
a decent place to stink in your flat rhythms
of ambition and disease
English, I know you, you are frightened by saliva
your adventure is the glass bricks of sociology

you are German with a licence to kill
I hate you but it is not in English
I love you but it is not in French
I speak to the devil but it is not about your punishment
I speak to the table but it is not about your plan
I kneel between the legs of the moon
in a vehicle of perfect stuttering
and you dare to interview me on the matter
of your loathsome destinies
you poor boobies of the north
who have set out for heaven with your mouths on fire
Surrender now surrender to each other
your loveliest useless aspects
and live with me in this and other voices
like the wind harps you were meant to be
Come and sleep in the mother tongue
and be awakened by a virgin
(O dead-hearted turds of particular speech)
be awakened by a virgin
into a sovereign state of common grace

Focus Questions

1. How do both Borduas and the FLQ interpret Québec's history to support their opinions? Can you provide a counter-interpretation of this same history?

    - Aware of compression
    - religion destroying everything for power
    - French were still stayed French.
    - isolation being trapped
    - reject all.

2. What did Borduas think was wrong with Québec in 1948, and how did he propose to solve its woes? How did the FLQ's definition of Quebec's problems, and their solutions, differ?

3. According to Lévesque, what did/does Quebec want? How did he think they would achieve it? Are there any similarities in his opinions to those of Borduas or the FLQ?

    - independence from Canada - protect French and the culture
      business world spoke English

    - church
    - English oppresses French
    - French against immigration

4. What is overall message of Cohen's poem? Does his presentation of the contrasts between these two languages alter your sense of their relative importance? Does he offer any sort of solution for the conflict?

5. Does the recent decision by the Federal Conservative Government of Stephen Harper to define Québec as a nation within the nation open the door for separatist agitation? Why or why not?

14

Aboriginal Policy after 1960: Red, White, Conflicted

Introduction

In recent years, the consequences of decades of neglect and indifference toward Canada's First Nations people have made frequent headlines in newspapers and television reports. Extreme poverty, unemployment, disease, alcoholism, drug addiction, despair, and high rates of suicide are the now too-common conditions on many reserves. Despite the conditions of life imposed and perpetuated by their historic, dysfunctional relationship to the federal government and non-Aboriginal Canadians, however, First Nations people are not a passive or hopeless group. Indeed, since the end of World War II, they have become increasingly vocal and assertive, pressing their demands for self government, for reparations and redress, and for recognition of their status. Like Pauline Johnson (see Chapter 7), they make a clear case about the causes of their poor condition of life—but unlike her, they demand more than sympathy.

This battle has been an uphill one, and has been perpetuated at times by an enormous gap between governmental and Aboriginal views of potential solutions. One instance of this sort of gap is revealed in the first two documents in this chapter. The first was written by Pierre Elliot Trudeau's Liberal Government in 1969. This so-called "White Paper" proposed that the 'Indian problem' was caused by their claim to special status. In the impassioned reply, *Citizens Plus* (commonly known as the Red Paper), this approach is fundamentally rejected. In a passive, though not altogether surprising move, the Government's only reaction to *Citizen's Plus* was to withdraw the proposals made in the White Paper.

In more recent years, however, passivity has become an increasingly difficult, and a decidedly less tolerable response. Clashes between Aboriginal and non-Aboriginal Canadians have become more common, and conditions of life on reserves have not improved. In some cases, they continue to deteriorate. In order to seek out the full range of causes and potential solutions to these problems, the federal government launched the Royal Commission on Aboriginal Peoples in the early 1990s. Tragically, however, their findings, published in 1996 and extracted for this chapter, have made very little appreciable impact on government policies or public attitudes. As was recently argued by Maragert Philp of *The Globe and Mail,* "The catastrophe of native life in Canada is old news. Decades pass, reports are drafted, articles are published, and nothing happens. Canadians have become as remote to the suffering as spouses in a stale marriage."[1] This situation is one which must change. As the authors of the Royal Commission have argued, "Canada's claim to be a fair and enlightened society depends on it."[2]

[1] Margaret Philp, "A slap in the face of every Canadian," *The Globe and Mail,* 3 February 2007.

[2] *Royal Commission on Aboriginal Peoples. People to People, Nation to Nation: Highlights from the Report of the Royal Commission on Aboriginal Peoples,* 1996.

The White Paper
Government of Canada
1969

Statement of the Government of Canada on Indian Policy

Presented to the First Session of the Twenty-eighth Parliament by the Honourable Jean Chretien, Minister of Indian Affairs and Northern Development

To be an Indian is to be a man, with all a man's needs and abilities. To be an Indian is also to be different. It is to speak different languages, draw different pictures, tell different tales and to rely on a set of values developed in a different world.

Canada is richer for its Indian component, although there have been times when diversity seemed of little value to many Canadians.

But to be a Canadian Indian today is to be someone different in another way. It is to be someone apart—apart in law, apart in the provision of government services and, too often a part in social contacts.

To be an Indian is to lack power—the power to act as owner of your lands, the power to spend your own money and, too often, the power to change your own condition.

Not always, but too often, to be an Indian is to be without—without a job, a good house, or running water; without knowledge, training or technical skill and, above all, without those feelings of dignity and self-confidence that a man must have if he is to walk with his head held high.

All these conditions of the Indians are the product of history and have nothing to do with their abilities and capacities. Indian relations with other Canadians began with special treatment by government and society, and special treatment has been the rule since Europeans first settled in Canada. Special treatment has made of the Indians a community disadvantaged and apart.

Obviously, the course of history must be changed.

To be an Indian must be to be free—free to develop Indian cultures in an environment of legal, social and economic equality with other Canadians.

Statement of the Government of Canada on Indian Policy. Ottawa: Indian and Northern Affairs Canada, 1969. Reproduced with the permission of the Minister of Public Works and Government Services Canada, 2006.

Forward

The Government believes that its policies must lead to the full, free and non-discriminatory participation of the Indian people in Canadian society. Such a goal requires a break with the past. It requires that the Indian people's role of dependence be replaced by a role of equal status, opportunity and responsibility , a role they can share with all other Canadians.

This proposal is a recognition of the necessity made plain in a year's intensive discussions with Indian people throughout Canada. The Government believes that to continue its past course of action would not serve the interests of either the Indian people or their fellow Canadians.

The policies proposed recognize the simple reality that the separate legal status of Indians and the policies which have flowed from it have kept the Indian people apart from and behind other Canadians. The Indian people have not been full citizens of the communities and provinces in which they live and have not enjoyed the equality and benefits that such participation offers.

The treatment resulting from their different status has been often worse, sometimes equal and occasionally better than that accorded to their fellow citizens. What matters is that it has been different.

Many Indians, both in isolated communities and in cities, suffer from poverty. The discrimination which affects the poor, Indian and non-Indian alike, when compounded with a legal status that sets the Indian apart, provides dangerously fertile ground for social and cultural discrimination.

In recent years there has been a rapid increase in the Indian population. Their health and education levels have improved. There has been a corresponding rise in expectations that the structure of separate treatment cannot meet . . .

The Government does not wish to perpetuate policies which carry with them the seeds of disharmony and disunity, policies which prevent Canadians from fulfilling themselves and contributing to their society. It seeks a partnership to achieve a better goal. The partners in this search are the Indian people, the governments of the provinces, the Canadian community as a whole and the Government of Canada. As all partnerships do, this will require consultation, negotiation, give and take, and co-operation if it is to succeed.

Many years will be needed. Some efforts may fail, but learning comes from failure and from what is learned success may follow. All the partners have to learn; all will have to change many attitudes.

Governments can set examples, but they cannot change the hearts of men. Canadians, Indians and non-Indians alike stand at the crossroads. For Canadian society the issue is whether a growing element of its population will become full participants contributing in a positive way to the general well-being or whether, conversely, the present social and economic gap will lead to their increasing frustration and isolation, a threat to the general well-being of society. For many Indian people, one road does exist, the only road that has existed since Confederation and before, the road of different status, a road which has led to a blind alley of deprivation and frustration. This road, because it is a separate road, cannot lead to full participation, to equality in practice as well as in theory. The Government has outlined a number of measures and a policy which it is convinced will offer another road for Indians, a road that would lead gradually away from different status to full social, economic and political participation in Canadian life. This is the choice.

Indian people must be persuaded, must persuade themselves, that this path will lead them to a fuller and richer life.

Canadian society as a whole will have to recognize the need for changed attitudes and a truly open society. Canadians should recognize the dangers of failing to strike down the barriers which frustrate Indian people. If Indian people are to become full members of Canadian society they must be warmly welcomed by that society.

The Government commends this policy for the consideration of all Canadians, Indians and non-Indians, and all governments in Canada.

1 Background

The Government has reviewed its programs for Indians and has considered the effects of them on the present situation of the Indian people. The review has drawn on extensive consultations with the Indian people, and on the knowledge and experience of many people both in and out of government.

This review was a response to things said by the Indian people at the consultation meetings which began a year ago and culminated in a meeting in Ottawa in April.

This review has shown that this is the right time to change long-standing policies. The Indian people have shown their determination that present conditions shall not persist . . .

The Government could press on with the policy of fostering further education; could go ahead with physical improvement programs now operating in reserve communities; could press forward in the directions of recent years, and eventually many of the problems would be solved. But progress would be too slow. The change in Canadian society in recent years has been too great and continues too rapidly for this to be the answer. Something more is needed. We can no longer perpetuate the separation of Canadians. Now is the time to change.

This Government believes in equality. It believes that all men and women have equal rights. It is determined that all shall be treated fairly and that no one shall be shut out of Canadian life, and especially that no one shall be shut out because of his race.

This belief is the basis for the Government's determination to open the doors of opportunity to all Canadians, to remove the barriers which impede the development of people, of regions and of the country.

Only a policy based on this belief can enable the Indian people to realize their needs and aspirations.

The Indian people are entitled to such a policy. They are entitled to an equality which preserves and enriches Indian identity and distinction; an equality which stresses Indian participation in its creation and which manifests itself in all aspects of Indian life.

The goals of the Indian people cannot be set by others; they must spring from the Indian community itself—but government can create a framework within which all persons and groups can seek their own goals.

2 The New Policy

True equality presupposes that the Indian people have the right to full and equal participation in the cultural, social, economic and political life of Canada.

The government believes that the framework within which individual Indians and bands could achieve full participation requires:

1. that the legislative and constitutional bases of discrimination be removed;
2. that there be positive recognition by everyone of the unique contribution of Indian culture to Canadian life;
3. that services come through the same channels and from the same government agencies for all Canadians;
4. that those who are furthest behind be helped most;
5. that lawful obligations be recognized;
6. that control of Indian lands be transferred to the Indian people.

The Government would be prepared to take the following steps to create this framework:

1. Propose to Parliament that the Indian Act be repealed and take such legislative steps as may be necessary to enable Indians to control Indian lands and to acquire title to them.
2. Propose to the governments of the provinces that they take over the same responsibility for Indians that they have for other citizens in their provinces. The take-over would be accompanied by the transfer to the provinces of federal funds normally provided for Indian programs, augmented as may be necessary.
3. Make substantial funds available for Indian economic development as an interim measure.
4. Wind up that part of the Department of Indian Affairs and Northern Development which deals with Indian Affairs. The residual responsibilities of the Federal Government for programs in the field of Indian affairs would be transferred to other appropriate federal departments.

. . . The new policy looks to a better future for all Indian people wherever they may be. The measures for implementation are straightforward. They require discussion, consultation and negotiation with the Indian people—individuals, bands and associations—and with provincial governments.

Success will depend upon the co-operation and assistance of the Indians and the provinces. The Government seeks this co-operation and will respond when it is offered . . .

Historical Background

The weight of history affects us all, but it presses most heavily on the Indian people. Because of history, Indians today are the subject of legal discrimination; they have grievances because of past undertakings that have been broken or misunderstood; they do not have full control of their lands; and a higher proportion of Indians than other Canadians suffer poverty in all its debilitating forms. Because of history too, Indians look to a special department of the Federal Government for many of the services that other Canadians get from provincial or local governments.

This burden of separation has its origin deep in Canada's past and in early French and British colonial policy. The elements which grew to weigh so heavily were deeply entrenched at the time of Confederation.

Before that time there had evolved a policy of entering into agreements with the Indians, of encouraging them to settle on reserves held by the Crown for their use and benefit, and of dealing with Indian lands through a separate organization—a policy of treating Indian people as a race apart.

After Confederation, these well-established precedents were followed and expanded . . .

This system—special legislation, a special land system and separate administration for the Indian people—continues to be the basis of present Indian policy. It has saved for the Indian people places they can call home, but has carried with it serious human and physical as well as administrative disabilities.

Because the system was in the hands of the Federal Government, the Indians did not participate in the growth of provincial and local services. They were not required to participate in the development of their own communities which were tax exempt. The result was that the Indians, persuaded that property taxes were an unnecessary element in their lives, did not develop services for themselves. For many years such simple and limited services as were required to sustain life were provided through a network of Indian agencies reflecting the authoritarian tradition of a colonial administration, and until recently these agencies had staff and funds to do little more than meet the most severe cases of hardship and distress.

The tradition of federal responsibility for Indian matters inhibited the development of a proper relationship between the provinces and the Indian people as citizens. Most provinces, faced with their own problems of growth and change, left responsibility for their Indian residents to the Federal Government. Indeed, successive Federal Governments did little to change the pattern. The result was that Indians were the almost exclusive concern of one agency of the Federal Government for nearly a century.

For a long time the problems of physical, legal and administrative separation attracted little attention. The Indian people were scattered in small groups across the country, often in remote areas. When they were in contact with the new settlers, there was little difference between the living standards of the two groups . . .

With the technological change of the twentieth century, society became increasingly industrial and complex, and the separateness of the Indian people became more evident. Most Canadians moved to the growing cities, but the Indians remained largely a rural people, lacking both education and opportunity. The land was being developed rapidly, but many reserves were located in places where little development was possible. Reserves were usually excluded from development and many began to stand out as islands of poverty. The policy of separation had become a burden.

The legal and administrative discrimination in the treatment of Indian people has not given them an equal chance of success. It has exposed them to discrimination in the broadest and worst sense of the term—a discrimination that has profoundly affected their confidence that success can be theirs. Discrimination breeds discrimination by example, and the separateness of Indian people has affected the attitudes of other Canadians towards them.

The Case for the New Policy

In the past ten years or so, there have been important improvements in education, health, housing, welfare and community development. Developments in leadership among the Indian communities have become increasingly evident. Indian people have begun to forge a new unity. The Government believes progress can come from these developments but only if they are met by new responses. The proposed policy is a new response.

The policy rests upon the fundamental right of Indian people to full and equal participation in the cultural, social, economic and political life of Canada.

To argue against this right is to argue for discrimination, isolation and separation.

No Canadian should be excluded from participation in community life, and none should expect to withdraw and still enjoy the benefits that flow to those who participate.

1 The Legal Structure

Legislative and constitutional bases of discrimination must be removed.

Canada cannot seek the just society and keep discriminatory legislation on its statute books. The Government believes this to be self-evident. The ultimate aim of removing the specific references to Indians from the constitution may take some time, but it is a goal to be kept constantly in view. In the meantime, barriers created by special legislation can generally be struck down . . .

In the long term, removal of the reference in the constitution would be necessary to end the legal distinction between Indians and other Canadians. In the short term, repeal of the Indian Act and enactment of transitional legislation to ensure the orderly management of Indian land would do much to mitigate the problem.

The ultimate goal could not be achieved quickly, for it requires a change in the economic circumstances of the Indian people and much preliminary adjustment with provincial authorities. Until the Indian people are satisfied that their land holdings are solely within their control, there may have to be some special legislation for Indian lands.

2 The Indian Cultural Heritage

There must be positive recognition by everyone of the unique contribution of Indian culture to Canadian society.

. . . For many years Canadians believed the Indian people had but two choices: they could live in a reserve community, or they could be assimilated and lose their Indian identity. Today Canada has more to offer. There is a third choice—a full role in Canadian society and in the economy while retaining, strengthening and developing an Indian identity which preserves the good things of the past and helps Indian people to prosper and thrive.

This choice offers great hope for the Indian people. It offers great opportunity for Canadians to demonstrate that in our open society there is room for the development of people who preserve their different cultures and take pride in their diversity . . .

Steps will be taken to enlist the support of Canadians generally. The provincial governments will be approached to support this goal through their many agencies operating in the field Provincial educational authorities will be urged to intensify their review of school curriculae and course content with a view to ensuring that they adequately reflect Indian culture and Indian contributions to Canadian development.

3 Programs and Services

Services must come through the same channels and from the same government agencies for all Canadians.

This is an undeniable part of equality. It has been shown many times that separation of people follows from separate services. There can be no argument about the principle of common services. It is right.

It cannot be accepted now that Indians should be constitutionally excluded from the right to be treated within their province as full and equal citizens, with all the responsibilities and all the privileges that this might entail. It is in the provincial sphere where social remedies are structured and applied, and the Indian people, by and large, have been non-participating members of provincial society.

Canadians receive a wide range of services through provincial and local governments, but the Indian people and their communities are mostly outside that framework. It is no longer acceptable that the Indian people should be outside and apart. The Government believes that services should be available on an equitable basis, except for temporary differentiation based on need. Services ought not to flow from separate agency established to serve particular groups, especially not to groups that are identified ethnically.

Separate but equal services do not provide truly equal treatment. Treatment has not been equal in the case of Indians and their communities. Many services require a wide range of facilities which cannot be duplicated by separate agencies. Others must be integral to the complex systems of community and regional life and cannot be matched on a small scale.

The Government is therefore convinced that the traditional method of providing separate services to Indians must be ended. All Indians should have access to all programs and services of all levels of government equally with other Canadians . . .

4 Enriched Services

Those who are furthest behind must be helped most.

There can be little argument that conditions for many Indian people are not satisfactory to them and are not acceptable to others. There can be little question that special services, and especially enriched services, will be needed for some time . . .

Additional funds would be available from a number of different sources; In an atmosphere of greater freedom, those who are able to do so would be expected to help themselves, so more funds would be available to help those who really need it. The transfer of Indian lands to Indian control should enable many individuals and groups to move ahead on their own initiative. This in turn would free funds for further enrichment of programs to help those who are furthest behind . . .

In many situations, the problems of Indians are similar to those faced by their non-Indian neighbours. Solutions to their problems cannot be found in isolation but must be sought within the context of regional development plan involving all the people. The consequence of an integrated regional approach is, that all levels of government—federal, provincial and local and the people themselves are involved. Helping overcome regional disparities in the economic well-being of Canadians is the main task assigned to the, Department of Regional Economic Expansion. The Government believes that the needs of Indian communities should be met within this framework.

5 Claims and Treaties

Lawful obligations must be recognized

Many of the Indian people feel that successive governments have not dealt with them as fairly as they should. They believe that lands have been taken from them in an improper manner, or without adequate compensation, that their funds have been improperly administered, that their treaty rights have been breached. Their sense of grievance influences their relations with governments and the community and limits their participation in Canadian life.

Many Indians look upon their treaties as the source of their rights to land, to hunting and fishing privileges, and to other benefits. Some believe the treaties should be interpreted to encompass wider services and privileges, and many believe the treaties have not been honoured . . .

The terms and effects of the treaties between the Indian people and the Government are widely misunderstood. A plain reading of the words used in the treaties reveals the limited and minimal promises which were included in them. As a result of the treaties, some Indians were given an initial cash payment and were promised land reserved for their exclusive use, annuities, protection of hunting, fishing and trapping privileges subject (in most cases) to regulation, a school or teachers in most instances and, in one treaty only, a medicine chest . . .

The significance of the treaties in meeting the economic, educational, health and welfare needs of the Indian people has always been limited and will continue to decline. The services that have been provided go far beyond what could have been foreseen by those who signed the treaties.

The Government and the Indian people must reach a common understanding of the future role of the treaties. Some provisions will be found to have been discharged; others will have continuing importance . Many of the provisions and practices of another century may be considered irrelevant the light of a rapidly changing society and still others may be ended by mutual agreement. Finally I once Indian lands are securely within Indian control, the anomaly of treaties between groups within society and the government of that society will require that these treaties be reviewed to—how they can be equitably ended . . .

6 Indian Lands

Control of Indian lands should be transferred to the Indian people.

Frustration is as great a handicap as a sense of grievance. True cooperation and participation can come only when the Indian people are controlling, the land which, makes up the reserves.

The reserve system has provided the Indian people with lands that generally have been protected against alienation without their consent. Widely scattered across Canada, the reserves total nearly 6,000,000 acres and are divided into about 2,200 parcels of varying sizes. Under the existing system, title to reserve lands is held either by the Crown in right of Canada or the Crown in right of one of the provinces. Administrative control and legislative authority are.1 however, vested exclusively in the Government l and the Parliament of Canada. It is a trust. As long as this trust exists, the Government, as a trustee, must supervise the business connected with the land.

The result of Crown ownership and the Indian Act has been to tie the Indian people to a land system that lacks flexibility and inhibits development. Indian people do not have control of their lands except as the Government allows and this is no longer acceptable to them. The Indians have made this clear at the consultation meetings. They now want real control, and this Government believes that they should have it. The Government recognizes that full and true equality calls for Indian control and ownership of reserve . . .

The Government believes that full ownership implies many things. It carries with it the free choice of use, of retention or of disposition. In our society it also carries with .it an obligation to pay for certain services. The Government recognizes that it may not be acceptable to put all lands into the provincial systems immediately and make them subject- to taxes. When the Indian people see that the only way they can own and fully control land is to accept taxation the way other Canadians do, they will make that decision . . .

The Government hopes to have the bulk of the policy in effect within five years and believes that the necessary financial and other arrangements can be concluded so that Indians will have full access to provincial services within that time. It will seek an immediate start to the many discussions that will need to be held with the provinces and with representatives of the Indian people . . .

A policy can never provide the ultimate solutions to all problems. A policy can achieve no more than is desired by the people it is intended to serve. The essential role of the Government's proposed new policy for Indians is that it acknowledges that truth' by recognizing the central and essential role of the Indian people in solving their own problems. It will provide for first time, a non-discriminatory framework within which, in an atmosphere of freedom, the Indian people could, with other Canadians, work out their own destiny.

Citizen's Plus
Indian Chiefs of Alberta
1969

A. The Preamble

To us who are Treaty Indians there is nothing more important than our Treaties, our lands and the well being of our future generation. We have studied carefully the contents of the Government White Paper on Indians and we have concluded that it offers despair instead of hope. Under the guise of land ownership, the government has devised a scheme whereby within a generation or shortly after the proposed Indian Lands Act expires our people would be left with no land and consequently the future generation would be condemned to the despair and ugly spectre of urban poverty in ghettos.

In Alberta, we have told the Federal Minister of Indian Affairs that we do not wish to discuss his White Paper with him until we reach a position where we can bring forth viable alternatives because we know that his paper is wrong and that it will harm our people. We refused to meet him on his White Paper because we have been stung and hurt by his concept of consultation.

In his White Paper, the Minister said, "This review was a response to things said by Indian people at the consultation meetings which began a year ago and culminated in a meeting in Ottawa in April." Yet, what Indians asked for land ownership that would result in Provincial taxation of our reserves? What Indians asked that the Canadian Constitution be changed to remove any reference to Indians or Indian lands? What Indians asked that Treaties be brought to an end? What group of Indians asked that aboriginal rights not be recognized'? What group of Indians asked for a Commissioner whose purview would exclude half of the Indian population in Canada? The answer is no Treaty Indians asked for any of these things and yet through his concept of "consultation," the Minister said that his White Paper was in response to things said by Indians.

We felt that with this concept of consultation held by the Minister and his department, that if we met with them to discuss the contents of his White Paper without being

From "The Preamble" and "The Counter-Policy" in *Citizens Plus,* A Presentation by the Indian Chiefs of Alberta to Right Honourable P. E. Trudeau, Prime Minister and the Government of Canada, June 1970. Reprinted by permission of Mel H. Buffalo on behalf of the Indian Association of Alberta.

fully prepared, that even if we just talked about the weather, he would turn around and tell Parliament and the Canadian public that we accepted his White Paper.

We asked for time to prepare a counter proposal. We have received assurances that the implementation process would not take place. However, the Federal rhetoric has not been substantiated by action. In fact, there is every indication that the implementation process is being carried as fast and as fully as possible. For example, the Departmental officials have prepared their budgets so as to make implementation possible. They rationalize this action by saying that if the White Paper on Indians is implemented their programs must be set whereby they can achieve the implementation within five years or if it does not come about that they can have better programs. Where is the moratorium that we have asked for on activities on the implement on the White Paper?

The Minister of Indian Affairs has stated publically that he is not attempting to throw the Indians over to the provinces in spite of what is contained in writing in his White Paper. Yet, while maintaining this contradictory position he writes a letter to the Premier of Alberta dated February 20, 1970 stating that the Federal Government would transfer funds to the Province for the extension of provincial services to reserves; but these funds would be gradually phased out with the assumption that at this point the Provincial Government would bear full financial responsibility for the provision of these services.

Where is the consistency of the Minister's position when he tells Indians verbally that their reserves will not come under the Provincial tax system but his White Paper and his letter of the Premier say otherwise.

B. The Counter Policy

B.1. Indian Status

The White Paper Policy said "that the legislative and constitutional bases of discrimination should be removed."

We reject this policy. We say that the recognition of Indian status is essential for justice.

Retaining the legal status of Indians is necessary if Indians are to be treated justly. Justice requires that the special history, rights and circumstances of Indian People be recognized. The Chretien Policy says, "Canada cannot seek the just society and keep **discriminatory** legislation on its statute books." That statement covers a faulty understanding of fairness. Professor L.C. Green found that in other countries minorities were given special status. Professor Green has concluded:

> "The 1969 Statement of the Government of Canada on Indian Policy is based on the assumption that any legislation which sets a particular segment of the population apart from the main stream of the citizenry is ipso facto conducive to a denial of equality and therefore discriminatory and to

be deplored. **Such an attitude indicates a complete lack of understanding of the significance of the concept of equality,** particularly in so far as the law concerning the protection of minorities is concerned.

"...It is perhaps not easy to define the distinction between the notions of equality in fact and equality in law; nevertheless. it may be said that the former notion excludes the idea of a merely formal equality . . ."

Equality in law precludes discrimination of any kind; **whereas equality in fact may involve the necessity of different treatment** in order to obtain a result which establishes an equilibrium between different situations . . .

"To attempt to maintain that the rights of the Indians result in discrimination against them or are evidence of a denial of their equality in the sense that their status is reduced thereby. is to indulge in an excessively **narrow view of the meaning of words. of the purpose of equality and of the nature of discrimination.**"[1]

The legal definition of registered Indians must remain. If one of our registered brothers chooses, he may renounce his Indian status, become "enfranchised", receive his share of the funds of the tribe, and seek admission to ordinary Canadian society. But most Indians prefer to remain Indians. We believe that to be a good useful Canadian we "must first be a good, happy and productive Indian.

B.2. The Unique Indian Culture and Contribution

The White Paper Policy said "that there should be positive recognition by everyone of the unique contribution of Indian culture to Canadian life.

We say that these are nice sounding words which are intended to mislead everybody. The only way to maintain our culture is for us to remain as Indians. To preserve our culture it is necessary to preserve our status, rights, lands and traditions. Our treaties are the bases of our rights.

There is room in Canada for diversity. Our leaders say that Canada should preserve her "pluralism", and encourage the culture of all her peoples. The culture of the Indian peoples are old and colorful strands in that Canadian fabric of diversity. We want our children to learn our ways, our history; our customs, and our traditions.

Everyone should recognize that Indians have contributed much to the Canadian community. When we signed the treaties we promised to be good and loyal subjects of the Queen. The record is clear—we kept our promises. We were assured we would not be required to serve in foreign wars; nevertheless many Indians volunteered in greater proportion than non-Indian Canadians for service in two world wars. We live and are agreeable to live within the framework of Canadian civil and criminal law.

We pay the same indirect and sales taxes that other Canadians pay. Our treaty rights cost Canada very little in relation to the Gross National Product or to the value of the lands ceded, but they are essential to us.

B.4. Enriched Services

We do not want different treatment for different tribes. These promises of enriched services are bribes to get us to accept the rest of the Policy. The Federal Government is trying to divide us Indian people so it can conquer us by saying that poorer reserves will be helped most.

All reserves and tribes need help in the economic social. recreational and cultural development.

B.5. Lawful Obligations

The White Paper Policy says "that lawful obligations should be recognized." If the Government meant what it said we would be happy. But it is obvious that the Government has never bothered to learn what the treaties are and has a distorted picture of them.

The Government shows that it is willfully ignorant of the bargains that were made between the Indians and the Queen's Commissioners.

The Government must admit its mistakes and recognize that the treaties are historic, moral and legal obligations. The redmen signed them in good faith, and lived up to the treaties. The treaties were solemn agreements. Indian lands were exchanged for the promises of the Indian Commissioners who represented the Queen. Many missionaries of many faiths brought the authority and prestige of whiteman's religion in encouraging Indians to sign,

In our treaties of 1876, 1877, 1899 certain promises were made to our people; some of these are contained in the text of the treaties, some in the negotiations, and some in the memories of our people. Our basic view is that all these promises are part of the treaties and must be honored.

Modernize the Treaties

The intent and spirit of the treaties must be our guide, not the precise letter of a foreign language. Treaties that run forever must have room for the changes in the conditions of life. The undertaking of the Government to provide teachers was a commitment to provide Indian children the educational opportunity equal to their white neighbors. The machinery and livestock symbolized economic development.

The White Paper Policy says "a plain reading of the words used in the treaties reveals the limited and minimal promises which were included in them. . . . and in one treaty only a medicine chest." But we know from the Commissioners' Reports that they told the Indians that medicine chests were included in all three.

Indians have the right to receive, without payment, all healthcare services without exception and paid by the Government of Canada.

The medicine chests that we know were mentioned in the negotiations for Treaties Six, Seven and Eight mean that Indians should now receive free medical, hospital and dental care—the same high quality services available to other Canadians,

We agree with the judgement of Policha, J. in **Regina** vs, Walter Johnston:

> "Referring to the 'Medicine chest' clause of Treaty Number Six, it is common knowledge that the provision for caring for the sick and injured in the areas inhabited by the Indians in 1876 were somewhat primitive compared to present day standards, It can be safely assumed that the Indians had limited knowledge of what provisions were available and" it is obvious that they were concerned that their people be adequately cared for. With that in view and possibly carrying the opinion of Angers, J. a step further. I can only conclude that the 'medicine chest' clause and the 'pestilence' clause in Treaty No.6 should be properly interpreted to mean that the Indians are entitled to receive all medical services, including medicines, drugs, medical supplies and hospital care free of charge, Lacking proper statutory provisions to the contrary, this entitlement would embrace all Indians within the meaning of the Indian Act, without exception."[2]

The principle thus laid down by Policha, J. is that all the provisions of the treaties arc to be interpreted in favour of the Indians with full regard given to changing social and economic conditions.

The Indian people see the treaties as the basis of all their rights and status. If the Government expects the co-operation of Indians in any new policy, it must accept the Indian viewpoint on treaties, This would require the Government to start all over on its new policy

B.6. Indian Control of Indian Lands

The White Paper Policy says "that control of Indian lands should be transferred to Indian people."

We agree with this intent but we find that the Government is ignorant of two basic points. The Government wrongly thinks that Indian Reserve lands are owned by the Crown, The Government is, of course, in error. These lands are held in trust by the Crown but they are Indian lands.

The Indians are the beneficial (actual) owners of the lands. The legal title has been held for us by the Crown to prevent the sale or breaking up of our land. We are opposed to any system of allotment that would give individuals ownership with rights to sell.

According to the **Indian Act** R.S,C. 1952 the land is safe and secure held in trust for the common use and benefit of the tribe. The land must never be sold. mortgaged or taxed.

The second error the Government commits is making the assumption that Indians can have control of the land only if they take ownership in the way that ordinary property is owned. The Government should either get some legal advice or get some brighter legal advisers. The advice we have received is that the Indian Act could be changed to give Indians control of lands without changing the fact that the title is now held in trust.

Indian lands must continue to be regarded in a different manner than other lands in Canada. It must be held forever in trust of the Crown because, as we say, "The true owners of the land are not yet born."

Conclusions

The Report of the Royal Commission on Aboriginal Peoples

1996

"I want to get rid of the Indian problem. I do not think as a matter of fact, that the country ought to continuously protect a class of people who are able to stand alone . . .

Our objective is to continue until there is not a single Indian in Canada that has not been absorbed into the body politic and there is no Indian question, and no Indian Department, that is the whole object of this Bill."[1]

Rarely Have The Prevailing assumptions underlying Canadian policy with regard to Aboriginal peoples been stated so graphically and so brutally. These words were spoken in 1920 by Duncan Campbell Scott, deputy superintendent general of Indian affairs, before a special parliamentary committee established to examine his proposals for amending the enfranchisement provisions of the *Indian Act*.

This statement, redolent of ethnocentric triumphalism, was rooted in nineteenth-century Canadian assumptions about the lesser place of Aboriginal peoples in Canada. Far from provoking fervent and principled opposition to the assimilationist foundation of his testimony, Scott's statements were generally accepted as the conventional wisdom in Aboriginal matters. Any dispute was over the details of his compulsory enfranchisement proposals, not over the moral legitimacy of assimilation as the principle guiding relations between the federal government and Aboriginal peoples.

That a Canadian official could speak such words before the representatives of the Canadian people in the twentieth century without arousing profound and vehement objections is equally noteworthy. It was taken for granted that Aboriginal peoples were simply a minority group of 'inferior' peoples, internal 'immigrants', in effect, in a country ready to accept them on equal terms only if they renounced their Aboriginal identity and demonstrated in terms acceptable to non-Aboriginal society that they were fit for the 'privileges' of enfranchisement and fuller participation in the more evolved, more 'civilized' society that had overtaken and grown up around them.[2] In other words, the false premises that underlay so much of government policy toward Aboriginal peoples were alive and well in the third decade of this century.

Impassioned opposition to Scott's proposal, from Indian interveners appearing before the special committee, was ignored, and the amendment allowing enfranchisement of Indians without their consent was passed with minor procedural modifications. Despite continuing Indian hostility to its destructive intent, it was given royal assent and became law on 1 July 1920.

Thus, on the day commemorating Canada's own emergence as a distinct political entity in the broader world community, Canada adopted a law whose avowed goal was the piecemeal but complete destruction of distinct social and political entities within the broader Canadian community. This relatively minor episode perhaps best encapsulates the core injustice that had been building for close to 100 years. That was the continuous and deliberate subversion of Aboriginal nations—groups whose only offence was their wish to continue living in their own communities and evolving in accordance with their own traditions, laws and aspirations.

In the first part of this volume, we traced the evolution of the relationship between Aboriginal peoples and the new arrivals from Europe, following it through four distinct but overlapping periods and trying to capture the experience and perspectives of Aboriginal peoples. We showed how, during the period we call displacement and assimilation, new philosophies that trumpeted the superiority of 'civilized' Europeans over 'uncivilized', even 'savage', Aboriginal peoples, swept the British Empire. The policies resulting from these ethnocentric philosophies—represented for the First Nations by enfranchisement and similar measures and for the Metis people by individual land allotments and subsequent land losses in the west—undermined the tripartite relationship between Aboriginal peoples, the colonies and the imperial Crown, and paved the way for the attempted destruction of Aboriginal societies.

Having come upon diverse societies possessing their own long-established laws and customs, the newcomers from Europe were forced to justify their failure to continue to accord Aboriginal nations the respect that initially guided relations between them. Former commercial and military allies, original full-fledged partners in a joint enterprise, Aboriginal peoples came to be seen by increasingly ethnocentric and intolerant colonial and Canadian authorities in an entirely different and contemptuous light.

It was a light, moreover, that seemed deliberately to leave in the shadows Aboriginal peoples' actual status as nations and as peoples and their legitimate demands to participate as constitutional equals to the colonies that eventually federated to become Canada. Only now have the shadows cast by the false assumptions of decades of Canadian Aboriginal policy begun to lift, to reveal the true contours of the Canadian federation.

The unflattering and misleading image of Aboriginal people promoted by the new generation of Canadian nation builders is nowhere better captured than in the annual report of the department of the interior for 1876, the year the first *Indian Act* was adopted. That image recast Aboriginal people in the role of wards or children of the state, requiring of federal officials that "every effort should be made to aid the Red man in lifting himself out of his condition of tutelage and dependence" because "that is clearly our wisdom and our duty, through education and other means, to prepare him for a higher civilization . . . ."[3]

Our focus in this second part of this volume has been on what transpired when the initial consensus supporting the alliance between Aboriginal nations and settler governments died, and the balance of power shifted decisively in favour of colonial and Canadian authorities. With the political and economic ascendency of the new Canadian state confirmed, there was no effective challenge to the validity of the false premises generated by the ethnocentric certainties of the nineteenth century.

These premises provided sufficient moral and philosophical foundation to justify the broad consensus, across all sectors of Canadian society, that put the actions examined in the last four chapters beyond challenge. This gave government the licence to treat a category of people in a way that would never have been tolerated, even in the more constrained political environment of the day, if it had been practised against the Canadian population as a whole. Such an orientation, it is clear to us today, was profoundly racist.

The legacy is still with us. The *Indian Act,* the centrepiece of federal legislation, continues to interfere profoundly in the lives, cultures and communities of First Nations peoples today. We believe there can be no real change within the confines of this act. We discuss more fully in Volume 2 what should replace it. We acknowledge the profound mistrust that causes many communities to hold onto the *Indian Act* in the absence of any process assuring them that their historical rights will be respected. We believe that recognition by the Canadian people of the profound injustices visited on Aboriginal peoples over the decades by this legislation will lead to a demand that governments commence a process that will lead to a new legal basis for the relationship.

No segment of our research aroused more outrage and shame than the story of the residential schools. Certainly there were hundreds of children who survived and scores who benefitted from the education they received. And there were teachers and administrators who gave years of their lives to what they believed was a noble experiment. But the incredible damage—loss of life, denigration of culture, destruction of self-respect and self-esteem, rupture of families, impact of these traumas on succeeding generations, and the enormity of the cultural triumphal ism that lay behind the enterprise—will deeply disturb anyone who allows this story to seep into their consciousness and recognizes that these policies and deeds were perpetrated by Canadians no better or worse intentioned, no better or worse educated than we are today. This episode reveals what has been demonstrated repeatedly in the subsequent events of this century: the capacity of powerful but grievously false premises to take over public institutions and render them powerless to mount effective resistance. It is also evidence of the capacity of democratic populations to tolerate moral enormities in their midst.

These were also acts of profound cruelty to individuals: children (now adults) and their families and communities. A public inquiry is urgently required to examine the origins, purposes and effects of residential school policies, to identify abuses, to recommend remedial measures and to begin the process of healing.

The history of relocations compounds the malaise and explains poignantly the social dysfunction that has become widespread in many Aboriginal communities. Again we see the impunity with which public institutions can act when buttressed by erroneous premises. . . . Aboriginal people were moved because they were moveable. The intentions of those who made the policies and those who implemented them may have been just in their own eyes, but Aboriginal peoples could be treated in this way only because different standards applied to them than to other Canadians. Decisions could be made for them—token consultation was all that was required. To do anything else would jeopardize the desired outcome. And these moves were undertaken, it is now apparent, with no understanding of their profound and debilitating impact on almost all aspects of the relocatees' lives.

As with the residential schools policy, profound damage was done to the human rights of Aboriginal Canadians in the course of many relocations. It is true that our sensitivity to and understanding of human rights has progressed significantly in recent decades. But many of these relocations occurred well after Canada's endorsement of the Universal Declaration of Human Rights in 1948. We believe that the right approach to accountability and compensation is a process of inquiry through the Canadian Human Rights Commission to assess each case on its own merits and judge, among other things, whether the accepted standards of the day were applied in the design and implementation of the relocation. Coupled with this process for redress, governments should adopt relocation guidelines that explicitly incorporate the highest standards of human rights.

The final chapter in this sad era of dispossession is equally poignant. Despite all that had gone before, Aboriginal men and women volunteered in remarkable numbers to serve in the armed forces in both world wars. Motivated in some cases by ancient traditions, a continuing sense of obligation to act when an ally is threatened, or the opportunity to earn a living, they found in wartime service acceptance and equality. They served with great distinction. But when they returned to private life, they again faced discrimination and deprivation. Many were denied access to assistance equivalent to that received by their comrades unless they abandoned their home communities. Valued by their comrades on the battlefield and hailed at home for their contributions to defense industries and wartime charities, when the peace was won, Aboriginal people were again relegated to the margins of society, with the apparent acquiescence of Canadians.

We believe that Canadians and their governments must recognize and honour these men and women for their extraordinary acts of patriotism on behalf of a country in which they were not yet, for the most part, full citizens. Canadians owe them a particular debt of gratitude and special recognition of their participation in the struggle for freedoms that they themselves were denied when they returned.

All who read these accounts will be disturbed. Many exposed to these events for the first time will urge us to forget the past: building for the future is what counts, they argue; preoccupation with past injustices and compensation can only continue to embroil the relationship in blame and confrontation.

But as Aboriginal people have told us, the past might be forgiven but it cannot be forgotten. It infuses the present and gives shape to Canadian institutions, attitudes and practices that seriously impede their aspirations to assume their rightful place in a renewed Canadian federation. Only if Canada admits to the fundamental contradiction of continuing colonialism, they assert, can true healing and true reconciliation take place.

The social, economic and political weaknesses of most modern Aboriginal communities stem from the failure of imperial, colonial and Canadian authorities to respond to Aboriginal peoples' request for the opportunity to evolve in harmony with the growth of the non-Aboriginal society emerging around them. Having willfully abandoned and marginalized Aboriginal peoples, and deliberately undermined their social and political cohesiveness, non-Aboriginal governments cannot now plead the passage of time and the institutional weaknesses of present-day Aboriginal nations as an excuse for inaction.

As we move through the current period of our shared journey together—the stage of negotiation and renewal—we urge governments and the Canadian people to undertake a comprehensive and unflinching assessment of the unstable foundations of the relationship that developed during the period of displacement and assimilation. We can no longer afford merely to 'manage' the continuing crisis in the relationship by mediating potential areas of conflict while leaving unaltered the foundation on which that conflict inevitably arises.

Endotes

1. Duncan Campbell Scott, deputy superintendent general of Indian affairs, testimony before the Special Committee of the House of Commons examining the Indian Act amendments of 1920, National Archives of Canada, Record Group 10, volume 6810, file 470-2-3, volume 7, pp. 55 (L-3) and 63 (N-3). See John Leslie, *The Historical Development of the Indian Act,* second edition (Ottawa: Department of Indian Affairs and Northern Development, Treaties and Historical Research Branch, 1978), p. 114.
2. Enfranchisement was referred to explicitly in the *Indian Act* as a privilege. See, for example, the *Indian Act,* R.S.C. 1906, chapter 81, section 108, regarding Indians of "sufficient intelligence to be qualified to hold land in fee simple, and otherwise to exercise all the rights and privileges of an enfranchised person."
3. Department of the Interior [Indian Affairs Branch], *Annual Report* (Ottawa: 1876), p. XIV. See Wayne Daugherty and Dennis Madill, *Indian Government under Indian Act Legislation,* 1868–1951 (Ottawa: Department of Indian Affairs and Northern Development, Research Branch, 1980), p. 3.

Focus Questions

1. What was the government proposing with the 1969 White Paper, and why? What sort of political ideals/ideas may have been motivating the government to propose this approach?

2. Who/what do you think the government blamed, in 1969, for the low quality of life experienced by Canada's Aboriginal people? Who/what did the Royal Commission blame in 1996?

3. How are the solutions offered by the Royal Commission different from those offered by the White Paper? Which solution do you think is correct, and why?

4. What solutions were offered by Natives themselves in the *Red Paper* of 1970? How are these solutions analogous to the Royal Commission findings?

5. Why does history play such a significant role for Native understanding and politics, and why do you think, as the Royal Commission states, that many Canadians want instead to *forget* the past, and move on?

15

The Charter of Rights and Freedoms: Unifying Force or Divisive Wedge?

Introduction

The Canadian Charter of Rights and Freedoms has become an important symbol of national identity. The time of its birth was one of enormous political upheaval in the country, crowned by Levesque's 1981 referendum on Quebec separation. In this environment, Pierre Trudeau's liberal government envisioned the Charter as a document that would unite Canadians from diverse regions, classes, ethnicities and cultures, by creating a sense of shared values. In many ways, this goal has been achieved. As the CRIC report contained here demonstrates, the Charter has become important to defining national identity for more Canadians, than even the flag or the national anthem.

The Charter, for Trudeau, and for the majority of Canadians at the time, represented a much needed step forward—a progressive recognition of the fundamental rights and freedoms of each individual person. It also contains within it protections for Aboriginal treaty rights and multiculturalism. But is the Charter exclusively a uniting force? And did—or do—Canadians really understand how it has affected their lives and the political foundations of the country? The 1981 cartoon by Roy Peterson, "the MacPatriation Brothers," suggests that, at least in the beginning, the answer to this question was probably 'No.'[1] At the time of the Charter's ten-year

---

[1]The caricatures in the cartoon represent Trudeau and his then-Minister of Justice (and later Liberal Prime Minister), Jean Chrétien. They were modeled after a very popular comedy skit on SCTV, "The Great White North," which featured Rick Moranis and Dave Thomas as two beer-guzzling, dim-witted "hosers," Bob and Doug Mackenzie. Ironically, the Mackenzie brothers were inspired by government regulations about visible Canadian content on television (see Chapter 18, David Taras, "Swimming against the Current").

anniversary, political scientist Peter Russell gave an equally ambiguous response—declaring himself, overall, 'agnostic' about the Charter's effects, whether good or bad. As this document was entrenched in the 1982 Constitution act, making it part of the highest law in the land and the document against which all court decisions and political manoeuvres are judged, its ramifications and ambiguities must be understood. Without this understanding, Peterson's cartoon is just as relevant today as it was over twenty-five years ago.

The MacPatriation Brothers

Roy Peterson

28 October 1981

Roy Peterson, Vancouver Sun. Reprinted by permission.

Canadian Charter of Rights and Freedoms
Constitution Act
1982

Whereas Canada is founded upon principles that recognize the supremacy of God and the rule of law:

Guarantee of Rights and Freedoms

1. The *Canadian Charter of Rights and Freedoms* guarantees the rights and freedoms set out in it subject only to such reasonable limits prescribed by law as can be demonstrably justified in a free and democratic society.

Fundamental Freedoms

2. Everyone has the following fundamental freedoms:
   a) freedom of conscience and religion;
   b) freedom of thought, belief, opinion and expression, including freedom of the press and other media of communication;
   c) freedom of peaceful assembly; and
   d) freedom of association.

Democratic Rights

3. Every citizen of Canada has the right to vote in an election of members of the House of Commons or of a legislative assembly and to be qualified for membership therein.
4. (1) No House of Commons and no legislative assembly shall continue for longer than five years from the date fixed for the return of the writs of a general election of its members.
   (2) In time of real or apprehended war, invasion or insurrection, a House of Commons may be continued by Parliament and a legislative assembly may be continued by the legislature beyond five years if such continuation is not opposed by the votes of more than one-third of the members of the House of Commons or the legislative assembly, as the case may be.
5. There shall be a sitting of Parliament and of each legislature at least once every twelve months

Mobility Rights

6. (1) Every citizen of Canada has the right to enter, remain in and leave Canada.
   (2) Every citizen of Canada and every person who has the status of a permanent resident of Canada has the right
       a) to move to and take up residence in any province; and
       b) to pursue the gaining of a livelihood in any province.
   (3) The rights specified in subsection (2) are subject to
       a) any laws or practices of general application in force in a province other than those that discriminate among persons primarily on the basis of province of present or previous residence; and
       b) any laws providing for reasonable residency requirements as a qualification for the receipt of publicly provided social services.
   (4) Subsections (2) and (3) do not preclude any law, program or activity that has as its object the amelioration in a province of conditions of individuals in that province who are socially or economically disadvantaged if the rate of employment in that province is below the rate of employment in Canada.

Legal Rights

7. Everyone has the right to life, liberty and security of the person and the right not to be deprived thereof except in accordance with the principles of fundamental justice.
8. Everyone has the right to be secure against unreasonable search or seizure.
9. Everyone has the right not to be arbitrarily detained or imprisoned.
10. Everyone has the right on arrest or detention
    a) to be informed promptly of the reasons therefor;
    b) to retain and instruct counsel without delay and to be informed of that right; and
    c) to have the validity of the detention determined by way of *habeas corpus* and to be released if the detention is not lawful.
11. Any person charged with an offence has the right
    a) to be informed without unreasonable delay of the specific offence;
    b) to be tried within a reasonable time;
    c) not to be compelled to be a witness in proceedings against that person in respect of the offence;
    d) to be presumed innocent until proven guilty according to law in a fair and public hearing by an independent and impartial tribunal;
    e) not to be denied reasonable bail without just cause;
    f) except in the case of an offence under military law tried before a military tribunal, to the benefit of trial by jury where the maximum punishment for the offence is imprisonment for five years or a more severe punishment;

g) not to be found guilty on account of any act or omission unless, at the time of the act or omission, it constituted an offence under Canadian or international law or was criminal according to the general principles of law recognized by the community of nations;

h) if finally acquitted of the offence, not to be tried for it again and, if finally found guilty and punished for the offence, not to be tried or punished for it again; and

i) if found guilty of the offence and if the punishment for the offence has been varied between the time of commission and the time of sentencing, to the benefit of the lesser punishment.

12. Everyone has the right not to be subjected to any cruel and unusual treatment or punishment.

13. A witness who testifies in any proceedings has the right not to have any incriminating evidence so given used to incriminate that witness in any other proceedings, except in a prosecution for perjury or for the giving of contradictory evidence.

14. A party or witness in any proceedings who does not understand or speak the language in which the proceedings are conducted or who is deaf has the right to the assistance of an interpreter.

Equality Rights

15. (1) Every individual is equal before and under the law and has the right to the equal protection and equal benefit of the law without discrimination and, in particular, without discrimination based on race, national or ethnic origin, colour, religion, sex, age or mental or physical disability.

(2) Subsection (1) does not preclude any law, program or activity that has as its object the amelioration of conditions of disadvantaged individuals or groups including those that are disadvantaged because of race, national or ethnic origin, colour, religion, sex, age or mental or physical disability.

Official Languages of Canada

16. (1) English and French are the official languages of Canada and have equality of status and equal rights and privileges as to their use in all institutions of the Parliament and government of Canada.

(2) English and French are the official languages of New Brunswick and have equality of status and equal rights and privileges as to their use in all institutions of the legislature and government of New Brunswick.

(3) Nothing in this Charter limits the authority of Parliament or a legislature to advance the equality of status or use of English and French.

16.1.

(1) The English linguistic community and the French linguistic community in New Brunswick have equality of status and equal rights and privileges, including the right to distinct educational institutions and such distinct cultural institutions as are necessary for the preservation and promotion of those communities.

(2) The role of the legislature and government of New Brunswick to preserve and promote the status, rights and privileges referred to in subsection (1) is affirmed.

17. (1) Everyone has the right to use English or French in any debates and other proceedings of Parliament.

(2) Everyone has the right to use English or French in any debates and other proceedings of the legislature of New Brunswick.

18. (1) The statutes, records and journals of Parliament shall be printed and published in English and French and both language versions are equally authoritative.

(2) The statutes, records and journals of the legislature of New Brunswick shall be printed and published in English and French and both language versions are equally authoritative.

19. (1) Either English or French may be used by any person in, or in any pleading in or process issuing from, any court established by Parliament.

(2) Either English or French may be used by any person in, or in any pleading in or process issuing from, any court of New Brunswick.

20. (1) Any member of the public in Canada has the right to communicate with, and to receive available services fi-01TI, any head or central office of an institution of the Parliament or government of Canada in English or French, and has the same right with respect to any other office of any such institution where

   a) there is a significant demand for communications with and services from that office in such language; or

   b) due to the nature of the office, it is reasonable that communications with and services from that office be available in both English and French.

(2) Any member of the public in New Brunswick has the right to communicate with, and to receive available services from, any office of an institution of the legislature or government of New Brunswick in English or French.

21. Nothing in sections 16 to 20 abrogates or derogates from any right, privilege or obligation with respect to the English and French languages, or either of them, that exists or is continued by virtue of any other provision of the Constitution of Canada.

22. Nothing in sections 16 to 20 abrogates or derogates from any legal or customary right or privilege acquired or enjoyed either before or after the coming into force of this Chmier with respect to any language that is not English or French.

Minority Language Educational Rights

23. (1) Citizens of Canada
    a) whose first language learned and still understood is that of the English or French linguistic minority population of the province in which they reside, or
    b) who have received their primary school instruction in Canada in English or French and reside in a province where the language in which they received that instruction is the language of the English or French linguistic minority population of the province, have the right to have their children receive primary and secondary school instruction in that language in that province.
    (2) Citizens of Canada of whom any child has received or is receiving primary or secondary school instruction in English or French in Canada, have the right to have all their children receive primary and secondary school instruction in the same language.
    (3) The right of citizens of Canada under subsections (1) and (2) to have their children receive primary and secondary school instruction in the language of the English or French linguistic minority population of a province
    a) applies wherever in the province the number of children of citizens who have such a right is sufficient to warrant the provision to them out of public funds of minority language instruction; and
    b) includes, where the number of those children so warrents, the right to have them receive that instruction in minority language educational facilities provided out of public funds.

Enforcement

24. (1) Anyone whose rights or freedoms, as guaranteed by this Charter, have been infringed or denied may apply to a court of competent jurisdiction to obtain such remedy as the court considers appropriate and just in the circumstances.
    (2) Where, in proceedings under subsection (1), a court concludes that evidence was obtained in a manner that infringed or denied any rights or freedoms guaranteed by this Charter, the evidence shall be excluded if it is established that, having regard to all the circumstances, the admission of it in the proceedings would bring the administration of justice into disrepute.

General

25. The guarantee in this Charter of certain rights and freedoms shall not be construed so as to abrogate or derogate from any aboriginal, treaty or other rights or freedoms that pertain to the aboriginal peoples of Canada including
    a) any rights or freedoms that have been recognized by the Royal Proclamation of October 7, 1763; and
    b) any rights or freedoms that now exist by way of land claims agreements or may be so acquired.
26. The guarantee in this Charter of certain rights and freedoms shall not be construed as denying the existence of any other rights or freedoms that exist in Canada.
27. This Charter shall be interpreted in a manner consistent with the preservation and enhancement of the multicultural heritage of Canadians.
28. Notwithstanding anything in this Charter, the rights and freedoms referred to in it are guaranteed equally to male and female persons.
29. Nothing in this Charter abrogates or derogates from any rights or privileges guaranteed by or under the Constitution of Canada in respect of denominational, separate or dissentient schools.(93)
30. A reference in this Charter to a Province or to the legislative assembly or legislature of a province shall be deemed to include a reference to the Yukon Territory and the Northwest Territories, or to the appropriate legislative authority thereof, as the case may be.
31. Nothing in this Charter extends the legislative powers of any body or authority.

Application of Charter

32. (1) This Charter applies
    a) to the Parliament and government of Canada in respect of all matters within the authority of Parliament including all matters relating to the Yukon Territory and Northwest Territories; and
    b) to the legislature and government of each province in respect of all matters within the authority of the legislature of each province.
    (2) Notwithstanding subsection (1), section 15 shall not have effect until three years after this section comes into force.
33. (1) Parliament or the legislature of a province may expressly declare in an Act of Parliament or of the legislature, as the case may be, that the Act or a provision thereof shall operate notwithstanding a provision included in section 2 or sections 7 to 15 of this Charter.
    (2) An Act or a provision of an Act in respect of which a declaration made under this section is in effect shall have such operation as it would have but for the provision of this Charter referred to in the declaration.

(3) A declaration made under subsection (1) shall cease to have effect five years after it comes into force or on such earlier date as may be specified in the declaration.

(4) Parliament or the legislature of a province may re-enact a declaration made under subsection (1).

(5) Subsection (3) applies in respect of a re-enactment made under subsection (4).

Citation

34. This Part may be cited as the *Canadian Charter of Rights and Freedoms*.

The Political Purposes of the Charter: Have They Been Fulfilled

Peter H. Russell

Ten years into charterland, the one clear consequence of the Charter is that it has produced an awful lot of Charter chatter by the chattering classes. In case you were wondering who belongs to this group, you need only look at the people attending this conference—those who have the time, the money, and the inclination to attend a decennial anniversary of an event which they must believe was significant for Canada, the adoption of a constitutional bill of rights.

As a charter member of the chattering classes I do not mean to sound ungrateful. For whatever the Charter has done for our fellow citizens, it has surely given us members of Canada's chattering classes a lot more to talk about, to write about, and, yes, to litigate about. Life for us has been much more interesting in charterland than it was in Canada without the Charter.

Still, grateful though we should be to the folks who brought us the Charter, I do not think they had the chattering classes in mind as its principal beneficiary. No, I believe that they had larger goals in mind. Unity, liberty, and equality—these were the larger purposes that animated the Charter's sponsors and supporters. It is in terms of those larger purposes that I wish to examine the first decade of life in the Canadian charterland.

Let me begin with the purpose of the Charter's political sponsors. By political sponsors I have in mind the politicians who took the lead in making the Charter a priority for constitutional reform in Canada. These sponsors were primarily the federal Liberals and above all their leader, Pierre Elliott Trudeau. There were other leaders and other parties who backed the project—in particular, the national NDP and its predecessor, the CCF, right back to the days of M. J. Coldwell and Frank Scott. But it was the Trudeau Liberals who, from the late 1960s on, made it their number one constitutional cause. They, more than any other politicians, are responsible for the birth of charterland ten years ago.

In making the Charter the first plank in their constitutional platform, the Trudeau Liberals aimed to counter the decentralizing thrust of Quebec's constitutional aspirations.[1] If constitutional reform was to take place, it should be directed

"The Political Purposes of the Charter: Have They Been Fulfilled? An Agnostic's Report Card" by Peter H. Russell in *Protecting Rights and Freedoms: Essays on the Charter's Place in Canada's Political, Legal, and Intellectual Life,* Philip Bryden, Steven Davis, John Russell, editors, University of Toronto Press, 1994. Reprinted by permission of Peter Russell.

towards changes that would pull the country together rather than demands emanating from Quebec and other provinces that threatened to pull it apart. Pre-eminent among such unifying proposals was a Charter of Rights crystallizing in Canada's highest law the common values of its people. For Trudeau's own people, the Québécois, such a Charter was designed to reorient their sense of national destiny: instead of remaining cooped up on a provincial reserve they would become citizens bearing equal rights, with full access to a bilingual and multicultural continental state.[2]

Trudeau, in his first public speech on the Charter (to the Canadian Bar Association in 1967), emphasized its unifying potential. In making a Charter of Rights the first priority of constitutional reform, he explained, "Essentially we will be testing—and hopefully, establishing—the unity of Canada."[3] Again in his final speech in the parliamentary debate on the Charter in 1981, he summed up his case for the Charter with these words: "Lest the forces of self-interest tear us apart, we must now define the common thread that binds us together."[4]

So now, after ten years of the Charter, what can be said about its consequences for national unity? Has it become "the common thread that binds us together"?

Undoubtedly the Charter has had a profound effect on how many Canadians think about the constitution and their participation in Canadian citizenship. The Charter's impact on civic consciousness is probably more significant than any of its more direct effects on public policy. No one has described this dimension of the Charter more insightfully than my political science colleague, Alan Cairns. In his writings, Cairns has shown how the Charter, by shifting the focus of Canadian constitutionalism from the powers of governments to the rights of citizens, tends to convert "a government's constitution to a citizen's constitution."[5] That the Charter has given citizens a greater stake in the constitution—indeed, a greater sense of constitutional proprietorship—is most evident in the demand for a more democratic form of constitution-making. A constitution that inscribes the rights of the people belongs to the people and is not to be altered by eleven first ministers meeting behind closed doors.

However profound the Charter's influence has been on how some Canadians think about their country and its constitution, that influence has not been felt evenly in all parts of Canada. To put the matter bluntly, as Cairns and all of us must observe in the aftermath of the Meech Lake debacle, the Charter did not "take" in Quebec the way it did in the rest of Canada.[6] The majority of French Quebeckers did not make Charter rights their fundamental constitutional value. The Trudeau vision of a Canada—composed of citizens bearing equal rights who resided in equal provinces with their prime allegiance to a bilingual/multicultural nation-state—did not capture the hearts and minds of the Québécois. Trudeau may be a constitutional hero in English Canada, but ironically he is not a constitutional hero for the majority in his home province, Quebec.

We should be clear about the asymmetry of charterphilia. It is not a case of Quebeckers being less civil libertarian, less supportive of fundamental Charter values than the rest of Canada. In 1987, four of us carried out a survey of Canadian attitudes to the Charter of Rights and its values. The survey was conducted through in-depth interviews with a representative sample of 2,000 Canadians and 500 of their elected politicians, including 85 members of the Parti Québécois. At that time, we found in both English and French Canada (including Péquiste politicians) a high level of support for the Charter and its fundamental values of political freedom, due process of law. and social equality. Our conclusion, in a nutshell, was that so far as civil liberties are concerned. Quebec is not a distinct society.[7]

The Charter became divisive only when it became involved as a contentious symbol in our constitutional politics. This occurred in the Meech Lake round, which began just as we were completing our survey. During the Meech round, for many citizens and politicians in English-speaking Canada, the Charter became an icon, a symbol of constitutional first principles.

This tendency came to a head in December 1988 when Quebec, in the wake of the Supreme Court's decision overturning its French-only sign law,[8] invoked the Charter's override clause to enact legislation reestablishing the French-only rule for outdoor advertising. In the hue and cry which then arose outside Quebec we could hear how the rhetoric of constitutional rights invests political discourse with a deep sense of moral rectitude. English-speaking Canadians who in the past simply disliked Quebec's language policy could now, as Roger Gibbons has observed, "wrap themselves in the flag of the Charter and come charging forward in defence of universal human rights."[9] There was no need to give any heed to French Quebeckers' beliefs about what was necessary for the survival of their culture. Clifford Lincoln's words, "Rights are rights and will always be rights," brought tears to his own and to English Canada's eyes. Freedom to advertise in the language of one's choice was now elevated to the status of a fundamental human right that must override any other human right or social interest. The Meech Lake Accord must die because its recognition of Quebec's distinct culture posed too severe a threat to fundamental rights.

The message the rest of Canada sent to Quebec—and Newfoundland's premier, Clyde Wells, was the chief messenger—was essentially this: "Quebec, you must choose: either our Charter or your distinct society. Show us that your first allegiance is to a Canadian nation defined by its Charter of Rights and Freedoms and not to a province in which the French majority have the power to preserve and promote their distinct culture."[10] Given that choice, it was clear which option the majority of Quebeckers would choose. They would stick with the original bargain of Confederation. A jurisdiction in which the French majority could maintain and develop its distinct identity would remain their fundamental constitutional value. And if that condition appeared unobtainable under a constitution shared with other Canadians, the majority of Quebeckers would prefer to be a separate people with their own constitution.

And so the Charter, at this moment of Canadian history, rather than realizing its political sponsors' aim of serving as an instrument of national unity, had become a major source, arguably the major source, of disunity. I say "at this moment" because the divisive effect of the Charter need not be a permanent condition. It is not the actual Charter but the Charter as political icon and Charter worship as a misguided political fundamentalism that render the Charter a source of disunity in Canada.

The actual Charter is a complex and highly textured document. It recognizes collective as well as individual rights. Its first section recognizes the need to balance Charter rights against other important concerns of a free and democratic society. Its legislative override clause wisely acknowledges that judges as well as legislators are fallible and that neither should have the last word in making decisions about the balance to be struck among competing rights and freedoms.[11] Section 23 of the Charter even provides for Quebec's distinctiveness by leaving discretion over the language régime for the schooling of Quebec immigrants to the government and legislature of Quebec.

The multidimensional, balanced nature of the Canadian Charter is equally evident in its interpretation by the courts. This is particularly true of the Supreme Court of Canada's jurisprudence, which is so crucial in fleshing out the Charter's meaning in concrete situations. In its decision on Quebec's sign law, for instance, the Court held that a law requiring predominantly (although not exclusively) French signs could be justified as a reasonable limit on freedom of expression in order to achieve the legitimate objective of maintaining Quebec's "visage linguistique." Bill 178's indoor/outdoor compromise may actually satisfy the Supreme Court's ruling.

In the present post-Meech "Canada Round" of constitutional politics, English-speaking Canadians seem much more willing to recognize Quebec's distinctness and incorporate it as a consideration that, like multiculturalism and aboriginal tradition, is to be given weight in interpreting the Charter. So I remain optimistic that we can have our Charter and our country too—provided that we abandon Charter patriotism for Charter realism.

The Canadian Charter of Rights and Freedoms does not owe its existence solely to politicians. The Charter's political sponsors were aided and abetted by a phalanx of academics and lawyers who believed a Charter was needed to enhance our freedom and secure our liberty. These civil libertarian advocates of a Charter I will call "the believers." Has the believers' faith in the Charter as a bastion against oppressive government been borne out by results?

On this front I cannot detect a great deal of change resulting from the Charter. However, I must confess that I am not well qualified to report in this area, as I do not think we Canadians were exactly in chains before the Charter, nor that the quality of freedom enjoyed by citizens in the great republic to the south through two centuries of living with a constitutional bill of rights was distinctly superior to our own.

Most of the laws limiting free expression have survived the first decade in charterland. In considering the challenges to these laws the courts have generally (and for the most part wisely) favoured the rights of those who can be seriously injured by various forms of communication—complainants in sexual assault cases,[12] the targets of publications intended to arouse race hatred,[13] children manipulated by television advertising[14] and those who are vulnerable to consumers of pornography celebrating sexual violence.[15] The main exception, it would seem, is the Supreme Court's decision in the *Edmonton Journal* case[16] permitting journalists to report the smutty details of divorce proceedings—hardly a great blow for freedom.

It is possible that the Charter's impact on the quality of political freedom may not be felt primarily through the courts' striking down oppressive laws but in its influence on public attitudes. The Charter's most emancipating effect could very well be its tendency, earlier noted, to foster expectations of a less elitist, more democratic form of constitution-making. While such a tendency may provide a civic culture more susceptible to genuine constitutional self-determination, it does not necessarily enhance the prospects of Canadian unity.[17] Canadians are learning in the post-Meech round that it is easier to use their political freedom to defeat an elitist accord than to negotiate a popular accord.

On this matter of popular attitudes, I must add, on a personal note, that as a university professor I do not find that ten years in charterland have made my working environment more tolerant or free from oppression. On the contrary, in thirty-five years of university teaching, I have never sensed as much pressure to conform to certain political positions as I do at the present time, particularly when objection is made to the expression of ideas that are offensive to certain groups. As this very presentation may all too dearly show, professors of political science cannot really function if they are not permitted to be offensive.

It is in the field of criminal justice that the Charter has its greatest potential for enhancing liberty and resisting state oppression. Most of the laws struck down by the courts on Charter grounds have been part of Canada's criminal law.[18] Most of these have been anachronistic elements of criminal law which no one should miss.[19] Most of the activities of the executive branch of government struck down or modified through Charter review in the courts are the practices and policies of prosecutors and the police.

It is also in the field of criminal justice that the Charter is most accessible to the individual Canadian. The Charter gives those who come under police surveillance or are charged with a criminal offence (provided that they retain legal counsel) an extra line of defence. Through legal aid, hundreds of thousands of Canadians have made effective use of professional legal advice and representation. The trench warfare of the criminal justice system is the everyday arena of Charter combat. Important victories have been recorded there. Laws that criminalized abortion[20] and imposed a seven-year mandatory prison term for drug importing have been struck down.[21] Judges have shown that they will throw out evidence obtained through an interrogation in which the police did not afford suspects a real opportunity to exercise their right to legal counsel.[22]

There have been losses in this arena too. The judiciary have on occasion. as for instance with impaired driving[23] and gun control laws,[24] given the nod to crime prevention and social order over individual liberty. For the avid civil libertarian, a single loss is one loss too many. Still, my impression is that, on balance, court decisions on the criminal justice dimension of the Charter have been relatively liberal. Indeed, a comparison with American jurisprudence in this area indicates that on a number of issues the contemporary Canadian Supreme Court has been more liberal than the U.S. Supreme Court even in the Warren court era.[25] As a result, Canada's criminal law and the rules governing its application are more sensitive to the claims of individual liberty than was the case before the Charter.

Even if this is so, it does not necessarily follow that Canada's criminal justice system is actually functioning in a more liberal and less oppressive manner. Jurisprudential triumphs do not automatically change the behaviour of the police and justice officials to whom they theoretically apply. Empirical research in the United States demonstrated that the police in several American cities coped with the Warren court's civil liberty decisions by avoiding the courts and administering their own brand of justice in the back alleys.[26] We simply do not know the extent of police compliance with the Supreme Court's Charter rulings because we have not looked. The answer is not to be found in the law report but through independent social science surveillance of the police and justice officials.

Even if we were to find out that Charter rulings have actually changed the behaviour of those who administer the criminal justice system, that in itself would not mean that the system as a whole has become much less oppressive. We know that the Americans with their hoary old Bill of Rights and we Canadians with our shiny new Charter continue to incarcerate a higher proportion of our populations than virtually any other liberal democracy.[27] Charters of rights do not change that condition, nor do they do much for the people in the prisons, aside from giving them the right to vote. If in the criminal justice field the Charter does no more than line the path to prison with procedural safeguards, it will indeed be a shallow victory for civil liberty.

There was another cluster of interest groups and ideologues besides the civil libertarians who were strong advocates of the Charter. These I would call "the hopers"; the egalitarians on the left who hoped the Charter would be an instrument for reforming society. Whereas the civil libertarians believed the Charter was essential for preserving liberty, the egalitarians hoped it would bring about social equality.

The egalitarian hopers must be much more disappointed with the results of the Charter than the civil libertarian believers. They ought to be more disappointed for the very good reason that a constitutional charter of rights is an ill-conceived instrument for promoting equality in civil society.[28] The Charter's aim is to restrain government, to protect the negative freedom of citizens—freedom from the strong arm of the state. The Charter is used to attack legislation and government programs for what they do—not what they fail to do. But those who seek equality of social and economic condition need a strong state that can and ill intervene in civil society to redistribute power and wealth and enhance the welfare of those most vulnerable to the free play of market forces. Government is to be attacked not for its sins of commission but for its sins of omission. For persons of this persuasion, particularly for those who flail about in the courts, the Charter of Rights was bound to be a disappointment.

And of course it has been: the Charter has done little to alter power relations, redistribute wealth, or promote social welfare within the Canadian version of welfare capitalism. The Supreme Court's interpretation of the Charter has minimized its impact on social and economic relations. I refer, in particular, to its decision in *Dolphin Delivery*[9] to exclude from the Charter's reach court enforcement of the common law in so-called private disputes, including labour disputes, in which government is not a party, as well as to the Court's interpretation of the Charter in a series of cases that have the effect of largely excluding from the Charter's ambit both the collective bargaining rights of labour[30] and the corporate economic rights of business.[31] A majority of Supreme Court justices have shown a determination to remain in the middle of the political spectrum on socio-economic issues—a pattern that must be more objectionable to those who want social change than to those content with the status quo.

The Charter's limited scope has not deterred lawyers representing social action groups from trying to use the Charter as a vehicle for social change. Their efforts have aroused the ire of critics on the right who fear that a "court party" led by charterphile lawyers will use Charter advocacy as an undemocratic means of advancing the interests of special interest groups.[32] Some left-wing critics have been equally aroused by the "court party" on the grounds that Charter litigation will fritter away the energy and resources of progressive social forces.[33]

There is little evidence thus far to support the concerns of charter-phobes on the right or left.[34] Right-wing critics of the court party can point to few instances where judicial review under the Charter has forced elected politicians to initiate policies or spend money against their wishes. Nor is there any evidence that feminists, anti-racists, the labour movement, environmentalists, or other groups working for social reform in Canada have decided to forsake direct political action for Charter litigation. Most interest groups are smart enough to work both sides of the street.

If the Charter is to have a fundamental effect on the distribution of wealth and power and the level of social welfare in Canada, it will not be through its application in the courts but through its influence on the political consciousness of citizens. If Charter idolatry were to persuade the vast majority of Canadians that the Charter really does embody their most fundamental rights and freedoms and that the key to social progress is restricting government activity, then indeed the Charter would have contributed mightily to a shift of the entire political spectrum to the right.

So let us add up my score card: for the political sponsors, up to now more disunity than unity; for the civil libertarian believers, a wee bit of liberty; for the egalitarian hopers, not much, if any, equality.

Personally, I remain doubtful about whether the Charter is a good or bad thing for Canada. The one feature of charterland I find difficult to stomach is Charter worship. I believe the country might choke on Charter patriotism too. The Charter has done little good for anything I care much about except to enrich the intellectual life of the chattering classes. For that, I know, I should be exceedingly thankful.

Notes

1. See Peter H. Russell, "The Political Purposes of the Canadian Charter of Rights and Freedoms," (1983) 61 *Canadian Bar Review* 30.
2. For an analysis of Trudeau's ideological use of the Charter and its failure, see Kenneth McRoberts, *English Canada and Quebec: Avoiding the Issue* (North York: York University Centre for Canadian Studies 1992).
3. Pierre Elliott Trudeau, *Federalism and the French Canadians* (Toronto: Macmillan, 1968) 54.
4. House of Commons Debates, 23 March 1981, 8519.
5. See, in particular, Alan C. Cairns, *Disruptions: Constitutional Struggles from the Charter to Meech Lake* (Toronto: McClelland and Stewart 1990).
6. See Alan C. Cairns, *The Charter Versus Federalism: The Dilemmas of Constitutional Reform* (Montreal: McGill-Queen's University Press 1992) chapter 4.
7. Paul Sniderman, Joseph Fletcher, Peter Russell, and Philip Tedock, "Liberty, Authority and Community: Civil Liberties and the Canadian Political Community," paper presented at the Annual Meeting of the Canadian Political Science Association, Windsor, Ontario, 9 June 1988.
8. *Ford v. A.-G. Quebec,* [1988] 2 SCR 712.
9. Roger Gibbons, "Constitutional Politics in the West and the Rest," in Robert Young, ed., *Confederation in Crisis* (Toronto: James Lorimer 1991), 23.
10. For an analysis of this ideological conflict see Charles Taylor, "Shared and Divergent Values," in Ronald L. Watts and Douglas M. Brown, eds., *Options for a New Canada* (Toronto: University of Toronto Press 1991), 53.
11. For an account of the wisdom of the override, see Peter H. Russell, "Standing Up for Notwithstanding," (1991) 29 *Alberta Law Review* 293.
12. *Canadian Newspapers Co. v. A.-G. Canada,* [1988] 2 SCR 112.
13. *R. v. Keegstra,* [1990] 3 SCR 697.
14. *Irwin Toy Ltd. v. A.-G. Quebec,* [1989] I SCR 927.
15. *R. v. Butler,* [1992] 1 SCR 452.
16. *Edmonton Journal v. A.-G. Alberta,* [1989] 2 SCR 1326.
17. This argument is more fully developed in Peter H. Russell, *Constitutional Odyssey: Can Canadians Become a Sovereign People?* (Toronto: University of Toronto Press 1992).
18. For a statistical analysis of the Supreme Court of Canada's first hundred Charter decisions, see F. L. Morton, Peter H. Russell, and Michael J. Withey, "Judging the Judges: The Supreme Court's First One Hundred Charter Decisions," in Paul Fox and Graham White, eds., *Politics: Canada,* 7th ed. (Toronto: McGraw-Hill Ryerson 1991).
19. For instance, the section of the Criminal Code making constructive murder culpable homicide which was struck down in *R. v. Vaillancourt,* [1987] 2 SCR 636.

20. *R. v. Morgentaler, Smoling and Scott,* [1988] 1 SCR 30.
21. *R. v. Smith,* [1987] 1 SCR 1045.
22. See, for instance, *R. v. Manninen,* [1987] 1 SCR 1233.
23. *R. v. Hufsky,* [1988] 1 SCR 621 and *R. v. Thomsem,* [1988] 1 SCR 640.
24. *R. v. Schwartz,* [1988] 1 SCR 640.
25. Robert Harvie and Hamer Foster, "Ties That Bind? The Supreme Court of Canada, American Jurisprudence and the Revision of Canadian Criminal Law Under the Charter," (1990) 28 *Osgoode Hall Law Journal* 729.
26. Jerome H. Skolnick, *Justice Without Trial* (New York: John Wiley 1967).
27. For Canada's high imprisonment rate among Western countries, see Curt T. Griffiths and Simon N. Verdun-Jones, *Canadian Criminal Justice* (Toronto: Butterworths 1989) 313.
28. For an elaboration of this argument, see Alan C. Hutchinson and Andrew Petter, "Private Rights/Public Wrongs: The Liberal Lie of the Charter," (1988) 38 *University of Toronto Law Journal* 1270.
29. *Dolphin Delivery Ltd. v. Retail, Wholesale & Department Store Union,* [1986] 1 SCR 573.
30. The leading case is *Reference Re Public Service Employees Relation Act and Police Officers Collective Bargaining Act of Alberta,* [1987] 1 SCR 313.
31. See, in particular, *Irwin Toy Ltd. v. A.-G. Quebec,* supra note 14.
32. See Rainer Knopff and F. L. Morton, *Charter Politics* (Toronto: Nelson 1992), chapter 4.
33. See Michael Mandel, *The Charter of Rights and the Legalization of Politics in Canada* (Toronto: Wall & Thompson 1989).
34. See Richard Sigurdson, "Left and Right-wing Charterphobia in Canada," paper presented at the annual meeting of the Canadian Political Science Association, Charlottetown, 31 May 1992.

The Charter: Dividing or Uniting Canadians?
Center for Research and Information on Canada
2002

Highlights

- The Canadian Charter of Rights and Freedoms is viewed favourably by large majorities in all regions, with the highest rate of approval in Quebec (91%), and the lowest in the West (86%). Approval of the Charter is higher than in previous years.
- 71 % say that the Court and not Parliament should have the final say when the Supreme Court declares a law unconstitutional because it conflicts with the Charter. This figure is higher than in previous years.
- A smaller majority (54%) opposes the Charter section that allows governments to override the courts and pass a law that the courts have declared unconstitutional. But a sizeable minority (41%) think that governments should have this power. In Quebec, 57% oppose the override.
- Despite its opposition in principle to the override clause, a majority (55%) thinks that the government should override the Supreme Court if the Court rules that the government's new anti-terrorism law violates some civil liberties.
- More generally, 66% agree that it is all right to suspend the usual civil rights, if the federal government says there is a national emergency, and a majority in Parliament agrees; 28 % disagree.
- A small majority of Canadians (56%) are prepared to give the police more power to detect and arrest criminals, even if it means the civil rights of some might not be respected. 41% take the opposite view.
- Significant numbers of Canadians are prepared to limit the protection of freedom of expression in certain circumstances, such as banning the spread of racial hatred (82%) or pornography that degrades women (68%).
- 61% feel that the Court was wrong to strike down the government's attempt to limit spending by interest groups on advertising supporting a party or candidate during an election campaign.

"Highlights" from *The CRIC Papers, The Charter: dividing or uniting Canadians,* April 2002. Reprinted by permission for The Center for Research and Information on Canada, a division of The Canadian Unity Council.

- 51 % agree with the Court that an outright ban on tobacco advertising is too severe a restriction on the right to freedom of expression; 47 % disagree.
- French-speaking families living outside Quebec should have the right to have their children educated in French, according to 86 % of Canadians outside Quebec. In Quebec, 88 % agree that English-speaking families should be able to have their children educated in English.
- Support for French-language education rights in western Canada (85 %) is as high as it is in Ontario.
- A majority (55 %) believes the Charter has united Canadians, making them more aware of common values, while 39 % say it has divided Canadians because we have become too willing to push for our own particular rights regardless of the views of other people.
- Canadians agree (78 %) with the courts that the Charter's prohibition of discrimination should be extended to gays and lesbians. 20 % disagree.
- Only 11 % say the Charter goes *too far* in protecting the rights of minority groups, and even fewer (6 %) say this is true in the case of the rights of women.
- 78 % agree with the Supreme Court's decision that refugee claimants on Canadian soil have a right to a fair hearing. When told that this decision means longer delays for determining whether refugee claimants should be allowed to stay in Canada, a majority (60 %) continues to support the Court.
- 86 % approve of the section in the Charter that calls for it to be interpreted consistent with the preservation and enhancement of Canada's multicultural heritage.

Preface

Canadians are deeply attached to the Charter of Rights and Freedoms. In recent years, nine out of ten surveyed have said the Charter is important to their sense of national identity. The Charter is seen as important to Canadian identity by more people than is the national anthem or the flag.[1]

But it is more than a symbol. Early advocates of a constitutionally entrenched charter of rights saw it as the best way to protect both individuals and minorities by imposing firm limits on "the tyranny of the majority" and the state's ability to interfere with personal freedom.

It also was hoped that a charter of rights would strengthen national unity in two important ways; unite Canadians of all origins through a powerful statement of shared political values; and defuse conflict between Anglophones and Francophones by providing constitutional protections for minority language and education rights.

"Preface" from *The CRIC Papers, The Charter: dividing or uniting Canadians,* April 2002. Reprinted by permission for The Center for Research and Information on Canada, a division of The Canadian Unity Council.

That the Charter was intended to protect rights and strengthen national unity is manifest in Prime Minister Pierre Trudeau's remarks at the ceremony where it was signed into law:

"I speak of a country where every person is free to fulfill himself or herself to the utmost, unhindered by the arbitrary actions of Government. ... If individuals and minorities do not feel protection against the possibility of the tyranny of the majority, if French-speaking Canadians or native peoples or new Canadians do not feel they will be treated with justice, it is useless to ask them to open their hearts and minds to their fellow Canadians."[2]

In the ensuing 20 years, Canadians have used the Charter frequently in defence of their rights and freedoms. In the process, however, the Charter has, on occasion, become the source of considerable controversy. It has provided the legal basis for court decisions on such divisive issues as abortion, assisted suicide, homosexuality, pornography, hate literature, police powers, the rights of the accused, and Quebec's French language laws. Moreover, the many successful court challenges of government actions have led some to argue that the courts have become too "activist" effectively displacing democratically elected legislatures as the forums in which key public policy disputes are settled.

5. Does the Charter Go too Far?

While Canadians are almost unanimous in saying that the Charter is a good thing for the country, some might also be anxious about the extent to which it has been used by certain groups to advance their particular interests. There may also be growing anxiety about how Canadian society and politics have changed as a result of the accentuated "rights consciousness" fostered by the Charter. This section explores these hypotheses.

Equality Rights

Canadians *do not* think the Charter unduly favours those groups who have relied on it to protect their equality rights. Respondents were asked whether the Charter goes too far, not far enough, or just far enough to protect the rights of minority groups and of women. In each case, a majority says the Charter goes just far enough, and a sizeable minority—between one-quarter and one-third—says it does not go far enough (see Figure 1). Very few people think the Charter goes too far in protecting the rights of minority groups or women.

Previous surveys by Environics have shown that most Canadians believe that the Charter has improved the rights of minority groups, but only a minority say the same

"Does the Charter Go too Far?" from *The CRIC Papers, The Charter: dividing or uniting Canadians,* April 2002. Reprinted by permission for The Center for Research and Information on Canada, a division of The Canadian Unity Council.

Figure 1 The Charter: Too Far, or not Far Enough

In your opinion, does the Charter of Rights and Freedoms go too far, not far enough, or just far enough to protect the rights or each of the following?

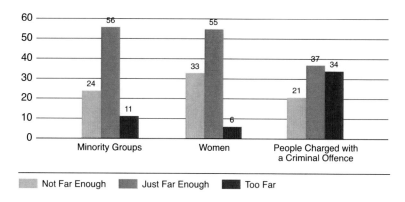

is true of their own personal rights.[3] The present survey adds that a majority of Canadians agree that the level of protection that the Charter has provided to minority groups is appropriate. In fact, 24% would like the Charter to go *further* in protecting these groups. Thus, if Canadians feel that the Charter has been of particular benefit to the rights of minority groups, it is likely that they believe that these groups are most in need of protection. Indeed, only 6% say the Charter goes too far in protecting the rights of women. This figure can be seen as a strong vote of confidence, especially in light of the publicity generated by Charter cases relating to matters such as human reproduction, pornography, and prosecution of those charged with sexual assault.

Legal Rights

Some of the harshest criticism leveled against the Charter and the courts' interpretations of its provisions relates to protections afforded to suspected criminals. Disbelief and outrage have been fueled by the occasional dismissal of charges against an accused on the basis of what many see as a "technicality," such as a minor transgression of Charter rights by the police or the prosecution. Such instances have prompted critics to argue that such court rulings have "transformed" criminal justice procedures "to the chagrin of the police and to the delight of criminal lawyers and their clients."[4]

As shown above in Figure 1, however, only one in three Canadians say that the Charter goes too far in protecting the rights of people charged with a criminal offence. Still, this represents many more than those who think that the Charter goes too far to protect minority groups or women, indicating that the issue of legal rights raises more concerns that does that of equality rights.

Figure 2 A Matter of Trust

Do you trust each of the following to do the right thing all the time, most of the time, some of the time, or hardly ever?

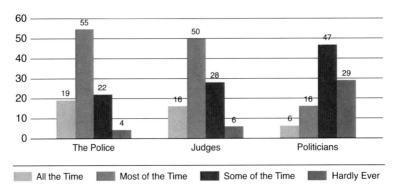

In fact, there is ample evidence that the public sympathizes with the police in the fight against crime:

- First, the public trusts the police more than judges and politicians. Almost three-quarters of Canadians trust the police to do the right thing either all or most of the time (see Figure 2).
- Second, 69% of Canadians agree with the statement that "one reason there is so much crime in Canada is that the police and the courts have to spend too much time worrying about the rights of criminals." Only 29% disagree.
- Finally, the most revealing finding is that a majority (56%) is prepared to give the police more power to detect and arrest criminals, *even if that means that the civil rights of some Canadians might not be respected.*. Forty-one percent take the opposite view, preferring that the police respect everyone's civil rights, even of that means that some criminals might escape detection.

These results support an earlier study which found "overwhelming evidence of opposition to judicial decisions" that had the effect of limiting the police's ability to obtain evidence against criminal suspects.[5] And the readiness to compromise on legal rights in order to empower the police contrasts sharply with the survey's finding of much stronger public support for Charter protections of minority or equality rights.

On the other hand, as we have seen, rather than thinking that criminal suspects as a rule have too many rights, a majority of Canadians (57%) say that the Charter either goes *just far enough or not far enough* to protect the rights of those charged with a criminal offence. Moreover, two out of five would prefer to see the police uphold civil rights, even at the cost some criminals going free. And, earlier in the paper, we noted that 78% percent of Canadians say that the police should not be allowed to enter and search someone's home or office without a search warrant. This question, however, was asked of only one-half of survey respondents.

The other half was asked about searches of a *suspected criminal's* home or office. In this case, 65 % say that police should not be allowed to search without a warrant. Although fewer people would restrict police powers in a case involving someone suspected of a crime, almost two thirds would prohibit what the courts would surely view as an unreasonable search of a suspect's home or office.

The Canadian Charter of Rights and Freedoms Section 8:
Everyone has the right to be secure against unreasonable search or seizure.

It is wrong to conclude, therefore, that the public does not support the Charter's protection of legal rights. It is perhaps more accurate to recognize that the public supports these rights in principle, but not always in practice. Canadians will continue to be frustrated in cases where they perceive that an overly legalistic interpretation of rights unduly limits the ability of the police and the courts to arrest, prosecute and convict genuine criminals. In the context of this frustration, they will be willing to compromise rights in return for security.

Common Values?

The Charter was intended to do more than protect rights and liberties. Many of its supporters hoped it would also "strengthen the country's unity by basing the sovereignty of the Canadian people on a set of values common to all."[6] But critics argue that, in practice, the Charter has been divisive, fracturing the country into rights-seeking groups who eschew political compromise in favour of winner-take-all court battles. The result has been to "embitter politics" and to leave Canadians "less of a single people" than we were before.[7]

In view of this argument, respondents were read the following two statements about the Charter, and asked to state which was closer to their own view:

1. the Charter's protection of our rights and freedoms has united Canadians because we have become more aware of the values that we have in common; or
2. the Charter of Rights and Freedoms has divided Canadians because we have become too willing to push for our own particular rights regardless of the views of other people.

A majority (55 %) says that the Charter has united Canadians by making us more aware of common values. However, 39 % say that it has divided us, as we have become too focused on our own particular rights. The modest majority seeing the Charter as more unifying than divisive contrasts with the overwhelming majority who would say that it is important to Canadian identity and that it is a good thing for the country.

Views about the unifying or divisive effect of the Charter are closely linked to attitudes about a wide range of specific issues relating to rights and freedoms.[8]

The tendency to say that the Charter has united Canadians is higher among those who:

- Insist that the police should respect civil rights, even if some criminals might escape arrest;
- Disagree that the Charter goes too far to protect the rights of minority groups;
- Favour allowing gay and lesbian couples to marry;
- Agree with the Court that the Charter should prohibit discrimination against gays and lesbians;
- Approve of the clause in the Charter relating to multiculturalism;
- Agree with the Court's decision to uphold Aboriginal treaty rights;
- Say that it is important to preserve English and French as Canada's two official languages;
- Agree that French Canadians living outside Quebec should have the right to federal government services available in French;
- Favour the constitutional recognition of Quebec's unique character.

Those who take the opposing view are more likely to say that the Charter has divided Canadians because we have become too willing to push for our own particular rights regardless of the views of others.

Thus, those who are less likely to say that the Charter has made us more aware of our "common values"—such as bilingualism, multiculturalism, equality rights, minority rights, and civil liberties—are precisely those who are less likely to agree that those values are in fact commonly held. There is a constituency of people within Canada who, because of their views, are concerned about the direction in which the Charter (and judicial interpretation of Charter rights) is taking the country. What the present study cannot tell us—and what future research should address—is whether this constituency is growing or shrinking with time.[9]

While this finding is important, it should not overshadow the strong overall support for the Charter and its provisions. Nor should it eclipse the majority view that the Charter does not "go too far," and, in fact, has united Canadians, making them more aware of common values.

National Unity Revisited

One of the most important findings of the survey is the lack of any significant regional differences of opinion on the Charter's legitimacy or the relationship between Parliament and the courts. Canadians in each of the country's major regions have the similar views on these key issues: whether the Charter is a good thing for Canada; whether Parliament or the Supreme Court should have the final say when

"National Unity Revisited" from *The CRIC Papers, The Charter: dividing or uniting Canadians,* April 2002. Reprinted by permission for The Center for Research and Information on Canada, a division of The Canadian Unity Council.

Figure 3 Opinion on the Charter and the Courts, by Region

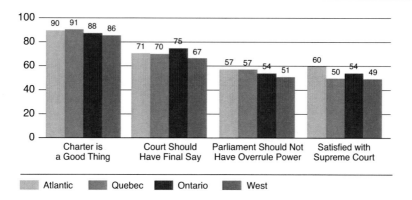

laws conflict with the Charter; whether Parliament should have the power to overrule the Court's decisions; and on whether the way the Supreme Court is working is satisfactory (see Figure 3).

It would appear that the Charter and the role of the courts are not regionally divisive issues. What's more, large majorities in every region support Charter principles relating to bilingualism and minority language education rights, multiculturalism, the acceptability of "reasonable limits" on freedom of expression, and the prohibition of police searches without a search warrant. The Charter does indeed speak to certain fundamental values upon which all Canadians can agree.

If we look more closely at the other results of the survey, however, some distinct regional patterns do emerge.

First, Quebecers tend to be more supportive of equality as a principle, and of groups seeking greater equality in practice. Quebecers are much more likely than other Canadians to say that equality is more important that personal freedom (see Table 1).

Quebecers are also more likely to favour allowing same-sex marriage, to support the prohibition of discrimination against gays and lesbians, and to say that the Charter has not gone far enough to protect minorities and women (see Figure 4). Western Canadians are least supportive of "gay rights," and are least likely to say the Charter has not gone far enough to protect minority groups and women. The degree of regional difference should not be exaggerated, however. In the case of Charter protection for gays and lesbians, for instance, a majority in all regions agree.

Quebecers also take a somewhat different view of police powers and civilliberties.[10] For example:

- 61% agree that one reason there is so much crime in Canada is that the police and the courts have to spend too much time worrying about the rights of criminals, compared to 72% of Canadians living in the other nine provinces;

Table 1   Freedom vs. Equality (Percentage Agreeing with either Statement)

	Atlantic	Quebec	Ontario	West
Both freedom and equality are important. But I consider personal freedom to be more important, that iS, everyone can live in freedom and develop without hindrance.	51	39	54	54
Both freedom and equality are important. But I consider equality to be more important, that is, nobody is underprivileged and social class differences are not so strong.	40	59	43	44

- 71% say that the police *should not* be allowed to enter and search a criminal suspect's home or office without a search warrant, compared with 63% of those outside Quebec;
- 57% think that it is all right for the federal government to suspend civil liberties in times of national emergency, compared with 68% outside Quebec;
- :• 85% agree with the court decision giving refugee claimants the right to a fair hearing, compared with 75% outside Quebec;

Quebecers are also much less trusting of the police and of judges than are other Canadians, and less likely to say that it is *very* important to strengthen respect and obedience to authority.

The tendency of Quebecers to be more supportive of civil liberties is apparent in all but two cases. The more widely held view in Quebec that the Charter goes too far to protect the rights of people charged with a criminal offence may be shaped by the ongoing debate in the province about whether the Charter places too many obstacles in the way of the fight against organized crime. And Quebecers are just as likely as other Canadians to agree that the government should have the power to overrule the courts, should the courts find that the new anti-terrorism law violates some civil liberties.

Finally, while it is true that there are no significant regional divisions in attitudes on the Charter, it is worth noting that western Canadians, particularly those living in the Prairie provinces, appear least satisfied. Only 48% of Prairie residents say that it has united Canadians by making them more aware of the values held in common, compared with 57% of those in the other provinces. Forty-eight percent of Prairie residents are satisfied with the way the Supreme Court is working while 43% are dissatisfied, whereas 53% of other Canadians are satisfied and 31% are dissatisfied. The question for future research is whether, in time, this difference of opinion will narrow or widen.

Figure 4 Attitudes on Equality, by Region

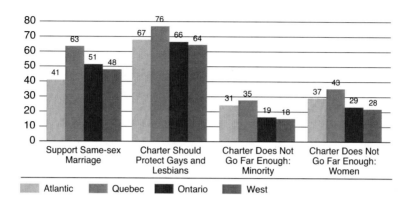

A Final Word

A central objective for the framers of the Charter was to strengthen national unity by focusing Canadians of all backgrounds on the political values they hold in common. The survey provides dramatic proof that they succeeded. The Charter speaks to values widely shared by Canadians, and in the space of two decades, it has become an important symbol of national identity. Moreover, what Canadians like most about the Charter are precisely those aspects that underpin the maintenance of unity—protection of official languages, multiculturalism, and equality rights. The Charter defines the very ideal of Canada: a pluralist, inclusive and tolerant country, one in which all citizens can feel equally at home.

Certainly, the Charter, and the courts' interpretations of its clauses, will generate ever more controversy. Modern societies currently are grappling with difficult issues: advances in medical research; the impacts of information technology; changes in family structure and relationships; the evolution of social mores; political mobilization of disadvantaged groups of citizens; and the growing sophistication of criminals and terrorists. Government attempts to confront these challenges inevitably will spark heated debates about appropriate limits to fundamental freedoms and equality rights. In Canada, these will revolve around the Charter. This raises a question: Will the Charter emerge from these debates as the same kind of rallying point for Canadians that it became during its first two decades?

"A Final Word" from *The CRIC Papers, The Charter: dividing or uniting Canadians,* April 2002. Reprinted by permission for The Center for Research and Information on Canada, a division of The Canadian Unity Council.

Endnotes

1. The exact question asked by Environics is: "How important are the following to the Canadian identity: very important, somewhat important, not very important or not at all important? The Charter of Rights and Freedoms." The same question was asked about other items, including the national anthem and the flag. In 2000, the most recent year in which the question was asked, 94 % of those surveyed said the Charter was important to the Canadian identity (source: Environics Research Group).

2. Pierre Trudeau, speech on Parliament Hill, April 17, 1982, as quoted in Thomas Walkom, "Rights Charter Lauded by PM", The Globe and Mail (Toronto), 19 April 1982, p. 10.

3. In 1999, for instance, 61 % said that the rights of minority groups had improved as a result of the Charter of Rights and Freedoms, while 20 % said they had not changed and only 7 % said they had deteriorated. When asked about their own personal rights, 26 % said they had improved, 40 % said they had not changed, and 15 % said they had deteriorated. Source: Environics Research Group.

4. Morton and Knopff, *Charter Revolution,* p. 20. Similarly, Alex Macdonald alleges that law enforcement officers "have had their daily work hamstrung" as the Charter rights of accused are "propped up to extraordinary heights" by judges allergic to common sense. Macdonald, *Outrage,* p. 29 and 56.

5. Fletcher and Howe, "Canadian Attitudes toward the Charter and the Courts," p. 37.

6. Pierre Elliott Trudeau, "The Values of a Just Society," in Thomas S. Axworthy and Pierre Elliott Trudeau, eds., Towards A Just Society: The Trudeau Yea15 (Markham: Viking, 1990), p. 363.

7. Morton and Knopff, Charter Revolution, pp. 150–51; 166.

8. Also, those who are less optimistic about the economy and less secure about their own employment are less likely to see the Charter as promoting unity.

9. There are indications, however, that over time, Canadians are becoming more supportive of some of the values just mentioned. For instance, Canadians as a whole are becoming more liberal in their attitudes towards homosexuality (see Bricker and Greenspon, *Searching for Certainty,* pp. 267–68). Note that, according to the survey under consideration here, support for a Charter prohibition against discrimination on the basis on sexual orientation is much greater than that measured by Environics in the mid-1990s. Environics also confirms that support for "bilingualism in all of Canada" is higher today than at any time in the previous 25 years (source: Environics Research Group).

10. Quebec is singled out for attention here because the responses of Quebecers *to these particular questions* are consistently different from those of Canadians in other regions. On these questions, Canadians from the Atlantic provinces, Ontario and the West give similar responses.

Focus Questions

1. What does the "MacPatriation Brothers" cartoon mean, and does it still have meaning today?

   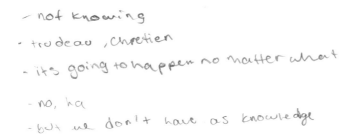

   - not knowing
   - trudeau, chretien
   - its going to happen no matter what
   - no, ha
   - but we don't have as knowledge

2. After reading the text of the Charter, which of its provisions do you think has had, or has the potential to make, the greatest change in the lives of individual Canadians?

   - legal Freedoms
   - eqcality

3. Do you think Trudeau made a mistake when he allowed Section 33 (the "notwithstanding" clause) to be included in the document? Why was the clause so important for the provinces?

   Regional identities

   "room for acomedation"

4. In what ways has the Charter united Canadians? In what ways has it divided them? Which of these two forces—uniting or dividing—has been strongest?

    - human basis
    - English / French
      Dividing
    - French / Canadians
    - not effectively used
    └ but what would it be like w out it.

5. According to Russell, how and why has the Charter altered Canadians' perceptions of their Constitution? Do you think this change has been for the better or worse?

    power
    - from Gov'n to citizens

      - a group of ppl that haven't faced
    what citizens
    └ we didn't appoint them

    └ democracy

6. What vital thing(s) has the Charter failed to do, and why?

16

From Nativism to Multiculturalism: Immigration and National Identity

Introduction

Many Canadians today enthusiastically support multiculturalism—that series of policies and programs designed to promote and celebrate the vast array of cultures and ethnicities which make up the Canadian mosaic. Multiculturalism does bring challenges, however, not the least of which is the fact that the concept rubs against the grain of history. In the not-too-distant past, English Canadians had difficulty with the idea of a *bi*-cultural nation (French and English), let alone a multicultural one. The presence of non-English speaking immigrants generated enormously hostile reactions from many Canadians, including some very prominent social and political figures. The first two readings in this chapter expose what were, in the early twentieth century, mainstream attitudes toward the presence of minority groups in Canada. The first of these is from renowned humorist Steven Leacock, and the second from Emily Murphy, a woman best known for her tireless campaigns on behalf of women's rights. Their opinions on immigrants from non-English speaking countries are clearly racist, and for those who look to these two individuals for a sense of Canada's noble past, they are also quite disturbing.

When multiculturalism became a topic for discussion and policy development in the 1960s, racist critiques like those offered by Leacock and Murphy became increasingly unacceptable. Indeed, many believed that the concept would promote the eventual disappearance of racism altogether. Ironically, current critics, including Neil Bissoondath, argue that multiculturalism has not eliminated racism, but instead has worked to entrench it further into the social and political landscape of the country.

Others remain committed to its principles, and sure of its value as both a political and social goal—even in the wake of the 9/11 attacks on the United States, when ethnic identity becomes a decidedly rocky and uncertain terrain. As these readings reveal, multiculturalism is seen by some as a laudable ideal, and by others as an undesirable one. It is simultaneously defined as a source of the nation's identity, and the reason for the lack thereof.

Economic Prosperity in the British Empire
Stephen Leacock
1930

[. . .] We must start, I say, from the fact that the emigrant, or local worker, with whom we are concerned possesses nothing; or, more likely, in the form of a dependent wife and children, possesses, economically less than nothing. We have to start from this. Any scheme of migration dealing with thrifty Scottish farmers who have saved a hundred pounds, or well-to-do Americans from Kansas, or young men whose people will pay a hundred pounds to get rid of them, is quite beside the mark.

The emigrant has nothing, except his capacity to work. If he is disabled and cannot work, his case lies outside of this book. But at present, let us say, he cannot find work; he is one of the 2,000,000 unemployed and the 5,000,000 under-employed of Great Britain.

Citizens of alien countries are not under consideration, do not fit into the scheme. The outer empire needs population and settlement. Part of it, like Canada, can only carry its" overhead" of transportation and capital investment on the condition that a stream of newcomers shall move in. If there were no available British to come, we should very likely have to take in others or drift into liquidation. But it so happens that there are British—millions of them. The others we only need as a second-best choice.

Canada, especially in its northwest provinces, is badly damaged in this respect. As a result of the great foreign immigration before the War, the last census of Canada showed among its inhabitants 459,000 people born in continental Europe, including 57,000 Austrians, 31,000 Galicians, 101,000 Russians, 21,000 Poles, 35,000 Italians, and various others.

From the point of view of the Russians and the Galicians, etc., this meant improvement for the northwest. Not so from others. Learning English and living under the British flag may make a British subject in the legal sense, but not in the real sense, in the light of national history and continuity. A few such people can easily be absorbed—over a large area many thousands can be absorbed. A little dose of them may even, by variation, do good, like a minute dose of poison in a medicine. But if you

From *Economic Prosperity in the British Empire* by Stephen Leacock, Toronto: The Macmillan Company of Canada, 1930.

get enough of them, you get absorbed yourself. What you called the British Empire turns into the Russian and Galician Empire.

I am not saying that we should absolutely shut out and debar the European foreigner, as we should and do shut out the Oriental. But we should in no way facilitate his coming. Not for him the free ocean transit, nor the free coffee of the immigrant shed, nor the free land, nor the found job, nor the guaranteed anything. He is lucky if he is let in "on his own,"

International Rings
Emily Murphy
1922

Concerning the operations of Drug Rings in Asia especially in relation to opium, Dr. Ruth states that the opium traffic in Asia has grown to immense proportions and has become one of the greatest industries in the world, being organized with Standard Oil efficiency. In Persia, Turkey and India, immense plantations are operated by powerful interests, while great banking institutions for financing the drug traffic are well established.

Among the pedlars who are the agents of the Ring, the traffic is chiefly in the hands of Americans, Canadians, Chinese, Negroes, Russians and Italians, although the Assyrians and Greeks are running closely in the race.

It is claimed also, but with what truth we cannot I say, that there is a well-defined propaganda among the aliens of color to bring about the degeneration of the white race.

Maybe, it isn't so, after all, the popular dictum which has something to do with a flag and a bulldog. *

Oh! yes! it is the one which declares, "What we have we'll hold." The trouble with most bulldogs is that their heads are only developed in the region of the jaw and that any yellow terrier can hamstring them from behind.

We have no very great sympathy with the baiting of the yellow races, or with the belief that these exist only to serve the Caucasian, or to be exploited by us.

Such a belief was exemplified in a film once shown at a five-cent theatre in Chicago, and was reported by Jane Addams.

In the pictures, a poor woman is surrounded by her several children, all of whom are desperately hungry, and hold out pleading hands for food. The mother sends one of the boys on the streets to beg but he steals a revolver instead, kills a Chinaman, robs him of several hundred dollars, and rushes home with the money to his mother.

The last scene portrays the woman and children on their knees in prayer thanking God for His care and timely rescue of them.

The Chinese, as a rule are Friendly people and have a fine sense of humor that puts them on an easy footing with our folk, as compared with the Hindu and others we might mention.

From *The Black Candle* by Emily F. Murphy, Toronto: Thomas Allen, 1922, pp. 186–189.

*The bulldog was a common image used to represent the British.

Ah Duck, or whatever we choose to call him, is patient, polite, and persevering. Also he inhales deeply. He has other peculiarities such as paying his debts and refraining from profanity. "You sabe?"

The population of china amounts to 426,000,000 or one-third of the human race. Yes! It was a New York citizen who, looking up from an encyclopedia exclaimed with deadly earnestness, "In this household, we shall not have more than three children seeing this book says every fourth child born in the world is a Chinaman."

Still, it behooves the people in Canada and the United States, to consider the desirability of these visitors—for they *are* visitors—and to say whether or not we shall be *"at home"* to them for the future.

A visitor may be polite, patient, persevering, as above delineated, but if he carries poisoned lollypops in his pocket and feeds them to our children, it might seem wise to put him out.

It is hardly credible that the average Chinese pedlar has any definite idea in his mind of bringing about the downfall of the white race, his swaying motive being probably that of greed, but in the hands of his superiors, he may become a powerful instrument to this very end.

In discussing this subject, Major Crehan of British Columbia has pointed out that whatever their motive, the traffic always comes with the Oriental, and that one would therefore be justified in assuming that it was their desire to injure the bright-browed races of the world.

Naturally, the aliens are silent on the subject, but an addict who died this year in British Columbia told how he was frequently jeered at as "a white man accounted for." This man belonged to a prominent family and, in 1917, was drawing a salary of six thousand dollars a year. He fell a victim to a drug "booster" till, ultimately, he became a ragged wreck living in the noisome alleys of Chinatown, "lost to use, and name and fame."

This man used to relate how the Chinese pedlars taunted him with their superiority at being able to sell the dope without using it, and by telling him how the yellow race would rule the world. They were too wise, they urged, to attempt to win in battle but would win by wits; would strike at the white race through "dope" and when the time was ripe would command the world.

"It may sound like a fantastic dream," writes the reporter, "but this was the story he told in one of the brief periods when he was free from the drug curse, and he told it in all sincerity."

Some of the Negroes coming into Canada—and they are no fiddle-faddle fellows either—have similar ideas, and one of their greatest writers has boasted how ultimately they will control the white men.

Many of these Negroes are law-abiding and altogether estimable, but contrariwise, many are obstinately wicked persons, earning their livelihood as free ranging pedlars of poisonous drugs. Even when deported, they make their way back to Canada carrying on their operations in a different part of the country.

EVERYONE'S A Critic
John Biles
2002

Criticising multiculturalism in Canada is a growth industry. For over thirty years Canadians, researchers, cultural commentators, politicians (or would-be politicians) of every stripe, and newspaper columnists along with their media brethren have railed against multiculturalism in Canada. Earnscliffe research noted in 1996 that, "opponents of multiculturalism seem to use the word [multiculturalism] to indicate their dislike of a number of changes occurring within Canada in the last three or four decades, with the nature of their criticism going well beyond the nominal target of official multiculturalism." In this essay I want to examine the critiques which have been thrown at multiculturalism

Before proceeding however, it is important to be clear on what exactly I mean by multiculturalism. Although I am a strong supporter of multiculturalism as public policy, and I believe that the federal policy has been key in the development of multiculturalism in Canada, I do not believe the federal policy is the be all and end all. Rather, it is one piece of a far larger exercise that Canadians have collectively pursued over the last thirty years, or longer if you believe the work of Joshee (1995), Pal (1993), Day (2000), or Biles and Panousos (1999). Every major public institution in the country has developed a policy on multiculturalism at one time or another, and every provincial and municipal government has tackled issues arising from our diversity. This great volume of policies and concomitant discussions has developed a commitment on the part of Canadians to a continual active discourse on issues arising from diversity. This is what Fleras and Elliott (1992) have dubbed, "multiculturalism as critical discourse."

Participation in this critical discourse occurs in a myriad of forms. Neil Bissoondath's claim that "few silences are as loaded in this country as the one encasing the cult that has grown up around our policy of multiculturalism" (1994: 4) rings· as false today as it did seven years ago. This animated discourse may be integral to the lived experience of individual Canadians or of Canadian communities; it may be shaped by legislative or judicial decisions; it may be used by various opinion leaders; or it may be printed in the media, in peer-reviewed academic literature, non-academic publications or vanity presses. They make take the form of brief editorials or newspaper commentaries (O'Sullivan 1999, Loney 1998, Frum 1999, Amiel 1998, Lakritz 1998, 1999); articles in academic journals (Abu-Laban and Stasiulis 1992, Das Gupta and Iacovetta 2000); dialectic collected works (Charlton and Barker 1994, Cohen, Howard and Nussbaum] 999, Griffiths 2000, Cardozo and Musto 1997); or in full-scale monographs (Gairdner 1990, Bibby 1990, Bissoondath 1994, Gwyn 1995, Loney 1998, Foster 1998, Sugunasiri 1999, Bannerji 2000, Day 2000). Whatever the form, four major critiques predominate: (1) the divisive nature of pluralism; (2) political expediency; (3) threat to the status quo; and (4) cultural relativism.

The Divisive Nature of Multiculturalism

The easiest and most often presented critique of multiculturalism in Canada is that it is divisive. This view is most clearly expressed by Martin Loney in his *The Pursuit of Division: Race, Gender and Preferential Hiritzg in Canada* (1998). Loney and others contend that multiculturalism is a centrifugal rather than centripetal force. This is nowhere more clear than in the most overworked of Canadian images—the mosaic. The mosaic as a central image for Canadian multiculturalism is disastrous. It conjures images of pretty little tiles which are cemented together to form a picture which can literally last millennia. It fails to capture the two-way nature of integration that has long been enshrined in the multiculturalism policy which was constitutionally entrenched through the *Canadian Charter of Rights and Freedoms (1982)*; which was legislated in the *Canadian Multiculturalism Act* (1988) and was recently recognized as a guiding principle of the *Immigration and Protection of Refugees Act* (2001). Perversely, the imagery of the melting pot seems much more applicable, even if its negative baggage renders it impolitic as an image of choice. In a melting pot the addition of every new ingredient alters the entire liquid—there is no cement! No belief in an immutable core.

Despite the inadequacy of the image, it persists and even flourishes today. John Porter's *The Veritical Mosaic:An Analysis of Social Class and Power in Canada* (1965) is kept company by Leo Driedger ed. *The Canadian Ethnic Mosaic: A Quest for Identity* (1978) and most recently by Kelley and Trebilcock's *The Making of the Canadian Mosaic: A History of Canadian Immigration Policy* (1998). In recent years a preoccupation with social cohesion suggests that governments are actively attempting to cement new mosaics into place (Jeannotte 2000).

In some part then, I want to argue that the conceptualization of multiculturalism as a mosaic by proponents of the approach, actually opened the doors to the critique that multiculturalism is divisive or forces minorities into ghettos. Going further, as Blommaert and Verschueren argue in their *debating diversity: Analysing the discourse of tolerance* (1998), even the most well-meaning can lapse into systemic discrimination if the starting point is flawed: one could even end up entombing inequality in the drying cement of social cohesion!

On the first count, the divisive nature of multiculturalism, Gairdner claims "Opinion polls in Canada, the U.S.A., and Australia consistently show strong to overwhelming majorities opposed to multiculturalism policies that erode the core culture." (Gairdner 1990: 389) I am left wondering why an Environics poll in 1996 found that multiculturalism is identified as a common Canadian symbol more often than our winter national sport—hockey (Environics 1996: 61). Every opinion poll I have seen since actually strongly supports multiculturalism. I also wonder if, in some sense, the very ubiquitous nature of public discourse on multiculturalism suggests that it actually unites Canadians. More work can, and should, be done in this regard to evaluate the extent to which multiculturalism represents a core belief of Canadians and respect for diversity as a core Canadian value. A periodic national opinion poll like that done by Angus Reid in 1991 would yield a wealth of information.

On the second critique, the forced ghettoization of minorities (Bissoondath 1994), more research can be brought to bear. A literal spatial interpretation can be evaluated through research initiatives like Metropolis (http://www.metropolis.net). Within Metropolis an incredible amount of research has been conducted in Canada and around the world on whether minority communities congregate in particular areas and why this might be the case (Lithman 1997, Blom 1997, Rose 1999). There is ample evidence that minorities choosing to live in close proximity to one another may not be harmful to the much-vaunted bridging capital Robert Putnam (1994) has written about. They may, indeed, choose to live together for much the same reason as any other group of Canadians - cost of housing, quality of life, access to sites of worship, schools, employment, proximity to public transportation and so forth. More negatively, research by Valerie Preston (2000) suggests environmental racism has a role to play in determining where people choose to live.

If we look at ghettoization in a less spatial sense and expand it to include the permanent "othering" in the social, economic, cultural and political spheres of Canadian society, we have a different range of research findings to consider. Small scale studies have been conducted in Canada on these topics, but future work to connect these disparate studies will be essential. Will Kymlicka cites a range of indicators in his *Finding Our Way: Rethinking Ethnocultural Relations in Canada* (1998) which include intermarriage, language acquisition and naturalization. Clearly others can be developed like the *Ethnic Diversity Survey* and the social capital and time use modules of cycle seventeen of the *General Social Survey* The promised development of an inclusion/ exclusion index by the multiculturalism program and Metropolis and continued work of the political participation network (http://www.canada.metropolis.net/pprn) will also continue to yield invaluable results.

Political Expediency

The political participation of ethnic, racial, religious, and linguistic minorities in Canada is frequently the subject of casual conversation, but seldom the subject of academic enquiry. The easiest off the cuff criticism to make of multiculturalism is that it is a means to "buy" the "ethnic vote." Closely allied to this critique is the language of the "special interest group" increasingly adopted by political figures on the centre right. Somehow, in the Canadian context, the significant body of work done on interest groups, most notably by Paul Pross in his *Group Politics and Public Policy* (1986) has morphed into a dichotomy of valid and invalid interest groups. It would appear that the Canadian Alliance and the Liberal parties of Canada, the Business Council on National Issues, and the CEOs of major banks constitute valid interests, whereas the Croatian-Canadians in Toronto or the Blacks in Halifax are "special interest groups" and, therefore, illegitimate.

At the core of this critique is something that smells a great deal like racism and/or discrimination. How else can we understand the pejorative language used to denigrate the interests of some Canadians? It also has a rather essentialist air to it that echoes that of the division critics mentioned earlier. This critique suggests that there is such a thing as THE Black community in Halifax and that it is a homogeneous entity. Decades of research show that any so-called community is, in fact, a heterogeneous collection of people with competing, and often conflicting, interests and agendas. Much of the work done by the Political Participation Research Network also suggests that any claims or accusations of an "ethnic vote" are, at the very least, exaggerated, and, in most cases, fictitious.

Perhaps the best indicator of the salience of "ethnic votes" may be the extent to which minorities are represented in the formal political system across the country. My own work in Ottawa (1998), Carolle Simard's in Montreal (2000) and Myer Siemiatycki's in Toronto (1998) demonstrates that the majority of minority communities are chronically under-represented at ALL levels of government. A decade after the *Royal Commission on Electoral Reform and Party Financing*, we are no closer to having a representative democracy. Once again, more can, and should, be done in this area and future analysis of the *Canadian Election Study* data set and the *Ethnic Diversity Survey* will yield more information.

As in the case with the earlier critiques, there is also a political expediency critique emanating from supporters of diversity. This critique is centred on the symbolic nature of multiculturalism. Most of us are familiar with the ubiquitous, derogatory comments about multiculturalism that center on the fluffy stuff: the song, dance, and food. I believe there are a number of problems with this critique.

First, and foremost, is the power of symbolism. I have heard the *Canadian Multiculturalism Act* referred to as a "legislated press release." Anyone examining legislation pertaining to multiculturalism, diversity or human rights will be familiar with the "toothless" critique that is thrown at every piece of legislation or governmental approach. For a toothless, merely symbolic policy, there is has been an incredible amount of discussion, analysis and action over the last thirty years.

Second, there is scant evidence to suggest that the expenditure of billions of dollars of public funds on the whole range of issues under the rubric of multiculturalism has achieved nothing. If we examine the two stock-taking reports prepared for the Canadian Secretariat for the World Conference Against Racism, Racial Discrimination, Xenophobia and Related Intolerance (Jedwab et. al. 2001, Davis and Brant Castellano 2001) we discover the depth of enquiry into diversity issues that has taken place over the last twenty years. If we expand further and examine the breadth of research, as represented by the inventory of graduate research compiled by Mulholland (2001), we see a clear commitment, on the part of Canadians and their governments, to know more about multiculturalism in Canada and to effect change for the better. The planned index of inclusion/exclusion will also provide concrete examples of change that can be tracked longitudinally.

Third, not all human beings are profit maximizers. To decry any activity that is not economically-focused is to omit an incredible portion of the lives of Canadians. In addition, in a perfect world, the social, cultural, economic and political arenas would be equally occupied by men and women. We do not live in a perfect world. Women are still disproportionately responsible for the social and cultural aspects of our lives and seniors are largely outside of the formal economic arena. To eliminate any serious consideration of cultural and social elements of our lives leads to the systemic underestimation and belittlement of the role of many women and seniors in Canadian society. The question posed by *Toronto Star* emeritus editor, Haroon Siddiqui at the Fifth National Metropolis Conference in October 2001, still rings in my ears:

"How do we value a grandmother?" She may not earn dollars, but she contributes extensively to the quality of life of her extended family, and she enables the parents of the grandchildren to participate in the economy or to pursue educational goals. Census questions on unpaid work could certainly be brought to bear on this interesting question. Issues of voluntarism also need to be explored further.

Threat to the Status Quo

The third major critique of multiculturalism that litters the discourse, is the threat diversity poses to the status quo. Critics are well represented here by Richard Gwynn's *Nationalism Without Walls: The Unbearable Lightness of Being Canadian* (1995) in which he decries the end of the "tram lines of Canadian history." Chapters by Gairdner (1990) "The Silent Destruction of English Canada: Multiculturalism, Bilingualism and Immigration" and Bissoondath (1994) "Losing the Centre" are just variations on a theme. This critique plays itself out in two large ways, one through the lament for "national" history, and the other through the evolution of "national" symbols. The history debate is most apparent around Canada Day when the Dominion Institute surveys on knowledge of select Canadians and Canadian events have become de rigeur in all major newspapers. It also reached a boil with Jack Granatstein's *Who Killed Canadian History?* (1998). In a link back to the first critique Granatstein wrote, "Now it may only be a coincidence that the turn away from national and political history took place at the same time that Canada began to fragment. Did the historians' shift to victimization and blame-seeking on the fringes, to a peoples' history, and to abstract, abstruse language lead Canada's plunge toward dissolution, or did it merely reflect what was happening in the body politic? ... Tragically, at a time when it was critical that Canadians understand their political and constitutional history, historians wanted to talk tiny, trivial subjects of little or no general interest" (1998: 77). His doomsday scenario fits well with the social cohesion perspective which suggests that diversity represents "fault-lines" which threaten the Canadian social fabric. A whole body of literature counters Granatstein's claim and suggests that a "national" history lost credibility because it omitted the stories of many Canadians and their communities. Timothy Stanley's "Why I Killed Canadian History: Conditions for an Anti - Racist History" (2000) rebuts Granatstein's view and argues that a meta-narrative is necessarily exclusionary and we would be better served by many small histories. His point is hammered home by work of historians like Jim Walker (1999), Constance Backhouse (1999), and Olive Dickason (1997) who unearth many elements of the Canadian experience overlooked by the "national" histories advocated by Granatstein.

The second major threat to the status quo surrounds the evolution of "national" symbols. This critique is best exemplified by the millinery issues which have exploded in the Canadian media over the last decade: the hijab in Quebec schools, and the turban in legion halls or as part of the Royal Canadian Mounted Police's dress uniform. If we consider the latter the illusion underpinning the critique is clear. The RCMP are a symbol of Canadian nationhood that harks back to pre-Confederation and to an era when Canadian society was overwhelmingly composed of people of British or French origin. However, as *Ottawa Citizen* journalist Tom Spears noted, "for a uniform that everybody recognizes, mountie garb has undergone an incredible number of changes over the years" (Spears 1998: A6). The key point to consider is that symbols emerge and evolve over time. This is always the case and a causal link to multiculturalism is dubious at best. Further research into the evolution of symbols would further enhance our knowledge in this area. Daniel Francis goes further and skewers many of our "long-standing" symbols in his enlightening *National Dreams: Myth, Memory and Canadian History* (1997). Tellingly, he observes that, "It turns out that many of our cherished myths were invented by government agencies or private corporations for quite specific, usually self-serving purposes. Canadians as a whole then embraced them because they seemed to express something that we wanted to believe about ourselves" (9). The question is what did we want to believe?

Canadians and their governments continually negotiate the limits on what is acceptable. What multiculturalism assures is that all Canadians will have a say in the rules by which we choose to collectively live.

Cultural Relativism or There are No Limits

The last of the major critiques is the argument put forward by Reginald Sibby in his *Mosaic Madness: The Poverty and Potential of Life in Canada* (I990), and by Bissoondath (I994) in a chapter entitled "The Limits of Diversity". The essence of this critique is that if all cultures and all cultural practices are equally valid, then society will cease to function because we will be unable distinguish between the good and the bad. The most well known example in this area is female genital operations/mutilation or female circumcision.

To me, at least, this appears to be the most specious of the critiques covered here. Alissa Levine (1999) also questions the Canadian approach on this issue. Even a superficial reading of the *Charter of Rights and Freedoms and the Criminal Code of Canada,* not to mention an entire body of legislation and judicial decisions, argue that this is not the case. Neil Bissoondath (1994) and Naomi Lakritz (1998) cite a number of examples of judges who overstepped the mark in decisions that can only be considered outliers as proof that multiculturalism knows no bounds.

From where I sit, there are boundaries. Yes, they are flexible and subject to change from legislation and judicial decisions, but how many legal parameters in Canada are not subject to change? It is my contention Canadians and their governments continually negotiate the limits on what is acceptable. What multiculturalism assures is that all Canadians will have a say in the rules by which we choose to collectively live. Far from a violation of democratic principles, I believe this kind of inclusion is fundamental to democracy.

Conclusions

Clearly there is work to be done. As a basic starting point the discourse surrounding multiculturalism needs to be informed. Critics and proponents need to bring research that substantiates their points of view to the discussion. It is easy to disparage critics who neglect to document any sources in their work, but it is equally important to hold proponents of multiculturalism to account for the generalities that they can spout with regularity.

Longitudinal research frameworks, which can form the spine of the endeavours in this field, must be developed and implemented. Initiatives like Metropolis, which bring key policy figures (federal, provincial and municipal), researchers from across the country (centres of excellence already exist in Vancouver, Edmonton, Toronto and Montreal, and an Atlantic Centre is expected to start April 1 , 2003), and practitioners together are a start. Data sources from Statistics Canada like *The Ethnic Diversity Survey* will yield more valuable information. The inclusion of ethnicity in survey design for government-wide data gathering instruments and on public opinion polling would both meet the requirements of the *Act* and provide knowledge to guide public discourse.

The much maligned Annual Report on the Operation of the Multiculturalism Act could be redesigned to enhance its efficacy. I believe that Bohdan Kordan (1997) has it wrong when he writes of the report, it "is unquestionably an inadequate instrument." By creating an index of inclusion/exclusion, which is presented and tested at the annual Metropolis and Policy Research Initiative Conferences, and is highlighted as the first chapter of the annual report, continuity could be established and priorities for enquiry in the coming year could be flagged. Equally, the connection to cross-government initiatives, be they skills and innovations or social cohesion, could be highlighted in the report each year. As the key source document on multiculturalism as official policy, the Annual Report is frequently referenced in research and policy design. It should, therefore, be part of an integrated longitudinal design to report on where we collectively find ourselves on a range of issues arising from diversity.

Finally, at the outset of official multiculturalism, regular conferences were designed to bring the key players from across the country together. A return to this format would enable key research findings, policy considerations and past practices to be shared broadly. If each conference focused on a particular issue (say, institutional development in health care), past practices and research could be used to design future work that would assist us all in dismantling the barriers which continue to persist in the social, economic, cultural and political realms of Canadian society. These conferences would also go a long way to ensuring that the heated discourse around multiculturalism is based on knowledge and not ignorance.

Testing "The Canadian Diversity Model": Hate, Bias and Fear After September 11th

John Biles and Humera Ibrahim

2002

In the 2001 annual report of the Canadian Human Rights Commission, Chief Commissioner Michelle Falardeau-Ramsay observed, "Canada has a reputation as a place where people from every corner of the world can live in harmony with mutual respect and tolerance that reputation is well-deserved. But in the fall of 2001, our respect for each other was put to the test. In some ways, our response was admirable; in other ways, not so" (Canadian Human Rights Commission 2002: 4).

The reputation to which the commissioner refers is one that has been built most extensively since the end of the Second World War (Dreisziger 1988, Jaworsky 1979; Joshee 1995, Pal 1 993, and Schiffer-Grahame 1989), but one which other researchers suggest has been developing for well over a century (Biles and Panousos 1999; Day 2000). While far from a coherent 'model' *per se*, the Canadian approach to fashioning a country composed of extremely diverse peoples does have some core elements: an emphasis on bringing Canadians of diverse backgrounds together; fostering a culture of inclusion; and a commitment to core values of equality, accommodation and acceptance.

This approach has been largely driven by Canadians themselves and is an amalgam of initiatives of individuals, communities, different levels of government and judicial decisions.

Of late there has been a number of attempts to meld this approach into an explicit "Canadian Diversity Model." Two of the most recognizable attempts are Prime Minister Jean Chretien's "Canadian Way" speech at a conference on "Progressive Governance for the 21st Century" in Berlin 2-3 June, 2000 and a paper commissioned by the Department of Canadian Heritage from the Canadian Policy Research Network (2001) entitled, "The 'Canadian Diversity Model': Repetoire in Search of a Framework."

These attempts to articulate a coherent model are matched by a number of stock-taking exercises in the field of diversity undertaken by the Multiculturalism Program

"Testing 'The Canadian Diversity Model' Hate, Bias and Fear After September 11th" by John Biles and Humera Ibrahim, *Canadian Issues,* September 2002. Reprinted with the permission of John Biles and Humera Ibrahim as well as the Association for Canadian Studies.

and other elements of the Department of Canadian Heritage. In preparation for the World Conference Against Racism, Racial Discrimination, Xenophobia and Related Intolerance (WCAR), two major exercises were undertaken. The first was a series of consultations with communities across the country, and the second was a pair of research studies that examined reports made to governments in Canada over the last twenty years in the broad field of diversity (Jedwab et. al. 2000, Davis and Brandt Castellano 2000). Each was designed to gauge the state of our "diversity model" and ascertain where future work needed to be targeted. In addition, a database of Canadian graduate work on diversity in the last twenty years was prepared for the Multiculturalism Program (Mulholland 2001). Collectively, these stock-taking exercises painted a picture of an actively engaged population.

Thus, many Canadians, non-governmental organizations and the Government of Canada were engaged in an exercise to refocus the "Canadian Diversity Model" to tackle new and emerging issues and to focus on entrenched issues that had not been successfully addressed. A sizeable Canadian delegation attended WCAR in Durban South Africa in early September 2001. Many of the delegation had not returned to Canada when all commercial air traffic ground to a halt in North America in the wake of the terrorist attacks on the twin towers in New York City, the Pentagon and in Pennsylvania.

Post-September 11th Backlash

Canadians and the Government of Canada were not resting upon their diversity laurels, but were actively trying to figure out how to proceed more effectively. Nevertheless, there was considerable confusion and several Canadian communities paid a price for that confusion. Muslim, Jewish, Hindu and Sikh Canadians all once again found themselves on the receiving end of unjust treatment meted out by their neighbours. Arab Canadians, and in at least one puzzling case Aboriginal Canadians, also found themselves victimized by hate and bias.

Hate and bias activity is notoriously difficult to monitor. Different police forces record incidents differently and there is no centralized reporting structure to allow a truly national comparison. (The Canadian Centre for Justice Statistics at Statistics Canada has examined the issue and has a forthcoming report on how this should be tackled in the future.) As a result, to examine the hate and bias incidents that followed the September 11th, terrorist attacks, we will use a combination of statistics, some collected by non-governmental organizations and others by police forces. The result is a portrait of some of the reported incidents; many more are likely to have gone unreported.

In addition, we will examine the sense of fear that gripped many Canadians following the events of September 11, and the hate crimes and bias activity that followed. This is essential since, as criminologist Julian Roberts notes, "The statistics fail to convey a sense of the true harm inflicted upon the individuals and groups that are the target of hate crimes" (Roberts 1995: 3).

Islamaphobia

As the community most commonly linked to Osama Bin Laden, Muslim Canadians bore the brunt of hate and bias incidents. Although generally those who engage in hate and bias activities are not terribly discerning. For example, a Hindu temple was burnt to the ground, Sikh Canadians reported prejudice and an Aboriginal man was attacked in British Columbia. Jewish Canadians, perennial targets of hate in Canada, were also targeted by hate and bias.

The Muslim Canadian community has settled in Canada in large numbers fairly recently (roughly 600,000 Muslims live in Canada according to community estimates, but most have arrived since the 1970s). As a result, the community is not as institutionally complete as the Jewish community (356,315 Jews lived in Canada in 1991. Jews have been in Canada since the 18th century, but the first big wave came to Winnipeg in the 1870s according to historians Abella (1999) and Tulchinsky (1992)). Nevertheless, a sizeable number of community organizations helped Muslim Canadians contend with the backlash aimed at them. These organizations included the Canadian Muslim Civil Liberties Association, Canadian Labour Congress, Council on American-Islamic Relations Canada, Canadian Council of Muslim Women, Canadian Race Relations Foundation, B'Nai Brith Canada, Canadian Arab Federation, Center for Research Action on Race Relations, Federation of Muslim Women, Canadian Association of Jews and Muslims, Council of Agencies Serving South Agencies, Afghan Women's Organization, Urban Alliance on Race Relations, Ontario Council of Agencies Serving Agencies, Chinese Canadian National Council, Jamaican Canadian Association, and the Canadian Islamic Congress.

The organization that took the lead in tracking hate and bias activities was the Council on American-Islamic Relations Canada (CAIR-CAN). In a press release on November 20, 2001 CAIR-CAN reported 110 anti-Muslim incidents across Canada in the two months following September 11th." When considering these figures, it should be noted that there is likely to be significant differences between incidents that will be reported to a non-governmental organization and those that will be reported to the police. The variance is probably especially pronounced among newcomers to Canada who may have negative perceptions of the justice system shaped by experiences in their country of origin, or by negative experiences with the Canadian justice system. Nevertheless, many incidents were reported to the Toronto Police Service: 57 hate and bias incidents aimed at Muslims were reported in Toronto in 2001: 1 arson, 13 assaults, 2 bomb threats, 5 criminal harassments, 20 mischief, 1 robbery and 15 threat incidents (Toronto Police Service 2001).

Anti-Semitism

The Canadian Jewish community has faced discrimination in Canada for over fifty years, most notably on the eve of the Second World War (Abella and Troper 1983). As a result, the community has developed solid infrastructure to tackle hate and bias. Indeed, much of Canada's hate crime legislation springs from the work of the Jewish community (Walker 2001).

The level of hate and bias is so consistent that B'Nai Brith Canada publishes an annual audit of anti-Semitic incidents. The 2001 Audit reported 286 anti-Semitic incidents in 2001, roughly the same level as 2000, but an increase of 35 % over the figures of five years ago. According to the report 35 % of all incidents were reported in the aftermath of September 11th'", with 20 % in the immediate aftermath and close to an additional 15 % in October (B'Nai Brith 2001).

For 2001, the Toronto Police Service reported 60 incidents of anti-Semitism: 1 mischief, 1 threat, 1 advocate for genocide, 3 assaults, 2 bomb threats, 7 criminal harassment, 7 mischief, 24 threats and 14 willful promotion of hate (Toronto Police Service 200 I). While there were more anti-Semitic incidents than anti-Muslim incidents reported by the Toronto Police Service, it is important to note that the Muslim community was much more likely to experience physical violence than their Jewish counterparts, especially assaults.

Hate and Bias

B'Nai Brith Canada reported that the various police reports across the country report "a spike in hate crimes in general during that volatile period [September-October 2001], targeting minority ethnic and religious groups" (B'Nai Brith 2001). This was reinforced by Krista Foss who reported in *The Globe and Mail* that police in Ottawa and Calgary confirmed that "hate crimes doubled in the 30-day period after the terrorist attacks and police confirmed that the incidents ranged 'from assaults, arson, death threats and bomb threats to slurs yelled out of passing cars, vandalism and venomous e-mails.' Police in Montreal, Calgary and Ottawa reported 40, 24 and 44 hate-related incidents respectively" (CAlR-CAN 2001, Foss 2001: A6).

The Toronto Police Service's "2001 Hate Bias Statistical Report" recorded an increase in reported hate crimes in Toronto from 204 in 2000 to 338 in 2001, a 66 percent increase. The report notes, "The Toronto Police Service received 121 hate occurrences directly related to the terrorist attacks. This figure represents 90 percent of the total increase in hate crimes from the year 2000" (Toronto Police Service 2001).

What stands out most clearly from the statistics is the clear predominance of religious and race related hate crime occurrences. Hate crimes based on religion ballooned from 35 incidents in 2000 to 118 in 2001, representing 36 percent of the total hate crime occurrences. While relatively less frequent, hate crime motivated by nationality also increased dramatically from 9 incidents to 35 in 2001.

Fear

Researchers examining hate and bias activity observe that the crime is against both the individual and the community in general through lingering fear. After September 11th fear gripped much of the western world and it preyed particularly heavily upon the minds of minority communities within western societies.

Allan Fotheringham, a senior journalist, went so far as to observe that the racism facing Canadians in the wake of September 11 was, in fact, terrorism by another name (Fotheringham 2001: 88). The fear felt by the Muslim Canadian community in particular manifested itself in closed schools, cautionary tips on websites, a wallet-sized card advising Canadians of their rights, and a number of children and youth carrying cell phones with a pre-programmed emergency number (Page 2001: A7). One Ottawa woman mused in the *Ottawa Citizen*, "I've always thought that Canada was the land of freedom and multiculturalism, but now it doesn't seem like it. Most Muslims came here seeking a better life, but why do we have to live in fear?" (Zeidan 2001).

Community fear in the immediate aftermath of September 11 came to a particularly ugly head on two occasions. First, when a Muslim teenager was pulled off his bike in Ottawa and badly beaten (Roman and Korn 2001: A4). Second, when a 50-year old Muslim woman was beaten up on a Toronto bus (Madaka 2002: 1). Fear from high profile cases like these two was compounded by a number of anthrax threats directed at the Jewish community. The Toronto Police Service reported 79 criminal biological threats, 19 including hate/bias motivation (Toronto Police Service 2001: 22).

During debate over the *Anti-Terrorism Act* (C-36) the fear felt by Arab and Muslim Canadians was highlighted repeatedly. For example, then president of the Canadian Arab federation, John Asfour, told a parliamentary committee "some members of the community are so afraid of mistreatment that they have stopped leaving their homes" (Tibbets 2001 b). Similarly, a spokesman for the Muslim Lawyers Association, Khalid Baksh told a senate committee "We have issues up and down the line because of this climate of fear . . . C-36 ratchets it up to an unbearable level that you can feel it every time you walk into the community" (Tibbetts 2001c). This fear may have been well-founded. Roco Galati, a lawyer renowned for defending Canadians accused of terrorism, estimated that 800 Muslims and Arabs were detained by Canadian immigration officials following the terrorist attacks (Tibbets 2001 b).

Fear of the state also manifested itself in many ways in the months following September 11. Restrictions on charities following the passage of the *Charities Registration (Security Information) Act* (C-16) led many Muslim Canadians to stop their charitable donations or remittances to "impoverished relatives overseas for fear of being investigated by police" (Tibbetts 2001c). Given the importance of remittances to international development (DeSipio 2000) this may prove to be an extremely harmful outcome. Various security alerts also increased fear in minority communities. For example, in January 2002, as the hunt continued for potential terrorist suspects, the announcement that a Tunisian suspect was sought led to a perceptible level of fear in Montreal's Tunisian community (Brooks 2002a; 2002b).

The extremely contentious issue of profiling was debated widely in public discourse. The announcement of a special police unit in Ontario to "hunt down illegal immigrants with outstanding deportation warrants and deport them" drew both then Premier Mike Harris and one of his security advisors, retired Major-General Lewis Mackenzie, into the debate. They both claimed that racial profiling was a problem and Mackenzie stated "I find that [profiling is] distasteful and only increases tensions," yet at the same time maintained that "closer scrutiny of particular ethnic groups at certain checkpoints is an aspect of security" (Schmidt 2001: A5).

Many proponents of profiling, especially newspaper editorials, argue that it is only common sense that it be allowed (National Post 16 February 2002: A17, Gillis 2001: AS, *Vancouver Sun* 7 June 2002: 13-14, Krauthammer 2002: 60, Morgan 2002: A 14). On the other hand, as political scientist Reg Whitaker pointed out, "[Profiling] inevitably involves actual injustice" (Gillis 2001: AS). This point of view was taken up by the New Democratic Party when it censored the government:

> Just as harmful, though not noted in the Report [Standing Committee on
> Citizenship and Immigration Report on border issues], is a more subtle
> mythology that has emerged that equates immigrants—especially
> refugees—with terrorism. The most disturbing manifestation of this is the
> association by some Canadians of specific groups with a terrorist threat
> based on race or religious beliefs. Incidents including vandalism, insults
> and assaults have been reported across Canada. This is unacceptable and
> a pro-active government response is necessary. Instead, the government
> has sent the exact opposite signal by sanctioning its officials' profiling of
> certain immigrant and refugee applicants . . . (Standing Committee on
> Citizenship and Immigration 2001: New Democratic Party Dissenting
> Opinion).

Critics of profiling argued that it would be ineffective (Berck 2002: A14), or that it put Canada on a slippery slope that would lead to greater racism and discrimination in Canada across the whole spectrum of activities (Hurst 2001: 1\30, Ovenden 2001: A1, Saloojee 2002: AI5).

When polled, Canadians appear almost evenly divided although slightly more in favour of profiling immediately after September 11. In an EKOS poll conducted from September 24-26, 2001, 50 percent of respondents agreed that it was acceptable for police and customs officials to give special attention to individuals of Arabic origin, while 34 percent disagreed and 15 percent opted for neither (Gwyn 2001: A6). However, two months later in an IPSOS-Reid poll only 37 percent of respondents agreed with racial profiling of people of Arab appearance at the border and 36 percent disagreed (Lindgren 2001: A1).

The largest spectre that raised its head over the last year has been the question of internment. The Prime Minister moved quickly to dispel fears, yet constant media references kept the concern in the centre of public discourse (Harper 2001: A8). Minorities in Canada decried the imposition of security measures that limited civil rights and argued that this was the slippery slope to internment (Cooper 2001: A17, Hebert 2001:AI5). The right wing critics of diversity argued that this might be a justifiable measure. Journalist Dan Gardner in the *Ottawa Citizen* noted that 'columnist Diane Francis called for mass arrests under the authority of the (long defunct) War Measures Act" (Gardner 2001: AI8). Even more frighteningly, however, journalist David Warren wrote in the *Ottawa Citizen,* "What I fear is that we are now moving instead in the direction of mass expulsions, and internment camps. And let me make this clear as day: this is not something that I want to see, it is something that I dread. It would represent the death of an important part of our old 'liberal dream' that is also my dream, a closing of the 'open society.' But how can it be prevented, given the way the world is now moving?" (Warren 200 I: A 14).

Mutual suspicion also fuelled fears. While communities were afraid of immigration officials, there was also a fear campaign targeted at then Minister of Citizenship and Immigration, Elinor Caplan, who received 15 to 20 pieces of hate mail per day following September 11th (Aubry 2001 b).

Conclusion

In any exercise as complex as the reaction of Canadians and the Government of Canada there are lessons to be learned that will guide future actions and allow society to handle future crises. This was definitely true post-September 11. To be sure, there were mistakes made, and there are knowledge gaps that need to be addressed. However, no domestic crises emerged that indicated any fundamental failures of "the Canadian diversity model." Indeed, much of the response commends the resilience of Canadians and their communities. In roundtables conducted with Canadian youth, D-Code found that "in the aftermath of September 11 our respondents became more aware of the importance of multiculturalism and tolerance not only in words, but, more importantly, in actions. They indicated that episodes of ethnic intolerance made them more adamant about the need to protect and support multiculturalism as a Core Canadian value" (D-Code 2002: 4). This response and that of Canadians and the Government of Canada suggests that our collective commitment to social inclusion in Canada may have been strengthened rather than weakened by the post-September 11 fallout. This is not to discount the hate, bias and fear that some Canadians experienced. Rather, it is to emphasize that a renewed commitment to eradicating these types of incidents is required.

The complete bibliography for this text can be found at http://www.acs-aec.caje_magazine.html

Focus Questions

1. Why were people like Emily Murphy and Stephen Leacock so concerned about Chinese/non-white immigration? Did their opinions surprise you, given both their relative fame and status and what you may have learned of them before this?

2. What are the current criticisms made about multiculturalism policy, and how do the policy's supporters counter these criticisms?

3. What do you think of the policy? Are you swayed by one side of the argument or another? Is it worth defending? Is it realistic?

4. What effect did 9/11 have on public support for multiculturalism? Why?

17

Us versus U.S.: Defining and Defending Canadian Culture

Introduction

Politicians, pundits, poets, philosophers, journalists, and historians, have frequently commented that while Canadians are never exactly sure of who they are, they are very sure of at least one thing—that they are not American. This assertion is made even in those places and at those times when the cultural and political similarities between the two countries vastly outnumber the differences. Indeed, in the early 1920s, American literary giant Ernest Hemmingway speculated poetically on what he "liked" about both Canadians and Americans, perhaps demonstrating that our differences are less real than imagined. His poems, reprinted in this chapter, first appeared in the *Toronto Star* in 1924, while he worked there as a reporter.

Beyond the poetics, how important are the differences between these two countries? While the economic and cultural clout of the Americans has made many Canadians, in the past and the present, very nervous, it also has led to speculation about whether or not Canada is, or can continue to be, a country independent of its southern neighbour. Consider, for example, the first reading in this chapter, the "Canadian Question," penned in 1891 by Goldwin Smith, one of Canada's foremost journalists and academics. Smith's review of Canada's situation at the end of the nineteenth century led him to believe that union with the United States was actually desirable, if not inevitable. Over a century later, David Taras pondered similar questions about Canadian independence, by exploring the contours of cultural similarity between the two countries, as well as the drive for cultural protection north of the 49th parallel. His essay, "Swimming Against the Current," concludes this chapter's brief, but century-spanning exploration of cultural differences and connections between "us" and the "U.S."

Canada and the Canadian Question
Goldwin Smith
1891

Whether the four blocks of territory constituting the Dominion can for ever be kept by political agencies united among themselves and separate from their Continent, of which geographically, economically, and with the exception of Quebec ethnologically, they are parts, is the Canadian question . . .

Let those who prophesy to us smooth things take stock of the facts. When one community differs from another in race, language, religion, character, spirit, social structure, aspirations, occupying also a territory apart, it is a separate nation, and is morally certain to pursue a different course, let it designate itself as it can. French Canada may be ultimately absorbed in the English-speaking population of a vast Continent; amalgamate with British Canada so as to form a united nation it apparently never can . . .

From British as well as from French Canada there is a constant flow of emigration to the richer country, and the great centres of employment. Dakota and the other new States of the American West are full of Canadian farmers; the great American cities are full of Canadian clerks and men of business, who usually make for themselves a good name. It is said that in Chicago there are 25,000. Hundreds of thousands of Canadians have relatives in the United States. Canadians in great numbers—it is believed as many as 40,000—enlisted in the American army during the civil war . . . A young Canadian thinks no more of going to push his fortune in New York or Chicago than a young Scotchman thinks of going to Manchester or London. The same is the case in the higher callings as in the lower: clergymen, those of the Church of England as well as those of other churches, freely accept calls to the other side of the Line. So do professors, teachers, and journalists. The Canadian churches are in full communion with their American sisters, and send delegates to each other's Assemblies. Cadets educated at a Military College to command the Canadian army against the Americans, have gone to practise as Civil Engineers in the United States. The Benevolent and National Societies have branches on both sides of the Line, and hold conventions in common. Even the Orange Order has now its lodges in the United States, where the name of President is substituted in the oath for that of the Queen. American labour organizations . . . extend to Canada. The American Science Association met the other day at Toronto. All the reforming and philanthropic movements, such as the Temperance movement, the Women's Rights' movement, and the Labour movements, with their conventions, are continental. Intermarriages between

Canadians and Americans are numerous, so numerous as scarcely to be remarked. Americans are the chief owners of Canadian mines, and large owners of Canadian timber limits. The railway system of the continent is one. The winter ports of Canada are those of the United States. Canadian banks trade largely in the American market, and some have branches there. There is almost a currency union, American bank-bills commonly passing at par in Ontario, while those of remote Canadian Provinces pass at par only by special arrangement. American gold passes at par, while silver coin is taken at a small discount: in Winnipeg even the American nickel is part of the common currency. The Dominion bank-bills, though payable in gold, are but half convertible, because what the Canadian banks want is not British but American gold. Canadians go to the American watering-places, while Americans pass the summer on Canadian lakes. Canadians take American periodicals, to which Canadian writers often contribute. They resort for special purchases to New York stores, or even those of the Border cities. Sports are international; so are the Base Ball organisations; and the Toronto "Nine" is recruited in the States. All the New-World phrases and habits are the same on both sides of the Line. The two sections of the English-speaking race on the American continent, in short, are in a state of economic, intellectual, and social fusion, daily becoming more complete. Saving the special connection of a limited circle with the Old Country, Ontario is an American State of the Northern type, cut off from its sisters by a customs line, under a separate government and flag . . .

The isolation of the different Canadian markets from each other, and the incompatibility of their interests, add in their case to the evils and absurdities of the protective system. What is meat to one Province is, even on the protectionist hypothesis, poison to another. Ontario was to be forced to manufacture; she has no coal; yet to reconcile Nova Scotia to the tariff a coal duty was imposed; in vain, for Ontario after all continued to import her coal from Pennsylvania. Manitoba and the North-West produced no fruit; yet they were compelled to pay a duty in order to protect the fruit-grower of Ontario 1500 miles away. Hardest of all was the lot of the North-West farmer. His natural market, wherein to buy farm implements, was in the neighbouring cities of the United States, where, moreover, implements were made most suitable to the prairie. But to force him to buy in Eastern Canada 25 per cent was laid on farm implements. As he still bought in the States, the 25 per cent was made 35 per cent . . .

Without commercial intercourse or fusion of population, the unity produced by a mere political arrangement can hardly be strong or deep . . .

The thread of political connection is wearing thin. This England sees, and the consequence is a recoil which has produced a movement in favour of Imperial Federation. It is proposed not only to arrest the process of gradual emancipation, but to reverse it and to reabsorb the colonies into the unity of the Empire. No definite plan has been propounded, indeed, any demand for a plan is deprecated, and we are adjured to embrace the principle of the scheme and leave the details for future revelation—to which we must answer that the principle of a scheme is its object, and that it is impossible to determine whether the object is practically attainable without a working plan. There is no one in whose eyes the bond between the colonies and the mother country is more precious than it is in mine. Yet I do not hesitate to say that, so far as Canada is concerned, Imperial Federation is a dream. The Canadian people will never part with their self-government. Their tendency is entirely the other way. They have recently . . . asserted their fiscal independence, and by instituting a Supreme Court of their own, they have evinced a disposition to withdraw as much as they can of their affairs from the jurisdiction of the Privy Council. Every association, to make it reasonable and lasting, must have some practical object. The practical objects of Imperial Federation would be the maintenance of common armaments and the establishment of a common tariff. But to neither of these, I am persuaded, would Canada ever consent; she would neither contribute to Imperial armaments nor conform to an Imperial tariff. Though her people are brave and hardy, they are not, any more than the people of the United States, military, nor could they be brought to spend their earnings in Asiatic or African wars . . . Remember that Canada is only in part British. The commercial and fiscal circumstances of the colony again are as different as possible from those of the mother country . . .

Annexation is an ugly word; it seems to convey the idea of force or pressure applied to the smaller State, not of free, equal, and honourable union, like that between England and Scotland. Yet there is no reason why the union of the two sections of the English-speaking people on this Continent should not be as free, as equal, and as honourable as the union of England and Scotland. We should rather say their reunion than their union, for before their unhappy schism they were one people. Nothing but the historical accident of a civil war ending in secession, instead of amnesty, has made them two . . .

That a union of Canada with the American Commonwealth, like that into which Scotland entered with England, would in itself be attended with great advantages cannot be questioned, whatever may be the considerations on the other side or the reasons for delay. It would give to the inhabitants of the whole Continent as complete a security for peace and immunity from war taxation as is likely to be attained by any community or group of communities on this side of the Millennium. Canadians almost with one voice say that it would greatly raise the value of property in Canada; in other words, that it would bring with it great increase of prosperity . . .

Again, Canadians who heartily accept democracy wish that there should be two experiments in it on this Continent rather than one, and the wish is shared by thoughtful Americans not a few. But we have seen that in reality the two experiments are not being made. Universal suffrage and party government are the same, and their effects are the same in both Republics. Differences there are, such as that between the Presidential and the Cabinet system, of a subordinate kind, yet not unimportant, and such as might make it worthwhile to forego for a time at least the advantages of union, supposing that the dangers and economical evils of separation were not too great, and if the territorial division were not extravagantly at variance with the fiat of Nature. The experiments of political science must be tried with some reference to terrestrial convenience. Besides, those who scan the future without prejudice must see that the political fortunes of the Continent are embarked in the great Republic, and that Canada will best promote her own ultimate interests by contributing without unnecessary delay all that she has in the way of political character and force towards the saving of the main chance and the fulfilment of the common hope. The native American element in which the tradition of self-government resides is hard pressed by the foreign element untrained to self-government, and stands in need of the reinforcement which the entrance of Canada into the Union would bring it . . .

In the present case there are, on one side, geography, commerce, identity of race, language, and institutions, which with the mingling of population and constant intercourse of every kind, acting in ever-increasing intensity, have brought about a general fusion, leaving no barriers standing but the political and fiscal lines. On the other side, there is British and Imperial sentiment, which, however, is confined to the British, excluding the French and Irish and other nationalities, and even among the British is livelier as a rule among the cultivated and those whose minds are steeped in history than among those who are working for their bread; while to set against it there is the idea, which can hardly fail to make way, of a great continent with an almost unlimited range of production forming the home of a united people, shutting out war and presenting the field as it would seem for a new and happier development of humanity . . .

I Like Americans
Ernest Hemmingway
December 15, 1923

I like Americans.
They are so unlike Canadians.
They do not take their policemen seriously.
They come to Montreal to drink.
Not to criticize.
They claim they won the war.
But they know at heart that they didn't.
They have such respect for Englishmen.
They like to live abroad.
They do not brag about how they take baths.
But they take them.
Their teeth are so good.
And they wear B.V.D.'s all the year round.
I wish they didn't brag about it.
They have the second-best navy in the world.
But they never mention it.
They would like to have Henry Ford for president.
But they will not elect him.
They saw through Bill Bryan.
They have gotten tired of Billy Sunday.
Their men have such funny haircuts.
They are hard to suck in on Europe.
They have been there once.
They produced Barney Google, Mutt and Jeff.
And Jiggs.
They do not hang lady murderers.
They put them in vaudeville.
They read *The Saturday Evening Post.*
And believe in Santa Claus.
And they make money.
They make a lot of money.
They are fine people.

"I Like Americans" by Ernest Hemingway, from *The Toronto Star Weekly,* December 15, 1923, as appeared in *Dateline: Toronto: The Complete Toronto Star Dispatches, 1920–1924,* edited by William White.

I Like Canadians
Ernest Hemmingway
December 15, 1923

I like Canadians.
They are so unlike Americans.
They go home at night.
Their cigarettes don't smell bad.
Their hats fit.
They really believe that they won the war.
They don't believe in Literature.
They think Art has been exaggerated.
But they are wonderful on ice skates.
A few of them are very rich.
But when they are rich they buy more horses
Than motorcars.
Chicago calls Toronto a puritan town.
But both boxing and horse racing are illegal
In Chicago.
Nobody works on Sunday.
Nobody.
That doesn't make me mad.
There is only one Woodbine.
But were you ever at Blue Bonnets?
If you kill somebody with a motorcar in Ontario
You are liable to go to jail.
So it isn't done.
There have been over 500 people killed by motorcars
In Chicago
So far this year.
It is hard to get rich in Canada.
But it is easy to make money.
There are too many tearooms.
But, then, there are no cabarets.

"I Like Canadians" by Ernest Hemingway, from *The Toronto Star Weekly*, December 15, 1923, as appeared in Dateline: *Toronto: The Complete Toronto Star Dispatches, 1920–1924,* edited by William White.

If you tip a waiter a quarter
He says "Thank you"
Instead of calling the bouncer.
They let women stand up in the streetcars.
Even if they are good-looking.
They are all in a hurry to get home to supper
And their radio sets.
They are fine people.
I like Canadians.

Swimming Against the Current: American Mass Entertainment and Canadian Identity
David Taras
2000

JOHN MEISEL, A much-respected Canadian scholar and a former chairman of the Canadian Radio-Television and Telecommunication Commission, once argued that "Inside every Canadian whether she or he knows it or not, there is, in fact, an American. The magnitude and effect of this American presence in us varies considerably from person to person, but it is ubiquitous and inescapable."[1] According to Meisel, many Canadians, especially heavy TV viewers, look to the United States for their cultural orientation. Their cultural compasses point south. They watch blockbuster Hollywood movies and hit TV shows, follow American celebrities, tune in to American talk TV and newsmagazines, cheer for US sports teams and plan dream vacations in theme cities such as Las Vegas, Orlando or Nashville. These Canadians tend to have little interest in Canadian programming and don't want their tax dollars spent defending or promoting Canadian culture.

According to Meisel, the degree of infatuation with, or better still submersion into, American culture, however, often depends on one's level of education. Those who are better educated, and thus less likely to watch television, are much more likely to be consumers of Canadian culture. One can even argue that these educated Canadians form a defensive wall preventing Canadian culture from being completely overrun.

Meisel was later to alter his position, arguing that Canadian culture could survive and even flourish amid the relentless pounding surf of American images, tastes and products because there are certain constituencies whose natural allegiance is to Canadian culture.[2] They exist and find their *raison d'etre* within a Canadian world. But Meisel's argument is still a chilling one. There are Canadians who inhabit media worlds that are largely American, and this, in the long run, may shape their commitments as Canadian citizens and voters.

This chapter will look at the differences between the Canadian and American media worlds. I will focus on the different structures and traditions in Canadian and American television and on the economic realities that underpin both systems. I will also compare the concentration of ownership in the Canadian newspaper industry with that found in the United States and discuss the particular problems that arise from the fact that the industry in Canada is controlled by a very few individuals and corporations. The chapter will also examine the controversy that surrounds "split runs" and what some observers see as an American assault on the Canadian magazine industry.

TV, magazines and newspapers are the central nervous systems of cultural transmission. Canadians watch on average 23 hours of television per week or, to put it differently, we spend nearly one full day out of every week glued to our TV sets. Magazines are devoured by millions of readers each week and over 5 million newspapers are sold every day in Canada. When scholars argue that Canada has a "media-constructed public sphere," they are making the point that public life in Canada, our sense of place and of society, comes to us through the mass media. If our media system fails us in some way, if our public spaces are closed off so that Canadians can't communicate with each other, then the society as a whole is weakened.

A central theme is that Canadians must come to terms with the sheer size and overwhelming power of the American media colossus. Unlike Asians or Europeans, we don't have the luxury of being able to observe the American media system from a safe and comfortable distance, and from behind the protective dikes of a different language and religion. The American system is our system as well. For better or worse, Canadians have to carve out their own identity while living within an American media bubble.

Hollywood and Canadian Broadcasting

It would be a mistake to view American network television as a distinct economic and social force. American TV networks are but spokes in much larger wheels. They are in every case part of what can only be described as huge entertainment or communication conglomerates. Disney owns ABC. General Electric controls NBC. The Fox network is part of Rupert Murdoch's giant News Corporation. Viacom, which controls Paramount Pictures, Blockbuster Video, and Simon and Schuster publishing among other companies, recently gobbled up CBS. The fledgling USA network is allied with and largely controlled by Seagram which owns Universal. And the newest kid on the block, Warner TV, is but an offshoot of AOL-Time Warner, a mammoth entertainment company that holds a large number of cable TV properties including CNN, Cinemax and HBO. American TV networks can only be understood within this wider context.

The Fox television network provides a good example of how the machinery of American television works. Fox Broadcasting is only a small part of Rupert Murdoch's News Corporation empire, an empire that includes almost all aspects of media production, distribution and publicity. The hub of the wheel is 20th Century Fox, a film and TV studio that has produced such hits as *Titanic, The Simpsons, South Park* and *The X-Files.* The distribution arm includes the TV network, a myriad of cable channels such as Fox News, a 24-hour all news channel, Fox Sports Net, and the Family Channel. In addition News Corporation owns flagship TV stations in New York, Los Angeles, Chicago, Washington, Philadelphia and Atlanta as well as in 15 other American cities, and satellite television systems in Asia and Europe. Murdoch also owns the world's largest newspaper chain, a bevy of magazines and supermarket tabloids and sports franchises such as the Los Angeles Dodgers and the LA Lakers and Kings. It would be a mistake therefore to see Fox Broadcasting as an entity that has to make money or survive on its own. Its TV programs are integrated into—are subsumed within—a larger corporate matrix.

The hit series, *The X-Files*, for instance, provides a vivid illustration of the way in which TV programs are used as a springboard for a host of other media productions and products. The program is, in effect, a brand name that is used and promoted, pumped and squeezed, by a number of arms within News Corporation. *The X-Files* has been the basis for a blockbuster movie, videos, a video game, books, various board games as well as calendars, posters, magazines and T-shirts. Murdoch's cohort of newspapers, magazines, and TV stations ensures that the program is endlessly promoted and some would argue continuously showered by favourable publicity.

The surface impression is that the major American TV networks are dying a slow death because they attract only a declining share of the audience. The explosion in the number of satellite and cable channels, competition from an increasing number of independent stations, the growing video rental market, and the Internet revolution have diverted and fragmented audiences. Where in the 1970s, the three US networks, CBS, NBC and ABC, commanded 98% of the audience, by the year 2000 their audience numbers had plunged to well below 50%. But this portrait is to some degree an optical illusion because it sees the US networks as stand-alone operations rather than as part of a wider corporate and media mix. The same companies that own the US networks also own lucrative cable franchises, and there is a great deal of cross-fertilization between network and cable operations. Disney, which owns ABC, also owns a number of cable gold mines such as ESPN, A&E and the Disney Channel. News Corporation, which owns the Fox network, also owns cable channels such as Fox News, Fox Sports Net and the Family Channel. NBC is linked with the powerful financial channel, CNBC, and to the cable and Internet broadcaster MSNBC that it owns together with Microsoft. Viacom's cable treasure trove includes MTV, Nickelodeon, Comedy Central, Showtime, Country Music Television and the Nashville Network in addition to its ownership of CBS.

When all is said and done, American TV networks have the advantage of economics of scale. With a domestic market that is roughly 10 times the size of Canada's, American TV producers have ample opportunity to recover their costs in their home market. This allows them to dominate the international market place by selling their programs at cut-rate prices. Canadian broadcasters can buy shows "off the shelf" Hollywood for between one-fifth and one-tenth of the costs of production.[3] It is cheaper to buy an American program than it is to produce a Canadian show from scratch.

The dominant position of US network shows is continually reinforced by the fact that Hollywood TV shows simply have more production value—they boast more production fire power—than Canadian, Australian or European programs. With budgets of $2-3 million (US) per episode or more, hit US shows can overpower the competition. They have been audience tested, have better technical quality, can afford more expensive sets, are buttressed by teams of highly paid writers and other talent, boast a cavalcade of recognizable stars, and are hyped and marketed by huge global media conglomerates that own newspapers, magazines and other media.

Canadian television is built on different foundations and has different objectives. The Canadian system is heavily subsidized by the federal government and has a crown corporation, the CBC-Radio-Canada, as one of its main engines. While American television does have a public component, the Corporation for Public Broadcasting, which controls the Public Broadcasting Service (PBS) and National Public Radio (NPR), receives far less government funding than the CBC and is heavily dependent on corporate sponsorships and membership drives.

The Canadian television system is a complex hybrid of very different options and entities. At the core is the publicly funded CBC-Radio-Canada. But there are also educational and community channels such as Now TV, TV Ontario and Radio-Quebec, which are supported by private cable operators or provincial governments. Private networks such as CTV, Global, the French-language TVA and a host of independent stations attract the lion's share of the audience. In addition there is a long picket fence of specialized cable services including such channels as TSN, Newsworld, YTV, History Television, Space: The Imagination Station, and Much Music as well as a tier of pay-per-view choices.

Even the CBC is a phalanx of networks and services. The CBC consists of the main English- and French-language TV channels, Radio One (AM) and Radio Two (FM) in both languages, Newsworld and the Reseau de L'Information, both 24-hour all-news networks, Newsworld International, which only broadcasts outside of Canada, northern services that broadcast in native languages, Radio Canada International, and a very extensive and impressive web site. The CBC remains the largest journalistic organization in Canada with almost one in five Canadian journalists working for the crown corporation. Roughly 70% of its schedule is devoted to what can be described as news and current affairs programming.

In 1997-98, the CBC had a total operating budget of $1,128 billion with two-thirds of that money coming from an annual grant from Parliament, a grant that has been reduced by approximately one-third over the last decade. The rest of the CBC's budget came from advertising, sales and other revenues. Unlike the American networks that are driven wholly by commercial imperatives and aim their programs at demographic groups that have high incomes, the CBC has a mandate geared to public needs and services. The mandate is enshrined in the Broadcasting Act of 1991 which stipulates that the public broadcaster must, among other duties:

1. offer programs that are uniquely Canadian
2. "contribute to shared national consciousness and identity"
3. give expression to regional and linguistic differences as well as reflect the country's multicultural spirit
4. provide programming that "informs, enlightens and entertains."

The CBC is also the broadcaster of record, covering the major events of the Canadian political calendar. The CBC is there to cover federal and provincial elections, the opening of Parliament, federal and provincial budgets, Canada Day festivities and Remembrance Day services, and events of national significance such as the signing of the Nisga'a Treaty or the funeral for Jean Drapeau, the legendary mayor of Montreal. While commercial broadcasters may cover some of these events they are unlikely to provide the wall-to-wall in-depth coverage that the CBC does. They are leery about any kind of programming that will not draw audiences and advertisers, the bread and butter of their existence. They are more than happy to leave this kind of public affairs coverage to the CBC.

In the last decade the CBC has been wounded by budget cuts that have made it far more difficult for the public broadcaster to fulfill its mandate. With its budget having been reduced by at least one-third, the CBC has been in a continual state of disarray. Thousands of employees have been let go, stations have been closed, major projects have been shelved, shows are broadcast repeatedly and schedules have been turned inside out. All of this bleeding has made the CBC less attractive and less competitive. The CBC's audience share plummeted from almost 22% in 1984-85 to less than 10% in 1999.[4]

Perhaps the most important provisions of the Broadcasting Act, what some consider its heart and soul, are the Canadian content requirements. "CanCon" applies to television as well as radio. TV broadcasters must set aside 60% of their daily schedule for Canadian content programs. Commercial broadcasters can reduce their CanCon programming to 50% during prime time (6 P.M. to midnight). But under recent changes, they must also provide at least eight hours of Canadian drama per week in that lucrative time period. To qualify as Can Con, Canadian programs are judged according to a point system. Points are awarded based on the citizenship of key production personnel—performers, editors, writers, and so on, and on the percentage of services supplied by Canadians. In all cases the producer must be Canadian. If a program receives a score of 10 out of 10 then, in effect, the board lights up and extra Can Con time credits are awarded.

Canadian content provisions have been criticized from a number of perspectives. W.T. Stanbury, a professor of business at the University of British Columbia believes that the imposing of Can Con requirements could be considered a violation of a citizen's right to freedom of expression.[5] His argument is that by dictating the nationality of the people that are allowed to make TV programs, the Broadcast Act has narrowed the choices available to citizens. Viewers have a right to be exposed to any and all views, and to all forms of cultural expression, to be open to the world of influences, regardless of borders and nationalities. Others argue, of course, that without Can Con commercial broadcasters in particular would have little incentive to air Canadian programs at all because they can make far more money buying programs in Hollywood than making original shows in Canada. Canadians would, in effect, be exposed to stories from across the globe but see little of our own reflection on TV.

Another problem is that Can Con as presently defined does not deal with program content. In what some see as the convoluted and twisted world of Can Con, a program can be about pollution on Australian beaches or gambling in Las Vegas and still qualify as Canadian content. The measure, the yard marker, is not whether Canadian themes or issues are being addressed but simply the citizenship of those who produce, act in or work on the program. If the TV show or film is over the high jump bar in terms of Canadian citizens, then the actual content doesn't matter. Theoretically a program could feature great Canadian divas such as Celine Dion or Shania Twain, and therefore qualify as CanCon, even though their songs might not mention Canada in any way.

Another problem is that with the advent of new information technologies, Can Con may become obsolete simply because such regulations will be impossible to enforce. In an era when all media are merging one into the other, when the telephone, cable, satellites and computer are all converging, the imposition of national standards may be impossible. For instance, it won't be long before virtually everything on the World Wide Web will be available on television. Viewers relaxing with their proverbial beer and chips will be able to access web sites from anywhere on the globe, and many of these sites will contain programming. In the new world, the defensive walls that were erected to defend cultural sovereignty are likely to come tumbling down. Some argue that CanCon's days are numbered.

The philosophy adopted by the Canadian Radio-television and Telecommunications Commission (CRTC), the body that regulates all aspects of Canada's electronic highway, is that everything should be done to make commercial broadcasting profitable. The presumption is that as broadcasters such as CTV, Global and TVA became stronger, they will spend more on Canadian programming. To ensure profits, however, governments have stepped into the breach, buttressing commercial broadcasters with subsidies, tax breaks and other advantages. It is also argued that broadcast regulations are weighted—are tilted—so that they favour commercial broadcasters.

First, commercial broadcasters are shielded to at least some degree from the full force, the full onslaught, of US network competition. Through what is known as simultaneous substitution, American TV signals are blocked, erased, when Canadian and American stations air the same programs at the same time. In fact, Canadian broadcasters often deliberately jig their schedules so that they broadcast hit series like

Frasier, E.R and *Friends* at the same times that the programs are being aired on American stations. Thus viewers receive Canadian feeds, and most crucially Canadian advertising, instead of signals from across the border. According to one estimate, simulcasting brings roughly $100 million annually into the coffers of Canadian networks.

Canadian broadcasters also benefit from provisions of the Income Tax Act which discourage Canadian companies from advertising on US border stations. Without this tax wall, TV stations in places like Plattsburg, N.Y, Buffalo, Detroit or Seattle, whose signals spill across the border, would draw tens of millions of dollars in advertising each year away from their Canadian competitors.

Canadian broadcasters, including the CBC, also benefit from an array of funding programs and tax breaks. The Canadian Television and Cable Production Fund (three-quarters of which comes from the federal government and the rest from the cable industry) and Telefilm Canada play a major role in launching TV and film projects. Their funding often mean the difference between life and death for a film or TV series. Without this crucial injection of capital, quite a number of important Canadian programs would never have seen the light of day. Programs such as *Cold Squad, Traders, Road to Avonlea, The Newsroom, More Tears, The City* and *Due South* among other shows were nurtured on a thick broth of public funds. Added to the mix are generous federal and provincial tax breaks that are used to offset a significant portion of labour and location costs. When all is said and done, public money often accounts for well over 50% of the costs of producing a Canadian film or TV series.

Critics argue that the existence of "hit" Canadian programs has done little to wean private broadcasters off American programming. The great irony is that the basic economics of the broadcasting industry run counter to and undermine the objectives of the federal government's policy. In order to become profitable and hence more Canadian, commercial broadcasters have first had to become more American. The bottom line is that it is far more profitable to buy shows in Hollywood—with their glitz and stars, almost guaranteed audiences and advertisers and heavy promotion in the US media—than to produce a Canadian program from scratch. Producing Canadian shows not only involves an enormous creative and financial effort, but it also entails tremendous risks. Unlike US shows that have the benefit of a large domestic market. Canadian producers have to sell their shows in the US and overseas in order to recoup their costs. And while big media empires can' afford to have a number of shows that flop, a couple of big misses can be catastrophic to—can sink—a Canadian company or even a network.

While Canadian broadcasters have made great strides in terms of bringing Canadian stories to the TV screen, they also know that American shows are their proverbial meat in the sandwich. According to statistics from one Canadian network, American TV shows bring in approximately $2 in revenue for every dollar that they cost. Canadian shows bring in roughly 62 cents for every dollar that is invested.[6] The deficit with regard to Canadian programming can be put another way: an hour of

Canadian drama usually costs broadcasters $200,000 in licence and rental fees. Advertising normally brings in only about $125,000 per hour.[7]

Small wonder that Canadian commercial TV showcases its US programs. In terms of audience share, which is the gold standard on which the TV industry is based, the top 20 programs in the Toronto market in spring 1998 were all big-ticket American shows.[8] If one factors in the programming from US border stations, cable channels and superstations, the harsh reality is that at least two-thirds of the shows watched by English Canadians are American. Among francophone viewers, who are sheltered by the protective cover of the French language, almost 70% of programs that they watch are Canadian. As Ivan Fecan, the president of CTV, once expressed the basic conundrum of Canadian TV: "People don't watch flags, they watch good shows."[9]

Moreover the situation may be worsening. While the explosion of new channels along the cable frontier has created many important opportunities for new initiatives, this has also led to a fragmentation of the audience. Cable channels have begun to drain viewers away from the main Canadian networks that are the main producers of Canadian television. Indeed in 1999 over 20% of the audience were glued to US and Canadian cable channels.[10] Even within the thick forest of cable offerings, the Canadian presence may be diminishing. The CRTC's decision to allow one new American cable channel in the door for every two Canadian cable services that have been established means that US cable titans such as CNN, HBO, CNBC, A&E and the Learning Channel have access to Canadian audiences.

While the Canadian television industry has had its share of successes and has emerged as an important player on the international stage, the problem of Canadians being saturated by US programs remains a serious one. In fact, to some degree the American media giants that dominate Hollywood are larger and more influential than they have ever been.

The Magazine Wars

To some degree the challenges that the Canadian magazine industry faces are the mirror image of those that have plagued Canadian television. Huge media conglomerates control much of the distribution and use magazines as part of a larger media strategy, American magazines dominate sales, and Canadian magazines are struggling to maintain their footholds in the Canadian market. The federal government, as is the case with television, has passed legislation to protect the magazine industry from the American invasion and provide subsidies to keep the industry afloat. The same drama, with the same actors—massive media empires, the federal government and a fragile vulnerable industry—is played out in a slightly different way.

American magazines, much like US TV networks, are part and parcel of the entertainment conglomerates within which they operate. AOL-Time Warner (AOL-TW), for instance, owns a whole stable of valuable magazine properties—*Time, People, Sports Illustrated, Fortune, Life, Entertainment Weekly, In Style*, and many more.

While these magazines are each expected to turn a profit, they are also promotional vehicles used to pump and spin other AOL-Time Warner media products. They cannot be seen as operating apart from Warner Brothers studios which produces blockbuster films and top-rated TV programs; cable holdings such as CNN, Cinemax and HBO; giant music labels such as Atlantic and Elektra; its impressive publishing arm, Warner Books; America Online, with its 20 million Internet subscribers; sports franchises that include the Atlanta Braves in baseball, the NHL's Atlanta Thrashers and the Atlanta Hawks in basketball, not to mention stadiums and theme parks. For instance, CNN has aggressively linked its programs and web sites with TW magazines. Its show *Sports Tonight* has been teamed with *Sports Illustrated* so that each feeds and supports the other.

In these circumstances, it's often difficult to know where journalism leaves off and self-promotion begins. When the movie *Eyes Wide Shut* was being released in the summer of 1999, *People* magazine featured the film's two stars, Tom Cruise and Nicole Kidman, on its front cover. In this case it was hard to discern whether the magazine was celebrating the release of an intriguing and sensational film, the last Stanley Kubrick epic, or whether the magazine was merely pumping a movie that had been made by Warner Brothers. Similarly when Ted Turner, a Time Warner Vice President, is featured on *Time's* front cover because of his contributions to charity, it's not clear whether the AOL-TW publicity machine is in full throttle or play is being given to a genuine news and human-interest story.

Rupert Murdoch's News Corporation also owns a bevy of important magazines as a result of buying Triangle publications from Walter Annenberg in 1988. Murdoch's holding's include such lucrative titles as *TV Guide, Elle, Seventeen,* and the *Daily Racing Form. TV Guide* is especially valuable since it can be used to promote programs on the Fox network and channels on Murdoch's cable and satellite empire. Apparently Murdoch goes to considerable lengths to ensure that his magazines have pride of place at check-out counters and at newsstands. It is difficult to compete with publications that "own" the prime magazine-buying locations.

The largest publisher of monthly magazines in the US is the Hearst Corporation. Founded by newspaper titan William Randolph Hearst, the subject of a brilliant portrayal by actor and director Orson Welles in the classic film, *Citizen Kane,* the Hearst Corporation has spread its wings into local TV and cable as well as magazines. Its mainstays include name brands such as *Cosmopolitan, Esquire, Popular Mechanics, Good Housekeeping,* and *Town & Country.* Significantly, Hearst has produced magazines and web sites that are offshoots of its cable TV properties—ESPN, The History Channel and Arts & Entertainment among others. A trip to the newsstand becomes an advertisement for other Hearst products.

Not every American magazine, of course, is part of a large media conglomerate. The prestigious Conde Nast is a company that has focused almost exclusively on magazine business. It has specialized in upscale publications such as *Vanity Fair, Vogue, GQ, Tatler,* and *The World of Interiors* that appeal to those with money to spend fashions, beauty products and vacations. And of course there are strong independent voices such as the *Atlantic Monthly, The New Republic,* and *The National Review* that are driven by intellectual or ideological causes.

The Canadian magazine industry is not structured in the same way as the American industry. While one company, Maclean Hunter, has a dominant position in the Canadian market producing such venerable and glossy titles as *Chatelaine, Maclean's, L'Actualite, Flare,* and *Canadian Business* among others, Maclean Hunter is a minor league player compared to its American rivals. It does not own a whole phalanx of other media properties and does not have the capacity to make inroads in the US in the same way that American magazines can flood the Canadian market.

As is the case with other Canadian publishers, Maclean Hunter believes that it is vulnerable and under attack. The problem is the relatively new practice by American magazines of producing "split-run" editions for the Canadian market. Split-runs are special Canadian editions of US publications that keep most of their American content but contain enough Canadian content to be able to qualify as a domestic publication. While *Time* and *Reader's Digest* have been allowed by special exemption to publish split-run editions because they both produced popular Canadian editions before legislation banning split-runs was put in place, it was *Sports Illustrated (SI)* that upset the apple cart when it began publishing split-run editions in 1993. Keeping their American edition largely intact, *SI* would insert articles on Blue Jays baseball or on the NHL into their "Canadian" edition. It would then use the leverage that it had as part of a megamedia corporation to undercut the advertising rates charged by Canadian magazines. Soon as many as 100 other American magazines were threatening to follow *SI's* strategy in leaping across the border.

Fearing that Canadian magazines would be decimated by the onslaught, in 1995, the federal government moved to impose an 80% tax on the advertising revenues garnered from split-run editions. What followed was a rough-and-tumble battle between the US and Canadian governments over access by American magazines to the Canadian market. When the World Trade Organization ruled in favour of Americans in 1997, the federal government responded by passing Bill C-55, a bill designed to limit the amount of Canadian advertising that could appear in a split-run. The American government immediately upped the ante, threatening what amounted to a full-scale trade war if Canada continued to resist the US magazine invasion. With the Americans threatening sanctions against Canadian exports of steel, apparel, wood and plastics, industries that accounted for almost $5 billion a year in exports, the Canadian government finally agreed to a compromise in May 1999. Bill C-55 was amended so that the amount of Canadian advertising that could go into split-runs could be limited to 18% of their total advertising space at the end of three years. If American magazines want to "go over the top" and attract more Canadian advertising, at least half of all of their editorial content will have to be Canadian.

Spokespeople for the Canadian magazine industry reacted to the agreement by predicting virtual doom for the industry. If all of the major US magazines that entered the country sold 18 % of their ad space to Canadian advertisers (and these are often thick book-like editions swollen with ads), there would be only the thinnest of pickings left over for Canadian magazines. Brian Segal, the editor of *Maclean's,* argued that the numbers just don't add up. According to Segal, the top 13 women's magazines in the US sell a total of 19,000 pages of advertising each month. The top seven Canadian women's magazines sell 4,800 pages. With the door open to split-runs, the American magazines would be allowed to eat up 3,000 pages in a small market that previously consisted of only 4,800 pages.[11] In addition, there are concerns that much of what Canadians will read about their own country will be produced by American magazine companies. Writers for magazines such as *Time, Newsweek, Cosmopolitan* or *Fortune,* even if they are Canadian, are likely, it is argued, to see Canada through an American view-finder, unselfconsciously imposing American priorities, styles and perspectives.

Even before this last magazine war, Canadian publishers felt that they were under considerable pressure. American and foreign publications already dominate Canadian newsstands. While Canadian magazines account for some 50 % of all magazine sales including those bought through subscriptions, American publications constitute 80 % of all newsstand sales.[12] Canadian publishers complain about having to fight for space, of being crowded out by the sheet number and popularity of glossy US brand-name magazines.

Following its decision to water down Bill C-55, the federal government faced a deluge of criticism from not only the magazine publishers but from Canadian nationalists generally. They accused the government of buckling under US pressure, of giving up the battle without firing a shot. The federal government's response followed an old familiar pattern. The government promised to provide subsidies to Canadian magazines so that they could withstand the wave of split-run editions that everybody now expects. One is reminded of the famous saying attributed to the ancient philosopher, Thucydides: "The strong do what they can, the weak suffer what they must."

Contending with the Power of Canada's Newspaper Barons

Although the television and magazine industries illustrate some of the differences between the Canadian and American media cultures, similar patterns seem to have emerged in the politics of both industries. Huge American conglomerates dominate much of the Canadian landscape while the federal government mounts protectionist policies that provide much of the oxygen that sustains the Canadian industries. The situation with regard to newspapers is very different. What distinguishes Canadian newspapers from their American counterparts is the enormous concentration of ownership that exists in the Canadian newspaper industry. Aproximately 70 % of Canadian newspaper circulation is controlled by only *three* chains— Hollinger/Southam, Thomson and Quebecor. In the US, 75 % of circulation is in the hands of 19 companies.[13] While some of the American chains are quite large and many American cities lack significant newspaper competition, no ownership group has a lock on entire provinces or segments of the market as is the case in Canada. Moreover, roughly 25 % of American newspapers are independendly owned, including family-run corporations like *The Washington Post* and *The New York Times*, arguably the two most powerful and innfluential newspapers in the United States, if not the world.[14] "In English Canada, only the Toronto Star—sizable media conglomerate in its own right—can be considered an independent voice. *La press"* and *Le Devoir,* arguably the two most influential newspapers in Quebec, can also be classified as being independent.

The name most identified with the Canadian newspaper industry is Conrad Black. Black, through his ownership of Bollinger/Southam, controls close to 60 Canadian newspapers including the newly founded national newspaper, the National Post, and most of the venerable old lions of the Canadian newspaper industry—the *Victoria Times Colonist,* the *Vancouver Sun,* the Vancover Province, the *Calgary Herald,* the *Edmonton Journal,* the *Windsor Star,* the *Ottawa Citizen* the *Gazette* (Monteal), *le Soleil* (Quebec City) and the *Halifax Daily News* among others. Black's newspapers reach approximately 2.4 million readers daily, almost 45 % of total Canadian circulation.[15] His companies own all of the major dailies in five provinces—British Columbia, Alberta, Saskatchewan, Prince Edward Island and Newfoundland. Black's Canadian holdings are only part of a newspaper empire that includes such landmark publications as the *Daily Telegraph* (London), the *Jerusalem post* and the *Chicago Sun Times.*

Black's near stranglehold on the Canadian newspaper industry has stirred considerable controversy. Black's critics argue that there is simply too much power in the hands of a single individual. They worry that Black's strong rightwing political beliefs and passions, and his penchant for right-leaning journalists and politicians, are inevitably reflected in the editorial content of the newspapers that he owns. Black hires in his own image, and his publishers are well aware of what will please and what will anger their boss. Critics also point out that Black, who is a British as well as a Canadian citizen, and who spends most of his time in London as a fixture of London high society, has shown a decreasing interest in Canada and tends to see the country as little more than a backwater. But it's the sheer lack of choice, the lack of alternative perspectives, that most concerns critics of the current situation. Not only are many readers trapped in one-newspaper towns, but in many Canadian cities, advertisers have to accept Bollinger/Southam rates or face the prospect of not being able to advertise in newspapers at all.

Observers are also concerned that while the *National Post* has offered competition to the *Globe and Mail* on the national level, thus adding to the editorial choices available to readers, Black has created a two-tiered system within his media empire. While the *National Post* has been made into a flagship newspaper which pays competitive salaries and gives writers a great deal of space for their articles and columns, the fear is that it has reduced other papers in the chain to minor league status. The *National*

Post often takes the best stories away from papers like the *Calgary Herald* or the *Halifax Daily News*, reducing them to reporting strictly local news or to news "lite" accounts of stories that receive greater play in the *Post*. Papers in the farm system are becoming less distinctive as they are forced to fit a "cookie-cutter" mold dictated by head office. Part of the model requires them to cut costs by hiring young reporters at reduced salaries, doing less investigative work and using more wire service copy. In the end, local newspapers have been weakened: some would say that they have been reduced to hollow shells.

Supporters of Conrad Black would dispute everyone of these charges. They would argue that Black is one of the few businessmen who had actually invested in the newspaper business in the last decade. The *National Post* has added to the mix of views available to newspaper readers, and as a national newspaper it has contributed to and strengthened awareness of Canadian arts and culture. And far from having weakened local papers, Black has saved quite a number of papers from extinction. Some papers were in critical condition before Black provided the financial oxygen that they needed to survive.

His supporters also contend that while he has strong—even fierce—political views, he does not meddle in editorial policy. And even if he did, a newspaper baron such as Black has far less influence in shaping public opinion today than was true in the heyday of American newspaper titans such as William Randolph Hearst or Walter Annenberg. They were able to flex raw political muscle by supporting some political leaders while ignoring or damning others. While the extraordinary nature of Black's power is seen as potentially dangerous by some, its also true that satellites, cable and the Internet have expanded horizons so that readers have access to a cacophony of news choices and views. They are not dependent on newspapers, in fact far from it. At the click of a mouse, readers can literally be almost anywhere on the globe. Moreover, there is speculation that newspapers will soon become an endangered species because new information technologies will drastically cut into their advertising and readership.

Those who believe that Black has a grip on too much power are also disturbed by the fact that other newspaper owners seem to share Black's staunch conservative views. Quebecor owns the Sun Media Corporation, with its fleet of tabloid newspapers in Toronto, Calgary, Edmonton, Winnipeg, and Ottawa. It also owns *Le Journal de Montreal,* which has the second largest circulation in Canada, the *London Free Press* and a smattering of other newspapers in Quebec and the Maritimes. Sun President and CEO, Paul Godfrey, a former elected politician, is a rock ribbed conservative. The *Suns'* rough-and-tumble reporting of and fascination with car crashes, celebrities, sports heroes and women's bodies belies an editorial slant that is unabashedly right of centre. The *Suns* are continually cheerleading for many of the same causes that have become the grist for the *National Post's* editorial mill. Critics can also gain little comfort from the editorial positions taken by the *Globe and Mail,* which is owned by the giant Thomson Corporation. The *Globe* is the *National Post's* deadly rival in the battle to remain Canada's national newspaper, and the two seemed locked in a contest for many of the same readers—upscale, business-oriented consumers. Although the *Globe* often focuses on charting social trends and is not afraid to ruffle the feathers of Ottawa politicians of every stripe, its editorial views tend to fall in line with those of the business community. The *Globe's* establishment credentials, its dark grey respectability, are hard to miss.

The issue is not that almost all newspapers tend to be conservative in their editorial policies. If newspapers were all left-leaning or liberal the question would be the same: are readers being given the full range of views that they need in order to make informed judgments about the nature of communities in which they live? Some observers believe that for all of the controversy about ownership, citizens are being provided with a rich smorgasbord of views and perspectives. Owners realize that readers will simply not read newspapers that continually take positions that irritate them, or that fail to provide them with the "spite and spit" that they expect from their newspapers. With so many other media to choose from, newspapers can be easily abandoned. Others claim that Canadians are getting a thin diet of views and have little choice in what to digest.

The structure of the newspaper industry differs considerably from that of television and magazines. Where Canadian television viewers and magazines readers are effectively part of a wider North American market in which Canadian content is a cherished and protected resource, newspapers remain one of Canada's great nationalizing institutions. While American news stories and American wire service copy are part of any newspaper, a national and local focus predominates. Hence newspapers play a critical role in offsetting the integrating power, the north-south gravitational pull, of other media. The future of Canadian cultural sovereignty is likely to be linked at least to some degree with the future of newspapers.

Conclusion

Canadians and Americans largely inhabit the same media universe. As a result, American images, products, priorities and values have become part of the way that Canadians see the world. The American experience as conveyed through the lens of the mass media has also become part of our experience. Yet a distinct, successful and powerful media tradition has taken root in Canada. Institutions like the CBC, *Maclean's, The Globe and Mail,* CTV and *La Presse* are part of the fabric of Canadian life. While each of these institutions is likely to face difficult challenges in the years ahead, especially as new information technologies begin to scramble, reorient and displace the old media, they each have established traditions and loyalties that will not easily be erased.

The issue perhaps is whether a distinct Canadian media system could stand on its own if it were not propped up by protectionist legislation, subsidies and tax breaks. Historically there have been two schools of thought on this question. One school believes that the Canadian media system is strong and vibrant enough to withstand any and all pressures from south of the border. If the protectionist walls were removed, Canadian media industries would still draw audiences and readers and produce distinctive and creative Canadian programs and magazines. Canadians will inevitably turn to their own cultural products, turn to images that reflect their identity and concerns. The more pessimistic position is that without protectionist barriers, the American invasion—the American conquest—would even be more complete than it is today. Canadians are simply, to use Pierre Trudeau's famous analogy, "lying in bed with an elephant." Even if the elephant is a friendly elephant, it still has the capacity to crush anyone who gets too close. Some feel that the elephant has already rolled on top of us, doing a great deal of damage to prospects for Canadian cultural independence.

The two media systems described in this article live in conflict and symbiosis with each other. They are not mutually exclusive, at least from the Canadian point of view. Living with and measuring our own sense of self against the values of American mass culture has long been one of the defining characteristics of being a Canadian. Scholars such as Seymour Martin Lipset argue that Canada emerged in part as a conservative reaction to and rejection of the values of the American Revolution.[16] The question posed by John Meisel is whether we are now so immersed in American culture that there is no longer a clear distinction between who they are and who we are?

Endnotes

1. John Meisel, "Escaping Extinction: Cultural Defence of an Undefended Border," in David Flaherty and William McKercher, eds., *Southern Exposure: Canadian Perspectives on the United States* (Toronto: McGraw-Hill Ryerson, 1986), 12.
2. John Meisel, "Extinction Revisited: Culture and Class in Canada," in Helen Holmes and David Taras, eds., *Seeing Ourselves: Media Power and Policy in Canada* (Toronto: Harcourt Brace Canada, 1996), 249–56.
3. See W.T. Stanbury, "Canadian Content Regulations: The Intrusive State at Work." *Fraser Forum* (August 1998), 49.
4. See *Report of the Mandate Review Committee-GBG, NFB, Telefilm* (Ottawa: Minister of Supply and Services Canada, 1996) and Canadian Broadcasting Corporation. *Annual Report 1997–98: A Summary.*
5. Stanbury. "Canadian Content Regulations," 7.
6. Liss Jeffrey, "Private Television and Cable," in Michael Dorland, ed., *The Cultural Industries in Canada: Problems, Policies and Prospects* (Toronto: Lorimer, 1996), 245.
7. Stanbury, "Canadian Content Regulations," 50.
8. Jacquie McNish and Janet McFarland, "Izzy Asper Ascends to TV's Throne," *Globe and Mail* (August 22, 1998), B5.
9. Quoted in Susan Gittens, *GTV: The Television Wars* (Toronto: Stoddart, 1999), 333.
10. "Canadian Media Director's Council, *Media Digest* 1997–98, 19.
11. Brian Segal quoted in Heather Scoffield, "Publishers Greet Split-run Deal with Dismay," *Globe and Mail* (May 27, 1999), B4.

12. Canada's Magazines," *Globe and Mail* (May 27, 1999), B1.
13. Gene Roberts, "Conglomerates and Newspapers," in Erik Barnouw et al., *Conglomerates and the Media* (New York: The New Press, 1997), 72.
14. Gene Roberts, "Conglomerates and Newspapers."
15. Statistics drawn from Tim Jones, "That Old Black Magic," *Columbia Journalism Review* (March–April 1998),40–43.
16. Seymour Martin Lipset, *Continental Divide: The Values and Institutions of the United States and Canada* (Toronto and Washington: C.D. Howe Institute and National Planning Association, 1990).

Focus Questions

1. What was Goldwin Smith's "Canadian Question" in 1891? Do you think his concerns still apply today? What has—or has not—changed? What were the benefits of annexation, according to Smith?

2. What sorts of contrasts does Hemmingway draw between these two cultures? Do you think his observations were meant to distinguish the two countries, or to point out more important similarities between them?

3. John Meisel, quoted here in David Taras's essay, wrote that "inside every Canadian, whether she or he knows it or not, there is in fact an American." Do you think this is true?

4. Why do so many Canadians react so strongly against the idea that we are simply Americans living on the north side of the 49th parallel?

5. Do you believe that the Canadian government should give financial support, and/or establish protectionist laws for Canadian media outlets? Why or why not? What do you think Goldwin Smith's opinion would be on this issue?

18

Canada on the World Stage: Peacekeeping

Introduction

Lester Bowles Pearson is one of the most well-known of Canada's former Prime Ministers—but not because of something he did while holding that office. At the height of the Suez Crisis in 1957, Pearson advocated for, and engineered the creation of, the United Nations Peacekeeping Force. His action generated international acclaim, and he was awarded the Nobel Peace Prize. As the text of his acceptance speech makes clear, he was devoted to the cause of peace, and acutely aware of the danger of allowing international tensions to devolve into armed conflict. He was, after all, living through the Cold War, when such conflict carried the very real threat of nuclear destruction. Since that time, Canadians have developed an international reputation for their skill and dedication to Peacekeeping. It has become a pillar of Canadian identity.

The end of the Cold War in the late 1980s did not bring an end to global tensions, but it did see the emergence of a very different *kind* of conflict. The threat of nuclear war between nations receded, while civil wars based on religious and ethnic differences, tore countries apart from the inside, out. Peacekeeping quickly became an exercise in *peacemaking,* bringing with it very different challenges and requirements. The second reading in this chapter is an excerpt from Canadian Lieutenant-General Romeo Dallaire's book, *Shake Hands with the Devil.* Dallaire experienced first-hand the inadequacies of Pearson's peacekeeping model to a post-Cold War world, even as Pearson's understanding of the requirements for peace held true. The methods and standards employed by the UN during the Cold War, have been ill-equipped to respond to new global realities, and the results have been catastrophic. Equally troubling, as Dallaire explains, is the western world's apparent indifference to the conflicts like that in Rwanda.

Dallaire's experiences have brought a new, and decidedly uncomfortable element into Canada's Peacekeeping identity. The extraordinary violence, unpredictability, and higher casualty rates of the modern Peacekeeping operation (PKO), have raised concerns about Canadians' continued participation in such activities. As David Pugliese's brief article explores, there has been a notable withdrawal of Canadian forces from PKOs in recent years, particularly as the costs—both human and financial—continue to rise.

The Four Faces of Peace
Lester Pearson
1957

I cannot think of anything more difficult than to say something which would be worthy of this impressive, and, for me, memorable occasion, and of the ideals and purposes which inspired the Nobel Peace Award.

I would like, at the very beginning, to pay my tribute to the memory of a great man, Alfred Nobel, who made this award—and others—possible. Seldom in history has any man combined so well the qualities of idealism and realism as he did, those of the poet and the practical man of business.

We know all about his dynamite and his explosives and how he lamented the use to which they would be put. Yet ideas can also be explosive, and he had many that were good and were deeply concerned with peace and war. He liked to write and talk about the "rights of man and universal brotherhood," and no one worked harder or more unselfishly to realize those ideals, still so far away.

At this moment I am particularly conscious of the wisdom of one of his observations, that "long speeches will not ensure peace."

A great gulf, has been opened between man's material advance and his social and moral progress, a gulf in which he may one day be lost if it is not closed or narrowed. Man has conquered outer space. He has not conquered himself. If he had, we would not be worrying today as much as we are about the destructive possibilities of scientific achievements. In short, moral sense and physical power are out of proportion. This imbalance may well be the basic source of the conflicts of our time, of the dislocations of this "terrible twentieth century."

All of my adult life has been spent amidst these dislocations, in an atmosphere of international conflict, of fear, and insecurity. As a soldier, I survived World War I when most of my comrades did not. As a civilian during the second war, I was exposed to danger in circumstances which removed any distinction between the man in and the man out of uniform. And I have lived since—as you have—in a period of cold war, during which we have ensured, by our achievements in the science and technology of destruction, that a third act in this tragedy of war will result in the peace of extinction. I have, therefore, had compelling reason, and some opportunity, to think about peace, to ponder over our failures since 1914 to establish it, and to shudder at the possible consequences if we continue to fail.

I remember particularly one poignant illustration of the futility and tragedy of war. It was concerned, not with the blood and sacrifice of battles from 1914–1918, but with civilian destruction in London in 1941 during its ordeal by bombing. It was a quiet Sunday morning after a shattering night of fire and death. I was walking past the smoking ruins of houses that had been bombed and burned during the night. The day before, they had been a neat row of humble, red brick, workmen's dwellings. They were now rubble except for the front wall of one building, which may have been some kind of community club, and on which there was a plaque that read, "Sacred to the memory of the men of Alice Street who died for peace during the Great War, 1914–18." The children and grandchildren of those men of Alice Street had now in their turn been sacrificed in the Greater War, 1939–45. For Peace? There are times when it does not seem so.

True there has been more talk of peace since 1945 than, I should think, at any other time in history. At least we hear more and read more about it, because man's words, for good or ill, can now so easily reach the millions. Very often the words are good and even inspiring, the embodiment of our hopes and our prayers for peace. But while we all pray for peace we do not always, as free citizens, support the policies that make for peace, or reject those which do not. We want our own kind of peace, brought about in our own way.

The choice, however, is as clear now for nations as it was once for the individual: peace or extinction. The life of states cannot, any more than the life of individuals, be conditioned by the force and the will of a unit, however powerful, but by the consensus of a group, which must one day include all states. Today the predatory state, or the predatory group of states, with power of total destruction, is no more to be tolerated than the predatory individual.

Our problem, then, so easy to state, so hard to solve, is how to bring about a creative peace and a security which will have a strong foundation. There have been thousands of volumes written by the greatest thinkers of the ages on this subject, so you will not expect too much from me in a few sketchy and limited observations. I cannot, I fear, provide you, in the words of Alfred Nobel, with "some lofty thought to lift us to the spheres."

My aim this evening is a more modest one. I wish to look at the problem in four of its aspects—my "four faces of peace." There is Peace and Trade, Peace and Power, Peace and Policy, Peace and People.

Peace And Trade

One face of peace is reflected in the prosperity of nations. This is a subject on which thought has changed greatly within the memories of most of us and is now, I submit, in process of rapid further change.

Not so long ago prominence was always given to economic factors as causes of war. That was at a time when people sought more assiduously than we now do for rational causation in human behavior. To the philosophers of the nineteenth century it seemed that there must be a motive of real self-interest, of personal gain, that led nations into conflict. To some extent there was. But in this century we have at least learned to understand more fully the complexity of motives that impel us both as individuals and as nations. We would be unwise to take any credit for that. The cynic might well remark that never has irrationality been so visible as in our times, and especially in relation to war.

We know now that in modern warfare, fought on any considerable scale, there can be no possible economic gain for any side. Win or lose, there is nothing but waste and destruction. Whatever it is that leads men to fight and suffer, to face mutilation and death, the motive is not now self-interest in any material sense.

If, however, we no longer stress so much economic factors as the direct cause of war, that does not lessen their importance in the maintenance of a creative and enduring peace. Men may not now go to war for trade, but lack of trade may help to breed the conditions in which men do go to war. The connection is not simple. Rich nations are not necessarily more peace-loving than poorer nations. You do not have to have poverty and economic instability, people do not have to be fearful about their crops or their jobs, in order to create the fears and frustrations and tensions through which wars are made. But poverty and distress—especially with the awakening of the submerged millions of Asia and Africa—make the risks of war greater.

It is already difficult to realize that a mere twenty years ago poverty was taken almost for granted over most of the earth's surface. There were always, of course, a few visionaries, but before 1939 there was little practical consideration given to the possibility of raising the living standards of Asia and Africa in the way that we now regard as indispensable. Perhaps only in North America every man feels entitled to a motor car, but in Asia hundreds of millions of people do now expect to eat and be free. They no longer will accept colonialism, destitution, and distress as preordained. That may be the most significant of all the revolutionary changes in the international social fabric of our times.

Until the last great war, a general expectation of material improvement was an idea peculiar to Western man. Now war and its aftermath have made economic and social progress a political imperative in every quarter of the globe. If we ignore this, there will be no peace. There has been a widening of horizons to which in the West we have been perhaps too insensitive. Yet it is as important as the extension of our vision into outer space.

Today continuing poverty and distress are a deeper and more important cause of international tensions, of the conditions that can produce war, than previously. On the other hand, if the new and constructive forces which are at work among areas and people stagnant and subdued only a few years ago can be directed along the channels of cooperation and peaceful progress, it should strengthen mankind's resistance to fear, to irrational impulse, to resentment, to war.

The higher the common man sets his economic goals, in this age of mass democracy, the more essential it is to political stability and peace that we trade as freely as possible together, that we reap those great benefits from the division of labor, with each man and each region doing what he and it can do with greatest relative efficiency, which were the economic basis of nineteenth-century thought and policy.

Just as we cannot in this day have a stable national democracy without progress in living standards and a sense that the community as a whole participates in those standards, without too great extremes of wealth and poverty, likewise we cannot have one world at peace without international social and economic progress in the same direction. We must have rising living standards in which all nations are participating to such a degree that existing inequalities in the international division of wealth are, at least, not increased. For substantial progress on those lines we need the degree of efficiency that comes only with the freest possible movement of commerce through the world, binding people together, providing the basis of international investment and expansion, and thereby, I hope, making for peace.

Peace and Power

I now come to Peace and Power.

Every state has not only the right but the duty to make adequate provision for its own defense in the way it thinks best, providing it does not do so at the expense of any other state. Every state denies and rejects any suggestion that it acquires military power for any other purpose than defense. Indeed, in a period of world tension, fear, and insecurity, it is easy for any state to make such denial sound reasonable, even if the ultimate aims and policies of its leaders are other than pacific.

No state, furthermore, unless it has aggressive military designs such as those which consumed Nazi leaders in the thirties, is likely to divert to defense any more of its resources and wealth and energy than seems necessary. The economic burden of armaments is now almost overpowering, and where public opinion can bring itself effectively to bear on government, the pressure is nearly always for the greatest possible amount of butter and the smallest possible number of guns.

Nevertheless, defense by power as a first obligation on a state has to be considered in relation to other things than economics. For one thing—and this is certainly true of smaller countries—such power, unless 'it is combined with the defense forces of other friendly countries, is likely to be futile, both for protection and for prevention, or for deterrence, as we call it. This in its turn leads to coalitions and associations of states. These may be necessary in the world in which we live, but they do extend the area of a possible war in the hope that greater and united power will prevent any war. When they are purely defensive in character, such coalitions can make for peace by removing the temptation of easy victory. But they can never be more than a second-best substitute for the great coalition of the whole United Nations, established to preserve the peace, but now too often merely the battle-ground of the cold war.

Furthermore, the force which you and your allies collect for your own security can, in a bad international climate, increase, or seem to increase, someone else's insecurity. A vicious chain reaction begins. In the past, the end result has always been, not peace, but the explosion of war. Arms, produced by fear, out of international tension, have never maintained peace and security except for limited periods. I am not arguing against their short-run necessity. I am arguing against their long-run effectiveness. At best they give us a breathing space during which we can search for a better foundation for the kind of security which would itself bring about arms reduction.

These coalitions for collective defense are limited in area and exclusive in character. And they provoke counter-coalitions. Today, for instance, we have now reached the point where two—and only two—great agglomerations of power face each other in fear and hostility, and the world wonders what will happen.

If the United Nations were effective as a security agency—which it is not—these more limited arrangements would be unnecessary and, therefore, undesirable. But pending that day can we not put some force behind the United Nations which—under the authorization of the Assembly—might be useful at least for dealing with some small conflicts and preventing them from becoming great ones.

Certainly the idea of an international police force effective against a big disturber of the peace seems today unrealizable to the point of absurdity. We did, however, take at least a step in the direction of putting international force behind an international decision a year ago in the Suez crisis. The birth of this force was sudden and it was surgical. The arrangements for the reception of the infant were rudimentary, and the mid wives—had no precedents or experience to guide them. Nevertheless, UNEF, the first genuinely international police force of its kind, came into being and into action.

It was organized with great speed and efficiency even though its functions were limited and its authority unclear. And the credit for that must go first of all to the Secretary-General of the United Nations and his assistants. Composed of the men of nine United Nations countries from four continents, UNEF moved with high morale and higher purpose between national military forces in conflict. Under the peaceful blue emblem of the United Nations, it brought, and has maintained, at least relative quiet on an explosive border. It has supervised and secured a cease-fire.

r do not exaggerate the significance of what has been done. There is no peace in the area. There is no unanimity at the United Nations about the functions and future of this force. It would be futile in a quarrel between, or in opposition to, big powers. But it may have prevented a brush fire from becoming an all-consuming blaze at the Suez last year, and it could do so again in similar circumstances in the future.

We made at least a beginning then. If, on that foundation, we do not build something more permanent and stronger, we will once again have ignored realities, rejected opportunities, and betrayed our trust. Will we never learn?

Today less than ever can we defend ourselves by force, for there is no effective defense against the all-destroying effect of nuclear missile weapons. Indeed their very power has made their use intolerable, even unthinkable, because of the annihilative retaliation in kind that such use would invoke. So peace remains, as the phrase goes, balanced uneasily on terror, and the use of maximum force is frustrated by the certainty that it will be used in reply with a totally devastating effect. Peace, however, must surely be more than this trembling rejection of universal suicide.

The stark and inescapable fact is that today we cannot defend our society by war, since total war is total destruction, and if war is used as an instrument of policy, eventually we will have total war. Therefore, the best defense of peace is not power, but the removal of the causes of war, and international agreements which will put peace on a stronger foundation than the terror of destruction.

Peace And Policy

The third face of peace, therefore, is policy and diplomacy. If we could, internationally, display on this front some of the imagination and initiative, determination and sacrifice, that we show in respect of defense planning and development, the outlook would be more hopeful than it is. The grim fact, however, is that we prepare for war like precocious giants and for peace like retarded pygmies.

Our policy and diplomacy—as the two sides in the cold war face each other—are becoming as rigid and defensive as the trench warfare of forty years ago, when two sides dug in, dug deeper, and lived in their ditches. Military moves that had been made previously had resulted in slaughter without gain, so for a time all movement was avoided. Occasionally there was almost a semblance of peace.

It is essential that we avoid this kind of dangerous stalemate in international policy today. The main responsibility for this purpose rests with the two great world powers, the United States and the USSR. No progress will be made if one side merely shouts "coexistence"—a sterile and negative concept—and "parleys at the summit," while the other replies "no appeasement," "no negotiation without proof of good faith."

What is needed is a new and vigorous determination to use every technique of discussion and negotiation that is available, or, more important, that can be made available, for the solution of the tangled, frightening problems that divide today, in fear and hostility, the two power-blocs and thereby endanger peace. We must keep on trying to solve problems, one by one, stage by stage, if not on the basis of confidence and cooperation, at least on that of mutual toleration and self-interest.

What I plead for 'is no spectacular meeting of a Big Two or a Big Three or a Big Four at the summit, where the footing is precarious and the winds blow hard, but for frank, serious" and complete exchanges of views—especially between Moscow and Washington—through diplomatic and political channels.

The time has come for us to make a move, not only from strength, but from wisdom and from confidence in ourselves; to concentrate on the possibilities of agreement, rather than on the disagreements and failures, the evils and wrongs, of the past.

It would be folly to expect quick, easy, or total solutions. It would be folly also to expect hostility and fears suddenly to vanish. But it is equal or even greater folly to do nothing: to sit back, answer missile with missile, insult with insult, ban with ban.

That would be the complete bankruptcy of policy and diplomacy, and it would not make for peace.

Peace and People

In this final phase of the subject, I am not thinking of people in what ultimately will be their most important relation to peace, the fact that more than thirty millions of them are added to our crowded planet each year. Nor am I going to dwell at any length on the essential truth that peace, after all, is merely the aggregate of feelings and emotions in the hearts and minds of individual people.

Spinoza said that "Peace is the vigor born of the virtue of the soul." He meant, of course, creative peace, the sum of individual virtue and vigor. In the past, however, man has unhappily often expressed this peace in ways which were more vigorous than virtuous. It has too often been too easy for rulers and governments to incite men to war. Indeed, when people have been free to express their views, they have as often condemned their governments for being too peaceful as for being too belligerent.

This may perhaps have been due to the fact that in the past men were more attracted by the excitements of conflict and the rewards of expected victory than they were frightened by the possibility of injury, pain, and death. Furthermore, in earlier days, the drama of war was the more compelling and colorful because it seemed to have a romantic separation from the drabness of ordinary life. Many men have seemed to like war—each time—before it began.

As a Canadian psychiatrist, Dr. G. H. Stevenson, put it once: "People are so easily led into quarrelsome attitudes by some national leaders. A fight of any kind has a hypotic influence on most men. We men like war. We like the excitement of it, its thrill and glamor, its freedom from restraint. We like its opportunities for socially approved violence. We like its economic security and its relief from the monotony of civilian toil. We like its reward for bravery, its opportunities for travel, its companionship of men in a man's world, its intoxicating novelty. And we like taking chances with death. This psychological weakness is a constant menace to peaceful behavior. We need to be protected against this weakness, and against the leaders who capitalize on this weakness."

Perhaps this has all changed now. Surely the glamor has gone out of war. The thin but heroic red line of the nineteenth century is now the production line. The warrior is the man with a test tube or the one who pushes the nuclear button. This should have a salutary effect on man's emotions. A realization of the consequences that must follow if and when he does push the button should have a salutary effect also on his reason.

Peace and People has another meaning. How can there be peace without people understanding each other, and how can this be, if they don't know each other? How can there be cooperative coexistence, which is the only kind that means anything, if men are cut off from each other, if they are not allowed to learn more about each other? So let's throw aside the curtains against contacts and communication.

I realize that contact can mean friction as well as friendship, that ignorance can be benevolent and isolation pacific. But I can find nothing to say for keeping one people malevolently misinformed about others. More contact and freer communication can help to correct this situation. To encourage it—or at least to permit it—is an acid test for the sincerity of protestations for better relations between peoples.

I believe myself that the Russian people—to cite one example—wish for peace. I believe also that many of them think that Americans are threatening them with war, that they are in danger of attack. So might I, if I had as little chance to get objective and balanced information about what is going on in the United States. Similarly, our Western fears of the Soviet Union have been partly based on a lack of understanding or of information about the people of that country.

Misunderstanding of this kind arising from ignorance breeds fear, and fear remains the greatest enemy of peace.

May I express one final thought. There can be no enduring and creative peace if people are unfree. The instinct for personal and national freedom cannot be destroyed, and the attempt to do so by totalitarian and despotic government will ultimately make not only for internal trouble but for international conflict. Authority under law must, I know, be respected as the foundation of society and as the protection of peace. The extension of state power, however, into every phase of man's life and thought is the abuse of authority, the destroyer of freedom, and the enemy of real peace.

In the end, the whole problem always returns to people; yes, to one person and his own individual response to the challenges that confront him.

Above all, we must find out why men with generous and understanding hearts, and peaceful instincts in their normal individual behavior, can become fighting and even savage national animals under the incitements of collective emotion.

That is the core of our problem: why men fight who aren't necessarily fighting men. It was posed for me in a new and dramatic way one Christmas Eve in London during World War II. The air raid sirens had given their grim and accustomed warning. Almost before the last dismal moan had ended, the anti-aircraft guns began to crash. In between their bursts I could hear the deeper, more menacing sound of bombs. It wasn't much of a raid, really, but one or two of the bombs seemed to fall too close to my room. I was reading in bed, and to drown out or at least to take my mind off the bombs, I reached out and turned on the radio. I was fumbling aimlessly with the dial when the room was flooded with the beauty and peace of Christmas carol music. Glorious waves of it wiped out the sound of war and conjured up visions of happier peace-time Christmases. Then the announcer spoke—in German. For it was a German station and they were Germans who were singing those carols. Nazi bombs screaming through the air with their message of war and death; German music drifting through the air with its message of peace and salvation. When we resolve the paradox of those two sounds from a single national source, we will, at last, be in a good position to understand and solve the problem of peace and war.

Shake Hands with the Devil: The Failure of Humanity in Rwanda
Roméo Dallaire
2003

From 1991 to 1993, my brigade sent more than four thousand troops on peacekeeping missions in places all over the world, from Cambodia to the Balkans to Kuwait. At one point I called the commander of the army to suggest that my whole brigade headquarters be moved overseas, since it felt like I was the only one left at home. He thanked me for the moment of levity, but told me I should prepare for even more UN taskings. I couldn't figure out where I would get the troops.

We were sending our soldiers, who were ready for classic Chapter six peacekeeping missions, into a world that seemed increasingly less amenable to such interventions. Chapter six of the UN Charter deals with threats to international peace and security. In the fifties, Lester Pearson, Canada's minister of foreign affairs at the time, had come up with a concept of peacekeeping that had been implemented in conflict areas throughout the Cold War (and had won Pearson a Nobel Peace Prize) In these operations, lightly-armed, multinational, blue helmeted, impartial and neutral peacekeepers were deployed and interposed between two former warring factions, with their consent, either to maintain the status quo, as in Sinai from 1956 to 1967, or to assist the parties in implementing a peace accord, as was at that time the case in Cambodia. The key principles of these operations are impartiality, neutrality and consent. Classic peacekeeping had worked well during the Cold War, where the two camps had used peacekeeping to diffuse conflicts that could draw in the major superpowers and lead to nuclear Armageddon. This was the type of peacekeeping that I had been trained in and the principles with which I was most familiar.

But we were increasingly less certain of the effectiveness of the classic approach. Not only were we stretched in finding enough personnel, but on top of everything else, we started to receive casualties—some even killed in action. On June 18, 1993, one of the soldiers from the brigade, Corporal Daniel Gunther, died on active duty in Bosnia. The report I was given at the time suggested that a mortar bomb had exploded near his armoured personnel carrier and that he had been killed by flying shrapnel. Beth and I attended his funeral, which I found simple to the point of disrespect. Corporal Gunther was buried with a minimum of peacetime honours, and he and his family were treated as if he had been killed in a road accident. I remember his devastated father coming up to me after the service and asking me what, if anything, his son had died for? I had no answer to offer him and the rest of the shocked and grieving family.

According to the often gut-wrenching testimony of my young troops, the situations they found themselves in the field were far more dangerous and complex than we were being led to expect. For instance, I found out much later that Gunther had actually been hit in the chest by an anti-tank rocket that had been fired from a shoulder-held grenade launcher. He had been deliberately targeted, and murdered. And yet the kind of training I was supposed to offer these troops before they went into the theatre was based on a hopelessly outdated model of lightly-armed blue berets monitoring a stable ceasefire. Lessons learned were slowly beginning to emerge, but not fast enough or with the force needed to stimulate any real changes. I was deeply concerned about the impact the combined effects of extreme stress and brutal violence encountered in the field were having on my troops. I harassed army headquarters to send some clinical psychology experts out to try to come up with solutions. The response that came back? Because of troop limitations, there were barely enough bayonets to do the job, let alone resources for such a low-priority effort. A commander should know how to do what needed to be done . . .

I confess that when General Roy called, I didn't know where Rwanda was or exactly what kind of trouble the country was in. The next day, he told me more about the tiny, heavily populated African nation. Rwanda was in the midst of negotiating a peace agreement to end a vicious two-and-a-half-year civil war between a rebel force, the Rwandese Patriotic Front (RPF), and the government. The rebel movement had grown out of a refugee population of Rwandans who had fled north to Uganda in the early sixties, after independence had changed the political balance in their homeland. In the early nineties, the rebel army had twice pushed into the northern region of Rwanda and was now hunkered down behind a demilitarized zone monitored by a group of neutral military observers under the auspices of the Organization of African *Unity* (OAU). While the parties negotiated the terms of a peace agreement in Arusha, Tanzania, the UN had been asked by the president of Uganda, Yoweri Museveni, to send in a small force to *monitor* the border to ensure that weapons and soldiers were not crossing from Uganda into Rwanda to reinforce the RPF.

This was to be my mission, dubbed the United Nations Observer Mission in Uganda and Rwanda (UNOMUR). General Roy described it as a classic peacekeeping operation, a confidence-building exercise designed to encourage the belligerents to get down to the serious business of peace. It was extremely modest in scope and size: I would have under my command a total of eighty-one unarmed military observers, who would operate on the Ugandan side of the border.

Why pick me to lead this tiny mission in a place I'd barely heard of? I was about to begin an unprecedented third year as commander of the 5ieme Brigade Group; in four days we were going to celebrate the twenty-fifth anniversary of its founding with more than a thousand troops on parade. The 5th still faced plenty of challenges, many of them in the area of peacekeeping. We were still too ad hoc in our preparation of troops for deployment on ever more challenging missions. Much of our training was still focused on classic war-fighting, even though the conflicts we were sending troops into usually were not unfolding like classic wars. As far as I was concerned, it wasn't yet time for me to leave, but I was being asked—ordered—to deploy. Whether it was a big force, a small force or just me alone, I was going over. Knowing that Major General Maurice Baril was heading up the military component of the UN Department of Peace-keeping Operations (DPKO), I surmised that there must be more to this mission than met the eye. In the end I decided that this was my chance to learn first-hand what would work in the changing nature of conflict in the post-Cold War world.

I set aside as my temporary headquarters the Artillery Room in the Garrison Club, which had been built in the 1820s by British engineers as their headquarters for the massive defensive works of the old capital. The windows look out toward the lush green of the Plains of Abraham, where generations of French, English and Canadian military leaders plotted campaigns, and beyond the plains to the St. Lawrence River. This room, with its heavy, old oak furniture and yellowing nineteenth-century prints depicting training and fighting scenes in the garrison, always sent a thrill through me. I could almost feel the presence of the military and political leaders who came before me, pacing in front of the fireplace as they pondered strategies and worked through knotty tactical problems.

My mission was hardly on the level of their campaigns, but still I was carried away by the romance of it, by the idea of adventure that Africa represented to me. Growing up Catholic in Quebec in the fifties, I had been captivated by missionary tales from "the dark continent." As a result, my notions of Africa were outdated and Eurocentric. I combed the library for anything I could find on Rwanda and the Great Lakes region of central Africa. There wasn't much. But serious work was afoot, and time was of the essence.

We tried to cram in as much knowledge about the Great Lakes region of central Africa as we could. Tiny, landlocked Rwanda was tucked between Zaire on the west and Tanzania on the east, with Uganda to the north and Burundi to the south. Rwanda had never been considered important enough by scholars in the West to war-rant extensive study. Brent and I managed to piece together a rough history from newspaper accounts and a few scholarly articles, which reduced a highly complex social and political situation to a simple inter-tribal conflict . . . with a confidence born of ignorance, we soldiered on.

We traced the roots of the current hostilities back to the early twentieth century and Belgian colonial rule. When the Belgians chased the Germans out of the territory in 1916, they discovered that two groups of people shared the land. The Tutsis, who were tall and quite light skinned, herded cattle; the shorter, darker Hutus farmed veg-etable plots. The Belgians viewed the minority Tutsis as closer in kind to Europeans and elevated them to positions of power over the majority Hutu, which exacerbated the feudal state of peasant Hutus and overlord Tutsis. Enlisting the Tutsis allowed the Belgians to develop and exploit a vast network of coffee and tea plantations without the inconvenience of war or the expense of deploying a large colonial service.

Rwanda achieved independence in 1962, after a popular uprising slaughtered or drove out the Tursi elite, and installed a Hutu-dominated government led by the charismatic Gregoire Kayibanda. Over the next decade, a series of violent pogroms further targeted the Tutsi population of Rwanda and many more fled to the neighbouring states of Uganda, Burundi and Zaire, where they led a precarious existence as stateless refugees.

In 1973, Major General Juvenal Habyarimana, a Hutu, toppled Kayibanda in a *coup d'etat* and began a twenty-year dictatorship. It led to a degree of stability in Rwanda that was envied in the volatile Great Lakes region. But the expulsion and persecution of the country's Tutsis sowed permanent seeds of discord. Slowly, the Tutsi diaspora became a force to be reckoned with. Fuelled by the continued oppression in Rwanda and harsh treatment at the hands of their reluctant host countries, the diaspora finally coalesced into the Rwandese Patriotic Front. A small but highly effective military and political movement, the RPF proved capable of engaging and defeating the French-backed Rwandese Government Forces (RGF). By 1991, the Rwandan government was caught between an increasingly formidable rebel army and international pressure for democratic reform. President Habyarimana began the on-again, off-again negotiations that formed the basis for the peace talks then taking place in Arusha, Tanzania.

A few short weeks of snatching at whatever material that came our way was not about to make Africanists of either one of us.

To Go Or To Stay?

I awoke at dawn on April 8 to the sound of heavy gunfire. Brent* had scrounged a cup of tea for me, and after I drank it, I washed and shaved using a glass of water. This would be my morning routine for the next hundred days. The city water supply had already been cut off, and we had to conserve as much as we could of our bottled water for drinking. None of us would see a shower or bath for months, and we were rationed to a single glass a day for keeping ourselves clean. We began to save rainwater in order to wash our uniforms—by hand, often without any soap—and all of us soon carried a very distinct and unpleasant odour.

With the dawn, the mobs were back on the streets, and firing was being reported across the city. The RPF's attack on the Presidential Guard compound had been repulsed, and the RPF was consolidating their positions around the end complex. Elements of the RGF and the Gendarmerie had joined the Presidential Guard and the Interahamwe in the rampages of the previous day, and it appeared that the power of the Third Force now extended well beyond the known extremist units.

---

*Major Brent Beardsley, RCR

All UN compounds were sheltering thousands of fearful Rwandans.

I needed clarification from New York as to what authority I had to protect these people, whose plight posed both a moral quandary and a logistics nightmare. How could I possibly keep them safe? In the meantime, we continued to open our gates to all those seeking sanctuary. At the first morning prayers of the war, I directed that everyone entering the compounds be searched and disarmed. I also directed that the few hundred Rwandans already in the Force HQ be escorted to the Amahoro stadium as soon as possible. The lack of water and food would take a toll over the next days and weeks. We protected these citizens from certain death at the hands of the extremists or the RPF, but then had to watch helplessly as some of them succumbed to dehydration, disease and ultimately hunger. Many of my troops living among them would also fall ill: they simply could not eat what little rations they had in front of starving people, especially children, and gave what they had at the expense of their own health. Humanitarian assistance was still a long way off . . .

Brent and a team of MILOBs had spent the day conducting rescue missions in one of the APCs. On the first effort, he'd picked up several UN civilian staff and their families and also the Canadian chargé d'affaires, Linda Carroll, who was able to provide him with a list of addresses of Canadian expatriates in Kigali.[2]

With Brent that day were Marek Pazik and Stefan Stec, both Polish officers who had briefly been billeted in the Gikondo Parish Church, known as the Polish Mission because it was run by priests from Poland. Pazik and Stefan had not lasted long under the austere regime at the mission, but two of their fellow Polish MILOBs had stayed on. That morning, a faint radio call had come from the men at the mission begging for help. The batteries on the radio were dying and all Brent could make out was that there had been killings at the church.

Not knowing what to expect, Brent, Pazik and Stec armed themselves and, hatches down, set off to Gikondo in the APC with a Bangladeshi officer and three men. Along the route, they passed through fighting between the RGF and the RPF, through Gendarmerie roadblocks and through the ever-increasing and chaotic militia roadblocks. They saw the bodies of men, women and children near these roadblocks. So many civilians were on the move, it looked like the entire population was abandoning Kigali.

At the church, they came to a halt and dismounted. Pazik and a Bangladeshi soldier went to the rectory to find the Polish MILOBs, while Brent and Stec confronted the first evidence of wholesale massacre. Across the street from the mission, an entire alleyway was littered with the bodies of women and children near a hastily abandoned school. As Brent and Stefan were standing there trying to take in the number of bodies, a truck full of armed men roared by. Brent and Stefan decided to head for the church. Stefan went inside while Brent stood by the door to cover him and to keep the APC in sight. They confronted a scene of unbelievable horror—the first such scene UNAMIR witnessed—evidence of the genocide, though we didn't yet know to call it that. In the aisles and on the pews were the bodies of hundreds of men, women and children. At least fifteen of them were still alive but in a terrible state. The priests were applying first aid to the survivors. A baby cried as it tried to feed on the breast of its dead mother, a sight Brent has never forgotten. Pazik found the two Polish MILOBs, who were in a state of grief and shock, hardly able to relate what had happened. The night before, they said, the RGF had cordoned off the area, and then the Gendarmerie had gone door to door checking identity cards. All Tutsi men, women and children were rounded up and moved to the church. Their screams had alerted the priests and the MILOBs, who had come running. The priests and officers were seized at the church doors and slammed up against the wall with rifle barrels at their throats. They were forced to watch at gunpoint as the gendarmes collected the adults' identity cards and burned them. Then the gendarmes welcomed in a large number of civilian militiamen with machetes and handed over the victims to their killers.

Methodically and with much bravado and laughter, the militia moved from bench to bench, hacking with machetes. Some people died immediately, while others with terrible wounds begged for their lives or the lives of their children. No one was spared. A pregnant woman was disembowelled and her fetus severed. Women suffered horrible mutilation. Men were struck on the head and died immediately or lingered in agony. Children begged for their lives and received the same treatment as their parents. Genitalia were a favourite target, the victims left to bleed to death. There was no mercy, no hesitation and no compassion. The priests and the MILaBs, guns at their throats, tears in their eyes, and the screams of the dying in their ears, pleaded with the gendarmes for the victims. The gendarmes' reply was to use the rifle barrels to lift the priests' and MILOBs' heads so that they could better witness the horror.

Killing with machetes is hard work, and sometime in the night the murderers became fatigued with their gruesome task and left the church, probably headed for some sleep before they moved on to the next location. The priests and MILOBs did what they could for the few survivors, who moaned or crawled from underneath the corpses that had sheltered them.

Both of the MILOBs were overwhelmed by emotion as they recounted the night's events. One fell completely silent while the other admitted that though he had served in places, such as Iraq and Cambodia, this was it, he was going home. The men needed to get our of there, to get back to the security of headquarters and regain their equilibrium, and they urged the priests to join them. But the fathers refused, saying they had to stay with the wounded, who were too many to carry in the APC Brent and the others gave the priests a radio and a charged battery, what water they had and a small first aid kit, and promised to report the incident and mount a rescue mission. They warned the priests that since it was already mid-afternoon, it was unlikely that a large armed escort with ambulances or heavy transport could be mounted and then negotiate the dozens of roadblocks before nightfall, but the priests were confident they could hide overnight, as the militia and gendarmes had surely finished with them.

Feeling like deserters, the UNAMIR group returned to Force HQ, and the Polish MILOBs were put to bed. Kigali Sector was directed to conduct a rescue mission, but as Brent had suspected, it couldn't comply until the next day—dozens of missions were already underway. Early the next morning, the priests called on the radio and reported that the militia had returned during the night. Our APC had been spotted at the church, and the killers had returned to destroy the evidence of the massacre. They had killed the wounded and removed and burned the bodies.

The decision to leave the priests and the victims had had disastrous consequences, but such are the decisions that soldiers make in war. Some days you make decisions and people live, other days people die. Those innocent men, women and children were simply Tutsi. That was their crime.

The massacre was not a spontaneous act. It was a well-executed operation involving the army, Gendarmerie, Interahamwe and civil service. The identity card system, introduced during the Belgian colonial period, was an anachronism that would result in the deaths of many innocent people. By the destruction of their cards, and of their records at the local commune office, these human beings were erased from humanity. They simply never existed. Before the genocide ended, hundreds of thousands of others would be erased. The men who organized and perpetrated these crimes knew they were crimes and not acts justified by war, and that they could be held accountable for them. The Interahamwe returned to destroy the evidence. The faceless bureaucrats who fed the names to the militias and destroyed the records also played a part. We were not in a war of victors and vanquished. We were in the middle of a slaughterhouse, though it was weeks before we could call it by its real name . . .

How could I spark the conscience of the world? We were diminished but determined to stay put and continue to tell the story of what was happening in Rwanda. I had to press the right buttons and I had to do it as fast as possible. Since my reports seemed to keep vanishing into the abyss of non-action in New York, I stepped up the media campaign. For those politicians and generals who distrust and avoid the free media, I can assure them that the media can be an ally and a weapon equal to battalions on the ground. With the Belgian departure, it appeared that Mark Doyle of the BBC might also leave. I called him into my office and made him an offer he could not refuse. He could live with us, be protected by us, be fed and sustained by us, and I would guarantee him a story a day and the means (my satellite phone) to get that story to the world. I did not care if his story was positive or negative about UNAMIR as long as it was accurate and truthful. The key was for him to become the voice of what was happening in Rwanda.

Mark agreed and in the coming days he did become that voice. Other news agencies noticed, and journalists began to flow into Rwanda to cover the slaughter. Jean-Guy Plante was on the case, helping them in any way he could. He loved to be around people, and he organized the reporters already in country, establishing a system of rotation of media between Nairobi and Kigali with the help of the Canadian movement staff in charge of the Hercules flights. Plante decided how long reporters would stay in theatre in order to permit a maximum of different media outfits and journalists to report what was going on in Rwanda. I wanted no stupid casualties. Plante had

UN vans, rooms in the Meridien, food cards, and electronic hookups in the Force HQ ready for them. He guaranteed them security, at least one story every day and delivery of their stories to Nairobi. This was achieved on occasion by UNMaO driving to the Ugandan border and handing the material to UNOMUR, who would take it by helicopter to Entebbe and beyond.

I also directed Brent to ensure each night that any journalist calling for an interview was given access to me. With our own national broadcasting network, the CBC, Brent exercised his initiative, with very positive results. The producer of *As It Happens*, an internationally well-regarded radio interview show listened to at home by hundreds of thousands of Canadians, finally secured our phone number and called to set up a live interview with the show's host, Michael Enright. Brent refused to put me on the line unless the producer provided the scores of the NHL (National Hockey League) playoff games. We had no news at all from home but knew the playoffs were on. Brent, a confirmed Toronto Maple Leafs fan at the time, and I, a resolute Montreal Canadiens fan, were grateful for this news. In the weeks that followed, we always got our scores, and Enright got his live interviews. In our conversations, Enright became the voice of home to me.

The media was the weapon I used to strike the conscience of the world and try to prod the international community into action. I would even risk the lives of my UNMIRs to ensure that the stories got out every day . . .

As far as I have been able to determine, on April 24 the NGO Oxfam became the first organization to use the term "genocide" to describe what was happening in Rwanda. Calling it "ethnic cleansing" just did not seem to be hitting the mark. After numerous telephone conversations with Oxfam personnel in London, we queried New York if what we were seeing in Rwanda could be labelled genocide. As far as I am aware, we never received a response, but we started to use the term sometime after April 24 in all of our communications. Little did I realize the storm of controversy this term would invoke in New York and in the capitals of the world. To me it seemed an accurate label at last . . .

The pressures on all of us were beyond extraordinary. The fighting around the airport, with the RGF and the RPF firing on each other and anything else that raised its head, curtailed the Hercules flights, cutting drastically the emergency supplies that could get in. We had little food, little medicine and much stress: the result was a sapping of will and commitment among my troops. On a daily basis I saw the increase in sick parade, as more and more soldiers went down with disease, especially malaria. I can't tell you how disgusting daily life could be; the corpse-eating dogs that we shot on sight now had no qualms about attacking the living. One day while I was driving in Kigali, a lone dog attacked my side window while the vehicle was on the move. If I had not had the window up, the dog would have ripped off my arm. Another time, several officers taking a short coffee break saw a strange-looking dog wandering in the compound, then realized it was a rat that had grown to the size of a terrier. One of the officers, who was from Ghana, said that he had seen this after natural disasters back home: the rats fed and fed on an inexhaustible supply of human flesh and grew to an unbelievable size.

We had completely run out of water and were unable to find a source inside the country. I called the new CAO in Nairobi, Allay Golo from Chad, and asked him why there was no water. [1] Golo was a career UN civilian administrator, and he responded that he was bound by UN rules. Even though we had had no water for days, he still had to conduct a call for proposals and then do an analysis of the three best bids. The minimum estimate was a million litres, but securing that much water would take weeks, and we didn't even have days. I told him that even twenty thousand litres would tide us over, but he insisted on following procedure. I couldn't wait, and instead arranged to bring water in from UNaMUR. Even so, all of us, including the people we were sheltering, went without water for two more days.

Mid-afternoon that day, to the now usual cacophony of small-arms fire and artillery noise, I completed my thirty-four-page reassessment of the situation and sent it off to New York. And then I found out that Captain Oiagne Mbaye of Senegal had been hit by mortar fragments fired by the RPF at an RGF roadblock while he was bringing back a message for me from Bizimungu. Oiagne was dead before he hit the dashboard. He was the MlLOB who had saved Prime Minister Agathe's children, and in the weeks since, he had personally saved the lives of dozens upon dozens of Rwandans. Braving direct and indirect fire, mines, mobs, disease and any number of other threats, he eagerly accepted any mission that would save lives. In our HQ we observed a minute of silence in his honour, and on June I we held a small parade for him at the airport, behind sandbags, with the sound of artillery fire in our ears. His body was flown home, wrapped in a blue refugee tarp, another hero of Rwanda. As one of his fellow MILOBs said, "He was the bravest of us all." The BBC's Mark Doyle, who considered Diagne a friend, recently wrote to me, "Can you imagine the blanket media coverage that a dead British or American peacekeeper of Mbaye's bravery and stature would have received? He got almost none." (Doyle did write about him much later in *Granta* magazine.) . . .

June 1. I decided to enlist the help of the Gendarmerie to go look for a safer west-ward route out of the city, one that would avoid the RPFgauntlet and the RGF no man's land. We took a fairly large loop through some pretty rough trails. The rain fell so hard during the rainy season that it didn't have time to sink in, eroding the roads and leaving behind inches of slippery mud. On our trek we reached a washout on the slope of a hill and tried to run it. One of the vehicles slid and tumbled away down the hill. Luckily, nobody was injured.

We abandoned the vehicle that had rumbled, taking the distributor cap out of it so it couldn't be easily appropriated. About a week later, one of my UNMOs saw the truck in the hands of the RPF. The vehicle had been smeared with mud to try to cam-ouflage the UN markings. The RGF also spotted the vehicle and concluded that this was simply another way that UNAMIR was favouring the RPF. Eight of our vehicles had been abandoned in various parts of the country by this point, and I had to com-mence a campaign of negotiation to get the RPF not to use them.

We continued along lanes and paths that often took us through the middle of villages that did not appear on any map. In one village, we stopped to wait for all the vehicles to catch up to us. The path we were on had been one of the exit trails used by people fleeing Kigali. There were remnants of a barrier here, and many people had been killed and thrown in the ditches and on the sides of the road. As I got out to wait, I looked at the bodies, which seemed relatively fresh. Just as I glimpsed the body of a child, it moved. I wasn't sure if it was my imagination, but I saw the twitching of the child and wanted to help. I leaned down to pick the child up, and suddenly I was holding a little body that was both tingling and mushy in my hands. In a second I realized that the movement was not the child but the action of maggots. I was frozen, not wanting to fling the child away from me but also not wanting to hold it for a second longer. I managed to set the body down and then stood there, shaky, not wanting to think about what was on my hands.

We carried on with the reconnaissance of the road. In the early afternoon we crested a hill and before us stretched a huge encampment of the internally displaced, people who had managed to pass through all the roadblocks out of Kigali. The sky was lowering with dark rain clouds, and a blue wave of refugee tarps rose up to greet it; it was as if we were looking out at an ocean of the displaced. We drove very slowly down the hill and up through the camp, heading for the aid station that was set up near the top of the next rise. There were so many people jammed together on these hills that every little motion caused ripples of movement in every direction. The masses were so great it was hard to perceive the individuality of the people—there were so many faces, so many eyes. Clothing that had once been bright was drained of colour and smeared with dirt so that everything was a uniform brown.

The Red Cross workers here were locals, and they were overwhelmed by the demands on them. I told them how courageous they were and how impressed I was that the Red Cross was able to deliver some assistance in all parts of Rwanda. One of the elders in the crowd surrounding us began to speak. He told me that many of them had had to leave in such haste that they had left behind essentials. Since they'd arrived here, he said, they had received aid in the form of maize, and he held out a bit to show me. It was cattle corn, recognizable by its large, hard, jagged kernels. He said that they did not have the tools they needed to grind the kernels. They did not have the pots to cook the corn in to make it softer. They didn't have the water to put into the pot or the wood to build a fire to heat it. The uncooked maize was not edible, yet some of the children were so hungry they ate it. The jagged kernels ripped their digestive tracts and caused internal bleeding. The children were dying of it, bleeding through their bowels. With an ineffably sad face, this man asked me what I could do. I couldn't find an answer. In shame, I went back to my vehicle and we drove back to Kigali.

The road back was just as difficult and circuitous as the road in, but it did provide me with time to think with bitterness about how slow the humanitarian response had been. Rome, Paris, Geneva and New York were still demanding assessment upon assessment. Instead of coming to the aid of roughly two million people, the international community and aid groups were still conducting analyses of what was really needed. That night at evening prayers, I received Yaache's report on the situation, along with one from the new UNREO representative, Charles Petrie. Petrie was in despair about the continuous demands for assessments. I turned to him and said that in his next assessment, he could quote me: "Tell them to send me food, fuel, medical supplies and water for two million people, and we will work out the details of distributing it, but for God's sake tell them to start sending it!"

A couple of years later I met some of those decision-makers and assessment-demanders, who took the opportunity to tell me that I had been looking at the situation in a "simplistic fashion."

Too many parties have focused on pointing the finger at others, beyond the perpetrators, as the scapegoats for our common failure in Rwanda. Some say that the example of Rwanda proves that the UN is an irrelevant, corrupt, decadent institution that has outlived its usefulness or even its ability to conduct conflict resolution. Others have blamed the Permanent Five of the Security Council, especially the United States and France, for failing to see beyond their own national self-interest to lead or even support international intervention to stop the genocide. Some have blamed the media for not telling the story, the NGOs for not reacting quickly and effectively enough, the peacekeepers for not showing more resolve, and myself for failing in my mission. When I began this book, I was tempted to make it an anatomy of my personal failures, which I was finally persuaded would be missing the point.

I have witnessed and also suffered my share of recriminations and accusations, politically motivated "investigations" and courts martial, Monday-morning quarterbacking, revisionism and outright lies since I got back to Canada in September 1994—none of that will bring back the dead or point the way forward to a peaceful future. Instead, we need to study how the genocide happened not from the perspective of assigning blame—there is too much to go around—but from the perspective of how we are going to take concrete steps to prevent such a thing from ever happening again. To properly mourn the dead and respect the potential of the living, we need accountability, not blame. We need to eliminate from this earth the impunity with which the genocidaires were able to act, and re-emphasize the principle of justice for all, so that no one for even a moment will make the ethical and moral mistake of ranking some humans as more human than others, a mistake that the international community endorsed by its indifference in 1994.

There is no doubt that the toxic ethnic extremism that infected Rwanda was a deep-rooted and formidable foe, built from colonial discrimination and exclusion, personal vendettas, refugee life, envy, racism, power plays, *coups d'etat* and the deep rifts of civil war. In Rwanda both sides of the civil war fostered extremism. The fanatical far right of the Huru ethnicity was concentrated in the MRND and its vicious wing in the CDR party, and was nurtured by an inner circle around the president, Juvenal Habyarimana, and his wife. The Tutsis also had their hard-liners, in the persons of some of the embittered refugees of the 1959 revolution, and sons and daughters raised in the poverty and double standards of Uganda, permanently gazing across the border to a homeland denied to them until they took it by force; among them also were vengeful Hutus who had been abused by the Habyarimana regime.

Together these extremists created the climate in which a slaughter of an entire ethnicity could be dreamed up—an attempt to annihilate every Tutsi who had a claim on Rwanda, carried out by Rwandans on Rwandans. The violent extremism was nurtured over decades of an armed peace, but it could have been controlled or even eradicated before Hutu Power enacted its "final solution." Through our indifference, squabbling, distraction and delays, we lost a great many opportunities to destabilize the genocidaires and derail the genocide. I can easily delineate the factors that might have guaranteed our success, beginning with having the political and cultural savvy from the start to ensure an effective military and civilian police presence on the ground in Rwanda as soon as the Arusha Peace Agreement was signed; providing UNAMIR with hard intelligence on the ex-belligerents' intentions, ambitions and goals so that we didn't have to fumble in the dark; providing the mission with the political and diplomatic muscle to outmanoeuvre the hard-liners and also to push the RPF into a few timely concessions; reasonable administrative and logistical support of the mission; a few more well-trained and properly equipped battalions on the ground; a more liberal and forceful application of the mandate; and to bring it all off, a budget increase of only about US $100 million.

Could we have prevented the resumption of the civil war and the genocide? The short answer is yes. If UNAMIR had received the modest increase of troops and capabilities we requested in the first week, could we have stopped the killings? Yes, absolutely. Would we have risked more UN casualties? Yes, but surely soldiers and peacekeeping nations should be prepared to pay the price of safeguarding human life and human rights. If UNAMIR 2 had been deployed on time and as requested, would we have reduced the prolonged period of killing? Yes, we would have stopped it much sooner.

If we had chosen to enhance the capabilities of UNAMIR in these ways, we could have wrested the initiative from the ex-belligerents in reasonably short order and stymied the aggression for enough time to expose and weaken the "third force." I truly believe the missing piece in the puzzle was the political will from France and the United States to make the Arusha accords work and ultimately move this imploding nation toward democracy and a lasting peace. There is no doubt that those two countries possessed the solution to the Rwandan crisis.

Let there be no doubt: the Rwandan genocide was the ultimate responsibility of those Rwandans who planned, ordered, supervised and eventually conducted it. Their extremism was the seemingly indestructible and ugly harvest of years of power struggles and insecurity that had been deftly played upon by their former colonial rulers. But the deaths of Rwandans can also be laid at the door of the military genius Paul Kagame, who did not speed up his campaign when the scale of the genocide became clear and even talked candidly with me at several points about the price his fellow Tutsis might have to pay for the cause. Next in line when it comes to responsibility are France, which moved in too late and ended up protecting the genocidaires and permanently destabilizing the region, and the U.S. government, which actively worked against an effective UNAMIR and only got involved to aid the same Hutu refugee population and the genocidaires, leaving the genocide survivors to flounder and suffer. The failings of the UN and Belgium were not in the same league.

My own *mea culpa* is this: as the person charged with the military leadership of UNAMIR, I was unable to persuade the international community that this tiny, poor, overpopulated country and its people were worth saving from the horror of genocide—even when the measures needed for success were relatively small. How much of that inability was linked to my inexperience? Why was I chosen to lead UNAMIR? My experience was in training Canadian peacekeepers to go into classic Cold War-style conflicts; I had never been in the field as a peacekeeper myself I had no political expertise, and no background or training in African affairs or manoeuvring in the weeds of ethnic conflicts in which hate trumps reason. I had no way to gauge the duplicity of the exbelligerents. The professional development of senior officers in matters of classic peacekeeping, let alone in the thickets of the post-modern version (which I prefer to call conflict resolution), has often been reduced to throwing officers into situations and seeing whether they can cope. While the numbers of UN troop-contributing nations has increased well beyond the more traditional contributors (among which Canada was a major player), there are still no essential prerequisites of formal education and training for the job. As the conflicts grow increasingly ugly and complex and the mandates fuzzy and restrictive, you end up with more force commanders like myself, whose technical and experiential limitations were so clear. There will continue to be a need for UN-led missions and these missions will continue to increase in complexity as well as have more international impact. As a global community, it is crucial that we develop an international pool of multidisciplinary, multi-skilled and humanist senior leaders to fill these force commander billets.

Still, at its heart, the Rwandan story is the story of the failure of humanity to heed a call for help from an endangered people.

The international community, of which the UN is only a symbol, failed to move beyond self-interest for the sake of Rwanda. While most nations agreed that something should be done, they all had an excuse why they should not be the ones to do it. As a result, the UN was denied the political will and material means to prevent the tragedy.

Like many governments and NGOs, the UN more or less muddled through the tumultuous 1990s, a decade marred by the proliferation of armed conflicts that defied the codes of former wars. My own country, Canada, was carried by altruistic impulses into operations in places such as the former Yugoslavia, Somalia, Cambodia and Mozambique. During the Cold War, peacekeeping missions generally monitored the implementation of peace agreements and prevented isolated incidents from leading to a resumption of conflict. In the nineties the focus shifted: the mission aim was to bring about a form of order, whether it be a system of humanitarian relief or an agreement forced on warring factions. UNAMIR started out as a classic Cold War-style peacekeeping mission but then found itself in the middle of a civil war and genocide. In all these situations, a humanitarian catastrophe was either the catalyst for the security problem or the result of it. Displaced and refugee populations were on the move, in numbers rarely ever witnessed, and were prey to extremists, warlords and armed bandits. More often than not, peacekeeping missions had to make ad hoc responses, mounting tardy attempts to assist in the resolution of both the conflicts and the humanitarian crisis.

How do we pick and choose where to get involved? Canada and other peacekeeping nations have become accustomed to acting if, and only if, international public opinion will support them-a dangerous path that leads to a moral relativism in which a country risks losing sight of the difference between good and evil, a concept that some players on the international stage view as outmoded. Some governments regard the use of force itself as the greatest evil. Others define "good" as the pursuit of human rights and will opt to employ force when human rights are violated. As the nineties drew to a close and the new millennium dawned with no sign of an end to these ugly little wars, it was as if each troubling conflict we were faced with had to pass the test of whether we could "care" about it or "identify" with the victims before we'd get involved. Each mission was judged as to whether it was "worth" risking soldiers' lives and a nation's resources. As Michael Ignatieff has warned us, "riskless warfare in pursuit of human rights is a moral contradiction. The concept of human rights assumes that all human life is of equal value. Risk-free warfare presumes that our lives matter more than those we are intervening to save." On the basis of my experience as force commander in Rwanda, *j'accuse.*

Endnotes

1. Christine de Liso, our acting CAO, had been relieved of her duties in early May. A fine human being, she had done everything humanly possible to aid UNAMIR despite the enormous restraints placed on her by the FOD.
2. Linda Carroll was the epitome of what a diplomat should be in a crisis. Since the president's plane went down, she had warned her area wardens, calmed everyone by radio, located most of the Canadians she knew to be in Kigali and managed to gather them in key locations. With assistance from our embassy in Nairobi and others, Brent and his team conducted dozens of missions over the next two weeks to rescue and evacuate not only Canadians but also Rwandans and other nationals. There was one large complicating factor. From her records, Linda believed there were only about 65 Canadian citizens in Kigali, but we evacuated over 195. Many travellers and expatriares do not take their security seriously and feel under no obligation to check in with their local embassies or consulates—which causes enormous effort and grief among the men and women who must try to save them when conflict breaks out.

Pearson's Peacekeeping Legacy
David Pugliese
2006

In a rapidly changing world, where mounting terrorist threats have confused our notion of war, will Canadian Forces keep the peace?

The stage was set in late October 1956 when Israeli troops invaded Egypt. They were soon followed by British and French forces in a combined bid to seize control of the Suez Canal. The Soviet Union was threatening to intervene and help the Egyptians.

At the United Nations, representatives from various countries struggled to end the growing crisis before it spiralled out of control. It was at an emergency meeting of the UN's General Assembly that Lester B. Pearson, then Canada's secretary of state for External Affairs, proposed the creation of a large UN military force to keep the peace between the warring factions while a political compromise was worked out. He offered Canadian troops for the job, and after an all-night session of the General Assembly, his plan was approved.

The United Nations Emergency Force (UNEF), led by Canadian general Edison Louis Millard Burns, was formed and the soldiers were sent to supervise the withdrawal of French, British, and Israeli troops from Egypt. Once this was accomplished, UNEF's role would then be to act as a buffer between the Egyptian and Israeli armies. Canadians would patrol the northern section of the Israeli-Egyptian border while Yugoslav troops were to handle the rest.

More than one-thousand Canadian military personnel took part in the mission.

The next year, Pearson won the Nobel Peace Prize, the only Canadian ever to do so. In making its selection, the peace prize committee said the Canadian politician had "saved the world" with his proposal to defuse the Suez crisis. Today, Lester B. Pearson's vision during that tumultuous time remains embedded in the Canadian consciousness—even though some argue that it is no longer relevant in the world's conflict zones.

Five decades later, the legacy of the Suez crisis still resonates. Canadians have come to see peacekeeping as part of their national identity. It is reflected in our monuments and even our currency. For example, in October 1992 the federal government unveiled the Peacekeeping Monument across from the National Gallery in downtown Ottawa. A rendition of the monument is etched into some of our one-dollar coins. As

"Pearson's Peacekeeping Legacy" by David Pugliese as appeared in *The Beaver,* Oct/Nov 2006. Reprinted by permission of the author.

well, an image of a peacekeeper armed only with binoculars is on Canada's ten-dollar bill. The government of Canada's website boasts that peacekeeping is an important aspect of the country's national heritage and a reflection of our fundamental beliefs. Schoolchildren who write letters to Canadian soldiers overseas often address them to "a peacekeeper."

In his book *Canada's Army: Waging War and Keeping Peace,* military historian Jack Granastein dispels the myth that peacekeeping was invented during the Suez crisis. He writes that the UN had already organized several small observer missions to monitor the progress of ceasefires between warring states. For instance, in 1949, Canada had sent a number of officers to help create a ceasefire line and monitor disagreements between Pakistan and Indian in Kashmir.

What was created by Suez, Granastein points out, was the belief that Canadian troops were somehow natural-born peacekeepers.

The Canadian public passionately embraced that image following the Suez crisis to become leading advocates for peacekeeping. Even when the government was reluctant to involve itself in some of the world's war zones, such as in the Congo in 1960, public pressure ensured that Canadian troops were sent.

Some observers have even suggested that Canadians have "peacekeeping in their DNA" or that because we are a nation of immigrants, who have had to resolve differences of opinion, that Canadians are inherent peacekeepers. After all, peace, order, and good government are reflected in our charter, notes Kathryn White, executive director of the United Nations Association in Canada.

Not everyone, however, is happy with the legacy of Suez. Talk to Canadian soldiers and many will tell you they dislike the peacekeeper label. Most soldiers like to think of themselves as combatants first; peacekeeping is a skill that, while useful, is not their first priority.

Retired major general Lewis MacKenzie maintains that peacekeeping has always been a sideline activity for the Canadian military. Canada may have sent thousands of soldiers on UN missions from the 1960s to the 1990s, but it had many more thousands assigned to a combat role within NATO, ready to go to war with the former Soviet Union if need be.

Some Canadian officers and defence analysts argue that traditional Pearsonian-style peacekeeping, as practised in the Suez and elsewhere, is dead. There is no peace to keep in a world where terrorists and insurgents, instead of standing armies, dominate the war zones of today.

But the UN still operates such missions. In other cases, such as in the Congo today, it has approved a more aggressive style of operation, which includes combat to rein in warring factions.

Yet, today the Canadian Forces are unlikely to be involved in either. Over the last several years, Canada has been in a full-scale retreat from UN operations. In March, it shut down its contribution to the Golan Heights, ending a thirty-two-year presence that started in the aftermath of the 1973 Yom Kippur War.

With the withdrawal from the Golan Heights, Canada drops to fiftieth place in the rank of those contributing to UN missions, according to a March 2006 *Globe and Mail* article by Walter Dorn, associate professor at the Canadian Forces College and co-chair of the Department of Security Studies. The country once known as the committed peacekeeper now has fewer than sixty military personnel assigned to the world body, putting it on par with Guatemala, the Philippines, and Sri Lanka. The Canadian Forces have also pulled out their senior representative from the UN's peacekeeping directorate, arguing that the officer is needed back in Ottawa to work on the future transformation of the military.

Last year the Canadian Forces declined to send four additional soldiers to help deal with the ongoing crisis in the Congo, a catastrophe that is killing more than one-thousand people a day. Instead, Canada has nine soldiers among the sixteen-thousand United Nations troops in the Congo.

The Canadian government also recently declined to commit troops to the Darfur region in Sudan, even as human rights observers warned of the growing genocide there. As an alternative, the Canadian Forces are focusing on what they call higher priority and higher threat missions, such as fighting insurgents in Afghanistan. Defence Minister Gordon O'Connor has said that the focus of Canada's overseas military commitment for the near future will be the NATO/U.S. mission in Afghanistan and there will be few troops left over to be sent elsewhere, either on UN or other operations.

But the continuing problem for the Canadian military and the federal government is that the public is still anchored to the image of UN peacekeeping made famous during the Suez crisis. That message has been consistently delivered over the years by public opinion polls, done both for the Canadian Forces and other agencies.

Typical is a 2004 survey for the Department of National Defence, which noted that about 57 percent of respondents favoured a military involved in a traditional peacekeeping role, while only 41 percent supported a peacemaking role, which might involve fighting alongside troops from other nations to force peace in a disputed area. "Although Canadians recognize the need for a versatile military force, and understand the need to be combat ready, their preferred role for the forces is as peacekeepers and deliverers of humanitarian and disaster assistance," a Defence Department analysis of the poll concluded.

Trying to change the public's support for peacekeeping in favour of more combat-oriented roles, such as that in Afghanistan, may be more difficult than the Canadian military and government thinks. Rightly or wrongly, fifty years after the end of the Suez crisis, Canadians still want their armed forces to play the role of the honest peace-broker on the world stage.

Focus Questions

1. What were Pearson's "four faces of peace," and how might they be applied to modern situations of conflict?

   Trade - war, economic gain - NO; only destruction
      Barriers disadvantage
   Power - talking bout globalizing
   Policy - possibilities of agreement, war is the easy way
   People - Free ppl, fear enemy of peace
         as they are what makes the unity

2. Why did Pearson believe that an international police force was necessary? Why was this particular kind of international cooperation so attractive to him?

   - life experience
   - force to the UN's back / enforce rules

3. What were the central challenges faced by Peacekeepers under Dallaire in Rwanda? What do these challenges reveal about the current (post-cold-war) state of peacekeeping?

   - lack of equipment

4. After reading the extract from Dallaire's book, what contrasts do you see between the kind of international situation he was forced to work with, and the kind which Pearson envisioned?

5. What arguments are made by those who say Canadians should pull out of Peacekeeping operations? How are they countered?

19

Canada as Landscape, Real and Imagined

Introduction

The readings in this final chapter are all based on an aspect of Canadian nationalism which many see as the only truly *national* characteristic—the one thing that all Canadians can supposedly identify with, and be identified by—the landscape. But identification with and by landscape is not simple or unproblematic. Historically, as Carl Berger argues, notions of Canada as a northern nation have been used to justify racist policies and attitudes. And perhaps they still do. In contemporary society, as Will Ferguson argues, landscape creates a hollow and unjustified "nationalism by proxy" which is neither useful nor helpful. And as Miriam Waddington's beautiful, but ambivalent poem reveals, the Canadian landscape is both confused and confusing, blurred and distinct—and one need only scratch the geography to reveal the blood of history.

The True North Strong and Free
Carl Berger
1966

Hail! Rugged monarch, Northern Winter, hail!
Come! Great Physician, vitalize the gale;
Dispense the ozone thou has purified,
With Frost and Fire, where Health and age reside,—
Where Northern Lights electrify the soul
Of Mother Earth, whose throne is near the Pole.

Why should the children of the North deny
The sanitary virtues of the sky?
Why should they fear the cold, or dread the snow,
When ruddier blood thro' their hot pulses flow?
. . .

We have the Viking blood, and Celtic bone,
The Saxons' muscled flesh, and scorn to groan,
Because we do not bask in Ceylon's Isle,
Where Heber said, that 'only man is vile'.
. . .

But we, as laymen, must get down to earth,
And praise the clime which gave our nation birth.
Kind Winter is our theme.

William Henry Taylor,
Canadian Seasons. Spring:
Summer: Autumn: Winter:
with a Medley of Reveries in verse and Prose
and Other Curios (Toronto, 1913)

EVERYBODY TALKS ABOUT the weather and the climate: seldom have these been exalted as major attributes of nationality. Yet from the days of the French explorers, who often remarked that the future inhabitants of northern America must necessarily be as hardy as their environment, to John Diefenbaker's invocation of the northern destiny of the nation, detached observers and patriotic spokesmen alike have fixed upon the northern character of Canada as one of the chief attributes of her nationality. Canadian national feeling, like the nationalist impulse in other countries, has expressed itself in myths and legends about the past and anticipations of noble mission in the future, as well as in distinctive economic and international policies. Such myths and symbols nourish and sustain the emotional taproot of nationalism, and impart to it an intellectual content which itself has an attractive power. The purpose of this paper is to describe the elements and savour the texture of one such recurrent theme in Canadian nationalist thought which flowered in the half century after Confederation and which is, in muted form, still with us—the idea that Canada's unique character derived from her northern location, her severe winters, and her heritage of 'northern races.'

The True North, Strong and Free

In the rhetoric of the day, Canada was the 'Britain of the North,' 'this northern kingdom,' the 'True North' in Tennyson's phrase, the 'Lady of the Snows' in Kipling's. 'Canada is a young, fair and stalwart maiden of the north.'[1] 'The very atmosphere of her northern latitude, the breath of life that rose from lake and forest, prairie and mountain, was fast developing a race of men with bodies enduring as iron and minds as highly tempered as steel.'[2] Canada was the 'Young giant nation of the North,' the 'Young scion of the northern zone'; her people, 'Our hardy northern race'; her location, those 'Stern latitudes.'[3] These images denote not merely geographical location or climatic condition but the combination of both, moulding racial character. The result of life in the northern latitudes was the creation and sustenance of self-reliance, strength, hardness—in short, all the attributes of a dominant race. 'Northern nations always excel southern ones in energy and stamina, which accounts for their prevailing power.'[4] In the north 'the race is compelled by nature to maintain its robust attributes, mental and physical, whereas in more sunny countries like Africa and Australia the tendency of the climate is toward deterioration.'[5] 'A constitution nursed upon the oxygen of our bright winter atmosphere,' exclaimed Governor General Dufferin, 'makes its owner feel as though he could toss about the pine trees in his glee . . .'[6] Just as 'northern' was synonymous with strength and self-reliance, so 'southern' was equated with degeneration, decay, and effeminacy. Our 'bracing northern winters,' declared the *Globe* in 1869, 'will preserve us from the effeminacy which naturally steals over the most vigorous races when long under the relaxing influence of tropical or even generally mild and genial skies.'[7] Moreover, it was believed that liberty originated among the tribes of northern Europe and was dependent upon those very characteristics which the northern environment called forth. Canada, then, was not only the true north, but also strong and free.

In origin, ideas about the relationship between climate and the character of 'races' and their institutions were rooted in myths and stereotypes in classical, medieval, and renaissance Europe, most of which viewed the southern Mediterranean peoples as gay, lively, and individualistic, and the northerners as stupid and dull barbarians.[8] The first coherent Canadian statement of the idea of the northern race came from an associate of the Canada First Movement who was also a Fellow of the Royal Society of Northern Antiquaries of Copenhagen, Robert Grant Haliburton. Lamenting the fact that Confederation had been created with as little excitement among the masses as if a joint-stock company had been formed, he asked, 'Can the generous flame of national spirit be kindled and blaze in the icy bosom of the frozen north?' Convinced that the indispensable attribute of a nation, a 'national spirit,' was the product of slow growth unless stimulated by a violent struggle, the memory of a glorious past, or the anticipation of a bright future. Haliburton added to the Canada First spirit the contention that Canada's future as a dominant nation was secure because of its northern character, 'We Are the Northmen of the New World,' his lecture to the Montreal Literary Club in 1869 on the men of the north and their place in history was the seedbed of the northern race idea. Ironically, Haliburton's poor health compelled him to spend his winters in tropical climates, where he devoted himself to ethnological and anthropological investigations. In 1887 he discovered the existence of a race of pygmies in North Africa.

Haliburton's declaration that Canadians were a northern race was expressed in the language of science and the rich imagery of romantic history. 'Our cornfields, rich though they are, cannot compare with the fertile prairies of the West, and our long winters are a drain on the profits of business, but may not our snow and frost give us what is of more value than gold or silver, a healthy, hardy, virtuous, dominant race?' The peculiar characteristic of the new dominion, he asserted, 'must ever be that it is a Northern country inhabited by the descendants of Northern races.' This claim to dominance rested on two assumptions: firstly, the hardy northern races of Europe are attracted to Canada. The British people themselves are 'but a fusion of many northern elements which are here again meeting and mingling, and blending together to form a new nationality.' This new nationality must comprise at once 'the Celtic, the Teutonic, and the Scandinavian elements, and embrace the Celt, the Norman French, the Saxon and the Swede.' Secondly, to Haliburton, the climate itself was a creative force. 'Is it climate that produces varieties in our race or must we adopt the views of some eminent authorities of science, who hold that the striking diversities now apparent in the languages, temperament, and capacities of nations, must have existed *ab initio?* The Mosaic chronology must be rejected and the period of man's life on earth must be extended to millions of years.' 'If climate has not had the effect of moulding races, how is it that southern nations have almost invariably been inferior to and subjugated by the men of the north?'

The stern climate would preserve in their pristine vigour the characteristics of the northern races and ensure that Canada would share the destiny of the northmen of the old world, who destroyed Rome after it 'had become essentially Southern in its characteristics.' Those northmen were not barbarians but the carriers of the germ of liberty, 'On investigating the history of out laws and of the rise of civil and political liberty in Europe,' Haliburton found them rooted in the elemental institutions of the northmen. 'Almost all the Northern nations had similar systems of regulating the rights of property and the remedies of wrongs. Their laws were traditions called by them their *customs,* an unwritten code which still exists in England where it is known as the Common law. . . . [and] it is a remarkable fact that wherever these unwritten laws have been preserved, civil and political liberty has also survived.' In Canada, 'the cold north wind that rocked the cradle of our race, still blows through our forests, and breathes the spirit of liberty into our hearts.'[9] Thus, because of the climate and because Canadians are sprung from these men of the north—the 'Aryan' family, Canada must be a pre-eminent power, the home of a superior race, the heir of both the historical destiny of the ancient Scandinavians and their spirit of liberty.

In the exuberant optimism of Canada First nationalism. Haliburton took the Canadian climate—since the days of Voltaire's famous disparagement, the symbol of sterility, inhospitality, and worthlessness—and turned it into the dynamic element of national greatness. Though he was to break with Haliburton over the issue of Canadian independence, to the end of his days the irrepressible Colonel Denison could boast that 'We are the Northmen of the new world.'[10] Charles Mair, too, thought that 'whilst the south is in a great measure a region of effeminacy and disease, the northwest is a decided recuperator of decayed function and wasted tissue.'[11] And William Foster, in his address on the new nationality in 1871, said that 'The old Norse mythology, with its Thor hammers and Thor hammerings, appeals to us,—for we are a Northern people,—as the true out-crop of human nature, more manly, more real than the weak marrow-bones superstition of an effeminate South.[12] It is no accident that members of this youthful and intellectual nationalist group should appeal to what Mair, in his poem on Foster's death, called 'the unconquered North,' that they should extol Alexander Morris's vision of 'the Great Britannic Empire of the North,' or that they should be remembered a generation later as exponents of the northern destiny of Canada. Their most practical achievement in politics was the agitation for Canadian acquisition of the northwest territory, the importance of which they contended had been obscured by tales of ice and snow falsely broadcast by Hudson's Bay Company officials to protect their fur domain from settlement.

Climatic or Racial Determinism?

While Haliburton's address included much that was to receive progressive elaboration by others, such as the notion that French and English were, in racial terms, one people, it contained an ambivalence that was to become more obvious as the idea of the northern race became enmeshed in a popularized Darwinism. This dichotomy was simply between an optimistic, idealistic meliorism which took climate as moulding desirable qualities irrespective of the racial origins of the people, and a scientific determinism which saw racial capacities as fixed, or changeable only to a limited degree. Haliburton avoided such subtleties by implying that all future immigration into Canada would consist of those races already inured and adapted to the northern environment. Later, more pessimistic writers were to see the climate as a 'barrier' to certain kinds of immigrant, rather than as an agency for totally transforming them. This dualism can be best illustrated by considering two different versions of the idea.

A most forceful statement of the view that assumed the complete malleability of character was made in 1877 by another Nova Scotian, Charles R. Tuttle. A self-educated schoolteacher who later made a career of journalism in Winnipeg and the United States, Tuttle produced a large number of now forgotten books including an imposing two-volume history of Canada. In this history he expressed the optimistic opinion that the institutions, soil, and climate of Canada would determine the character of the people. The immigrants, he wrote, come from the monarchical countries of Europe, 'ignorant, rude, and unmannerly,' but their character is transformed, they become self-reliant, and exhibit a 'manly independence,' under the influence of British institutions and the 'broad rivers, boundless prairies, high mountains, and pathless woods.'[13]

In Tuttle, a romantic ruralism was mixed with the conviction that man's capacity for improvement was infinite and, in a favourable environment, inevitable. Where he saw the 'ignorant, rude, and unmannerly' being formed into independent and hardy yeomen by the natural features of the country and British institutions, more pessimistic observers, while not denying the potent influence of environment, nevertheless emphasized rather the inherent and unchangeable aptitudes of the 'northern races.' That the northern climate constituted a national blessing because it excluded 'weaker' races was the persistent theme of the writings and orations of the Canadian imperialist George Parkin. A native of New Brunswick, Parkin was one of the most forceful and idealistic spokesmen of the Imperial Federation League, Principal of Upper Canada College during the late 1890s, and subsequently one of the organizers of the Cecil Rhodes scholarship trust. Heavily influenced by the social Darwinism of the time, and acknowledging his debt to the historian Buckle for the idea of climatic influence upon the life of nations, Parkin called the Canadian climate 'one of our greatest blessings.' The 'severe winter climate of Canada,' he said, 'is perhaps the most valuable asset that the country has.' A temperature of twenty degrees below zero which he found at Winnipeg 'seemed to give an added activity to people's steps and a buoyancy to their spirits.' The climate necessitates vigorous effort; 'it teaches foresight; it cures or kills the shiftless and improvident; history shows that in the long run it has made strong races.'

Where Tuttle viewed the capacity for self-government as the product of the environment, Parkin contended that fitness for self-government was itself the inherent function of the northern races. Without race vanity, he asserted, we may attribute to the Anglo-Saxon race a unique aptitude for self-government. The special importance of the Canadian climate, therefore, was not merely that it sustained the hardy character of the stronger races, but that it also constituted, in Darwinian terms, 'a persistent process of natural selection.' The northern winters ensured that Canada would have no Negro problem, 'which weighs like a troublesome nightmare upon the civilization of the United States'; and it seemed that nature itself had decreed that Canada would have no cities 'like New York, St. Louis, Cincinnati, or New Orleans which attract even the vagrant population of Italy and other countries of Southern Europe.' 'Canada,' Parkin emphasized, 'will belong to the sturdy races of the North-Saxon, and Celt, Scandinavian, Dane and Northern German, fighting their way under conditions sometimes rather more severe than those to which they have been accustomed in their old homes.' The climate 'is certain, in short, to secure for the Dominion and perpetuate there the vigour of the best northern races.'[14]

The Advantages of Northernness

To recapitulate and detail the elements of this concept is to indicate the basis of its credibility and the nature of its appeal. First of all, the very fact of northernness connoted strength and hardihood, vigour and purity. 'Strength and power,' ran the familiar refrain, 'have ever been with the Northern peoples.'[15] In the struggle for existence, the northern conditions called forth the virtues of self-reliance and strength: only the fittest survived. On the other hand, the 'south' conjured up the image of enervation, of abundance stifling the Victorian values of self-help, work, and thrift of effeminacy, of voluptuous living, and consequently of the decay and degeneration of character.

A whole series of desirable national characteristics were derived from Canada's northern location. It was implied that northern peoples expressed their hard individualism in an individualistic religion, stripped of the gorgeous luxuries congenial to southern Catholicism. The climate said Parkin, imparts 'a Puritan turn of mind which gives moral strenuousness.'[16] A Methodist clergyman and editor, who attended the American centennial exhibition in 1876 and saw a representative collection of European paintings, reported his disgust with the Catholic art of the south, a reaction he attributed to the lax morals of the 'Latin' races. 'I must,' he wrote, 'record my protest against the sensuous character of many of the foreign paintings, especially of France, Austria, and Spain. In this respect they are in striking contrast with the almost universal chaste and modest character of the English and American pictures, and those of Rothern (*sic,* Northern) Europe. I attribute this difference partly to the only partial moral restraints of the Roman Catholic religion, and partly to a survival, in the old Latin races, of the ancient pagan characteristics which created the odious art and literature, and social corruptions of the effete and dying Roman Empire.'[17] These impurities, of course, were due to much else besides climate, but the clear, cold, and frosty air itself seemed an insulation against lax morality. Another clergyman found in the Canadian winter the impulse to cultural and mental improvement. The winter 'is prophetic . . . of a race, in mind and body and moral culture, of the highest type.' Applying to Canada the remarks that Sir Charles Dilke had made in reference to Scotland, the Reverend F. A. Wightman cited with approval the opinion that the ' "long winters cultivate thrift, energy and fore-thought, without which civilization would perish, and at the same time give leisure for reading and study. So the Scottish, the Icelanders, the Swedes, and the northern races generally, are much better educated than the Latin and southern races.'"[18]

The Canadian winter was not only considered to be conducive to mental improvement: in maintaining physical health and stimulating robustness, according to one of the foremost Canadian physicians of the day, it was unsurpassed. A belief in the healthful qualities of the climate was expressed in much of the literature on the northern theme, but it was left to a surgeon at the Hôtel-Dieu in Montreal to impart to this idea the authority of medical knowledge and statistical proof. William Hales Hingston had studied medicine at McGill and Edinburgh, as well as Berlin, Heidelberg, and Vienna; in 1854 he began practice in Montreal and was for many years surgeon at the largest hospital in Canada and a professor of clinical surgery at the Montreal School of Medicine. In 1884 Hingston published a series of papers under the title, *The Climate of Canada and its Relation to Life and Health.* Employing statistics provided by the surgeons at British and American army stations, he ascertained that as one passed northward the salubrity of the climate increased, that the ratios of mortality from digestive, respiratory, and nervous disorders decreased in a northward progression. After considering practically every known malady from diarrhoe to dysentery, consumption to cataract, he emphasized that there are no diseases indigenous to the country. The dry air and cold winter, moreover, are decided recuperators of disease. 'Indeed,' he concluded, 'in considering the few diseases which here afflict humanity relatively to elsewhere, we have great reason to be thankful to the All-powerful Controller of the seasons as of our fate. . . . He keeps us in health, comfort and safety.' If only such pernicious social habits as intemperance could be avoided, the climate was most 'favourable to the highest development of a hardy, long-lived, intelligent people'; the tendency 'is unmistakably in favour of increased muscular development'; 'the future occupants of the soil will be taller, straighter, leaner people—hair darker and drier and coarser; muscles more tendinous and prominent and less cushioned . . .' These future occupants of the soil will be, emphatically, a *Canadian* people,' for the distinct nationalities of Europe will blend here into a homogeneous race, the predominating characteristics of which will be determined 'after the fashion described by Darwin as the struggle for existence.' To this people 'will belong the privilege, the great privilege, of aiding in erecting, in what was so lately a wilderness, a monument of liberty and civilization, broader, deeper, firmer, than has ever yet been raised by the hand of man.'[19] There was much in Hingston's book—description of the variety of the climate, reflections on social habits, and the straight faced observation that those frozen to death display on their visages a look of contentment achieved only by successful religious mystics—but its central burden was that the northern location will breed a distinctive, superior, and healthy people.

It seemed that scarcely any advantages accruing to Canada from the winter season went unnoticed or unsung. The winter snow covers and protects fall crops; the frost acts as a solvent on the soil, ploughing the ground and leaving it in springtime 'completely pulverized'; the cold freezes newly-killed livestock and preserves them for market. It makes possible the commercial activity of lumbering, for the 'frost makes bridges without a cent of cost; the snow provides the best roads,' 'the whole face of the country being literally Macadamized by nature.' Winter makes possible sleighing, tobogganing, snowshoeing, and skating. 'Jack Frost effectually and gratuitously guards us on three thousand miles of our northern coast, and in this he does us a distinct service, greatly relieving national expenditure and contributing much to our sense of security.'[20]

A Basis for Racial Unity

While Canada's northernness implied these desirable national advantages, in its second aspect it underlined the fundamental unity of the French and British Canadians. According to most definitions of nationality offered in the late nineteenth century, a nation was held together by the ties of race, religion, and language, as well as by a general similarity in political and social institutions. The very existence of the French Canadians, however, and the 'racial conflict' and disunity their distinctive social and religious institutions helped to engender, seemed to belie the contention that Canada was a nation.

But the French Canadians, by the very facts of their colonization, settlement, and multiplication, had demonstrated their fitness to cope with the inhospitable northern environment. The stern climate and the winds of winter were uniform on both sides of the Ottawa River. The 'geographical contour of our Country,' said F. B. Cumberland, Vice-President of the National Club of Toronto, 'assists by creating a Unity of Race. Living throughout in a region wherein winter is everywhere a distinct season of the year, inuring the body and stimulating to exertion, we are by nature led to be a provident, a thrifty, and a hardy people; no weakling can thrive among us, we must be as vigorous as our climate.' Through the 'natural selection' of immigration, only the northern races, including the 'Norman French,' have settled here, and what selective immigration has effected 'nature is welding together into Unity and by this very similarity of climate creating in Canada a homogeneous Race, sturdy in frame, stable in character, which will be to America what their forefathers, the Northmen of old, were to the continent of Europe.'[21]

It was argued, moreover, that 'there is no real or vital difference in the origin of these two races; back beyond the foreground of history they were one.'[22] This identification of the common racial origin of both the British and French Canadians rested on the results of the research of genealogists, like Benjamin Sulte and Cyprien Tanguay, who had inquired into the origins of the original immigrants to New France. Between 1871 and 1890 Tanguay compiled no less than seven volumes of his *Dictionnaire généologique des familles canadiennes* and demonstrated that the majority of French Canadians were descended from immigrants who had come from Brittany and Normandy. The 'French Canadian type,' declared Sulte, 'is Norman, whether its origin be pure Norman, mixed Norman, Gascon or French-English.'[23] Since the Normans themselves were descendants of the Scandinavian invaders of the ninth and tenth centuries who had gone to conquer Britain, it could be claimed that both British and French were a northern race, or at least that both contained elements of the northern strains. It is an interesting fact, asserted the historian William Wood, 'that many of the French-Canadians are descended from the Norman-Franks, who conquered England seven hundred years before the English conquered La Nouvelle France, and that, however, diverse they are now, the French and British peoples both have some Norman stock in common.'[24]

That the 'Norman blood' was a positive unifying force in Canada was emphasized by George Bourinot in his constitutional histories, and in 1925 G. M. Wrong, Professor of History in the University of Toronto, told the Canadian Historical Association that 'There is in reality no barrier of race to keep the English and French apart in Canada: the two peoples are identical in racial origins.'[25] As late as 1944, Abbé Arthur Maheux, Professor of History at Laval University, after condemning those 'people who think along the lines of blood, so being Hitlerites without knowing it,' pointed out that 'the Norman blood, at least, is a real link between our two groups.' The French people, the Abbé explained, 'is a mixture of different bloods: the Gaul, the Briton, the Romans, the Norman each gave their share. The same is true with the English people, the Celt, the Briton, the Roman, the Saxon, the Dane, the Norman each gave their share of blood. It is easy to see that the elements are about the same and in about the same proportions in each of these two nations. Both are close relatives by blood from the very beginning of their national existences. And both Canadian groups have the same close kinship.'[26]

A Rationale for Anti-Americanism

The Canadian people were thus not only collectively a superior race, but their 'northernness' was constantly compared to the 'southernness' of the United States. The third use of the idea was a vigorous statement of the separateness of the two countries. When the annexationists asked 'why should the schism which divided our race on this continent 100 years ago, be perpetuated? . . . What do we gain by remaining apart?' and answered their own question by saying that 'Union would be the means of ultimately cementing the Anglo-Saxon race throughout the world,'[27] the usual retort was to deny that the Republic was an Anglo-Saxon country and to elaborate Canadian virtues derived from its northernness against the degeneration of 'the south.' While the northern climate of Canada was both moulding the northern elements and rejecting weaker, southern immigration, thus creating a homogeneous race, the southern climate of the United States was sapping the energies of even those descendants of vigorous races at the same time that it was attracting multitudes of the weaker races from Southern Europe, in addition to providing a hospitable home to the large Negro element. This destruction of the homogeneity of the Republic was regarded as 'diluting' its strength, as a species of 'deterioration.' This was because the southern immigrants were neither formed by a hardy climate in their homeland nor forced to adapt to one in the States. In Canada, Principal Falconer of the University of Toronto reassured his readers, 'the rigour of the northern climate has been, and will continue to be, a deterrent for the peoples of Southern Europe.'[28] Our climate, contended Parkin, excludes the lower races, 'squeezed out by that 30 or 40 degrees below zero.' Canada attracts 'the stronger people of the northern lands. That is the tendency to squeeze out the undesirable and pump in, as Kipling says, . . . the strong and desirable.' 'We have an advantage, this northern race, of a stern nature which makes us struggle for existence.' The 'submerged tenth,' the weaker members of even the stronger races, are also excluded, and hence Canada does not suffer from the American labour troubles. Labour problems are unknown in Canada partly because of the abundance of land and partly because the 'Canadian winter exercises upon the tramp a silent but well-nigh irresistible persuasion to shift to a warmer latitude.' The United States itself thus serves as a 'safety-valve' for labour questions in the Dominion. The climate 'is a fundamental political and social advantage which the Dominion enjoys over the United States.' It ensures stability and ordered development as well as superiority.[29]

Northernness and Liberty

The notion of strength and superiority inhering in the quality of northernness included a fourth, and perhaps the most important, element of the general idea. Expressed in the words of Emerson, it was that 'Wherever snow falls, there is usually civil freedom.'[30] Not only did the northern climate foster exactly those characteristics without which self-government could not work, but it was held that, historically, the 'germs' of the institutions of liberty originated among the northern peoples and that northern races, inured by centuries of struggles with the elements and acquaintance with these institutions of self-government, enjoyed a superior capacity for governing themselves. Liberty itself depended upon self-reliance, a rugged independence, instilled by the struggle for existence. Thus to the equation of 'northern' with strength and the strenuous virtues, against 'southern' with degeneration and effeminacy, was added the identification of the former with liberty and the latter with tyranny.

Because 'liberty' was itself somehow the major stimulant to 'progress,' the comparison was often made in terms of progress and regression. In a book review, the editor of the *Canadian Methodist Magazine* contrasted the result of Anglo-Saxon development in North America with that of the Latin races in South America. 'On the one side,' he wrote, 'a forward motion of society and the greatest development of agriculture, commerce and industry; on the other, society thrown backward and plunged to grovel in a morass of idle, unproductive town life, and given up to officialism and political revolutions. In the North we have the rising of the future, in the

South the crumbling and decaying past.'[31] Wherein, asked a pamphleteer, lies the secret of such marvelous progress? 'It springs largely from the fact that the country was peopled by the Anglo-Saxon race.... When Rome was overshadowing the nations of Southern and Central Europe with its greatness, in the cheerless, uninviting north, a people was undergoing hardy discipline, on land and sea, in constant strife and endless foray, which produced a nobler type of manhood than Rome.... It is from these fearless freemen of North Germany, England is indebted in a large measure for her political liberties.'[32]

The idea that it was in the north 'that the liberties of the world had their birth' was sustained by the political science of the day. Influenced by the 'comparative politics' of E. A. Freeman in England and H. B. Adams in the United States, the constitutional and political writings of George Bourinot detailed the operations of the Teutonic germ theory in Canada. In biological analogy, freedom was a 'seed,' a 'germ,' which originated in the tribal assemblies of the ancient Scandinavians, was transplanted to England and subsequently to New England, and then to Canada by the migration of descendants of these Teutonic races. Wherever the favoured race appeared, its early institutional life was repeated and amplified because 'freedom' was in 'the blood.' Conversely, southern non-Teutonic peoples were either 'untutored' in self-government but were educable, or were incapable of governing themselves altogether. In the bracing climate of the north, so resembling freedom's original home, liberty, it was thought, would flourish in a purer form.[33]

It was this identification of liberty with northernness that gave such force to the anti-American emotion that Canadian, or 'British,' liberty was far superior to the uproarious democracy of the United States. It was a charge taken directly from pessimistic American racists. The 'new immigration' coming from southern and southeastern Europe became the object of concern and then dread in the late 1880s, partly because it coincided with political and social disturbances arising from the transition from an agrarian to an industrial civilization. It was thought that this immigration not only destroyed the homogeneity of the American people, but also threatened the very existence of Anglo-Saxon leadership and Anglo-Saxon values. Commenting editorially on an article by Henry Cabot Lodge, the chief immigration restrictionist in the Senate, the *Empire* agreed that the old-stock families in the United States were losing their hold, that immigration and the multiplication of 'the dregs of the old world population' were increasing too rapidly for assimilation. 'The Anglo-Saxon element, the real strength of the nation, is not proportionally as influential now as it once was.'[34] Even earlier, Goldwin Smith feared that 'the Anglo-American race is declining in numbers; ... The question is whether its remaining stock of vitality is sufficient to enable it, before it loses its tutelary ascendancy, to complete the political education of the other races.'[35] What Smith viewed with apprehension, others relished in the conviction that Canada was preserved from such a fate. 'Take the fact that one million two hundred thousand people passed through Ellis Island into the port of New York last year. Who were they,' asked Parkin, 'Italians, Greeks, Armenians, Bulgarians, the

Latin races of the South. People unaccustomed to political freedom, unaccustomed to self-government, pouring in. . . . They did not come to Canada.'[36] In Canada, because of the climate, there were no Haymarket riots, no lynchings, no assassinations of public men. 'The United States,' declared the *Dominion Illustrated* in 1891, 'are welcome to the Hungarians, Poles, Italians and others of that class; they are, as a rule, wretchedly poor, make very poor settlers, and bring with them many of the vices and socialistic tendencies which have caused much trouble to their hosts already. Renewed efforts should . . . be made by our government to induce more of the hardy German and Norwegian races to remain here.'[37]

The Imperialism of the Northern Race

For the imperialist the idea of the northern race had an importance which transcended its purely Canadian application. It supported the notion of the tutelary role of the stronger races in extending order and liberty to southern peoples who, either because of their climate alone, or because of their inherent weakness, could neither generate progress unassisted nor erect the institutions of self-government. Imperialists like Parkin had an immense pride in their native Canada: it alone, of all the Dominions, lay above the forty-fifth parallel. Because of the vigour implied in its northernness, Canada could exercise within the imperial framework a dynamic influence on the future, perhaps even exceeding that of the homeland. Because of the inevitable deterioration that was creeping over the urbanized and industrialized Englishman, cut off from the land. Canada was to be a kind of rejuvenator of the imperial blood. For all their rhetoric about the citizens of Canada regarding South Africa or Australia as their own country, this notion of northernness bolstered their feeling of a unique connection between Canada and Britain.

The imperial role of Canada depended on the character of the race, and it was with 'character' that imperialists like Parkin and Kipling were most concerned. Their apprehensions that the character of the imperial race had deteriorated, that the instinct of adventure and self-sacrifice which had been the motive force of imperial expansion had decayed, were coupled with the pervasive fear that the race was becoming 'soft,' that it no longer manifested 'hardness'—hardness meaning not callousness but the stoical acceptance of the strenuous life and the performance of duty irrespective of rewards. It was this concern that lay at the bottom of their advocacy of a manly athleticism, their praise for what seemed to some a martial arrogance, and their exhortations to uplift the weaker races, not so much because they believed that the weaker races could be transformed but because the imperial race's assumption of the burden was in itself a test and an exaltation of their race's 'character.' The motive was as much self-regeneration as altruism. The northern race idea is subtly related to this concern, at least psychologically. In Canada, said Kipling, 'there is a fine, hard, bracing climate, the climate that puts iron and grit into men's bones.'[38] In moulding character this climate was a permanent fixture, unlike an abundance of free land. It instilled exactly those characteristics upon which the imperialists themselves placed the most value—hardness, strenuousness, endurance—so vital to dominance.

The aspect of northernness was associated with the historic imperialism of the northern races. The British Isles were conquered by the northmen, who transmitted to the Anglo-Saxons their love of the sea as well as their genius for self-government. 'The English came to America,' wrote the secretary of the Navy League in Quebec, 'in obedience to the same racial sea-faring instincts that led their ancestors to England itself.'[39] One of the reasons for British primacy, explained another historian, was that 'our northern climate has produced a race of sailors and adventurers from the days of the Vikings to the present, inured to all the perils of the sea and the rigours of climate.' The Icelandic sagas, he continued, 'are an interesting part of the native literature of our race, which owes much of its hardihood and enterprise to the admixture of northern blood.'[40] The celebrations of 1892 and 1897 of the voyages of Columbus and Cabot deepened interest in the Norsemen who had preceded both of them, an interest sometimes associated with the arguments of the navalists in the Navy League. Like liberty, the 'seafaring instincts' were racial properties. Parkin said that imperial expansion was not haphazard but the inevitable result of 'racial instincts' as well as national necessities. The mind which viewed expansive and hardy racial character as northern products saw the Norse voyages as something more than interesting details at the beginning of Canadian history books. 'Though nothing came of these Norse discoveries,' wrote Charles G. D. Roberts, 'they are interesting as the first recorded contact of our race with these lands which we now occupy. They are significant, because they were a direct result of that spirit of determined independence which dwells in our blood.'[41]

Moreover, this northernness of the imperial race was connected with the notion of the tendency of world power to shift northward as the phases of evolution proceeded. Parkin, who confessed finding confirmation and amplification of his own beliefs in Benjamin Kidd's *Social Evolution,* must have read with approval Kidd's prediction that northward the march of Empire makes its way:

> The successful peoples have moved westwards for physical reasons: the seat of power has moved continuously northwards for reasons connected with the evolution in character which the race is undergoing. Man, originally a creature of a warm climate and still multiplying most easily and rapidly there, has not attained his highest development where the conditions of existence have been easiest. Throughout history the centre of power has moved gradually but surely to the north into those stern regions where men have been trained for the rivalry of life in the strenuous conflict with nature in which they have acquired energy, courage, integrity, and those characteristic qualities which contribute to raise them to a high state of social efficiency . . .[42]

Especially after 1890, the northern-race concept was frequently explained in the language of a popularized social Darwinism which imparted to it a scientific credibility surpassing in authority either vague rhetoric or poetic allusions. Parkin often employed the terminology of evolutionary science when expressing the notion, but it was left to an obscure writer in a university magazine to place the idea in the general context of 'The Theory of Evolution.' Beginning with a curt dismissal of the Mosaic account of creation as 'a mixture of Hebrew folk-lore and Christian teaching,' he stated that 'man himself does not stand apart from the rest of living things as a separate creation, but has had a common origin with them and is governed by the same laws.' One of these laws is the progressive evolution of man which accompanied his migration from the tropical to the northern zones. 'The most primitive type of man at present existing is the Negro, who, like the Apes most nearly allied to Man, is essentially a tropical animal, and does not flourish in cold countries.' 'As the negro race, however, spread, it gradually reached the temperate regions, and here the struggle with Nature became fiercer and the whole civilization underwent development and a higher type of man—the yellow or Mongolian race was evolved.' This race, which included the Red Indians, Peruvians, Chinese, and Japanese, also came into contact with a more vigorous climate, either by expanding northward, or meeting the Ice Age as it moved southward. The result was progressive evolution: 'the struggle for the necessities of life, the need for bravery, endurance, and all the manly virtues, reached its climax, and the highest type of man was evolved—the Nordic type or white man, whose original home was on the fringe of the ice-sheet.' Subsequently, from Scandinavia and Russia, the Nordic race conquered Britain and temperate Europe. From this capsule history, 'as determined by zoological methods,' the writer drew several 'comforting conclusions as to the future of Canada.' For one thing, the Canadian must be 'the conquering type of man,' and this included the 'French-speaking fellow countrymen who, so far as they are of Norman descent, belong to the same race.' Moreover, the 'Nordic man is essentially an arctic animal and only flourishes in a cold climate—whilst in a warmer region he gradually loses virility and vitality. So that from a zoological point of view the outlook is bright for Canada.'[43]

The Northern Myth in Canadian Art

The image of Canada as a northern country with a strenuous and masterful people was reinforced and sustained in the novels, travelogues, and works of scientific exploration that abounded in the period. The adventure stories centering on life in the isolated Hudson Bay posts and the exploits of the lonely trapper had long been the staple themes of the novels of Robert M. Ballantyne and the boys' books of J. Macdonald Oxley. But after 1896, when the northwest became the locus of immigration and investment, imaginative writers found in that region not only a picturesque setting and indigenous historical incidents and themes but also an area which a large number of their readers had never experienced. Certainly it is significant that a number of the best-selling writers in the decade before the First World War, Ralph Connor, Robert Service, and William Fraser, not only set their works in the northerly setting but also lived there.

The very titles of these books are indicative of their focus: Agnes Laut's story of the fur-trader, *Lords of the North* (1900), and her history—*Canada, the Empire of the North* (1909); Gilbert Parker's *An Adventure of the North* (1905); H. A. Cody's life of Bishop Bompas, *An Apostle of the North* (1905); Ralph Connor's many manly novels set in the northwest, like *Corporal Cameron* (1912) with its inevitable blizzard; travelogues like Agnes D. Cameron's description of her journey through the Athabasca and Mackenzie River region of the Arctic, *The New North* (1909); chronicles of exploration, J. W. Tyrrell's *Across the Sub-Arctics of Canada* (1897), and Vilhjalmur Stefansson's *My Life with the Eskimo* (1913). In 1926, a literary critic complained that the 'whole of Canada has come to be identified with her northernmost reaches,' and in 'modern folk-geography Canada means the North.'[44]

This image was strengthened by the paintings of the 'national movement,' in Canadian art, the Group of Seven. While some of the most characteristic work of men like A. Y. Jackson and J. E. H. Macdonald was done in the post-war decades, it was during the years before 1914 that their nationalism was inspired and their determination made to express the essence of Canada through her landscape. Some of them were directly influenced by a Scandinavian art exhibition in 1912 which 'impressed them as an example of what other northern countries could do in art.' A member of the group admitted that in their minds Canada was 'a long, thin strip of civilization on the southern fringe of a vast expanse of immensely varied, virgin land reaching into the remote north. Our whole country is cleansed by the pristine and replenishing air which sweeps out of that great hinterland. It was the discovery of this great northern area as a field of art which enticed and inspired these painters.' But the north—with its sparkling clear air and sharp outlines which could never be apprehended with the techniques of Old World art—was much more than a field of art: it was the mirror of national character. After a trip into the Arctic with A. Y. Jackson, Lawren Harris reported that 'We came to know that it is only through the deep and vital experience of its total environment that a people identifies itself with its land and gradually a deep and satisfying awareness develops. We were convinced that no virile people could remain subservient to and dependent upon the creations in art of other peoples. . . . To us there was also the strange brooding sense of another nature fostering a new race and a new age.' Though they displayed a variety of personal styles and attitudes, the group was united in the effort to portray the rugged terrain of the Canadian Shield and the changing seasons in the northern woods. While present in J. E. H. Macdonald's *The Solemn Land* (1921) and other early works, the theme of northernness culminated in A. Y. Jackson's *The North Shore of Baffin Island* (c. 1929) and Lawren Harris's *Bylot Island* (1930) both of which exude the crystalline cold and seem themselves to be a part of the stark northern wastes.[45]

The Northern Theme in Retrospect

In retrospect, the northern theme, as it was expressed in the first half-century after Confederation, must be regarded as a myth, for not only did the observations it exalted conflict with objective appraisal, but its primary, intellectual assumptions became suspect. While it rested on the truism, confirmed by modern human geography, that certain climates are stimulating to human exertion, it too frequently glossed over the variety of climatic regions within Canada, and it tended to identify the whole country with that region of it which contained the fewest of her people. It was related and sustained, moreover, by the ebullient faith in the progress of the northwest, in the lusty but mistaken hopes of the wheat-boom years that the northern zone would become the home of millions of happy yeomen. The northern theme also assumed a racist aspect, holding that the capacity for freedom and progress were inherent in the blood of northern races. Not only was this belief progressively undermined by modern anthropological scholarship, but the identification of the Teutonic race with the spirit of liberty appeared especially specious after the First World War. In addition, the appeal of the northern-race idea was limited in the post-war period because its main usefulness had been to underline the differences between Canada and the United States. In the 1920s the focus of nationalist thought shifted, and one of its dominant preoccupations came to be the definition of Canadian character in terms of North American experience, to emphasize the similarities between Canada and the United States.

Intellectual styles change but the permanent facts they seek to interpret and render meaningful do not. As long as there exists a nationalist impulse in Canada the imagination of men will be challenged by the very existence of the fascinating north. Though racism and crude environmentalism have now largely been discredited, the effort to explain Canadian uniqueness in terms of the north has not. As late as 1948, Vincent Massey found several differences between the United States and Canada, such as 'the air of moderation in Canadian habits' to be derived from climate and race:

> Climate plays a great part in giving us our special character, different from that of our southern neighbours. Quite apart from the huge annual bill our winter imposes on us in terms of building construction and clothing and fuel, it influences our mentality, produces a sober temperament. Our racial composition—and this is partly because of our climate—is different, too. A small percentage of our people comes from central or southern Europe. The vast majority springs either from the British Isles or

Northern France, a good many, too, from Scandinavia and Germany, and it is in northwestern Europe that one finds the elements of human stability highly developed. Nothing is more characteristic of Canadians than the inclination to be moderate.[46]

Apart from the muted tone, these observations do not really differ in substance from the remarks made in ringing rhetoric and with scientific certainly in the late nineteenth century by George Parkin, who was, incidentally, Massey's father-in-law.

Very different, however, and of high political potency, was the emotional appeal to the Canadian northern mission evoked by John Diefenbaker in the election of 1958. Seizing upon a theme which his native northwest had inspired in poets and nationalists since Confederation, he declared, suitably enough at Winnipeg, that 'I see a new Canada'—not orientated east and west, but looking northward, responding to the challenges of that hinterland, its energies focused on the exploration and exploitation of the Arctic—'A CANADA OF THE NORTH!' To this compelling theme, which runs so persistently through Canadian nationalist thought since the days of D'Arcy McGee, Canadians responded eagerly and with conviction.[47]

On a more sober and scholarly plane, but not less pungent and appealing, is another recent exposition of the northern theme articulated by a president of the Canadian Historical Association, W. L. Morton, also a native of the northwest. In an address delivered in 1960, Professor Morton fixed upon Canada's 'northern character,' her origins in the expansion of a northern, maritime frontier, and her possession of a distinctive, staple economy, as factors which explained a substantial aspect of her development, her historical dependence upon Britain and the United States, the character of her literature, even the seasonal rhythm of Canadian life.[48]

The concept of Canada as a northern nation, like the idea that the unique character of the United States was shaped by the westward movement, is as important for understanding the intellectual content and emotional appeal of nationalism as it is for explaining the objective determinants of historical development. From the time of Benjamin Franklin, Americans saw 'the west' not so much as a geographical fact but as a symbol, around which they grouped the leading tenets of their nationalist faith—that their movement westward was carrying the American further and further away from effete Europe, that 'the garden' would become the home of an independent yeomanry in which alone reposed true Republican virtue, that the frontier was a safety valve which kept social conditions in the new world from ever approximating those in decadent, classridden Europe. Like the American symbol of the west, the Canadian symbol of the north subsumed a whole series of beliefs about the exalted past, the national character and the certain future. Unlike the American frontier of free land, however, the north itself was inexhaustible: as A. R. M. Lower has recently reminded us, it is a perpetual breath of fresh air.

If Canadian nationalism is to be understood, its meaning must be sought and apprehended not simply in the sphere of political decisions, but also in myths, legends, and symbols like these. For while some might think that Canadians have happily been immune to the wilder manifestations of the nationalist impulse and rhetoric, it seems that they too have had their utopian dreamers, and that they are not totally innocent of a tradition of racism and a falsified but glorious past, tendencies which have always been the invariable by-products of nationalism. For by its very nature, nationalism must seize upon objective dissimilarities and tendencies and invest them in the language of religion, mission, and destiny.

Notes

1. William Pitman Lett, *Annexation and British Connection, Address to Brother Jonathan* (Ottawa, 1889), p. 10.
2. Walter R. Nursey, *The Story of Isaac Brock* (Toronto), 1909, p. 173.
3. Joseph Pope, *The Tour of Their Royal Highnesses the Duke and Duchess of Cornwall and York through the Dominion of Canada in the Year 1901* (Ottawa, 1903), p. 259; Hon. George W. Ross, *The Historical Significance of the Plains of Abraham, Address Delivered Before the Canadian Club of Hamilton, April 27th, 1908* (n.p., n.d.), p. 18; *The Canadian Military Gazette*, xv (January 2, 1900), p. 15; Silas Alward, *An Anglo-American Alliance* (Saint John, N.B. 1911).
4. G. D. Griffin, *Canada Past, Present, Future, and New System of Government* (n.p. 1884), p. ii.
5. George Parkin, address to the Canadian Club and Board of Trade in Saint John, N.B., reported in *The Daily Telegraph*, Saint John, N.B., *March 6, 1907.* Clipping in *Parkin Papers, vol. 82 (Public Archives of Canada, hereinafter PAC).*
6. William Leggo, *History of the Administration of the Earl of Dufferin in Canada* (Toronto, 1878), p. 599.
7. *Weekly Globe,* April 2, 1869.
8. For a fascinating sketch of these myths see J. W. Johnson, " 'Of Differing Ages and Climes.'" *Journal of the History of Ideas,* XXI (Oct.–Dec., 1960) pp. 465–80.
9. R. G. Haliburton, *The Men of the North and their place in history. A Lecture delivered before the Montreal Literary Club, March 31st, 1869,* (Montreal, 1869) pp. 2, 8, 16.
10. Clipping from *The Globe,* December 8, 1904, in *Denison Scrapbook 1897–1915,* p. 167. *Denison Papers* (PAC).
11. Charles Mair, 'The New Canada: its natural features and climate.' *Canadian Monthly Magazine* VIII (July, 1875), p. 5.
12. *Canada First: A Memorial of the late William A. Foster* (Toronto, 1890), p. 25.
13. Charles R. Tuttle, *Popular History of the Dominion of Canada,* 2 vols., Boston 1877 and 1879, vol. 1, p. 28.
14. G. R. Parkin, *The Great Dominion, Studies of Canada,* London, 1895, pp. 25, 211–15: 'The Railway Development of Canada.' *The Scottish Geographical Magazine* (May, 1909), p. 249, reprint in *Parkin Papers* vol. 66 (PAC), address to Canadian Club and Board of Trade in Saint John. New Brunswick, reported in *The Daily Telegraph,* March 6, 1907. Clipping in *Parkin Papers,* vol. 82 (PAC).
15. Edward Harris. *Canada, The Making of a Nation* (n.p., ca 1907), p. 7.

16. G. R. Parkin, *The Great Dominion,* p. 216.

17. W. H. Withrow, 'Notes of a Visit to the Centennial Exhibition,' *Canadian Methodist Magazine* (December, 1876) p. 530.

18. Rev. F. A. Wightman, *Our Canadian Heritage, Its Resources and Possibilities* (Toronto, 1905). p. 46.

19. W. H. Hingston, *The Climate of Canada and its Relation to Life and Health* (Montreal, 1884). pp. xviii, 94, 126–7, 260, 263, 265–6.

20. Wightman, *Our Canadian Heritage,* pp. 280, 44–5; J. Sheridan Hogan. *Canada, An Essay: to which was awarded the first prize by the Paris Exhibition Committee of Canada* (Montreal, 1855). pp. 53–4.

21. F. B. Cumberland, 'Introduction,' *Maple Leaves: being the papers read before the National Club of Toronto at the 'National Evenings,' during the Winter 1890–1* (Toronto, 1891). pp. vii–viii.

22. Wightman, as cited, p. 221.

23. Benjamin Suite, *Origin of the French Canadian. Read before the British Association, Toronto, August 1897* (Ottawa, 1897), p. 14. See also his essay of 1897. 'Défense de nos Origines' in *Mélanges historiques,* compiled by Gérard Malchelosse, vol. 17 (Montreal, 1930).

24. *The Storied Province of Quebec, Past and Present,* W. Wood (ed.) vol. 1 (Toronto, 1931), p. 3.

25. G. M. Wrong, *The Two Races in Canada, a Lecture delivered before the Canadian Historical Association, Montreal, May 21st, 1925* (Montreal, 1925), pp. 4–5.

26. Abbé Arthur Maheux, *Canadian Unity: What Keeps Us Apart* (Quebec, 1944), pp. 22, 23, 25.

27. *Canada's Future! Political Union With the U.S. Desirable* (1891), pp. 2–3.

28. Principal R. A. Falconer. 'The Unification of Canada,' *University Magazine,* VII (February, 1908), pp. 4–5.

29. George Parkin, 'Canada and the United States on the American Continent,' reported in *Yarmouth Herald,* March 3, 1908. Clipping in *Parkin Papers,* vol. 84, (PAC): *The Great Dominion,* p. 214.

30. Cited in Charles and Mary Beard, *The American Spirit, A Study of the Civilization of the United States* (New York, 1962), p. 173.

31. *Canadian Methodist Magazine* (December, 1898) pp. 566–7.

32. Silas Alward, as cited, pp. 8–10.

33. See especially, J. G. Bourinot, *Canadian Studies in Comparative Politics* (Montreal, 1890).

34. *The Empire,* January 24, 1891.

35. *The Week,* January 1, 1885.

36. G. Parkin, in *Yarmouth Herald,* March 3, 1908.

37. *Dominion Illustrated,* VI (April 11, 1891).

38. Cited in *Canadian Methodist Magazine* (June, 1899), p. 536.

39. William Wood, *The Fight for Canada* (Boston, 1906), p. 33.

40. Rev. W. P. Creswell, *History of the Dominion of Canada* (Oxford, 1890), pp. 11, 15.

41. Charles G. D. Roberts, *A History of Canada* (Boston, 1897), p. 3.

42. Benjamin Kidd, *Social Evolution* (London, 1895), pp. 61–2.

43. E. W. MacBride, 'The Theory of Evolution,' *The McGill University Magazine,* 1 (April, 1902), pp. 244–62.

44. Lionel Stevenson, *Appraisals of Canadian Literature* (Toronto, 1926), pp. 245–53.

45. R. H. Hubbard, *The Development of Canadian Art* (Ottawa, 1964), p. 88; L. Harris, 'The: Group of Seven in Canadian History.' *Canadian Historical Association Report* (1948) pp. 30, 36–7.
46. Vincent Massey, *On Being Canadian* (Toronto, 1948), pp. 29–30.
47. Peter Newman, *Renegade in Power: The Diefenbaker Years* (Toronto, 1964), p. 218.
48. W. L. Morton, 'The Relevance of Canadian History' in *The Canadian Identity* (Toronto, 1961), pp. 88–114.

Canadians
Mariam Waddington
1972

Here are
our signatures:
geese, fish, eskimo
faces, girl-guide
cookies, ink-drawings
tree-plantings, summer
storms and winter
emanations.

We look
like a geography but
just scratch us
and we bleed
history, are full
of modest misery
are sensitive
to double-talk double-take
(and double-cross)
in a country
too wide
to be single in.

Are we real or
did someone invent
us, was it Henry
Hudson Etienne Brûlé
or a carnival
of village girls?
Was it
a flock of nuns

"Canadians" from *Driving Home: Poems New and Selected* by Miriam Waddington. Reprinted by permission of Jonathan Waddington.

a pity of indians
a gravyboat of
fur-traders, professional
explorers or those
amateur map-makers
our Fathers
of Confederation?

Wherever you are
Charles Tupper Alexander
Galt Darcy McGee George
Cartier Ambrose Shea
Henry Crout Father
Ragueneau Lord Selkirk
and John A.—however
far into northness
you have walked—
when we call you
turn around please and
don't look so
surprised.

An Inordinate Pride in Mountains: The Myth of the Natural Canadian
Will Ferguson
1997

What is the Deal with the Rocky Mountains?

Why are Canadians so damn proud of them? It's not like we *earned* them, right? It's not as though we built them ourselves. They were already there. We just showed up. So why this inordinate, proprietorial sense of pride?

When I travel through the North or through the Rockies, I am awed by the sheer majesty and scope of Canada. But I don't revel in personal glory and I certainly don't feel *proud* of them. Bragging to the world about your landscape is a little like bragging about your spouse's cooking. It's pride by proxy, reflected glory. And yet, Canadians are obsessed with geography and size.

Personally, I blame Mercator.

Gerardus Mercator was a sixteenth-century Flemish cartographer and mathematician. His great claim to fame is that he solved one of mapmaking's most persistent problems: how to reproduce a lumpy, spherical, three-dimensional world on a flat sheet of paper. The Mercator Projection, as it is known, stretches the world at either end, keeping the shapes accurate, but wildly exaggerating the scale—especially as you go further north.

The Mercator Projection has warped our view of the world. On a Mercator map, Greenland looks larger than South America, and Alaska looks larger than Mexico. The Mercator method is only now being abandoned—or at least tinkered with—but in Canada this four-hundred-year-old mathematical solution to a cartographical conundrum still has a certain nostalgic, nationalistic charm. It is a bit like looking at a fun-house mirror that expands your biceps or bust-line to cartoonlike proportions: it's an ego stroke. Using Mercator's method, Canada looms across the northern hemisphere like some large looming thing. A behemoth or something. On the old maps, the Commonwealth countries were always shown in pink, and Canada looked positively huge, especially when compared to—you guessed it—the U.S. of A. *Ha ha!* They might have more guns and larger penises, but just look at all that pink we own!

Make no mistake: maps are works of interpretive fiction. They are subjective and selective, and they colour our outlook more than we realize. I saw this first-hand while living in Japan, where world maps are divided not down the Pacific but down the Atlantic—a technique which just happens to place Japan in the very centre. Fair enough. Putting Japan smack dab in the heart of everything shows the nation's relation to the rest of the world much better. Harder to explain, however, is why Japan is the only country coloured red on Japanese maps. It creates this warped perception of the world, where Japan is utterly unique and central—and small. By positioning itself in the centre, Japan is surrounded by the largest nations on earth: China, Russia, Australia, the United States and Canada. This has a desirable effect in Japan, where the citizens prefer to see themselves as a "tiny but powerful" nation, outgunned and outsized, yet still succeeding through sheer will power and racial purity. Japan is, in fact, *not* a small country. The main island of Japan alone is larger than "Great" Britain. If Japan were in Europe, it would dominate the continent.

Canada is just the opposite. Because of Mercator's optical illusion, Canada appears much larger than it actually is. True, we are—and if you say it fast enough, you can get it out in one breath—*thesecondbiggestcountryintheworld.*

Or, even more straw-graspingly, *thelargestcountryintheWesternHemisphere.* The message being, What we lack in depth we make up in sheer size.

It is very adolescent, this fixation we have on size. What is the *third* largest country in the world? Canadians don't have a clue. All that matters is that we are number two. And for the record, number three is not the United States. It's China, which is virtually the same size as Canada. But here's the kicker: so is the United States. Forget Mercator. Canada and the U.S. are—for all intents and purposes—the same size. Canada covers 9,976,139 km^2 and the U.S. 9,372,614 km^2, a difference of 6 per cent. That's right, Canada is a whopping 6 per cent bigger than the United States. *Yeeehaw!*

On Mercator it looks like this: In real life, like this:

Depressing, isn't it? We looked so large on those Fun-House Maps that we started to believe they were accurate in their portrayal. It gets worse. When you consider that almost 50 per cent of Canada is permanently frozen, and that there are approximately 225,000,000 more Americans than there are Canadians, we are left with little to celebrate. Even now I can hear your chests deflate like leaky balloons. It may be hard to face, but the truth must come out! We are, effectively, a much, much smaller nation than the United States.

Not that we are a small country in general. No sir. We have geography coming out the wazoo, we have vast reaches of tundra, trees and muskeg, and more empty land than those namby-pamby mamma's-boys over in Europe can ever hope for, but what's the point, right? It is only the U.S. we are really interested in beating. The fact that New Brunswick is larger than Ireland, or that you could drop the U.K. into Alberta with room to spare is hardly cause for a flush of national pride.

So why this obsession with geography? Mainly, I suppose, it's because we do have a lot of it, and as noted earlier, people tend to glorify whatever their particular specialty happens to be. The Scots are dead proud of the moors and the Highlands, rejoicing in what is in essence a large deforested midge-infested bog. In Canada it is the Rocky Mountains, "the snow-capped Rockies, shiny white in the setting sun!" The Rockies are *the* definitive image of Canada, both abroad and at home, and they have a powerful effect. Jean Chrétien, for one, is especially fond of appealing to the Rockies in the name of national unity. "Da Rockies dey are my Rockies and everybuddy's Rockies!" This may be a bit embarrassing, but it's not unusual. Landscape has long been used as a tool of nationalism.

Classically, there are two ways in which landscapes are exploited by nationalists, but I have added a third way—one more common among Canadians:

1. as a sacred "homeland"
2. as source of communion
3. as an object of personal pride.

In his study, *National Identity*, Professor Anthony D. Smith of the London School of Economics outlines the appeal of the homeland as the cradle of a culture, "the repository of historic memories and associations."

> Its rivers, coasts, lakes, mountains and cities become "sacred"—places of veneration and exaltation whose inner meanings can be fathomed only by the initiated, that is, the self-aware members of the nation.

"Nationalism is about *land*," writes Smith. "Both in terms of possessing and of belonging."

This mystical, profound attachment to one's homeland is a powerful force indeed. But this is not what inspires the average Hoser's pride in the Rockies. The key element, "self-aware," is usually missing.

The second method is more private: landscape as source of personal communion. The classic example of this is Pierre "Still Virile After These Years" Trudeau, last seen sliding out of the mist in his canoe and buckskin jacket. When he was just twenty-five years old, Trudeau penned a stirring essay entitled *Exhaustion and Fulfilment: The Ascetic in a Canoe,* which ends with the following observation:

> I know a man whose school could never teach him patriotism, but who acquired that virtue when he felt in his bones the vastness of his land, and the greatness of those who founded it.

This is certainly the type of relationship that most Canadian nationalists allude to: an immediate and sublime connection between the individual and the land he or she inhabits. This is landscape as an extension of self. This is the spirit of the voyageur—and Trudeau was undoubtedly the Last of the Voyageurs. But let's face it, Trudeau is a cut above the rest of us mere mortals. He haunts us still, *yaddah-yaddah-yaddah.*

The average Canadian isn't delving as deep as Pierre Trudeau when he or she boasts about the Rockies. Canadians like to think they have a special affinity with nature, but statistics show otherwise. Canada is a hopelessly urban society whose average citizen couldn't pick a moose out of a police lineup. Yet still we wax poetic about majestic forests and open tundra. This has nothing to do with communion; it has everything to do with ego.

Here's a test: when was the last time you, a noble and natural Canadian, really communed with nature? (Riding a bicycle through Stanley Park does not count.)

In days of yore, it was the Canadian frontier that drew our hearty pioneer forefathers (and foremothers and forecousins and foreoxen) westward, ever westward, inveigled as they were with promises of free land and open space. And it is the frontier—be it the Rockies or the Arctic of the Canadian Shield—that is still being trumpeted as a cause for Canadian patriotism. But "frontier" is just another word for colony. Frontiers are invented solely to be tamed.

So why the love of frontier? Partly, I suppose, it comes back to that tin-can allure of potential. The promise of future greatness. Partly too, it comes from patterns embedded deep in the Canadian psyche. Commentators call it "the garrison mentality," bred in the bone as we huddled in small pockets of civilization, surrounded by forests primeval thick with Windigos and wolves and Wacoustas and all the rest. But that is far too heroic. What we have today is not a Garrison Mentality but a Mall Mentality, a climate-controlled, consumer-oriented cocoon.

The Natural Canadian no longer exists. We no longer experience the Canadian wilderness as pioneers but as spectators. At best, we are backwoods dilettantes, spending the long weekend in our cottages in Kenora before scurrying back to the sanctity of the suburbs and the safety of shopping malls. I do not claim to be any better than this, but at least I am upfront about it. I don't take any personal pride from our rugged outdoors. The Rockies are a magnificent range of mountains, but they would be magnificent no matter who was living here. We are merely tenants.

It was that great grey blob of a prime minister, Mackenzie King, who made the oft-repeated quip: "If some countries have too much history, we have too much geography." I don't mean to suggest that His Royal Blandness was wrong, but here in Canada we have plenty of history. Tons. We have history to spare. It is just vastly underappreciated, in much the same way that our geography is vastly *over*appreciated. The problem lies not with Canada but with Canadians. We have elevated real estate at the expense of history. We are proud for all the wrong reasons.

The flaw is this: By predicating national pride on our landscape, we remove Canadians from the equation. I grew up in northern Canada and trust me—tundra is overrated. Instead of boasting about our landscape, we should be asking ourselves what we, as Canadians, have achieved. What difference would it make to the world if we had never existed? What do we have to show for ourselves?

I prefer my landscapes inhabited.

It is in the cities and towns and villages of Canada that I feel most Canadian. It is there that Canadians have shaped a culture and a way of life: in Old Québec, in ramshackle St. John's, in Ragged Ass Road, in impossibly twee Victoria, in my own dear Loyalist town of St. Andrews.

Not far from where I live is a Loyalist graveyard, lying quiet among the autumn leaves and bracketed on either side by noisy schoolyards: an elementary school on one side, a high school on the other. This quiet Loyalist burial ground contains memories, ghosts and small personal epics. That graveyard, with its tangled tales of love and betrayal, with its collection of lives lived, surrounded on both sides by unruly schoolchildren—that is a landscape that stirs my soul. I am proud to be part of a country that created St. Andrews. I am proud of both our graves and our schoolyards. This too is pride by proxy—all nationalism is—but it is at least a living, human pride. We must not forget the critical part of Trudeau's epiphany, "the vastness of his land, and *the greatness of those who founded it.*" As Canadians, our true connection to Canada is primarily with the people who came before us and those who will come after, and not the wild indifferent landscape against which those human epics were set.

The Rockies are magnificent, but far more stirring to me *as a Canadian* are the rolling hills and small villages of Prince Edward Island. Here is the interplay of people and land: the cliffs of Cavendish, blood-red in the sunset, the winding lanes, the vermilion roads, the farms, the endless procession of churches, the lighthouse on the far cape.

Writing-on-Stone National Park in southern Alberta is the site of ancient Blackfoot pictographs that delineate tribal territory and call forth great events of the past. It is the writing and not the stone that gives this landscape resonance. And the challenge for Canadians is to decipher and learn to appreciate not the stone, but the writing—faded, half-lost, evocative.

Focus Questions

1. How and why was Canadian nationalism in the first part of the 20th century, as described by Berger, influenced by ideas about climate and geography?

- Due to the climate and Geography Canadians were stronger
- moral superiority

2. What are the positive and negative consequences of this brand of nationalism? How much of this early 20th century nationalist vision remains in place today?

positive
↳ strong workers
↳ fundamental unity
negative
↳ racist - northern pole
   are better than
      southern ppl

Yes - hockey
↳ Canadian Tire commercial

3. In her 1972 poem "Canadians," Merriam Waddington asks that "however/far into northness/[they] have walked," the Fathers of Confederation should turn around when called, but not look so surprised. What do you think they would have been surprised by?

- Surprised at the Canadians identifing themselves w
the geography
- we don't

4. Waddington describes Canada as something that looks "like a geography but/just scratch us/and we bleed history. . . ." What do you think this means?

- geography is superficial
  ↳ what is real is our ppl, our history

5. What is the "Inordinate Pride in Mountains," and why does it inspire Canadian writer Will Ferguson to declare that he "hates Canadians"? [the title of the original book in which this Chapter appears is called *Why I Hate Canadians*.]

6. All three of these readings focus on Canadians' geographic sensibilities and pride. Why does geography matter so much for nationalism, and if it is ever eventually removed from nationalist sensibilities, what is left?